FEEL THE FORCE

Win that SPRINT!

Forces in Sport

Angela Royston

raintree
a Capstone company — publishers for children

Raintree is an imprint of Capstone Global Library Limited, a company incorporated in England and Wales having its registered office at 7 Pilgrim Street, London, EC4V 6LB – Registered company number: 6695582

www.raintreepublishers.co.uk
myorders@raintreepublishers.co.uk

Edited by Helen Cox Cannons and Holly Beaumont
Designed by Philippa Jenkins
Original illustrations © Capstone Global Library Ltd
Illustrated by HL Studios, Witney, Oxon; page 7 Medi-mation; page 16 Barry Atkinson
Picture research by Tracy Cummins
Production by Helen McCreath
Originated by Capstone Global Library Ltd
Printed and Bound in China by Leo Paper Group

ISBN 978 1 406 29646 4
19 18 17 16 15
10 9 8 7 6 5 4 3 2 1

British Library Cataloguing in Publication Data
A full catalogue record for this book is available from the British Library.

Acknowledgements
We would like to thank the following for permission to reproduce photographs: Adidas-Salomon AG: 36; Capstone Press: Barry Atkinson, 16, HL Studios, 6 Top, Karon Dubke, 10, 11, 18, 19, 22, 23, Medi-mation, 7; Corbis: 237/Robert Daly/Ocean, 34; Dreamstime: Amy S. Myers, 38, James Phelps Jr, 35, Photographerlondon, 24, 43 Middle, Sarah Dusautoir, 25; Getty Images: Asad Zaidi/Bloomberg, 37; iStockphotos: technotr, 14, 42 Bottom; Shutterstock: Andrey Myagkov, Design Element, bikeriderlondon, 20, 31, Diego Barbieri, 15, ev radin, 41, FCG, 12, 42 Top, Gustavo Miguel Fernandes, 17, Herbert Kratky, 28, Iurii Osadchi, 27, Jacek Chabraszewski, 13, Michael Mitchell, 6 Bottom, 43 Top, muzsy, 29, Natursports, 39, oliveromg, 26, Paolo Bona, 33, Pete Saloutos, Front Cover, Peter Bernik, 8, 9, 42 Middle; Thinkstock: Daniel Hurst, 4, Dilip Vishwanat, 32, 43 Bottom, Yie Sandison, 5.

We would like to thank Patrick O'Mahony for his invaluable help in the preparation of this book.

Every effort has been made to contact copyright holders of material reproduced in this book. Any omissions will be rectified in subsequent printings if notice is given to the publisher.

Contents

Some words are shown in bold, **like this**. You can find out what they mean by looking in the glossary.

What makes a winner?

Sport is a good way to exercise and become healthier, but competing to win is what makes sport so exciting. Athletes and teams pit their strength and skill against each other. The winners are those who can best use their bodies to produce **forces** and control them.

Making it happen

A force is needed to get something moving and to keep it moving, but forces can do much more than that. They can make an object change direction. They can make it change speed or stop moving. Forces can even make an object change shape. Every movement or change in movement needs a force to make it happen.

Who wins the race? Generally, the fastest runner is the person who can produce the strongest force to push them across the finish line first.

FORCES IN ACTION

A force is either a push or a pull. When you hit or throw a ball, you push it in the direction you want it to go. In swimming, you pull yourself through the water. As you compete in a race or game, you are generating and using many different forces to get the result you want.

A player throws the ball accurately to score a goal. To do this he has to control the force that makes the ball move.

Forces in sport

In most sports, the competitors produce the forces needed for every movement in the race or game. Athletes race to see who can run, jump or swim the fastest. Many ball games, such as football, basketball and rugby, involve two teams playing against each other. In tennis, cricket and other games, the players hit the ball with a racket or a bat. This book looks at how athletes use different forces to make sport fast and skilful.

How does your body produce forces?

To move your body you have to move your bones. Bones, however, cannot move by themselves, and so they are attached to **muscles** that **contract**, or become shorter, to produce the force to pull the bones.

The main muscles you use to throw are in your shoulder and arm, although you also use muscles in your stomach, back and legs.

Shoulder

Muscles in upper arm move lower arm up and down

Elbow

Shoulder muscles move upper arm around in a circle

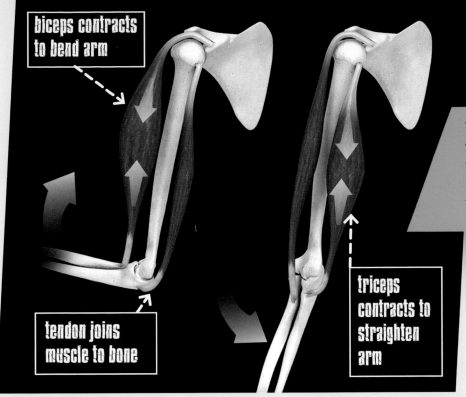

biceps contracts to bend arm

tendon joins muscle to bone

triceps contracts to straighten arm

The **biceps** and **triceps** work together as a pair to bend and straighten the arm.

Bones and joints

Your legs and arms are each made up of three long bones, one in the upper leg or arm and two in the lower leg or arm. A **joint** is the place where bones meet and it allows particular parts of the body to move. For example, the elbow is a joint that allows your lower arm to move, while your shoulder joint allows your upper arm to move.

Muscles

Muscles cannot push a bone, they can only pull it. They move a bone by pulling it across a joint. For example, two muscles in your upper arm move the bones in your lower arm to bend and straighten your elbow. To throw a ball, muscles in the back and shoulders pull your arm around in a big circle, before muscles in the upper arm straighten the arm as you throw.

Practice

Exercise makes the muscles and bones stronger and helps the joints to move more easily. Top athletes spend many hours a day exercising and practising, but exercise makes everyone fitter and healthier.

How do sprinters run so fast?

A sprint is a fast race over a short distance. Sprinters launch themselves from the starting blocks, accelerate to top speed and pound down the track. The fastest sprinters cover 100 metres (328 feet) in less than 10 seconds. The winner is the person who can best use their muscles and coordinate the movement of their legs and arms to propel themselves forward.

The starting blocks

Before the race begins, sprinters take their place at the start. They crouch down with each foot against a sloping starting block, and bend forward with their fingertips on the start line. As the starting pistol fires, the sprinters push against the blocks and use their thighs, **hips** and **glutes** (from the Latin name *gluteus maximi*, for the muscles that form the buttocks) to force themselves upwards and forwards.

A sprinter waits on the starting blocks for the starter's pistol to fire. Their muscles are tense, ready to propel them towards the finish line.

The sprint

At every stride, the runner pushes backwards against the ground with one foot while the hip, glutes and thigh muscles lift and drive the other leg forwards. As the lifted leg stretches forwards and touches down, the calf muscles bend the foot, ready to push off with the next stride. One leg after the other repeats the sequence, while the opposite arms swing to keep the body balanced.

A sprinter uses the muscles in her thighs, calves, buttocks, hips, shoulders and upper arms to reach top speed from the start.

GETTING A GRIP

Muscle power is not the only force that runners rely on. They could not use their feet to grip and push off the ground without a force called **friction**. Friction slows down or prevents one surface moving against another. Without friction, the runners' feet would slip as they pushed backwards. Friction is greater or lesser depending on how rough or smooth the surfaces are.

ACTIVITY: Measuring friction

Use a **force meter** to measure the force of friction. Compare the amount of friction produced by rough- and smooth-soled shoes, and discover if dry or wet surfaces produce more. Remember, friction increases with weight, so to make this a fair test you'll need to make the shoes weigh the same.

1 Use the force meter to weigh each shoe and make a note of the weights.

2 Put marbles inside the lighter shoes until all the shoes weigh the same.

3 Place one of the shoes on the smooth surface and hook the force meter to the top of the heel. Measure and record the force needed to move the shoe. Repeat with the other two shoes. Which shoe needs most force?

4 Wet the surface and measure the forces again. Are the forces larger or smaller than before? Record your results.

Conclusion

The training shoe has a rubbery sole with grooves running through it. It should have needed the largest force to make it move. The smoothest sole should have needed the least force. Water reduces friction, so less force should have been needed on the wet surface. The grooves help the shoe to grip in the wet, however, so the training shoe may still have taken a large force to make it move.

What makes a good long-distance runner?

While top sprinters are big and muscular, long-distance runners are usually slim and lightweight. They have strong running muscles and lots of **stamina** – the ability to keep going for a long time.

Fuelling the muscles

Muscles burn fuel to release **energy**. This energy can be used to create a force. The fuel is sugar, which comes from the food you eat and drink. The **oxygen** needed to burn the fuel comes from the air you breathe into your **lungs**. To keep working, the muscles need a constant supply of fuel and oxygen.

A marathon race is 42.2 kilometres (26.2 miles) long. Runners drink energy drinks as they run to keep their muscles topped up with energy food.

Heart and lungs

Long-distance runners develop strong hearts and good lungs. The heart is made up of muscles that contract and relax to pump blood all around the body. On the way, the blood collects sugar and **nutrients** from the **digestive system** and oxygen from the lungs. It then delivers these to the muscles and other parts of the body.

Improving delivery

Athletes increase their stamina by exercising their heart and lungs during **aerobic** exercise. Long-distance runners breathe in more air with every breath and their heart pushes more blood around the body with every beat. They can do this because the muscles that control breathing and form the heart are large and very strong.

Running is brilliant exercise. It strengthens the muscles and makes the heart and lungs work better. The more you practise running, the faster and further you will be able to go.

How can I jump further and higher?

Jumping uses muscle power to push the body into the air. Long jumpers push themselves up and forwards. High jumpers try to push themselves high enough to clear a bar. To jump they have to overcome the force of **gravity**, the force that pulls everything towards the ground.

GRAVITY

Gravity is a force of attraction between two objects. The larger an object is, the greater the force. Earth is so large that its gravity overpowers other forces and pulls everything towards the ground. A jumper has to overcome the force of gravity to rise into the air. After their momentum drops to zero, gravity pulls them down again.

A long jumper brings both arms and legs forward to help her travel further before gravity succeeds in bringing her down to the ground.

The run-up

Both long jumpers and high jumpers run up to the jump. Running helps them to go on moving through the air. This force is called **momentum** and is a combination of an object's **mass** and speed. Long jumpers and high jumpers run forwards before taking off so that their momentum will carry them further or higher.

The jump

When they reach the point of take-off, they bend the take-off leg and push down with the foot. As they straighten the leg, they push off into the air. A long jumper stretches their feet forwards and tries to pull the rest of the body forwards before they land. A high jumper uses their momentum to travel upwards. They twist their body in the air so that their head goes over the bar first, followed by their back and legs. It is vital that a high jumper has a safe place to land.

This style of high jump is called the Fosbury Flop, after the high jumper Dick Fosbury who used it to win a gold medal in the 1968 Olympic Games.

Pole-vaulting

The highest jumpers are pole-vaulters. Top high jumpers can clear over 2.4 metres (nearly 8 feet), but top pole-vaulters reach over 6 metres (20 feet). They could not do it without a pole, which stores their energy and **levers** them over the bar.

LEVERS

A lever uses a force, called the **effort**, to lift a **load**. The lever turns around a point called the **pivot** and this is what makes the force more effective. A first-class lever has the pivot between the effort and the load. A pole vault pole acts as a second-class lever. The effort comes from the vaulter pushing upwards with their foot and upper hand.

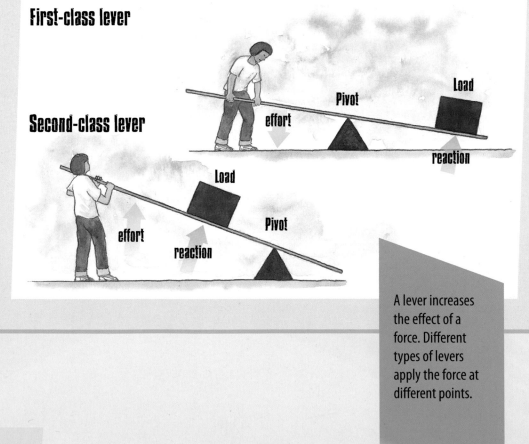

First-class lever

Second-class lever

A lever increases the effect of a force. Different types of levers apply the force at different points.

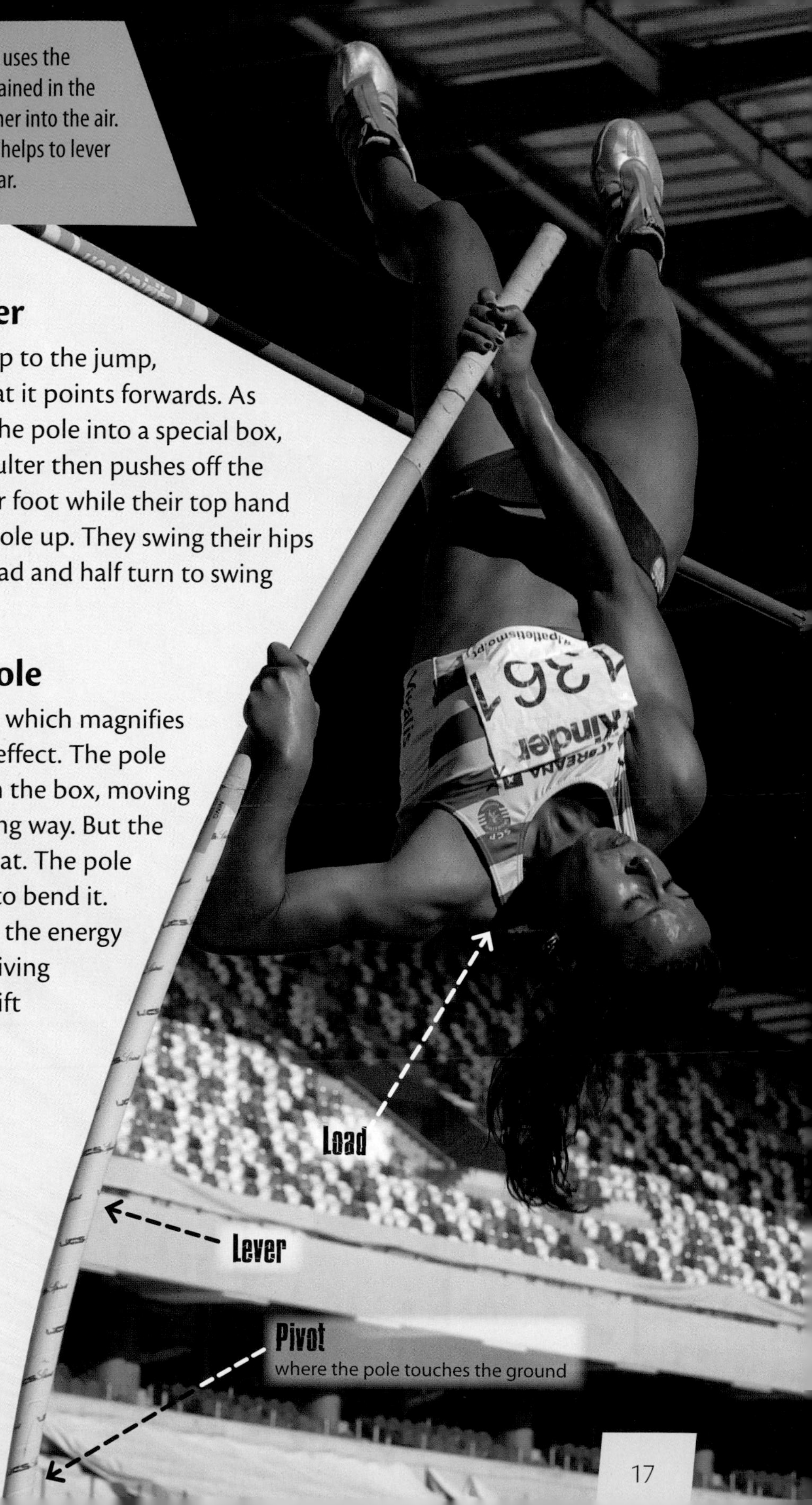

Higher and higher

First, the vaulter runs up to the jump, carrying the pole so that it points forwards. As they slide the front of the pole into a special box, the pole bends. The vaulter then pushes off the ground with their lower foot while their top hand pushes the top of the pole up. They swing their hips and legs above their head and half turn to swing over the bar.

The role of the pole

The pole acts as a lever, which magnifies a force to give a bigger effect. The pole turns around the end in the box, moving the top of the pole a long way. But the pole does more than that. The pole stores the energy used to bend it. As the pole straightens, the energy returns to the vaulter, giving them an extra push to lift themselves higher.

Load

Lever

Pivot
where the pole touches the ground

17

ACTIVITY: How a vaulter's pole works

Use rulers to show how a pole vaulter's pole works. Vaulters use the pole to give themselves as much height as possible, but this experiment uses bendy rulers to give distance. Measure how far different rulers project a pen top to find out which one works best.

You will need:
- three rulers of different lengths and bendiness
- a pen top
- a measuring tape
- a pen and paper

SAFETY! When you release the ruler, take care not to hit yourself, or anyone else with the pen top.

1 Mark a starting point on a table top or on the floor. Put the shortest ruler upright on the mark and place the pen top at the top of the ruler so that the pointed end is facing forwards. Bend the ruler back.

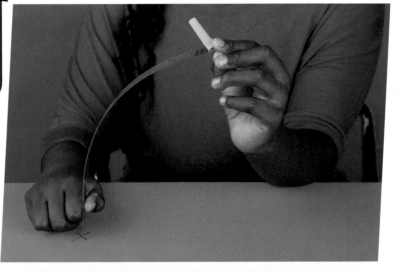

2 Release the top of the ruler so that the pen top is projected through the air. Measure how far the pen top travelled. Have three goes and record the result each time.

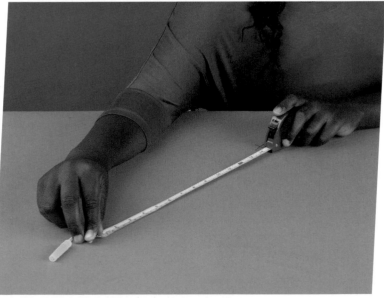

3 Repeat with the middle-sized ruler. Does the pen top travel further or less far than before?

4 Repeat with the longest ruler. Does it catapult the pen top further or less far? Which ruler is best of all? Is it longer or shorter, bendier or more rigid than the other rulers?

Conclusion

Long levers require less force than shorter levers, so the longest ruler may fire the pen top further. The bendiest ruler will store more energy than more rigid rulers. However, the bendiest ruler may fire the pen top at too steep an angle, so that it goes up rather than along. The best ruler will be the one that fires the pen top at an angle about half-way between the floor and the upright. Pole-vaulters have to get their angles right too!

Why is swimming slower than running?

Straight arm enters water

Body is streamlined and head is in line with body

Arm pushes back along body

Legs kick water away

In backstroke, the arms and hands push the water towards your feet, pushing you forwards.

EQUAL RESISTANCE

Isaac Newton (1643–1727) was a brilliant scientist who worked out the laws of forces and motion and published them in 1687. His third law states that "for every action there is an equal and opposite **reaction**". This means that the greater the force you can produce to push the water backwards, the greater the force with which the water will push you forwards.

In swimming, you use your arms as well as your legs to move forwards, so why can you run faster than you can swim? The answer is that **water resistance** holds you back. As you move through the water, it pushes back against you, slowing you down. Air also pushes back when you run, but **air resistance** is weaker than water resistance.

Water resistance

Water resistance acts against any movement through water and slows you down. **Streamlining** helps to reduce water resistance. A fish has a streamlined shape because its body curves smoothly from its head to its tail and allows the water to flow easily around it.

Increasing speed

Streamlining helps you swim faster. In breaststroke, you move both hands forward together, so they cut through the water like the pointed bow of a boat. In all swimming strokes, you should keep your head in the water, in line with the rest of your body so that the water can flow smoothly over and around you. The exceptions are breaststroke and butterfly, when your head comes out of the water as your arms go back, allowing you to breathe.

ACTIVITY: Water resistance

Explore the effects of water resistance and get hands-on with modelling clay to find the most streamlined shape for moving through the water fastest.

You will need:
- a large plastic container or large, empty drinks bottle with the top cut off
- a chunk of modelling clay
- a stopwatch
- some water

1 Use the modelling clay to make a round ball about 2.5 centimetres (1 inch) across. Hold the ball above the lip of the container and time how long it takes to fall from the top to the bottom of the empty container.

2 Fill the container with water and time how long the ball takes to drop the same distance.

3 Now use the same chunk of clay to make the shape of a shark, whale or torpedo, which is pointed at one end. Time how long it takes to drop it through the water.

4 Change the shape of the modelling clay to make a flat "S" shape. How long does it take to drop down through the water? Which shape sank fastest? Which one sank slowest? Test other shapes to see if you can find one that is even faster.

Conclusion

The round ball should take longer to drop through water than through air, because water is more resistant than air. The pointed end of the cylinder shape makes it streamlined, like a shark or a torpedo, so it should fall fastest. The bent, flat "S" shape is like a person swimming with their head out of the water and their legs drooping. It should take longer to fall. Did you find a faster shape? Could you copy that shape when you swim?

What muscles and joints do I use to swim?

Swimming is one of the healthiest sports because it uses all the main groups of muscles. The muscles in the shoulders, back and upper arms move the arms, and those in the hips, glutes and legs move the legs. In front crawl and backstroke, the arms move one at a time. In breaststroke, both arms and then both legs move together.

Moving your arms

In front crawl, you bend one arm, turn it forwards and straighten the elbow to stretch the arm as it enters the water. As you pull the arm through the water, the lower arm flexes your wrist so that the palm of your hand is flat against the water. As one arm moves through the water, the other arm repeats the movement.

This swimmer is making herself as streamlined as possible. Her outstretched arm cuts through the water and one leg pushes water down, while the rest of her body stays in a straight line.

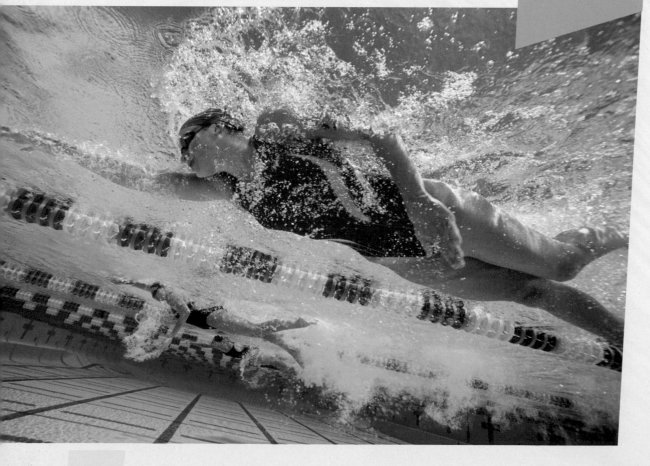

Moving your legs

The movement of the legs also drives the swimmer forwards. In front crawl, you bend and straighten first one knee and then the other. As the leg straightens, you pull the thigh down to increase the force pushing the water away.

Pushing off or diving in

Top swimmers achieve extra speed by diving forwards into the water at the start of a race and so gain extra momentum. In a swimming pool, you can also get extra momentum by pushing off from the edge of the pool.

At the start of a race, swimmers dive in, their streamlined shapes slicing through the water.

Why do sledges move so fast?

Sledging is thrilling, both to do and to watch as a sport. The fastest sledges are bobsleighs. These speed down a narrow, icy slope, going fastest where the slope is steepest. Two natural forces help sledges to go fast: the force of gravity increases and maintains their speed, while the slippery ice decreases friction, keeping the sledge moving.

Sledging on a snowy hill is fun. Some people have proper toboggans but others use any smooth surface, such as a kitchen tray or plastic bag!

A bobsleigh team pushes off at the top of the slope then jump quickly into their sleigh before it rockets down the track.

Pushing off

Human power provides the force to get a sledge moving. Ordinary sledgers sit on the sledge and push off with their feet, or are given a push by a friend. With a bobsleigh, the sleigh is pushed by the riders who run forward with it before jumping on board.

Fast track

A modern bobsleigh track is extremely smooth and includes a straight section as well as 15 or more bends. The track is made of concrete covered with ice, and the sleigh can travel at over 130 kilometres (80 miles) per hour. Riders bend down to make a more streamlined shape. They wear crash helmets and other protective clothes, but the sport is still dangerous.

REDUCING FRICTION

Friction is less between smooth surfaces than between rough surfaces. Sledges move on smooth runners over slippery ice, which reduces friction between them. In other situations, such as car engines, oil is used as a **lubricant**. This means that a film of oil is spread between two surfaces to make them smoother and so reduce friction.

How does ice skating work?

Ice skaters can move fast, spin on the spot and glide on one skate. Ice hockey is an extremely fast game, played between two teams with sticks and a rubber puck. Ice hockey and skating competitions usually take place on ice rinks, where the ice is smooth and slippery. The blades of ice skates are also smooth, reducing friction further.

Ice skating requires power and balance, strong leg muscles and stretchy joints.

FAST ICE

Ice is more slippery than any other smooth surface because it is covered with an extremely thin layer of water, and water is a lubricant. Even very cold ice has this water-like layer. The amount of water increases as the blade slides over the ice, partly because of friction and because the weight of the skater melts the ice beneath the blades. Skaters talk about fast ice, which is hard ice, and soft ice, which is slushier. Soft ice is slower for skating on than hard ice.

Ice hockey players move fast and use their sticks to hit the puck to pass and to score goals. As the game goes on, the ice becomes softer and slushier.

Moving on skates

To skate, you push the blades of the skates against the ice to move yourself in the opposite direction. As one skate pushes, the other glides. The muscles in the thigh bend the knee and straighten it to push off. The glutes and hip muscles give more power, and the muscles around the stomach keep the skater stable.

Ice hockey

Top ice hockey players need to have quick reactions as well as strong muscles. One moment they are speeding in one direction, the next they have stopped and are dodging opposing players before passing the puck. A player leans forward and digs his skates into the ice to accelerate.

How can I throw further?

Games such as cricket, rounders and netball involve throwing a ball, and athletes compete to throw a javelin, discus and shot the furthest. The greater the force behind the throw the further the object will go. The forces that work against the throw are air resistance and gravity.

The throw

To throw a ball forwards, you push it with force from your muscles (see page 6). Taking your arm back first means that as you swing your arm forwards you are applying the force for a longer time. Flexing your wrist as you release puts extra force behind the ball. Running up to make the throw passes more momentum to the ball.

The forces against

Air resistance is the force of the air pushing against a moving ball or object. Air resistance slows the ball while gravity pulls it towards the ground. To **counteract** gravity, you need to throw the ball upwards as well as forwards. If you throw it too steeply, the ball will go up instead of forwards. If you throw it straight ahead, gravity will soon bring it down to the ground. You need to throw the ball halfway between the vertical and the horizontal – at an angle of about 45 degrees.

Path of the ball

As the ball travels forwards, its path makes an arc through the air. It rises most steeply at first and then flattens out. As it falls, it continues to move forwards, until it hits the ground.

To throw a ball well, the thrower has to coordinate the movement of their entire body with the movement of their throwing arm.

Ball is released at the top of the forward swing

As throwing arm swings forwards, the other arm swings back to balance movement

Standing with feet far apart aids stability as weight moves from back to front foot

Catch that ball!

To catch a ball you have to stop it moving, and then hold on to it without dropping it or letting it bounce out of your hands. To stop a force you have to meet it with an equal force in the opposite direction. The good news is that the force of friction is on your side when you catch a ball, and you can use it to make catching easier.

Catching gloves

In football, the goalkeeper wears thick gloves on both hands, but in baseball, the catcher has one cupped glove. The gloves are rough, which increases the friction between the surface of the ball and the gloves. Friction makes it easier to grip the ball and hold on to it.

The catcher gets himself into the right position, with the open end of the glove tilted to recover and grip the ball.

The catch

To make a successful catch you first have to get yourself in the right place. This involves judging the arc of the ball and positioning yourself so that you can catch the ball before it hits the ground. If you are catching with two hands, hold your hands pressed together just below the wrists so that the ball does not slip between them. As you catch the ball, pull it towards you. This takes some of the energy out of the ball as it slows down and stops.

Hard to catch

Wet balls are more slippery than dry ones, which means it is harder for goalkeepers to catch a ball when it is raining or the pitch is wet. Rugby balls are oval, not round. It is extra hard to catch them after they have bounced because then it is difficult to predict which way they will go!

What makes a ball bounce?

Many games or points in games are won or lost on the bounce of the ball. Most objects, such as books, tomatoes and shoes, hardly bounce at all, but round balls can bounce back almost to the point they started from. What is it that makes a ball so different?

Storing energy

When a ball hits a surface such as the ground, the surface pushes back with an equal but opposite force to send the ball in the opposite direction. A ball, however, is slightly squashy. The part that touches the surface is squashed, or **compressed**, as the ball comes to a rapid halt. The energy used to compress the ball is stored. As the ball returns to its original shape, the energy becomes a force that bounces the ball in the opposite direction.

Spinning and slicing

If you hit or kick an approaching ball flat in the middle, it will return and bounce along the same path. However, if you hit or kick the ball forward but off-centre, the ball will spin, making it curve and bounce to the left or right after it hits the ground. Tennis players often hit up and over the ball. This is called topspin and it brings the ball down sooner and makes it bounce higher.

The bottom of a bouncy ball is flattened as the ball hits the ground. This will give it extra energy on the rebound.

In tennis, a player hits a slice or underspin by hitting under the ball. This stroke slows the ball down and makes it change direction after it bounces.

CHANGING DIRECTION

If a ball is travelling fast, holding a bat or racket in its way stops the ball, and makes it **rebound** in the direction the bat or racket is pointing. Moving or swinging the racket or bat as it connects with the ball makes the ball rebound with added speed.

How is a football made?

It takes a lot of careful design and engineering to produce a football that will stand up to strong forces and perform reliably when it is kicked. Such a ball needs to be perfectly round to reduce air resistance and completely waterproof. It also has to be hard-wearing and tough. To achieve all of these things, a modern football is made of several layers.

The outer cover of the ball is made of moulded shapes that fit together.

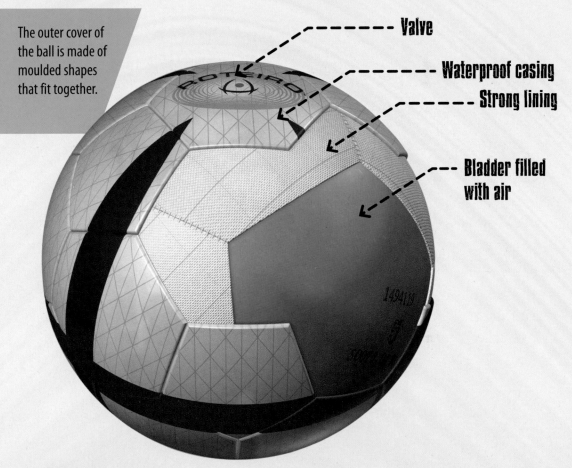

Valve

Waterproof casing

Strong lining

Bladder filled with air

Inside the ball

The core of the ball is a round **bladder** made of **latex**, which is filled with air. Latex is made from rubber or is a **synthetic** material that acts like rubber. The bladder is covered by a strong fabric lining that helps the ball to keep its shape when it is kicked.

The outer cover

The outer cover is made of strong synthetic material that is cut into shapes that fit together to make a perfectly round ball. In the past, the shapes were sewn together by hand, but modern footballs use a technique called **thermal bonding**. The shapes are fitted into a mould and then heat is used to glue them together. The result is a hard-wearing, waterproof cover.

Testing

The modern design was tested by a robotic football boot to make sure that the ball always performed the same way when it was kicked. Then it was tested by people. They found that the ball was too smooth. As a result, the outer cover was made slightly rough so that it would move more accurately through the air. The next time you play with a football, test how it reacts to the different types of force you use to kick it.

Good ball control

What are the most important skills a footballer needs? To score a goal, it helps to kick the ball fast and accurately, while a goalkeeper uses force to clear the ball far up the field. However, football is a team sport and controlling the ball and passing between players is every bit as important as kicking it with great force.

Passing

Controlling the ball means keeping it close to your feet and passing accurately before you are tackled. First, you have to stop the ball without it rebounding to a player on the other team. Then you use many small forces to keep the ball close to your feet. Before passing, you need to judge how hard to kick the ball and in what direction so that your team mate can run forward on to the ball.

Dribbling and tackling

You may decide to dribble the ball up the field. Then you kick it forwards with a light force and run after it. You may dodge an opposing player by kicking it to one side of them or between their legs. The tackling player tries to get their foot to the ball with enough force to stop the ball and send it in another direction.

Footballers use their hip, knee and ankle joints the most. They need strong muscles in their thighs, glutes, hips and calves.

A player prepares to take a free kick. If he can get the ball past the opposing wall of players, his team may score a goal.

Taking a free kick

Sometimes a free kick is awarded just in front of the goal. Several of the opposing team stand side by side between the ball and the goal to form a "wall". The best kickers can curve the ball by putting a spin on it as they kick, so that the ball goes around the wall and into the goal!

How many different forces?

In most sports and games, several forces are in action at the same time. The result is the sum of all the different forces. In football, gravity, air resistance and wind affect the path of the ball as well as the force and direction of the kick. In tennis, the action and reaction of the racket add another set of forces.

Driving force

The serve is the most powerful force in professional tennis. The action is a bit like that for throwing a ball forwards, but the racket increases the speed. Top players can serve the ball at over 250 kilometres (155 miles) per hour. Ground strokes, where the player hits a forehand or backhand after the ball has bounced, can be powerful too. The player hits a winner when they put the ball beyond the reach of their opponent.

Ball and racket

Tennis balls are filled with air. Hard balls, in which the air is under most pressure, travel furthest and fastest. When a racket hits a fast ball, both the racket strings and the ball are pushed out of shape. Part of the ball is compressed and the strings bend. Both store energy, which returns to the ball to give it extra force for the return.

Fast reactions

Like all sports, tennis involves many skills. The players have to react quickly to guess the path of the ball and be in the right place in time to choose the right stroke. Players use their eyes and brains as well as their muscles and joints to win the game.

direction and speed of ball

Muscles tighten
to produce force
to hit the ball

gravity

Serena Williams watches
the ball closely as it speeds
towards her. She is ready to
hit under the ball, to send it
spinning back over the net.

Quiz

1 Which of these things is not necessary to run a marathon?
   a) good lungs
   b) big feet
   c) a strong heart
   d) strong muscles

2 The pole in a pole vault stores energy when it is bent. This energy:
   a) seeps out of the bottom of the pole into the ground
   b) makes the pole shake as the pole-vaulter rises into the air
   c) returns to the pole-vaulter to give them an extra push
   d) stays in the pole

3 Why should a football be perfectly round?
   a) to make it more streamlined
   b) to make it bounce
   c) to make it waterproof
   d) to make it bend when you kick it

4 Which joints does a sprinter use most?
   a) elbow, neck and knee
   b) shoulder, wrist and ankle
   c) hip, elbow and neck
   d) hip, knee and ankle

5 The force of friction is stronger:
   a) on a rough surface
   b) on a wet surface
   c) going uphill
   d) on a smooth surface

6 What forces are acting on a long jumper when he or she is in the air?
   a) forward momentum from pushing off the ground and air resistance
   b) force of friction from pushing off the ground and gravity
   c) gravity and air resistance
   d) forward momentum from pushing off the ground, gravity and air resistance

7 Which muscle or muscles are used to straighten your elbow when you throw a ball?
- a) the muscles in your lower arm
- b) the biceps, the muscle at the front of the upper arm
- c) the triceps, the muscle at the back of the upper arm
- d) the muscles in the shoulder

8 In swimming, why does pushing back the water push you in the opposite direction?
- a) because you use the flat of your hand
- b) because when you push the water it pushes back with an equal force in the opposite direction
- c) because water resistance pushes against gravity
- d) because water resistance is stronger than the force pushing the water back

9 Which force helps you to catch and hold on to a ball?
- a) gravity
- b) friction
- c) air resistance
- d) water resistance

10 Streamlining:
- a) reduces gravity
- b) increases water resistance and air resistance
- c) increases friction
- d) reduces water resistance and air resistance

Glossary

aerobic requiring extra oxygen. Aerobic exercise makes you breathe deeper and faster.

air resistance force that slows down the movement of an object through the air

biceps muscle in the upper arm that contracts to bend the arm at the elbow joint

bladder stretchy bag. The core of a football is called a bladder because originally a pig's bladder was used.

compressed squashed or squeezed by a force

contract become shorter

counteract act against a force to reduce its effect

digestive system parts of the body that break down food into the different nutrients that the body needs to survive

effort in a lever, the force used to move the load

energy ability to do work

force force is a push or a pull on an object. A force gives energy to an object.

force meter machine for measuring force. It can also be used to weigh something, since weight is a measure of the force of gravity.

friction force produced when one surface moves over another surface. Friction acts to slow down the movement.

glutes short for *gluteus maximi*, the muscles in the buttocks, the soft parts that cushion your bottom

gravity force of attraction between two objects. On Earth, gravity pulls everything towards the ground. This is because Earth's mass is much greater than everything around it.

hip joint that links the top of the thigh bone to the pelvis, the bone that cradles your lower belly

joint place where two bones meet and fit together. The shape of the joint determines how the bones move.

latex rubbery material that is bendy and slightly stretchy

lever simple machine that magnifies the effect of a force. A lever is a rod or pole that moves around a point to make something move.

load weight that a lever moves

lubricant liquid or grease that makes surfaces smoother and so reduces friction

lungs parts of the body where oxygen from the air moves into the blood and waste carbon dioxide moves from the blood into the air that is breathed out

mass amount of matter, or physical substance, something has. Weight is related to mass because weight measures the force of gravity on the mass of an object.

momentum force of a moving body or object due to its movement. Momentum increases with mass and speed.

muscle soft part of the body that shortens to move a particular bone or part of the body

nutrients parts of food that a living thing needs to grow and be healthy

oxygen one of the gases in the air

pivot point around which a lever turns

reaction force produced in response to another force; reaction is also the way a person responds to an event

rebound bounce in the opposite direction

stamina ability to keep doing something before becoming too tired

streamlined shaped so that air or water moves easily around an object

synthetic material made by people from another material, such as oil

thermal bonding joining two pieces together by coating the edges with glue and heating them so that they melt and become securely attached

triceps muscle at the back of the upper arm that straightens the arm

water resistance force that slows down the movement of an object through water

Find out more

Books

Crushed! Explore Forces and Use Science to Survive (Science Adventures), Louise and Richard Spilsbury (Franklin Watts, 2013)

Cycling (Sports Science), James Bow (Franklin Watts, 2013)

Forces and Motion (Essential Physical Science), Angela Royston (Raintree, 2014)

Websites

www.bbc.co.uk/education/clips/z8jc87h
Go to this section of the BBC's Learning Zone to see how a squash ball is flattened by the force of hitting the wall of the court. Go to the Physical Education section to find lots more information about different sports and sportspeople.

www.fun-facts.org.uk/human_body/muscles.htm
Find out more about muscles and how you use them to move your body.

pbskids.org/sid/funwithfriction.html
Play the game that explores friction on different surfaces with Sid the Science Kid.

www.sciencekids.co.nz/sports.html
The Sports Science for Kids website includes experiments, games, videos and fun facts about various sports and the human body. Click on the rugby video to find out why a rugby scrum is the most dangerous moment in sport.

www.sciencemuseum.org.uk/educators/teaching_resources/activities.aspx
This Science Museum website has lots of science activities, including how to make your own rocket mouse.

Places to visit

Science Museum
Exhibition Road
South Kensington
London SW7 2DD
www.sciencemuseum.org.uk

This is the world's largest science museum of its kind. It has 40 galleries that explore scientific breakthroughs and include hands-on exhibits.

Glasgow Science Centre
50 Pacific Quay
Glasgow G51 1EA
www.glasgowsciencecentre.org

This museum is informative and entertaining. It includes interactive exhibits, workshops, shows and activities. Even the buildings are amazing!

Wimbledon Lawn Tennis Museum
All England Lawn Tennis Club
Church Road
London SW19 5AE
www.wimbledon.com/museum

Wimbledon, the most famous tennis tournament in the world, is played on these courts. The museum includes interactive galleries, film and video of exciting matches and much more.

Football Stadium Tours
Most major football clubs offer tours of their stadium and pitch.

Further research

- You can explore for yourself the important part forces play in any sport. Go to your local library and look online for information about how particular sports are played. See if you can find out how the athletes use and control the various forces.

- Collect as many different types of ball as you can, such as a squash ball, ping-pong ball, golf ball, rugby ball as well as a football and tennis ball. Compare how each one bounces and how they vary in size and weight. See if you can find out why a tennis ball is slightly furry.

- Go to your local sports centre and try one of the sports in this book. Can you use your knowledge of how forces work to improve your technique?

- Go to your local swimming pool and practise making different shapes as you swim. Try keeping your head in line with your back, and your back level. Time yourself to see which shape results in the fastest time.

Index

The Human Genome

Edited by
Carina Dennis and Richard Gallagher

Foreword by
James D. Watson

nature ✳ palgrave

Acknowledgements

For invaluable input, constructive suggestions and general support during the preparation of this book, we should like to thank Barbara Cohen, Francis Collins, Elizabeth Dennis, Daniel Drell, Mark Guyer, Mark Hirst, Michael Hopkin, Ian Jones, Michael Kilborn, John MacFarlane, Joseph McInerney, Richard Nathan, Hemai Parthasarathy and Peter Wrobel. We also wish to thank Jane Ades, Barbara Izdebska, Betty Mansfield, Majo Xeridat, the National Human Genome Research Institute (NHGRI), the Department of Energy (DOE) and the Wellcome Trust for their help in illustrating the text.

Note

A version of the article which appears on pp. 4–7 was also published in *A Passion for DNA: Genes, Genomes, and Society* by James D. Watson, Cold Spring Harbor Laboratories (2001).

First published 2001 by
PALGRAVE
Houndmills, Basingstoke, Hampshire RG21 6XS and
175 Fifth Avenue, New York, N.Y. 10010
Companies and representatives throughout the world

PALGRAVE is the new global academic imprint of
St. Martin's Press LLC Scholarly and Reference Division and
Palgrave Publishers Ltd (formerly Macmillan Press Ltd).

ISBN 0-333-97143-4

This book is printed on paper suitable for recycling and made from fully managed and sustained forest sources.

A catalogue record for this book is available from the British Library.

Library of Congress Cataloging-in-Publication Data
The human genome/Carina Dennis, Richard Gallagher.
    p. cm.
  Includes bibliographical references and index.
  ISBN 0-333-97143-4
  1. Human genome. 2. Human gene mapping.
  3. Human Genome Project. I. Dennis,
  Carina II. Gallagher, Richard B.
  QH447.H835 2001
  599.93'5–dc21   2001133051

10 9 8 7 6 5 4 3 2 1
10 09 08 07 06 05 04 03 02 01

Produced in association with
Book Production Consultants plc, Cambridge, UK
Printed and bound in Italy

Contents

The human genome revealed

James D. Watson

Seeing the Human Genome Project's draft sequence of the human genome is highly satisfying. The way in which its 3 billion bases have been determined closely follows the course outlined more than a decade ago by the National Academy of Sciences (NAS) Committee on Mapping and Sequencing the Human Genome. Bruce Alberts, now the President of the NAS, was its chairman and I was one of its 14 other members. The predictions in our 1988 report that the human genome could be sequenced over a 15-year period for a cost of US$3 billion were more accurate than we dared guess. Two more years of work, to fill in gaps and correct mistakes, will result in an almost errorless genetic script for human existence.

That the human script would become available within our lifetimes never passed through my mind, or that of Francis Crick, when we found the double helix in 1953. Then, just learning how cells read the genetic instructions within DNA seemed a tall order. Happily, progress was faster than expected and by 1966 we knew how the genetic code utilizes groups of three DNA bases to specify the amino acid constituents of proteins – the main actors in the plays of life. Things speeded up even more after the recombinant DNA procedures of Stanley Cohen and Herb Boyer burst onto the scene in 1973. Gene cloning and manipulation metamorphosed from being dreams to becoming facts of life. Simultaneously, Fred Sanger and Walter Gilbert each developed a powerful way to determine the order of bases along DNA molecules. This meant that humans, like cells, could read the messages of genes. The way was open to ascertain the complete genetic instructions, that is to sequence the genome, of any

organism (subject to the usual constraints of money, personnel and technology).

Viral genomes were the first to be tackled, beginning with genomes of just several thousand bases. By the early 1980s, viral genomes containing more than 100 000 bases had been sequenced and bacterial genomes containing more than a million bases became realistic objectives. The completion of such genomes would tell us the number of different proteins necessary for bacterial existence. Back then I thought that the human genome, at several billion bases long, was much, much too large to take on. Soon, however, I became a strong proponent of an international Human Genome Project (HGP), believing that the large-scale mapping and sequencing resources that it would command would hasten our discovery of the genetic underpinnings of many important human diseases.

Our NAS committee wasted little time on whether or not we needed an HGP; instead, we focused on how it should be organized and financed. It seemed best to begin modestly and end with a sequencing crescendo, hopefully fuelled by much lower sequencing costs. We agreed unanimously that the first big sequencing efforts should not focus on human DNA but on DNA from the model organisms of genetics, such as baker's yeast or the fruit fly. We knew that many human genes were likely to be homologous to those of model organisms.

We proposed a 15-year-long effort, reflecting our belief that those starting the project should also be part of the finishing team. Richard Gibbs, Eric Lander, Maynard Olson, John Sulston, Bob Waterston and Jean Weissenbach all stayed the course, running increasingly larger megabase sequencing labs. Only one of our original NAS committee is no longer in science. Sadly, Dan Nathans died three years ago at the age of 70, of leukemia. During our committee deliberations, no-one proposed a shorter timeframe – technology had to be improved too much. Later, I learned that Congress likes big projects to be finished within ten years so that key initial backers are still in Washington when the achievement is celebrated. Luckily, Tom Harkin recently became that Congress rarity, a three-term Democratic Senator from Iowa, so that he and New Mexico's Republican Senator Pete Domenici will see the HGP from its commencement to its conclusion.

The improvements in technology that the HGP needed for its success materialized almost on schedule. They largely involved modifications of pre-existing methods, as opposed to great leaps forward that generate Nobel-Prize-like rewards. The current DNA sequencing machines, the workhorses of our big sequencing labs, are 1000-fold-improved descendants of the original sequencing machine put together by Mike Hunkapiller and Lloyd Smith in Lee Hood's Caltech lab. The computers and software that now compare new raw DNA sequences to pre-existing ones also do their tasks 1000 times faster than was possible when the HGP started.

A major obstacle for the correct assembly of the human genome was the vast amount of repetitive DNA (~50%), so the HGP labs decided early on to sequence DNA from known chromosomal locations. Their map-based approach, however, was challenged in May 1998 by a new company, Celera, led by Craig Venter. Celera proposed an alternative strategy whereby the genome is randomly shredded into pieces that are sequenced and then reassembled in a single process without the construction of a map, a strategy known as 'whole-genome shotgun'. Key to their approach were 300 of the new high-capacity capillary DNA sequencers that were about to be launched onto the market, as well as proprietary shotgun assembly software for use on high-powered computers. So armed, Celera promised a first draft of the human genome in only two years.

I first heard of Celera in a phone call from my former associate, Richard Roberts. Rich told me that Celera would blow the international consortium out of the water, and asked me to consider joining him on its scientific advisory

board. Expecting to learn more about Celera's game plan at the soon-to-be-held Spring Genome Meeting, I reported to the National Institutes of Health (NIH) and the Wellcome Trust that Celera had marked them out for obsolescence. Later that week, Craig Venter visited NIH to tell Harold Varmus and Francis Collins that HGP's future effort might best be devoted to sequencing the mouse.

From the moment of Rich Roberts's call, I found it unthinkable that a private company should effectively control much of the human genome through key patents. This was a gene power-play that, at all costs, had to be matched. To my relief, the Wellcome Trust's immediate response was to double the budget for human genome sequencing at the Sanger Centre. Though the merits of each approach were yet to be tested, Celera's 'super shotgun' method caught the fancy of the serious press, who reported that HGP was off course. In fact, at the spring 1996 Bermuda meeting, HGP leaders had discussed Jim Weber's proposal for a low-resolution, whole-genome shotgun effort to complement the high-resolution map approach. There, Phil Green's off-the-cuff calculations, later redone and published, indicated that human DNA is too repetitive for a pure shotgun approach to assemble the genome correctly.

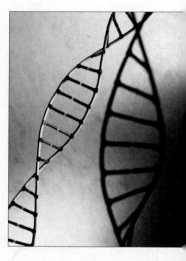

In September 1998 I returned to Washington to tell key congressional leaders that expanded federal support of the publicly funded sequencing efforts was necessary to prevent a monopoly on human genetic information. Many large pharmaceutical companies rooted for the public HGP, believing that Celera's future databases could only be validated through checking with publicly obtained sequences. To my relief, Congress increased public sequencing moneys significantly. So encouraged, HGP announced that it, like Celera, would complete a rough draft of the human genome in the spring of 2000 and, unlike Celera, it would pursue a highly accurate final product.

The February 2001 publication of drafts of the human genome by HGP and Celera represents a milestone in human history, revealing the basic features of the human genetic script. The drafts will allow us to identify most of the genes that underlie human existence. Using the genetic code to translate their message into protein products, we now have the first comprehensive overview of the molecules that make up our bodies. And it is immediately obvious that these are very similar to the molecular building blocks of other forms of life. Darwinian evolution can be increasingly described through incremental changes in underlying DNA scripts.

It is, however, unclear whether either draft is accurate enough for confident protein structure predictions. In fact proteome predictions from the two human drafts may be seriously misleading; only a virtually errorless 'gold standard' human DNA script will confidently move us into proteome waters. That so much more sequencing needs to be done, however, should in no way lessen our admiration for what both groups have accomplished.

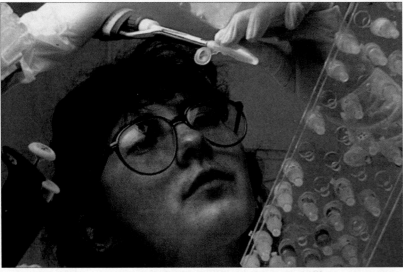

National Human Genome Research Institute, NIH

Until we saw the DNA text that underlies multicellular existence it seemed natural that increasing organismal complexity would involve corresponding increases in gene numbers. So I, and virtually all my scientific peers, were surprised last year when the number of genes of the fruit fly *Drosophila melanogaster* was found to be much lower than that of a less complex animal, the roundworm *Caenorhabditis elegans* (13 500 versus 18 500). More shocking still was the recent finding that the small mustard plant *Arabadopsis thaliana* contains many thousands more genes (~28 000) than *C. elegans*. Now we are jolted again, by the conclusion that the number of human genes is not much more than 30 000. Until a year ago, I anticipated that human existence would require 70 000 to 100 000 genes.

Why organismal complexity fails to correlate with gene numbers is not fully clear. It may be due in part to RNA splicing events which generate multiple protein products from single genes; vertebrate genes give rise to more splicing products than invertebrate genes. But the quality of respective nervous systems may be equally relevant. The roundworm, being dumber than the fruit fly, may need more specific proteins (and therefore genes) to respond to enemies or changes in its environment – the fruit fly's more advanced nervous system lets it respond to potential enemies and stresses by flying away. Plants, being totally dumb, must continually evolve new genes to respond to new enemies and climatic changes.

Many more vertebrate genomes need to be sequenced before we have a sense of how often the generation of new genes has underlain evolutionary change. We also need to know why vertebrate genomes contain so many more repetitive sequences than invertebrates. Most human repetitive sequences appear to have arisen as the result of the generation and movement of transposable genetic elements. Conceivably, many of the mutations that underlie vertebrate evolution arise from transposon movements into regulatory regions, changing gene expression patterns. The very high levels of repetitive DNA in amphibians and lungfish may reflect past needs to evolve fast for survival in their ever-changing ecological niches.

It should be possible to test the idea that changes in regulatory segments, as opposed to changes in protein-coding segments, have dominated vertebrate evolution. For example, sequence information from morphologically different breeds of dog may be informative, and hopefully funds will be made available to produce draft genomes of several breeds. How soon we shall be able to compare the chimpanzee genome with ours remains unclear. Obviously we should like to know the genetic changes that make possible the larger and more powerful human brain.

Of the many new facts emerging from the draft human genome, I am most excited by the finding that repetitive sequences are almost absent from the four clusters of homeobox genes. Unlike most functionally related human genes, the chromosomal order of homeobox genes exactly reflects their temporal expression patterns during embryonic development. In this respect, they resemble the genes of bacterial operons that are transcribed from single messenger RNA molecules; genes located at the start of bacterial operons are transcribed first by RNA polymerase molecules moving along the respective DNA. Conceivably, much of early developmental timing in humans is a reflection of the time needed for RNA polymerase molecules to transcribe the lengthy introns of homeobox genes. If so, insertions of sizeable transposable sequences into them would lethally mis-set key timing events in embryonic development.

Many, many more unanticipated observations and hypotheses will emerge as the reading of the human script extends beyond those individuals who produced it to the much larger world of interested biologists. Even the heartiest of them, however, will find themselves stretched if they take on too much. Most triumphs of the near future will probably come from focusing on the human homologues of genes of known function in one or more model organisms.

Eventually, even more important dividends will come from focusing on ourselves as human beings and making sense of the oft seemingly intractable relations between nature and nurture. There is much more to human life than interactions between its DNA script and the RNA and protein actors that carry out its instructions. The culturally derived facts and traditions that our brains pass on from one generation to the next equally affect our lives.

Our genomes, thus, can never accurately predict our futures. But we would be more than silly if we did not use their information to the fullest. The human genetic script that we are now finalizing will be regarded as the most important book ever to be read.

Remarks from the Editor of *Nature*

Philip Campbell

Occasionally, a scientific advance enraptures a particular field, sends waves of excitement through other areas of research and percolates through to the general public. The publication of the first draft and analysis of the human genome is just such an event. It provides the first meaningful look at the molecular and genetic content of what lies at the heart of every one of the trillions of cells in our bodies: the DNA that comprises our chromosomes. This book is an opportunity to experience the biological drama of the human genome, and to marvel at what it already tells us about ourselves, about our relatives in the kingdoms of life, and about those who went before us.

Often, the great breakthroughs in science appear in the pages of *Nature*. Why do researchers choose to publish in *Nature*, and what functions does it, and scientific journals in general, serve? There are several important roles. Journals offer a forum for scientists to present and debate their findings, and provide a permanent record of the progress of scientific endeavour. They offer a stamp of validation, or at least of assessment, through 'peer review', which is a thorough, formal appraisal of submitted research papers. The experts that carry out this appraisal are selected by the journal's editors, and they perform their task without recognition or financial reward. As with all research published in *Nature*, the papers on the human genome were reviewed, and greatly strengthened, by scientific peers. I salute their contribution. At *Nature*, we are also proud of the roles that our own staff play in selecting the most interesting science, coordinating its peer review, improving the clarity of its presentation and illustration, and adding complementary commentary.

The genome sequence data are made available on the Internet on a daily basis, thanks to the Human Genome Project's policy of instant accessibility. But the papers, and especially the wonderfully expressed article about the sequence that is reproduced in this book, made the meaning of all of those Cs, As, Gs and Ts clear to a huge audience. We were pleased to join in the spirit of the project and make the papers freely available to all-comers on the Internet. It was a privilege to assess the publicly funded work and to assist in making its significance as clear as possible.

Preface

For the first time in history we can read the complete set of instructions for making human beings.

Such a profound development inevitably evokes intense positive and negative reactions, sometimes both in the same individual. On the one hand, it is a pinnacle of self-knowledge, realized by a society driven by a desire to understand itself and the world around it; it is also an astonishing technical achievement. It promises practical dividends – an era of disease diagnosis, therapy and prevention that will surpass any previous development in medical science. On the other hand, the potential to 'mess with nature' through the genetic modification of plants, animals and humans induces a visceral reaction in many people. And there is a deep and widespread unease about the impact the new knowledge will have on society, indeed upon the very essence of what it means to be human.

In the words of UK Prime Minister Tony Blair, the way forward is 'to focus on the possibilities, develop them and then face up to the hard ethical and moral questions that are inevitably posed by such an extraordinary scientific discovery'. To achieve this requires a basic understanding of what a genome is and of genomics – the science of sequencing, analysing and drawing conclusions from genomes. The purpose of this book is to assist that basic understanding. It is not intended to be comprehensive. Rather, we hope it will serve as an introduction to, or a continuation of, an exploration of the human genome. We have purposefully avoided the politics and personalities involved in the project, focusing instead on the genome itself.

At the heart of the book is the scientific article describing the first assembly and analysis of our genetic code, the product of more than a decade of work by the thousands of researchers worldwide. Accompanying that article is a series of essays from leading researchers, which provides the scientific context, a sense of the excitement and a critical evaluation of the work. These essays and the scientific article are reprinted from the journal *Nature*.

To open up the Human Genome Project to a wider audience, we have written a series of introductory chapters to outline the scientific concepts and technological advances behind the project. The book begins with a definition of the genome, a description of its building blocks, the information embedded within its sequence and how each of us is a subtle genetic variation on a theme. It continues with a guide to sequencing, describing the technology that enabled scientists to sequence the genome and build the maps needed to navigate around the genome landscape. A timeline follows, tracking the project from initial stirrings to its development into a massive international mission. As a companion to the research article itself, there is an overview of the main findings that emerged from the analysis. In the final chapters, the implications of genetic information for the individual and society are considered, along with highlights from the media coverage.

This is just our first glimpse of the human genome – a so-called 'working draft'. There are still gaps to fill in and ambiguities in the sequence to resolve that will keep scientists busy until at least 2003. All the secrets of the genome are not likely to be given up for many, many years. But we have reached a landmark, the first view of the entire genome, and this is an achievement to celebrate.

Carina Dennis and Richard Gallagher
Washington and London August 2001

An owner's guide to the genome

The human genome sequence has been described as the most precious collection of information imaginable. But what exactly is the genome? What does it do? To what extent is it unique? And what do we learn from having the sequence of the genome revealed? As the owner of a unique version of the genome, you may be curious to know. In this opening chapter, we set the genome in its biological context and explain some of the concepts needed to understand the impact that the discoveries of the Human Genome Project (HGP) will have.

The big picture

Your genome is your genetic constitution. It is the information that you inherited from your parents and, in part, it directs your life. It comprises 3 billion (3 000 000 000) pieces of data in the form of deoxyribonucleic acid (DNA). The individual pieces of information are called nucleotides or bases, and these are the units of DNA. Nucleotides are linked together in tremendously long strings and their order along these strings is the DNA sequence.

What does the genome do? If you think of the body as a complex biochemical machine full of interacting chemicals, molecules and macromolecules, the genome is the blueprint for the machine. It includes the instructions for the assembly of macromolecular components; these instructions are the genes and the working components that they encode are mostly proteins. Genes influence our physical characteristics – such as eye colour, height and hair colour – as well as susceptibility to some illnesses.

However, the genome is much more than a list of component parts; it also incorporates information that controls when and where the parts should be made. Consider the miraculous early development of an embryo from a single cell to a multicellular organism – the series of transformations that brings this about requires highly coordinated expression of an enormous cast of genes. Even much more simple activities, such as fighting an infection, require elaborate patterns of gene interaction to marshal the appropriate defences. So the genome is not just a collection of genes working in isolation, but rather it encompasses the global and highly coordinated control of information to carry out a range of cellular functions. One of the great advantages of knowing the genome sequence is that we can begin to understand the regulation of cellular functions.

Your own genome is at least 99.9 per cent identical to anyone else's on the planet; compare it with that of someone closely related to you and the figure is even higher. A difference of

DNA crystals. DNA in a liquid crystalline state forms exquisite conical-shaped and fan-like structures. [Courtesy of Michael W. Davidson, Florida State University, Tallahassee]

> "I've seen a lot of exciting biology emerge over the past 40 years. But chills still ran down my spine when I first read the paper that describes the outline of our genome."
>
> *David Baltimore, California Institute of Technology*

0.1 per cent might not seem a particularly impressive amount of uniqueness, but it translates to about three million differences embedded in our genetic code, which gives plenty of scope for individuality. Some of the differences have no apparent effect, but others influence our appearance, behaviour, vulnerability to disease, and responses to medication. In essence, we are all hewn from the same genetic script, but our fine individual distinctions matter greatly.

"To see the entire sequence of a human chromosome for the first time is like seeing an ocean liner emerging out of the fog, when all you've ever seen before are rowboats."

Francis Collins, National Human Genome Research Institute

That being said, individuals cannot be reduced to their genetic characteristics; we are much more than simply the products of our genomes. Issues of what we share and how we differ, and of what our genes do and do not define, are complex. The Universal Declaration on the Human Genome and Human Rights, by the United Nations Educational, Scientific and Cultural Organization, provides a wonderful expression of this concept. In calling for respect for human uniqueness and diversity, the declaration states that: 'The human genome underlies the fundamental unity of all members of the human family, as well as the recognition of their inherent dignity and diversity. In a symbolic sense, it is the heritage of humanity.'

What are the practical benefits of determining the sequence of the human genome? For scientists, they are enormous and immediate. Virtually every field of biology, from biochemistry to behavioural psychology, palaeontology to parasitology, conservation to cancer research, will gain new insight. One application of the sequence will be to open a window on our history, providing a biological scroll of how our ancestors dispersed and settled around the world.

Humans: bipedal primate mammals distinguished by a highly developed brain and by an erect body carriage that frees the hands for manipulation. Vital statistics include an average adult weight range of 36–95 kg; average height of 1.7 m; and an average lifespan of 75 years.
[The cover image, by Eric Lander, was created by Runaway Technology, Inc. (www.photomosaic.com) using PhotoMosaic by Robert Silvers from original artwork by Darryl Leja. It is used courtesy of the Whitehead Institute for Biomedical Research.]

The benefits from the sequence will extend far beyond the research community, to revolutionize medicine. Our genetic make-up influences our susceptibility to disease. Most common human diseases, such as cardiovascular disease, rheumatoid arthritis and diabetes, involve several genes and are also influenced by environmental factors. The genetic basis of these complex diseases, which are known as 'multifactorial' or 'polygenic', is difficult to decipher. How will genomics help? In addition to identifying all the genes, researchers have been cataloguing variation within the genome, pinpointing the locations and types of genetic differences between individuals. This will help to identify genetic profiles that are prevalent in complex diseases. Not only will this lead to early detection and treatment of disease, but it will also propel us towards a new era of prevention, which, as the saying goes, is better than cure. Knowing the sequence of the genome and how it varies between individuals will also shed light on why some people with a particular disease respond better than others to drug treatment. And it will reveal new targets for the development of medicines.

The sequencing of the genome is only the first step on a long journey to full understanding of the biology of humans. However, although there is still much to learn, we are already gaining great insight into the nature of the genome and what makes us different from other organisms.

Zooming in on the genome

Before plunging into the details of our genome sequence, it helps to have a sense of biological scale. Here we start with the human body and break it down into progressively smaller components.

The first level of division is the ten interdependent systems that make up the body. These are the skeletal, muscular, circulatory, nervous, respiratory, digestive, excretory, endocrine, reproductive and immune systems. Each of these is composed of a network of interacting tissues and organs which, in turn, are made up of a unique composition of cell types.

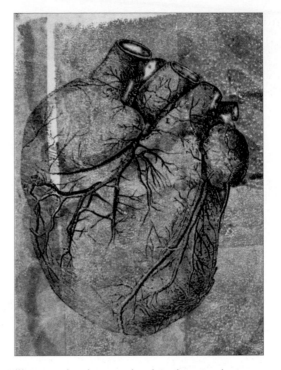

The heart is the pump of the circulatory system. Like all organs, it has a unique composition and function. It contains a wide range of specialized cell types that interact to provide structure and function.

"Let us be in no doubt about what we are witnessing today: a revolution in medical science whose implications far surpass even the discovery of antibiotics, the first great technological triumph of the 21st century."

UK Prime Minister Tony Blair

Cells are the basic units of all forms of life. The number of cells in an organism can range from one to trillions. The simplest forms of life are free-living, single-celled organisms such as bacteria, whereas humans are estimated to be made up of some 75 trillion (75 000 000 000 000) cells. Cells can vary greatly in size: the typical human cell is around 20 micrometres (0.00002 m) in diameter, whereas some nerve cells are over a metre in length. Although all cells of the human body have a similar basic structure, they display tremendous diversity. There are more than 200 different types of human cells, all varying in appearance, lifespan and function. And yet each cell of an individual contains the same genetic information. It is the selective expression of that information, through the switching on and off of genes, that

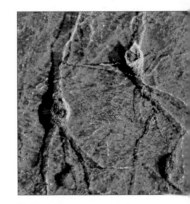

All living things are made of cells. Shown here is a confocal microscopy image of the brain showing the nerve cells in yellow. [Medical Microscopy Science / Wellcome Photo Library]

"The availability of genome sequence is just the beginning. Scientists now want to understand the genes and the role they play in the prevention, diagnosis and treatment of disease."

Randy Scott, President of Incyte Genomics

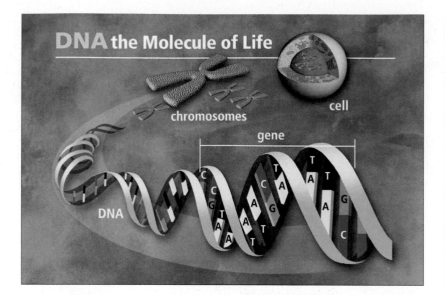

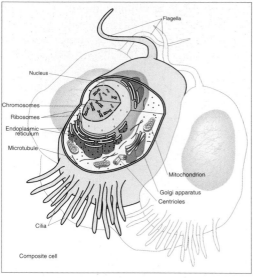

Inside the cell. Above right: some of the many organelles of a cell, each of which has its own distinct functions (NHGRI). DNA is found within the nucleus, tightly packaged into chromosomes, as illustrated above. [NHGRI, NIH]

provides the variety. An analogy to the genome would be a well-stocked kitchen; just as different combinations of ingredients can be used to concoct a host of different dishes, so various patterns of gene expression can produce a variety of cell types.

Each cell is further subdivided into structures called organelles (meaning 'small organs'). They are dedicated to specific tasks

inside the cell; for example, mitochondria are the power generators, ribosomes are protein factories, lysosomes act as waste-disposal units, and the endoplasmic reticulum labels, sorts and transports molecules. The organelle that concerns us here is the nucleus, which could be considered the headquarters of the cell – the nucleus houses the DNA.

Inside the nucleus the long, slender threads

A spectral karyotype of human chromosomes

Chromosomes (meaning 'coloured bodies') can be readily stained with certain dyes. The differences in size and banding pattern allow the chromosomes to be distinguished from each other, an analysis called karyotyping. Here, each chromosome is labelled with a different colour, a technique that is useful for identifying chromosome abnormalities. Some human diseases are caused by major chromosomal abnormalities, including missing or extra copies of chromosomes or breaking and rejoining of parts of chromosomes (called translocations). For example, Down syndrome results from a third copy of chromosome 21. [NHGRI, NIH]

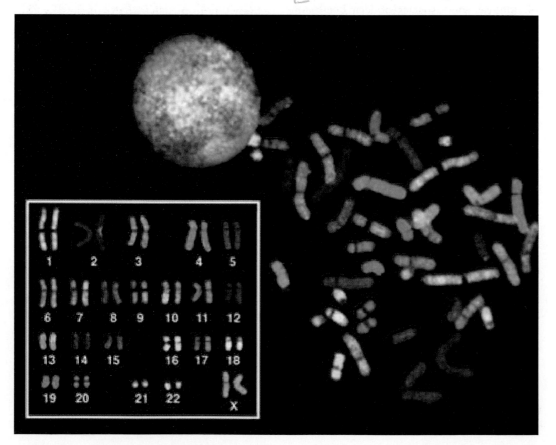

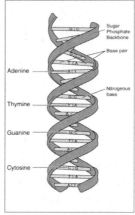

Structure of DNA. The double-helical structure of DNA is shown above left [c. Pete Artymiuk/Wellcome Picture Library]. Above, base pairing is illustrated. The binding of two nucleotides forms a base pair. Cytosine and guanine are bound together by three hydrogen bonds, whereas adenine and thymine are bound by two hydrogen bonds. Therefore the link between cytosine and guanine is much stronger than the link between adenine and thymine. [NHGRI, NIH]

of DNA are tightly coiled into distinct, rod-like structures called chromosomes. Each species packages its DNA into a particular number of chromosomes, of characteristic size and shape. A mosquito has just 6, a pea plant makes do with 14, whereas some species of fern boast over 1000. Cats and dogs have 38 and 78 respectively, and chimpanzees have 48. Humans have 46 chromosomes arranged in 23 pairs, 22 of which are called autosomes. They are numbered 1–22, in decreasing order of size (except for chromosome 21, which is actually smaller than chromosome 22). The remaining pair is the sex chromosomes. Normal males have an X and a Y chromosome, whereas normal females have two X chromosomes. Y is the smallest chromosome of the human genome, being little more than a stump.

Defining DNA

The basic unit of DNA – the nucleotide – is composed of a sugar molecule, a phosphate molecule and a nitrogenous base. The base is the information-carrying element and exists in four different versions: adenine, cytosine, guanine and thymine. These are abbreviated to A, C, G and T, the four letters of the genetic alphabet.

Strings of nucleotides are joined together to form an incredibly long strand of DNA; unwound and joined together, the DNA from a single cell would be almost 2 metres long but only 50 trillionths of a centimetre wide. In cells, DNA molecules consist of two strands that wrap around each other to resemble a twisted ladder, the famous double helix. The sides of the ladder are made of sugar and phosphate molecules, and the 'rungs' are formed by pairs of bases, one on each strand. A remarkable feature of DNA is the way in which the pairs of bases are held together: A only pairs with T, and G with C. These pairings are termed 'base pairs'.

The linear order of the bases along a DNA strand represents its sequence. The genome size of an organism is usually stated as the total number of base pairs; the human genome contains roughly 3 billion. There is little correlation between the complexity of an organism and the size of its genome. Although the human genome contains at least 200 times more DNA than that of yeast, and is comparable to that of frogs and sharks, it is dwarfed by the genome of the newt, which has 15 billion base pairs and, extraordinarily, by that of a single-celled micro-organism, *Amoeba dubia*, which is 200 times bigger than the human genome.

The slice of life

Throughout life, cells are constantly being replaced and replenished. This is possible because most cells are able to replicate. Before a cell divides, it first copies its genome so that identical genetic material can be distributed to each of its daughter cells.

➤18

DNA: an icon

Photomicrograph of high-density liquid crystalline DNA. [Courtesy of Michael W. Davidson, Florida State University, Tallahassee]

The history of how DNA was discovered, its importance recognized, and its structure revealed is extraordinary. It has filled the pages of entire books, recounting the fascinating discoveries and equally fascinating people behind the science. To appreciate how DNA went from being considered a 'boring molecule' to being hailed as a modern-day icon, it is worth recapping a few of the highlights along the way.

In a less-than-auspicious beginning, DNA was first identified in cells of pus from discarded surgical bandages. This was in 1869, when the Swiss biochemist Friedrich Miescher described a substance that could not be broken down by protein-digesting enzymes and therefore 'cannot belong among any of the protein substances known hitherto'. Because it came from the nucleus, Miescher named it nuclein, but it was later found to have acidic properties and was renamed nucleic acid. There are two varieties of nucleic acid which, depending on the presence of one of two types of sugar – ribose and deoxyribose – are called ribonucleic acid (RNA) and deoxyribonucleic acid (DNA).

Clues that DNA can transmit information came from studies of the bacterium pneumococcus, the agent of pneumonia, which was a widespread killer at the time. In the 1920s, Frederick Griffiths described two strains, a virulent one that was lethal when injected into mice, and a non-virulent one. Neither the non-virulent strain nor a preparation of the virulent strain that had been killed by heating was lethal. But when the heat-killed virulent bacteria were injected together with the untreated non-virulent strain, the mice died. Somehow, the dead virulent strain had conferred lethality on the non-virulent strain. In 1943, Oswald Avery and colleagues revealed DNA to be the transforming factor that was at work. Using about 20 gallons (76 litres) of bacteria, the team purified DNA that was free from all other substances, and showed that it alone was responsible for the transformation.

At the time, the work received little attention. DNA was thought to be too simple a molecule, especially in comparison to proteins, to contain all of the genetic information for an organism. Definitive evidence that DNA is the hereditary material was finally provided by Alfred Hershey and Martha Chase in 1952. They carried out experiments using bacteriophages (literally meaning 'eaters of bacteria'), which are viruses that infect and seize control of bacteria, hijacking the cell's machinery to produce more virus particles. Bacteriophages contain both protein and DNA, but which of these mediates the takeover? Hershey and Chase labelled two cultures of bacteriophages: one with radioactive phosphorus, which tags DNA; and one with radioactive sulphur, which tags proteins. They then infected different colonies of bacteria with the different bacteriophage populations, and tracked the location of the radioactive material. Radioactive sulphur (and therefore the protein) remained outside the bacteria, whereas radioactive phosphorus (and therefore the DNA) was on the inside. Furthermore, newly produced bacteriophages contained radioactive phosphorus. These results firmly established DNA as the material of heredity.

The acceptance of DNA as the chemical basis of heredity inspired many scientists to attempt to discover its structure. One of these was Rosalind Franklin, a chemist at University College London. She used X-ray crystallography, a technique in which an X-ray beam is fired at a crystal of the substance of interest and the resulting scattering of the X-rays is used to build up a picture of the structure. Franklin and her colleague Maurice Wilkins obtained great insight into the structure of DNA, notably its helical nature. But it was James Watson and Francis Crick, two maverick intellectuals working in Cambridge, UK, who finally uncovered the elusive structure of DNA.

It is one of the most frequently told stories of science, not least because, as later recounted by Watson, it is a tale of boundless ambition, impatience with authority and disdain for conventional wisdom. The pair's first attempt at solving the structure (at the end of 1951) went badly wrong; because of a muddled

No. 4356 **April 25, 1953** **NATURE** 737

equipment, and to Dr. G. E. R. Deacon and the captain and officers of R.R.S. *Discovery II* for their part in making the observations.

[1] Young, F. B., Gerrard, H., and Jevons, W., *Phil. Mag.*, **40**, 149 (1920).
[2] Longuet-Higgins, M. S., *Mon. Not. Roy. Astro. Soc., Geophys. Supp.*, **5**, 285 (1949).
[3] Von Arx, W. S., Woods Hole Papers in Phys. Oceanog. Meteor., **11** (3) (1950).
[4] Ekman, V. W., *Arkiv. Mat. Astron. Fysik. (Stockholm)*, **2** (11) (1905).

MOLECULAR STRUCTURE OF NUCLEIC ACIDS

A Structure for Deoxyribose Nucleic Acid

WE wish to suggest a structure for the salt of deoxyribose nucleic acid (D.N.A.). This structure has novel features which are of considerable biological interest.

A structure for nucleic acid has already been proposed by Pauling and Corey[1]. They kindly made their manuscript available to us in advance of publication. Their model consists of three inter-twined chains, with the phosphates near the fibre axis, and the bases on the outside. In our opinion, this structure is unsatisfactory for two reasons : (1) We believe that the material which gives the X-ray diagrams is the salt, not the free acid. Without the acidic hydrogen atoms it is not clear what forces would hold the structure together, especially as the negatively charged phosphates near the axis will repel each other. (2) Some of the van der Waals distances appear to be too small.

Another three-chain structure has also been suggested by Fraser (in the press). In his model the phosphates are on the outside and the bases on the inside, linked together by hydrogen bonds. This structure as described is rather ill-defined, and for this reason we shall not comment on it.

We wish to put forward a radically different structure for the salt of deoxyribose nucleic acid. This structure has two helical chains each coiled round the same axis (see diagram). We have made the usual chemical assumptions, namely, that each chain consists of phosphate di-ester groups joining β-D-deoxy-ribofuranose residues with 3′,5′ linkages. The two chains (but not their bases) are related by a dyad perpendicular to the fibre axis. Both chains follow right-handed helices, but owing to the dyad the sequences of the atoms in the two chains run in opposite directions. Each chain loosely resembles Furberg's[2] model No. 1 ; that is, the bases are on the inside of the helix and the phosphates on the outside. The configuration of the sugar and the atoms near it is close to Furberg's 'standard configuration', the sugar being roughly perpendicular to the attached base. There

This figure is purely diagrammatic. The two ribbons symbolize the two phosphate—sugar chains, and the horizontal rods the pairs of bases holding the chains together. The vertical line marks the fibre axis

is a residue on each chain every 3·4 A. in the z-direction. We have assumed an angle of 36° between adjacent residues in the same chain, so that the structure repeats after 10 residues on each chain, that is, after 34 A. The distance of a phosphorus atom from the fibre axis is 10 A. As the phosphates are on the outside, cations have easy access to them.

The structure is an open one, and its water content is rather high. At lower water contents we would expect the bases to tilt so that the structure could become more compact.

The novel feature of the structure is the manner in which the two chains are held together by the purine and pyrimidine bases. The planes of the bases are perpendicular to the fibre axis. They are joined together in pairs, a single base from one chain being hydrogen-bonded to a single base from the other chain, so that the two lie side by side with identical z-co-ordinates. One of the pair must be a purine and the other a pyrimidine for bonding to occur. The hydrogen bonds are made as follows : purine position 1 to pyrimidine position 1 ; purine position 6 to pyrimidine position 6.

If it is assumed that the bases only occur in the structure in the most plausible tautomeric forms (that is, with the keto rather than the enol configurations) it is found that only specific pairs of bases can bond together. These pairs are : adenine (purine) with thymine (pyrimidine), and guanine (purine) with cytosine (pyrimidine).

In other words, if an adenine forms one member of a pair, on either chain, then on these assumptions the other member must be thymine ; similarly for guanine and cytosine. The sequence of bases on a single chain does not appear to be restricted in any way. However, if only specific pairs of bases can be formed, it follows that if the sequence of bases on one chain is given, then the sequence on the other chain is automatically determined.

It has been found experimentally[3,4] that the ratio of the amounts of adenine to thymine, and the ratio of guanine to cytosine, are always very close to unity for deoxyribose nucleic acid.

It is probably impossible to build this structure with a ribose sugar in place of the deoxyribose, as the extra oxygen atom would make too close a van der Waals contact.

The previously published X-ray data[5,6] on deoxy-ribose nucleic acid are insufficient for a rigorous test of our structure. So far as we can tell, it is roughly compatible with the experimental data, but it must be regarded as unproved until it has been checked against more exact results. Some of these are given in the following communications. We were not aware of the details of the results presented there when we devised our structure, which rests mainly though not entirely on published experimental data and stereo-chemical arguments.

It has not escaped our notice that the specific pairing we have postulated immediately suggests a possible copying mechanism for the genetic material.

Full details of the structure, including the conditions assumed in building it, together with a set of co-ordinates for the atoms, will be published elsewhere.

We are much indebted to Dr. Jerry Donohue for constant advice and criticism, especially on inter-atomic distances. We have also been stimulated by a knowledge of the general nature of the unpublished experimental results and ideas of Dr. M. H. F. Wilkins, Dr. R. E. Franklin and their co-workers at

Oliver Burston/Wellcome Picture Library

Watson and Crick's paper published in *Nature* in April 1953.

King's College, London. One of us (J. D. W.) has been aided by a fellowship from the National Foundation for Infantile Paralysis.

J. D. WATSON
F. H. C. CRICK

Medical Research Council Unit for the Study of the Molecular Structure of Biological Systems, Cavendish Laboratory, Cambridge. April 2.

[1] Pauling, L., and Corey, R. B., *Nature*, **171**, 346 (1953) ; *Proc. U.S. Nat. Acad. Sci.*, **39**, 84 (1953).
[2] Furberg, S., *Acta Chem. Scand.*, **6**, 634 (1952).
[3] Chargaff, E., for references see Zamenhof, S., Brawerman, G., and Chargaff, E., *Biochim. et Biophys. Acta*, **9**, 402 (1952).
[4] Wyatt, G. R., *J. Gen. Physiol.*, **36**, 201 (1952).
[5] Astbury, W. T., Symp. Soc. Exp. Biol. 1, Nucleic Acid, 66 (Camb. Univ. Press, 1947).
[6] Wilkins, M. H. F., and Randall, J. T., *Biochim. et Biophys. Acta*, **10**, 192 (1953).

Molecular Structure of Deoxypentose Nucleic Acids

NATURE April 25,

James Watson (left) and Francis Crick (right) with their model of the DNA double helix. [A. Barrington Brown/Science Photo Library]

to others, Watson and Crick made another attempt. Watson was able to examine the X-ray evidence from Franklin and Wilkins in January 1953, at which point he and Crick went into a frenzy of model building, using large, three-dimensional models that were one of the keys to their success. On 7 March 1953 they were ready to announce to fellow patrons of the Eagle pub in Cambridge that they had found 'the secret of life'.

'We wish to suggest a structure for the salt of deoxyribose nucleic acid (D.N.A.),' they announced in an article in *Nature* on 25 April 1953, continuing: 'This structure has novel features which are of considerable biological interest.' The paper, a model of clarity, precision and understatement, is reproduced on the previous page. What Watson and Crick suggested was a winding double helix in which the nucleotide bases on each strand are interlocked (A with T, and C with G), holding the two strands together. Each DNA molecule in the double helix thus forms a template for the other, immediately suggesting how DNA would replicate itself.

The model had great beauty and simplicity, and fitted the experimental data available, so it was soon accepted as correct. Max Delbruck, a theoretical physicist who became a principal figure in genetics, wrote: 'It might be said that Watson and Crick's discovery of the DNA double helix in 1953 did for biology what many physicists hoped in vain could be done for atomic physics: it solved all the mysteries in terms of classical models and theories, without forcing us to abandon our intuitive notions about truth and reality.'

recollection of a lecture that Franklin had given, they came up with a three-chain model with the backbone on the inside. Undaunted, and despite being instructed by the head of their laboratory to leave DNA structure

For this achievement, Watson, Crick and Wilkins won the 1962 Nobel Prize for physiology/medicine. Franklin, whose work greatly contributed to the discovery, had died of cancer several years earlier at the age of 37.

What do an interior design company, a group of musicians, an electronic magazine and a nightclub in San Francisco have in common? DNA! The double helix has taken its place as a modern icon. Some of its many uses in science, art, leisure and advertising are illustrated on the facing page. Here, in their own words, is why this disparate collection of entities chose DNA as a symbol.

 "We used the name and DNA image as being the ultimate building blocks and blueprint in design that, hopefully, reflects the way we work. The double helix has a strong simple visual impact, but is complex and detailed in the way that it is generated, a perfect representation of our company. As an image it is open to lots of opportunities for us to express our creative abilities."
Chris Page, DNA Design
(http://subscriber.scoot.co.uk/dna_design/)
A pair of Christmas cards from DNA Design is shown.

"The name of our electronic band 'Freaky DNA' references DNA as a way to symbolize the dichotomy which is often assumed between the

 ideals of the scientific and the artistic. Anything which has its origins in freaky DNA is likely to evolve into something new and unexpected, sometimes mutated and sometimes beautiful but always with a life of its own, much like our goals when we create music."
Leonard Paul (http://www.sfu.ca/~leonardp/)

 "What I had in mind was a magazine which would explore the unique and/or the unknown, and of course with the intention of an alternative perception of things around us. And that was exactly DNA: something unique, a code man has not yet broken, a new perspective leading us to another dimension!

DNA magazine tries to include everything an alien from another world would like to know about this one. In other words, our essence."
George Drakakis
(http://www.dnamag.gr/index.htm)

 "DNA is the fundamental building block of all life on earth, and I wanted the club to be the fundamental building block of club life in San Francisco. Even in 1985 the term DNA and the double helix symbol were widely recognized, and 'not too scary' – for the general public. Finally I wanted a name that was inviting – 'a place where your DNA can lounge'.
Barry Synoground, DNA Lounge, San Francisco (http://www.dnalounge.com)

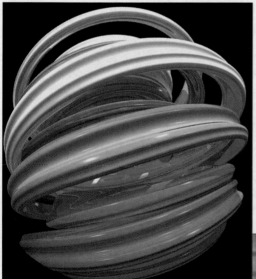

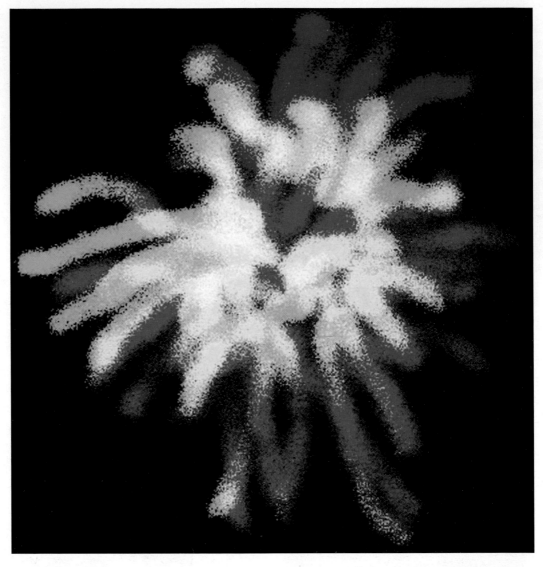

Cell division. Before cells divide, they copy their chromosomes. A copy of each chromosome is then pulled to either end of the cell so that, upon division, each progeny cell receives the full complement of chromosomes. This picture shows a cell about to divide, with its chromosomes stained with a dye that binds specifically to DNA. [Rachel Errington, Sally Davies and Paul J. Smith/ Wellcome Trust Medical Photographic Library]

The process of duplicating and dividing the genetic material of a cell is called mitosis. It happens as follows: the parent cell makes copies of all its chromosomes, which line up along the midline of the cell and are then pulled apart, so that each end of the cell contains a copy of every chromosome. A membrane then forms through the middle of the cell, dividing it in two, with each daughter cell containing an identical and complete set of chromosomes.

How are the chromosomes copied? Existing DNA molecules are used as templates to copy new ones, a process known as DNA replication. The double helix along the stretch of DNA to be copied is unwound and the weak bonds between the base pairs break, allowing the strands to separate. A DNA-copying molecule, called DNA polymerase, then binds to each strand and moves along it. DNA polymerase makes an exact replica of the old strand that used to be paired with the template strand. It takes new bases, which float freely inside the nucleus, and inserts them into the growing strand, strictly obeying the base-pairing rules. A is only inserted opposite T and C opposite G, ensuring that the new strand is an exact copy of the old one. Once the copying is complete, the strands rewind and the helices reform, resulting in two double-stranded molecules of DNA (each containing one original strand and one new strand) which are divided between the two daughter cells.

From genes to proteins

The gene is the fundamental unit of inheritance. It is a stretch of sequence in a specific position on a DNA strand that carries the instructions for making a particular protein. Proteins are the building blocks of life; they provide the structural architecture of cells and tissues, enzymes for essential biochemical reactions, and signalling molecules to coordinate cellular activities. When a cell is making a protein, the gene is said to be 'expressed', 'active' or 'switched on'. As discussed earlier, all cells in an organism contain the same genes but the subset of genes that are expressed defines the physical nature of a given cell as well as its function in the body.

In more complicated organisms than bacteria, genes are divided into sections that code for proteins, called exons (meaning 'expressed sequences'), interrupted by non-coding spacers

"The gene is by far the most sophisticated program around."

Bill Gates, CEO Microsoft

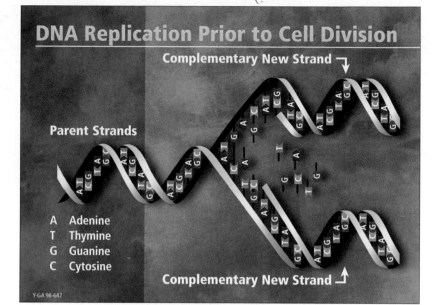

DNA Replication Prior to Cell Division

Complementary New Strand

Parent Strands

A Adenine
T Thymine
G Guanine
C Cytosine

Complementary New Strand

Y-GA 98-647

DNA replication. To replicate before cell division, the DNA double helix unwinds and each strand acts as a template for making a new complementary strand. A new strand is the mirror image of the template strand according to the rules of base pairing: A with T, and G with C. This results in two DNA molecules (each consisting of one old and one new DNA strand), whose sequences are identical to those of the original DNA. [DOE Human Genome Program]

called introns (meaning 'intervening sequences'). Human genes vary greatly in length; whereas the average protein-coding sequence of a gene is about 1000 to 2000 base pairs, long stretches of non-coding sequence interspersed between exons can extend the boundaries by 20 000–100 000 base pairs. The largest known human gene, which encodes dystrophin (an important protein in the scaffolding of muscle cells), is 2.4 million base pairs long, of which only 14 000 actually code for the protein.

A single gene can be used by a cell to make more than one protein. This can be done by splicing together different combinations of exons within a gene. Alternatively, the protein made by a gene can be modified after it is produced, by adding different chemical groups that change its properties. So there are many more proteins than genes, but no-one knows exactly how many yet. There are now thought to be 30 000–40 000 human genes, and some scientists estimate that there could be more than 120 000 different proteins in the human body.

Proteins are made up of long chains of subunits called amino acids, of which there are 20 different kinds. How do the 4 letters of the DNA alphabet translate to the 20 different building blocks of proteins? Like many good things, the genetic code happens in threes. Each specific sequence of three DNA bases (called a 'codon') codes for one amino acid. For example, the base sequence GCA codes for the amino acid alanine, and AGA codes for arginine. The genetic code is thus a series of 3-base codons

that tell the cell's protein-synthesizing machinery the order in which to construct a string of amino acids to make a particular protein.

The genetic code, like the English language, has a bit of flexibility in its usage – there are several ways to say the same thing. There are 64 possible codons (4×4×4) but only 20 amino acids, so more than 1 codon may code for a single amino acid. For example, CGC, CGA and CGG all code for arginine.

The information for making proteins is not handed directly from the DNA to the cell's protein manufacturers. Rather, there is an intermediary called messenger ribonucleic acid (mRNA). RNA is very similar to a single strand of DNA, except that it has a different base in place of thymine, called uracil (abbreviated to U). The RNA molecule is a copy of the protein-coding information of a gene, and is copied

"Most of biology happens at the protein level, not the DNA level."

Craig Venter, President of Celera Genomics

from the DNA template by a process known as transcription. Think of it like a photocopier – keeping the master copy safe but reeling out one, ten or a thousand copies of different genes in different cells. The mRNA is then shuttled out of the nucleus to special organelles (called the rough endoplasmic reticulum) where the protein-making machines, which are termed ribosomes, are located. The protein-synthesizing

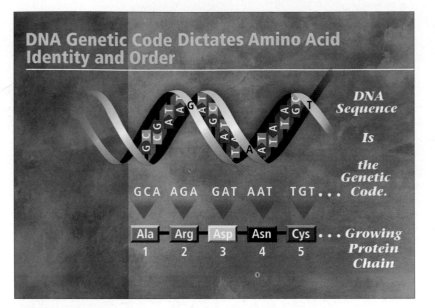

DNA Genetic Code Dictates Amino Acid Identity and Order

DNA Sequence Is the Genetic Code.

GCA AGA GAT AAT TGT...

Ala — Arg — Asp — Asn — Cys ... *Growing Protein Chain*
1   2   3   4   5

The genetic code. The language of DNA and its intermediary message, mRNA, consists of just 4 characters, which are translated to the 20-character language of proteins. The genetic code consists of a linear series of nucleotides read three at a time – these triplets are called 'codons'. Each codon specifies a particular amino acid to be added to the end of the growing protein chain. This process of converting the genetic code into protein is called 'translation'. [DOE Human Genome Program]

machinery translates the codons of the RNA strand into a string of amino acids. This progression of DNA to RNA to protein is known as the central dogma of genetics.

The genetic language is universal; our DNA speaks the same language as the DNA in a plant or a fly. There are slight differences in dialect, but our cells would have no problem in making a protein encoded by a gene from just about any organism on Earth! This is the reason why genetic modification works so well and why the ability to transfer genes between species is now routine in research. A further practical benefit is that if we know the genes of one organism, we can use this information to search for genes in another.

Less than 2 per cent of the human genome is made up of protein-coding sequences. To think of it another way, this means that genetic instructions take up just a few centimetres of the 2-metre strand of DNA that is packed inside every cell. The remainder has been labelled as 'junk' DNA. The function of these vast tracts of non-coding sequence is still largely obscure, but they do seem to contain instructions that help to control what proteins are expressed where, and when.

Personal genomes

Clearly, we are all unique at many levels, including the level of the genome. To understand how we differ from each other, we need to understand how a parent's genome is transmitted to his or her children. Genetic material is passed to the next generation through the sex cells,

sperm and egg. Whereas most cells of the human body possess pairs of each of the 23 chromosomes, the sex cells contain only a single copy. When an egg and sperm unite during fertilization, the resulting embryo inherits half a copy of each parent's genome to restore the normal number of chromosomes.

Sex cells (or gametes) are created by meiosis, a special kind of cell division that only happens in the egg-producing cells of the ovaries and the sperm-producing cells of the testes. The chromosomes are copied as in normal cell division (mitosis), but the cells divide twice rather than just once. This produces four sex cells, each of which contains only one set of the 23 chromosomes.

The chromosomes inherited are not simply standard copies from our parents. Instead, during the first round of division, the pairs of homologous chromosomes swap pieces of their genetic material. Pairs of chromosomes come together, break at identical points along their length, exchange equivalent pieces of DNA,

"Man with all his noble qualities ... still bears in his bodily frame the indelible stamp of his lowly origin."

Charles Darwin 1809–82, natural historian; The Descent of Man *(1871), closing words*

and then rejoin. This shuffling is known as 'recombination', and it produces chromosomes with new combinations of genes – and therefore traits – that may not have been present in either parent. Children thus inherit 'patchwork' chromosomes, consisting of alternate portions of the chromosomes that originated in their grandparents.

Most differences between individual human genomes are very small – a few bases missing here, a few extra inserted there. The overwhelming majority of variation has no effect, as it occurs in parts of the genome that do not code for genes, but occasionally these small changes give rise to altered proteins. The most common variations are single-base substitutions, known as 'single-nucleotide polymorphisms' or SNPs (pronounced 'snips'). An example of a SNP that could affect the structure of a protein is a change from A to C in the sequence CAT. CAT encodes the amino acid histidine, whereas CCT gives proline.

How do such changes in the human genome sequence come about? Well, nobody – and nothing in biology – is perfect. Although the cell generally copies its DNA accurately, occasionally a wrong base is inserted into the new DNA sequence, or some bases are inadvertently skipped or added. This slip-up in DNA copying can occur in the sex-producing cells, and hence be inherited by a child and passed down through subsequent generations. Alternatively, genetic changes can occur during division of normal cells of the body and are not passed on to the next generation – these are known as 'somatic' changes.

Our genomes are therefore a combination of old and new changes. Cumulative alterations can be passed down through the generations, which is why we are genetically more similar to our relatives. Changes that occurred in distant human ancestors are likely to be present in many groups of people around the world, whereas recent changes will be found in more localized populations.

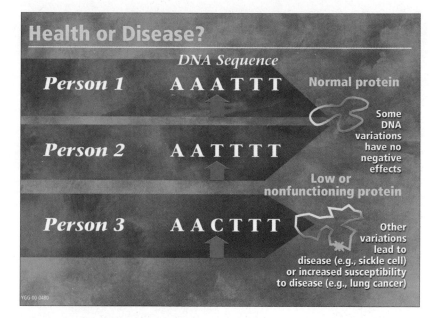

Robert Boston / Washington University School of Medicine in St Louis

Genetic variation and disease

Genetic variation is a double-edged sword. Changes in the genome sequence create diversity and allow any population, including humans, to have a broader range of attributes that help it adapt to changing environments. Some genetic changes, or 'mutations', however, can be disadvantageous in that they cause disease.

Errors in single genes are responsible for more than 4000 hereditary diseases, including cystic fibrosis, Tay-Sachs disease, sickle-cell anaemia and Duchenne muscular dystrophy. Most hereditary diseases are rare, but collectively they affect a substantial proportion of the population. You probably know or have heard about someone who is affected by an inherited genetic disease. Stephen Hawking, one of the world's great cosmologists, suffers from amyotrophic lateral sclerosis (ALS), the hereditary disease that took the lives of baseball player Lou Gehrig and actor David Niven. Huntington disease claimed the life of songwriter Woody Guthrie. But genetic disease takes its heaviest toll among the young, causing a substantial percentage of all infant mortalities.

Our chromosomes exist in pairs and we have two copies of most genes (the exception being some genes on the sex chromosomes; males

Genetic variation. Most variation in the human genome arises from substitutions of individual nucleotides, called single-nucleotide polymorphisms (SNPs), which are like typographical errors. In the example illustrated here, A, C or T can occupy the same position in the genome sequence. Fortunately, most of the genetic changes (or 'mutations') are harmless because they do not occur in parts of the DNA that contain instructions for making a protein. Sometimes, however, a mutation in a gene can affect the structure or function of the protein encoded by the gene, and this can alter how cells behave in the body and lead to disease. [DOE Human Genome Program]

"Now, for the first time, we have an historical anthology of ourselves, some of it passed down for a billion years. We're just learning how to read the story, and it's sure to enthral us for decades to come."

Eric Lander, Whitehead Institute

have a single X chromosome so they will have only one copy of some X-linked genes where there is no equivalent counterpart on the Y chromosome). Alternative forms of our genes are called 'alleles', and a single allele of each gene is inherited separately from each parent. Different alleles produce variation in inherited characteristics such as hair colour and blood type.

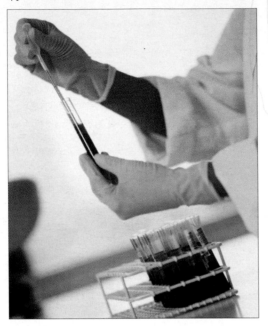

"It would surprise me enormously if in 20 years the treatment of cancer had not been transformed."

Mike Stratton, Cancer Genome Project

When a mutation inactivates one copy of a gene, the second copy can sometimes act as a back-up and compensate for the deficiency. So some genetic diseases do not develop unless a person has two defective copies of the gene – such diseases are termed 'recessive'. Cystic fibrosis is an example of a recessive trait; it arises from a mutation in the gene encoding a protein that serves as a channel through which chloride ions enter and leave cells. About 1 in 20 people carries the cystic-fibrosis mutation in one copy of the gene. It is only when two defective copies

are inherited that the disease develops. For other conditions, however, a change in just one copy of a gene is enough to cause disease. This form of inheritance is called 'dominant' because the flawed copy dominates the normal copy of the gene. An example is Huntington disease, which is caused by an unusual repetition of a triplet of bases, CAG, in the gene that encodes the protein huntingtin (the normal function of which is still unclear). In unaffected people CAG may be repeated 11–34 times, but in an affected patient the triplet is repeated many more times, sometimes more than 80. This results in the production of an abnormal huntingtin protein, which disrupts the function of nerve cells.

The examples given above are inherited genetic diseases, in which a genetic mutation is passed from parents to offspring through the parents' sex cells. Genetic changes in somatic cells – that is, normal cells of the body that are not passed on to the next generation – can also cause disease. Cancer, for the most part, is caused by somatic mutations that result in uncontrolled cell growth and cell division. Cancer typically arises from the accumulation of mutations in not one but several genes. It starts with a single mutation in a cell that is transmitted to all its daughter cells through mitosis. Some divisions later, a second mutation occurs which is also transmitted to daughter cells, and so on. Cancer-causing mutations typically give a cell a 'growth advantage' over normal cells, enabling it to divide more quickly. Thus, the disease often arises from mutations in three types of gene: 'oncogenes', which promote cell growth and division; 'tumour-suppressor genes', which keep cell division in check; and DNA-repair genes, which fix damaged genes.

Knowing the complete sequence of human DNA has transformed the process of identifying genes that are responsible for hereditary diseases. And now that the catalogue of human variation is rapidly being compiled, important studies are being undertaken to link the common complex diseases with underlying genome variation. The revolution is under way.

"This is the outstanding achievement, not only of our lifetime, but in terms of human history. I say this because the Human Genome Project does have the potential to impact on the life of every person on this planet."

Michael Dexter, Wellcome Trust

The art of DNA sequencing

The Human Genome Project (HGP) has often been compared to the space programme. Both have attracted much public and media attention; and both have been characterized by curiosity, a spirit of adventure and a high degree of interdisciplinary collaboration, as well as by competition and controversy. Their respective end products – the sequencing of the human genome and the landing of people on the moon – are landmark achievements in science and technology. Just as our admiration for space exploration is deepened by an awareness of the hurdles that were overcome, so an understanding of the technical challenges of genome sequencing gives a better appreciation of the venture into our molecular selves. This chapter explains how the human genome was sequenced, recounts the historic breakthroughs that made it possible and describes the technical developments that accelerated the project towards its goal.

The recipe for genome sequencing

DNA sequencing is the term used to describe the laboratory process of reading the order of the four letters of the genetic alphabet (A, C, G and T) along a strand of DNA. Sequencing a genome therefore means reading every single letter of an organism's DNA. Let's start with an overview of how a genome is sequenced:

Step 1 – select your organism.

Step 2 – isolate the DNA from cells and prepare large samples of high quality.

Step 3 – cut the purified DNA at random into manageably sized, overlapping pieces.

Step 4 – insert the DNA pieces into packages for the production of limitless copies (or 'clones').

Step 5 – read the order of bases for each DNA piece.

Step 6 – determine the overlap of each piece and assemble the sequences to give the final genome sequence.

Reading the genetic script

There are a couple of different approaches to DNA sequencing, the most popular of which is the 'chain-termination method'. This takes advantage of a naturally occurring DNA polymerase, a protein that plays a central role in replicating the genetic information of a cell. This process is essential as it ensures that every time a cell divides, both new cells contain their own set of DNA. DNA polymerase molecules attach to both strands and use them as templates to string together new, complementary strands from single nucleotides. The result is two sets of double-stranded DNA – one set for each new cell. This DNA-copying process is astonishingly accurate and the strict rules of base pairing – that A pairs only with T, and G with C – ensure that two exact copies are replicated from the parent cell.

To sequence DNA, this copying process is re-created in the laboratory, with a twist. Along with all of the ingredients needed to make new DNA – which include a DNA template to be copied, DNA polymerase and single A, C, G and T nucleotides – modified versions of the nucleotides known as 'terminator nucleotides' are also included. DNA polymerase can add terminator nucleotides to the new growing strand of DNA, after which no further nucleotides can be added, so the polymerase stops in its tracks. As the addition of a terminator nucleotide (instead of a normal nucleotide) is a random process, the result is a collection of incompletely copied fragments that all start at the same point but differ in length by a single base, depending on how far the polymerase got

How to sequence DNA

a) DNA polymerase copies a strand of DNA.

b) The insertion of a terminator base into the growing strand halts the copying process. This is a random event that results in a series of fragments of different lengths, depending on the base at which the copying stopped. The fragments are separated by size by running them through a gel matrix, with the shortest fragments at the bottom, largest at the top.

c) The terminators are labelled with different fluorescent dyes, so each fragment will fluoresce a particular colour depending on whether it ends with a A, C, G or T.

d) The sequence is 'read' by a computer. It generates a 'sequence trace', as shown here, with the coloured hillocks corresponding to fluorescent bands read from bottom to top of one lane of the gel. The computer translates these fluorescent signals to DNA sequence as illustrated across the top of the plot.

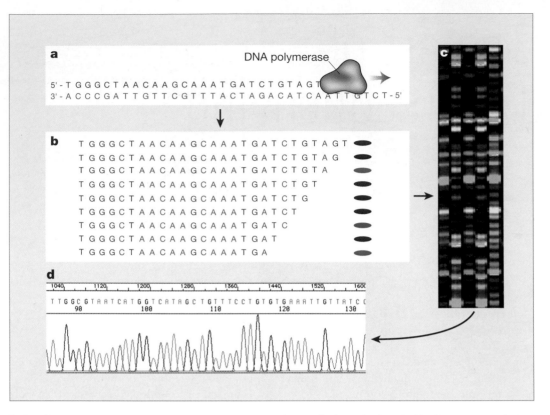

before inserting a terminator. Each of the terminator bases can be labelled with differently coloured dyes (for example, green, blue, yellow or red), which is important for distinguishing the fragments later.

Fragments of DNA can be separated according to their size. This is achieved by propelling the DNA through either a very thin sheet or a tiny capillary of acrylamide gel, a substance that is like firm jelly (or Jell-O). After the DNA samples are put onto the gel, an electric current is applied and the DNA fragments migrate towards the positive pole because the DNA itself has a negative charge – this process is known as gel electrophoresis. The gel is a densely packed meshwork through which the shorter fragments can move faster than the longer ones. After a few hours, this creates a ladder of DNA fragments spaced out along the gel, with the shortest at the bottom. Moving up the gel, each fragment is bigger than the previous one by just a single base.

How does this ladder of fragments translate into the sequence? Each fragment is tagged at its end with one of the four terminators labelled with different dyes. Gels used for sequencing are mounted onto specialized equipment and, as the fragments move through the gel, they pass a laser beam at a set point, which excites the dye, causing it to fluoresce in its particular colour. This fluorescent signal is captured by detectors and displayed as a coloured band on a computer monitor – the pattern thus looks like a 'ladder' of red, green, yellow and blue bands. The computer interprets the two pieces of information that it has for each band: the position (which indicates its length) and the colour (which identifies the base at the end of that fragment) and converts this information into the order of bases of the sequence.

Gel electrophoresis is limited by the number of bands that it can clearly resolve. For any sequencing reaction only about 500–800 bases can be read, so the DNA must first be cut into tiny pieces to be sequenced.

Getting automated – fast, faster, fastest

Technical wizardry, combined with intensive automation, has transformed the pace of DNA sequencing. Robots and computers are now used in every aspect of the process: performing the sequencing reactions, transferring the reactions onto gels, separating the fragments by electrophoresis, and reading the order of bases. Work that once took many days and many people can now be done in minutes, and a few staff members can keep the whole operation ticking 24 hours a day.

This is a far cry from the mid-1980s, when state-of-the-art laboratories could sequence only about 500 bases a day. Then Leroy Hood and his colleagues began to automate the process – their first sequencing machine could read up to 15 000 bases in a single day. The DNA-sequencing machines of today are even more powerful, and some can accurately sequence up to 400 000 bases per day. This has led to spectacu-

The origins of sequencing

Fred Sanger (left) and Walter Gilbert (below) shared the 1980 Nobel Prize for chemistry for their independently developed methods of sequencing DNA. For Sanger this was a second Nobel Prize, a feat achieved by only four people; his first was awarded in 1958 for work on the structure of proteins, in particular insulin. Sanger's chain-termination method (also known as the 'dideoxy' method after the chemistry of the terminator bases used in the reaction) is the most widely used today. Gilbert, together with Allan Maxam, developed an alternative strategy that uses chemical agents to cleave DNA specifically at A, C, G or T bases. The fragments, which are radioactively labelled, are separated by size on gels and exposed to film, and the resulting ladder is used to determine the sequence.

The Sanger Centre, near Cambridge, UK, is named after Fred Sanger. It is one of the largest sequencing centres in the world and deciphered roughly one-third of the human genome.

Walter Gilbert is notable for his entrepreneurial spirit, having launched several biotechnology companies. He also proposed the sequencing of the human genome as a commercial venture – more than ten years before the company Celera Genomics pursued this very goal.

lar progress: researchers of the HGP sequenced 90 per cent of the human genome in just 15 months.

The technology revolution triggered dramatic growth. Over the past decade the amount of

The sequence rainbow. The output from an automated DNA sequencing machine used to determine the complete human genome sequence. Each vertical lane shows the sequence of bases in a given stretch of DNA. Each of the four different bases is labelled with one of the four coloured dyes. The order of the bases is analysed by a computer and assembled to give the continuous base sequence for a segment of the genome. [Sanger Centre/Wellcome Photo Library]

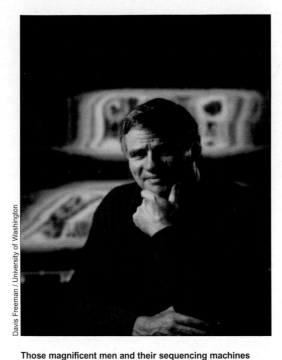

Davis Freeman / University of Washington

Those magnificent men and their sequencing machines

The first automated DNA-sequencing machine was invented by Leroy Hood (above), Lloyd Smith and Mike Hunkapiller (below) in 1985. They also improved Sanger's sequencing method by replacing unstable and hazardous radioisotope tags with fluorescent dyes of different colours to tag each of the four DNA terminator bases. Hood and Hunkapiller (and several others) set up Applied Biosystems Incorporated to market the gene-sequencing machine the following year.

In 1998, Hunkapiller's group at PE Biosystems developed a new sequencer, the ABI Prism 3700 DNA Analyzer, which was faster and even more automated than previous sequencers.

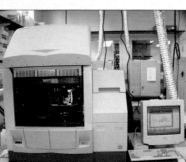

[Both images: Dr Eric Green National Human Genome Research Institute, NIH]

Most of the human genome was sequenced using two state-of-the-art sequencing machines: the ABI Prism 3700 DNA Analyzer (above left), and MegaBACE 1000 DNA Sequencing System (left), a product of Amersham Pharmacia Biotech.

sequence data collected worldwide has doubled every 18 months, while the cost of sequencing has halved. Thus sequencing volume is increasing, and the cost of sequencing is coming down by a factor of 10 every five years. This is reminiscent of the doubling of microprocessor speed every 18 months, which in the computing industry is known as Moore's law (named after Gordon Moore, co-founder of Intel), despite the fact that it's an observation rather than an actual law. The cost of sequencing has come down, from more than US$10 per base in the late 1980s to about 10 cents per base in 2001. These trends have not just accelerated the sequencing of the human genome; they have also fuelled genome projects for a wide range of animal, plant and microbial species.

Inside the molecular biologist's toolbox

Sequencing requires short stretches of DNA, so genomes must be cut into very small pieces, which are then copied in sufficient amounts for sequencing. Here we look at the tools required to chop up the genome and copy the pieces.

As scissors to clip DNA molecules at specific sites, scientists use proteins called 'restriction enzymes'. These proteins are produced naturally by bacteria as a defence against viral infection. Bacterial DNA is protected by a process known as methylation so that only foreign (viral) DNA is affected – chopping up the viral genome halts the infection. More than 3000 such enzymes have been isolated from different bacteria, each of which recognizes short stretches of DNA, typically 4–8 bases long. By using combinations of restriction enzymes, scientists can tailor the size of the DNA fragments that they desire.

The next step is to produce the large quantities of genomic fragments required for sequencing. This involves making copies (or 'clones') of the fragments. Most restriction enzymes don't leave nice, neat edges as they slice through double-stranded DNA. Instead, a few unpaired bases trail from one of the strands; the sequence of this overhang is specific to the particular restriction enzyme used. These bases can attach to complementary overhangs on other DNA molecules cut by the same enzyme, like flaps of Velcro sticking together. This allows the creation of new combinations, known as 'recombinant' molecules. An enzyme that welds the ends together – a so-called 'DNA ligase' – is used to prevent the recombinant molecules from becoming unfastened.

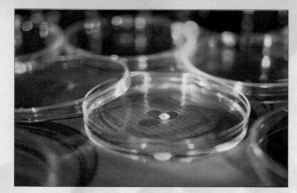

Tools of the trade. In 1970, Hamilton Smith purified the first restriction enzyme, a molecule that cuts DNA at specific sites. Smith shared a Nobel Prize in 1978 with Werner Arber and Daniel Nathans for the discovery of restriction enzymes and their application to molecular biology. Their work added 'molecular scissors' to the toolkit for manipulating DNA and paved the way for the development of genetic engineering.

In 1972, Paul Berg and Herbert Boyer cut and pasted together two DNA strands to create the first recombinant DNA molecule. The following year, Boyer, together with Stanley Cohen, created the first recombinant organism by splicing together sections of viral and bacterial DNA and transferring the resulting recombinant DNA molecule into a bacterial host. On the heels of this discovery, they cloned the first animal gene. They fused a frog gene that encodes ribosomal RNA (part of the cell's protein-synthesizing machinery) to DNA from a bacterium and put the recombinant DNA molecule back into a bacterial cell, where it produced the frog ribosomal RNA.

In 1977, a human gene was cloned by the first genetic engineering company, Genentech, which was co-founded by Herbert Boyer. The gene encoding somatostatin (an inhibitor of human growth hormone) was inserted into bacteria, which began making somatostatin. This was the first time a human protein had ever been produced by a living creature outside the human body. The following year, Genentech cloned human insulin which, when marketed in 1992, became the first recombinant-DNA drug.

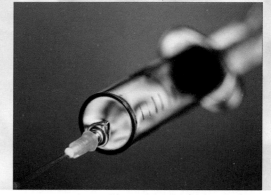

This approach is used to insert (or 'splice') the genomic DNA of interest into bacterial plasmids. Plasmids are tiny rings of DNA found inside bacteria that are copied independently of the bacterium's main genome. They can be manipulated in the laboratory and are easily isolated. The recombinant plasmid, bearing the inserted genomic DNA, is returned to its bacterial host, where it is copied as the bacterium divides. Thus, the bacteria can be thought of as tiny biological 'factories', making endless clones of the genomic DNA fragment.

The creation of recombinant molecules and their cloning into micro-organisms are much used techniques in molecular biology. The cloning of a DNA fragment should not be confused with the cloning of animals, such as Dolly, the famous cloned sheep. Cloning in molecular biology is simply the use of micro-organisms to reproduce limitless quantities of a DNA fragment – a sort of biological photocopying. The organisms used are usually bacteria, particularly the species *Escherichia coli*, which is a favourite workhorse of biologists.

Plasmids can comfortably carry small inserts of DNA but, as we shall see, bigger fragments are required for some purposes. To hold these, another type of package (or vector) called an artificial chromosome can be used. These can be inserted into bacteria or yeast, where they are replicated in the same way as normal chromosomes and are therefore termed bacterial or yeast artificial chromosomes (BACs or YACs) respectively. Inserts of more than 1 000 000 base pairs of genomic DNA can be carried by YACs, but these can be unstable, so BACs that hold up to 300 000 base pairs are more commonly used.

To ensure that the whole genome of the organism is sequenced, researchers produce DNA libraries. A DNA library is a collection of individually cloned fragments which together constitute the entire genome of the organism. These have a role analogous to that of conventional book libraries – storing an entire collection of information in a convenient, well-catalogued set of packages as a resource that can be used by anyone in the community.

Constructing an overlapping clone library. A collection of clones of chromosomal DNA, called a library, has no obvious order indicating the original positions of the cloned pieces on the uncut chromosome. To establish the order of cloned fragments, libraries of clones containing partly overlapping regions must be constructed. These clone libraries are ordered by dividing the inserts into smaller fragments and determining which clones share common DNA sequences.

Importantly, because of the way in which the cloned fragments are originally generated, many of the clones are partially overlapping so that the information is found in many entries.

Sequencing many overlapping entries might sound like a waste of time, but it actually serves two purposes: it ensures high accuracy in the final sequence, and the overlaps allow the fragment information to be reassembled into a single, complete set of information that represents the entire genome.

Piecing together the genome puzzle

Sequencing a genome is like doing an enormous jigsaw puzzle. First, the genome is cut into small pieces; next, the individual pieces are sequenced; and, finally, the pieces are put back together in the correct order. As noted above, the reason that the pieces can be put back together is that they are partially overlapping, allowing one fragment to be exactly fitted to the correct neighbour, just as the unique curves of jigsaw-puzzle pieces allow only one possible assembly of the puzzle.

The human genome poses a particularly daunting brainteaser. At roughly 3.2 gigabases (3 200 000 000 bases) it is 25 times larger than any previously sequenced genome; indeed, it is bigger than the combined number of bases sequenced in all previous genome projects by a factor of 8. Moreover, the abundance of DNA sequences that are repeated many times over – comprising over half of the genome – also poses a significant technical challenge, as one region could easily be mistaken for another when the sequence is assembled.

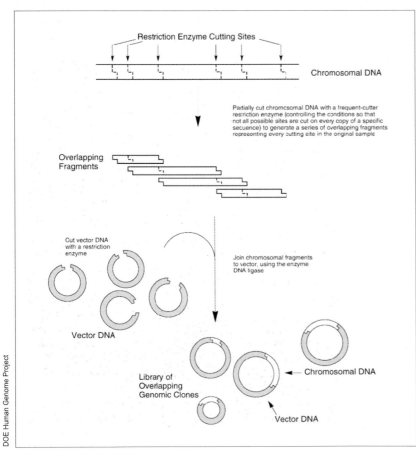

➤32

Making maps

Genome maps are constructed by determining the order of thousands of landmarks scattered across the DNA, and are usually needed before embarking on the sequencing of the genome. To explain mapping, let's try an analogy. Suppose that sequencing of the human genome is like flying across a continent, taking photographs that each cover 10 square miles. Assembly is equivalent to piecing these photographs together to get an accurate picture of the continent as a whole. Some landscapes and cityscapes would be easy to piece together because they contain recognizable landmarks – think of the Eiffel Tower, the Grand Canyon or the Great Pyramids – but others would be extremely difficult, such as deserts, featureless farmland or miles of suburbia. But imagine that before taking the photographs, every sector was labelled with a distinctive landmark. Now entire continents could be pieced together relatively easily. Different types of landmarks (or markers) can be used in genome mapping, but they must be unique sites that identify specific coordinates on a chromosome.

Aiding the map-making process, the human genome already naturally exists in smaller segments, namely the chromosomes. We have 22 pairs plus either two X chromosomes (in the case of females) or an X and a Y (for males). Each chromosome can be broken down into smaller maps that vary in the level of resolution, the type of marker used or the way in which the distances between markers are measured. Genome maps can be broadly classified as either genetic or physical.

During the formation of the sex cells, pairs of chromosomes break at specific sites and exchange equivalent pieces of DNA. If two sites on the DNA are close together, then the chance of their being separated and reshuffled during the formation of the sex cells is less than if they were far apart. This provides the conceptual basis for genetic (or linkage) maps. Such maps determine the order of specific DNA markers along a chromosome by examining how they are inherited through generations. Genetic maps only give the relative positions of markers, not their physical locations in the genome or actual distances, but their great power is in identifying genes that underlie physiological or morphological traits. They have proved extremely useful in the identification of important disease genes, including those involved in cystic fibrosis and sickle-cell anaemia.

Physical maps, on the other hand, determine the precise physical locations of landmarks in the genome; the distance from one landmark to the next is measured in base pairs. Some landmarks are variations in the DNA sequence that can be distinguished by whether they are cleaved by specific restriction enzymes – such landmarks are called 'restriction-fragment-length polymorphisms' (RFLPs). Other landmarks are short, repeated sequences that vary in the number of repeated units, and are known as 'variable number of tandem repeats' (VNTRs). Modern maps typically use short sequences of about 200–500 base pairs that occur only once in the genome; these are called 'sequence-tagged sites' (STSs).

The Human Genome Project

What is the Human Genome Project?
The Human Genome Project (HGP) is an international research programme that was set up to characterize the genomes of humans and other organisms; to develop the new technology needed to do so; and to address the ethical, legal and social implications of this new information. All the data produced are widely and freely available.
When did it start? The possibility of sequencing the human genome was first discussed in the mid-1980s. The HGP officially started in 1990 with a 15-year plan to map and sequence the human genome.
What was the plan? The HGP was launched with the aim of developing genomic tools and resources, and of mapping and sequencing the human and other genomes. Throughout the project, maps of human chromosomes have been made; sequencing technology has been improved; computational tools have been designed; and strategies for collecting, analysing and storing data have been developed. The study of the effect on society of large amounts of new genetic knowledge and technology, and the recommendation of policy to maximize the benefits and minimize the risks, have been an integral part of the HGP since its inception.

Initial efforts were focused on the genomes of laboratory organisms such as yeast (*Saccharomyces cerevisiae*) and the

Who is sequencing the human genome?
The group of scientists within the HGP that is sequencing the human genome is known as the International Human Genome Sequencing Consortium (IHGSC). It is composed of more than 2000 scientists at 20 institutions in 6 countries. The institutes are listed below in order of total genomic sequence contributed, with the first five centres producing the bulk (about 85%) of the sequence.

1. Whitehead Institute for Biomedical Research, Center for Genome Research, Cambridge, Massachusetts, USA
2. The Sanger Centre, Cambridge, UK
3. Washington University Genome Sequencing Center, St Louis, Missouri, USA
4. US Department of Energy Joint Genome Institute, Walnut Creek, California, USA
5. Baylor College of Medicine Human Genome Sequencing Center, Houston, Texas, USA
6. RIKEN Genomic Sciences Center, Yokohama, Japan
7. Genoscope and CNRS UMR-8030, Evry, France
8. GTC Sequencing Center, Waltham, Massachusetts, USA
9. Department of Genome Analysis, Institute of Molecular Biotechnology, Jena, Germany
10. Beijing Genomics Institute/Human Genome Center, Beijing, China
11. Multimegabase Sequencing Center, Institute for Systems Biology, Seattle, Washington, USA
12. Stanford Genome Technology Center, Stanford, California, USA
13. Stanford Human Genome Center, Stanford, California, USA
14. University of Washington Genome Center, Seattle, Washington, USA
15. Department of Molecular Biology, Keio University School of Medicine, Tokyo, Japan
16. University of Texas Southwestern Medical Center, Dallas, Texas, USA
17. University of Oklahoma Advanced Center for Genome Technology, Norman, Oklahoma, USA
18. Max Planck Institute for Molecular Genetics, Berlin, Germany
19. Cold Spring Harbor Laboratory, Lita

What is the 'working draft'? The working draft is an intermediate stage in the generation of the true goal of the HGP, a high-quality, 'finished' sequence of the human genome. In the working draft, each letter of the genetic code has been read at least four to five times (4–5× coverage). Although the draft sequence is very useful, it still has some gaps and ambiguities. The ultimate goal of the HGP is to produce a completely finished sequence, with no gaps and at least 99.99 per cent accuracy (which will require about 9× coverage). A finished, high-quality sequence is expected to be completed by the end of year 2003, two years earlier than originally planned.
Why 'finish' the sequence? The working draft has allowed a first view of the whole human genome. But a completely accurate, finished sequence is needed to compile a comprehensive inventory of genes and to identify the sequences involved in control mechanisms, which are embedded in the vast stretches of non-coding regions between genes.

An accurate reference sequence will also help to determine the variation that exists between the DNA of different individuals, how the sequence varies in distinct populations around the world, and how our DNA is different from that of our ancestors and closest relatives in the animal kingdom.
How fast do HGP scientists sequence?
Twenty years ago, deciphering 12 000 bases would have taken a year or more. Three years ago, when pilot sequencing projects to evaluate the feasibility of human DNA sequencing were initiated, sequencing 12 000 bases took 20 minutes. Today, the consortium churns out 1 000 bases of raw sequence per second, or 12 000 bases of 'working draft' per minute.

In 1990, when the HGP began, DNA sequencing probably cost at least US$10 per base. The process has been streamlined and automated to read sequences faster and more cheaply, reducing the cost to roughly 10 cents per base.
Whose DNA is being sequenced? The human reference sequence does not correspond to any one person's genome. The sequence is derived from the DNA of a large number of volunteers, who responded to local public advertisements near the laboratories where the DNA 'libraries' were being prepared. Researchers collected blood (male and female) or sperm samples (male only, obviously) from a large number of donors from diverse populations. About five to ten times as many volunteers donated samples as were eventually used and all identification was removed before samples were selected, so neither donors nor scientists know whose DNA has been sequenced.
Who has access to the human DNA sequence? Anyone who can log on to the Internet has full access to the sequence data held in public databases. Sequence assemblies of 1000–2000 bases are deposited into the databases within 24 hours of completion, and the data can be accessed without any restriction. The code of practice for rapid data release was agreed upon at a meeting of the HGP held in Bermuda in February 1996 and is known as the 'Bermuda principles'.

roundworm (*Caenorhabditis elegans*). These projects helped to refine DNA-sequencing technology and the conceptual strategies needed to tackle more complex genomes, and at the same time provided crucial information for interpreting the human sequence. Only a very small amount – as little as 1.5 per cent – of the human genome encodes proteins. Comparing human DNA with that of other organisms helps to identify human genes amongst the sea of sequences and also provides clues as to their function.

In 1996 a series of pilot sequencing projects was initiated to test the feasibility of deciphering the human genome. Within a couple of years, these efforts were deemed successful, and the large-scale (or 'high-throughput') effort to sequence the human genome was launched in March 1999. Around this time, the HGP adopted a strategy that would first generate a 'working draft', so that scientists would have useful data covering the entire genome as soon as possible, rather than having to wait for the sequence to be 'finished'.

With the infrastructure and resources in place, productivity skyrocketed, and more than 90 per cent of the sequence was produced in just 15 months. In February 2001, HGP scientists published the sequence, assembly and analysis of the working draft of the human genome.

Annenberg Hazen Genome Center, New York, USA
20. GBF German Research Centre for Biotechnology, Braunschweig, Germany

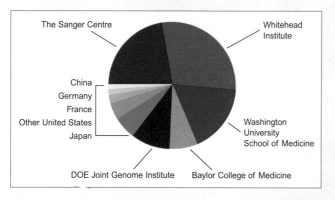

How much does it cost, and who pays?
About US$300 million has been spent world-wide to generate the draft sequence. The 15-year HGP effort has a total projected funding of US$3 billion (1990–2005), which encompasses a wide range of scientific activities related to genomics – the sequencing of the human genome represents only a fraction of the overall effort. Investment has been made in developing the technology and creating the resources to make large-scale sequencing feasible, allowing the sequencing of genomes of other organisms, the training of scientists, and the examination of the societal implications of genome research.

The project is funded by grants from government agencies and public charities in the various countries. These include the US National Institutes of Health (NIH), the US Department of Energy (DOE), the Wellcome Trust in the UK and the UK Medical Research Council, as well as agencies in Japan, France, Germany and China.

Where is it stored? There are international public nucleotide-sequence databases in the United States (GenBank), Europe (the European Bioinformatics Institute) and Japan (the DNA Database of Japan). These databases exchange information daily, so that all sequence information is available from any of the three.

As well as sequence data for the human genome, these databases contain the complete genome sequences of 'model' organisms (those most frequently used in the laboratory) such as yeast, worm, fruit fly and many microbes, as well as DNA sequences from other genomes that are currently being sequenced. Scientists in their thousands access the databases every day.

Links to the databases as well as other human-genome resource sites can be found at:

http://www.ensembl.org/genome/central
and
http://www.ncbi.nlm.nih.gov/genome/central

Also see Box 2 on page 88

There are two basic approaches to solving the puzzle of genome sequencing. One is the 'map-based' or 'clone-by-clone' method. This is a hierarchical process in which the genome is broken up into progressively smaller segments. The sequence of the smallest pieces is determined and the pieces are then reassembled into progressively larger segments until the entire genome has been pieced back together. The first set of large segments is used to build a physical map, which determines the origin of each segment within the genome and the position of each of the segments relative to all the others. Then each of these segments is diced into small,

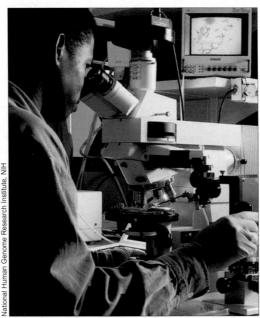

National Human Genome Research Institute, NIH

overlapping pieces and sequenced, a process that has been termed 'shotgun sequencing'. Once all the sequences have been determined, the overlaps are used to reconstruct the continuous sequence of the large segment and these are then assembled to give the whole genome. The overall approach is also known as the hierarchical shotgun method.

An alternative strategy is to shatter the entire genome and sequence all of the tiny pieces directly, completely bypassing the construction of a physical map. Computer programs assemble the millions of sequenced fragments into continuous stretches, ultimately reassembling the full genome. These programs consist of a staggered series of mathematical steps that sort, edit and assemble fragments, and are typically designed so that the easier steps are done first, followed by the harder moves. This

strategy is called the whole-genome shotgun method.

How do the two methods compare, using the jigsaw-puzzle analogy? Blank side up, all the pieces look roughly the same. Turning them over (sequencing) shows you the picture on each piece. After this, they can be assembled in two different ways. One is by comparing the pieces with the picture on the box; for example by gathering and piecing together all the blue and white bits that make up the sky. This is equivalent to a map-based method, with the picture serving the function of the map. The alternative is to take each piece individually and figure out which other pieces or clusters it fits with. This is analogous to the whole-genome shotgun method.

Both approaches have been used successfully. A map-based method was used to sequence the first eukaryotic genome, the baker's yeast *Saccharomyces cerevisiae*, and for the first animal genome, the roundworm *Caenorhabditis elegans*. The first free-living microbe to be sequenced, the bacterium *Haemophilus influenzae*, was sequenced using a whole-genome shotgun method, as was the genome of the fruit fly *Drosophila melanogaster*.

The two methods each have their advantages and disadvantages. The map-based approach is reliable, and the maps have other uses besides sequence assembly. Much of the sequencing technology in use today was developed in laboratories that used this method in the late 1980s and 1990s, providing a valuable foundation for much of the work on the human genome. But the construction of maps is time consuming, particularly for a genome the size of a human's. On the other hand, whole-genome shotgunning is (potentially) very fast, but the reconstruction of a genome from so many tiny pieces poses obvious challenges.

Which method was used on the human genome? The answer is both. Researchers of the HGP, on which we concentrate here, primarily used the map-based approach, constructing a physical map of the whole genome that was used to assemble the sequence. However, whole-genome shotgun data were an important aspect of their strategy. And whole-genome shotgunning was the primary technique used by the company Celera Genomics, although its assembly also incorporated map-based data. In other words, as with solving jigsaw puzzles, a mixed strategy can often be best.

Celera Genomics

WHAT IS CELERA?

As indicated by its name (meaning 'swift' in Latin) and its slogan 'Discovery can't wait', Celera is very much about speed. Launched in 1998 in Rockville, Maryland, with J. Craig Venter at the helm, the company set out with an ambitious plan to sequence the human genome in just three years.

Celera's first major project was the sequencing of the fruit fly *Drosophila melanogaster* genome. Upon successful completion, sequencing of the human genome began in September 1999. The sequence was generated over nine months and, together with the sequence data made freely available by the Human Genome Project (HGP), Celera assembled the genome. In a joint announcement on 26 June 2000, the HGP and Celera celebrated their respective first assemblies of the human genome. Celera went on to publish its initial analysis in the 16 February 2001 issue of *Science*, the same week that the public effort reported their findings in *Nature*.

WHAT WAS CELERA'S APPROACH?

Celera used whole-genome shotgunning (WGS) to sequence the human genome. Chromosomes were randomly sheared into millions of pieces of 2 000 and 10 000 base pairs in length. The pieces were inserted into plasmid vectors (to create DNA 'libraries') and propagated in *E. coli* to produce millions of copies of each fragment. A key feature of Celera's approach is that both ends of each fragment of DNA are sequenced (called 'paired-end sequencing') to help determine the order and orientation of the fragments during assembly.

Combining Celera's sequence and the HGP's data, computer algorithms assembled the millions of sequenced fragments into a continuous stretch of the human genome. Two methods of assembly were used: a whole-genome assembly algorithm and compartmentalized shotgun assembly (CSA), whereby the genome data are divided into segments or compartments, which are then assembled. The CSA assembly was used for the annotation reported in *Science*. Comparing the two assemblies served as an accuracy check of the assembly process.

WHOM DID CELERA SEQUENCE?

To sequence the human genome, Celera used DNA samples collected from five donors who identified themselves as Hispanic, Asian, African-American or Caucasian. The five people (two men and three women) whose genomes were used were selected from a pool of twenty-one individuals, who volunteered in response to newspaper advertisements and outreach efforts.

SEQUENCING POWER, COMPUTING POWER

The speed of Celera's genomic sequencing is dependent upon a powerful, highly automated sequencing machine, called ABI Prism 3700 DNA Analyzer. With 300 of these sequencers running day and night, it isn't surprising that Celera clocked up an electricity bill of around US$1 million a year!

Computers played a huge role in the genome assembly. Celera relied on high-performance computer technology to manage the more than 80 terabytes of data and to perform what are believed to be some of the most complex computations in the history of supercomputing. The calculation to perform the initial assembly involved 500 million trillion sequence comparisons requiring over 20 000 CPU (central processor unit) hours on Celera's supercomputer. Celera's final assembly computations required 64 gigabytes of memory.

Assembling the human genome

The members of the HGP created a high-resolution map to help to assemble the genome sequence. They derived the physical map using the following strategy. Human DNA was cut into fragments of 100 000–200 000 base pairs using restriction enzymes, after which the fragments were cloned into bacterial artificial chromosomes (BACs) and inserted into bacteria, which stored and replicated the human DNA so that it could be prepared in sufficient quantities for sequencing. A collection of clones containing an entire genome is called a BAC library – it took about 20 000 BAC clones to store the human genome.

The BAC clones were then 'fingerprinted'; that is, they were cut with a restriction enzyme to generate a unique pattern of fragments. By comparing the fingerprints of different clones, it was possible to identify ones that overlap with each other (because they contain a similar subset of fragments) and thus to order the BAC clones. Each BAC clone was also 'mapped' to determine where its human DNA came from within the set of human chromosomes. This was done by looking for recognizable

Genome Gallery

A selection of notable genomes that have been sequenced.

Φ X 174
(1977) 5386 bp
First genome sequenced, a bacteriophage

Haemophilus influenzae
(1995) 1 830 000 bp
First genome of a free-living organism

Mycoplasma genitalium
(1995) 580 000 bp
Smallest genome of any free-living organism

David Scharf / Science Photo Library

Saccharomyces cerevisiae
(1996) 12 100 000 bp
First genome of a 'eukaryotic' (nucleus-containing) organism, the yeast used by brewers and bakers

Methanococcus jannaschii
(1996) 1 660 000 bp
The first genome from the third kingdom, *Archae*, which comprises microbes that live in harsh environments, for example thermal springs

Escherichia coli
(1997) 4 670 000 bp
Workhorse bacterium for biologists

Helicobacter pylori
(1997) 1 660 000 bp
Bacterium associated with gastric disease

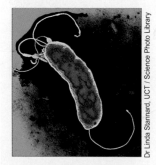
Dr Linda Stannard, UCT / Science Photo Library

Genome Gallery

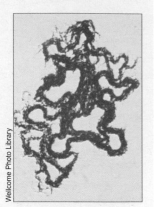

Mycobacterium tuberculosis
(1998) 4 400 000 bp
Cause of the disease
tuberculosis

Caenorhabditis elegans
(1998) 97 000 000 bp
The first genome sequence
of an animal, the roundworm

Deinococcus radiodurans
(1999) 2 600 000 bp Highly
radiation-resistant bacterium

First human chromosomes
(1999 and **2000)**
Chromosomes 22,
48 000 000 bp and 21,
45 000 000 bp respectively

Drosophila melanogaster
(2000) 180 000 000 bp
Fruit fly, an important laboratory organism in genetics

genomic landmarks in each BAC clone. Integration of all this information generated a physical map of the genome, from which the precise genomic location of the sequence from each clone, and its spatial relation to the human DNA in other BAC clones, could be determined.

For sequencing, each BAC clone was cut into smaller, overlapping fragments of about 2000 base pairs in length. These were inserted into plasmids and a sequencing reaction was performed at each end of the plasmid clones. The full sequence of the BAC clone was derived by piecing together the sequences from all these tiny fragments, first to form longer-sequence 'contigs' (short for 'contiguous sequences'), and eventually to obtain a single-sequence contig representing the entire human fragment carried by the BAC in question. As the order and overlap of BAC clones were known from the physical map, even longer stretches of sequence could then be assembled. Ultimately, the contigs were fitted together to assemble whole chromosomes and eventually the entire sequence of the human genome.

Going from a sequence of 500 base pairs produced by a sequencing machine to a genome of 3 200 000 000 base pairs is a mind-boggling leap that requires huge computing power. Literally millions of sequence reads are generated, and the data are then fed into 'assembler' programs, which identify and merge overlaps in the sequence.

Quality control is obviously very important. Software has been developed to monitor the quality of the raw sequence data and to assess the likelihood that the base identified by the 'base-calling' program is the correct one. Sequence reads that contain a lot of errors or ambiguities are weeded out before they are fed into the assembly programs. PHRED (pronounced 'Fred') is the standard software program used to assign quality values to each base read by the sequencing machine. The standard computer program that then assembles overlapping sequences is called PHRAP (pronounced 'Frap'). Both of these programs were developed by Phil Green and colleagues at the University of Washington.

Although assembly computer programs can sift through conflicting information and make predictions about which sequence is likely to be correct, the assembly and final polishing are done by humans. Experts, known as finishers, painstakingly identify every gap and ambiguity,

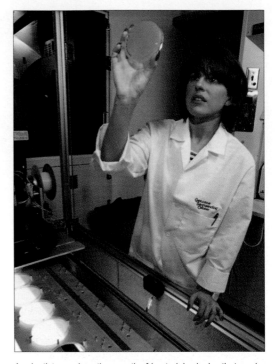

A scientist examines the growth of bacterial colonies that can be used as 'factories' for making many copies of human genomic fragments. [Robert Boston / Washington University School of Medicine in St Louis]

and work out what experiments need to be done to fill in the missing pieces and resolve the discrepancies. The genome sequence must be read many times over to be sure that no base has been missed or misread by the sequencing machines. Some stretches are easy to read and need to be sequenced only a few times to determine the order of the bases accurately. For other regions, the sequence must be read many times to generate a high-quality sequence. The number of times that a genome sequence is re-read is called the 'depth of coverage'.

The goal of the HGP is to generate a high-quality 'finished' sequence for the human genome. The agreed standard for the finished sequence is that each letter should be designated as 99.99 per cent accurate, which means there will be no more than 1 error per 10 000 bases. To achieve this, each base must be read an average of nine times (that is, it will have 9× depth of coverage). This level of accuracy is needed to recognize all genes and their regulatory components, and to detect variation between different human genomes.

The human genome sequence published in February 2001 is a working draft – in other words, it isn't finished yet. In all, it encompasses over 90 per cent of the euchromatic region of the genome – some 2 950 000 000 base pairs – in which most genes are found and where the DNA adopts a relatively 'open' conformation. (Other portions of the genome, known as heterochromatic regions, which include the centres and ends of chromosomes, are considered to be in a 'closed' conformation.) Each base of the working draft has at least 4–5× coverage, and has an accuracy of at least 99.9 per cent. But some regions have been read many more times and, in fact, roughly one-third was already in 'finished' form, including two entire chromosomes (21 and 22), at the time of publication.

The working draft contains many gaps and ambiguities. It's like having a book with some pages missing, some words in the wrong order or on the wrong page, and lots of typographical errors. What causes gaps and misassemblies? Often they occur because the chemical properties of particular stretches of DNA make them harder to clone and sequence. Repetitive regions of DNA, of which the human genome has many, can be especially difficult to handle. They can be troublesome to clone because of their instability; they can be difficult to sequence because they confuse DNA polymerase; and they can complicate the assembly because identical-looking regions can be mistaken for one another.

The human genome sequence will be finished when all the gaps are closed and ambiguities resolved (as far as current technology allows). The goal of the HGP is to produce a finished version of the human genome sequence by the year 2003 – hopefully in time for the 50th anniversary of the discovery of the structure of DNA by Watson and Crick.

Making sense of the sequence

An assembled genome sequence can amount to little more than a long, featureless string of letters. To be of real value it must be 'annotated', meaning that information about genes, the proteins they encode, and other interesting features are ascribed to specific stretches of the sequence. Making sense of a DNA sequence the size of the human genome is a more formidable task than the sequencing itself.

Researchers enlist the power of computers to scrutinize the jumble of bases. These reveal patterns suggestive of genes or other features that help to deduce how the genome is wired. The development of computer-driven methods for extracting biological information from sequences is part of a rapidly expanding field of science known as bioinformatics, which straddles the boundaries of biology, computer science and mathematics. It involves the storage, retrieval, analysis and integration of biological data to identify genes, determine their structures and predict their functions. Analysis of DNA sequences is just one part of the field, which also encompasses analysis of protein structure, gene and protein functions, pre-clinical and clinical trial information, and studies of metabolic pathways in numerous species.

Finding human genes can be a difficult task. Not only do they make up a tiny percentage of the genome, but they tend to be split into a multitude of small coding 'exons' (the instructions for making proteins), separated by much longer stretches of non-coding sequence called 'introns'. There are several ways to identify genes in a long sequence. One is to look for the tell-tale signatures of gene structures. Another is to look for sequences that match known gene sequences from other organisms on the assumption that, if they have been conserved through evolution, such sequences are likely to be functional. A third approach is to search for evidence that a DNA sequence is copied into messenger RNA, suggesting that the sequence encodes a real gene. Although each of these approaches has limitations, they are powerful in combination.

The 'working draft' provides a good first view of the landscape of the human genome. It allows new genes to be identified and tentative predictions to be made about the functions of genes or families of genes. It can also be used to learn about the types and distribution of repeated elements in the human genome, to characterize duplications and to identify so-called 'pseudogenes', which are genes that no longer function but can provide insights into genetic evolution. At present, the speed at which sequence data are being acquired greatly exceeds our capacity to understand it and to put it into a proper biological context. Furthermore, as with the translation of a vast and complex script in an unknown language, there is potential for multiple interpretations. Researchers have designed annotation programs that can create significantly different genome schematics. The challenge of the future will be to resolve these differences and to refine our view of the genome.

Genome Gallery

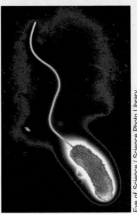

Vibrio cholerae
(2000) 4 030 000 bp
Cause of the disease cholera

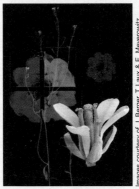

Arabidopsis thaliana
(2000) 120 000 000 bp
The first genome of a plant, the mustard weed

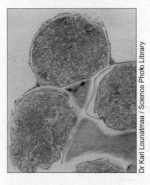

Mycobacterium leprae
(2001) 3 270 000 bp
Cause of the disease leprosy

Timeline of the human genome project

The completion of the draft human genome sequence by the HGP is the culmination of more than a decade of work, involving 20 sequencing centres in six countries. Here are some of the key moments.

Mid 1980s

Scientists begin to discuss plans for a mammoth project to sequence the complete human genome. Charles DeLisi, then director of health and environmental research at the Department of Energy (DOE), also explores the feasibility of such a project and DOE funding begins in 1987.

1988

The National Institutes of Health (NIH) establishes the Office of Human Genome Research in September 1988. Renamed the National Centre for Human Genome

Peter Menzel / Science Photo Library

Research (NCHGR) a year later, its director is James Watson, co-discoverer of the double helix structure of DNA. Watson's testimony to the US Congress, in which he pledged to devote a small fraction of the project's budget to 'ethical, legal and social' issues, had proved instrumental in garnering political support.

Early 1990s

With sequencing still slow and expensive, the genome project adopts a 'map-first, sequence-later' strategy. In the early 1990s, two Parisian laboratories, the Centre d'Etude du Polymorphisme Humain and Généthon, have an integral role in

mapping – underlining the project's international character. The labs' driving forces are Daniel Cohen and Jean Weissenbach. Later, the genome project constructs a higher-resolution map that is used to sequence and assemble the human genome.

1992

In April 1992, Watson resigns as head of NCHGR after clashing with then-NIH director Bernadine Healy over the patenting of gene fragments. Francis Collins (below)

NIH

of the University of Michigan is appointed director of NCHGR in April 1993.

In June 1992, Craig Venter leaves NIH to set up The Institute for Genomic Research (TIGR) in Rockville, Maryland. TIGR later sequences a host of bacterial genomes, starting with *Haemophilus influenzae*, the first free-living organism to be sequenced.

1996

In February 1996, at a meeting in Bermuda, international partners in the genome project agree to formalize the

SUPER MODELS

The complete genome sequences of model organisms are proving immensely valuable to biologist working on these species, and will also help interpret the human genome sequence. Published highlights to date include the yeast *Saccharomyces cerevisiae* (May 1997), the nematode *Caenorhabditis elegans* (December 1998), the fruit fly *Drosophila melanogaster* (March 2000, above), and the plant *Arabidopsis thaliana* (December 2000, right).

AVP, LSHTM/Wellcome Photo Library

Images courtesy of J. Berger, T. Laux & E. Meyerowitz

DOE

conditions of data access, including release of sequence data into public databases within 24 hours. These came to be known as the 'Bermuda principles'.

1998

In May 1998, Craig Venter (left) forms a company to sequence the human genome within three years. The company, later named Celera, will use an ambitious 'whole-genome shotgun' method, which involves assembling the genome without using maps. But its data release policy will not follow the Bermuda principles.

1999

The public project responds to Venter's challenge. By early 1999, it is on track to produce a draft genome sequence by 2000. Increasingly, the bulk of the

sequencing takes place in five huge centres dubbed the 'G5': at the Whitehead Institute for Biomedical Research in Cambridge Massachusetts; the Sanger Centre near Cambridge, UK; Baylor College of Medicine in Houston; Washington University in St Louis; and the DOE's Joint Genome Institute (JGI) in

Walnut Creek, California. Here, Robert Waterson of Washington University in St Louis and John Sulston of the Sanger Centre are pictured in a rare moment of relaxation. Trevor Hawkins and Elbert Branscomb of JGI prepare samples (below).

1999–2000

The first sequence of a human chromosome – number 22 – is published in December 1999. Chromosome 21 follows in May 2000, a collaborative effort led by German and Japanese groups.

2000

On 26 June 2000, leaders of the public project and Celera announce completion of a working draft of the human genome sequence. Collins and Venter are seen

here on television with Ari Patrinos of the DOE, who cut through the animosity between the rival projects to broker the joint announcement at the White House in Washington.

2001

The assembly and analysis of the drafts of the human genome are published by the public project in *Nature* on 15 February and by Celera in *Science*'s 16 February issue.

We are grateful for contributions and input from Francis Collins, Richard Gibbs, Eric Green, Trevor Hawkins, Victor McKusick and John McPherson.

TECHNICAL GURUS

Without advances in sequencing technology, we would still be waiting to unveil our genetic blueprint. Double Nobel laureate Fred Sanger (pictured) of the Laboratory of Molecular Biology in Cambridge invented the now commonly used technique of gene sequencing back in the 1970s. In 1986, Leroy Hood, then at the California Institute of Technology in Pasadena, introduced the first automated sequencing machine. During the 1990s, the development of high-throughput capillary sequencing machines enabled the rapid sequencing progress of the past two years. Assembling fragments of the genome into a complete sequence, meanwhile, depended heavily on computer programs developed by Philip Green of the University of Washington in Seattle.

Highlights of our genome

Twenty-four chromosomes, 3.2 billion bases and around 31 000 genes – some theories confirmed, a few surprises and a hatful of mysteries. Welcome to your genome. In this chapter, we highlight the key discoveries from the genome sequence so far, as reported in the seminal paper by the International Human Genome Sequencing Consortium, which is reproduced later in this book.

What do we have in hand? A map and a 'working draft' sequence for most of the 'euchromatic' region of the genome, comprising 2.95 billion bases of the 3.2-billion total. Most of the genes are located here and the DNA is in an 'open' conformation. The small remainder of the genome is composed of 'heterochromatin' – large blocks of densely packaged sequence that are commonly found at the centres and ends of chromosomes and consist almost entirely of repetitive DNA.

The term 'draft' may underplay the status of the work – in all it encompasses over 90 per cent of the genome, each base being sequenced with at least 99.9 per cent accuracy. At the time of publication, about one-third of the genome sequence was 'finished'; that is, sequenced at 99.99 per cent accuracy (less than 1 error in every 10 000 bases). The missing bits are mostly regions that have proved difficult to clone and/or sequence. So although there are acknowledged holes and ambiguities scattered across this vast four-letter scroll, the sequence provides an invaluable new resource.

Where are all the genes?

If a fly, a worm and a mustard weed can get by with 13 000, 18 000 and 26 000 genes respectively, how many genes are needed to make a human being? Previously, numbers up to and

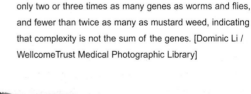

Complexity is not in gene numbers. Humans seem to have only two or three times as many genes as worms and flies, and fewer than twice as many as mustard weed, indicating that complexity is not the sum of the genes. [Dominic Li / WellcomeTrust Medical Photographic Library]

Human	Thale cress	Nematode worm	Fruit fly	Yeast	Tuberculosis microbe
31 000	26 000	18 000	13 000	6 000	4 000

beyond 150000 have been bandied about. However, in something of a blow to our collective ego, it seems that there are only 30000–40000 human genes.

The proteins encoded by these genes can be grouped into families on the basis of their similarity to one another, and it turns out that we share most of the same protein families with worms, flies and plants – although the numbers of family members are greater in humans. This expansion is particularly evident in the genes that drive development by signalling between cells. Humans have thirty fibroblast growth-factor genes, whereas flies and worms have two each; similarly, humans have forty-two transforming growth-factor genes, of which flies and worms have nine and six respectively. Such differences are also apparent in the proteins of the immune system: humans have 765 genes that encode immunoglobulin subunits or 'domains' (such as those in antibodies), whereas the fly has 140, the worm has 64, and the mustard weed and yeast have none at all.

The remaining extra human genes are not primarily the result of the invention of new types of protein in vertebrates – only 7 per cent of identified protein and protein-domain families are truly unique to vertebrates. Rather, new proteins arise from reshuffling the number and order of protein domains, a process that is analogous to making different structures with the same Lego pieces.

If the increasing complexity of humans isn't due to a significant increase in gene numbers, then what might explain it? No single dominant property stands out. Instead, a mixed bag of features combines to enhance innovation greatly. One example is 'alternative splicing' of RNA; once RNA has been copied from a gene sequence, the non-coding intron sequences are spliced out to bring the coding sequences of the exons next to one another. By skipping an exon here and there, the splicing machinery can create new products. Around 60 per cent of human genes are predicted to have two or more alternatively spliced RNAs, compared, for example, with only 22 per cent in the worm. So instead of producing only one protein, the average human gene produces several.

Another factor is the lavish supply of proteins – called 'transcription factors' – that switch genes on or off. Some families of transcription factors, such as the 'zinc-finger' family, have expanded independently in humans, yeast, flies

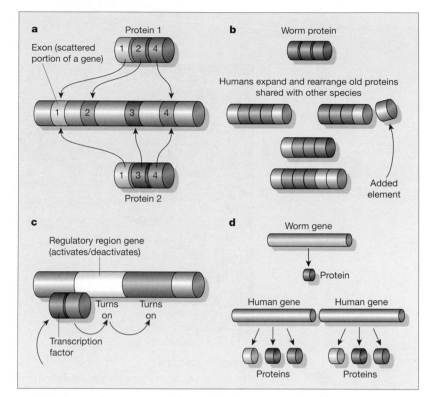

Manufacturing complexity

Although humans do not have many times more genes than simpler creatures, a variety of processes has created layers of complexity.

a) More than one protein can be made from the same gene by a process known as alternative splicing. The separate protein-encoding sections of genes, known as exons, can be skipped, giving rise to an assortment of proteins that either lack or contain the specific protein domains encoded by different exons.

b) Rather than creating entirely new protein domains, humans have rearranged the number and order of protein domains encoded within genes to come up with new combinations.

c) Humans have created unique patterns of gene expression by using different ways to modulate the times and places genes are turned on, including expanding the repertoire of transcription factors that control gene expression.

d) Simpler organisms, such as the worm, produce only one protein per gene. In contrast, an average human gene produces several different proteins, and sometimes as many as five. This is done by alternative splicing, as well as by modification of proteins after they are made, for example by addition of fats, sugars or chemical groups.

[Majo Xeridat]

and worms – but humans still have twice as many zinc-finger proteins as flies and almost five times as many as worms. Meanwhile, proteins themselves can be modified, for example by enzymes snipping bits off, or by the addition of sugars or fats that alter their activity.

This builds into a picture of complex and exquisite control of genes and proteins, with genes being turned on and off, and up and down, with extraordinary subtlety. This finely tuned regulation of our gene activity drives our development from fertilized egg to adult, and maintains and repairs our bodies during the rigours of daily life.

Genome cartography

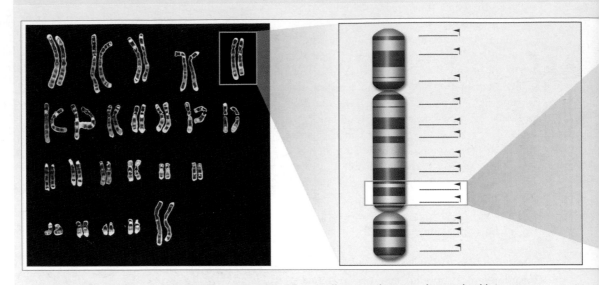

Above: Zooming in on the genome. [The Wellcome Trust]

Sequencers and mappers informed each other of their efforts throughout the Human Genome Project, thereby building up a contoured geography of the chromosomes. The sequence-analysis paper was accompanied by a series of different maps of the genome. What do the more panoramic views of the genome landscape tell us?

At the highest magnification, of course, there is the almost endless stream of As, Cs, Gs and Ts.

From a distance, these can be resolved into gene structures, regulatory regions and other recognizable genetic features. One of the maps, showing single-nucleotide polymorphisms (SNPs), charts the naturally occurring genomic variation in the human population.

Zooming further out, the physical map provides a surveyor's chart of the whole genome, with almost every sequence captured in a cloned fragment. Finally, the bird's-eye view is of whole chromosomes decorated with tags at regular

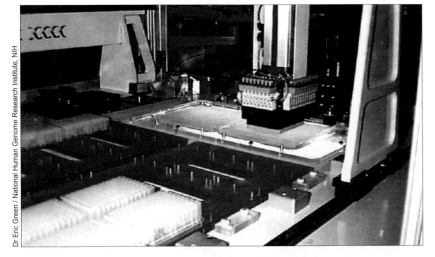

Genome terrain

The general arrangement of the genome provides another startling jolt. In some ways it may resemble your garage/bedroom/refrigerator/life: highly individualistic and unkempt, with little evidence of organization and much accu-

mulated clutter (referred to as 'junk' DNA). Virtually nothing is ever discarded, and the few patently valuable items are scattered indiscriminately, apparently carelessly.

These patently valuable items are the genes themselves. The actual sequence that codes for proteins, the exons, takes up only a few per cent of the genome, whereas the intervening sequences, the introns, account for 24 per cent. Genes are unevenly scattered across the genome and typically stick together, prompting geneticists to call the topography of our genome 'lumpy'. Some genes crowd together in particular regions like dense urban centres, whereas others are dotted across vast expanses of desolate 'deserts' of sequence. This exaggerated terrain of the human genome is distinct from that of other organisms, such as the fly, worm and mustard weed, in which the genes are much more regularly spaced.

Roughly half of the human genome consists of repetitive sequences, with the vast majority of

Genome cartography

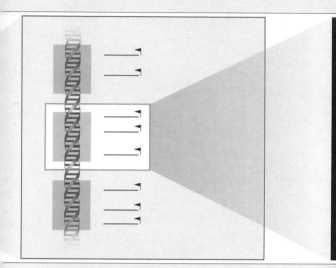

```
ATTAGAGGCTCACCGATTCATGTCGGAGATGGTCAGAAAAC
CGTTTCAGAAGCAACCTTGGGCTTAGTCCCACCCTTTTTAGGC
GTGCCTAGAAAGATGACAACTCAAGCACCGACGTTTACGCAG
GTACTGGAGGGTAGTACCGCAACCTTTGAGGCTCACATTAGT
GTGAGCTGGTTTAGGGATGGCCAGGTGATTTCCACTTCCACTC
TCCTTTAGCGATGGCCGCGCTAAACTGACGATCCCCGCCGTGA
CGATATTCCCTGAAAGCCACCAATGGATCTGGACAAGCGACT
GTGAAAGCTGAGACAGCACCACCCAACTTCGTTCAACGACTG
CAAGGAAGCCAAGTGAGACTCCAAGTGAGAGTGACTGGAATC
TTCTACCGGGATGGAGCCGAAATCCAGAGCTCCCTTGATTTCC
GACCTCTACAGCTTACTGATTGCAGAAGCATACCCTGAGGACT
AATGCCACCAATAGCGTTGGAAGAGCTACTTCGACTGCTGAAT
GAGAAGTACCTGCTAAAAAGACAAAGACAATTGTTTCGACT
AGACAAACCCGAATTGAAAAGAAGATTGAAGCCCACTTTGAT
GTTGAGATGGTCATAGATGGTGCCGCTGGGCAACAGCTGCCAC
ATTCCTCCGATCATAGA
```

intervals; this is the cytogenic map, the anchor at the whole-genome level upon which the sequence and clone maps depend.

During the formation of the sex cells, each of the twenty-three pairs of chromosomes briefly come together and exchange equivalent segments in the process of recombination. The advantage of this interchange is that it mixes the gene pool, allowing the creation of new combinations of traits. Analysis of the genome sequence reveals that the rate of recombination varies strikingly across the genome: short chromosome arms have a higher rate of recombination than long arms or the central regions of the chromosomes. Within this general pattern are recombination 'deserts', where recombination is sparse, and 'jungles', where exchange is frequent. Understanding these patterns of recombination frequency across the genome will be important for mapping the genes that cause disease.

A diverse genome landscape

Below: A look at the composition of our genome reveals a rich terrain. About 41 per cent is made up of either G or C bases; the rest is composed of A and T. Roughly half of our genome is repeat sequences. The majority of repeated sequences are transposable 'parasitic' elements, such as LINEs and SINEs, the most prolific member of the latter being Alu elements. About 5 per cent of the genome is made up of large duplicated regions. Genes occupy about a quarter of the genome, but only about 1.5 per cent encodes for proteins, the rest being non-coding stretches of DNA called introns that separate the protein-coding exons. [The Wellcome Trust]

these (around 45%) accounted for by repeats derived from 'parasitic' DNA sequences known as transposable elements, or transposons. These elements propagate by replicating and then inserting a new copy of themselves into another site in the genome. The sheer number of repeated elements is unprecedented in any other sequenced genome; repeats account for just 1.5 per cent of a typical bacterial genome and 3 per cent in the fly, 7 per cent in the worm and 11 per cent in the mustard weed.

Curiously, much of the repeat content of our genome represents ancient remnants of 'long-dead' transposons; in contrast, the fly and mouse genomes harbour large numbers of younger, more active elements. Only two mobile elements are known still to be active in the human genome: they are called long interspersed element 1 (LINE1) and Alu. Together, LINE1 and Alu account for more than 60 per cent of all repeated sequences in our genome. The sequence of LINE1 encodes the machinery it needs to copy itself. Alu, however, cannot replicate by itself; it uses the machinery of LINE1 elements to reproduce and is therefore something of a freeloader. And a very successful freeloader it is: Alu is the most abundant transposable element, with a million copies littering the human genome.

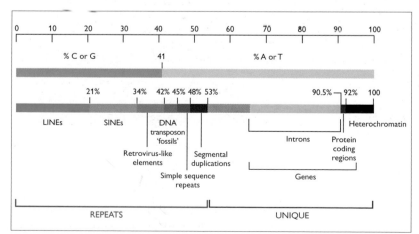

Most transposable elements entered our ancestral genome more than 100 million years ago, long before mammals with placentas (eutherian mammals) evolved. Some types of transposons flourished, such as LINE1 and Alu elements. Others seem to have found the environment unsavoury; for example, only faint traces of another group of transposable elements called LTR retrotransposons are detectable in the human genome – although they are alive and kicking in the mouse genome. DNA transposons, another type of repeat, have marked our genome with two bursts of activity: before and after the evolution of placental mammals.

Most repetitive elements are not under strict pressure to maintain the integrity of sequence as the genome is passed through generations,

T J McMaster / Wellcome Trust Medical Photographic Library

Robert Boston / Washington University School of Medicine in St Louis

because they do not code for a functional product. So these repeats accumulate mutations and their sequences diverge over time. Tracking the migration of repetitive elements (by tracing the sequence changes) as they wandered through the genome during human evolution opens a

fascinating window on our past. Genetic archaeologists are sifting through the repeat sequences to figure out the pattern and timing of genetic changes in order to reconstruct the history of our genome and of the evolution of our species.

Why does the genome carry such a heavy load of parasitic DNA? Are we unusually sloppy at cleaning out the ancient debris of past invaders? Could we be considered simply as vehicles for the proliferation of these selfish elements? Or do we retain them because they serve some useful purpose? It is likely that there is some truth in each of these propositions. There is evidence that transposons shaped the evolution of the genome and mediated the creation of new genes. Fragments of transposons are found in the regulatory sequences that control the expression of several hundred genes. So it is not inconceivable that, at least in part, transposons are retained because they help to regulate the expression of certain genes.

Just as our genes are unevenly distributed, so too are the repeat elements. Most elements, including LINE1, are found in portions of the genome that are rich in A and T. This tends to separate them from genes, which usually congregate in areas of high GC content. Thus, the mobile elements are relegated to areas where they are less likely to disrupt gene sequences and damage their hosts. In contrast, Alu repeats are more common in GC-rich regions. The reason for this preferential distribution has puzzled geneticists, but it suggests that Alu may positively influence genes and contribute favourably towards their expression or evolution.

Seeing double

Duplications also seem to have played a significant role in genome evolution, as roughly 5 per cent of the sequence has arisen through duplication of large blocks (more than 10 000 base pairs) within and between chromosomes. This is a much more prevalent feature in the human genome than in the fly, worm and yeast genomes. Duplications enable one copy of a gene to relocate to a new site, where it may take on a distinct physiological function.

Duplicated regions are likely to have contributed much to the expansion of gene families in humans. The family of genes that encodes the olfactory receptors responsible for detecting smell provides an extreme example. In all, there are about a thousand olfactory genes scattered throughout the genome, which demonstrates the importance of smell to most mammals. Yet in humans about 60 per cent are non-functional pseudogenes, illustrating our reduced dependency on smell compared with other mammals.

Although duplication offers a means of increasing gene numbers, it can also cause problems. During the production of sperm or eggs, pairs of equivalent chromosomes swap DNA (a process called recombination), creating new combinations of traits in offspring. This process of DNA shuffling can be confused by chunks of almost identical sequence – leading to the deletion of large pieces of genome, which can result in human disease. Examples include DiGeorge and velocardiofacial syndromes, in which most patients harbour a deletion from chromosome 22 that is thought to have been mediated by duplicated sequences flanking the deleted region. As a result, several genes from this region are not present in patients with DiGeorge syndrome, causing a range of clinical symptoms including abnormal facial characteristics, heart defects, and immune and endocrine abnormalities. Similarly, duplications are thought to predispose to the rearrangement and deletion in the region of chromosome 7 associated with Williams–Beuren syndrome, in which patients have a characteristic facial appearance, heart and blood-vessel problems, dental and kidney abnormalities, and sensitive hearing.

Y under siege

The X and Y chromosomes were once a matching pair, like the other twenty-two pairs of chromosomes in the human genome. However, since the evolution of sexual differences in mammals, which is thought to have begun when one of the pair of chromosomes acquired a gene for 'maleness', the sex chromosomes have grown apart. As they diverged over time, the Y chromosome lost the ability to exchange segments with the X chromosome (except at the very tips) during recombination. As a consequence, many of the

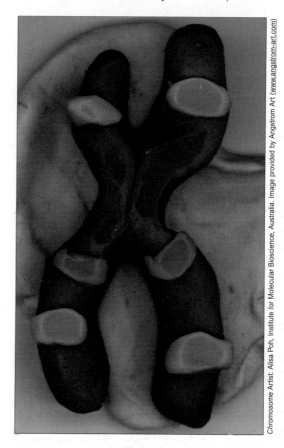

Chromosome Artist: Alisa Poh, Institute for Molecular Bioscience, Australia. Image provided by Angstrom Art (www.angstrom-art.com)

genes on the Y that are not essential have accumulated mutations and have either been shut down or lost. Now, the Y chromosome is reduced to a stump, clinging onto the genes that offer males a competitive advantage.

The Y chromosome has some other striking features. It has a large number of repeated chunks that are so similar that they are almost impossible to tell apart. Many of the male specific genes lie in these regions, such as those involved in testes development and sperm production. It is possible that these duplications are an attempt to ensure that the genes aren't lost (safety in numbers!).

Another surprise is a large stretch of sequence, around 3.5 million bases, which is in one orientation in some males, and in the opposite orientation in others. It is feasible, although merely a speculation, that this large inversion, as well as other variations in the number and orientation of the duplicated blocks, may underlie variations in male fertility and virility.

Mutations in the male genome are more common than in the female. Indeed, sperm cells are the main source of human genetic mutation, with mutation rates that are twice as high as in eggs. The reason for this is not known, but it may be because of the numerous cell divisions that occur during continuous sperm production throughout adult male life, whereas females undergo only a single round of egg production during development. Every time a cell divides, there is the potential for a mistake to occur when the DNA is copied. Sometimes these mutations can be a source of innovation that aids survival in changing environments; however, they can also disrupt gene function and cause disease.

Bacterial footprints

Have bacteria left their mark on our genome? Remarkably, a couple of hundred genes that are found in humans seem to be more similar to bacterial genes than to any in yeast, worms, flies or plants. This observation suggested that some genes might have been transferred from various bacterial genomes directly to vertebrate genomes.

Could it be a case of bacterial genes hitching an evolutionary ride, or is there something in it for us? Most of the bacterially derived genes encode enzymes and have been sequestered into specific pathways, such as stress responses and the metabolism of environmental chemicals, suggesting that they have been adapted to important physiological functions.

Since the publication of the human genome sequence, studies by others have provided evidence that at least some of these genes are unlikely to have been transferred from bacteria. Instead, they were probably present in an ancestral species and were lost in some lineages, such as those of worms and flies, but were retained in vertebrates. Both hypotheses are presently being debated, but the matter is unlikely to be settled until extensive sequence data from the genomes of other organisms have been acquired.

Hunting down disease genes

The draft genome sequence has already had a considerable impact on the identification of disease genes. Previously, the identification of a candidate gene in the absence of sequence and biochemical information was time consuming, costly and tedious. Now candidate genes can be readily detected using computers to interrogate public sequence databases, and confirmed by mutation screening of plausible candidates. The entire process can be completed in a matter of months.

With the aid of the draft genome sequence, more than thirty genes have already been identified, including genes involved in breast cancer, muscle disease, deafness and blindness. Meanwhile, the search for the many genes that underlie common chronic ailments, such as cardiovascular disease, arthritis, osteoporosis and cancer, will be greatly assisted by a knowledge of the sites in the genome that vary between individuals. The most common type of sequence variation is a change of an individual base, known as a single-nucleotide polymorphism (SNP). On average, there is likely to be one SNP in every 1000–2000 bases. The SNP Consortium – a collaboration between researchers, private companies and a charity — has gone a long way towards documenting human variation by constructing a map of 1.42

million SNPs, which was published in the same issue of *Nature* as the report of the human genome sequence.

Looking further ahead, a complete catalogue of genes opens up opportunities for drug development. Currently, our entire drug cabinet is derived from fewer than 500 targets. Even if a small proportion of genes and gene products prove to be valid targets, the genome sequence will provide enormous possibilities for new therapies. For example, when classic drug-target proteins were used to search the genome sequence database, more than a dozen new relatives were found, including neurotransmitter receptors and growth factors.

Collaboration, competition and conclusions

The Human Genome Project (HGP) is responsible for one of two draft sequences that were published contemporaneously. The other, from Celera Genomics, appeared in the journal *Science*. Was it, as some have argued, a waste of money to undertake two genome projects? Can a winner and a loser in the 'sequence race' be identified?

Our answer to both of these questions is 'no'. The two groups took different approaches to the sequencing of the genome, spurring developments in technology. Both were successful – the HGP independently and Celera in combining the (publicly accessible) HGP's data with its own major sequencing effort. The availability of two draft sequences inspires confidence in the conclusions drawn about the genome (which are, by and large, in close agreement). And the two groups provide a range of tools with which to analyse and exploit the sequence.

Beyond practical application, what does it mean to know the sequence of our genome? We have a description of our own inheritance, a glimpse into eons of gradual change. The genome is clearly not a well-ordered, tightly executed instruction manual, as some over-simplistic metaphors may have implied. Even with the genetic read-out in front of us, we have only tantalizing hints of how our genes work together, with extraordinary complexity, to build a human being. We are left with a sense of the quirkily human nature of the genome, with all its wonderful ingredients, that gets more interesting the deeper into it we go.

The genome in the news

There were two great waves of coverage of the human genome in the media. The first was in late June 2000, following press conferences at the White House and 10 Downing Street to announce that the genome had been sequenced. This was headline news and the coverage was celebratory in tone, epitomized by the use of colourful metaphors as political and scientific leaders sought to put the achievement into context. Remarkably, the publication of the research papers in February 2001 received still greater coverage in the media.

"President Clinton called the information 'the most important, most wondrous map ever produced'. He said that 'it outstripped in importance the map with which Lewis and Clarke opened America's way to the West'."

Other comparisons floated were to Galileo's discoveries in the solar system, the invention of the printing press, the race to develop the atomic bomb, and the space programme that put men on the moon.

The Boston Globe again:

"As a scientific enterprise, the race to map the human genome bears resemblance to the Manhattan Project, the furious World War II rush to develop an atomic bomb ..."

Richard Dawkins, quoted in the UK's *The Daily Telegraph*, went beyond the sciences for inspiration:

Groundbreaking 'map' to human genome due today

Genetic decoding holds surprise: Proteins seen playing major role

By Maggie Fox
REUTERS NEWS AGENCY

Our future may not lie in our genes, after all.

Two separate teams of researchers will report today that they have taken the first in-depth look at the human genetic code and found about half what they expected to find. Instead of 60,000 to 80,000 genes, humans have only 30,000 to 40,000. Both teams agree this means

that, in humans anyway, it is proteins that matter — much more so than genes.

The human body, it seems, is set up to adapt to its environment by cutting up and recombining the protein "products" of genes to make a protein suitable for the circumstance.

Each gene makes one protein — this is the basic function of any cell. Researchers had known

see ROLE, *page A10*

By Patricia Reaney
REUTERS NEWS AGENCY

Scientists will publish the initial sequence of the human genome today in a breakthrough that promises to revolutionize the understanding and treatment of diseases.

The sequencing of 3.1 billion letters of DNA shows humans are made up of about 30,000 to 40,000 genes, considerably fewer than earlier estimates of 60,000 to 100,000 genes, and only about twice as many as the earthworm and fruit fly.

Scientists say identifying all the genes and what they do will herald a new age in science and medicine, vastly expanding human knowledge and accelerating the diagno-

Holds key to aging, intractable illness

sis and treatment, as well as potential preventions and cures, for disease.

"It is going to revolutionize science and medicine," said Tim Hubbard of the Sanger Centre in Cambridge, England, who worked on the project.

"Everything about us is in the sequence."

The Human Genome Project, the publicly funded international collaboration of 20 groups of scientists from the United States, Britain, Japan, France, Germany and China, completed the working draft of the human genetic code in

June.

All the information has now been arranged and appears in the scientific journal Nature with a dizzying array of reports, maps and analyses to explain what it all means.

Celera Genomics Inc. of Rockville, the privately owned company that raced to produce the first draft, reports its findings in the journal Science.

The sequence is just the beginning and will not be fully finished for several years, but it is already revealing its secrets — far fewer genes, where they come from, the complexity of proteins and what makes us different from other organisms.

see GENOME, *page A10*

This time the analysis was weightier, focusing on what was learned from the sequence, rather than on the achievement itself. Here's a selection of what was on offer.

Grappling with the concept

The sequencing of the genome is not an easy sell in news terms. How was it presented to bring out the significance?

The Boston Globe went for a winning combination of political clout and the appeal of history:

"Along with Bach's music, Shakespeare's sonnets and the Apollo Space Programme, the Human Genome Project is one of those achievements of the human spirit that makes me proud to be human."

Others, such as Japanese Prime Minister Yoshiro Mori, quoted in *The Washington Post*, got straight to the point:

"An immense step forward for humanity in deciphering the makeup of life itself."

Political leaders around the world concurred. French Research Minister Roger-Gerard Schwartzenberg said:

"The deciphering of the book of life, is a milestone in science."

Chinese President Jiang Zemin commented that it was:

"A great scientific project in the scientific history of human beings and one of vital importance to the development of life sciences, medicine and pharmaceutical study".

But for sheer bravado, the Director of the Wellcome Trust, quoted in *The Financial Times*, was unmatched:

"Mike Dexter ... said the breakthrough could have longer-lasting significance than the wheel. In fact, while the wheel might one day be obsolete, the genome would be useful so long as there were humans on this – or any other – planet."

A humbling gene number

If there was a stand-out finding, it was the dramatically lower estimate for gene number than had been anticipated. This was widely interpreted as a severe knock to the human ego. For example, *The Daily Telegraph* lamented:

"It took about only 12 000 more genes than a worm and around 17 000 more genes than a fruit fly to build Einstein ..."

Warming to a similar theme, *The New York Times* considered that:

"The human genome, besides being only just out of the worm league, seems to have almost too much in common with many other kinds of animal genomes."

Taking the theme of self-deprecation a stage further was Robert Waterston, one of the leaders of the Human Genome Project (HGP). Talking to *The Washington Post*, he said:

"It's a humbling perspective. You can't study the genome for very long before you start feeling that you're just a transient vehicle for making more DNA."

Not absolutely everyone, however, was angst-ridden over the revelation on gene numbers. Martin Bobrow, a professor of medical genetics, was sanguine in *The Daily Telegraph*:

"Knowing a fly only has slightly fewer genes than me doesn't make me feel degraded – they are pretty complex things; they have four wings and can fly – I can't do that."

Once the initial shock was overcome, the media regrouped to provide some sensible explanations for our biological complexity despite the dearth of genes. Australia's *Sydney Morning Herald* suggested that:

"What sets us apart from flies and worms is the complexity of our proteins. Our extra genes do not make lots of new kinds of proteins. Rather, they reshuffle the different bits of old protein in novel ways ...

What makes us human is our intricate mechanism for switching genes on and off at various stages of life."

SOURCES: Celera Genomics; Human Genome Project   AP/GLOBE GRAPHIC

First genome reading holds some surprises
Scientists find DNA of humans similar to that of 'lower' animals

By Richard Saltus
GLOBE STAFF

Humbled by their first look at man's complete set of genes, scientists yesterday said it will take years to understand how humankind evolved from a DNA blueprint that is remarkably similar to so-called "lower" animals.

That striking similarity was the biggest surprise to scientists from public and private teams who released the first readout of the complete set of DNA instructions in human cells — the "human genome."

At press conferences in Washington and in other countries, the scientists said the genome — likened to a recipe

book or parts list for the human body — contains only about 30,000 genes, or separate messages — only about one-third as many as had been predicted and only about twice as many as fruit flies.

And it turns out there's nothing so special about human genes. The common mouse has genes that are similar to all but some 300 human genes, reported Craig Venter, leader of the private-sector genome effort. The two teams largely agreed on what the genome messages say.

"The abiding mystery of the genome is how we became so complex with such a relatively

Continued on next page

Startling finds in genome analysis
Refute long-held 'facts' of genetics carried in today's textbooks

By August Gribbin
THE WASHINGTON TIMES

The world's leading genetic scientists yesterday formally announced the first detailed analysis of the human genome — the so-called "blueprint of life" — they produced in June.

Their analysis held surprises. Although it's difficult for the nonscientist to grasp the full significance of the startling finds the genome sequencing and its interpretation facilitate, most of the discoveries are immensely important.

They help researchers identify the lines of inquiry that ultimately

are expected to revolutionize medicine and lead to new therapies and cures for devastating diseases like Alzheimer's, Parkinson's, diabetes and others.

There is no way of predicting when such cures might come. But Peter Bruns, a geneticist and vice president at Bethesda's Howard Hughes Medical Institute, said, "I think we'll see the scientific findings put to some practical uses very quickly. Not years. Days."

Even before the genome was sequenced, gene research had linked certain genes with specific illnesses like prostate cancer, glaucoma, muscular atrophy, hardening of the arteries of the heart and

more.

And in Boston, physicians last summer successfully injected genes into the hearts of chronically ill heart-attack patients and provoked the growth of new blood vessels. Increasingly, medical pioneers are developing similar gene-based therapies.

Mr. Bruns says such work will be speeded because, "Now the findings are all on the Internet. It's like having a map of a city that's so detailed, you can see which homes have refrigerators and what kind.

"If there is spoiled food, you can look to see if it was caused by the

see GENOME, page A10

These views were backed up by Francis Collins, who was quoted in *The New York Times*:

"The main invention seems to have been cobbling things together to make a multitasked protein. Maybe evolution designed most of the basic folds that proteins could use a long time ago, and the major advances in the last 400 million years have been to figure out how to shuffle those in interesting ways. That gives another reason not to panic."

Far from panicking, another set of reports seized on gene number to make bold assertions about the human condition. These were spearheaded by the British Sunday newspaper, *The Observer*. A somewhat overstated lead story opined that:

"The discovery of our meagre gene numbers ... reveals that environmental influences are vastly more powerful in shaping the way humans act."

It speculated that:

"The discovery has critical implications for our understanding of the idea of free will".

Other papers, such as Italy's *La Repubblica*, acknowledged nature–nurture interaction in more balanced terms:

Tiny Gene Disparities Go a Long Way

■ Science: DNA of people of different races is unexpectedly alike, new genome findings show.

By ROSIE MESTEL
TIMES MEDICAL WRITER

The first detailed survey of the human genetic code is revealing many striking things about the blueprint for making a human being. Among them: how similar we all are to each other. And how different.

The findings, to be formally announced today and published later this week, reveal for instance that members of two different racial groups can be more alike than members of the same group.

The studies also reveal that two unrelated people are unexpectedly alike, differing on average at just 1 out of every 1,000 sites in our DNA.

Yet even that small difference adds up to roughly 3 million places in DNA where tiny disparities exist between two people's genetic codes. That's enough to create all the known genetic variety, from simple traits such as eye color to more complicated ones such as higher risks for depression or heart disease, according to the new findings published by two groups, the Human Genome Project and a privately funded group. The genome project was funded largely by the U.S. government and a British charity.

Today, because of the genome effort, places in our DNA where those differences occur have been cataloged in detail unimaginable just a few years ago. This new in-
Please see GENES, A5

"The French geneticist Jean-Michel Claverie writes in *Science* that such a low number of genes could represent a paradigm shift that could radically change our understanding of the complexity of organisms and of evolution. This paradigm shift would force us to re-examine the importance of genetic control on who we are and what we do, rescuing the role of the environment and its interaction with the genome."

Undermining racism

Another point picked up throughout the world was our extraordinary similarity at the genetic level. For instance, the UK's *The Independent* reported:

"The notion that skin colour is a useful method of predicting physical or mental variations between human beings has been refuted by the genome maps. Every person on earth shares 99.9% of the same genetic code and the differences within racial groups are often greater than those between people of different colours ..."

Hope was expressed that these findings could reduce racial prejudice. According to *The Daily Telegraph*:

"Prof Svante Paabo, of the Max Planck Institute of Evolutionary Anthropology in Leipzig, Germany, is optimistic that as we learn more about the genetic similarities and differences between individuals, this knowledge will encourage social tolerance and compassion.

It is already apparent that the gene pool in Africa contains more variation than elsewhere, and that the genetic variation found outside Africa contains only a subset of that found in Africa. 'From that perspective, all humans are therefore Africans, either residing in Africa or in recent exile,' he said.

He believes that studies of genetic variation in human populations may not be so easy to abuse, in terms of using the data as 'scientific support' for racism and other forms of bigotry. 'If anything, such studies will have the opposite effect because prejudice, oppression and racism feed on ignorance.'

The impact on health and society

Many newspapers described the possible impact that the genome sequence could have on health. They highlighted the potential for new medical approaches, as in the case of the UK's *The Guardian:*

"The human genome could open an era of a new kind of medicine – one tailored to a patient's unique genetic makeup".

And they covered target diseases, as reported in Spain's *El Pais*:

"For scientists, the publication of the sequence ... opens the door to a new era for medicine and biology, as well as for finding a cure to a large number of diseases that have a hereditary component such as cancer, Alzheimer or diabetes ..."

The *China People's Daily* commented:

"In addition to genetic disease, the knowledge of human biochemistry that is contained in the human genome could hold new insights into tackling infectious diseases such as AIDS and tuberculosis."

Bill Clinton drew up a rough timeframe for developments, as quoted in *The Financial Times*:

"It is conceivable that our children's children will know the term Cancer only as a constellation of stars."

Others were less sure of this timetable, with *The Washington Post* warning that:

"It will take the best part of the 21st century to fulfil the grand promises made at the announcement of the complete human blueprint."

Some unease about the practical consequences was also expressed. Displaying mixed emotions was *The Irish Times*:

"The effort has raised both immense hopes for curing diseases and stopping birth defects along with fears of genetic discrimination and selective breeding."

Discomfort registered a further notch in *The Boston Globe*:

"Hanging over the whole day, however, was the sense that the world had entered uncharted ethical waters. Will people be discriminated against based on their genes? Will babies be genetically engineered?"

The Hindustan Times was of like mind:

"However, many are concerned about the resulting risk of discrimination in insurance and employment, leading to 'nightmare' dilemmas about whether such tests should be permitted by employers, lenders and health insurers."

These thorny issues were grasped by UK Prime Minister Tony Blair, quoted in *The Financial Times*:

"The powerful information now at our disposal [must] be used to transform medicine, not abused to make man his own creator or invade individual privacy."

There was also concern from developing countries about access to advances for all peoples. *The Namibian Times*, for instance, said:

"Disabled people fear the information will be used to create perfect people and some scientists claim the benefits of the achievement will only be enjoyed by people living in wealthy countries."

The sequence and society

Like other great scientific advances, the sequence of the human genome can be harnessed for good or bad purposes. There are several factors that make human genomic information stand out. One is its personal nature – it deals with our fundamental make-up. Another is the power of its application – information about our genes potentially affects all of us in our daily lives, transforming medicine but also providing new knowledge that can be used outside the clinical context. Add the aspect of immediacy, namely that practical use of the sequence is already a reality, and it is clear that there is an urgent need for society to understand, debate and decide on the appropriate settings for the use of genetic information.

Fortunately, there has been a considerable amount of foresight and planning for these new developments in genetic science. Many countries are already grappling with complex ethical, social and legal issues in the light of growing genome knowledge. Expert committees have been set up, politicians have played an important role in fostering debate, and media interest has been invaluable in bringing concerns to the attention of the wider public. In this chapter, we consider some of the societal conundrums that the availability of the genome sequence raises.

Dealing with genetic risk

Genetic knowledge offers great hope for early detection, more accurate diagnosis and

Joe Heller, Wisconsin - *The Green Bay Press-Gazette*

The ELSI Program

The architects of the Human Genome Project (HGP) recognized that, in parallel with striving towards the scientific and technological goal of sequencing the human genome, it would be imperative to address the impact of this new science on individuals, families and society. To address these issues they established, in 1990, the Ethical, Legal and Social Implications (ELSI) Program, which receives 3–5 per cent of the annual HGP budgets of the US Department of Energy (DOE) and the National Human Genome Research Institute (NHGRI). This represents the world's largest bioethics programme. It is complemented by similar initiatives around the world.

The ELSI Program funds research in ethics, law, economics and other related fields to anticipate and address the issues arising from new genetic information and technology, and from their applications. In several instances, this has led to policy recommendations and proposed legislative solutions. Some of the specific topics include fair use of genetic information, maintaining the privacy and confidentiality of genetic information, issues of informed consent for genetic testing, commercialization of genetic research discoveries, and education of health professionals and policy-makers. Information about ELSI can be obtained at the NHGRI or DOE websites: www.nhgri.nih.gov; or www.ornl.gov/hgmis.

mine whether a person carries a gene mutation that could affect his or her children. To do a gene test, a DNA sample isolated from the blood or tissue of a patient is scanned for a specific mutation linked to a particular disorder.

Although there are several hundred genetic tests for different conditions, fewer than 100 tests are available commercially, and most are for rare disorders caused by a mutation in just a single gene. For instance, individuals with a family history of a genetic condition such as Huntington disease, an adult-onset neurodegenerative condition, may desire a genetic test because they want to know their chances of developing the disease later in life. Couples who

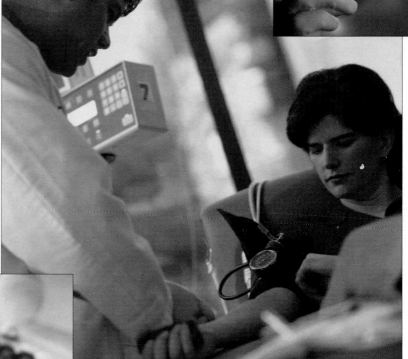

improved treatment of a variety of medical conditions. It is also likely to bring preventive medicine to the fore. Researchers will begin to understand how DNA variations underlie individual susceptibilities to certain diseases and responses to medical treatments. It may also be possible to design customized drugs that are more effective for particular groups of patients.

Genetic testing (or DNA-based testing) is one of the first commercial applications of genetic discoveries to medicine. It can be used, for example, to diagnose a condition, to estimate the likelihood of developing one, or to deter-

are asymptomatic but suspect that they may carry a disease-causing mutation may use genetic tests to find out the risk of passing on the condition to their children. Prenatal diagnosis, involving the testing of a foetus during pregnancy, can be used to diagnose a number of conditions, including Tay–Sachs disease, a fatal neurological disorder of early childhood.

Genetic tests present a number of personal dilemmas and ethical issues. Should a test be taken? What action should be taken in response to the results? How should the new information be handled, both individually and within the family? A further problem is that in some cases diagnosis has outpaced treatment. For an adult-onset disorder where a test for a genetic disorder is available but a treatment is not, is it preferable not to know and live in hope, or to be rid of the uncertainty?

Single-gene disorders are rare and account for only a very small percentage of all diseases. For the majority of common diseases – such as cancer, heart disease, asthma, obesity and diabetes – the causes are much more complex and are thought to involve a variety of gene mutations, perhaps acting in combination with each other and together with certain environmental factors. Untangling the genetic and environmental contributions to these complex diseases will ultimately offer opportunities to develop diagnostic markers for predisposition to certain conditions.

Knowing your genetic susceptibility to common diseases can offer some advantages. It might help you to make better choices about lifestyle and behaviour. For example, people who are genetically predisposed to heart problems may be able to lower their chances of developing symptoms by not smoking, eating healthy foods, exercising regularly and taking certain medicines. For diseases such as colorectal cancer, where early detection can significantly improve prognosis, knowing one's genetic disposition can alert an individual to the need for close monitoring and regular check-ups.

There are concerns about how people will handle the uncertainty that surrounds genetic susceptibility to common diseases. Testing positive for a genetic indicator of disease predisposition only indicates a risk of developing the disorder; it does not mean that the condition will automatically develop. It may only be in the context of other gene mutations as well as the influence of specific environmental factors that the disease will occur. Conversely, a negative result for a genetic test does not necessarily mean an individual won't eventually develop the disease.

It is difficult to predict how different people will react to learning that they are genetically predisposed to a certain condition. Some may use this information to make better decisions about their lifestyle and habits. For others, however, it may provoke anxiety and stress. Learning that one is at risk, even a slight risk, of developing a particular disease could give way to 'genetic fatalism', whereby a person believes that genes alone determine future health, irrespective of changes to diet and behaviour.

All of us carry some variations that are potentially detrimental in particular contexts and environments. The degree of risk can vary for individuals in different populations and can be influenced by a host of factors, some of which are within a person's control and others outside any sort of control. Given that it will be possible to identify our individual genetic susceptibilities to disease in the not-too-distant future, it is essential that people are educated about the meaning of genetic risk, how best to handle this risk, and how to live with the uncertainty.

While genetic information is deeply personal, it is not just about an individual. It may reveal information about another family member. People contemplating genetic tests need to consider the consequences not only for them-

Genetic testing of children

- Genetic testing of children can confirm a medical diagnosis or make a predictive diagnosis.
- Often a child's health will greatly benefit from early detection and treatment of a genetic disorder.
- Genetic testing of children raises unique ethical concerns. For instance, 'informed consent' of the patient is required prior to genetic testing; obviously this presents difficulties in the case of a child.
- Telling a child about his or her genetic susceptibilities raises difficult issues, such as at what age and level of maturity to do so.
- While parents may believe that having a specific genetic test is in the best interests of the child, it is hard to predict how the child will deal with this information later in life.
- The testing of children for adult-onset disorders, such as Huntington disease, where there is no intervention that can decrease risk or prevent disease onset, is controversial and is typically not permitted.

selves but also for their relatives. Should other members of a family be informed of the test results, which may reveal their own risk of getting a particular disease?

As more genetic tests become available, mechanisms to assure the accuracy and reliability of such tests must be put in place. There is currently little regulation of tests but it is urgently needed. There is also a need to ensure equitable access to genetic tests and counselling. At present, genetic tests can range in cost from hundreds to thousands of dollars. There needs to be the infrastructure to enable everyone, regardless of their socioeconomic or other circumstances, to have the opportunity to take advantage of the beneficial information that genetic testing potentially offers.

Genetic discrimination and privacy

The potential abuse of genetic information, such as in the workplace or in the provision of health insurance, raises grave concern. There is a real danger that a genetic 'underclass' might develop.

Based on genetic information, employers might try to avoid hiring workers who they believe are likely to take sick leave, resign or retire early for health reasons. Cases of discrimination could occur even where an individual

The importance of genetic counselling

Because of the dilemmas it can present, genetic testing should always be contemplated and conducted with the support of genetic counselling. Professionally trained counsellors help people to understand the limitations of genetic tests, to anticipate how different test results might affect them, and to explain the choices available in the light of the results. The value of genetic counselling is not to make the decision for the patient, but rather to help them make informed decisions regarding all the possible implications.

Currently, medical geneticists in conjunction with trained genetic counsellors provide genetic testing. However, as it becomes cheaper, easier to perform and more readily available, genetic testing may be carried out by primary health-care providers. It is essential to establish practices that continue to ensure that people undergoing genetic testing are fully informed of the implications. All health-care providers will have to be equipped with the skills to provide appropriate counselling. And there needs to be knowledge on both sides – the patient and the health-care provider – so they can work together to enable the patient to reach the most informed decision and realize when additional, more specialized counselling should be sought.

may never show signs of disease, or where their genetic condition has no effect on their ability to perform work. Substantial gaps in the laws of many countries leave open the potential for employees to be discriminated against on the basis of genetic information. While existing anti-discrimination laws, such as those protecting people with disabilities, could be interpreted to include genetic discrimination, specific legislation is desirable.

There are concerns too about the health insurance industry using genetic information to discriminate against individuals. Cases have been reported where individuals with a genetic disorder or predisposition have been refused health insurance, or had their enrolment cancelled or premiums increased. There are fears that medical expenses for those suffering from genetic conditions will not be covered and children may be excluded from coverage because they are at risk of inheriting a genetic disease.

Information about genetic make-up is personal. Furthermore, it may not just reveal information about an individual but also about other family members. And yet it could be made available without a person's knowledge, or even against his or her wishes. For instance, an employer or insurance provider may require access to medical records which include the results of genetic tests. Disclosure of genetic information may be considered an invasion of privacy.

Many argue that holders of genetic information should be prohibited from releasing it without the individual's prior authorization and, to protect against information being used for purposes other than what it was originally collected for, an individual's consent should be required for each disclosure. While it may not be realistic to expect confidential genetic profiles of individuals never to be disclosed in an electronic information age, this underscores the need to have policies in place that serve not only to deter but also to penalize the inappropriate collection, disclosure and abuse of this information.

DNA to the defence

"DNA aids the search for truth by exonerating the innocent. The criminal justice system is not infallible"

Janet Reno, US Attorney General during President Clinton's administration

Forensic DNA technology can help convict the guilty as well as exonerate the innocent. A number of factors can contribute to a wrongful conviction, such as mistaken eyewitnesses, incompetent counsel and erroneous laboratory results from other biological markers. But DNA testing provides scientific and irrefutable proof of innocence.

An example is the Innocence Project, founded in 1992 by attorneys Barry Scheck and Peter Neufeld – a programme operating out of the Benjamin N. Cardozo School of Law in New York. This programme provides free assistance to help wrongly convicted prison inmates prove their innocence through DNA tests.

Since the advent of forensic DNA testing in the late 1980s, more than 63 people in the United States have been exonerated and subsequently set free after DNA testing of the evidence. Some of these people had been convicted of capital crimes and were incarcerated or on death row. The Innocence Project represented or assisted in over 36 of these cases, and is presently handling over 200 cases, with a further 1000 or more pending evaluation.

Efforts such as this have been credited with expanding awareness amongst law-enforcement authorities, prosecutors, judges, politicians and the public that not only is DNA testing an important tool to fight crime, but it also provides a means for ensuring that the criminal justice system works fairly.

The DNA files

DNA technology has revolutionized forensic science and the criminal justice system. DNA has been a key 'witness' in numerous trials, helping police and the courts to identify the perpetrators of violent crimes with a very high degree of confidence. But, just as it can point the finger at the guilty, it can also exonerate the wrongly accused.

DNA fingerprinting, or DNA typing, involves comparing sections of DNA between samples – if all the sections match, mathematical formulae are used to estimate the odds that both samples come from the same person. DNA typing cannot absolutely prove a match, but it can come very close. Although DNA typing can't be used to prove guilt definitively – because there is always a chance, no matter how remote, that a suspect's DNA profile is a very close match to that of the real offender – it can nevertheless support corroborating evidence. DNA typing, however, can prove innocence because it can indisputably determine whether a person's genetic profile does not match the DNA evidence of the crime.

Hair, blood, saliva, semen, skin, teeth and nail clippings all contain cells with DNA, which can be used to provide useful information about a person, such as their sex or whether two people are related. Aside from its use in criminal cases, DNA typing can also help identify missing persons and murder or accident victims. It has also been used to prove or

disprove paternity, that is whether a man is the father of a particular child.

Although DNA typing is a powerful tool for forensics, it does raise questions about the protection of privacy. DNA information collected by the police is stored in law-enforcement agencies' DNA databanks. While this information is typically only obtained for serious crimes, increasingly DNA is being collected and stored for anyone convicted of a crime, and some agencies are considering collecting DNA from all those arrested, in much the same way that fingerprints are currently taken. Some concerns have been raised about the confidentiality of this information and whether it could be used for purposes other than that for which it was collected.

Genes for cure

Genetic knowledge is being applied to diagnosis, treatment, cure and prevention of health problems. Genetic engineering of medicines and genetic testing provide two approaches – gene therapy is another. Gene therapy involves changing genes within a person's cells. It can be used, for example, to replace missing or defective proteins, or to introduce gene products that destroy cancer cells or render them more vulnerable to treatment.

The transfer of genes into cells of the body, other than sex cells (sperm or eggs), is called somatic gene therapy. It is still at an experimental stage and is usually only tried with patients who have diseases for which there is no cure. The technical challenges are enormous: a gene must be introduced into the appropriate cells of the body, and the cells must express the gene product in an active form, at the right time and in the right quantities. Hundreds of gene-therapy trials have been undertaken or are presently under way. Although there have been a number of promising studies, none has so far been able to achieve complete success.

There are also many ethical concerns with gene-therapy applications. The benefits of treating serious diseases may be very clear-cut, but for other conditions it may raise questions about what is a disorder or disability and what is normal. An example of this is growth disorders. Also, gene therapy is, and will probably remain, very expensive, raising questions about who will have access to these therapies and who will pay.

Even more contentious than somatic therapy is germline gene therapy. This involves changing genes in sex cells, that is the sperm and egg, so that the altered DNA is passed on to offspring. Germline gene therapy offers the potential for permanently ridding a family of an

Czar Nicholas II and his family
DNA analysis can also uncover history – and controversy. It has been at the centre of the debate over whether US President Thomas Jefferson fathered children with his slave Sally Hemings. And it has confirmed that the bodies in a mass grave were those of Czar Nicholas II and his family, who were murdered during the Russian Revolution. [Bettmann/CORBIS]

inherited genetic disorder. There are a number of concerns about this form of gene therapy, one of which is the potentially detrimental impact that new genes could have on foetal development. Another concern is the ethical implications of changing the genes of future generations without assurances of safety, not to mention the lack of consent of all the potentially affected persons. So controversial is the issue of germline gene therapy that it is not being actively researched. At the very least, its development should await a better understanding of all the implications.

Genetic enhancement

Eugenics left an indelible stain on the twentieth century. Eugenics (derived from the Greek word meaning 'wellborn') is the use of genetics to improve the quality of humankind. It became popular in North America and Europe during the early to mid-1900s. The eugenics movement led to the endorsement of the sterilization of thousands of individuals considered 'genetically unfit' (which included people deemed 'feebleminded'). This type of thinking reached a shameful peak in the desire for racial purity in Nazi Germany. But even today eugenic ideas are being applied. For example, in China a law forbids mentally disabled people from marrying unless they have been sterilized.

The ideas, and many of the experiments, of

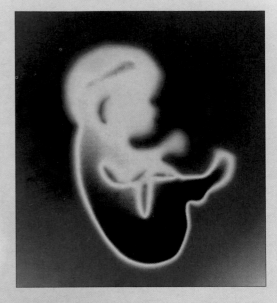

the original eugenicists have been largely discredited. However, there are fears that a new form of eugenics could emerge, whereby people might be tempted to tinker with genes on a wide scale in an attempt to select for 'desirable' traits for their children, such as physical attributes, IQ and personality. This raises the prospect of so-called 'designer babies'.

Fortunately, there are several barriers blocking such development. First, there are the technical hurdles. It is extremely difficult to select for several genes at once. Figuring out exactly which genes, in which combinations, create the complement of desired traits remains in the realm of science fiction, at least with current knowledge and technology. Also, environment and upbringing, and even experiences in the womb, play a big part in how a child develops.

While it may be technologically out of reach for some time, the issue of genetic enhancement of our future generations warrants ethical concern. Many would see the merits of using genetic knowledge and technology to help fix a faulty gene that would otherwise result in children being born with a painful, devastating disease that claims their lives early. However, we will inevitably reach the blurry boundaries between disease and normal variation.

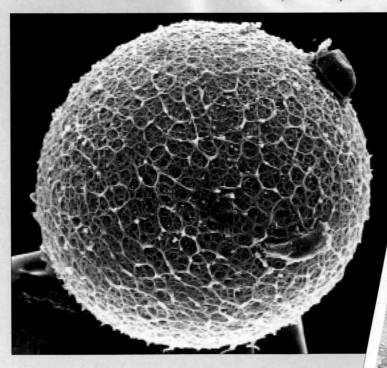

Colour-enhanced scanning electron micrograph of a human egg. [Yorgos Nikas / Wellcome Trust Medical Photographic Library]

Who 'owns' our genes?

A patent is a legal agreement that gives an inventor rights over the invention for a period (typically 20 years), during which time others cannot make, use or sell the invention unless the inventor licenses it to them to do so. Patents were developed to make information about inventions publicly available, to encourage investment and to reward inventiveness.

Patenting of genes has, however, been controversial. Should a naturally occurring entity, such as a gene, be viewed as an invention? Should the genome be treated like property or stocks and shares, being divided up, bought, sold and traded?

Patenting offers an incentive for the research and development necessary to translate genetic discoveries into genetic medicines. However, there are concerns that excessive licensing charges could impede the development of genetic diagnostic and therapeutic products. This could be exacerbated by the fact that a novel diagnostic or therapeutic product might involve many distinct patents, each owned by a different individual or company. A single DNA sequence can be patented in several different ways, triggering fears that the requirement for payments to multiple patent owners or licensees

might discourage the development of genetic tests and medicines. Others argue that cross-licensing agreements will be developed to overcome this potential obstacle.

The patenting of genetic tests can raise concerns for patients. Patients and their families often cooperate in the search for disease genes, providing blood samples and medical information about themselves and their families. However, when the gene discovery is commercialized, the very same families may be required to pay what they perceive to be unreasonable costs for tests and treatments derived from the gene that they helped identify.

In a recent example, a US patient advocacy group for Canavan disease has filed a lawsuit against the hospital and researcher who patented the gene that is mutated in the degenerative brain disorder. They claim that the gene was discovered using the genetic information and financial resources provided by Canavan families, and that the hospital charged royalties that limited the availability of testing for the disease. In contrast, the patient advocacy group for sufferers of pseudoxanthoma elasticum (a genetic disorder that causes connective tissue in the skin, eyes and arteries to calcify) played a significant role in organizing the research on

DNA crystals display conical and striated fan textures, and have a colour pattern that shifts through a range of different colours, such as from yellow to purple as illustrated in this photomicrograph. [Courtesy of Michael W. Davidson, Florida State University, Tallahassee]

Knowing our genetic selves

How does the human genome sequence affect the way we think about ourselves? The genome sequence will reveal a lot about each of us at an individual level, but it can also reveal a lot about our communities, our history and our species.

We shall learn about the 'sameness' and 'otherness' of people. Our genomes are about 99.9 per cent identical to each other. Identifying and deciphering that mere 0.1 per cent of genetic code that varies between humans will help us understand how genes influence our appearance, behaviour and susceptibility to disease.

The human genome sequence also potentially breaks down national and cultural boundaries; there are more genetic differences within a given population than between different populations. History lessons may require revision as scrutiny of the DNA sequence of different people resolves ambiguities in ancestral family trees, or records of the wanderings of earlier travellers. By extensive comparisons of human genomes, we shall be able to generate a higher-resolution picture of our cultural and geographical origins.

It also throws new light on how our species evolved and our relatedness to other species. We share about 99 per cent DNA sequence similarity with chimpanzees. Furthermore, at least 10 per cent of our genes have relatives in flies and worms. More refined comparison of the genetic differences between us and other animals will inevitably challenge notions of the uniqueness of the human species.

the disorder, and thereby garnered a place for their leader as an inventor on a patent application describing the gene discovery. This unique alliance provides a model for handling intellectual property emerging from collaboration between patients' groups and researchers.

A call for education

Genetics is a complex science, involving inferences from patterns of inheritance, some

knowledge of statistics and sophisticated technologies. This presents challenges in understanding the enormous promise of the Human Genome Project as well as the allied concerns. It is therefore imperative to translate the genetic science into understandable terms and concepts for the general public.

As genetic information begins to influence mainstream medical practice, the need to educate both practitioners and the public on its implications for health care will escalate. The public's expectations are high and, as a result of the electronic information flow of the worldwide web, some patients may be better informed than their physicians. The basic principles of genetics, as well as an awareness of current trends and recent developments, will need to be integrated into fundamental levels of training for all health-care practitioners, and also into continuing medical education.

Aside from the clinical setting, genomic knowledge is being used in other contexts, for example in the courtrooms and in evaluations of health and life insurance. It is incumbent on those who can act on the basis of this information to have a solid grounding in genetics.

It is imperative to guard against extreme reactions to the sequencing of the genome, both the unreasonably negative and the unrealistically positive. The issues relating to the use (or abuse) of genetic knowledge are complex and concerns from all sides must be discussed openly. Many of the worries relate to application of the science rather than to the science itself. Despite the pessimism of some, many of these concerns appear to have potential remedies. Nonetheless, a major feature in resolving doubts and fears will be ensuring that the public is educated about the science and has a say in how it is utilized.

At the other extreme, it is essential to keep expectations at a realistic level. Deciphering the human genome sequence is just a start; the hard part now begins as we try to understand what genes do, how they interact and what goes awry during disease. It will be many years before the full benefits are realized. If this message fails to get through, then widespread disappointment may result and, worse still, create a backlash against genetic science.

There are numerous benefits in the genomic era. But it will require an educated, prepared and receptive society to realize this potential fully.

The genome and beyond

"... the more we learn about the human genome, the more there is to explore."

International Human Genome Sequencing Consortium; penultimate sentence of the paper describing the human genome sequence

The Human Genome Project is continuing apace. The plan is to have all gaps closed and all ambiguities resolved by the year 2003. Using this completely 'finished' sequence, a comprehensive inventory of genes and sequence diversity should be well within reach. But identifying all human genes is only the first step; equipped with this new information, scientists aim to discover how genes and their protein products work and how they influence human health and disease.

Traditional methods of deciphering gene function typically work on a 'one gene in one experiment' basis. Now, thanks to the development of 'high-throughput' technologies, the functions of thousands of genes and the proteins they encode can be studied simultaneously. This large-scale analysis of the genome and its products is known as 'functional genomics'; it includes the study of where and when genes are expressed, and the process of determining the structure and function of proteins.

Learning from others

Genetically speaking, we are very much like other organisms. The structure of DNA, and the code that translates proteins from genes, are virtually identical across all life forms. So we can learn a lot about ourselves by studying non-human organisms.

Comparing DNA sequences of different species – an approach called 'comparative genomics' – can identify genes and provide clues as to their function. The concept is simple: DNA segments that have a function are more likely to retain their sequence during evolution than non-functional segments. Laboratory experiments using less complex organisms test these predictions. Yeast, for example, has been studied extensively. Most of the genes that control yeast cell division have been identified. By looking for their relatives in the human genome, a role in cell division can tentatively be assigned to those human genes and then be tested through specific experiments. A wide range of basic biological processes – such as DNA replication, repair, protein manufacturing, and general cell housekeeping – are shared by virtually all life forms, including single-celled organisms like bacteria and yeast.

Humans, of course, are far more complex than single-cell organisms. But insight into how our trillions of cells communicate and work together to form a human being can be gained from simpler animals. The worm *C. elegans*, for example, has one of the least complex nervous systems – it has only 302 neurons compared with about a hundred billion neurons in a human brain. Nonetheless, the development and function of the worm's nervous system can shed light on the workings of more complex brains.

Finding function

Knowing when and where genes are expressed can provide clues about function. This information can be gathered using microarrays, also known as 'DNA chips', thumbnail-sized glass or silicon wafers to which thousands of unique

Protein structures can give important clues about function, and can aid in the design of new drugs. [Wellcome Medical Photographic Library]

fragments of genes are attached. Microarrays enable scientists to monitor the expression levels of thousands of genes at a time.

To look at gene expression in a particular tissue at a particular time, scientists extract messenger RNA (mRNA) sequences, which are the transcribed intermediaries between DNA and proteins. The solution containing mRNAs is then washed over the microarray. The mRNA complementary to the fragments on the DNA chip 'sticks' to the microarrays and indicates which genes are expressed in the cells. By labelling mRNA samples with coloured dyes, it is possible to compare gene expression in different cells and tissues directly in one experiment.

An example of where microarrays have revealed useful information is in the study of cancer. By comparing expression profiles of tumour versus normal cells, it is possible to identify genes that may play a role in the development or progression of cancer. Tumours, even of the same cancer type, can vary in terms of how quickly they grow, how they respond to treatment and their likelihood of metastasis. While they can be indistinguishable by microscopy, specific patterns of gene expression can serve as markers to classify tumours and predict prognosis and response to treatment.

Profiling proteins

With the human genome nearly complete, scientists are increasingly turning their attention to proteins. The emerging field of 'proteomics' encompasses the study of the location, interaction, structure and function of proteins. Proteins are more challenging to work with than DNA. They often have complicated three-dimensional structures that determine their function. A suite of tools is being developed to characterize the full complement of proteins within a given cell, known as the 'proteome'.

'Protein chips', equivalent to DNA chips, are currently under development. These can measure changes in the quantities of proteins in a cell in response to drug treatment, or identify proteins with particular enzymatic properties.

The location of a protein within a cell provides clues to its function. A protein found on the cell surface, for example, may function as a receptor, while one sequestered in the nucleus may modulate gene expression. Using tagging and tracing techniques, the cellular locations of proteins are rapidly being discovered, building up a picture of the cellular landscape.

The binding partners of proteins provide another piece of the functional puzzle. If the function of a protein is known, it becomes possible to infer the function of proteins to which it binds. Techniques exist in which proteins are used as 'bait' to 'fish' for interacting partners in the cellular pond. Cataloguing these interactions provides an overview of protein networks and biological processes in a cell. Once again, model organisms such as yeast, in which the physical interactions between every protein have been mapped, provide invaluable templates to delineate similar networks in human cells.

One of the most powerful ways to analyse a protein is to determine its three-dimensional structure. This can provide insight into how proteins work at the molecular level and can aid rational drug design. Determining the structures of all human proteins presents an even greater challenge than sequencing the genome and a similar industrial-scale approach is under way.

Integrating information

The effort to unravel the functions of the genome is multidisciplinary, drawing in scientists from many fields – including biology, medicine, chemistry, physics, mathematics, engineering and computer science. The greatest promise lies in the integration of all this information to create a detailed picture of biological processes, and find out how these processes go awry in disease. Integral to this is 'bioinformatics', a new field of science that manages and analyses data to extract biological meaning. Databases and software tools will need to become much more sophisticated to help scientists make sense of the staggering amount of emerging computational and laboratory data.

While the potential is enormous, we are still a long way from a full understanding of biological processes. And it will be considerably longer before genome-based information delivers the anticipated practical solutions to medical problems. In the meantime, preparation and debate on the responsible use of genetic information are required. So, while pushing ahead with the research and technology, parallel steps are needed to ensure that public awareness and understanding – as well as attention to ethical, legal and societal concerns – keep pace with the science. The sequencing of the human genome is only a beginning.

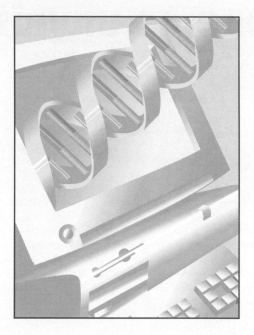

The research papers

The following section is reprinted directly from the pages of the human genome issue of *Nature* published on 15 February 2001. The centrepiece is the main research paper from the International Human Genome Sequencing Consortium, which describes the assembly and analysis of the human genome. It is the first comprehensive survey of the human genome sequence and summarizes more than a decade of work.

There is tradition, rigour and protocol in how scientists publish their discoveries. Research papers are submitted to scientific journals such as *Nature* for review and evaluation by editors and scientific peers; papers are accepted for publication only when the reviewers' queries have been satisfied. While the readership of *Nature* is primarily scientists, the authors went to some lengths to present the paper in a language and style that are as accessible as possible, within the constraints of a scientific journal. It is the longest scientific report ever published in the 132 years of the journal's existence. We are delighted to reproduce the work here, not only as a historic document but also as a fine example of scientific communication.

The engaging series of News and Views articles that introduced the scientific work is also reprinted here. *Nature*'s News and Views articles, introduced into the journal in 1927, provide context and accessibility for key findings. They are contributed by prominent independent researchers who have the expertise to comment on the relevance and impact of the research.

Our genome unveiled

David Baltimore

The draft sequences of the human genome are remarkable achievements. They provide an outline of the information needed to create a human being and show, for the first time, the overall organization of a vertebrate's DNA.

've seen a lot of exciting biology emerge over the past 40 years. But chills still ran down my spine when I first read the paper that describes the outline of our genome and now appears on page 860 of this issue[1]. Not that many questions are definitively answered — for conceptual impact, it does not hold a candle to Watson and Crick's 1953 paper[2] describing the structure of DNA. Nonetheless, it is a seminal paper, launching the era of post-genomic science.

This milestone of biology's megaproject is the long-promised draft DNA sequence from the International Human Genome Sequencing Consortium (the public project). The sequence itself is available to all those connected to the Internet[3]. In the paper in this issue, we are presented with a description of the strategy used to decipher the structures of the huge DNA molecules that constitute the genome, and with analyses of the content encoded in the genome. It is the achievement of a coordinated effort involving 20 laboratories and hundreds of people around the world. It reflects the scientific community at its best: working collaboratively, pooling its resources and skills, keeping its focus on the goal, and making its results available to all as they were acquired.

Simultaneously, another draft sequence is being published[4]. It is less freely available because it was generated by a company, Celera Genomics, that hopes to sell the information. This week's *Science* contains an account of the history of that project and the analyses of its data, while another of the papers in this issue contains a comparison of the quality of the two sequences[5]. To those who saw this as a competitive sport, the papers make it appear to be roughly a tie. However, it is important to remember that Celera had the advantage of all of the public project's data. Nevertheless, Celera's achievement of producing a draft sequence in only a year of data-gathering is a testament to what can be realized today with the new capillary sequencers, sufficient computing power and the faith of investors.

Answers

What have we learned from all of these AGCTs? The best way to answer the question is to read the analytical sections of the papers. I will only make some general comments. It is important to remember that no statements can be made with high precision because the draft sequences have holes and imperfections, and the tools for analysis remain limited (as described in a further paper[6] in this issue, page 828). However, the answers provided by the draft will be of interest to many investigators, and the value of having the draft published in its imperfect form is unquestionable.

The sequences are about 90% complete for the euchromatic (weakly staining, gene-rich) regions of the human chromosomes. The estimated total size of the genome is 3.2 Gb (that is gigabases, the latest escalation of units needed to contain the fruits of modern technology). Of that, about 2.95 Gb is euchromatic. Only 1.1% to 1.4% is sequence that actually encodes protein; that is just 5% of the 28% of the sequence that is transcribed into RNA. Over half of the DNA consists of repeated sequences of various types: 45% in four classes of parasitic DNA elements, 3% in repeats of just a few bases, and about 5% in recent duplications of large segments of DNA. The amounts in the first and third classes will certainly grow as our ability to characterize them increases in effectiveness and we examine the darkly staining, heterochromatin regions of chromosomes. As the co-discoverer of reverse transcriptase (the enzyme that reverses the common mode of information transfer from DNA to RNA), I find it striking that most of the parasitic DNA came about by reverse transcription from RNA. In places, the genome looks like a sea of reverse-transcribed DNA with a small admixture of genes.

Repeats

By contrast, the puffer fish — another vertebrate — has a genome that contains very few repeats. But it encodes a perfectly functional creature, so it seems likely that most of the repeats are simply parasitic, selfish DNA elements that use the genome as a convenient host. People call this 'junk DNA', but from the DNA's point of view it deserves more respect. In most places in the human genome the selfish elements are tolerated, and in some places —near the ends of chromosomes, for instance, or near the chromosome constrictions called centromeres — it builds up to form huge segments. However, the repeated DNA may have both negative and positive effects. For instance, the paucity of repeats in certain highly regulated regions of the genome suggests that insertions there can disrupt gene regulation and are deleterious. Conversely, the enrichment of the so-called Alu class of repeated sequences in the gene-rich, high-GC regions of the genome implies that they have a positive function. The repeats can also be fodder for evolving new functions and act as loci for gene rearrangements.

In humans, virtually all of the parasitic DNA repeats seem old and enfeebled, with little evidence of continuing reinsertions. However, there has been very little evolutionary scouring of these repeats from the human genome, making it a rich record of evolutionary history. The mouse genome, by contrast, has many actively reinserting parasitic sequences and is scoured more intensely, making it a much younger and more dynamic genome. This difference might reflect the shorter generation time of mice or something about their physiology, but I find it an intriguingly enigmatic observation.

Much of what we learn about the global organization of the genome is an elaboration of previous notions. For instance, we knew that the genome had regions with a relatively high content of GC bases and regions high in AT, but now we have a very complete appreciation of this architecture. What maintains the patchiness of the GC/AT ratio in the genome remains an unanswered question. As was expected, most genes are located outside the hete-rochromatic regions; interestingly, however, in regions of the genome rich in GC bases, the gene density is greater and the average intron size is lower. These introns — made up of largely meaningless sequence that breaks up the protein-coding sequences (exons) of genes — are much longer in human DNA than in the genomes previously sequenced. Their dilution of the coding sequence is one element that makes finding genes by computer so difficult in human DNA.

A major interest of the genome sequence to many biologists will be the opportunity it provides to discover new genes in their favourite systems — for instance, cell biologists will search for new genes for signalling proteins, and neurobiologists will look for new ion channels. This data-mining exercise was carried out by various groups which report their initial findings in papers that appear on pages 824–859 of this issue. They found some new and interesting genes, but surprisingly few, and occasionally could not find the full extent of genes that they knew were there. The paucity of discoveries reflects their concentration on systems that were previously heavily studied.

Gene-regulatory sequences are now there for all to see, but initial attempts to find them were also disappointing. This is where the genomic sequences of other species — in which the regulatory sequences, but not the functionally insignificant DNA, are likely to be much the same — will open up a cornucopia. Basically, the human sequence at its present level of analysis allows us to answer many global questions fairly well, but the detailed questions remain open for the future.

What interested me most about the genome? The number of genes is high on the list. The public project estimates that there are 31,000 protein-encoding genes in the human genome, of which they can now provide a list of 22,000. Celera finds about 26,000. There are also about 740 identified genes that make the non-protein-coding RNAs involved in various cell housekeeping duties, with many more to be found. The number of coding genes in the human sequence compares with 6,000 for a yeast cell, 13,000 for a fly, 18,000 for a worm and 26,000 for a plant. None of the numbers for the multicellular organisms is highly accurate because of the limitations of gene-finding programs. But unless the human genome contains a lot of genes that are

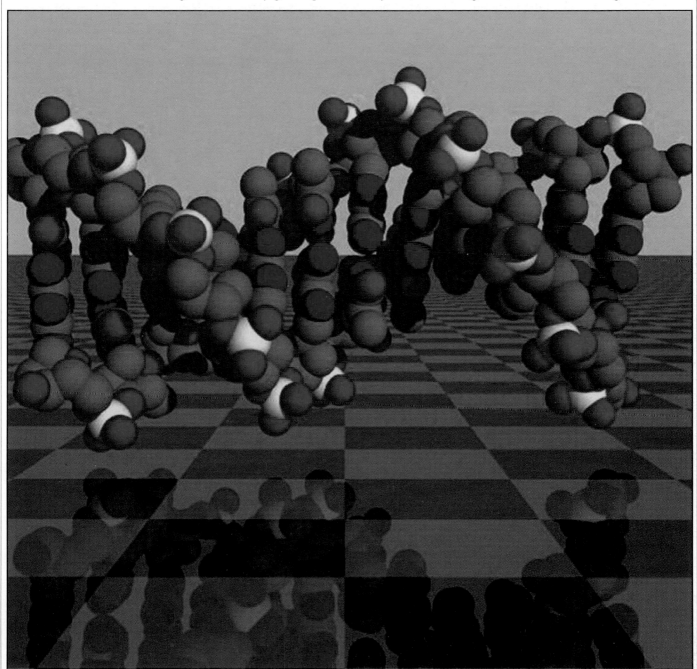

opaque to our computers, it is clear that we do not gain our undoubted complexity over worms and plants by using many more genes. Understanding what does give us our complexity — our enormous behavioural repertoire, ability to produce conscious action, remarkable physical coordination (shared with other vertebrates), precisely tuned alterations in response to external variations of the environment, learning, memory… need I go on? — remains a challenge for the future.

Complexity

Where do our genes come from? Mostly from the distant evolutionary past. In fact, only 94 of 1,278 protein families in our genome appear to be specific to vertebrates. The most elementary of cellular functions — basic metabolism, transcription of DNA into RNA, translation of RNA into protein, DNA replication and the like — evolved just once and have stayed pretty well fixed since the evolution of single-celled yeast and bacteria. The biggest difference between humans and worms or flies is the complexity of our proteins: more domains (modules) per protein and novel combinations of domains. The history is one of new architectures being built from old pieces. A few of our genes seem to have come directly from bacteria, rather than by evolution from bacteria — apparently bacterial genomes can be direct donors of genes to vertebrates. So DNA chimaeras consisting of the genes from several organisms can arise naturally as well as artificially (opponents of 'genetically modified foods' take note).

The most exciting new vista to come from the human genome is not tackling the question "What makes us human?", but addressing a different one: "What differentiates one organism from another?". The first question, imprecise as it is, cannot be answered by staring at a genome. The second, however, can be answered this way because our differences from plants, worms and flies are mainly a consequence of our genetic endowments. The Celera team[4] presents the more detailed analysis of the numbers of different protein motifs and protein types, in extensive tables. From them, it is easy to see what types of proteins and motifs have been amplified for specific types of organisms. In vertebrates, not surprisingly, we see elaboration and the *de novo* appearance of two types of genes: those for specific vertebrate abilities (such as neuronal complexity, blood-clotting and the acquired immune response), and those that provide increased general capabilities (such as genes for intra- and intercellular signalling, development, programmed cell death, and control of gene transcription). Someday soon we will have the mouse genome, and then those of fish and dogs, and probably the kangaroo genome from the Australians. Each of these will fill in a piece of the evolutionary puzzle and will provide exciting comparisons.

We wait with bated breath to see the chimpanzee genome. But knowing now how few genes humans have, I wonder if we will learn much about the origins of speech, the elaboration of the frontal lobes and the opposable thumb, the advent of upright posture, or the sources of abstract reasoning ability, from a simple genomic comparison of human and chimp. It seems likely that these features and abilities have mainly come from subtle changes — for example, in gene regulation, in the efficiency with which introns are spliced out of RNA, and in protein–protein interactions — that are not now easily visible to our computers and will require much more experimental study to tease out. Another half-century of work by armies of biologists may be needed before this key step of evolution is fully elucidated.

What is next? Lots of hard work, but with new tools and new aims. First, we have to stay the course and get the most precise representation of the genome that we can: this is a matter of filling the cracks, cleaning up the errors, and getting rid of the uncertainties that plague each of the analytical methods. Second, we need to see more genomes, with each one giving us a deeper insight into our own. Third, we need to learn how to take advantage of this book of life. Tools for scanning the activity levels of genes in different cells, tissues and settings are becoming available and are already revolutionizing how we do biological investigation. But we will have to move back from the general to the particular, because each gene is a story in itself and its full significance can be learned only from concentrating on its particular properties.

Fourth, we need to turn our new genomic information into an engine of pharmaceutical discovery. Individual humans differ from one another by about one base pair per thousand. These 'single nucleotide polymor-

phisms' (SNPs) are markers that can allow epidemiologists to uncover the genetic basis of many diseases. They can also provide information about our personal responses to medicines — in this way, the pharmaceutical industry will get new targets and new tools to sharpen drug specificity. Moreover, the analysis of SNPs will provide us with the power to uncover the genetic basis of our individual capabilities such as mathematical ability, memory, physical coordination, and even, perhaps, creativity.

Biology today enters a new era, mainly with a new methodology for answering old questions. Those questions are some of the deepest and simplest: "Daddy, where did I come from?"; "Mommy, why am I different from Sally?". As these and other questions get robust answers, biology will become an engine of transformation of our society. Instead of guessing about how we differ one from another, we will understand and be able to tailor our life experiences to our inheritance. We will also be able, to some extent, to control that inheritance. We are creating a world in which it will be imperative for each individual person to have sufficient scientific literacy to understand the new riches of knowledge, so that we can apply them wisely. ■

David Baltimore is at the California Institute of Technology, 1200 East California Boulevard, Mail Code 204-31, Pasadena, California 91125, USA.
e-mail: baltimo@caltech.edu

1. International Human Genome Sequencing Consortium *Nature* **409**, 860–921 (2001).
2. Watson, J. D. & Crick, F. H. C. *Nature* **171**, 737–738 (1953).
3. http://genome.cse.ucsc.edu/
4. Venter, J. C. *et al. Science* **291**, 1304–1351 (2001).
5. Aach, J. *et al. Nature* **409**, 856–859 (2001).
6. Birney, E., Bateman, A., Clamp, M. E. & Hubbard, T. J. *Nature* **409**, 827–828 (2001).

The maps

Clone by clone by clone

Maynard V. Olson

The public project's sequencing strategy involved producing a map of the human genome, and then pinning sequence to it. This helps to avoid errors in the sequence, especially in repetitive regions.

This issue of *Nature* celebrates a halfway point in the implementation of the 'map first, sequence later' strategy adopted by the Human Genome Project in the mid-1980s[1]. The results suggest that the strategy was basically sound. It led, as hoped, to a project that could be distributed internationally across many genome-sequencing centres, and that would allow sequenced fragments of the human genome to be anchored to mapped genomic landmarks long before the complete sequence coalesced

into one long string of Gs, As, Ts and Cs.

The centrepiece of the suite of mapping papers in this issue is on page 934, where the International Human Genome Mapping Consortium describes a 'clone-based' physical map of the human genome[2]. A map like this not only charts the genome, giving a structure on which to hang sequence data, but also provides a starting point for sequencing. Figure 1 shows the basics of the approach. I drew this figure in 1981, using India ink and a Leroy lettering set. Both

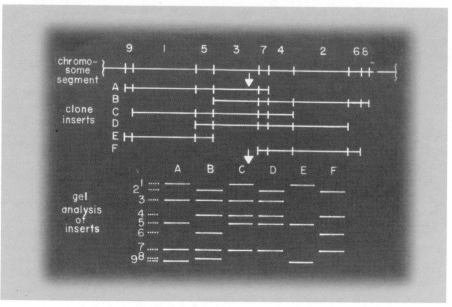

Figure 1 Clone-based physical mapping. The top line shows the location of 'restriction' sites (vertical bars) in a particular region of the genome. Restriction sites are places at which a site-specific restriction endonuclease cleaves DNA. The fragments produced by cleavage at every possible point in this region are numbered 1 to 9. Below the line are several clones with random end points, labelled A to F. Clones are produced by first partially digesting many copies of the genome with different restriction endonucleases; the resulting large segments are then inserted into bacteria and replicated (cloned). Each clone is digested with a restriction endonuclease, and the resulting fragments are separated, by size, on an electrophoretic gel ('gel analysis of inserts'). This process yields a distinctive pattern ('fingerprint') for each clone. The map-assembly problem requires working backwards (upwards in this figure) from the fingerprints to a clone-overlap map and restriction-site map of the chromosome segment. To finish the analysis of this region of the genome, the natural choice of clones to sequence would be A and B.

graphical and mapping technologies have come a long way since then, but the principles behind clone-based physical mapping have not changed.

The clone-based approach works as follows. Many copies of the genome are cut up into segments of about 150,000 base pairs by partial digestion with site-specific restriction endonucleases — enzymes that cleave DNA in specific places. ('Partial' digestion means that the reaction is not carried out for long enough to allow every possible cleavage to be made.) The large DNA segments are plugged into bacterial 'artificial chromosomes' (BACs) and inserted into bacteria, where they are copied exactly each time the bacteria divide. The process produces 'clones' of identical DNA molecules that can be purified for further analysis. Next, each clone is completely digested with a restriction endonuclease, chosen to produce a characteristic pattern of small fragments, or a 'fingerprint', for each clone. Comparison of the patterns reveals overlap between the clones, allowing them to be lined up in order, while the sites in the genome at which the restriction endonuclease cleaves are charted. The result is a physical map.

Individual BAC clones are then sheared into smaller fragments and cloned; the resulting 'small-insert' subclones are sequenced. The sequence of an individual

BAC clone is assembled from the sequences of an 'oversampled' set of subclones (in other words, enough subclones are sequenced to ensure that each part of the original clone is analysed several times). Finally, the whole genome sequence is assembled by melding together the sequences of a set of BACs that spans the genome.

This approach is similar to that used in the 1980s and early 1990s to map and sequence the genomes of the nematode *Caenorhabditis elegans* and the yeast *Saccharomyces cerevisiae*[3,4]. What is new in the human project is its staggering scale, and the speed with which it has been completed. By way of comparison, although the nematode and yeast genomes are, respectively, only 3% and 0.5% the size of the human genome, these early mapping projects spanned the better part of a decade, as opposed to two years for the much larger human project.

One weakness of clone-based physical mapping is that the maps often have poor continuity. For example, there is not always a BAC clone to cover every part of the genome; and overlaps between clones can be obscured by data errors or the presence of large-scale repeats in the genome. The current map[2] has more than 1,000 discontinuities. These will cause some difficulties as the Human Genome Project moves to its next phase, which will involve ensuring accuracy and

filling in any gaps in the sequence. Nonetheless, the current map typically maintains continuity for several million base pairs at a stretch. These continuous segments are big enough to allow the clone-based map to be overlaid on various lower-resolution maps. In this way, the mapped segments can be ordered and orientated, much as a discontinuous patchwork of high-resolution maps of the Earth's surface can be orientated by overlaying them on a satellite photograph of the whole Earth.

Two particularly interesting low-resolution maps are the genetic and cytogenetic maps, on pages 951 and 953 of this issue[5,6]. The genetic map[5] is based on the probability of the occurrence of recombination — the swapping of corresponding, nearly identical segments of DNA between maternally and paternally derived chromosomes as the genome is passed from one generation to the next. The cytogenetic map[6] is based on subtle variations in the staining properties of different regions of the genome, as viewed by light microscopy. Yet more papers describe different approaches to clone-based mapping[7–9]. These methods were applied to particular chromosomes simply because different sequencing centres chose to rely on the whole-genome map to different degrees.

But was all this cartography even necessary? Another draft of the human genome sequence is described in this week's *Science* by Celera Genomics[10]. This group adopted a different approach, which involved preparing small-insert clones directly from genomic DNA rather than from mapped BACs. The major rationale for the BAC-by-BAC approach[2] was to make easier the finishing phase of the Human Genome Project, which lies ahead. The consortium now plans to upgrade the 30,000 BAC sequences by sequencing more subclones from each BAC (the 'topping-up' phase) and then resolving internal gaps and discrepancies (the 'finishing' phase). Segmenting the finishing phase into BAC-sized portions provides an enormous advantage in dealing with blocks of sequence that are repeated at many different places within the genome. The power of this strategy is nicely illustrated by the mapping of the Y chromosome, whose repetitive structure is unusually complex (page 943 of this issue[11]).

Nature readers should not expect any real answer to the question of which of these two approaches is the better one. But it is likely that the only players still on the field when the toughest finishing issues are confronted will be the public consortium's BAC brigade. In the future, as genome sequencing moves on to other mammals, the context will have changed; the human sequence will provide an invaluable guide to assembling long stretches of sequence that are shared among all mammalian genomes. So the sequencing of the human genome is likely to be the only large sequencing project carried to completion by the methods described in this issue. Genome sequencing will get easier from here.

Looking ahead, there are two threats to producing a quality finished product. One is simple exhaustion on the part of the consortium's members: each new round of press conferences announcing that the human genome has been sequenced saps the morale of those who must come to work each day actually to do what they read in the newspapers has already been done.

We may also expect to hear the argument that the current sequence is good enough for most purposes, and that remaining problems should be resolved by users as the need for accurate sequence in specific regions arises. What we have now is certainly a lot better than what we had yesterday. But biologists in the future will be comparing vast data sets to the reference sequence of the human genome. They must be able to do so with confidence that the discrepancies they encounter are due to the limitations of their

own data or, more interestingly, to biology. They should not need to expend time, energy and imagination compensating for a failure now to pursue the Human Genome Project to a grand conclusion. We must move on and finish the job, even as the bright lights of media attention shift elsewhere. ∎

Maynard V. Olson is in the Departments of Medicine and Genetics, Fluke Hall, Mason Road, University of Washington, Seattle, Washington 98195-2145, USA.
e-mail: mvo@u.washington.edu

1. National Research Council *Mapping and Sequencing the Human Genome* (National Academy Press, Washington DC, 1988).
2. The International Human Genome Mapping Consortium *Nature* **409**, 934–941 (2001).
3. Coulson, A., Sulston, J., Brenner, S. & Karn, J. *Proc. Natl Acad. Sci. USA* **83**, 7821–7825 (1986).
4. Olson, M. V. *et al. Proc. Natl Acad. Sci. USA* **83**, 7826–7830 (1986).
5. Yu, A. *et al. Nature* **409**, 951–953 (2001).
6. The BAC Resource Consortium *Nature* **409**, 953–958 (2001).
7. Montgomery, K. T. *et al. Nature* **409**, 945–946 (2001).
8. Brüls, T. *et al. Nature* **409**, 947–948 (2001).
9. Bentley, D. R. *et al. Nature* **409**, 942–943 (2001).
10. Venter, J. C. *et al. Science* **291**, 1304–1351 (2001).
11. Tilford, C. A. *et al. Nature* **409**, 943–945 (2001).

The draft sequences

Filling in the gaps

Peer Bork and Richard Copley

Two rough drafts of the human genome sequence are now published. Completion of the sequences lies ahead, but the implications for studying human diseases and for biotechnology are already profound.

With the publication of the human genome sequence — described and analysed on page 860 of this issue[1] and in this week's *Science*[2] — we cross a border on the route to a better understanding of our biological selves. But unlike the previously published sequences of human chromosomes 21 and 22 (refs 3,4), the present sequences of the whole human genome are not considered complete. The bulk of the data make up what is called a 'rough draft'. So what is all the fuss about? What exactly does 'rough draft' mean, and what can we learn from sequences such as this?

In the draft from the publicly funded International Human Genome Sequencing Consortium[1], around 90% of the gene-rich — euchromatic — portion of the genome has been sequenced and 'assembled', the term used to describe the process of using a computer to join up bits of sequence into a larger whole. Each base pair of this 90% was sequenced four times on average, ensuring reasonable precision. Only about a quarter of the whole genome is considered 'finished' — another bit of genomics jargon, which basically means that each base pair has been sequenced eight to ten times on average, with gaps in the sequence existing only because of the limitations of present technology. Nonetheless, the sequence of base pairs in

the draft is very accurate, and is unlikely to change much; 91% of the euchromatin sequenced has an error rate of less than one base in 10,000 (ref. 1).

For the other draft, that produced by Celera Genomics[2], a variety of methods suggest that between 88% and 93% of the euchromatin has been sequenced and assembled. But direct comparison of these numbers with the public consortium's draft is almost impossible — different procedures and measures were used to process the data and to estimate accuracy. Both projects also have sequence data that were not used in the assembly process, raising the real level of coverage by a few percentage points.

These numbers might seem rather arbitrary, but even when the first genome of an animal species was published[5], it was clear that simple, practical finish lines do not exist (Box 1, Fig. 1). The present level of coverage of the human genome reflects the point where a shift of focus occurs, from sequencing the genome many times over to producing a high-quality, continuous sequence[6]. There is some way to go yet.

Essentially, 'rough draft' refers to the fact that the sequences are not continuous — there are gaps (Box 1). If there are too many gaps, it can be impossible to order and orientate the many small strings of bases that are the raw products of genome sequencing. This might, for example, hamper projects that seek to identify genes involved in inherited diseases. A first step to finding such genes is to work out which region of which chromosome they are on. The complete genome sequence should be immensely useful for the next step — identifying the relevant gene at that region. But gaps and errors in ordering and placing the strings of sequence will make this difficult.

Another problem of incompleteness is that it is difficult to make definitive

---

Box 1 What makes a completely sequenced genome?

When is sequencing work on a genome complete? No genome for a eukaryotic organism — roughly, those organisms whose cells contain a nucleus — has been sequenced to 100%. There are regions, often highly repetitive, that are difficult or impossible to clone (one of the initial steps in a sequencing project) or sequence with current technology. Fortunately, such regions are expected to contain relatively few protein-coding genes[4,10].

The extent of these regions varies widely in different species. So, rather than applying a universal gold standard, each sequencing project has made pragmatic decisions as to what constitutes a sufficient level of coverage for a particular genome. For example, as much as one-third of the sequence of the fruitfly *Drosophila melanogaster* was not stable in the cloning systems used, and so was not sequenced. But 97% of the so-called euchromatic portion — where most genes are thought to reside — was sequenced[11] (Fig. 1).

For the human genome, one definition of 'finished' is that fewer than one base in 10,000 is incorrectly assigned[6]; more than 95% of the euchromatic regions are sequenced; and each gap is smaller than 150 kilobases[12]. Such standards represent realistic goals given current technology. By this standard, over a quarter of the public consortium's sequence[1] is considered finished at present, including the previously published long arms of chromosomes 21 and 22 (refs 3,4; Fig. 1). The Celera sequences of chromosomes 21 and 22 are slightly more gappy than those from the public consortium, but the converse seems to be true for the other chromosomes[2]. But again, as different protocols were used, it is not easy to compare the overall status of the two assemblies. In the longer term, as much of the heterochromatin — which is harder to sequence, and contains few genes — as possible must be sequenced, because we might otherwise miss important features.

P.B. & R.C.

Organism	Year	Millions of bases sequenced	Total coverage (%)	Coverage of euchromatin (%)	Predicted number of genes	Number of genes per million bases sequenced
Saccharomyces cerevisiae	1996	12	93	100	5,800	483
Caenorhabditis elegans	1998	97	99	100	19,099	197
Drosophila melanogaster	2000	116	64	97	13,601	117
Arabidopsis thaliana	2000	115	92	100	25,498	221
Human chromosome 21	2000	34	75	100	225	7
Human chromosome 22	1999	34	70	97	545	16
Human genome rough draft (public sequence)	2001	2,693	84	90	31,780	12
Human genome rough draft (Celera sequence)	2001	2,654	83	88—93	39,114	15

Figure 1 **Sequenced eukaryotic genomes. Total coverage uses an estimate of the total genome size and includes heterochromatin (condensed genomic areas that were originally characterized by staining techniques, and are thought to be highly repetitive and gene-poor). The gene-rich areas make up euchromatin. Gene numbers are taken from the original sequence publications[1-6,14,15]; most numbers have since changed slightly and different sources give different estimates depending on protocols. The data for the public consortium's rough draft of the human genome are taken from ref. 1, Table 8, page 872. The estimate of total coverage for the Celera data is based on the public consortium's estimate of the full genome size (3,200 million base pairs); the percentage of euchromatin covered is taken from ref. 2. The predicted numbers of human genes are discussed further in the text.**

How many genes are encoded in the human genome? This is a simple question without — as yet — a straightforward answer[13]. The density of genes in the human genome is much lower than for any other genome sequenced so far (Fig. 1), making it particularly difficult to predict where genes are.

Both Celera and the public sequencing consortium used computational algorithms to model genes and make predictions, but such methods are far from perfect. Not only can the start and end positions of a predicted gene be wrong, but exons (the coding parts of a gene) can be missed entirely or wrongly predicted to exist. To reduce this latter effect, the public sequencing consortium required the exons of predicted genes to be 'confirmed', by showing significant similarity to a known sequence (DNA or protein) in a database. But this requirement might be too conservative, making it difficult to predict the presence of new gene families. Celera has required similar confirmation of predictions, but its mouse-genome sequencing project may have provided evidence for further vertebrate-specific genes.

Spurious prediction is also a problem. All genes are expressed by being copied (transcribed) into messenger RNA; most messenger RNAs are then translated into proteins. But even evidence that a stretch of DNA is transcribed does not definitively show that stretch to be a gene. We do not know how efficiently cells control transcription; indeed, it seems likely that non-gene DNA sequences are transcribed relatively frequently[12]. Nor do we know how well the cell identifies transcripts that cannot be translated into a functioning protein. Moreover, proteins that cannot serve any useful function (for example, because they cannot fold correctly) could be made, but rapidly removed. To arrive at a true set of protein-encoding genes, we cannot rely on computational techniques alone, but must continue to characterize proteins and their functions.

These problems provide scope for estimates of human gene number to vary widely. Although recent estimates are converging in the 30,000–40,000 range (as opposed to earlier estimates of 100,000 or so), it could be many years before we have the final answer. P.B & R.C.

statements about which genes are unique to other species and do not have relatives in the human genome. So it might be prudent not to place too much emphasis on such 'missing' genes at this stage. Even so, they are running out of places to hide, particularly because the level of coverage of the human genome is probably higher than reported here[1,2] — there are other chunks of unassembled genome sequence in public databases, such as in independent collections of so-called expressed sequence tags.

But ensuring high quality and high coverage are only two aspects of producing a finished genome. For most biologists, the real interest is in the genes themselves. Here, the picture is less rosy, although the problems are caused not so much by the draft nature of the sequence as by the difficulty in finding genes among the other genomic DNA (Box 2).

Even coming up with a rough count of the number of genes is not straightforward. The public consortium's initial set contains about 32,000 genes, made up of around 15,000 known genes and 17,000 predictions. But these 32,000 genes are estimated to come from around 24,500 actual genes — some predicted genes could be 'pseudogenes', or just fragments of real genes. On the other hand, the sensitivity of prediction tends to be only about 60%, so it is reasonable to assume that another 6,800 or so genes (40% of

17,000) have been overlooked. This is how the present estimate of about 31,000 genes (6,800 plus 24,500) was reached[1]. Celera predicts that there are around 39,000 genes, but warns that the evidence for some 12,000 of these is weak[2]. The two groups use different gene-identification techniques, so these numbers are not directly comparable. Minor changes in procedures or data could alter either figure considerably. For example, such changes led to a recent estimate being lowered[7,8] from 120,000 to fewer than 81,000 — and both now seem untenable. Much is a matter of interpretation.

Fortunately, there is every reason to believe that the quality of gene prediction will rapidly improve, and an experimental technique for doing so is discussed on page 922 (ref. 9). With the sequencing of the genomes of other vertebrates, our ability to detect genes by their similarity to known sequences will get better. This is because, thanks to natural selection, gene sequences tend to be altered less during evolution than the DNA surrounding them. In a couple of years we should have at least a more complete list of testable gene candidates.

Despite all this, the information now available has profound implications. For example, there are already many heavily hunted disease-associated genes that have been identified using the public draft (ref. 1, Table 26, page 912). Together with studies of

single nucleotide polymorphisms — the base differences from human to human — the draft also provides a framework for understanding the genetic basis and evolution of many human characteristics.

With the draft in hand, researchers have a new tool for studying the regulatory regions and networks of genes. Comparisons with other genomes should reveal common regulatory elements, and the environments of genes shared with other species may offer insight into function and regulation beyond the level of individual genes. The draft is also a starting point for studies of the three-dimensional packing of the genome into a cell's nucleus. Such packing is likely to influence gene regulation.

On a more applied note, the information can be used to exploit technologies such as chips made using DNA or proteins, complementing more traditional approaches. Such chips could now, for instance, contain all the members of a protein family, making it possible to find out which are active in particular diseased tissues. A new world of biotechnology will provide tools and information by exploiting genome data.

Sequencing the tough leftovers of the human genome will be essential. Without a finished sequence, we will not know what we are missing. Each missed gene is potentially a missed drug target, and even gene-poor areas might be critical for gene regulation. Nevertheless, we must now confront the fact that the era of rapid growth in human genomic information is over. The challenge we face is nothing less than understanding how this comparatively small set of genes creates the diversity of phenomena and characteristics that we see in human life. The human genome lies before us, ready for interpretation. ∎

Peer Bork and Richard Copley are at EMBL, Meyerhofstrasse 1, 69012 Heidelberg, Germany.
Peer Bork is at the Max-Delbrück Center for Molecular Medicine, Robert-Rössle-Strasse 10, 13125 Berlin-Buch, Germany.
e-mails: Peer.Bork@EMBL-Heidelberg.de
Richard.Copley@EMBL-Heidelberg.de

1. International Human Genome Sequencing Consortium *Nature* **409**, 860–921 (2001).
2. Venter, J. C. *et al. Science* **291**, 1304–1351 (2001).
3. Dunham, I. *et al. Nature* **402**, 489–495 (1999).
4. The Chromosome 21 Mapping and Sequencing Consortium *Nature* **405**, 311–319 (2000).
5. The *C. elegans* Sequencing Consortium *Science* **282**, 2012–2018 (1998).
6. Collins, F. S. *et al. Science* **282**, 682–689 (1998).
7. Liang, F. *et al. Nature Genet.* **25**, 239–240 (2000).
8. Liang, F. *et al. Nature Genet.* **26**, 501 (2000).
9. Shoemaker, D. D. *et al. Nature* **409**, 922–927 (2001).
10. The Arabidopsis Sequencing Consortium *Cell* **100**, 377–386 (2000).
11. Adams, M. D. *et al. Science* **287**, 2185–2195 (2000).
12. Normile, D. & Pennisi, E. *Science* **285**, 2038–2039 (1999).
13. Aparicio, S. *Nature Genet.* **25**, 129–130 (2000).
14. Goffeau, A. *et al. Nature* **387** (suppl.), 1–105 (1997).
15. The Arabidopsis Genome Initiative *Nature* **408**, 796–815 (2000).

The draft sequences

Comparing species

Gerald M. Rubin

Comparing the human genome sequences with those of other species will not only reveal what makes us genetically different. It may also help us understand what our genes do.

How are the differences between humans and other organisms reflected in our genomes? How similar are the numbers and types of proteins in humans, fruitflies, worms, plants and yeast? And what does all of this tell us about what makes a species unique? With the publication of the draft human genome sequences, on page 860 of this issue[1] and in this week's *Science*[2], we can start to compare the sequences of vertebrate, invertebrate and plant genomes in an attempt to answer these questions.

An obvious place to start our comparison is the total number of genes in each species. Here is a real surprise: the human genome probably contains between 25,000 and 40,000 genes, only about twice the number needed to make a fruitfly[3], worm[4] or plant[5]. We know that there is a higher degree of 'alternative splicing' in humans than in other species. In other words, there are often many more ways in which a gene's protein-coding sections (exons) can be joined together to create a functional messenger RNA molecule, ready to be translated into protein. So more proteins are encoded per gene in humans than in other species.

Even so, we cannot escape the conclusion — drawn previously from comparisons of simpler genomes[6] — that physical and behavioural differences between species are not related in any simple way to gene number. Many researchers, struck by the fact that there are four times as many genes in some gene families in the human genome compared with fruitflies[7], extrapolated from these cases and suggested that the human genome might be the product of two doublings of the whole of a simpler genome found in the common ancestor of fruitflies and humans. But, as the analyses of the human genome show[1,2], if such doublings did occur, the evidence for them has since been obscured by massive gene loss and amplification of particular gene families in the human genome.

Individual proteins often feature discrete structural units, called domains, that are conserved in evolution. More than 90% of the domains that can be identified in human proteins are also present in fruitfly and worm proteins, although they have been shuffled to create nearly twice as many different arrangements in humans[1,2]. Thus, vertebrate evolution has required the invention of few new domains. Of the human proteins that are predicted to exist, 60% have some sequence similarity to proteins from other species whose genomes have been sequenced. Just over 40% of the predicted human proteins share similarity with fruitfly or worm proteins. And 61% of fruitfly proteins, 43% of worm proteins and 46% of yeast proteins have sequence similarities to predicted human proteins.

But what about the proteins whose sequences show no strong similarity to known proteins from other species? Over a third of the yeast, fruitfly, worm and human proteins fall into this class. These proteins might retain similar functions, even though their sequences have diverged. Or they might have acquired species-specific functions.

Alternatively, we may need to entertain the possibility that the open reading frames that encode these proteins are maintained in a new way, one that is independent of the precise amino-acid sequence and thus is free to evolve rapidly. (An open reading frame is the part of a gene encoding the amino-acid sequence of its protein product.) After all, we know that cells have at least one mechanism, called nonsense-mediated decay of mRNA, for detecting imperfect open reading frames irrespective of the amino-acid sequence that they encode[8].

It will be interesting to see the extent to which the number of human proteins in this rapidly evolving class decreases as the genomes of other vertebrates, such as mice, are sequenced. This will give us an indication of just how fast these proteins are changing. Indeed, there is already evidence from studies of flies[9] and worms[10] that these rapidly evolving proteins are less likely to have essential functions, consistent with their being less likely to be conserved during evolution.

Such comparisons of distantly related genomes are fascinating from an evolutionary point of view. But comparison of closely related genomes will be much more important in addressing the key problem now facing genomics — determining the function of individual DNA segments. The concept is simple: segments that have a function are more likely to retain their sequence during evolution than non-functional segments. So DNA segments that are conserved between species are likely to have important functions. The ideal species for comparison are those whose form, physiology and behaviour are as similar as possible, but whose genomes have evolved sufficiently that non-functional sequences have had time to diverge. In practice, there may be no one ideal species, because different genes and regulatory sites evolve at different rates. Nevertheless, this approach has a long history of success, and becomes progressively more efficient as the cost of DNA sequencing declines.

One use of such sequence comparisons is

to determine the structure of genes — which parts (the exons) make their way into a functional mRNA molecule and which do not (the introns). The high degree of alternative splicing in vertebrates makes this comparative approach particularly important. Gene-finding computational algorithms cannot easily predict the existence of alternative forms of an mRNA without experimental information, but this information is difficult to come by in the case of rare mRNAs. For example, an exon that is used in only a few cells of the human brain might never be experimentally detected in an mRNA. But that exon's sequence would probably be conserved in the mouse genome.

Comparing the genomes of closely related species can also help in identifying gene-control regions. This approach has been used for over two decades[11], and has been validated by showing that the conserved sequences indeed correspond to functional control elements in individual genes[12]. But this computational problem is more difficult than identifying exons, and it will be challenging to scale up to a genome-wide level. The proteins that control gene expression by recognizing regulatory regions often detect sequence features that elude the best computer algorithms, and may use information from contacts with other proteins that is difficult to model. Proteins are simply cleverer than computers.

That said, our knowledge of the DNA-binding properties of individual proteins, as well as the structural features of the DNA sites to which they bind, continues to increase. Moreover, we can use experimental evidence; for example, genes that are expressed together might be expected to share control elements. And, as methods for comparing sequences continue to improve, we can expect to learn more about elusive features of the genome, such as genes encoding RNAs that do not encode proteins[13], start points of DNA replication, and genetic elements that control chromosome structure.

Gerald M. Rubin is in the Department of Molecular and Cell Biology, University of California at Berkeley, Berkeley, California 94708-3200, and the Howard Hughes Medical Institute, 4000 Jones Bridge Road, Chevy Chase, Maryland 20815-6789, USA.
e-mail: gerry@fruitfly.berkeley.edu

1. International Human Genome Sequencing Consortium *Nature* **409**, 860–921 (2001).
2. Venter, J. C. *et al. Science* **291**, 1304–1351 (2001).
3. Adams, M. D. *et al. Science* **287**, 2185–2195 (2000).
4. The *C. elegans* Sequencing Consortium *Science* **282**, 2012–2018 (1998).
5. The Arabidopsis Genome Initiative *Nature* **408**, 796–815 (2000).
6. Rubin, G. M. *et al. Science* **287**, 2204–2215 (2000).
7. Spring, J. *FEBS Lett.* **400**, 2–8 (1997).
8. Hentze, M. W. & Kulozik, A. E. *Cell* **96**, 307–310 (1999).
9. Ashburner, M. *et al. Genetics* **153**, 179–219 (1999).
10. Fraser, A. G. *et al. Nature* **408**, 325–330 (2000).
11. Ravetch, J. V., Kirsch, I. R. & Leder, P. *Proc. Natl Acad. Sci. USA* **77**, 6734–6738 (1980).
12. Fortini, M. E. & Rubin, G. M. *Genes Dev.* **4**, 444–463 (1990).
13. Lee, R. C., Feinbaum, R. L. & Ambros, V. *Cell* **75**, 843–854 (1993).

Single nucleotide polymorphisms

From the evolutionary past...

Mark Stoneking

Single nucleotide polymorphisms are the bread-and-butter of DNA sequence variation. They provide a rich source of information about the evolutionary history of human populations.

Studies of genetic variation in human populations began inauspiciously[1]. The first such study — of ABO blood-group frequencies — was carried out by two Polish immunologists, Ludwik and Hanka Hirszfeld, at the end of the First World War. This work was notable for its broad coverage of the world's populations, large sample sizes and scrupulous attention to anthropological details. Yet the Hirszfelds still ran into difficulties in publishing in *The Lancet*, the premier medical journal of the time. The editor could not see the relevance of their work, and so this seminal study of human genetic variation first appeared in an obscure anthropological journal[2]. The relevance became abundantly clear when Felix Bernstein subsequently used the Hirszfelds' data to demonstrate that the ABO blood-group frequencies were better explained by a single gene with three variants (alleles), and not —

as prevailing wisdom then held — two genes each with two alleles[3].

Happily, times have changed, diversity is now all the rage[4,5], and editors have become more appreciative of the importance of human genetic variation. The latest evidence of that is the paper on page 928 of this issue[6], which reports the identification and mapping of 1.4 million single nucleotide polymorphisms (SNPs, pronounced 'snips') in the human genome. The paper is the result of the labours of a large collaboration, The International SNP Map Working Group.

So, what are SNPs? Quite simply, they are the bread-and-butter of DNA sequence variation — polymorphism, to those in the business. A DNA sequence is a linear combination of four nucleotides; compare two sequences, position by position, and wherever you come across different nucleotides at the same position, that's a SNP (see Fig. 1 on

page 823). So SNPs reflect past mutations that were mostly (but not exclusively) unique events, and two individuals sharing a variant allele are thereby marked with a common evolutionary heritage. In other words, our genes have ancestors, and analysing shared patterns of SNP variation can identify them.

However, the real importance of SNPs is that there are so many of them. One estimate[7] is that comparing two human DNA sequences results in a SNP every 1,000–2,000 nucleotides. That may not sound like much until you realize that there are 3.2 billion nucleotides in the human genome, which translates into 1.6 million–3.2 million SNPs. And that's just from comparing two sequences — the total number of SNPs in humans is obviously much more. Most human variation that is influenced by genes can be traced to SNPs, especially in such medically (and commercially) important traits as how likely you are to become afflicted with a particular disease, or how you might respond to a particular pharmaceutical treatment, as discussed by Chakravarti[8] on the following page. And even when a SNP is not directly responsible, the sheer number of SNPs means they can also be used to locate genes that influence such traits.

The deluge of SNPs reported by the SNP working group[6] also promises great things for those of us who analyse patterns of molecular genetic variation to reconstruct the evolutionary history of human populations. Our genes contain the signature of an expansion from Africa within the past 150,000 years or so[9]. But there is still debate as to whether the modern humans from Africa completely replaced archaic non-African populations with no interbreeding, or whether we perhaps carry the vestiges of Neanderthal or other archaic non-African genes.

Demonstrating a recent African origin for every single one of our 3.2 billion nucleotides goes beyond the bounds of reason or necessity, but there is still much to be learned. For a start, most of our insights into molecular anthropology arise from DNA in mitochondria and (more recently) polymorphisms of the Y chromosome. This is because these DNA sequences are haploid — that is, represented just once in each cell, in contrast to the other chromosomes, which are represented twice — and they are inherited from just one parent, so they do not undergo the usual sequence shuffling (recombination) during egg and sperm production. This makes them easier to analyse and extremely informative. But both suffer from the drawback that, in the absence of recombination, they behave as single genes, and the history of any single gene can differ from that of a population or species because of natural selection or chance events involving that gene.

Accurate inferences concerning population history demand the analysis of several genes, with the most promising approach involving haplotypes[10], which consist of several closely spaced (linked) polymorphisms. The advantage of haplotypes over simply analysing polymorphisms at random is that there is valuable information in the associations between linked polymorphisms — the whole is greater than the sum of the parts. So the 1.4 million SNPs are a welcome resource that will greatly help in identifying haplotypes for tracing human evolutionary history, especially those that might reveal archaic non-African ancestry.

However, answering all of our questions about human evolutionary history will not be as simple as mining the SNP database and determining haplotypes in a representative sample of worldwide populations. There are four main reasons for that.

First, to be really useful, the SNPs in the database should really be SNPs, and not errors or artefacts, and they should be polymorphic in other samples, not just the sample of individuals used to find the SNPs. An important aspect of the SNP working group's data is that 1,585 SNPs were chosen for further verification, of which about 95% turned out to be true SNPs, which is good news indeed. Moreover, 1,276 SNPs were tested on additional population samples and at least 82% were polymorphic, which is reassuring.

Second, one might ask why only 0.1% of the 1.4 million SNPs were verified and tested. The answer is that our ability to determine allele frequencies efficiently and inexpensively for large numbers of SNPs lags behind our ability to simply identify them. This situation is reminiscent of the beginnings of the Human Genome Project, when developing technology was a primary concern and it was not at all clear how the 3.2 billion nucleotides were going to be determined. But human ingenuity won out then, and given the number of bright and capable minds now wrestling with the SNP-typing problem, one or more solutions should soon be at hand (especially with the motivation of lucrative commercial applications).

Third, a problem known as ascertainment bias can complicate the interpretation of results based on SNPs. For example, SNPs that were found to be polymorphic in European populations will overestimate genetic diversity in European as opposed to non-European populations. Moreover, the probability of finding a SNP, and the frequency of polymorphism at a SNP, depends on how many times a particular DNA segment was sequenced, and from how many individuals. The SNP working group report some intriguing preliminary findings regarding how SNP diversity is apportioned among chromosomes. But further work is required to see if these are truly biological differences, or if they instead reflect

ascertainment biases. Ascertainment bias is not an insurmountable problem — statistical geneticists love this sort of challenge and are already coming up with creative solutions[11]. Even so, SNP-finders must keep careful track of how their SNPs were ascertained.

Fourth, the emphasis in the SNP database is on SNPs where both of the alleles occur at high frequency, because these will be most useful for disease-association studies. In general, the higher the frequency of a SNP allele, the older the mutation that produced it, so high-frequency SNPs largely predate human population diversification. But many questions in human evolution involve specific migrations (such as the colonization of Polynesia or the Americas) for which population-specific alleles are most informative — indeed, this is one of the attractions of mitochondrial-DNA and Y-chromosome analyses for such questions, because population-specific alleles can be readily found. It is unlikely that Polynesian-specific SNPs are present in the database, so more work will be required to find such informative, population-specific SNPs.

Still, one can imagine that in the not-too-distant future the details of human population history will have been fleshed out, at least to the extent possible by analysing genetic variation in extant populations. What then? One area that is receiving increasing attention is the detection of the effects of natural selection in human populations[12]. Using SNPs to find chromosomal regions with abnormally low levels of varia-

tion is a particularly promising way of detecting the genomic signature of selection for favourable mutations[13].

Another area of increasing interest is identifying the molecular genetic basis of 'normal' phenotypic variation[4] — that is, variation of the old-fashioned, morphological kind, which is a traditional concern of anthropology. Molecular anthropology has for the most part concentrated on the molecules and what their diversity tells us about human evolution. With the advent of the human genome sequence and the SNP database, the ultimate in molecular tools, we are ironically now poised to focus on phenotypes and what their diversity tells us about human evolution — thereby bringing the anthropology back into molecular anthropology.

Mark Stoneking is at the Max Planck Institute for Evolutionary Anthropology, Inselstrasse 22, D-04103 Leipzig, Germany.
e-mail: stoneking@eva.mpg.de

1. Mourant, A. E. *Blood Relations* p.13 (Oxford Univ. Press, 1983).
2. Hirszfeld, L. & Hirszfeld, H. *Anthropologie* **29**, 505–537 (1919).
3. Crow, J. F. *Genetics* **133**, 4–7 (1993).
4. Weiss, K. M. *Genome Res.* **8**, 691–697 (1998).
5. Collins, F. S., Brooks, L. D. & Chakravarti, A. *Genome Res.* **8**, 1229–1231 (1998).
6. The International SNP Map Working Group *Nature* **409**, 928–933 (2001).
7. Li, W. H. & Sadler, L. A. *Genetics* **129**, 513–523 (1991).
8. Chakravarti, A. *Nature* **409**, 822–823 (2001).
9. Stoneking, M. *Evol. Anthropol.* **2**, 60–73 (1993).
10. Tishkoff, S. A. *et al. Science* **271**, 1380–1387 (1996).
11. Kuhner, M. K., Beerli, P., Yamato, J. & Felsenstein, J. *Genetics* **156**, 439–447 (2000).
12. Przeworski, M., Hudson, R. R. & Di Rienzo, A. *Trends Genet.* **16**, 296–302 (2000).
13. Nurminsky, D., De Aguiar, D., Bustamante, C. D. & Hartl, D. L. *Science* **291**, 128–130 (2001).

Single nucleotide polymorphisms

...to a future of genetic medicine

Aravinda Chakravarti

Single base differences between human genomes underlie differences in susceptibility to, or protection from, a host of diseases. Hence the great potential of such information in medicine.

The beginning of the Human Genome Project, over a decade ago, was accompanied by a cantankerous debate over whose genome was to be sequenced. Would it be a single individual? A celebrity, perhaps (widely rumoured to be Jim Watson, co-discoverer of the structure of DNA)? Or would several genomes, from many individuals, be studied? The discussion struck at the very heart of genetics. As the study of inherited variation between individuals, genetics might not immediately benefit from the sequence of a single genome. But even one genome would be immensely revealing to the science of deciphering the molecular blueprint of a species. Fortunately, geneticists were not forced to make this choice. Papers in this issue describe not only a single,

history-making human genome sequence, composed of little bits from many humans[1] (page 860), but also some 1.4 million sites of variation mapped along that reference sequence[2] (page 928).

But why this preoccupation with sequence variation, with the fact that no two humans (except identical twins) are genetically the same? The answer is that such variations, or 'polymorphisms', are markers of genes and genomes with which researchers perform genetic analysis in an outbred species where matings cannot be controlled. The fields of human and medical genetics simply cannot exist without understanding this variation.

It has become clear that the two 'genomes' that each of us carry, inherited

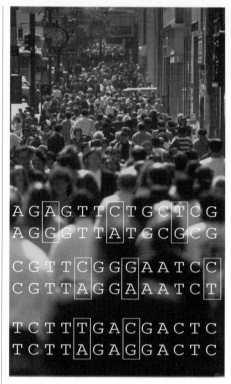

Figure 1 The most common sources of variation between humans are single nucleotide polymorphisms (SNPs) — single base differences between genome sequences. Fragments of two sequences, with eight SNPs, are shown.

from our parents, most often differ — from each other, and from the genomes of other humans — in terms of single base changes[1] (Fig. 1). The twentieth century saw the identification of only a few thousand of these so-called single nucleotide polymorphisms (SNPs, or 'snips' to the streetwise). In just the first year of the new century, this number has been increased one-thousand-fold[2]. Beyond the numbers, the excitement today comes from precise knowledge of where these sites of variation are in the genome[2]. The 1.42 million known SNPs are found at a density of one SNP per 1.91 kilobases. This means that more than 90% of any stretches of sequence 20 kilobases long will contain one or more SNPs. The density is even higher in regions containing genes. The International SNP Map Working Group[2] estimates that they have identified 60,000 SNPs within genes ('coding' SNPs), or one coding SNP per 1.08 kilobases of gene sequence. Moreover, 93% of genes contain a SNP, and 98% are within 5 kilobases of a SNP. For the first time, nearly every human gene and genomic region is marked by a sequence variation.

These data provide interesting first glimpses into the pattern of variation across the genome. Variation is commonly assessed by nucleotide diversity — the number of base differences between two genomes, divided by the number of base pairs compared. Nucleotide diversity is a sensitive indicator of biological and historical factors that have affected the human genome[3]. The nucleotide diversity in gene-containing regions has been estimated to be 8 differences per 10 kilobases[4,5]; we now know that the genome-wide average is similar, 7.51 differences per 10 kilobases (ref. 2). The variation between individual non-sex chromosomes is small, and lies in the range 5.19 (for chromosome 21) to 8.79 (for chromosome 15) differences per 10 kilobases (ref. 2).

Strikingly, humans vary least in their sex chromosomes. The variation between different X chromosomes is about 4.69 differences per 10 kilobases, and it is very much lower for the Y chromosome (1.51 differences per 10 kilobases). This is because the sex chromosomes have patterns of mutation and recombination (the swapping of similar DNA segments during the generation of eggs and sperm) that differ both from each other and from the non-sex chromosomes. Moreover, fewer ancestors have contributed to the sex chromosomes, which are therefore less variable than the non-sex chromosomes.

Perhaps not surprisingly, some genomic regions have significantly lower or higher diversity than the average. For example, the HLA locus, which encodes proteins that present antigens to the immune system, shows the greatest diversity. Such comparisons within genomes will be essential to our understanding of how variation shapes biochemical and cellular functions, and in illuminating past human evolution, as discussed in ref. 3, and by Stoneking in the preceding article (page 821; ref. 6).

But the main use of the human SNP map will be in dissecting the contributions of individual genes to diseases that have a complex, multigene basis. Knowledge of genetic variation already affects patient care to some degree. For example, gene variants lead to tissue and organ incompatibility, affecting the success of transplants. And the mainstay of medical genetics has been the study of the rare gene variants that lie behind inherited diseases such as cystic fibrosis.

But variations in genome sequences underlie differences in our susceptibility to, or protection from, all kinds of diseases; in the age of onset and severity of illness; and in the way our bodies respond to treatment. For example, we already know that single base differences in the *APOE* gene are associated with Alzheimer's disease, and that a simple deletion within the chemokine-receptor gene *CCR5* leads to resistance to HIV and AIDS. The benefit of the SNP map is that it covers the entire genome. So, by comparing patterns and frequencies of SNPs in patients and controls, researchers can identify which SNPs are associated with which diseases[7–9]. Such research will bring about 'genetic medicine', in which knowledge of our uniqueness will alter all aspects of medicine, perceptibly and forever.

Studies of SNPs and diseases will become more efficient when a few more problems are solved[3]. First, although 82% of SNP variants are found at a frequency of more than 10% in the global human population, the 'micro-distribution' of SNPs in individual populations is not known. Second, not all SNPs are created equal, and it will be essential to know as much as possible about their effects from computational analyses before studying their involvement in disease. For example, each SNP can be classified by whether it is coding or not. Coding SNPs can be classified by whether they alter the sequence of the protein encoded by the altered gene. Changes that alter protein sequences can be classified by their effects on protein structure. And non-coding SNPs can be classified according to whether they are found in gene-regulating segments of the genome[10] — many complex diseases may arise from quantitative, rather than qualitative, differences in gene products. Third, the technology for assaying thousands of SNPs, in thousands of patients and controls[7], is not yet fully developed, although there are some creative ideas around.

In the twentieth century, humans were not the geneticists' species of choice. The emphasis then was on understanding gene structure and function. Now, geneticists will concentrate increasingly on understanding physical and behavioural characteristics. Here, our species, with its obsession with self-examination, will make a superior subject. We will also see more studies of how natural variation leads to each one of our qualities. To some, there is a danger of genomania, with all differences (or similarities, for that matter) being laid at the altar of genetics[11]. But I hope this does not happen. Genes and genomes do not act in a vacuum, and the environment is equally important in human biology. By identifying variation across the whole genome, the SNP map[2] may be our best route yet to a better understanding of the roles of nature and (not versus) nurture. ∎

Aravinda Chakravarti is at the McKusick–Nathans Institute of Genetic Medicine, Johns Hopkins University School of Medicine, 600 North Wolfe Street, Jefferson Street Building 2-109, Baltimore, Maryland 21287, USA.
e-mail: aravinda@jhmi.edu

1. International Human Genome Sequencing Consortium *Nature* **409**, 860–921 (2001).
2. The International SNP Map Working Group *Nature* **409**, 928–933 (2001).
3. Chakravarti, A. *Nature Genet.* **21** (suppl.), 56–60 (1999).
4. Halushka, M. K. *et al. Nature Genet.* **22**, 239–247 (1999).
5. Cargill, M. *et al. Nature Genet.* **22**, 231–238 (1999).
6. Stoneking, M. *Nature* **409**, 821–822 (2001).
7. Risch, N. & Merikangas, K. *Science* **273**, 1516–1517 (1996).
8. Lander, E. S. *Science* **274**, 536–539 (1996).
9. Collins, F. S., Guyer, M. S. & Chakravarti, A. *Science* **278**, 1580–1581 (1997).
10. Loots, G. G. *et al. Science* **288**, 136–140 (1999).
11. Lewontin, R. *It Ain't Necessarily So: The Dream of the Human Genome and Other Illusions* (New York Review of Books, 2000).

Initial sequencing and analysis of the human genome

International Human Genome Sequencing Consortium*

* A partial list of authors appears on the opposite page. Affiliations are listed at the end of the paper.

The human genome holds an extraordinary trove of information about human development, physiology, medicine and evolution. Here we report the results of an international collaboration to produce and make freely available a draft sequence of the human genome. We also present an initial analysis of the data, describing some of the insights that can be gleaned from the sequence.

The rediscovery of Mendel's laws of heredity in the opening weeks of the 20th century[1-3] sparked a scientific quest to understand the nature and content of genetic information that has propelled biology for the last hundred years. The scientific progress made falls naturally into four main phases, corresponding roughly to the four quarters of the century. The first established the cellular basis of heredity: the chromosomes. The second defined the molecular basis of heredity: the DNA double helix. The third unlocked the informational basis of heredity, with the discovery of the biological mechanism by which cells read the information contained in genes and with the invention of the recombinant DNA technologies of cloning and sequencing by which scientists can do the same.

The last quarter of a century has been marked by a relentless drive to decipher first genes and then entire genomes, spawning the field of genomics. The fruits of this work already include the genome sequences of 599 viruses and viroids, 205 naturally occurring plasmids, 185 organelles, 31 eubacteria, seven archaea, one fungus, two animals and one plant.

Here we report the results of a collaboration involving 20 groups from the United States, the United Kingdom, Japan, France, Germany and China to produce a draft sequence of the human genome. The draft genome sequence was generated from a physical map covering more than 96% of the euchromatic part of the human genome and, together with additional sequence in public databases, it covers about 94% of the human genome. The sequence was produced over a relatively short period, with coverage rising from about 10% to more than 90% over roughly fifteen months. The sequence data have been made available without restriction and updated daily throughout the project. The task ahead is to produce a finished sequence, by closing all gaps and resolving all ambiguities. Already about one billion bases are in final form and the task of bringing the vast majority of the sequence to this standard is now straightforward and should proceed rapidly.

The sequence of the human genome is of interest in several respects. It is the largest genome to be extensively sequenced so far, being 25 times as large as any previously sequenced genome and eight times as large as the sum of all such genomes. It is the first vertebrate genome to be extensively sequenced. And, uniquely, it is the genome of our own species.

Much work remains to be done to produce a complete finished sequence, but the vast trove of information that has become available through this collaborative effort allows a global perspective on the human genome. Although the details will change as the sequence is finished, many points are already clear.

● The genomic landscape shows marked variation in the distribution of a number of features, including genes, transposable elements, GC content, CpG islands and recombination rate. This gives us important clues about function. For example, the developmentally important HOX gene clusters are the most repeat-poor regions of the human genome, probably reflecting the very complex coordinate regulation of the genes in the clusters.

● There appear to be about 30,000–40,000 protein-coding genes in the human genome—only about twice as many as in worm or fly. However, the genes are more complex, with more alternative splicing generating a larger number of protein products.

● The full set of proteins (the 'proteome') encoded by the human genome is more complex than those of invertebrates. This is due in part to the presence of vertebrate-specific protein domains and motifs (an estimated 7% of the total), but more to the fact that vertebrates appear to have arranged pre-existing components into a richer collection of domain architectures.

● Hundreds of human genes appear likely to have resulted from horizontal transfer from bacteria at some point in the vertebrate lineage. Dozens of genes appear to have been derived from transposable elements.

● Although about half of the human genome derives from transposable elements, there has been a marked decline in the overall activity of such elements in the hominid lineage. DNA transposons appear to have become completely inactive and long-terminal repeat (LTR) retroposons may also have done so.

● The pericentromeric and subtelomeric regions of chromosomes are filled with large recent segmental duplications of sequence from elsewhere in the genome. Segmental duplication is much more frequent in humans than in yeast, fly or worm.

● Analysis of the organization of Alu elements explains the long-standing mystery of their surprising genomic distribution, and suggests that there may be strong selection in favour of preferential retention of Alu elements in GC-rich regions and that these 'selfish' elements may benefit their human hosts.

● The mutation rate is about twice as high in male as in female meiosis, showing that most mutation occurs in males.

● Cytogenetic analysis of the sequenced clones confirms suggestions that large GC-poor regions are strongly correlated with 'dark G-bands' in karyotypes.

● Recombination rates tend to be much higher in distal regions (around 20 megabases (Mb)) of chromosomes and on shorter chromosome arms in general, in a pattern that promotes the occurrence of at least one crossover per chromosome arm in each meiosis.

● More than 1.4 million single nucleotide polymorphisms (SNPs) in the human genome have been identified. This collection should allow the initiation of genome-wide linkage disequilibrium mapping of the genes in the human population.

In this paper, we start by presenting background information on the project and describing the generation, assembly and evaluation of the draft genome sequence. We then focus on an initial analysis of the sequence itself: the broad chromosomal landscape; the repeat elements and the rich palaeontological record of evolutionary and biological processes that they provide; the human genes and proteins and their differences and similarities with those of other

Genome Sequencing Centres (Listed in order of total genomic sequence contributed, with a partial list of personnel. A full list of contributors at each centre is available as Supplementary Information.)

Whitehead Institute for Biomedical Research, Center for Genome Research: Eric S. Lander[1]*, Lauren M. Linton[1], Bruce Birren[1]*, Chad Nusbaum[1], Michael C. Zody[1], Jennifer Baldwin[1], Keri Devon[1], Ken Dewar[1], Michael Doyle[1], William FitzHugh[1]*, Roel Funke[1], Diane Gage[1], Katrina Harris[1], Andrew Heaford[1], John Howland[1], Lisa Kann[1], Jessica Lehoczky[1], Rosie LeVine[1], Paul McEwan[1], Kevin McKernan[1], James Meldrim[1], Jill P. Mesirov[1]*, Cher Miranda[1], William Morris[1], Jerome Naylor[1], Christina Raymond[1], Mark Rosetti[1], Ralph Santos[1], Andrew Sheridan[1], Carrie Sougnez[1], Nicole Stange-Thomann[1], Nikola Stojanovic[1], Aravind Subramanian[1] & Dudley Wyman[1]

The Sanger Centre: Jane Rogers[2], John Sulston[2]*, Rachael Ainscough[2], Stephan Beck[2], David Bentley[2], John Burton[2], Christopher Clee[2], Nigel Carter[2], Alan Coulson[2], Rebecca Deadman[2], Panos Deloukas[2], Andrew Dunham[2], Ian Dunham[2], Richard Durbin[2]*, Lisa French[2], Darren Grafham[2], Simon Gregory[2], Tim Hubbard[2]*, Sean Humphray[2], Adrienne Hunt[2], Matthew Jones[2], Christine Lloyd[2], Amanda McMurray[2], Lucy Matthews[2], Simon Mercer[2], Sarah Milne[2], James C. Mullikin[2]*, Andrew Mungall[2], Robert Plumb[2], Mark Ross[2], Ratna Shownkeen[2] & Sarah Sims[2]

Washington University Genome Sequencing Center: Robert H. Waterston[3]*, Richard K. Wilson[3], LaDeana W. Hillier[3]*, John D. McPherson[3], Marco A. Marra[3], Elaine R. Mardis[3], Lucinda A. Fulton[3], Asif T. Chinwalla[3]*, Kymberlie H. Pepin[3], Warren R. Gish[3], Stephanie L. Chissoe[3], Michael C. Wendl[3], Kim D. Delehaunty[3], Tracie L. Miner[3], Andrew Delehaunty[3], Jason B. Kramer[3], Lisa L. Cook[3], Robert S. Fulton[3], Douglas L. Johnson[3], Patrick J. Minx[3] & Sandra W. Clifton[3]

US DOE Joint Genome Institute: Trevor Hawkins[4], Elbert Branscomb[4], Paul Predki[4], Paul Richardson[4], Sarah Wenning[4], Tom Slezak[4], Norman Doggett[4], Jan-Fang Cheng[4], Anne Olsen[4], Susan Lucas[4], Christopher Elkin[4], Edward Uberbacher[4] & Marvin Frazier[4]

Baylor College of Medicine Human Genome Sequencing Center: Richard A. Gibbs[5]*, Donna M. Muzny[5], Steven E. Scherer[5], John B. Bouck[5]*, Erica J. Sodergren[5], Kim C. Worley[6]*, Catherine M. Rives[5], James H. Gorrell[5], Michael L. Metzker[5], Susan L. Naylor[6], Raju S. Kucherlapati[7], David L. Nelson[5], & George M. Weinstock[8]

RIKEN Genomic Sciences Center: Yoshiyuki Sakaki[9], Asao Fujiyama[9], Masahira Hattori[9], Tetsushi Yada[9], Atsushi Toyoda[9], Takehiko Itoh[9], Chiharu Kawagoe[9], Hidemi Watanabe[9], Yasushi Totoki[9] & Todd Taylor[9]

Genoscope and CNRS UMR-8030: Jean Weissenbach[10], Roland Heilig[10], William Saurin[10], Francois Artiguenave[10], Philippe Brottier[10], Thomas Bruls[10], Eric Pelletier[10], Catherine Robert[10] & Patrick Wincker[10]

GTC Sequencing Center: Douglas R. Smith[11], Lynn Doucette-Stamm[11], Marc Rubenfield[11], Keith Weinstock[11], Hong Mei Lee[11] & JoAnn Dubois[11]

Department of Genome Analysis, Institute of Molecular Biotechnology: André Rosenthal[12], Matthias Platzer[12], Gerald Nyakatura[12], Stefan Taudien[12] & Andreas Rump[12]

Beijing Genomics Institute/Human Genome Center: Huanming Yang[13], Jun Yu[13], Jian Wang[13], Guyang Huang[14] & Jun Gu[15]

Multimegabase Sequencing Center, The Institute for Systems Biology: Leroy Hood[16], Lee Rowen[16], Anup Madan[16] & Shizen Qin[16]

Stanford Genome Technology Center: Ronald W. Davis[17], Nancy A. Federspiel[17], A. Pia Abola[17] & Michael J. Proctor[17]

Stanford Human Genome Center: Richard M. Myers[18], Jeremy Schmutz[18], Mark Dickson[18], Jane Grimwood[18] & David R. Cox[18]

University of Washington Genome Center: Maynard V. Olson[19], Rajinder Kaul[19] & Christopher Raymond[19]

Department of Molecular Biology, Keio University School of Medicine: Nobuyoshi Shimizu[20], Kazuhiko Kawasaki[20] & Shinsei Minoshima[20]

University of Texas Southwestern Medical Center at Dallas: Glen A. Evans[21]†, Maria Athanasiou[21] & Roger Schultz[21]

University of Oklahoma's Advanced Center for Genome Technology: Bruce A. Roe[22], Feng Chen[22] & Huaqin Pan[22]

Max Planck Institute for Molecular Genetics: Juliane Ramser[23], Hans Lehrach[23] & Richard Reinhardt[23]

Cold Spring Harbor Laboratory, Lita Annenberg Hazen Genome Center: W. Richard McCombie[24], Melissa de la Bastide[24] & Neilay Dedhia[24]

GBF—German Research Centre for Biotechnology: Helmut Blöcker[25], Klaus Hornischer[25] & Gabriele Nordsiek[25]

* **Genome Analysis Group (listed in alphabetical order, also includes individuals listed under other headings):** Richa Agarwala[26], L. Aravind[26], Jeffrey A. Bailey[27], Alex Bateman[2], Serafim Batzoglou[1], Ewan Birney[28], Peer Bork[29,30], Daniel G. Brown[1], Christopher B. Burge[31], Lorenzo Cerutti[28], Hsiu-Chuan Chen[26], Deanna Church[26], Michele Clamp[2], Richard R. Copley[30], Tobias Doerks[29,30], Sean R. Eddy[32], Evan E. Eichler[27], Terrence S. Furey[33], James Galagan[1], James G. R. Gilbert[2], Cyrus Harmon[34], Yoshihide Hayashizaki[35], David Haussler[36], Henning Hermjakob[28], Karsten Hokamp[37], Wonhee Jang[26], L. Steven Johnson[32], Thomas A. Jones[32], Simon Kasif[38], Arek Kasprzyk[28], Scot Kennedy[39], W. James Kent[40], Paul Kitts[26], Eugene V. Koonin[26], Ian Korf[3], David Kulp[34], Doron Lancet[41], Todd M. Lowe[42], Aoife McLysaght[37], Tarjei Mikkelsen[38], John V. Moran[43], Nicola Mulder[28], Victor J. Pollara[1], Chris P. Ponting[44], Greg Schuler[26], Jörg Schultz[30], Guy Slater[28], Arian F. A. Smit[45], Elia Stupka[28], Joseph Szustakowski[38], Danielle Thierry-Mieg[26], Jean Thierry-Mieg[26], Lukas Wagner[26], John Wallis[3], Raymond Wheeler[34], Alan Williams[34], Yuri I. Wolf[26], Kenneth H. Wolfe[37], Shiaw-Pyng Yang[3] & Ru-Fang Yeh[31]

Scientific management: National Human Genome Research Institute, US National Institutes of Health: Francis Collins[46]*, Mark S. Guyer[46], Jane Peterson[46], Adam Felsenfeld[46]* & Kris A. Wetterstrand[46]; **Office of Science, US Department of Energy:** Aristides Patrinos[47]; **The Wellcome Trust:** Michael J. Morgan[48]

organisms; and the history of genomic segments. (Comparisons are drawn throughout with the genomes of the budding yeast *Saccharomyces cerevisiae*, the nematode worm *Caenorhabditis elegans*, the fruitfly *Drosophila melanogaster* and the mustard weed *Arabidopsis thaliana*; we refer to these for convenience simply as yeast, worm, fly and mustard weed.) Finally, we discuss applications of the sequence to biology and medicine and describe next steps in the project. A full description of the methods is provided as Supplementary Information on *Nature*'s web site (http://www. nature.com).

We recognize that it is impossible to provide a comprehensive analysis of this vast dataset, and thus our goal is to illustrate the range of insights that can be gleaned from the human genome and thereby to sketch a research agenda for the future.

Background to the Human Genome Project

The Human Genome Project arose from two key insights that emerged in the early 1980s: that the ability to take global views of genomes could greatly accelerate biomedical research, by allowing researchers to attack problems in a comprehensive and unbiased fashion; and that the creation of such global views would require a communal effort in infrastructure building, unlike anything previously attempted in biomedical research. Several key projects helped to crystallize these insights, including:
(1) The sequencing of the bacterial viruses ΦX174[4,5] and lambda[6], the animal virus SV40[7] and the human mitochondrion[8] between 1977 and 1982. These projects proved the feasibility of assembling small sequence fragments into complete genomes, and showed the value of complete catalogues of genes and other functional elements.
(2) The programme to create a human genetic map to make it possible to locate disease genes of unknown function based solely on their inheritance patterns, launched by Botstein and colleagues in 1980 (ref. 9).
(3) The programmes to create physical maps of clones covering the yeast[10] and worm[11] genomes to allow isolation of genes and regions based solely on their chromosomal position, launched by Olson and Sulston in the mid-1980s.

(4) The development of random shotgun sequencing of complementary DNA fragments for high-throughput gene discovery by Schimmel[12] and Schimmel and Sutcliffe[13], later dubbed expressed sequence tags (ESTs) and pursued with automated sequencing by Venter and others[14-20].

The idea of sequencing the entire human genome was first proposed in discussions at scientific meetings organized by the US Department of Energy and others from 1984 to 1986 (refs 21, 22). A committee appointed by the US National Research Council endorsed the concept in its 1988 report[23], but recommended a broader programme, to include: the creation of genetic, physical and sequence maps of the human genome; parallel efforts in key model organisms such as bacteria, yeast, worms, flies and mice; the development of technology in support of these objectives; and research into the ethical, legal and social issues raised by human genome research. The programme was launched in the US as a joint effort of the Department of Energy and the National Institutes of Health. In other countries, the UK Medical Research Council and the Wellcome Trust supported genomic research in Britain; the Centre d'Etude du Polymorphisme Humain and the French Muscular Dystrophy Association launched mapping efforts in France; government agencies, including the Science and Technology Agency and the Ministry of Education, Science, Sports and Culture supported genomic research efforts in Japan; and the European Community helped to launch several international efforts, notably the programme to sequence the yeast genome. By late 1990, the Human Genome Project had been launched, with the creation of genome centres in these countries. Additional participants subsequently joined the effort, notably in Germany and China. In addition, the Human Genome Organization (HUGO) was founded to provide a forum for international coordination of genomic research. Several books[24-26] provide a more comprehensive discussion of the genesis of the Human Genome Project.

Through 1995, work progressed rapidly on two fronts (Fig. 1). The first was construction of genetic and physical maps of the human and mouse genomes[27-31], providing key tools for identification of disease genes and anchoring points for genomic sequence. The second was sequencing of the yeast[32] and worm[33] genomes, as

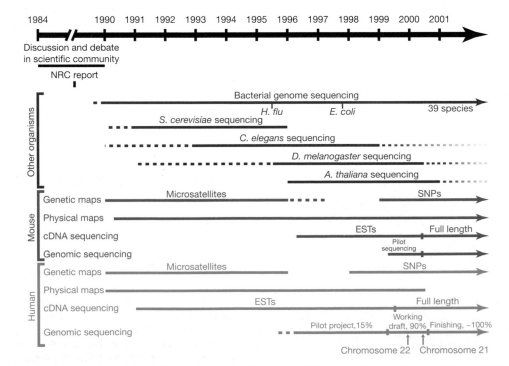

Figure 1 Timeline of large-scale genomic analyses. Shown are selected components of work on several non-vertebrate model organisms (red), the mouse (blue) and the human (green) from 1990; earlier projects are described in the text. SNPs, single nucleotide polymorphisms; ESTs, expressed sequence tags.

well as targeted regions of mammalian genomes[34-37]. These projects showed that large-scale sequencing was feasible and developed the two-phase paradigm for genome sequencing. In the first, 'shotgun', phase, the genome is divided into appropriately sized segments and each segment is covered to a high degree of redundancy (typically, eight- to tenfold) through the sequencing of randomly selected subfragments. The second is a 'finishing' phase, in which sequence gaps are closed and remaining ambiguities are resolved through directed analysis. The results also showed that complete genomic sequence provided information about genes, regulatory regions and chromosome structure that was not readily obtainable from cDNA studies alone.

In 1995, genome scientists considered a proposal[38] that would have involved producing a draft genome sequence of the human genome in a first phase and then returning to finish the sequence in a second phase. After vigorous debate, it was decided that such a plan was premature for several reasons. These included the need first to prove that high-quality, long-range finished sequence could be produced from most parts of the complex, repeat-rich human genome; the sense that many aspects of the sequencing process were still rapidly evolving; and the desirability of further decreasing costs.

Instead, pilot projects were launched to demonstrate the feasibility of cost-effective, large-scale sequencing, with a target completion date of March 1999. The projects successfully produced finished sequence with 99.99% accuracy and no gaps[39]. They also introduced bacterial artificial chromosomes (BACs)[40], a new large-insert cloning system that proved to be more stable than the cosmids and yeast artificial chromosomes (YACs)[41] that had been used previously. The pilot projects drove the maturation and convergence of sequencing strategies, while producing 15% of the human genome sequence. With successful completion of this phase, the human genome sequencing effort moved into full-scale production in March 1999.

The idea of first producing a draft genome sequence was revived at this time, both because the ability to finish such a sequence was no longer in doubt and because there was great hunger in the scientific community for human sequence data. In addition, some scientists favoured prioritizing the production of a draft genome sequence over regional finished sequence because of concerns about commercial plans to generate proprietary databases of human sequence that might be subject to undesirable restrictions on use[42-44].

The consortium focused on an initial goal of producing, in a first production phase lasting until June 2000, a draft genome sequence covering most of the genome. Such a draft genome sequence, although not completely finished, would rapidly allow investigators to begin to extract most of the information in the human sequence. Experiments showed that sequencing clones covering about 90% of the human genome to a redundancy of about four- to fivefold ('half-shotgun' coverage; see Box 1) would accomplish this[45,46]. The draft genome sequence goal has been achieved, as described below.

The second sequence production phase is now under way. Its aims are to achieve full-shotgun coverage of the existing clones during 2001, to obtain clones to fill the remaining gaps in the physical map, and to produce a finished sequence (apart from regions that cannot be cloned or sequenced with currently available techniques) no later than 2003.

Strategic issues

Hierarchical shotgun sequencing

Soon after the invention of DNA sequencing methods[47,48], the shotgun sequencing strategy was introduced[49-51]; it has remained the fundamental method for large-scale genome sequencing[52-54] for the past 20 years. The approach has been refined and extended to make it more efficient. For example, improved protocols for fragmenting and cloning DNA allowed construction of shotgun

libraries with more uniform representation. The practice of sequencing from both ends of double-stranded clones ('double-barrelled' shotgun sequencing) was introduced by Ansorge and others[37] in 1990, allowing the use of 'linking information' between sequence fragments.

The application of shotgun sequencing was also extended by applying it to larger and larger DNA molecules—from plasmids (~4 kilobases (kb)) to cosmid clones[37] (40 kb), to artificial chromosomes cloned in bacteria and yeast[55] (100–500 kb) and bacterial genomes[56] (1–2 megabases (Mb)). In principle, a genome of arbitrary size may be directly sequenced by the shotgun method, provided that it contains no repeated sequence and can be uniformly sampled at random. The genome can then be assembled using the simple computer science technique of 'hashing' (in which one detects overlaps by consulting an alphabetized look-up table of all k-letter words in the data). Mathematical analysis of the expected number of gaps as a function of coverage is similarly straightforward[57].

Practical difficulties arise because of repeated sequences and cloning bias. Small amounts of repeated sequence pose little problem for shotgun sequencing. For example, one can readily assemble typical bacterial genomes (about 1.5% repeat) or the euchromatic portion of the fly genome (about 3% repeat). By contrast, the human genome is filled ($>50\%$) with repeated sequences, including interspersed repeats derived from transposable elements, and long genomic regions that have been duplicated in tandem, palindromic or dispersed fashion (see below). These include large duplicated segments (50–500 kb) with high sequence identity (98–99.9%), at which mispairing during recombination creates deletions responsible for genetic syndromes. Such features complicate the assembly of a correct and finished genome sequence.

There are two approaches for sequencing large repeat-rich genomes. The first is a whole-genome shotgun sequencing approach, as has been used for the repeat-poor genomes of viruses, bacteria and flies, using linking information and computational

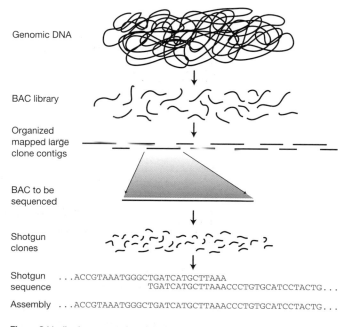

Hierarchical shotgun sequencing

Genomic DNA

BAC library

Organized mapped large clone contigs

BAC to be sequenced

Shotgun clones

Shotgun sequence . . . ACCGTAAATGGGCTGATCATGCTTAAA
                             TGATCATGCTTAAACCCTGTGCATCCTACTG . . .

Assembly . . . ACCGTAAATGGGCTGATCATGCTTAAACCCTGTGCATCCTACTG . . .

Figure 2 Idealized representation of the hierarchical shotgun sequencing strategy. A library is constructed by fragmenting the target genome and cloning it into a large-fragment cloning vector; here, BAC vectors are shown. The genomic DNA fragments represented in the library are then organized into a physical map and individual BAC clones are selected and sequenced by the random shotgun strategy. Finally, the clone sequences are assembled to reconstruct the sequence of the genome.

analysis to attempt to avoid misassemblies. The second is the 'hierarchical shotgun sequencing' approach (Fig. 2), also referred to as 'map-based', 'BAC-based' or 'clone-by-clone'. This approach involves generating and organizing a set of large-insert clones (typically 100–200 kb each) covering the genome and separately performing shotgun sequencing on appropriately chosen clones. Because the sequence information is local, the issue of long-range misassembly is eliminated and the risk of short-range misassembly is reduced. One caveat is that some large-insert clones may suffer rearrangement, although this risk can be reduced by appropriate quality-control measures involving clone fingerprints (see below).

The two methods are likely to entail similar costs for producing finished sequence of a mammalian genome. The hierarchical approach has a higher initial cost than the whole-genome approach, owing to the need to create a map of clones (about 1% of the total cost of sequencing) and to sequence overlaps between clones. On the other hand, the whole-genome approach is likely to require much greater work and expense in the final stage of producing a finished sequence, because of the challenge of resolving misassemblies. Both methods must also deal with cloning biases, resulting in under-representation of some regions in either large-insert or small-insert clone libraries.

There was lively scientific debate over whether the human genome sequencing effort should employ whole-genome or hierarchical shotgun sequencing. Weber and Myers[58] stimulated these discussions with a specific proposal for a whole-genome shotgun approach, together with an analysis suggesting that the method could work and be more efficient. Green[59] challenged these conclusions and argued that the potential benefits did not outweigh the likely risks.

In the end, we concluded that the human genome sequencing effort should employ the hierarchical approach for several reasons. First, it was prudent to use the approach for the first project to sequence a repeat-rich genome. With the hierarchical approach, the ultimate frequency of misassembly in the finished product would probably be lower than with the whole-genome approach, in which it would be more difficult to identify regions in which the assembly was incorrect.

Second, it was prudent to use the approach in dealing with an outbred organism, such as the human. In the whole-genome shotgun method, sequence would necessarily come from two different copies of the human genome. Accurate sequence assembly could be complicated by sequence variation between these two copies—both SNPs (which occur at a rate of 1 per 1,300 bases) and larger-scale structural heterozygosity (which has been documented in human chromosomes). In the hierarchical shotgun method, each large-insert clone is derived from a single haplotype.

Third, the hierarchical method would be better able to deal with inevitable cloning biases, because it would more readily allow targeting of additional sequencing to under-represented regions. And fourth, it was better suited to a project shared among members of a diverse international consortium, because it allowed work and responsibility to be easily distributed. As the ultimate goal has always been to create a high-quality, finished sequence to serve as a foundation for biomedical research, we reasoned that the advantages of this more conservative approach outweighed the additional cost, if any.

A biotechnology company, Celera Genomics, has chosen to incorporate the whole-genome shotgun approach into its own efforts to sequence the human genome. Their plan[60,61] uses a mixed strategy, involving combining some coverage with whole-genome shotgun data generated by the company together with the publicly available hierarchical shotgun data generated by the International Human Genome Sequencing Consortium. If the raw sequence reads from the whole-genome shotgun component are made available, it may be possible to evaluate the extent to which the sequence of the human genome can be assembled without the need

for clone-based information. Such analysis may help to refine sequencing strategies for other large genomes.

Technology for large-scale sequencing

Sequencing the human genome depended on many technological improvements in the production and analysis of sequence data. Key innovations were developed both within and outside the Human Genome Project. Laboratory innovations included four-colour fluorescence-based sequence detection[62], improved fluorescent dyes[63–66], dye-labelled terminators[67], polymerases specifically designed for sequencing[68–70], cycle sequencing[71] and capillary gel electrophoresis[72–74]. These studies contributed to substantial improvements in the automation, quality and throughput of collecting raw DNA sequence[75,76]. There were also important advances in the development of software packages for the analysis of sequence data. The PHRED software package[77,78] introduced the concept of assigning a 'base-quality score' to each base, on the basis of the probability of an erroneous call. These quality scores make it possible to monitor raw data quality and also assist in determining whether two similar sequences truly overlap. The PHRAP computer package (http://bozeman.mbt.washington.edu/phrap.docs/phrap.html) then systematically assembles the sequence data using the base-quality scores. The program assigns 'assembly-quality scores' to each base in the assembled sequence, providing an objective criterion to guide sequence finishing. The quality scores were based on and validated by extensive experimental data.

Another key innovation for scaling up sequencing was the development by several centres of automated methods for sample preparation. This typically involved creating new biochemical protocols suitable for automation, followed by construction of appropriate robotic systems.

Coordination and public data sharing

The Human Genome Project adopted two important principles with regard to human sequencing. The first was that the collaboration would be open to centres from any nation. Although potentially less efficient, in a narrow economic sense, than a centralized approach involving a few large factories, the inclusive approach was strongly favoured because we felt that the human genome sequence is the common heritage of all humanity and the work should transcend national boundaries, and we believed that scientific progress was best assured by a diversity of approaches. The collaboration was coordinated through periodic international meetings (referred to as 'Bermuda meetings' after the venue of the first three gatherings) and regular telephone conferences. Work was shared flexibly among the centres, with some groups focusing on particular chromosomes and others contributing in a genome-wide fashion.

The second principle was rapid and unrestricted data release. The centres adopted a policy that all genomic sequence data should be made publicly available without restriction within 24 hours of assembly[79,80]. Pre-publication data releases had been pioneered in mapping projects in the worm[11] and mouse genomes[30,81] and were prominently adopted in the sequencing of the worm, providing a direct model for the human sequencing efforts. We believed that scientific progress would be most rapidly advanced by immediate and free availability of the human genome sequence. The explosion of scientific work based on the publicly available sequence data in both academia and industry has confirmed this judgement.

Generating the draft genome sequence

Generating a draft sequence of the human genome involved three steps: selecting the BAC clones to be sequenced, sequencing them and assembling the individual sequenced clones into an overall draft genome sequence. A glossary of terms related to genome sequencing and assembly is provided in Box 1.

The draft genome sequence is a dynamic product, which is regularly updated as additional data accumulate en route to the ultimate goal of a completely finished sequence. The results below are based on the map and sequence data available on 7 October 2000, except as otherwise noted. At the end of this section, we provide a brief update of key data.

Clone selection

The hierarchical shotgun method involves the sequencing of overlapping large-insert clones spanning the genome. For the Human Genome Project, clones were largely chosen from eight large-insert libraries containing BAC or P1-derived artificial chromosome (PAC) clones (Table 1; refs 82–88). The libraries were made by partial digestion of genomic DNA with restriction enzymes. Together, they represent around 65-fold coverage (redundant sampling) of the genome. Libraries based on other vectors, such as cosmids, were also used in early stages of the project.

The libraries (Table 1) were prepared from DNA obtained from anonymous human donors in accordance with US Federal Regulations for the Protection of Human Subjects in Research (45CFR46) and following full review by an Institutional Review Board. Briefly, the opportunity to donate DNA for this purpose was broadly advertised near the two laboratories engaged in library

---

Box 1

Genome glossary

Sequence

Raw sequence   Individual unassembled sequence reads, produced by sequencing of clones containing DNA inserts.

Paired-end sequence   Raw sequence obtained from both ends of a cloned insert in any vector, such as a plasmid or bacterial artificial chromosome.

Finished sequence   Complete sequence of a clone or genome, with an accuracy of at least 99.99% and no gaps.

Coverage (or depth)   The average number of times a nucleotide is represented by a high-quality base in a collection of random raw sequence. Operationally, a 'high-quality base' is defined as one with an accuracy of at least 99% (corresponding to a PHRED score of at least 20).

Full shotgun coverage   The coverage in random raw sequence needed from a large-insert clone to ensure that it is ready for finishing; this varies among centres but is typically 8–10-fold. Clones with full shotgun coverage can usually be assembled with only a handful of gaps per 100 kb.

Half shotgun coverage   Half the amount of full shotgun coverage (typically, 4–5-fold random coverage).

Clones

BAC clone   Bacterial artificial chromosome vector carrying a genomic DNA insert, typically 100–200 kb. Most of the large-insert clones sequenced in the project were BAC clones.

Finished clone   A large-insert clone that is entirely represented by finished sequence.

Full shotgun clone   A large-insert clone for which full shotgun sequence has been produced.

Draft clone   A large-insert clone for which roughly half-shotgun sequence has been produced. Operationally, the collection of draft clones produced by each centre was required to have an average coverage of fourfold for the entire set and a minimum coverage of threefold for each clone.

Predraft clone   A large-insert clone for which some shotgun sequence is available, but which does not meet the standards for inclusion in the collection of draft clones.

Contigs and scaffolds

Contig   The result of joining an overlapping collection of sequences or clones.

Scaffold   The result of connecting contigs by linking information from paired-end reads from plasmids, paired-end reads from BACs, known messenger RNAs or other sources. The contigs in a scaffold are ordered and oriented with respect to one another.

Fingerprint clone contigs   Contigs produced by joining clones inferred to overlap on the basis of their restriction digest fingerprints.

Sequenced-clone layout   Assignment of sequenced clones to the physical map of fingerprint clone contigs.

Initial sequence contigs   Contigs produced by merging overlapping sequence reads obtained from a single clone, in a process called sequence assembly.

Merged sequence contigs   Contigs produced by taking the initial sequence contigs contained in overlapping clones and merging those found to overlap. These are also referred to simply as 'sequence contigs' where no confusion will result.

Sequence-contig scaffolds   Scaffolds produced by connecting sequence contigs on the basis of linking information.

Sequenced-clone contigs   Contigs produced by merging overlapping sequenced clones.

Sequenced-clone-contig scaffolds   Scaffolds produced by joining sequenced-clone contigs on the basis of linking information.

Draft genome sequence   The sequence produced by combining the information from the individual sequenced clones (by creating merged sequence contigs and then employing linking information to create scaffolds) and positioning the sequence along the physical map of the chromosomes.

N50 length   A measure of the contig length (or scaffold length) containing a 'typical' nucleotide. Specifically, it is the maximum length L such that 50% of all nucleotides lie in contigs (or scaffolds) of size at least L.

Computer programs and databases

PHRED   A widely used computer program that analyses raw sequence to produce a 'base call' with an associated 'quality score' for each position in the sequence. A PHRED quality score of X corresponds to an error probability of approximately $10^{-X/10}$. Thus, a PHRED quality score of 30 corresponds to 99.9% accuracy for the base call in the raw read.

PHRAP   A widely used computer program that assembles raw sequence into sequence contigs and assigns to each position in the sequence an associated 'quality score', on the basis of the PHRED scores of the raw sequence reads. A PHRAP quality score of X corresponds to an error probability of approximately $10^{-X/10}$. Thus, a PHRAP quality score of 30 corresponds to 99.9% accuracy for a base in the assembled sequence.

GigAssembler   A computer program developed during this project for merging the information from individual sequenced clones into a draft genome sequence.

Public sequence databases   The three coordinated international sequence databases: GenBank, the EMBL data library and DDBJ.

Map features

STS   Sequence tagged site, corresponding to a short (typically less than 500 bp) unique genomic locus for which a polymerase chain reaction assay has been developed.

EST   Expressed sequence tag, obtained by performing a single raw sequence read from a random complementary DNA clone.

SSR   Simple sequence repeat, a sequence consisting largely of a tandem repeat of a specific k-mer (such as $(CA)_{15}$). Many SSRs are polymorphic and have been widely used in genetic mapping.

SNP   Single nucleotide polymorphism, or a single nucleotide position in the genome sequence for which two or more alternative alleles are present at appreciable frequency (traditionally, at least 1%) in the human population.

Genetic map   A genome map in which polymorphic loci are positioned relative to one another on the basis of the frequency with which they recombine during meiosis. The unit of distance is centimorgans (cM), denoting a 1% chance of recombination.

Radiation hybrid (RH) map   A genome map in which STSs are positioned relative to one another on the basis of the frequency with which they are separated by radiation-induced breaks. The frequency is assayed by analysing a panel of human–hamster hybrid cell lines, each produced by lethally irradiating human cells and fusing them with recipient hamster cells such that each carries a collection of human chromosomal fragments. The unit of distance is centirays (cR), denoting a 1% chance of a break occuring between two loci.

---

construction. Volunteers of diverse backgrounds were accepted on a first-come, first-taken basis. Samples were obtained after discussion with a genetic counsellor and written informed consent. The samples were made anonymous as follows: the sampling laboratory stripped all identifiers from the samples, applied random numeric labels, and transferred them to the processing laboratory, which then removed all labels and relabelled the samples. All records of the labelling were destroyed. The processing laboratory chose samples at random from which to prepare DNA and immortalized cell lines. Around 5–10 samples were collected for every one that was eventually used. Because no link was retained between donor and DNA sample, the identity of the donors for the libraries is not known, even by the donors themselves. A more complete description can be found at http://www.nhgri.nih.gov/Grant_info/Funding/Statements/RFA/human_subjects.html.

During the pilot phase, centres showed that sequence-tagged sites (STSs) from previously constructed genetic and physical maps could be used to recover BACs from specific regions. As sequencing expanded, some centres continued this approach, augmented with additional probes from flow sorting of chromosomes to obtain long-range coverage of specific chromosomes or chromosomal regions[89–94].

For the large-scale sequence production phase, a genome-wide physical map of overlapping clones was also constructed by systematic analysis of BAC clones representing 20-fold coverage of the human genome[86]. Most clones came from the first three sections of the RPCI-11 library, supplemented with clones from sections of the RPCI-13 and CalTech D libraries (Table 1). DNA from each BAC clone was digested with the restriction enzyme HindIII, and the sizes of the resulting fragments were measured by agarose gel electrophoresis. The pattern of restriction fragments provides a 'fingerprint' for each BAC, which allows different BACs to be distinguished and the degree of overlaps to be assessed. We used these restriction-fragment fingerprints to determine clone overlaps, and thereby assembled the BACs into fingerprint clone contigs.

The fingerprint clone contigs were positioned along the chromosomes by anchoring them with STS markers from existing genetic and physical maps. Fingerprint clone contigs were tied to specific STSs initially by probe hybridization and later by direct search of the sequenced clones. To localize fingerprint clone contigs that did not contain known markers, new STSs were generated and placed onto chromosomes[95]. Representative clones were also positioned by fluorescence in situ hybridization (FISH) (ref. 86 and C. McPherson, unpublished).

We selected clones from the fingerprint clone contigs for sequencing according to various criteria. Fingerprint data were reviewed[86,90] to evaluate overlaps and to assess clone fidelity (to bias against rearranged clones[83,96]). STS content information and BAC end sequence information were also used[91,92]. Where possible, we tried to select a minimally overlapping set spanning a region. However, because the genome-wide physical map was constructed concurrently with the sequencing, continuity in many regions was low in early stages. These small fingerprint clone contigs were nonetheless useful in identifying validated, nonredundant clones

Table 1 Key large-insert genome-wide libraries

Library name*	GenBank abbreviation	Vector type	Source DNA	Library segment or plate numbers	Enzyme digest	Average insert size (kb)	Total number of clones in library	Number of fingerprinted clones†	BAC-end sequence (ends/clones/ clones with both ends sequenced)‡	Number of clones in genome layout§	Sequenced clones used in construction of the draft genome sequence		
											Number‖	Total bases (Mb)¶	Fraction of total from library
Caltech B	CTB	BAC	987SK cells	All	HindIII	120	74,496	16	2/1/1	528	518	66.7	0.016
Caltech C	CTC	BAC	Human sperm	All	HindIII	125	263,040	144	21,956/ 14,445/ 7,255	621	606	88.4	0.021
Caltech D1 (CITB-H1)	CTD	BAC	Human sperm	All	HindIII	129	162,432	49,833	403,589/ 226,068/ 156,631	1,381	1,367	185.6	0.043
Caltech D2 (CITB-E1)		BAC	Human sperm	All									
				2,501–2,565	EcoRI	202	24,960						
				2,566–2,671	EcoRI	182	46,326						
				3,000–3,253	EcoRI	142	97,536						
RPCI-1	RP1	PAC	Male, blood	All	MboI	110	115,200	3,388		1,070	1,053	117.7	0.028
RPCI-3	RP3	PAC	Male, blood	All	MboI	115	75,513			644	638	68.5	0.016
RPCI-4	RP4	PAC	Male, blood	All	MboI	116	105,251			889	881	95.5	0.022
RPCI-5	RP5	PAC	Male, blood	All	MboI	115	142,773			1,042	1,033	116.5	0.027
RPCI-11	RP11	BAC	Male, blood	All		178	543,797	267,931	379,773/ 243,764/ 134,110	19,405	19,145	3,165.0	0.743
				1	EcoRI	164	108,499						
				2	EcoRI	168	109,496						
				3	EcoRI	181	109,657						
				4	EcoRI	183	109,382						
				5	MboI	196	106,763						
Total of top eight libraries							1,482,502	321,312	805,320/ 484,278/ 297,997	25,580	25,241	3,903.9	0.916
Total all libraries								354,510	812,594/ 488,017/ 100,775	30,445	29,298	4,260.5	1

* For the CalTech libraries[82], see http://www.tree.caltech.edu/lib_status.html; for RPCI libraries[83], see http://www.chori.org/bacpac/home.htm.
† For the FPC map and fingerprinting[84–86], see http://genome.wustl.edu/gsc/human/human_database.shtml.
‡ The number of raw BAC end sequences (clones/ends/clones with both ends sequenced) available for use in human genome sequencing. Typically, for clones in which sequence was obtained from both ends, more than 95% of both end sequences contained at least 100 bp of nonrepetitive sequence. BAC-end sequencing of RPCI-11 and of the CalTech libraries was done at The Institute for Genomic Research, the California Institute of Technology and the University of Washington High Throughput Sequencing Center. The sources for the Table were http://www.ncbi.nlm.nih.gov/genome/clone/BESstat.shtml and refs 87, 88.
§ These are the clones in the sequenced-clone layout map (http://genome.wustl.edu/gsc/human/Mapping/index.shtml) that were pre-draft, draft or finished.
‖ The number of sequenced clones used in the assembly. This number is less than that in the previous column owing to removal of a small number of obviously contaminated, combined or duplicated projects; in addition, not all of the clones from completed chromosomes 21 and 22 were included here because only the available finished sequence from those chromosomes was used in the assembly.
¶ The number reported is the total sequence from the clones indicated in the previous column. Potential overlap between clones was not removed here, but Ns were excluded.

that were used to 'seed' the sequencing of new regions. The small fingerprint clone contigs were extended or merged with others as the map matured.

The clones that make up the draft genome sequence therefore do not constitute a minimally overlapping set—there is overlap and redundancy in places. The cost of using suboptimal overlaps was justified by the benefit of earlier availability of the draft genome sequence data. Minimizing the overlap between adjacent clones would have required completing the physical map before undertaking large-scale sequencing. In addition, the overlaps between BAC clones provide a rich collection of SNPs. More than 1.4 million SNPs have already been identified from clone overlaps and other sequence comparisons[97].

Because the sequencing project was shared among twenty centres in six countries, it was important to coordinate selection of clones across the centres. Most centres focused on particular chromosomes or, in some cases, larger regions of the genome. We also maintained a clone registry to track selected clones and their progress. In later phases, the global map provided an integrated view of the data from all centres, facilitating the distribution of effort to maximize coverage of the genome. Before performing extensive sequencing on a

Figure 3 The automated production line for sample preparation at the Whitehead Institute, Center for Genome Research. The system consists of custom-designed factory-style conveyor belt robots that perform all functions from purifying DNA from bacterial cultures through setting up and purifying sequencing reactions.

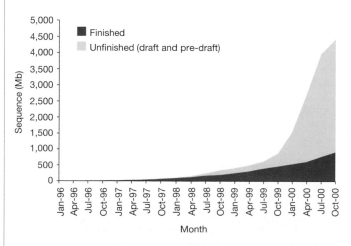

Figure 4 Total amount of human sequence in the High Throughput Genome Sequence (HTGS) division of GenBank. The total is the sum of finished sequence (red) and unfinished (draft plus predraft) sequence (yellow).

clone, several centres routinely examined an initial sample of 96 raw sequence reads from each subclone library to evaluate possible overlap with previously sequenced clones.

Sequencing

The selected clones were subjected to shotgun sequencing. Although the basic approach of shotgun sequencing is well established, the details of implementation varied among the centres. For example, there were differences in the average insert size of the shotgun libraries, in the use of single-stranded or double-stranded cloning vectors, and in sequencing from one end or both ends of each insert. Centres differed in the fluorescent labels employed and in the degree to which they used dye-primers or dye-terminators. The sequence detectors included both slab gel- and capillary-based devices. Detailed protocols are available on the web sites of many of the individual centres (URLs can be found at www.nhgri.nih.gov/genome_hub). The extent of automation also varied greatly among the centres, with the most aggressive automation efforts resulting in factory-style systems able to process more than 100,000 sequencing reactions in 12 hours (Fig. 3). In addition, centres differed in the amount of raw sequence data typically obtained for each clone (so-called half-shotgun, full shotgun and finished sequence). Sequence information from the different centres could be directly integrated despite this diversity, because the data were analysed by a common computational procedure. Raw sequence traces were processed and assembled with the PHRED and PHRAP software packages[77,78] (P. Green, unpublished). All assembled contigs of more than 2 kb were deposited in public databases within 24 hours of assembly.

The overall sequencing output rose sharply during production (Fig. 4). Following installation of new sequence detectors beginning in June 1999, sequencing capacity and output rose approximately eightfold in eight months to nearly 7 million samples processed per month, with little or no drop in success rate (ratio of useable reads to attempted reads). By June 2000, the centres were producing raw sequence at a rate equivalent to onefold coverage of the entire human genome in less than six weeks. This corresponded to a continuous throughput exceeding 1,000 nucleotides per second, 24 hours per day, seven days per week. This scale-up resulted in a concomitant increase in the sequence available in the public databases (Fig. 4).

A version of the draft genome sequence was prepared on the basis of the map and sequence data available on 7 October 2000. For this version, the mapping effort had assembled the fingerprinted BACs into 1,246 fingerprint clone contigs. The sequencing effort had sequenced and assembled 29,298 overlapping BACs and other large-insert clones (Table 2), comprising a total length of 4.26 gigabases (Gb). This resulted from around 23 Gb of underlying raw shotgun sequence data, or about 7.5-fold coverage averaged across the genome (including both draft and finished sequence). The various contributions to the total amount of sequence deposited in the HTGS division of GenBank are given in Table 3.

Table 2 Total genome sequence from the collection of sequenced clones, by sequence status

Sequence status	Number of clones	Total clone length (Mb)	Average number of sequence reads per kb*	Average sequence depth†	Total amount of raw sequence (Mb)
Finished	8,277	897	20–25	8–12	9,085
Draft	18,969	3,097	12	4.5	13,395
Predraft	2,052	267	6	2.5	667
Total					23,147

* The average number of reads per kb was estimated based on information provided by each sequencing centre. This number differed among sequencing centres, based on the actual protocols used.
† The average depth in high quality bases (≥99% accuracy) was estimated from information provided by each sequencing centre. The average varies among the centres, and the number may vary considerably for clones with the same sequencing status. For draft clones in the public databases (keyword: HTGS_draft), the number can be computed from the quality scores listed in the database entry.

By agreement among the centres, the collection of draft clones produced by each centre was required to have fourfold average sequence coverage, with no clone below threefold. (For this purpose, sequence coverage was defined as the average number of times that each base was independently read with a base-quality score corresponding to at least 99% accuracy.) We attained an overall average of 4.5-fold coverage across the genome for draft clones. A few of the sequenced clones fell below the minimum of threefold sequence coverage or have not been formally designated by centres as meeting draft standards; these are referred to as predraft (Table 2). Some of these are clones that span remaining gaps in the draft genome sequence and were in the process of being sequenced on 7 October 2000; a few are old submissions from centres that are no longer active.

The lengths of the initial sequence contigs in the draft clones vary as a function of coverage, but half of all nucleotides reside in initial sequence contigs of at least 21.7 kb (see below). Various properties of the draft clones can be assessed from instances in which there was substantial overlap between a draft clone and a finished (or nearly finished) clone. By examining the sequence alignments in the overlap regions, we estimated that the initial sequence contigs in a draft sequence clone cover an average of about 96% of the clone and are separated by gaps with an average size of about 500 bp.

Although the main emphasis was on producing a draft genome sequence, the centres also maintained sequence finishing activities during this period, leading to a twofold increase in finished sequence from June 1999 to June 2000 (Fig. 4). The total amount of human sequence in this final form stood at more than 835 Mb on 7 October 2000, or more than 25% of the human genome. This includes the finished sequences of chromosomes 21 and 22 (refs 93, 94). As centres have begun to shift from draft to finished sequencing in the last quarter of 2000, the production of finished sequence has increased to an annualized rate of 1 Gb per year and is continuing to rise.

In addition to sequencing large-insert clones, three centres generated a large collection of random raw sequence reads from whole-genome shotgun libraries (Table 4; ref. 98). These 5.77 million successful sequences contained 2.4 Gb of high-quality bases; this corresponds to about 0.75-fold coverage and would be statistically expected to include about 50% of the nucleotides in the human genome (data available at http://snp.cshl.org/data). The primary objective of this work was to discover SNPs, by comparing these random raw sequences (which came from different individuals) with the draft genome sequence. However, many of these raw sequences were obtained from both ends of plasmid clones and thereby also provided valuable 'linking' information that was used in sequence assembly. In addition, the random raw sequences provide sequence coverage of about half of the nucleotides not yet represented in the sequenced large-insert clones; these can be used as probes for portions of the genome not yet recovered.

Assembly of the draft genome sequence

We then set out to assemble the sequences from the individual large-insert clones into an integrated draft sequence of the human genome. The assembly process had to resolve problems arising from the draft nature of much of the sequence, from the variety of clone sources, and from the high fraction of repeated sequences in the human genome. This process involved three steps: filtering, layout and merging.

The entire data set was filtered uniformly to eliminate contamination from nonhuman sequences and other artefacts that had not already been removed by the individual centres. (Information about contamination was also sent back to the centres, which are updating the individual entries in the public databases.) We also identified instances in which the sequence data from one BAC clone was substantially contaminated with sequence data from another (human or nonhuman) clone. The problems were resolved in most instances; 231 clones remained unresolved, and these were eliminated from the assembly reported here. Instances of lower levels of cross-contamination (for example, a single 96-well microplate misassigned to the wrong BAC) are more difficult to detect; some undoubtedly remain and may give rise to small spurious sequence contigs in the draft genome sequence. Such issues are readily resolved as the clones progress towards finished sequence, but they necessitate some caution in certain applications of the current data.

The sequenced clones were then associated with specific clones on the physical map to produce a 'layout'. In principle, sequenced clones that correspond to fingerprinted BACs could be directly assigned by name to fingerprint clone contigs on the fingerprint-based physical map. In practice, however, laboratory mixups occasionally resulted in incorrect assignments. To eliminate such problems, sequenced clones were associated with the fingerprint clone contigs in the physical map by using the sequence data to calculate a

---

Table 3 Total human sequence deposited in the HTGS division of GenBank

Sequencing centre	Total human sequence (kb)	Finished human sequence (kb)
Whitehead Institute, Center for Genome Research*	1,196,888	46,560
The Sanger Centre*	970,789	284,353
Washington University Genome Sequencing Center*	765,898	175,279
US DOE Joint Genome Institute	377,998	78,486
Baylor College of Medicine Human Genome Sequencing Center	345,125	53,418
RIKEN Genomic Sciences Center	203,166	16,971
Genoscope	85,995	48,808
GTC Sequencing Center	71,357	7,014
Department of Genome Analysis, Institute of Molecular Biotechnology	49,865	17,788
Beijing Genomics Institute/Human Genome Center	42,865	6,297
Multimegabase Sequencing Center; Institute for Systems Biology	31,241	9,676
Stanford Genome Technology Center	29,728	3,530
The Stanford Human Genome Center and Department of Genetics	28,162	9,121
University of Washington Genome Center	24,115	14,692
Keio University	17,364	13,058
University of Texas Southwestern Medical Center at Dallas	11,670	7,028
University of Oklahoma Advanced Center for Genome Technology	10,071	9,155
Max Planck Institute for Molecular Genetics	7,650	2,940
GBF – German Research Centre for Biotechnology	4,639	2,338
Cold Spring Harbor Laboratory Lita Annenberg Hazen Genome Center	4,338	2,104
Other	59,574	35,911
Total	4,338,224	842,027

Total human sequence deposited in GenBank by members of the International Human Genome Sequencing Consortium, as of 8 October 2000. The amount of total sequence (finished plus draft plus predraft) is shown in the second column and the amount of finished sequence is shown in the third column. Total sequence differs from totals in Tables 1 and 2 because of inclusion of padding characters and of some clones not used in assembly. HTGS, high throughput genome sequence.
*These three centres produced an additional 2.4 Gb of raw plasmid paired-end reads (see Table 4), consisting of 0.99 Gb from Whitehead Institute, 0.66 Gb from The Sanger Centre and 0.75 Gb from Washington University.

Table 4 Plasmid paired-end reads

	Total reads deposited*	Read pairs†	Size range of inserts (kb)
Random-sheared	3,227,685	1,155,284	1.8–6
Enzyme digest	2,539,222	761,010	0.8–4.7
Total	5,766,907	1,916,294	

The plasmid paired-end reads used a mixture of DNA from a set of 24 samples from the DNA Polymorphism Discovery Resource (http://locus.umdnj.edu/nigms/pdr.html). This set of 24 anonymous US residents contains samples from European-Americans, African-Americans, Mexican-Americans, Native Americans and Asian-Americans, although the ethnicities of the individual samples are not identified. Informed consent to contribute samples to the DNA Polymorphism Discovery Resource was obtained from all 450 individuals who contributed samples. Samples from the European-American, African-American and Mexican-American individuals came from NHANES (http://www.cdc.gov/nchs/nhanes.htm); individuals were recontacted to obtain their consent for the Resource project. New samples were obtained from Asian-Americans whose ancestry was from a variety of East and South Asian countries. New samples were also obtained for the Native Americans; tribal permission was obtained first, and then individual consents. See http://www.nhgri.nih.gov/Grant_info/Funding/RFA/discover_polymorphisms.html and ref. 98.
*Reflects data deposited with and released by The SNP Consortium (see http://snp.cshl.org/data).
† Read pairs represents the number of cases in which sequence from both ends of a genomic cloned fragment was determined and used in this study as linking information.

partial list of restriction fragments *in silico* and comparing that list with the experimental database of BAC fingerprints. The comparison was feasible because the experimental sizing of restriction fragments was highly accurate (to within 0.5–1.5% of the true size, for 95% of fragments from 600 to 12,000 base pairs (bp))[84,85]. Reliable matching scores could be obtained for 16,193 of the clones. The remaining sequenced clones could not be placed on the map by this method because they were too short, or they contained too many small initial sequence contigs to yield enough restriction fragments, or possibly because their sequences were not represented in the fingerprint database.

An independent approach to placing sequenced clones on the physical map used the database of end sequences from fingerprinted BACs (Table 1). Sequenced clones could typically be reliably mapped if they contained multiple matches to BAC ends, with all corresponding to clones from a single genomic region (multiple matches were required as a safeguard against errors known to exist in the BAC end database and against repeated sequences). This approach provided useful placement information for 22,566 sequenced clones.

Altogether, we could assign 25,403 sequenced clones to fingerprint clone contigs by combining *in silico* digestion and BAC end sequence match data. To place most of the remaining sequenced clones, we exploited information about sequence overlap or BAC-end paired links of these clones with already positioned clones. This left only a few, mostly small, sequenced clones that could not be placed (152 sequenced clones containing 5.5 Mb of sequence out of 29,298 sequenced clones containing more than 4,260 Mb of sequence); these are being localized by radiation hybrid mapping of STSs derived from their sequences.

The fingerprint clone contigs were then mapped to chromosomal locations, using sequence matches to mapped STSs from four human radiation hybrid maps[95,99,100], one YAC and radiation hybrid map[29], and two genetic maps[101,102], together with data from FISH[86,90,103]. The mapping was iteratively refined by comparing the order and orientation of the STSs in the fingerprint clone contigs and the various STS-based maps, to identify and refine discrepancies (Fig. 5). Small fingerprint clone contigs (< 1 Mb) were difficult to orient and, sometimes, to order using these methods. In all, 942 fingerprint clone contigs contained sequenced clones. (An additional 304 of the 1,246 fingerprint clone contigs did not contain sequenced clones, but these tended to be extremely small and together contain less than 1% of the mapped clones. About one-third have been targeted for sequencing. A few derive from the Y chromosome, for which the map was constructed separately[89]. Most of the remainder are fragments of other larger contigs or represent other artefacts. These are being eliminated in subsequent versions of the database.) Of these 942 contigs with sequenced clones, 852 (90%, containing 99.2% of the total sequence) were localized to specific chromosome locations in this way. An additional 51 fingerprint clone contigs, containing 0.5% of the sequence, could be assigned to a specific chromosome but not to a precise position.

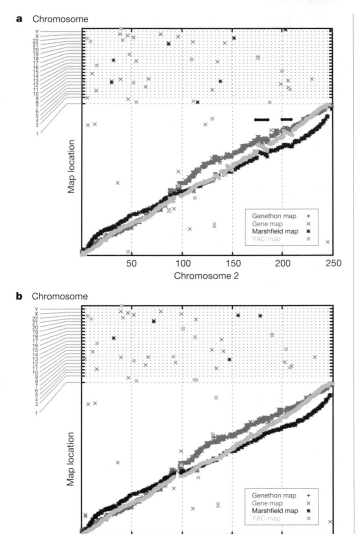

Figure 5 Positions of markers on previous maps of the genome (the Genethon[101] genetic map and Marshfield genetic map (http://research.marshfieldclinic.org/genetics/genotyping_service/mgsver2.htm), the GeneMap99 radiation hybrid map[100], and the Whitehead YAC and radiation hybrid map[29]) plotted against their derived position on the draft sequence for chromosome 2. The horizontal units are Mb but the vertical units of each map vary (cM, cR and so on) and thus all were scaled so that the entire map spans the full vertical range. Markers that map to other chromosomes are shown in the chromosome lines at the top. The data sets generally follow the diagonal, indicating that order and orientation of the marker sets on the different maps largely agree (note that the two genetic maps are completely superimposed). In **a**, there are two segments (bars) that are inverted in an earlier version draft sequence relative to all the other maps. **b,** The same chromosome after the information was used to reorient those two segments.

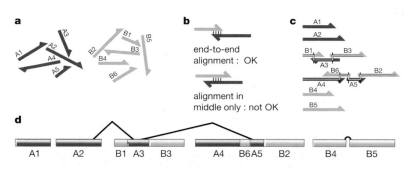

Figure 6 The key steps (**a–d**) in assembling individual sequenced clones into the draft genome sequence. A1–A5 represent initial sequence contigs derived from shotgun sequencing of clone A, and B1–B6 are from clone B.

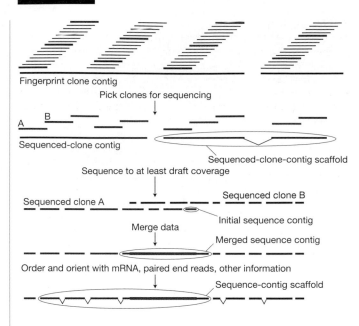

Figure 7 Levels of clone and sequence coverage. A 'fingerprint clone contig' is assembled by using the computer program FPC[84,451] to analyse the restriction enzyme digestion patterns of many large-insert clones. Clones are then selected for sequencing to minimize overlap between adjacent clones. For a clone to be selected, all of its restriction enzyme fragments (except the two vector-insert junction fragments) must be shared with at least one of its neighbours on each side in the contig. Once these overlapping clones have been sequenced, the set is a 'sequenced-clone contig'. When all selected clones from a fingerprint clone contig have been sequenced, the sequenced-clone contig will be the same as the fingerprint clone contig. Until then, a fingerprint clone contig may contain several sequenced-clone contigs. After individual clones (for example, A and B) have been sequenced to draft coverage and the clones have been mapped, the data are analysed by GigAssembler (Fig. 6), producing merged sequence contigs from initial sequence contigs, and linking these to form sequence-contig scaffolds (see Box 1).

The remaining 39 contigs containing 0.3% of the sequence were not positioned at all.

We then merged the sequences from overlapping sequenced clones (Fig. 6), using the computer program GigAssembler[104]. The program considers nearby sequenced clones, detects overlaps between the initial sequence contigs in these clones, merges the overlapping sequences and attempts to order and orient the sequence contigs. It begins by aligning the initial sequence contigs from one clone with those from other clones in the same fingerprint clone contig on the basis of length of alignment, per cent identity of the alignment, position in the sequenced clone layout and other factors. Alignments are limited to one end of each initial sequence contig for partially overlapping contigs or to both ends of an initial sequence contig contained entirely within another; this eliminates internal alignments that may reflect repeated sequence or possible misassembly (Fig. 6b). Beginning with the highest scoring pairs, initial sequence contigs are then integrated to produce 'merged sequence contigs' (usually referred to simply as 'sequence contigs'). The program refines the arrangement of the clones within the fingerprint clone contig on the basis of the extent of sequence overlap between them and then rebuilds the sequence contigs. Next, the program selects a sequence path through the sequence contigs (Fig. 6c). It tries to use the highest quality data by preferring longer initial sequence contigs and avoiding the first and last 250 bases of initial sequence contigs where possible. Finally, it attempts to order and orient the sequence contigs by using additional information, including sequence data from paired-end plasmid and BAC reads, known messenger RNAs and ESTs, as well as additional linking information provided by centres. The sequence contigs are thereby linked together to create 'sequence-contig scaffolds' (Fig. 6d). The process also joins overlapping sequenced clones into sequenced-clone contigs and links sequenced-clone contigs to form sequenced-clone-contig scaffolds. A fingerprint clone contig may contain several sequenced-clone contigs, because bridging clones remain to be sequenced. The assembly contained 4,884 sequenced-clone

Table 5 The draft genome sequence

Chromosome	Sequence from clones (kb)			Sequence from contigs (kb)		
	Finished clones	Draft clones	Pre-draft clones	Contigs containing finished clones	Deep coverage sequence contigs	Draft/predraft sequence contigs
All	826,441	1,734,995	131,476	958,922	840,815	893,175
1	50,851	149,027	12,356	61,001	78,773	72,461
2	46,909	167,439	7,210	53,775	81,569	86,214
3	22,350	152,840	11,057	26,959	79,649	79,638
4	15,914	134,973	17,261	19,096	66,165	82,887
5	37,973	129,581	2,160	48,895	61,387	59,431
6	75,312	76,082	6,696	93,458	28,204	36,428
7	94,845	47,328	4,047	103,188	14,434	28,597
8	14,538	102,484	7,236	16,659	47,198	60,400
9	18,401	77,648	10,864	24,030	42,653	40,230
10	16,889	99,181	11,066	21,421	54,054	51,662
11	13,162	111,092	4,352	16,145	65,147	47,314
12	32,156	84,653	7,651	37,519	43,995	42,946
13	16,818	68,983	7,136	22,191	38,319	32,429
14	58,989	27,370	565	78,302	3,267	5,355
15	2,739	67,453	3,211	3,112	34,758	35,533
16	22,987	48,997	1,143	27,751	20,892	24,484
17	29,881	36,349	6,600	33,531	14,671	24,628
18	5,128	65,284	2,352	6,656	40,947	25,160
19	28,481	26,568	369	32,228	7,188	16,003
20	54,217	5,302	976	56,534	1,065	2,896
21	33,824	0	0	33,824	0	0
22	33,786	0	0	33,786	0	0
X	77,630	45,100	4,941	83,796	14,056	29,820
Y	18,169	3,221	363	20,222	333	1,198
NA	2,434	1,858	844	2,446	122	2,568
UL	2,056	6,182	1,020	2,395	1,969	4,894

The table presents summary statistics for the draft genome sequence over the entire genome and by individual chromosome. NA, clones that could not be placed into the sequenced clone layout. UL, clones that could be placed in the layout, but that could not reliably be placed on a chromosome. First three columns, data from finished clones, draft clones and predraft clones. The last three columns break the data down according to the type of sequence contig. Contigs containing finished clones represent sequence contigs that consist of finished sequence plus any (small) extensions from merged sequence contigs that arise from overlap with flanking draft clones. Deep coverage sequence contigs include sequence from two or more overlapping unfinished clones; they consist of roughly full shotgun coverage and thus are longer than the average unfinished sequence contig. Draft/predraft sequence contigs are all of the other sequence contigs in unfinished clones. Thus, the draft genome sequence consists of approximately one-third finished sequence, one-third deep coverage sequence and one-third draft/pre-draft coverage sequence. In all of the statistics, we count only nonoverlapping bases in the draft genome sequence.

contigs in 942 fingerprint clone contigs.

The hierarchy of contigs is summarized in Fig. 7. Initial sequence contigs are integrated to create merged sequence contigs, which are then linked to form sequence-contig scaffolds. These scaffolds reside within sequenced-clone contigs, which in turn reside within fingerprint clone contigs.

The draft genome sequence

The result of the assembly process is an integrated draft sequence of the human genome. Several features of the draft genome sequence are reported in Tables 5–7, including the proportion represented by finished, draft and predraft categories. The Tables also show the numbers and lengths of different types of contig, for each chromosome and for the genome as a whole.

The contiguity of the draft genome sequence at each level is an important feature. Two commonly used statistics have significant drawbacks for describing contiguity. The 'average length' of a contig is deflated by the presence of many small contigs comprising only a small proportion of the genome, whereas the 'length-weighted average length' is inflated by the presence of large segments of finished sequence. Instead, we chose to describe the contiguity as a property of the 'typical' nucleotide. We used a statistic called the 'N50 length', defined as the largest length L such that 50% of all nucleotides are contained in contigs of size at least L.

The continuity of the draft genome sequence reported here and the effectiveness of assembly can be readily seen from the following: half of all nucleotides reside within an initial sequence contig of at least 21.7 kb, a sequence contig of at least 82 kb, a sequence-contig scaffold of at least 274 kb, a sequenced-clone contig of at least 826 kb and a fingerprint clone contig of at least 8.4 Mb (Tables 6, 7). The cumulative distributions for each of these measures of contiguity are shown in Fig. 8, in which the N50 values for each measure can be seen as the value at which the cumulative distributions cross 50%. We have also estimated the size of each chromosome, by estimating the gap sizes (see below) and the extent of missing heterochromatic sequence[93,94,105-108] (Table 8). This is undoubtedly an oversimplification and does not adequately take into account the sequence status of each chromosome. Nonetheless, it provides a useful way to relate the draft sequence to the chromosomes.

Quality assessment

The draft genome sequence already covers the vast majority of the genome, but it remains an incomplete, intermediate product that is regularly updated as we work towards a complete finished sequence. The current version contains many gaps and errors. We therefore sought to evaluate the quality of various aspects of the current draft genome sequence, including the sequenced clones themselves, their assignment to a position in the fingerprint clone contigs, and the assembly of initial sequence contigs from the individual clones into sequence-contig scaffolds.

Nucleotide accuracy is reflected in a PHRAP score assigned to each base in the draft genome sequence and available to users through the Genome Browsers (see below) and public database entries. A summary of these scores for the unfinished portion of the genome is shown in Table 9. About 91% of the unfinished draft genome sequence has an error rate of less than 1 per 10,000 bases (PHRAP score > 40), and about 96% has an error rate of less than 1 in 1,000 bases (PHRAP > 30). These values are based only on the quality scores for the bases in the sequenced clones; they do not reflect additional confidence in the sequences that are represented in overlapping clones. The finished portion of the draft genome sequence has an error rate of less than 1 per 10,000 bases.

Individual sequenced clones. We assessed the frequency of misassemblies, which can occur when the assembly program PHRAP joins two nonadjacent regions in the clone into a single initial sequence contig. The frequency of misassemblies depends heavily on the depth and quality of coverage of each clone and the nature of the underlying sequence; thus it may vary among genomic regions and among individual centres. Most clone misassemblies are readily corrected as coverage is added during finishing, but they may have been propagated into the current version of the draft genome sequence and they justify caution for certain applications.

We estimated the frequency of misassembly by examining instances in which there was substantial overlap between a draft clone and a finished clone. We studied 83 Mb of such overlaps, involving about 9,000 initial sequence contigs. We found 5.3 instances per Mb in which the alignment of an initial sequence contig to the finished sequence failed to extend to within 200 bases

---

Table 6 Clone level contiguity of the draft genome sequence

Chromosome	Sequenced-clone contigs		Sequenced-clone-contig scaffolds		Fingerprint clone contigs with sequence	
	Number	N50 length (kb)	Number	N50 length (kb)	Number	N50 length (kb)
All	4,884	826	2,191	2,279	942	8,398
1	453	650	197	1,915	106	3,537
2	348	1,028	127	3,140	52	10,628
3	409	672	201	1,550	73	5,077
4	384	606	163	1,659	41	6,918
5	385	623	164	1,642	48	5,747
6	292	814	98	3,292	17	24,680
7	224	1,074	86	3,527	29	20,401
8	292	542	115	1,742	43	6,236
9	143	1,242	78	2,411	21	29,108
10	179	1,097	105	1,952	16	30,284
11	224	887	89	3,024	31	9,414
12	196	1,138	76	2,717	28	9,546
13	128	1,151	56	3,257	13	25,256
14	54	3,079	27	8,489	14	22,128
15	123	797	56	2,095	19	8,274
16	159	620	92	1,317	57	2,716
17	138	831	58	2,138	43	2,816
18	137	709	47	2,572	24	4,887
19	159	569	79	1,200	51	1,534
20	42	2,318	20	6,862	9	23,489
21	5	28,515	5	28,515	5	28,515
22	11	23,048	11	23,048	11	23,048
X	325	572	181	1,082	143	1,436
Y	27	1,539	20	3,290	8	5,135
UL	47	227	40	281	40	281

Number and size of sequenced-clone contigs, sequenced-clone-contig scaffolds and those fingerprint clone contigs (see Box 1) that contain sequenced clones; some small fingerprint clone contigs do not as yet have associated sequence. UL, fingerprint clone contigs that could not reliably be placed on a chromosome. These length estimates are from the draft genome sequence, in which gaps between sequence contigs are arbitrarily represented with 100 Ns and gaps between sequence clone contigs with 50,000 Ns for 'bridged gaps' and 100,000 Ns for 'unbridged gaps'. These arbitrary values differ minimally from empirical estimates of gap size (see text), and using the empirically derived estimates would change the N50 lengths presented here only slightly. For unfinished chromosomes, the N50 length ranges from 1.5 to 3 times the arithmetic mean for sequenced-clone contigs, 1.5 to 3 times for sequenced-clone-contig scaffolds, and 1.5 to 6 times for fingerprint clone contigs with sequence.

of the end of the contig, suggesting a possible false join in the assembly of the initial sequence contig. In about half of these cases, the potential misassembly involved fewer than 400 bases, suggesting that a single raw sequence read may have been incorrectly joined. We found 1.9 instances per Mb in which the alignment showed an internal gap, again suggesting a possible misassembly; and 0.5 instances per Mb in which the alignment indicated that two initial sequence contigs that overlapped by at least 150 bp had not been merged by PHRAP. Finally, there were another 0.9 instances per Mb with various other problems. This gives a total of 8.6 instances per Mb of possible misassembly, with about half being relatively small issues involving a few hundred bases.

Some of the potential problems might not result from misassembly, but might reflect sequence polymorphism in the population,

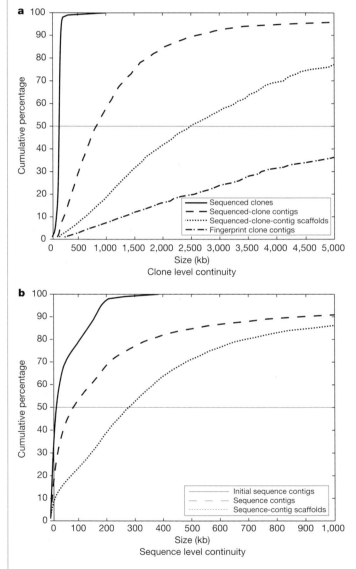

small rearrangements during growth of the large-insert clones, regions of low-quality sequence or matches between segmental duplications. Thus, the frequency of misassemblies may be overstated. On the other hand, the criteria for recognizing overlap between draft and finished clones may have eliminated some misassemblies.

Layout of the sequenced clones. We assessed the accuracy of the layout of sequenced clones onto the fingerprinted clone contigs by calculating the concordance between the positions assigned to a sequenced clone on the basis of *in silico* digestion and the position assigned on the basis of BAC end sequence data. The positions agreed in 98% of cases in which independent assignments could be made by both methods. The results were also compared with well studied regions containing both finished and draft genome sequence. These results indicated that sequenced clone order in the fingerprint map was reliable to within about half of one clone length (~100 kb).

A direct test of the layout is also provided by the draft genome sequence assembly itself. With extensive coverage of the genome, a correctly placed clone should usually (although not always) show sequence overlap with its neighbours in the map. We found only 421 instances of 'singleton' clones that failed to overlap a neighbouring clone. Close examination of the data suggests that most of these are correctly placed, but simply do not yet overlap an adjacent sequenced clone. About 150 clones appeared to be candidates for being incorrectly placed.

Alignment of the fingerprint clone contigs. The alignment of the fingerprint clone contigs with the chromosomes was based on the radiation hybrid, YAC and genetic maps of STSs. The positions of most of the STSs in the draft genome sequence were consistent with these previous maps, but the positions of about 1.7% differed from one or more of them. Some of these disagreements may be due to errors in the layout of the sequenced clones or in the underlying

Figure 9 Overview of features of draft human genome. The Figure shows the occurrences of twelve important types of feature across the human genome. Large grey blocks represent centromeres and centromeric heterochromatin (size not precisely to scale). Each of the feature types is depicted in a track, from top to bottom as follows. (1) Chromosome position in Mb. (2) The approximate positions of Giemsa-stained chromosome bands at the 800 band resolution. (3) Level of coverage in the draft genome sequence. Red, areas covered by finished clones; yellow, areas covered by predraft sequence. Regions covered by draft sequenced clones are in orange, with darker shades reflecting increasing shotgun sequence coverage. (4) GC content. Percentage of bases in a 20,000 base window that are C or G. (5) Repeat density. Red line, density of SINE class repeats in a 100,000-base window; blue line, density of LINE class repeats in a 100,000-base window. (6) Density of SNPs in a 50,000-base window. The SNPs were detected by sequencing and alignments of random genomic reads. Some of the heterogeneity in SNP density reflects the methods used for SNP discovery. Rigorous analysis of SNP density requires comparing the number of SNPs identified to the precise number of bases surveyed. (7) Non-coding RNA genes. Brown, functional RNA genes such as tRNAs, snoRNAs and rRNAs; light orange, RNA pseudogenes. (8) CpG islands. Green ticks represent regions of ~ 200 bases with CpG levels significantly higher than in the genome as a whole, and GC ratios of at least 50%. (9) Exofish ecores. Regions of homology with the pufferfish *T. nigroviridis*[292] are blue. (10) ESTs with at least one intron when aligned against genomic DNA are shown as black tick marks. (11) The starts of genes predicted by Genie or Ensembl are shown as red ticks. The starts of known genes from the RefSeq database[110] are shown in blue. (12) The names of genes that have been uniquely located in the draft genome sequence, characterized and named by the HGM Nomenclature Committee. Known disease genes from the OMIM database are red, other genes blue. This Figure is based on an earlier version of the draft genome sequence than analysed in the text, owing to production constraints. We are aware of various errors in the Figure, including omissions of some known genes and misplacements of others. Some genes are mapped to more than one location, owing to errors in assembly, close paralogues or pseudogenes. Manual review was performed to select the most likely location in these cases and to correct other regions. For updated information, see http://genome.ucsc.edu/ and http://www.ensembl.org/.

Figure 8 Cumulative distributions of several measures of clone level contiguity and sequence contiguity. The figures represent the proportion of the draft genome sequence contained in contigs of at most the indicated size. **a**, Clone level contiguity. The clones have a tight size distribution with an N50 of ~ 160 kb (corresponding to 50% on the cumulative distribution). Sequenced-clone contigs represent the next level of continuity, and are linked by mRNA sequences or pairs of BAC end sequences to yield the sequenced-clone-contig scaffolds. The underlying contiguity of the layout of sequenced clones against the fingerprinted clone contigs is only partially shown at this scale.

b, Sequence contiguity. The input fragments have low continuity (N50 = 21.7 kb). After merging, the sequence contigs grow to an N50 length of about 82 kb. After linking, sequence-contig scaffolds with an N50 length of about 274 kb are created.

Table 7 Sequence level contiguity of the draft genome sequence

Chromosome	Initial sequence contigs		Sequence contigs		Sequence-contig scaffolds	
	Number	N50 length (kb)	Number	N50 length (kb)	Number	N50 length (kb)
All	396,913	21.7	149,821	81.9	87,757	274.3
1	37,656	16.5	12,256	59.1	5,457	278.4
2	32,280	19.9	13,228	57.3	6,959	248.5
3	38,848	15.6	15,098	37.7	8,964	167.4
4	28,600	16.0	13,152	33.0	7,402	158.9
5	30,096	20.4	10,689	72.9	6,378	241.2
6	17,472	43.6	5,547	180.3	2,554	485.0
7	12,733	86.4	4,562	335.7	2,726	591.3
8	19,042	18.1	8,984	38.2	4,631	198.9
9	15,955	20.1	6,226	55.6	3,766	216.2
10	21,762	18.7	9,126	47.9	6,886	133.0
11	29,723	14.3	8,503	40.0	4,684	193.2
12	22,050	19.1	8,422	63.4	5,526	217.0
13	13,737	21.7	5,193	70.5	2,659	300.1
14	4,470	161.4	829	1,371.0	541	2,009.5
15	13,134	15.3	5,840	30.3	3,229	149.7
16	10,297	34.4	4,916	119.5	3,337	356.3
17	10,369	22.9	4,339	90.6	2,616	248.9
18	16,266	15.3	4,461	51.4	2,540	216.1
19	6,009	38.4	2,503	134.4	1,551	375.5
20	2,884	108.6	511	1,346.7	312	813.8
21	103	340.0	5	28,515.3	5	28,515.3
22	526	113.9	11	23,048.1	11	23,048.1
X	11,062	58.8	4,607	218.6	2,610	450.7
Y	557	154.3	140	1,388.6	106	1,439.7
UL	1,282	21.4	613	46.0	297	166.4

This Table is similar to Table 6 but shows the number and N50 length for various types of sequence contig (see Box 1). See legend to Table 6 concerning treatment of gaps. For sequence contigs in the draft genome sequence, the N50 length ranges from 1.7 to 5.5 times the arithmetic mean for initial sequence contigs, 2.5 to 8.2 times for merged sequence contigs, and 6.1 to 10 times for sequence-contig scaffolds.

Table 8 Chromosome size estimates

Chromosome*	Sequenced bases† (Mb)	FCC gaps‡		SCC gaps‖		Sequence gaps#		Heterochromatin and short arm adjustments** (Mb)	Total estimated chromosome size (including artefactual duplication in draft genome sequence)†† (Mb)	Previously estimated chromosome size‡‡ (Mb)
		Number	Total bases in gaps§ (Mb)	Number	Total bases in gaps¶ (Mb)	Number	Total bases in gaps☆ (Mb)			
All	2,692.9	897	152.0	4,076	142.7	145,514	80.6	212	3,289	3,286
1	212.2	104	17.7	347	12.1	11,803	6.5	30	279	263
2	221.6	50	8.5	296	10.4	12,880	7.1	3	251	255
3	186.2	71	12.1	336	11.8	14,689	8.1	3	221	214
4	168.1	39	6.6	343	12.0	12,768	7.1	3	197	203
5	169.7	46	7.8	337	11.8	10,304	5.7	3	198	194
6	158.1	15	2.6	275	9.6	5,225	2.9	3	176	183
7	146.2	27	4.6	195	6.8	4,338	2.4	3	163	171
8	124.3	41	7.0	249	8.7	8,692	4.8	3	148	155
9	106.9	19	3.2	122	4.3	6,083	3.4	22	140	145
10	127.1	14	2.4	163	5.7	8,947	5.0	3	143	144
11	128.6	29	4.9	193	6.8	8,279	4.6	3	148	144
12	124.5	26	4.4	168	5.9	8,226	4.6	3	142	143
13	92.9	12	2.0	115	4.0	5,065	2.8	16	118	114
14	86.9	13	2.2	40	1.4	775	0.4	16	107	109
15	73.4	18	3.1	104	3.6	5,717	3.2	17	100	106
16	73.1	55	9.4	102	3.6	4,757	2.6	15	101	98
17	72.8	41	7.0	95	3.3	4,261	2.4	3	88	92
18	72.9	22	3.7	113	4.0	4,324	2.4	3	86	85
19	55.4	49	8.3	108	3.8	2,344	1.3	3	72	67
20	60.5	7	1.2	33	1.2	469	0.3	3	66	72
21	33.8	4	0.1	0	0.0	0	0.0	11	45	50
22	33.8	10	1.0	0	0.0	0	0.0	13	48	56
X	127.7	141	24.0	182	6.4	4,282	2.4	3	163	164
Y	21.8	6	1.0	19	0.7	113	0.1	27	51	59
NA	5.1	0	0	134	0.0	577	0.3	0	0	0
UL	9.3	38	0	7	0.0	566	0.3	0	0	0

* NA, sequenced clones that could not be associated with fingerprint clone contigs. UL, clone contigs that could not be reliably placed on a chromosome.
† Total number of bases in the draft genome sequence, excluding gaps. Total length of scaffold (including gaps contained within clones) is 2.916 Gb.
‡ Gaps between those fingerprint clone contigs that contain sequenced clones excluding gaps for centromeres.
§ For unfinished chromosomes, we estimate an average size of 0.17 Mb per FCC gap, based on retrospective estimates of the clone coverage of chromosomes 21 and 22. Gap estimates for chromosomes 21 and 22 are taken from refs 93, 94.
‖ Gaps between sequenced-clone contigs within a fingerprint clone contig.
¶ For unfinished chromosomes, we estimate sequenced clone gaps at 0.035 Mb each, based on evaluation of a sample of these gaps.
# Gaps between two sequence contigs within a sequenced-clone contig.
☆ We estimate the average number of bases in sequence gaps from alignments of the initial sequence contigs of unfinished clones (see text) and extrapolation to the whole chromosome.
** Including adjustments for estimates of the sizes of the short arms of the acrocentric chromosomes 13, 14, 15, 21 and 22 (ref. 105), estimates for the centromere and heterochromatic regions of chromosomes 1, 9 and 16 (refs 106, 107) and estimates of 3 Mb for the centromere and 24 Mb for telomeric heterochromatin for the Y chromosome[108].
†† The sum of the five lengths in the preceding columns. This is an overestimate, because the draft genome sequence contains some artefactual sequence owing to inability to correctly to merge all underlying sequence contigs. The total amount of artefactual duplication varies among chromosomes; the overall amount is estimated by computational analysis to be about 100 Mb, or about 3% of the total length given, yielding a total estimated size of about 3,200 Mb for the human genome.
‡‡ Including heterochromatic regions and acrocentric short arm(s)[105].

Figure 9

Note: The diagrams of the chromosomes span more than one page. For ease of reference, the end of a chromosome segment on one page is repeated on the following page, so that the segments overlap by 2–4 megabases at each end.

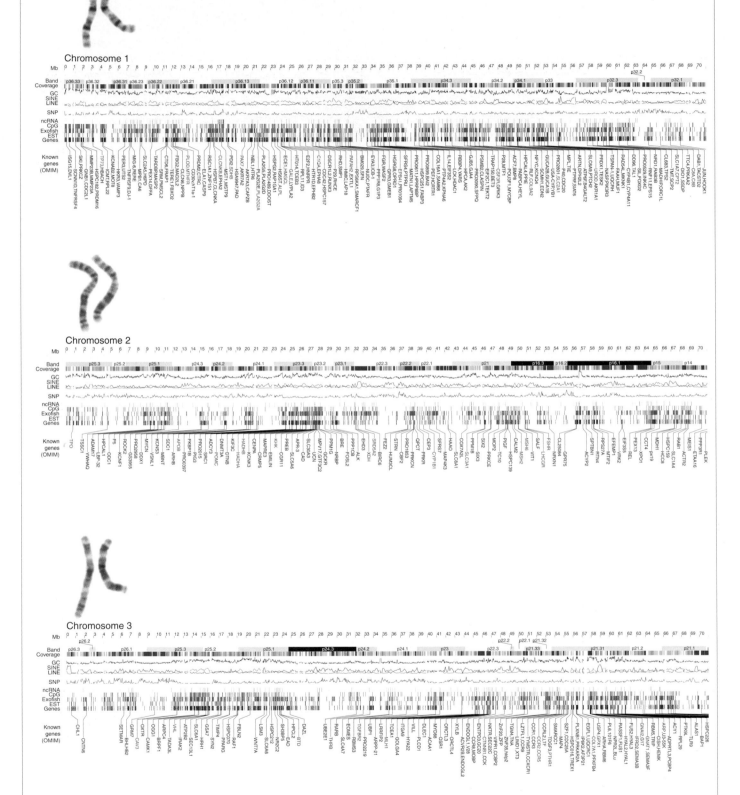

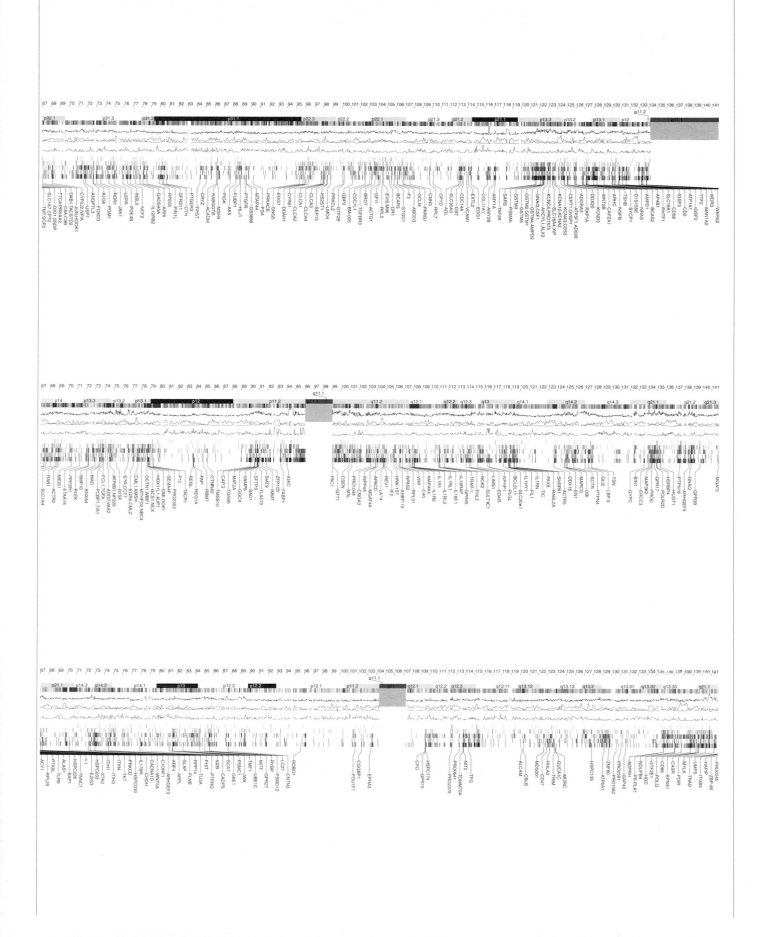

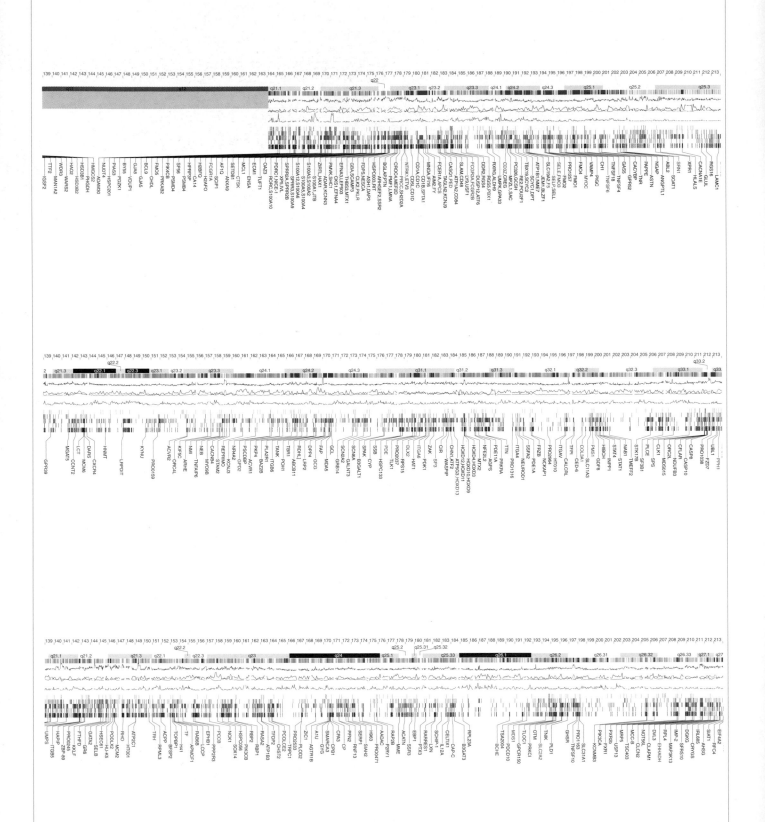

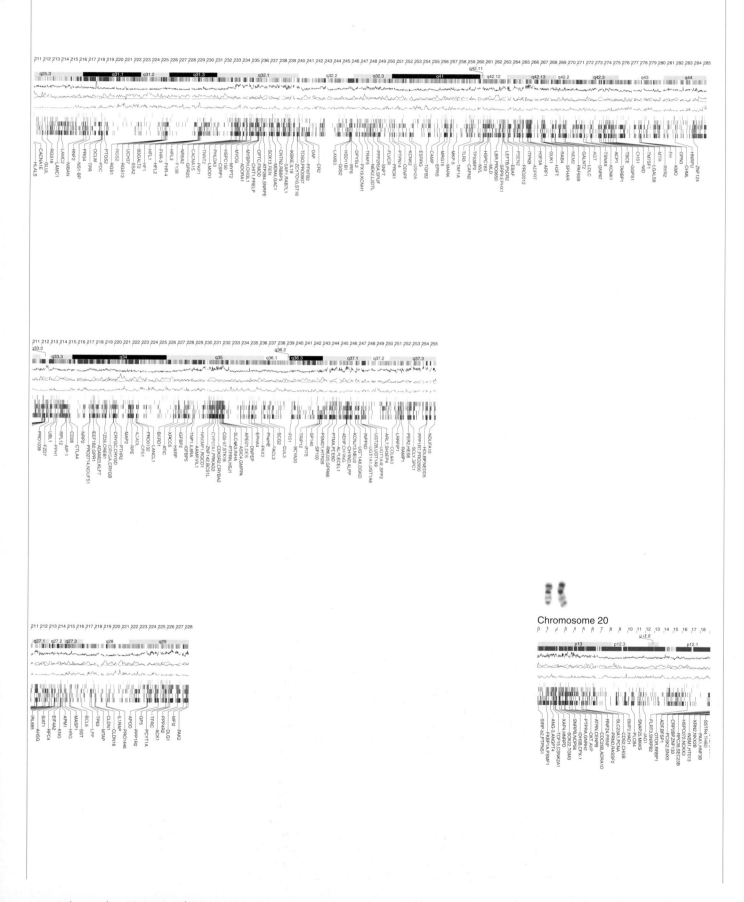

Chromosome 20

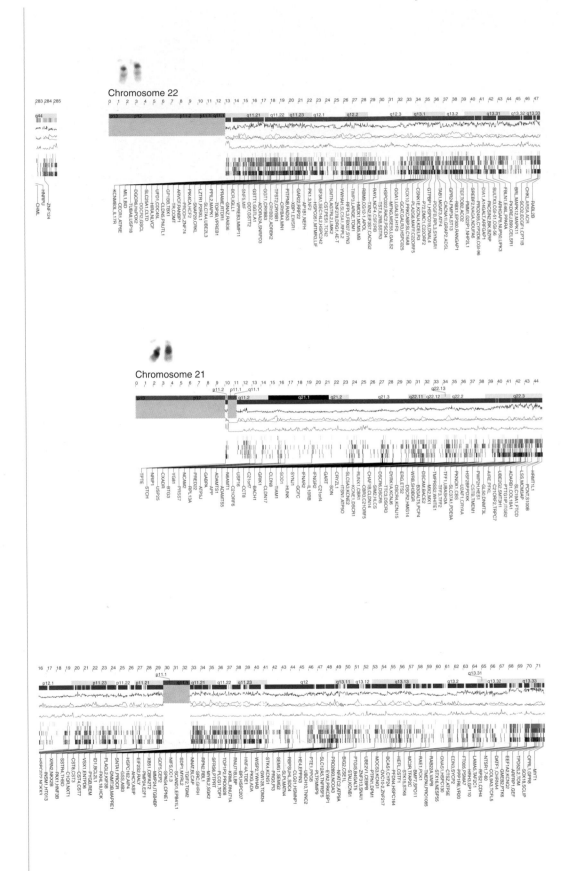

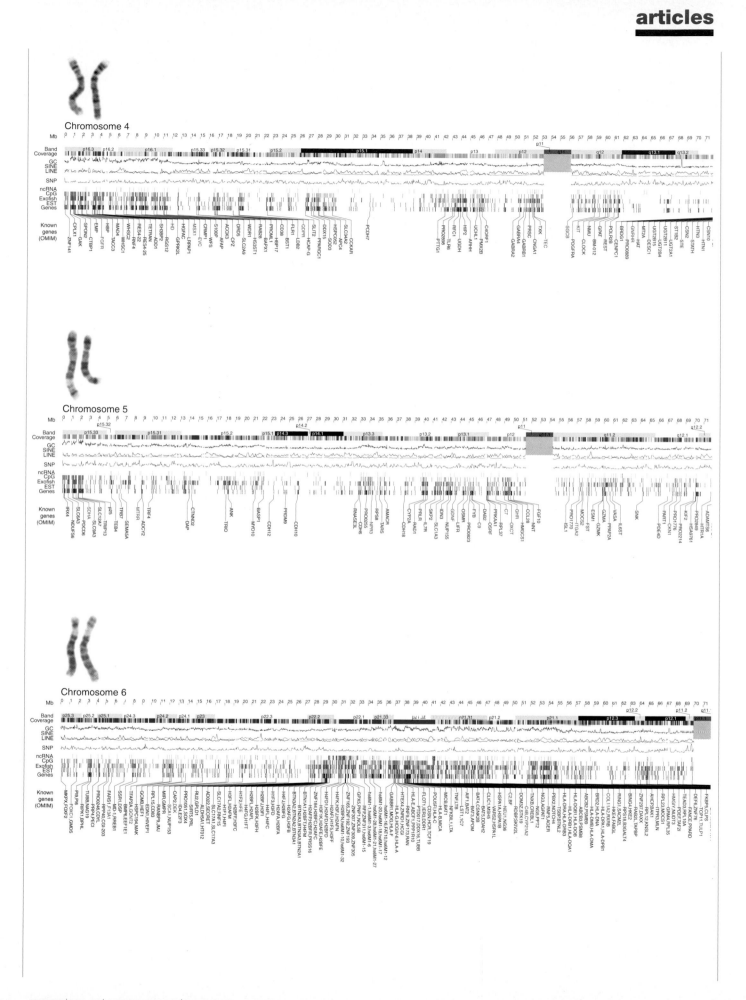

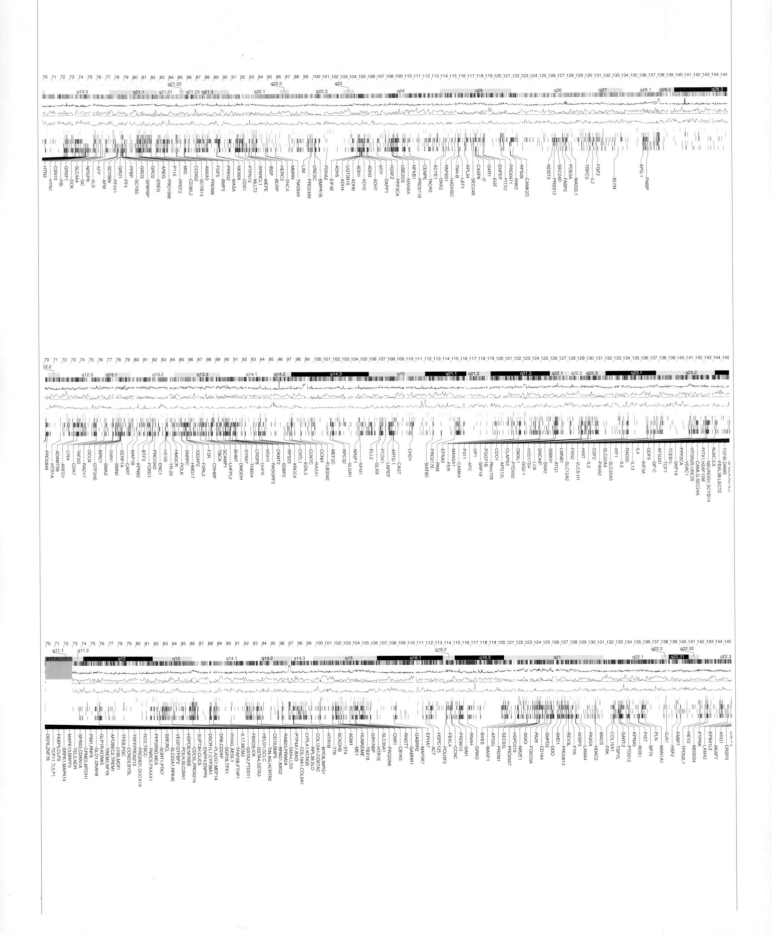

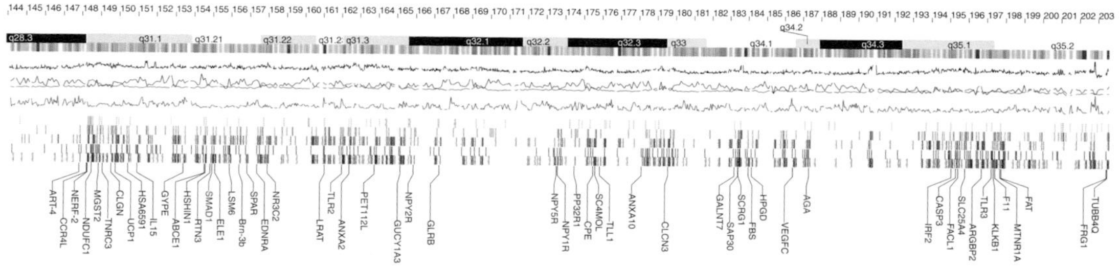

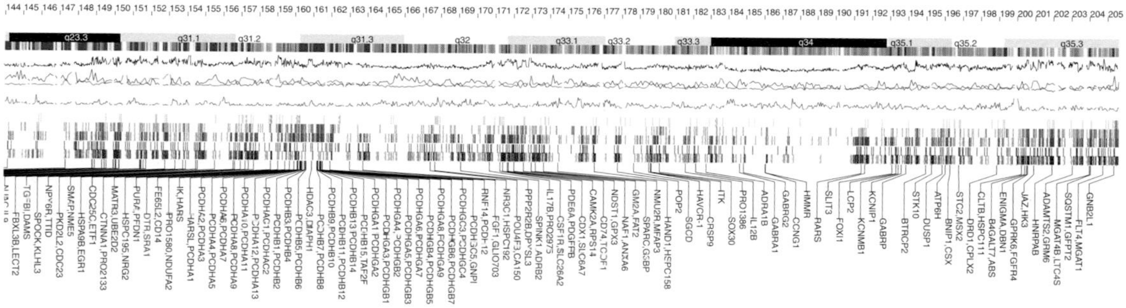

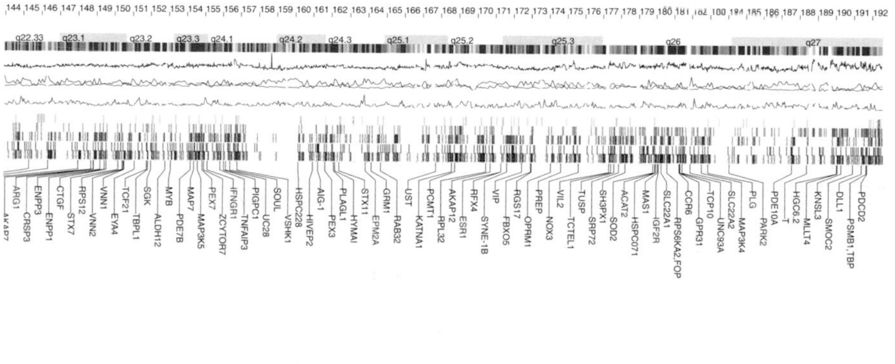

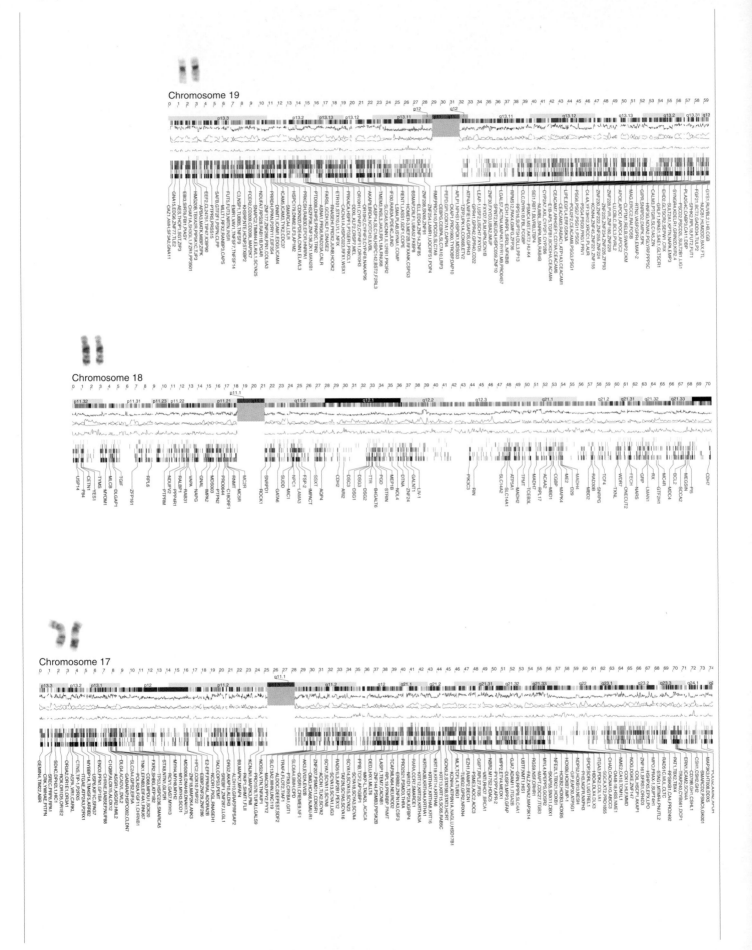

57 58 59 60 61 62 63 64 65 66 67 68 69 70 71 72 73 74 75 76

q13.31 q13.32 q13.33 q13.41 q13.42 q13.43

68 69 70 71 72 73 74 75 76 77 78 79 80 81 82 83 84 85 86 87

q22.1 q22.2 q22.3 q23

72 73 74 75 76 77 78 79 80 81 82 83 84 85 86 87 88 89 90

q24.1 q24.2 q24.3 q25.1 q25.2 q25.3

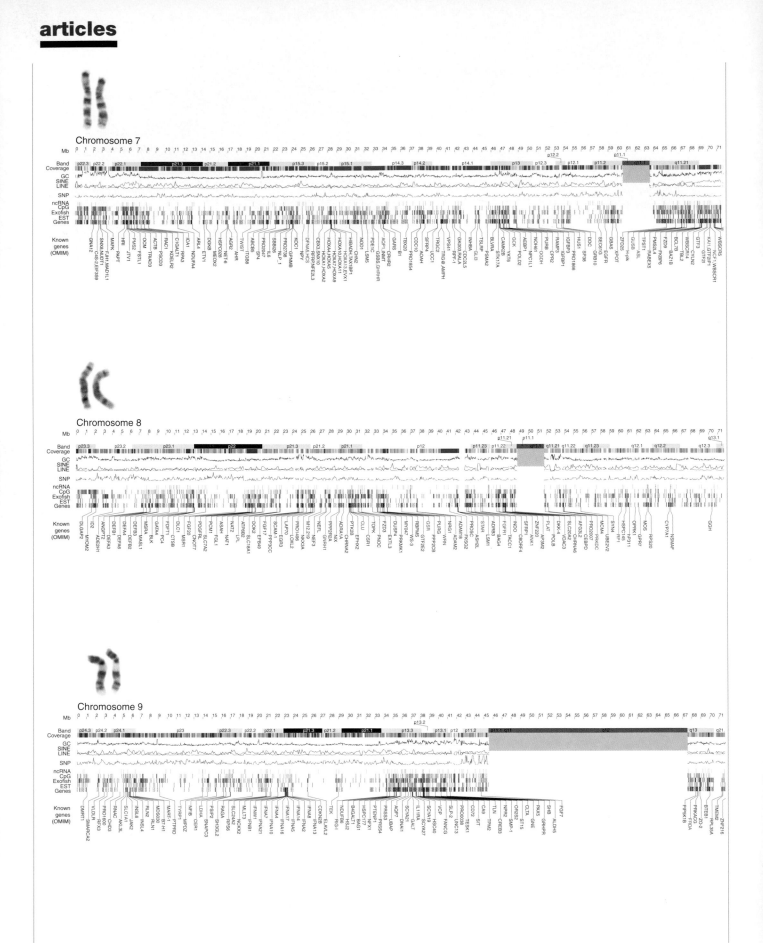

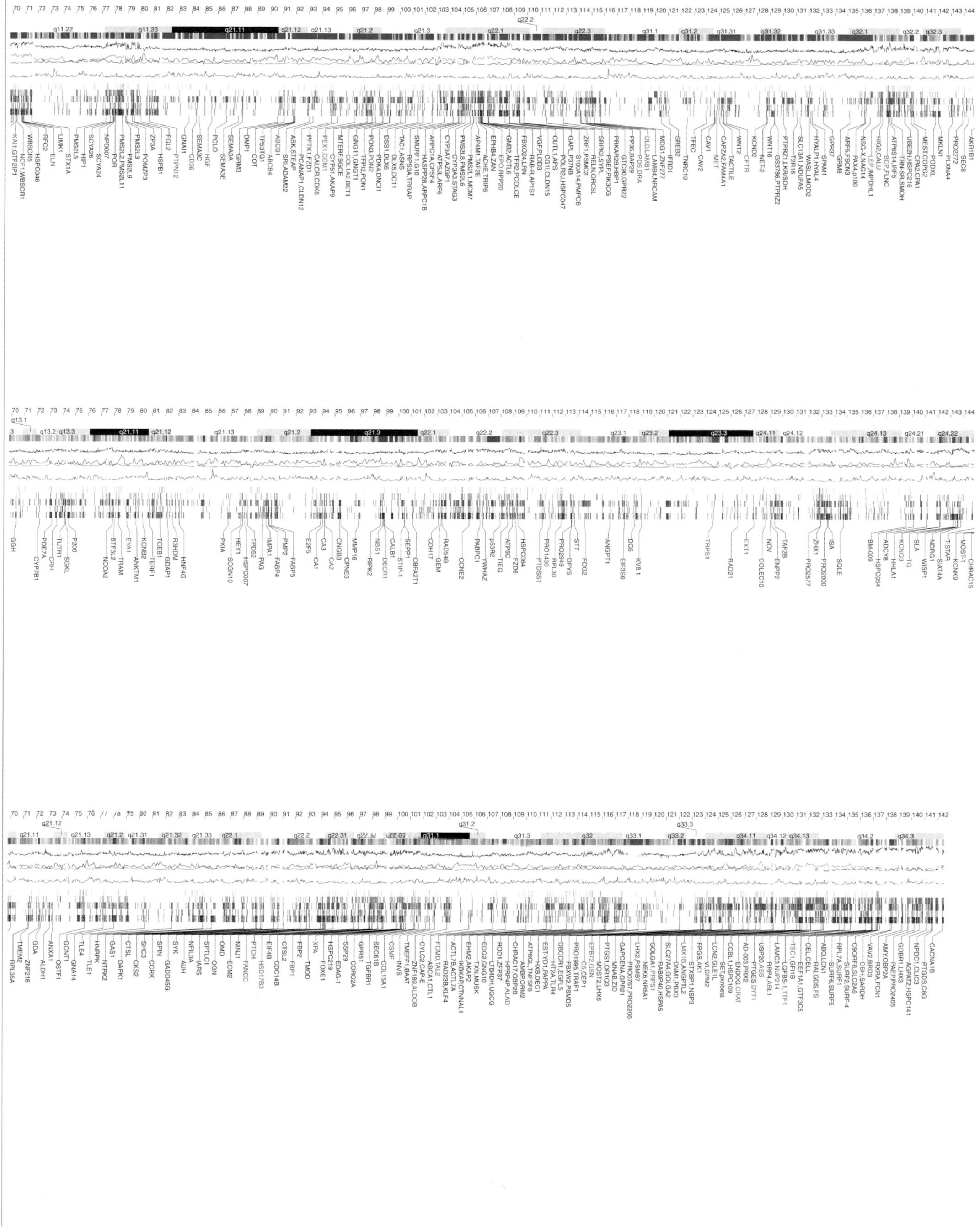

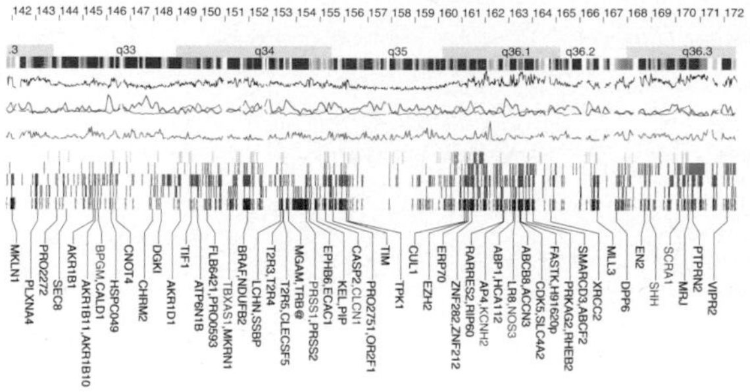
142 143 144 145 146 147 148 149 150 151 152 153 154 155 156 157 158 159 160 161 162 163 164 165 166 167 168 169 170 171 172
q33
q34
q35
q36.1
q36.2
q36.3
MKLN1
PLXNA4
PRO2272
SEC8
AKR1B1
AKR1B11,AKR1B10
BPGM,CALD1
HSPC049
CNOT4
CHRM2
DGKI
AKR1D1
TIF1
ATP6N1B
FLB6421,PRO0593
TBXAS1,MKRN1
BRAF,NDUFB2
LCHN,SSBP
T2R3,T2R4
T2R5,CLECSF5
MGAM,TRB@
PRSS1,PRSS2
EPHB6,ECAC1
KEL,PIP
CASP2,CLCN1
PRO2751,OR2F1
TIM
TPK1
CUL1
EZH2
ERP70
ZNF282,ZNF212
RARRES2,RIP60
AP4,KCNH2
ABP1,HCA112
LR8,NOS3
ABCB8,ACCN3
CDK5,SLC4A2
FASTK,H91620p
PRKAG2,RHEB2
SMARCD3,ABCF2
XRCC2
MLL3
DPP6
EN2
SHH
SCRA1
MRJ
PTPRN2
VIPR2

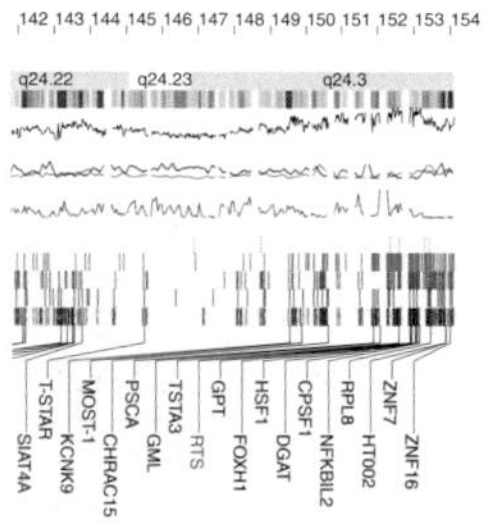
142 143 144 145 146 147 148 149 150 151 152 153 154
q24.22
q24.23
q24.3
SIAT4A
T-STAR
KCNK9
MOST-1
CHRAC15
PSCA
GML
TSTA3
RTS
GPT
FOXH1
HSF1
DGAT
CPSF1
NFKBIL2
RPL8
HT002
ZNF7
ZNF16

Chromosome 16

Chromosome 15

Chromosome 14

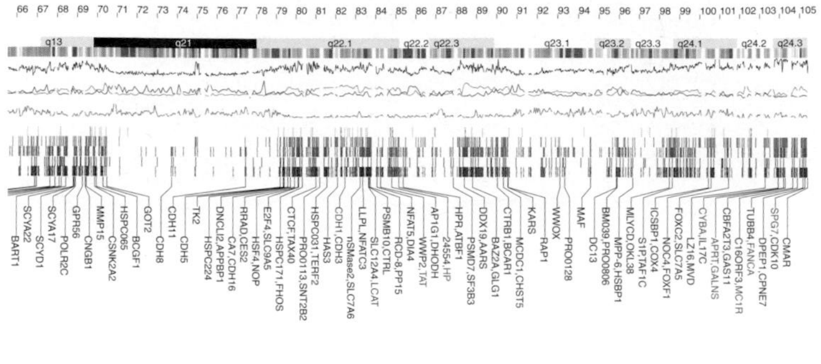

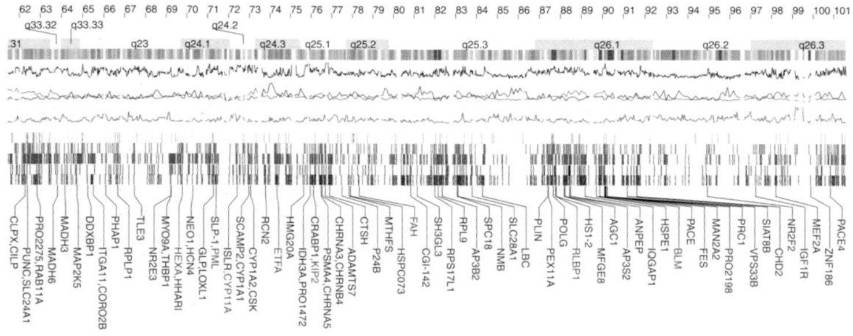

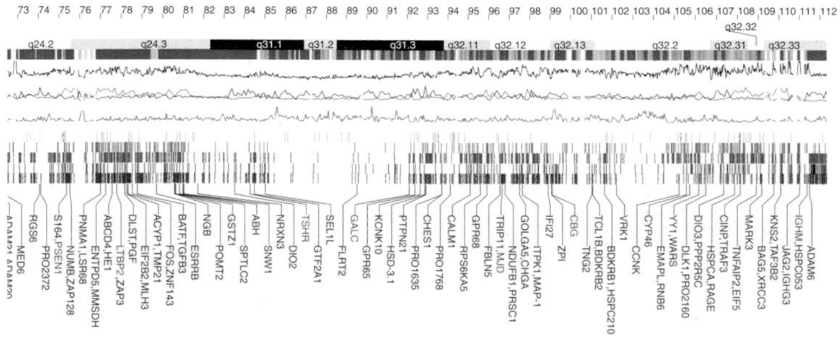

Chromosome 10

Chromosome 11

Chromosome X

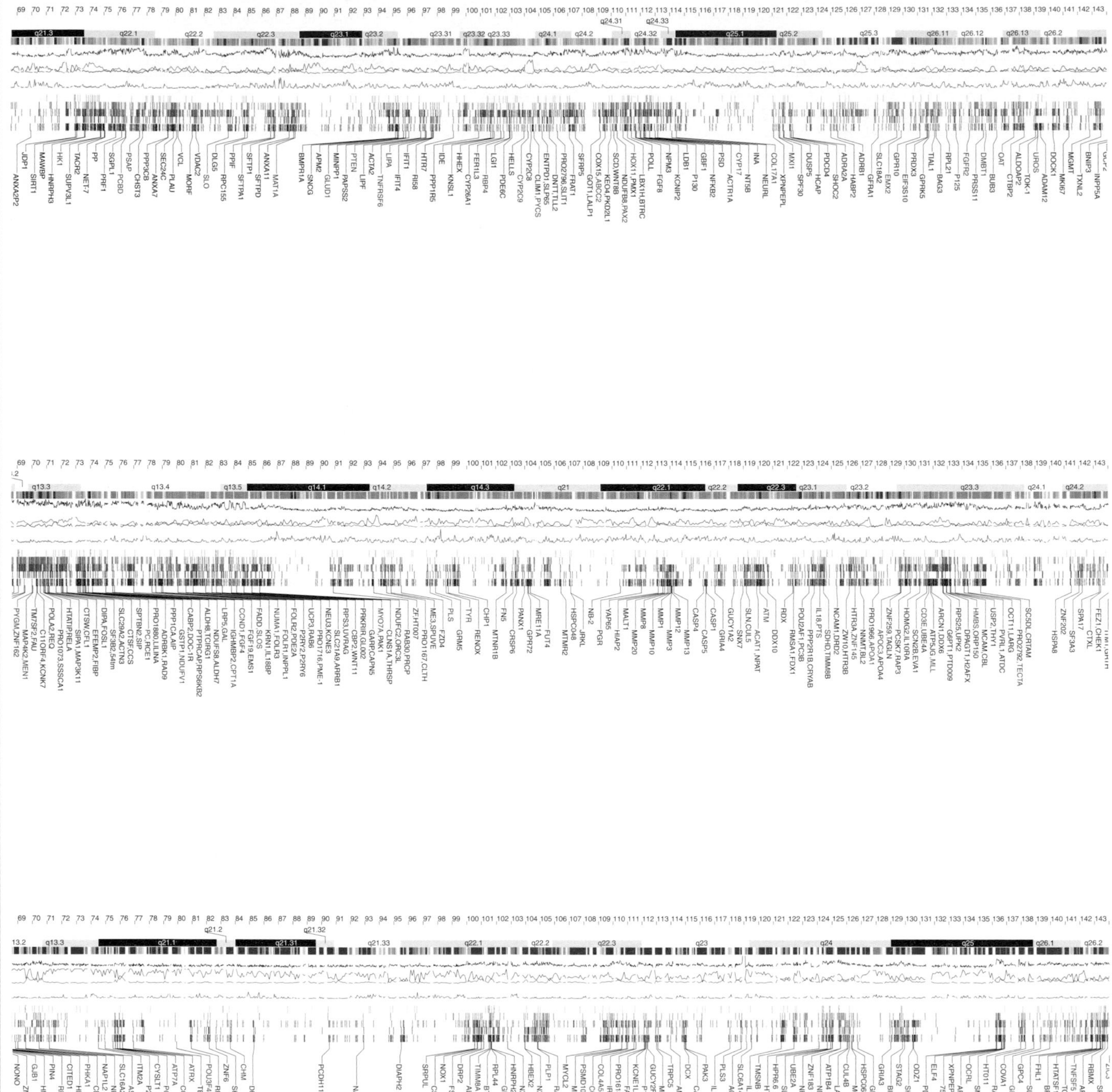

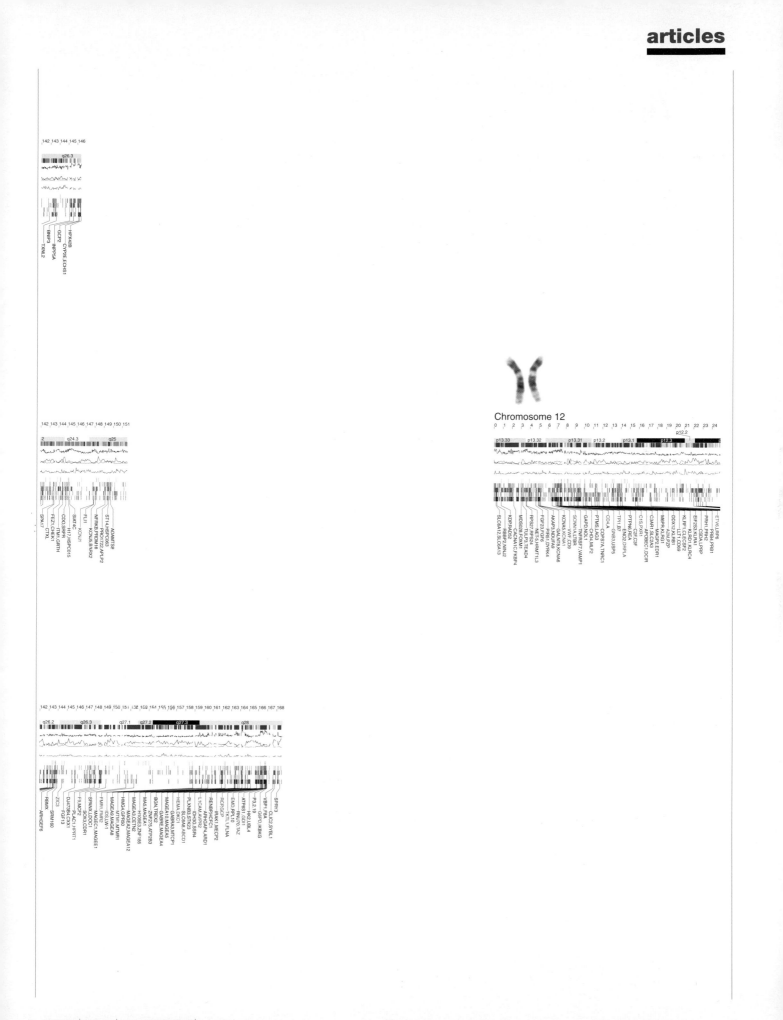

Chromosome 13

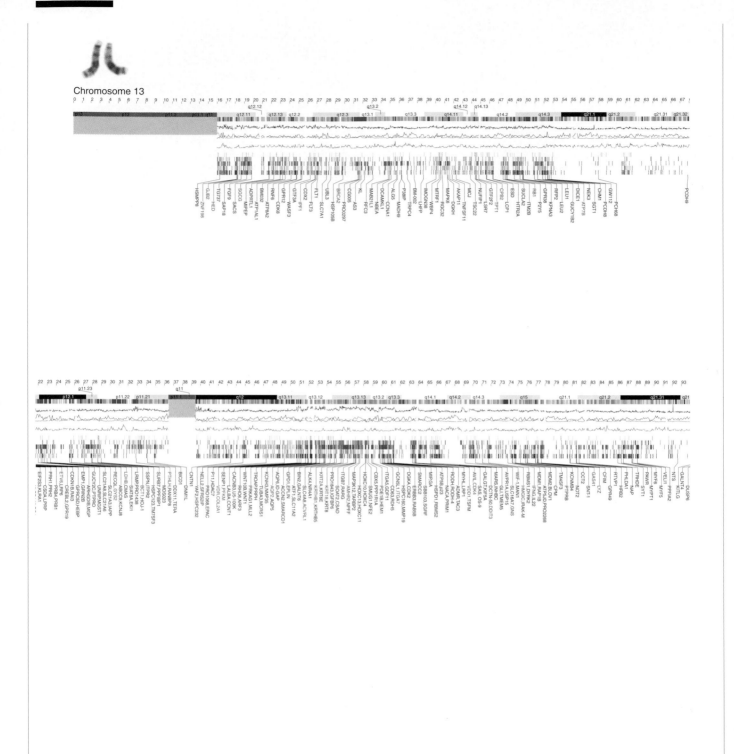

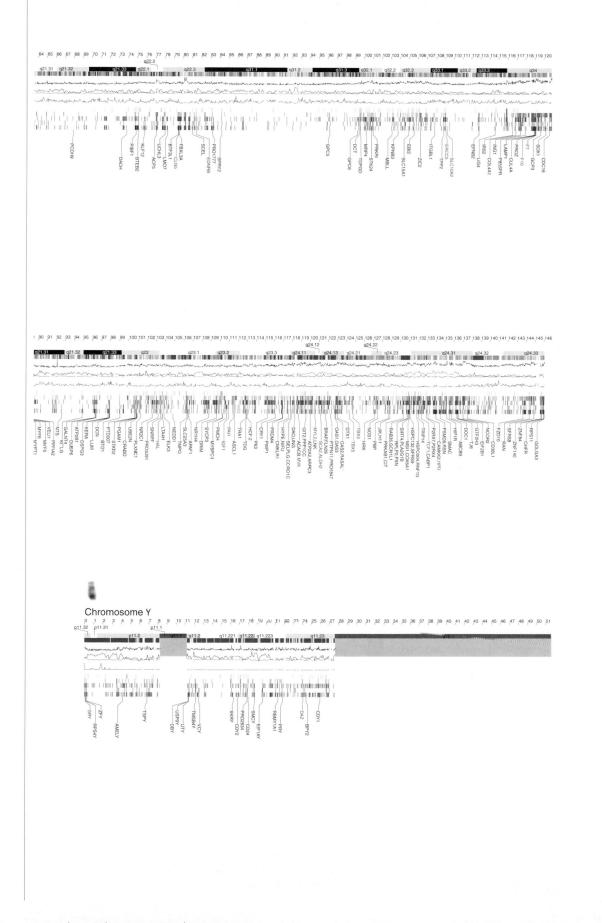

fingerprint map. However, many involve STSs that have been localized on only one or two of the previous maps or that occur as isolated discrepancies in conflict with several flanking STSs. Many of these cases are probably due to errors in the previous maps (with error rates for individual maps estimated at 1–2%[100]). Others may be due to incorrect assignment of the STSs to the draft genome sequence (by the electronic polymerase chain reaction (e-PCR) computer program) or to database entries that contain sequence data from more than one clone (owing to cross-contamination).

Graphical views of the independent data sets were particularly useful in detecting problems with order or orientation (Fig. 5). Areas of conflict were reviewed and corrected if supported by the underlying data. In the version discussed here, there were 41 sequenced clones falling in 14 sequenced-clone contigs with STS content information from multiple maps that disagreed with the flanking clones or sequenced-clone contigs; the placement of these clones thus remains suspect. Four of these instances suggest errors in the fingerprint map, whereas the others suggest errors in the layout of sequenced clones. These cases are being investigated and will be corrected in future versions.

Assembly of the sequenced clones. We assessed the accuracy of the assembly by using a set of 148 draft clones comprising 22.4 Mb for which finished sequence subsequently became available[104]. The initial sequence contigs lack information about order and orientation, and GigAssembler attempts to use linking data to infer such information as far as possible[104]. Starting with initial sequence contigs that were unordered and unoriented, the program placed 90% of the initial sequence contigs in the correct orientation and 85% in the correct order with respect to one another. In a separate test, GigAssembler was tested on simulated draft data produced from finished sequence on chromosome 22 and similar results were obtained.

Some problems remain at all levels. First, errors in the initial sequence contigs persist in the merged sequence contigs built from them and can cause difficulties in the assembly of the draft genome sequence. Second, GigAssembler may fail to merge some overlapping sequences because of poor data quality, allelic differences or misassemblies of the initial sequence contigs; this may result in apparent local duplication of a sequence. We have estimated by various methods the amount of such artefactual duplication in the assembly from these and other sources to be about 100 Mb. On the other hand, nearby duplicated sequences may occasionally be incorrectly merged. Some sequenced clones remain incorrectly placed on the layout, as discussed above, and others (< 0.5%) remain unplaced. The fingerprint map has undoubtedly failed to resolve some closely related duplicated regions, such as the Williams region and several highly repetitive subtelomeric and pericentric regions (see below). Detailed examination and sequence finishing may be required to sort out these regions precisely, as has been done with chromosome Y[89]. Finally, small sequenced-clone contigs with limited or no STS

landmark content remain difficult to place. Full utilization of the higher resolution radiation hybrid map (the TNG map) may help in this[95]. Future targeted FISH experiments and increased map continuity will also facilitate positioning of these sequences.

Genome coverage

We next assessed the nature of the gaps within the draft genome sequence, and attempted to estimate the fraction of the human genome not represented within the current version.

Gaps in draft genome sequence coverage. There are three types of gap in the draft genome sequence: gaps within unfinished sequenced clones; gaps between sequenced-clone contigs, but within fingerprint clone contigs; and gaps between fingerprint clone contigs. The first two types are relatively straightforward to close simply by performing additional sequencing and finishing on already identified clones. Closing the third type may require screening of additional large-insert clone libraries and possibly new technologies for the most recalcitrant regions. We consider these three cases in turn.

We estimated the size of gaps within draft clones by studying instances in which there was substantial overlap between a draft clone and a finished clone, as described above. The average gap size in these draft sequenced clones was 554 bp, although the precise estimate was sensitive to certain assumptions in the analysis. Assuming that the sequence gaps in the draft genome sequence are fairly represented by this sample, about 80 Mb or about 3% (likely range 2–4%) of sequence may lie in the 145,514 gaps within draft sequenced clones.

The gaps between sequenced-clone contigs but within fingerprint clone contigs are more difficult to evaluate directly, because the draft genome sequence flanking many of the gaps is often not precisely aligned with the fingerprinted clones. However, most are much smaller than a single BAC. In fact, nearly three-quarters of these gaps are bridged by one or more individual BACs, as indicated by linking information from BAC end sequences. We measured the sizes of a subset of gaps directly by examining restriction fragment fingerprints of overlapping clones. A study of 157 'bridged' gaps and 55 'unbridged' gaps gave an average gap size of 25 kb. Allowing for the possibility that these gaps may not be fully representative and that some restriction fragments are not included in the calculation, a more conservative estimate of gap size would be 35 kb. This would indicate that about 150 Mb or 5% of the human genome may reside in the 4,076 gaps between sequenced-clone contigs. This sequence should be readily obtained as the clones spanning them are sequenced.

The size of the gaps between fingerprint clone contigs was estimated by comparing the fingerprint maps to the essentially completed chromosomes 21 and 22. The analysis shows that the fingerprinted BAC clones in the global database cover 97–98% of the sequenced portions of those chromosomes[86]. The published sequences of these chromosomes also contain a few small gaps (5 and 11, respectively) amounting to some 1.6% of the euchromatic sequence, and do not include the heterochromatic portion. This suggests that the gaps between contigs in the fingerprint map contain about 4% of the euchromatic genome. Experience with closure of such gaps on chromosomes 20 and 7 suggests that many of these gaps are less than one clone in length and will be closed by clones from other libraries. However, recovery of sequence from these gaps represents the most challenging aspect of producing a complete finished sequence of the human genome.

As another measure of the representation of the BAC libraries, Riethman[109] has found BAC or cosmid clones that link to telomeric half-YACs or to the telomeric sequence itself for 40 of the 41 non-satellite telomeres. Thus, the fingerprint map appears to have no substantial gaps in these regions. Many of the pericentric regions are also represented, but analysis is less complete here (see below).

Representation of random raw sequences. In another approach to measuring coverage, we compared a collection of random raw sequence reads to the existing draft genome sequence. In principle,

Table 9 Distribution of PHRAP scores in the draft genome sequence

PHRAP score	Percentage of bases in the draft genome sequence
0–9	0.6
10–19	1.3
20–29	2.2
30–39	4.8
40–49	8.1
50–59	8.7
60–69	9.0
70–79	12.1
80–89	17.3
>90	35.9

PHRAP scores are a logarithmically based representation of the error probability. A PHRAP score of X corresponds to an error probability of $10^{-X/10}$. Thus, PHRAP scores of 20, 30 and 40 correspond to accuracy of 99%, 99.9% and 99.99%, respectively. PHRAP scores are derived from quality scores of the underlying sequence reads used in sequence assembly. See http://www.genome.washington.edu/UWGC/analysistools/phrap.htm.

the fraction of reads matching the draft genome sequence should provide an estimate of genome coverage. In practice, the comparison is complicated by the need to allow for repeat sequences, the imperfect sequence quality of both the raw sequence and the draft genome sequence, and the possibility of polymorphism. Nonetheless, the analysis provides a reasonable view of the extent to which the genome is represented in the draft genome sequence and the public databases.

We compared the raw sequence reads against both the sequences used in the construction of the draft genome sequence and all of GenBank using the BLAST computer program. Of the 5,615 raw sequence reads analysed (each containing at least 100 bp of contiguous non-repetitive sequence), 4,924 had a match of ≥ 97% identity with a sequenced clone, indicating that 88 ± 1.5% of the genome was represented in sequenced clones. The estimate is subject to various uncertainties. Most serious is the proportion of repeat sequence in the remainder of the genome. If the unsequenced portion of the genome is unusually rich in repeated sequence, we would underestimate its size (although the excess would be comprised of repeated sequence).

We examined those raw sequences that failed to match by comparing them to the other publicly available sequence resources. Fifty (0.9%) had matches in public databases containing cDNA sequences, STSs and similar data. An additional 276 (or 43% of the remaining raw sequence) had matches to the whole-genome shotgun reads discussed above (consistent with the idea that these reads cover about half of the genome).

We also examined the extent of genome coverage by aligning the cDNA sequences for genes in the RefSeq dataset[110] to the draft genome sequence. We found that 88% of the bases of these cDNAs could be aligned to the draft genome sequence at high stringency (at least 98% identity). (A few of the alignments with either the random raw sequence reads or the cDNAs may be to a highly similar region in the genome, but such matches should affect the estimate of genome coverage by considerably less than 1%, based on the estimated extent of duplication within the genome (see below).)

These results indicate that about 88% of the human genome is represented in the draft genome sequence and about 94% in the combined publicly available sequence databases. The figure of 88% agrees well with our independent estimates above that about 3%, 5% and 4% of the genome reside in the three types of gap in the draft genome sequence.

Finally, a small experimental check was performed by screening a large-insert clone library with probes corresponding to 16 of the whole genome shotgun reads that failed to match the draft genome sequence. Five hybridized to many clones from different fingerprint clone contigs and were discarded as being repetitive. Of the remaining eleven, two fell within sequenced clones (presumably within sequence gaps of the first type), eight fell in fingerprint clone

contigs but between sequenced clones (gaps of the second type) and one failed to identify clones in the fingerprint map (gaps of the third type) but did identify clones in another large-insert library. Although these numbers are small, they are consistent with the view that the much of the remaining genome sequence lies within already identified clones in the current map.

Estimates of genome and chromosome sizes. Informed by this analysis of genome coverage, we proceeded to estimate the sizes of the genome and each of the chromosomes (Table 8). Beginning with the current assigned sequence for each chromosome, we corrected for the known gaps on the basis of their estimated sizes (see above). We attempted to account for the sizes of centromeres and heterochromatin, neither of which are well represented in the draft sequence. Finally, we corrected for around 100 Mb of artefactual duplication in the assembly. We arrived at a total human genome size estimate of around 3,200 Mb, which compares favourably with previous estimates based on DNA content.

We also independently estimated the size of the euchromatic portion of the genome by determining the fraction of the 5,615 random raw sequences that matched the finished portion of the human genome (whose total length is known with greater precision). Twenty-nine per cent of these raw sequences found a match among 835 Mb of nonredundant finished sequence. This leads to an estimate of the euchromatic genome size of 2.9 Gb. This agrees reasonably with the prediction above based on the length of the draft genome sequence (Table 8).

Update. The results above reflect the data on 7 October 2000. New data are continually being added, with improvements being made to the physical map, new clones being sequenced to close gaps and draft clones progressing to full shotgun coverage and finishing. The draft genome sequence will be regularly reassembled and publicly released.

Currently, the physical map has been refined such that the number of fingerprint clone contigs has fallen from 1,246 to 965; this reflects the elimination of some artefactual contigs and the closure of some gaps. The sequence coverage has risen such that 90% of the human genome is now represented in the sequenced clones and more than 94% is represented in the combined publicly available sequence databases. The total amount of finished sequence is now around 1 Gb.

Broad genomic landscape

What biological insights can be gleaned from the draft sequence? In this section, we consider very large-scale features of the draft genome sequence: the distribution of GC content, CpG islands and recombination rates, and the repeat content and gene content of the human genome. The draft genome sequence makes it possible to integrate these features and others at scales ranging from individual

Figure 10 Screen shot from UCSC Draft Human Genome Browser. See http://genome.ucsc.edu/.

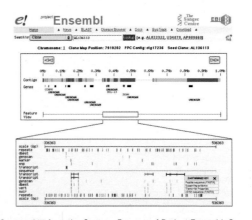

Figure 11 Screen shot from the Genome Browser of Project Ensembl. See http://www.ensembl.org.

nucleotides to collections of chromosomes. Unless noted, all analyses were conducted on the assembled draft genome sequence described above.

Figure 9 provides a high-level view of the contents of the draft genome sequence, at a scale of about 3.8 Mb per centimetre. Of course, navigating information spanning nearly ten orders of magnitude requires computational tools to extract the full value. We have created and made freely available various 'Genome Browsers'. Browsers were developed and are maintained by the University of California at Santa Cruz (Fig. 10) and the EnsEMBL project of the European Bioinformatics Institute and the Sanger Centre (Fig. 11). Additional browsers have been created; URLs are listed at www.nhgri.nih.gov/genome_hub. These web-based computer tools allow users to view an annotated display of the draft genome sequence, with the ability to scroll along the chromosomes and zoom in or out to different scales. They include: the nucleotide sequence, sequence contigs, clone contigs, sequence coverage and finishing status, local GC content, CpG islands, known STS markers from previous genetic and physical maps, families of repeat sequences, known genes, ESTs and mRNAs, predicted genes, SNPs and sequence similarities with other organisms (currently the pufferfish *Tetraodon nigroviridis*). These browsers will be updated as the draft genome sequence is refined and corrected as additional annotations are developed.

In addition to using the Genome Browsers, one can download

Box 2

Sources of publicly available sequence data and other relevant genomic information

http://genome.ucsc.edu/
University of California at Santa Cruz
Contains the assembly of the draft genome sequence used in this paper and updates

http://genome.wustl.edu/gsc/ human/Mapping/
Washington University
Contains links to clone and accession maps of the human genome

http://www.ensembl.org
EBI/Sanger Centre
Allows access to DNA and protein sequences with automatic baseline annotation

http://www.ncbi.nlm.nih.gov/ genome/guide/
NCBI
Views of chromosomes and maps and loci with links to other NCBI resources

http://www.ncbi.nlm.nih.gov/ genemap99/
Gene map 99: contains data and viewers for radiation hybrid maps of EST-based STSs

http://compbio.ornl.gov/channel/index.html
Oak Ridge National Laboratory
Java viewers for human genome data

http://hgrep.ims.u-tokyo.ac.jp/
RIKEN and the University of Tokyo
Gives an overview of the entire human genome structure

http://snp.cshl.org/
The SNP Consortium
Includes a variety of ways to query for SNPs in the human genome

http://www.ncbi.nlm.nih.gov/Omim/
Online *Mendelian Inheritance in Man*
Contain information about human genes and disease

http://www.nhgri.nih.gov/ELSI/ and http://www.ornl.gov/hgmis/elsi/elsi.html
NHGRI and DOE
Contains information, links and articles on a wide range of social, ethical and legal issues

---

from these sites the entire draft genome sequence together with the annotations in a computer-readable format. The sequences of the underlying sequenced clones are all available through the public sequence databases. URLs for these and other genome websites are listed in Box 2. A larger list of useful URLs can be found at www.nhgri.nih.gov/genome_hub. An introduction to using the draft genome sequence, as well as associated databases and analytical tools, is provided in an accompanying paper[111].

In addition, the human cytogenetic map has been integrated with the draft genome sequence as part of a related project. The BAC Resource Consortium[103] established dense connections between the maps using more than 7,500 sequenced large-insert clones that had been cytogenetically mapped by FISH; the average density of the map is 2.3 clones per Mb. Although the precision of the integration is limited by the resolution of FISH, the links provide a powerful tool for the analysis of cytogenetic aberrations in inherited diseases and cancer. These cytogenetic links can also be accessed through the Genome Browsers.

Long-range variation in GC content

The existence of GC-rich and GC-poor regions in the human genome was first revealed by experimental studies involving density gradient separation, which indicated substantial variation in average GC content among large fragments. Subsequent studies have indicated that these GC-rich and GC-poor regions may have different biological properties, such as gene density, composition of repeat sequences, correspondence with cytogenetic bands and recombination rate[112–117]. Many of these studies were indirect, owing to the lack of sufficient sequence data.

The draft genome sequence makes it possible to explore the variation in GC content in a direct and global manner. Visual inspection (Fig. 9) confirms that local GC content undergoes substantial long-range excursions from its genome-wide average of 41%. If the genome were drawn from a uniform distribution of GC content, the local GC content in a window of size n bp should be $41 \pm \sqrt{((41)(59)/n)}\%$. Fluctuations would be modest, with the standard deviation being halved as the window size is quadrupled — for example, 0.70%, 0.35%, 0.17% and 0.09% for windows of size 5, 20, 80 and 320 kb.

The draft genome sequence, however, contains many regions with much more extreme variation. There are huge regions (> 10 Mb) with GC content far from the average. For example, the most distal 48 Mb of chromosome 1p (from the telomere to about STS marker D1S3279) has an average GC content of 47.1%, and chromosome 13 has a 40-Mb region (roughly between STS marker A005X38 and

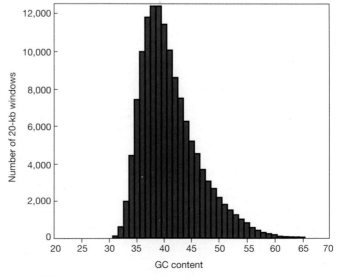

Figure 12 Histogram of GC content of 20-kb windows in the draft genome sequence.

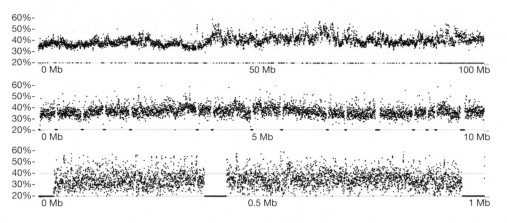

Figure 13 Variation in GC content at various scales. The GC content in subregions of a 100-Mb region of chromosome 1 is plotted, starting at about 83 Mb from the beginning of the draft genome sequence. This region is AT-rich overall. Top, the GC content of the entire 100-Mb region analysed in non-overlapping 20-kb windows. Middle, GC content of the first 10 Mb, analysed in 2-kb windows. Bottom, GC content of the first 1 Mb, analysed in 200-bp windows. At this scale, gaps in the sequence can be seen.

stsG30423) with only 36% GC content. There are also examples of large shifts in GC content between adjacent multimegabase regions. For example, the average GC content on chromosome 17q is 50% for the distal 10.3 Mb but drops to 38% for the adjacent 3.9 Mb. There are regions of less than 300 kb with even wider swings in GC content, for example, from 33.1% to 59.3%.

Long-range variation in GC content is evident not just from extreme outliers, but throughout the genome. The distribution of average GC content in 20-kb windows across the draft genome sequence is shown in Fig. 12. The spread is 15-fold larger than predicted by a uniform process. Moreover, the standard deviation barely decreases as window size increases by successive factors of four—5.9%, 5.2%, 4.9% and 4.6% for windows of size 5, 20, 80 and 320 kb. The distribution is also notably skewed, with 58% below the average and 42% above the average of 41%, with a long tail of GC-rich regions.

Bernardi and colleagues[118,119] proposed that the long-range variation in GC content may reflect that the genome is composed of a mosaic of compositionally homogeneous regions that they dubbed 'isochores'. They suggested that the skewed distribution is composed of five normal distributions, corresponding to five distinct types of isochore (L1, L2, H1, H2 and H3, with GC contents of < 38%, 38–42%, 42–47%, 47–52% and > 52%, respectively).

We studied the draft genome sequence to see whether strict isochores could be identified. For example, the sequence was divided into 300-kb windows, and each window was subdivided into 20-kb subwindows. We calculated the average GC content for each window and subwindow, and investigated how much of the variance in the GC content of subwindows across the genome can be statistically 'explained' by the average GC content in each window. About three-quarters of the genome-wide variance among 20-kb windows can be statistically explained by the average GC content of 300-kb windows that contain them, but the residual variance among subwindows (standard deviation, 2.4%) is still far too large to be consistent with a homogeneous distribution. In fact, the hypothesis of homogeneity could be rejected for each 300-kb window in the draft genome sequence.

Similar results were obtained with other window and subwindow sizes. Some of the local heterogeneity in GC content is attributable to transposable element insertions (see below). Such repeat elements typically have a higher GC content than the surrounding sequence, with the effect being strongest for the most recent insertions.

These results rule out a strict notion of isochores as compositionally homogeneous. Instead, there is substantial variation at many different scales, as illustrated in Fig. 13. Although isochores do not appear to merit the prefix 'iso', the genome clearly does contain large regions of distinctive GC content and it is likely to be

worth redefining the concept so that it becomes possible rigorously to partition the genome into regions. In the absence of a precise definition, we will loosely refer to such regions as 'GC content domains' in the context of the discussion below.

Fickett et al.[120] have explored a model in which the underlying preference for a particular GC content drifts continuously throughout the genome, an approach that bears further examination. Churchill[121] has proposed that the boundaries between GC content domains can in some cases be predicted by a hidden Markov model, with one state representing a GC-rich region and one representing an AT-rich region. We found that this approach tended to identify only very short domains of less than a kilobase (data not shown), but variants of this approach deserve further attention.

The correlation between GC content domains and various biological properties is of great interest, and this is likely to be the most fruitful route to understanding the basis of variation in GC content. As described below, we confirm the existence of strong correlations with both repeat content and gene density. Using the integration between the draft genome sequence and the cytogenetic map described above, it is possible to confirm a statistically significant correlation between GC content and Giemsa bands (G-bands). For example, 98% of large-insert clones mapping to the darkest G-bands are in 200-kb regions of low GC content (average 37%), whereas more than 80% of clones mapping to the lightest G-bands are in regions of high GC content (average 45%)[103]. Estimated band locations can be seen in Fig. 9 and viewed in the context of other genome annotation at http://genome.ucsc.edu/goldenPath/mapPlots/ and http://genome.ucsc.edu/goldenPath/hgTracks.html.

CpG islands

A related topic is the distribution of so-called CpG islands across the genome. The dinucleotide CpG is notable because it is greatly under-represented in human DNA, occurring at only about one-fifth of the roughly 4% frequency that would be expected by simply multiplying the typical fraction of Cs and Gs (0.21×0.21). The deficit occurs because most CpG dinucleotides are methylated on the cytosine base, and spontaneous deamination of methyl-C residues gives rise to T residues. (Spontaneous deamination of ordinary cytosine residues gives rise to uracil residues that are readily recognized and repaired by the cell.) As a result, methyl-CpG dinucleotides steadily mutate to TpG dinucleotides. However, the genome contains many 'CpG islands' in which CpG dinucleotides are not methylated and occur at a frequency closer to that predicted by the local GC content. CpG islands are of particular interest because many are associated with the 5′ ends of genes[122–127].

We searched the draft genome sequence for CpG islands. Ideally, they should be defined by directly testing for the absence of cytosine methylation, but that was not practical for this report. There are

Table 10 Number of CpG islands by GC content

GC content of island	Number of islands	Percentage of islands	Nucleotides in islands	Percentage of nucleotides in islands
Total	28,890	100	19,818,547	100
>80%	22	0.08	5,916	0.03
70–80%	5,884	20	3,111,965	16
60–70%	18,779	65	13,110,924	66
50–60%	4,205	15	3,589,742	18

Potential CpG islands were identified by searching the draft genome sequence one base at a time, scoring each dinucleotide (+17 for GC, –1 for others) and identifying maximally scoring segments. Each segment was then evaluated to determine GC content (≥50%), length (>200) and ratio of observed proportion of GC dinucleotides to the expected proportion on the basis of the GC content of the segment (>0.60), using a modification of a program developed by G. Micklem (personal communication).

various computer programs that attempt to identify CpG islands on the basis of primary sequence alone. These programs differ in some important respects (such as how aggressively they subdivide long CpG-containing regions), and the precise correspondence with experimentally undermethylated islands has not been validated. Nevertheless, there is a good correlation, and computational analysis thus provides a reasonable picture of the distribution of CpG islands in the genome.

To identify CpG islands, we used the definition proposed by Gardiner-Garden and Frommer[128] and embodied in a computer program. We searched the draft genome sequence for CpG islands, using both the full sequence and the sequence masked to eliminate repeat sequences. The number of regions satisfying the definition of a CpG island was 50,267 in the full sequence and 28,890 in the repeat-masked sequence. The difference reflects the fact that some repeat elements (notably Alu) are GC-rich. Although some of these repeat elements may function as control regions, it seems unlikely that most of the apparent CpG islands in repeat sequences are functional. Accordingly, we focused on those in the non-repeated sequence. The count of 28,890 CpG islands is reasonably close to the previous estimate of about 35,000 (ref. 129, as modified by ref. 130). Most of the islands are short, with 60–70% GC content (Table 10). More than 95% of the islands are less than 1,800 bp long, and more than 75% are less than 850 bp. The longest CpG island (on chromosome 10) is 36,619 bp long, and 322 are longer than 3,000 bp. Some of the larger islands contain ribosomal pseudogenes, although RNA genes and pseudogenes account for only a small proportion of all islands (< 0.5%). The smaller islands are consistent with their previously hypothesized function, but the role of these larger islands is uncertain.

The density of CpG islands varies substantially among some of the chromosomes. Most chromosomes have 5–15 islands per Mb, with a mean of 10.5 islands per Mb. However, chromosome Y has an

unusually low 2.9 islands per Mb, and chromosomes 16, 17 and 22 have 19–22 islands per Mb. The extreme outlier is chromosome 19, with 43 islands per Mb. Similar trends are seen when considering the percentage of bases contained in CpG islands. The relative density of CpG islands correlates reasonably well with estimates of relative gene density on these chromosomes, based both on previous mapping studies involving ESTs (Fig. 14) and on the distribution of gene predictions discussed below.

Comparison of genetic and physical distance

The draft genome sequence makes it possible to compare genetic and physical distances and thereby to explore variation in the rate of recombination across the human chromosomes. We focus here on large-scale variation. Finer variation is examined in an accompanying paper[131].

The genetic and physical maps are integrated by 5,282 polymorphic loci from the Marshfield genetic map[102], whose positions are known in terms of centimorgans (cM) and Mb along the chromosomes. Figure 15 shows the comparison of the draft genome sequence for chromosome 12 with the male, female and sex-averaged maps. One can calculate the approximate ratio of cM per Mb across a chromosome (reflected in the slopes in Fig. 15) and the average recombination rate for each chromosome arm.

Two striking features emerge from analysis of these data. First, the average recombination rate increases as the length of the chromosome arm decreases (Fig. 16). Long chromosome arms have an average recombination rate of about 1 cM per Mb, whereas the shortest arms are in the range of 2 cM per Mb. A similar trend has been seen in the yeast genome[132,133], despite the fact that the physical scale is nearly 200 times as small. Moreover, experimental studies have shown that lengthening or shortening yeast chromosomes results in a compensatory change in recombination rate[132].

The second observation is that the recombination rate tends to be suppressed near the centromeres and higher in the distal portions of most chromosomes, with the increase largely in the terminal

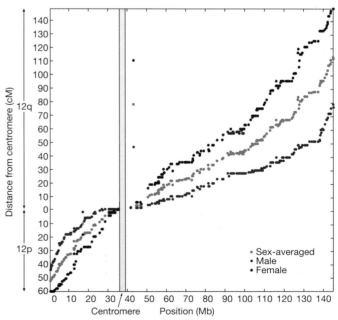

Figure 15 Distance in cM along the genetic map of chromosome 12 plotted against position in Mb in the draft genome sequence. Female, male and sex-averaged maps are shown. Female recombination rates are much higher than male recombination rates. The increased slopes at either end of the chromosome reflect the increased rates of recombination per Mb near the telomeres. Conversely, the flatter slope near the centromere shows decreased recombination there, especially in male meiosis. This is typical of the other chromosomes as well (see http://genome.ucsc.edu/goldenPath/mapPlots). Discordant markers may be map, marker placement or assembly errors.

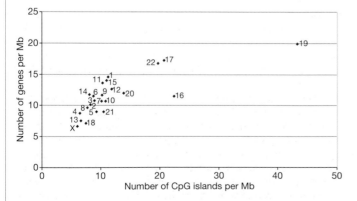

Figure 14 Number of CpG islands per Mb for each chromosome, plotted against the number of genes per Mb (the number of genes was taken from GeneMap98 (ref. 100)). Chromosomes 16, 17, 22 and particularly 19 are clear outliers, with a density of CpG islands that is even greater than would be expected from the high gene counts for these four chromosomes.

20–35 Mb. The increase is most pronounced in the male meiotic map. The effect can be seen, for example, from the higher slope at both ends of chromosome 12 (Fig. 15). Regional and sex-specific effects have been observed for chromosome 21 (refs 110, 134).

Why is recombination higher on smaller chromosome arms? A higher rate would increase the likelihood of at least one crossover during meiosis on each chromosome arm, as is generally observed in human chiasmata counts[135]. Crossovers are believed to be necessary for normal meiotic disjunction of homologous chromosome pairs in eukaryotes. An extreme example is the pseudoautosomal regions on chromosomes Xp and Yp, which pair during male meiosis; this physical region of only 2.6 Mb has a genetic length of 50 cM (corresponding to 20 cM per Mb), with the result that a crossover is virtually assured.

Mechanistically, the increased rate of recombination on shorter chromosome arms could be explained if, once an initial recombination event occurs, additional nearby events are blocked by positive crossover interference on each arm. Evidence from yeast mutants in which interference is abolished shows that interference plays a key role in distributing a limited number of crossovers among the various chromosome arms in yeast[136]. An alternative possibility is that a checkpoint mechanism scans for and enforces the presence of at least one crossover on each chromosome arm.

Variation in recombination rates along chromosomes and between the sexes is likely to reflect variation in the initiation of meiosis-induced double-strand breaks (DSBs) that initiate recombination. DSBs in yeast have been associated with open chromatin[137,138], rather than with specific DNA sequence motifs. With the availability of the draft genome sequence, it should be possible to explore in an analogous manner whether variation in human recombination rates reflects systematic differences in chromosome accessibility during meiosis.

Repeat content of the human genome

A puzzling observation in the early days of molecular biology was that genome size does not correlate well with organismal complexity. For example, *Homo sapiens* has a genome that is 200 times as large as that of the yeast *S. cerevisiae*, but 200 times as small as that of *Amoeba dubia*[139,140]. This mystery (the C-value paradox) was largely resolved with the recognition that genomes can contain a large quantity of repetitive sequence, far in excess of that devoted to protein-coding genes (reviewed in refs 140, 141).

In the human, coding sequences comprise less than 5% of the genome (see below), whereas repeat sequences account for at least 50% and probably much more. Broadly, the repeats fall into five classes: (1) transposon-derived repeats, often referred to as interspersed repeats; (2) inactive (partially) retroposed copies of cellular genes (including protein-coding genes and small structural RNAs), usually referred to as processed pseudogenes; (3) simple sequence repeats, consisting of direct repetitions of relatively short *k*-mers such as $(A)_n$, $(CA)_n$ or $(CGG)_n$; (4) segmental duplications, consisting of blocks of around 10–300 kb that have been copied from one region of the genome into another region; and (5) blocks of tandemly repeated sequences, such as at centromeres, telomeres, the short arms of acrocentric chromosomes and ribosomal gene clusters. (These regions are intentionally under-represented in the draft genome sequence and are not discussed here.)

Repeats are often described as 'junk' and dismissed as uninteresting. However, they actually represent an extraordinary trove of information about biological processes. The repeats constitute a rich palaeontological record, holding crucial clues about evolutionary events and forces. As passive markers, they provide assays for studying processes of mutation and selection. It is possible to recognize cohorts of repeats 'born' at the same time and to follow their fates in different regions of the genome or in different species. As active agents, repeats have reshaped the genome by causing ectopic rearrangements, creating entirely new genes, modifying and reshuffling existing genes, and modulating overall GC content. They also shed light on chromosome structure and dynamics, and provide tools for medical genetic and population genetic studies.

The human is the first repeat-rich genome to be sequenced, and so we investigated what information could be gleaned from this majority component of the human genome. Although some of the general observations about repeats were suggested by previous studies, the draft genome sequence provides the first comprehensive view, allowing some questions to be resolved and new mysteries to emerge.

Transposon-derived repeats

Most human repeat sequence is derived from transposable elements[142,143]. We can currently recognize about 45% of the genome as belonging to this class. Much of the remaining 'unique' DNA must also be derived from ancient transposable element copies that have diverged too far to be recognized as such. To describe our analyses of interspersed repeats, it is necessary briefly to review the relevant features of human transposable elements.

Classes of transposable elements. In mammals, almost all transposable elements fall into one of four types (Fig. 17), of which three transpose through RNA intermediates and one transposes directly as DNA. These are long interspersed elements (LINEs), short interspersed elements (SINEs), LTR retrotransposons and DNA transposons.

LINEs are one of the most ancient and successful inventions in eukaryotic genomes. In humans, these transposons are about 6 kb long, harbour an internal polymerase II promoter and encode two open reading frames (ORFs). Upon translation, a LINE RNA assembles with its own encoded proteins and moves to the nucleus, where an endonuclease activity makes a single-stranded nick and the reverse transcriptase uses the nicked DNA to prime reverse transcription from the 3′ end of the LINE RNA. Reverse transcription frequently fails to proceed to the 5′ end, resulting in many truncated, nonfunctional insertions. Indeed, most LINE-derived repeats are short, with an average size of 900 bp for all LINE1 copies, and a median size of 1,070 bp for copies of the currently active LINE1 element (L1Hs). New insertion sites are flanked by a small

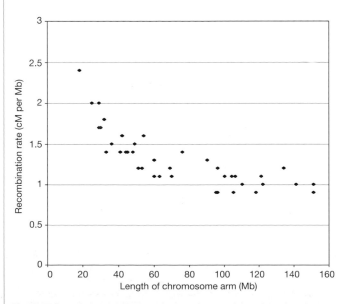

Figure 16 Rate of recombination averaged across the euchromatic portion of each chromosome arm plotted against the length of the chromosome arm in Mb. For large chromosomes, the average recombination rates are very similar, but as chromosome arm length decreases, average recombination rates rise markedly.

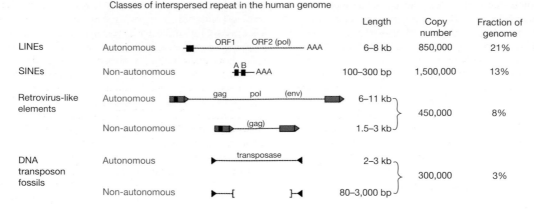

Figure 17 Almost all transposable elements in mammals fall into one of four classes. See text for details.

target site duplication of 7–20 bp. The LINE machinery is believed to be responsible for most reverse transcription in the genome, including the retrotransposition of the non-autonomous SINEs[144] and the creation of processed pseudogenes[145,146]. Three distantly related LINE families are found in the human genome: LINE1, LINE2 and LINE3. Only LINE1 is still active.

SINEs are wildly successful freeloaders on the backs of LINE elements. They are short (about 100–400 bp), harbour an internal polymerase III promoter and encode no proteins. These non-autonomous transposons are thought to use the LINE machinery for transposition. Indeed, most SINEs 'live' by sharing the 3' end with a resident LINE element[144]. The promoter regions of all known SINEs are derived from tRNA sequences, with the exception of a single monophyletic family of SINEs derived from the signal recognition particle component 7SL. This family, which also does not share its 3' end with a LINE, includes the only active SINE in the human genome: the Alu element. By contrast, the mouse has both tRNA-derived and 7SL-derived SINEs. The human genome contains three distinct monophyletic families of SINEs: the active Alu, and the inactive MIR and Ther2/MIR3.

LTR retroposons are flanked by long terminal direct repeats that contain all of the necessary transcriptional regulatory elements. The autonomous elements (retrotransposons) contain *gag* and *pol* genes, which encode a protease, reverse transcriptase, RNAse H and integrase. Exogenous retroviruses seem to have arisen from endogenous retrotransposons by acquisition of a cellular *envelope* gene (*env*)[147]. Transposition occurs through the retroviral mechanism with reverse transcription occurring in a cytoplasmic virus-like particle, primed by a tRNA (in contrast to the nuclear location and chromosomal priming of LINEs). Although a variety of LTR retrotransposons exist, only the vertebrate-specific endogenous retroviruses (ERVs) appear to have been active in the mammalian genome. Mammalian retroviruses fall into three classes (I–III), each comprising many families with independent origins. Most (85%) of the LTR retroposon-derived 'fossils' consist only of an isolated LTR, with the internal sequence having been lost by homologous recombination between the flanking LTRs.

DNA transposons resemble bacterial transposons, having terminal inverted repeats and encoding a transposase that binds near the inverted repeats and mediates mobility through a 'cut-and-paste' mechanism. The human genome contains at least seven major classes of DNA transposon, which can be subdivided into many families with independent origins[148] (see RepBase, http://www.girinst.org/~server/repbase.html). DNA transposons tend to have short life spans within a species. This can be explained by contrasting the modes of transposition of DNA transposons and LINE elements. LINE transposition tends to involve only functional elements, owing to the *cis*-preference by which LINE proteins assemble with the RNA from which they were translated. By contrast, DNA transposons cannot exercise a *cis*-preference: the encoded transposase is produced in the cytoplasm and, when it returns to the nucleus, it cannot distinguish active from inactive elements. As inactive copies accumulate in the genome, transposition becomes less efficient. This checks the expansion of any DNA transposon family and in due course causes it to die out. To survive, DNA transposons must eventually move by horizontal transfer to virgin genomes, and there is considerable evidence for such transfer[149–153].

Transposable elements employ different strategies to ensure their evolutionary survival. LINEs and SINEs rely almost exclusively on vertical transmission within the host genome[154] (but see refs 148, 155). DNA transposons are more promiscuous, requiring relatively frequent horizontal transfer. LTR retroposons use both strategies, with some being long-term active residents of the human genome (such as members of the ERVL family) and others having only short residence times.

Table 11 Number of copies and fraction of genome for classes of interspersed repeat

	Number of copies (× 1,000)	Total number of bases in the draft genome sequence (Mb)	Fraction of the draft genome sequence (%)	Number of families (subfamilies)
SINEs	1,558	359.6	13.14	
Alu	1,090	290.1	10.60	1 (~20)
MIR	393	60.1	2.20	1 (1)
MIR3	75	9.3	0.34	1 (1)
LINEs	868	558.8	20.42	
LINE1	516	462.1	16.89	1 (~55)
LINE2	315	88.2	3.22	1 (2)
LINE3	37	8.4	0.31	1 (2)
LTR elements	443	227.0	8.29	
ERV-class I	112	79.2	2.89	72 (132)
ERV(K)-class II	8	8.5	0.31	10 (20)
ERV (L)-class III	83	39.5	1.44	21 (42)
MaLR	240	99.8	3.65	1 (31)
DNA elements	294	77.6	2.84	
hAT group				
MER1-Charlie	182	38.1	1.39	25 (50)
Zaphod	13	4.3	0.16	4 (10)
Tc-1 group				
MER2-Tigger	57	28.0	1.02	12 (28)
Tc2	4	0.9	0.03	1 (5)
Mariner	14	2.6	0.10	4 (5)
PiggyBac-like	2	0.5	0.02	10 (20)
Unclassified	22	3.2	0.12	7 (7)
Unclassified	3	3.8	0.14	3 (4)
Total interspersed repeats		1,226.8	44.83	

The number of copies and base pair contributions of the major classes and subclasses of transposable elements in the human genome. Data extracted from a RepeatMasker analysis of the draft genome sequence (RepeatMasker version 09092000, sensitive settings, using RepBase Update 5.08). In calculating percentages, RepeatMasker excluded the runs of Ns linking the contigs in the draft genome sequence. In the last column, separate consensus sequences in the repeat databases are considered subfamilies, rather than families, when the sequences are closely related or related through intermediate subfamilies.

Census of human repeats. We began by taking a census of the transposable elements in the draft genome sequence, using a recently updated version of the RepeatMasker program (version 09092000) run under sensitive settings (see http://repeatmasker. genome.washington.edu). This program scans sequences to identify full-length and partial members of all known repeat families represented in RepBase Update (version 5.08; see http://www. girinst.org/~server/repbase.html and ref. 156). Table 11 shows the number of copies and fraction of the draft genome sequence occupied by each of the four major classes and the main subclasses.

The precise count of repeats is obviously underestimated because the genome sequence is not finished, but their density and other properties can be stated with reasonable confidence. Currently recognized SINEs, LINEs, LTR retroposons and DNA transposon copies comprise 13%, 20%, 8% and 3% of the sequence, respectively. We expect these densities to grow as more repeat families are recognized, among which will be lower copy number LTR elements and DNA transposons, and possibly high copy number ancient (highly diverged) repeats.

Age distribution. The age distribution of the repeats in the human genome provides a rich 'fossil record' stretching over several hundred million years. The ancestry and approximate age of each fossil can be inferred by exploiting the fact that each copy is derived from, and therefore initially carried the sequence of, a then-active transposon and, being generally under no functional constraint, has accumulated mutations randomly and independently of other copies. We can infer the sequence of the ancestral active elements by clustering the modern derivatives into phylogenetic trees and building a consensus based on the multiple sequence alignment of a cluster of copies. Using available consensus sequences for known repeat subfamilies, we calculated the per cent divergence from the inferred ancestral active transposon for each of three million interspersed repeats in the draft genome sequence.

The percentage of sequence divergence can be converted into an approximate age in millions of years (Myr) on the basis of evolutionary information. Care is required in calibrating the clock, because the rate of sequence divergence may not be constant over time or between lineages[139]. The relative-rate test[157] can be used to calculate the sequence divergence that accumulated in a lineage after a given timepoint, on the basis of comparison with a sibling species that diverged at that time and an outgroup species. For example, the substitution rate over roughly the last 25 Myr in the human lineage can be calculated by using old world monkeys (which diverged about 25 Myr ago) as a sibling species and new world monkeys as an outgroup. We have used currently available calibrations for the human lineage, but the issue should be revisited as sequence information becomes available from different mammals.

Figure 18a shows the representation of various classes of trans-

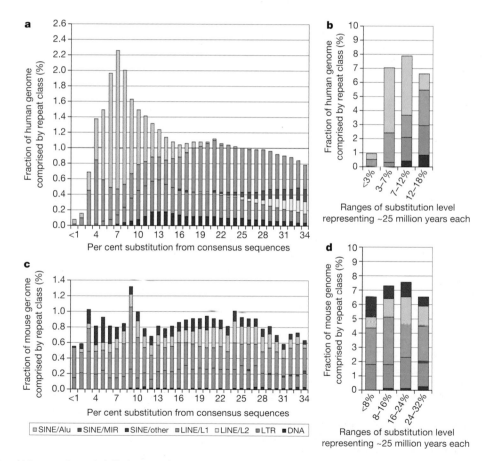

Figure 18 Age distribution of interspersed repeats in the human and mouse genomes. Bases covered by interspersed repeats were sorted by their divergence from their consensus sequence (which approximates the repeat's original sequence at the time of insertion). The average number of substitutions per 100 bp (substitution level, K) was calculated from the mismatch level p assuming equal frequency of all substitutions (the one-parameter Jukes–Cantor model, $K = -3/4\ln(1 - 4/3p)$). This model tends to underestimate higher substitution levels. CpG dinucleotides in the consensus were excluded from the substitution level calculations because the C→T transition rate in CpG pairs is about tenfold higher than other transitions and causes distortions in comparing transposable elements with high and low CpG content. **a**, The distribution, for the human genome, in bins corresponding to 1% increments in substitution levels. **b**, The data grouped into bins representing roughly equal time periods of 25 Myr. **c,d**, Equivalent data for available mouse genomic sequence. There is a different correspondence between substitution levels and time periods owing to different rates of nucleotide substitution in the two species. The correspondence between substitution levels and time periods was largely derived from three-way species comparisons (relative rate test[139,157]) with the age estimates based on fossil data. Human divergence from gibbon 20–30 Myr; old world monkey 25–35 Myr; prosimians 55–80 Myr; eutherian mammalian radiation ~100 Myr.

posable elements in categories reflecting equal amounts of sequence divergence. In Fig. 18b the data are grouped into four bins corresponding to successive 25-Myr periods, on the basis of an approximate clock. Figure 19 shows the mean ages of various subfamilies of DNA transposons. Several facts are apparent from these graphs. First, most interspersed repeats in the human genome predate the eutherian radiation. This is a testament to the extremely slow rate with which nonfunctional sequences are cleared from vertebrate genomes (see below concerning comparison with the fly).

Second, LINE and SINE elements have extremely long lives. The monophyletic LINE1 and Alu lineages are at least 150 and 80 Myr old, respectively. In earlier times, the reigning transposons were LINE2 and MIR[148,158]. The SINE MIR was perfectly adapted for reverse transcription by LINE2, as it carried the same 50-base sequence at its 3′ end. When LINE2 became extinct 80–100 Myr ago, it spelled the doom of MIR.

Third, there were two major peaks of DNA transposon activity (Fig. 19). The first involved Charlie elements and occurred long before the eutherian radiation; the second involved Tigger elements and occurred after this radiation. Because DNA transposons can produce large-scale chromosome rearrangements[159-162], it is possible that widespread activity could be involved in speciation events.

Fourth, there is no evidence for DNA transposon activity in the past 50 Myr in the human genome. The youngest two DNA transposon families that we can identify in the draft genome sequence (MER75 and MER85) show 6–7% divergence from their respective consensus sequences representing the ancestral element (Fig. 19), indicating that they were active before the divergence of humans and new world monkeys. Moreover, these elements were relatively unsuccessful, together contributing just 125 kb to the draft genome sequence.

Finally, LTR retroposons appear to be teetering on the brink of extinction, if they have not already succumbed. For example, the most prolific elements (ERVL and MaLRs) flourished for more than 100 Myr but appear to have died out about 40 Myr ago[163,164]. Only a single LTR retroposon family (HERVK10) is known to have transposed since our divergence from the chimpanzee 7 Myr ago, with only one known copy (in the HLA region) that is not shared between all humans[165]. In the draft genome sequence, we can identify only three full-length copies with all ORFs intact (the final total may be slightly higher owing to the imperfect state of the draft genome sequence).

More generally, the overall activity of all transposons has declined markedly over the past 35–50 Myr, with the possible exception of LINE1 (Fig. 18). Indeed, apart from an exceptional burst of activity of Alus peaking around 40 Myr ago, there would appear to have been a fairly steady decline in activity in the hominid lineage since the mammalian radiation. The extent of the decline must be even greater than it appears because old repeats are gradually removed by random deletion and because old repeat families are harder to recognize and likely to be under-represented in the repeat databases. (We confirmed that the decline in transposition is not an artefact arising from errors in the draft genome sequence, which, in principle, could increase the divergence level in recent elements. First, the sequence error rate (Table 9) is far too low to have a significant effect on the apparent age of recent transposons; and second, the same result is seen if one considers only finished sequence.)

What explains the decline in transposon activity in the lineage leading to humans? We return to this question below, in the context of the observation that there is no similar decline in the mouse genome.

Comparison with other organisms. We compared the complement of transposable elements in the human genome with those of the other sequenced eukaryotic genomes. We analysed the fly, worm and mustard weed genomes for the number and nature of repeats (Table 12) and the age distribution (Fig. 20). (For the fly, we analysed the 114 Mb of unfinished 'large' contigs produced by the whole-genome shotgun assembly[166], which are reported to represent euchromatic sequence. Similar results were obtained by analysing 30 Mb of finished euchromatic sequence.) The human genome stands in stark contrast to the genomes of the other organisms.
(1) The euchromatic portion of the human genome has a much higher density of transposable element copies than the euchromatic DNA of the other three organisms. The repeats in the other organisms may have been slightly underestimated because the repeat databases for the other organisms are less complete than for the human, especially with regard to older elements; on the other hand, recent additions to these databases appear to increase the repeat content only marginally.
(2) The human genome is filled with copies of ancient transposons, whereas the transposons in the other genomes tend to be of more recent origin. The difference is most marked with the fly, but is clear for the other genomes as well. The accumulation of old repeats is likely to be determined by the rate at which organisms engage in 'housecleaning' through genomic deletion. Studies of pseudogenes

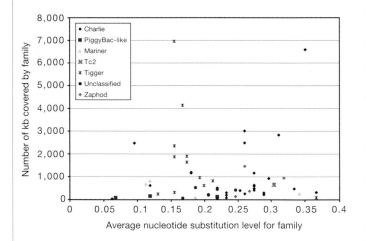

Figure 19 Median ages and per cent of the genome covered by subfamilies of DNA transposons. The Charlie and Zaphod elements were hobo-Activator-Tam3 (hAT) DNA transposons; Mariner, Tc2 and Tigger were Tc1-like elements. Unlike retroposons, DNA transposons are thought to have a short life span in a genome. Thus, the average or median divergence of copies from the consensus is a particularly accurate measure of the age of the DNA transposon copies.

Table 12 Number and nature of interspersed repeats in eukaryotic genomes

	Human		Fly		Worm		Mustard weed	
	Percentage of bases	Approximate number of families	Percentage of bases	Approximate number of families	Percentage of bases	Approximate number of families	Percentage of bases	Approximate number of families
LINE/SINE	33.40%	6	0.70%	20	0.40%	10	0.50%	10
LTR	8.10%	100	1.50%	50	0.00%	4	4.80%	70
DNA	2.80%	60	0.70%	20	5.30%	80	5.10%	80
Total	44.40%	170	3.10%	90	6.50%	90	10.50%	160

The complete genomes of fly, worm, and chromosomes 2 and 4 of mustard weed (as deposited at ncbi.nlm.nih.gov/genbank/genomes) were screened against the repeats in RepBase Update 5.02 (September 2000) with RepeatMasker at sensitive settings.

have suggested that small deletions occur at a rate that is 75-fold higher in flies than in mammals; the half-life of such nonfunctional DNA is estimated at 12 Myr for flies and 800 Myr for mammals[167]. The rate of large deletions has not been systematically compared, but seems likely also to differ markedly.

(3) Whereas in the human two repeat families (LINE1 and Alu) account for 60% of all interspersed repeat sequence, the other organisms have no dominant families. Instead, the worm, fly and mustard weed genomes all contain many transposon families, each consisting of typically hundreds to thousands of elements. This difference may be explained by the observation that the vertically transmitted, long-term residential LINE and SINE elements represent 75% of interspersed repeats in the human genome, but only 5–25% in the other genomes. In contrast, the horizontally transmitted and shorter-lived DNA transposons represent only a small portion of all interspersed repeats in humans (6%) but a much larger fraction in fly, mustard weed and worm (25%, 49% and 87%, respectively). These features of the human genome are probably general to all mammals. The relative lack of horizontally transmitted elements may have its origin in the well developed immune system of mammals, as horizontal transfer requires infectious vectors, such as viruses, against which the immune system guards.

We also looked for differences among mammals, by comparing the transposons in the human and mouse genomes. As with the human genome, care is required in calibrating the substitution clock for the mouse genome. There is considerable evidence that the rate of substitution per Myr is higher in rodent lineages than in the hominid lineages[139,168,169]. In fact, we found clear evidence for different rates of substitution by examining families of transposable elements whose insertions predate the divergence of the human and mouse lineages. In an analysis of 22 such families, we found that the substitution level was an average of 1.7-fold higher in mouse than human (not shown). (This is likely to be an underestimate because of an ascertainment bias against the most diverged copies.) The faster clock in mouse is also evident from the fact that the ancient LINE2 and MIR elements, which transposed before the mammalian radiation and are readily detectable in the human genome, cannot be readily identified in available mouse genomic sequence (Fig. 18).

We used the best available estimates to calibrate substitution levels and time[169]. The ratio of substitution rates varied from about 1.7-fold higher over the past 100 Myr to about 2.6-fold higher over the past 25 Myr.

The analysis shows that, although the overall density of the four transposon types in human and mouse is similar, the age distribution is strikingly different (Fig. 18). Transposon activity in the mouse genome has not undergone the decline seen in humans and proceeds at a much higher rate. In contrast to their possible extinction in humans, LTR retroposons are alive and well in the

mouse with such representatives as the active IAP family and putatively active members of the long-lived ERVL and MaLR families. LINE1 and a variety of SINEs are quite active. These evolutionary findings are consistent with the empirical observations that new spontaneous mutations are 30 times more likely to be caused by LINE insertions in mouse than in human (~3% versus 0.1%)[170] and 60 times more likely to be caused by transposable elements in general. It is estimated that around 1 in 600 mutations in human are due to transpositions, whereas 10% of mutations in mouse are due to transpositions (mostly IAP insertions).

The contrast between human and mouse suggests that the explanation for the decline of transposon activity in humans may lie in some fundamental difference between hominids and rodents. Population structure and dynamics would seem to be likely suspects. Rodents tend to have large populations, whereas hominid populations tend to be small and may undergo frequent bottlenecks. Evolutionary forces affected by such factors include inbreeding and genetic drift, which might affect the persistence of active transposable elements[171]. Studies in additional mammalian lineages may shed light on the forces responsible for the differences in the activity of transposable elements[172].

Variation in the distribution of repeats. We next explored variation in the distribution of repeats across the draft genome sequence, by calculating the repeat density in windows of various sizes across the genome. There is striking variation at smaller scales.

Some regions of the genome are extraordinarily dense in repeats. The prizewinner appears to be a 525-kb region on chromosome Xp11, with an overall transposable element density of 89%. This region contains a 200-kb segment with 98% density, as well as a segment of 100 kb in which LINE1 sequences alone comprise 89% of the sequence. In addition, there are regions of more than 100 kb with extremely high densities of Alu (> 56% at three loci, including one on 7q11 with a 50-kb stretch of > 61% Alu) and the ancient transposons MIR (> 15% on chromosome 1p36) and LINE2 (> 18% on chromosome 22q12).

In contrast, some genomic regions are nearly devoid of repeats. The absence of repeats may be a sign of large-scale *cis*-regulatory elements that cannot tolerate being interrupted by insertions. The four regions with the lowest density of interspersed repeats in the human genome are the four homeobox gene clusters, HOXA, HOXB, HOXC and HOXD (Fig. 21). Each locus contains regions of around 100 kb containing less than 2% interspersed repeats. Ongoing sequence analysis of the four HOX clusters in mouse, rat and baboon shows a similar absence of transposable elements, and reveals a high density of conserved noncoding elements (K. Dewar and B. Birren, manuscript in preparation). The presence of a complex collection of regulatory regions may explain why individual HOX genes carried in transgenic mice fail to show proper regulation.

It may be worth investigating other repeat-poor regions, such as a region on chromosome 8q21 (1.5% repeat over 63 kb) containing a gene encoding a homeodomain zinc-finger protein (homologous to mouse pID 9663936), a region on chromosome 1p36 (5% repeat over 100 kb) with no obvious genes and a region on chromosome 18q22 (4% over 100 kb) containing three genes of unknown function (among which is KIAA0450). It will be interesting to see whether the homologous regions in the mouse genome have

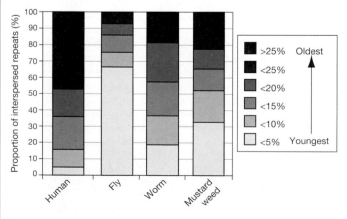

Figure 20 Comparison of the age of interspersed repeats in eukaryotic genomes. The copies of repeats were pooled by their nucleotide substitution level from the consensus.

Figure 21 Two regions of about 1 Mb on chromosomes 2 and 22. Red bars, interspersed repeats; blue bars, exons of known genes. Note the deficit of repeats in the HoxD cluster, which contains a collection of genes with complex, interrelated regulation.

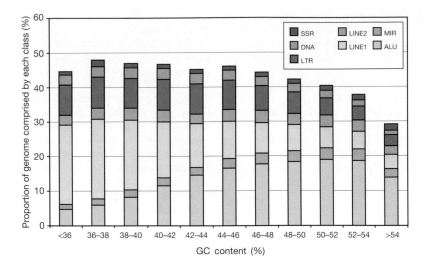

Figure 22 Density of the major repeat classes as a function of local GC content, in windows of 50 kb.

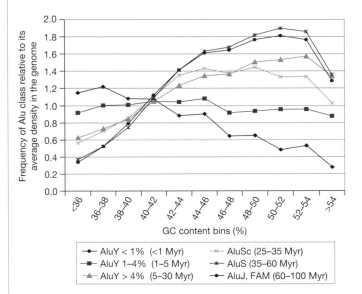

Figure 23 Alu elements target AT-rich DNA, but accumulate in GC-rich DNA. This graph shows the relative distribution of various Alu cohorts as a function of local GC content. The divergence levels (including CpG sites) and ages of the cohorts are shown in the key.

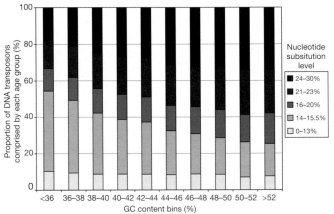

Figure 24 DNA transposon copies in AT-rich DNA tend to be younger than those in more GC-rich DNA. DNA transposon families were grouped into five age categories by their median substitution level (see Fig. 19). The proportion attributed to each age class is shown as a function of GC content. Similar patterns are seen for LINE1 and LTR elements.

similarly resisted the insertion of transposable elements during rodent evolution.

Distribution by GC content. We next focused on the correlation between the nature of the transposons in a region and its GC content. We calculated the density of each repeat type as a function of the GC content in 50-kb windows (Fig. 22). As has been reported[142,173–176], LINE sequences occur at much higher density in AT-rich regions (roughly fourfold enriched), whereas SINEs (MIR, Alu) show the opposite trend (for Alu, up to fivefold lower in AT-rich DNA). LTR retroposons and DNA transposons show a more uniform distribution, dipping only in the most GC-rich regions.

The preference of LINEs for AT-rich DNA seems like a reasonable way for a genomic parasite to accommodate its host, by targeting gene-poor AT-rich DNA and thereby imposing a lower mutational burden. Mechanistically, selective targeting is nicely explained by the fact that the preferred cleavage site of the LINE endonuclease is TTTT/A (where the slash indicates the point of cleavage), which is used to prime reverse transcription from the poly(A) tail of LINE RNA[177].

The contrary behaviour of SINEs, however, is baffling. How do

SINEs accumulate in GC-rich DNA, particularly if they depend on the LINE transposition machinery[178]? Notably, the same pattern is seen for the Alu-like B1 and the tRNA-derived SINEs in mouse and for MIR in human[142]. One possibility is that SINEs somehow target GC-rich DNA for insertion. The alternative is that SINEs initially insert with the same proclivity for AT-rich DNA as LINEs, but that the distribution is subsequently reshaped by evolutionary forces[142,179].

We used the draft genome sequence to investigate this mystery by comparing the proclivities of young, adolescent, middle-aged and old Alus (Fig. 23). Strikingly, recent Alus show a preference for AT-rich DNA resembling that of LINEs, whereas progressively older Alus show a progressively stronger bias towards GC-rich DNA. These results indicate that the GC bias must result from strong pressure: Fig. 23 shows that a 13-fold enrichment of Alus in GC-rich DNA has occurred within the last 30 Myr, and possibly more recently.

These results raise a new mystery. What is the force that produces the great and rapid enrichment of Alus in GC-rich DNA? One explanation may be that deletions are more readily tolerated in gene-poor AT-rich regions than in gene-rich GC-rich regions, resulting in older elements being enriched in GC-rich regions. Such an enrichment is seen for transposable elements such as

DNA transposons (Fig. 24). However, this effect seems too slow and too small to account for the observed remodelling of the Alu distribution. This can be seen by performing a similar analysis for LINE elements (Fig. 25). There is no significant change in the LINE distribution over the past 100 Myr, in contrast to the rapid change seen for Alu. There is an eventual shift after more than 100 Myr, although its magnitude is still smaller than seen for Alus.

These observations indicate that there may be some force acting particularly on Alus. This could be a higher rate of random loss of Alus in AT-rich DNA, negative selection against Alus in AT-rich DNA or positive selection in favour of Alus in GC-rich DNA. The first two possibilities seem unlikely because AT-rich DNA is

gene-poor and tolerates the accumulation of other transposable elements. The third seems more feasible, in that it involves selecting in favour of the minority of Alus in GC-rich regions rather than against the majority that lie in AT-rich regions. But positive selection for Alus in GC-rich regions would imply that they benefit the organism.

Schmid[180] has proposed such a function for SINEs. This hypothesis is based on the observation that in many species SINEs are transcribed under conditions of stress, and the resulting RNAs specifically bind a particular protein kinase (PKR) and block its ability to inhibit protein translation[181–183]. SINE RNAs would thus promote protein translation under stress. SINE RNA may be well suited to such a role in regulating protein translation, because it can be quickly transcribed in large quantities from thousands of elements and it can function without protein translation. Under this theory, there could be positive selection for SINEs in readily transcribed open chromatin such as is found near genes. This could explain the retention of Alus in gene-rich GC-rich regions. It is also consistent with the observation that SINE density in AT-rich DNA is higher near genes[142].

Further insight about Alus comes from the relationship between Alu density and GC content on individual chromosomes (Fig. 26). There are two outliers. Chromosome 19 is even richer in Alus than predicted by its (high) GC content; the chromosome comprises 2% of the genome, but contains 5% of Alus. On the other hand, chromosome Y shows the lowest density of Alus relative to its GC content, being higher than average for GC content less than 40% and lower than average for GC content over 40%. Even in AT-rich DNA, Alus are under-represented on chromosome Y compared with other young interspersed repeats (see below). These phenomena may be related to an unusually high gene density on chromosome 19 and an unusually low density of somatically active genes on chromosome Y (both relative to GC content). This would be consistent with the idea that Alu correlates not with GC content but with actively transcribed genes.

Our results may support the controversial idea that SINEs actually carn their keep in the genome. Clearly, much additional work will be needed to prove or disprove the hypothesis that SINEs are genomic symbionts.

Biases in human mutation. Indirect studies have suggested that nucleotide substitution is not uniform across mammalian

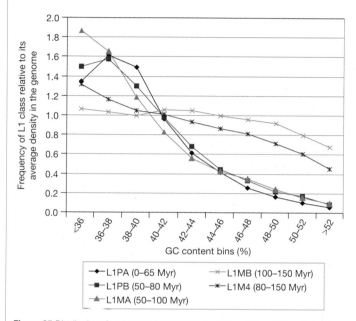

Figure 25 Distribution of various LINE cohorts as a function of local GC content. The divergence levels and ages of the cohorts are shown in the key. (The divergence levels were measured for the 3′ UTR of the LINE1 element only, which is best characterized evolutionarily. This region contains almost no CpG sites, and thus 1% divergence level corresponds to a much longer time than for CpG-rich Alu copies).

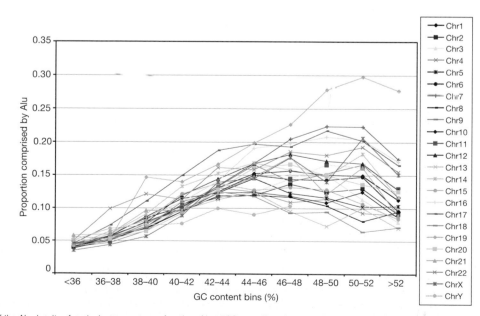

Figure 26 Comparison of the Alu density of each chromosome as a function of local GC content. At higher GC levels, the Alu density varies widely between chromosomes, with chromosome 19 being a particular outlier. In contrast, the LINE1 density pattern is quite uniform for most chromosomes, with the exception of a 1.5 to 2-fold over-representation in AT-rich regions of the X and Y chromosomes (not shown).

genomes[184–187]. By studying sets of repeat elements belonging to a common cohort, one can directly measure nucleotide substitution rates in different regions of the genome. We find strong evidence that the pattern of neutral substitution differs as a function of local GC content (Fig. 27). Because the results are observed in repetitive elements throughout the genome, the variation in the pattern of nucleotide substitution seems likely to be due to differences in the underlying mutational process rather than to selection.

The effect can be seen most clearly by focusing on the substitution process $\gamma \leftrightarrow \alpha$, where γ denotes GC or CG base pairs and α denotes AT or TA base pairs. If K is the equilibrium constant in the direction of α base pairs (defined by the ratio of the forward and reverse rates), then the equilibrium GC content should be $1/(1 + K)$. Two observations emerge.

First, there is a regional bias in substitution patterns. The equilibrium constant varies as a function of local GC content: γ base pairs are more likely to mutate towards α base pairs in AT-rich regions than in GC-rich regions. For the analysis in Fig. 27, the equilibrium constant K is 2.5, 1.9 and 1.2 when the draft genome sequence is partitioned into three bins with average GC content of 37, 43 and 50%, respectively. This bias could be due to a reported tendency for GC-rich regions to replicate earlier in the cell cycle than AT-rich regions and for guanine pools, which are limiting for

DNA replication, to become depleted late in the cell cycle, thereby resulting in a small but significant shift in substitution towards α base pairs[186,188]. Another theory proposes that many substitutions are due to differences in DNA repair mechanisms, possibly related to transcriptional activity and thereby to gene density and GC content[185,189,190].

There is also an absolute bias in substitution patterns resulting in directional pressure towards lower GC content throughout the human genome. The genome is not at equilibrium with respect to the pattern of nucleotide substitution: the expected equilibrium GC content corresponding to the values of K above is 29, 35 and 44% for regions with average GC contents of 37, 43 and 50%, respectively. Recent observations on SNPs[190] confirm that the mutation pattern in GC-rich DNA is biased towards α base pairs; it should be possible to perform similar analyses throughout the genome with the availability of 1.4 million SNPs[97,191]. On the basis solely of nucleotide substitution patterns, the GC content would be expected to be about 7% lower throughout the genome.

What accounts for the higher GC content? One possible explanation is that in GC-rich regions, a considerable fraction of the nucleotides is likely to be under functional constraint owing to the high gene density. Selection on coding regions and regulatory CpG islands may maintain the higher-than-predicted GC content. Another is that throughout the rest of the genome, a constant influx of transposable elements tends to increase GC content (Fig. 28). Young repeat elements clearly have a higher GC content than their surrounding regions, except in extremely GC-rich regions. Moreover, repeat elements clearly shift with age towards a lower GC content, closer to that of the neighbourhood in which they reside. Much of the 'non-repeat' DNA in AT-rich regions probably consists of ancient repeats that are not detectable by current methods and that have had more time to approach the local equilibrium value.

The repeats can also be used to study how the mutation process is affected by the immediately adjacent nucleotide. Such 'context effects' will be discussed elsewhere (A. Kas and A. F. A. Smit, unpublished results).

Fast living on chromosome Y. The pattern of interspersed repeats can be used to shed light on the unusual evolutionary history of chromosome Y. Our analysis shows that the genetic material on

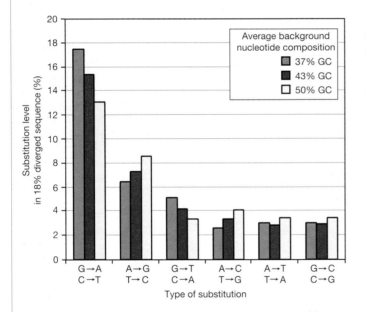

Figure 27 Substitution patterns in interspersed repeats differ as a function of GC content. We collected all copies of five DNA transposons (Tigger1, Tigger2, Charlie3, MER1 and HSMAR2), chosen for their high copy number and well defined consensus sequences. DNA transposons are optimal for the study of neutral substitutions: they do not segregate into subfamilies with diagnostic differences, presumably because they are short-lived and new active families do not evolve in a genome (see text). Duplicates and close paralogues resulting from duplication after transposition were eliminated. The copies were grouped on the basis of GC content of the flanking 1,000 bp on both sides and aligned to the consensus sequence (representing the state of the copy at integration). Recursive efforts using parameters arising from this study did not change the alignments significantly. Alignments were inspected by hand, and obvious misalignments caused by insertions and duplications were eliminated. Substitutions ($n = 80,000$) were counted for each position in the consensus, excluding those in CpG dinucleotides, and a substitution frequency matrix was defined. From the matrices for each repeat (which corresponded to different ages), a single rate matrix was calculated for these bins of GC content ($< 40\%$ GC, 40–47% GC and $> 47\%$ GC). Data are shown for a repeat with an average divergence (in non-CpG sites) of 18% in 43% GC content (the repeat has slightly higher divergence in AT-rich DNA and lower in GC-rich DNA). From the rate matrix, we calculated log-likelihood matrices with different entropies (divergence levels), which are theoretically optimal for alignments of neutrally diverged copies to their common ancestral state (A. Kas and A. F. A. Smit, unpublished). These matrices are in use by the RepeatMasker program.

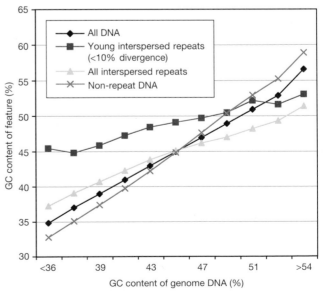

Figure 28 Interspersed repeats tend to diminish the differences between GC bins, despite the fact that GC-rich transposable elements (specifically Alu) accumulate in GC-rich DNA, and AT-rich elements (LINE1) in AT-rich DNA. The GC content of particular components of the sequence (repeats, young repeats and non-repeat sequence) was calculated as a function of overall GC content.

chromosome Y is unusually young, probably owing to a high tolerance for gain of new material by insertion and loss of old material by deletion. Several lines of evidence support this picture. For example, LINE elements on chromosome Y are on average much younger than those on autosomes (not shown). Similarly, MaLR-family retroposons on chromosome Y are younger than those on autosomes, with the representation of subfamilies showing a strong inverse correlation with the age of the subfamily. Moreover, chromosome Y has a relative over-representation of the younger retroviral class II (ERVK) and a relative under-representation of the primarily older class III (ERVL) compared with other chromosomes. Overall, chromosome Y seems to maintain a youthful appearance by rapid turnover.

Interspersed repeats on chromosome Y can also be used to estimate the relative mutation rates, α_m and α_f, in the male and female germlines. Chromosome Y always resides in males, whereas chromosome X resides in females twice as often as in males. The substitution rates, μ_Y and μ_X, on these two chromosomes should thus be in the ratio $\mu_Y{:}\mu_X = (\alpha_m){:}(\alpha_m + 2\alpha_f)/3$, provided that one considers equivalent neutral sequences. Several authors have estimated the mutation rate in the male germline to be fivefold higher than in the female germline, by comparing the rates of evolution of X- and Y-linked genes in humans and primates. However, Page and colleagues[192] have challenged these estimates as too high. They studied a 39-kb region that is apparently devoid of genes and resides within a large segmental duplication from X to Y that occurred 3–4 Myr ago in the human lineage. On the basis of phylogenetic analysis of the sequence on human Y and human, chimp and gorilla X, they obtained a much lower estimate of $\mu_Y{:}\mu_X = 1.36$, corresponding to $\alpha_m{:}\alpha_f = 1.7$. They suggested that the other estimates may have been higher because they were based on much longer evolutionary periods or because the genes studied may have been under selection.

Our database of human repeats provides a powerful resource for addressing this question. We identified the repeat elements from recent subfamilies (effectively, birth cohorts dating from the past 50 Myr) and measured the substitution rates for subfamily members on chromosomes X and Y (Fig. 29). There is a clear linear relationship with a slope of $\mu_Y{:}\mu_X = 1.57$ corresponding to $\alpha_m{:}\alpha_f = 2.1$. The estimate is in reasonable agreement with that of Page et al., although it is based on much more total sequence (360 kb on Y, 1.6 Mb on X) and a much longer time period. In particular, the discrepancy with earlier reports is not explained by recent changes in the human lineage. Various theories have been proposed for the higher mutation rate in the male germline, including the greater number of cell divisions in the formation of sperm than eggs and different repair mechanisms in sperm and eggs.

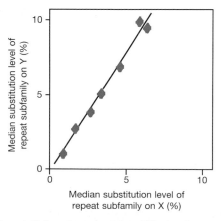

Figure 29 Higher substitution rate on chromosome Y than on chromosome X. We calculated the median substitution level (excluding CpG sites) for copies of the most recent L1 subfamilies (L1Hs–L1PA8) on the X and Y chromosomes. Only the 3′ UTR of the L1 element was considered because its consensus sequence is best established.

Active transposons. We were interested in identifying the youngest retrotransposons in the draft genome sequence. This set should contain the currently active retrotransposons, as well as the insertion sites that are still polymorphic in the human population.

The youngest branch in the phylogenetic tree of human LINE1 elements is called L1Hs (ref. 158); it differs in its 3′ untranslated region (UTR) by 12 diagnostic substitutions from the next oldest subfamily (L1PA2). Within the L1Hs family, there are two subsets referred to as Ta and pre-Ta, defined by a diagnostic trinucleotide[193,194]. All active L1 elements are thought to belong to these two subsets, because they account for all 14 known cases of human disease arising from new L1 transposition (with 13 belonging to the Ta subset and one to the pre-Ta subset)[195,196]. These subsets are also of great interest for population genetics because at least 50% are still segregating as polymorphisms in the human population[194,197]; they provide powerful markers for tracing population history because they represent unique (non-recurrent and non-revertible) genetic events that can be used (along with similarly polymorphic Alus) for reconstructing human migrations.

LINE1 elements that are retrotransposition-competent should consist of a full-length sequence and should have both ORFs intact. Eleven such elements from the Ta subset have been identified, including the likely progenitors of mutagenic insertions into the factor VIII and dystrophin genes[198–202]. A cultured cell retrotransposition assay has revealed that eight of these elements remain retrotransposition-competent[200,202,203].

We searched the draft genome sequence and identified 535 LINEs belonging to the Ta subset and 415 belonging to the pre-Ta subset. These elements provide a large collection of tools for probing human population history. We also identified those consisting of full-length elements with intact ORFs, which are candidate active LINEs. We found 39 such elements belonging to the Ta subset and 22 belonging to the pre-Ta subset; this substantially increases the number in the first category and provides the first known examples in the second category. These elements can now be tested for retrotransposition competence in the cell culture assay. Preliminary analysis resulted in the identification of two of these elements as the likely progenitors of mutagenic insertions into the β-globin and RP2 genes (R. Badge and J. V. Moran, unpublished data). Similar analyses should allow the identification of the progenitors of most, if not all, other known mutagenic L1 insertions.

L1 elements can carry extra DNA if transcription extends through the native transcriptional termination site into flanking genomic DNA. This process, termed L1-mediated transduction, provides a means for the mobilization of DNA sequences around the genome and may be a mechanism for 'exon shuffling'[204]. Twenty-one per cent of the 71 full-length L1s analysed contained non-L1-derived sequences before the 3′ target-site duplication site, in cases in which the site was unambiguously recognizable. The length of the transduced sequence was 30–970 bp, supporting the suggestion that 0.5–1.0% of the human genome may have arisen by LINE-based transduction of 3′ flanking sequences[205,206].

Our analysis also turned up two instances of 5′ transduction (145 bp and 215 bp). Although this possibility had been suggested on the basis of cell culture models[195,203], these are the first documented examples. Such events may arise from transcription initiating in a cellular promoter upstream of the L1 elements. L1 transcription is generally confined to the germline[207,208], but transcription from other promoters could explain a somatic L1 retrotransposition event that resulted in colon cancer[206].

Transposons as a creative force. The primary force for the origin and expansion of most transposons has been selection for their ability to create progeny, and not a selective advantage for the host. However, these selfish pieces of DNA have been responsible for important innovations in many genomes, for example by contributing regulatory elements and even new genes.

Twenty human genes have been recognized as probably derived

from transposons[142,209]. These include the RAG1 and RAG2 recombinases and the major centromere-binding protein CENPB. We scanned the draft genome sequence and identified another 27 cases, bringing the total to 47 (Table 13; refs 142, 209). All but four are derived from DNA transposons, which give rise to only a small proportion of the interspersed repeats in the genome. Why there are so many DNA transposase-like genes, many of which still contain the critical residues for transposase activity, is a mystery.

To illustrate this concept, we describe the discovery of one of the new examples. We searched the draft genome sequence to identify the autonomous DNA transposon responsible for the distribution of the non-autonomous MER85 element, one of the most recently (40–50 Myr ago) active DNA transposons. Most non-autonomous elements are internal deletion products of a DNA transposon. We identified one instance of a large (1,782 bp) ORF flanked by the 5′ and 3′ halves of a MER85 element. The ORF encodes a novel protein (partially published as pID 6453533) whose closest homologue is the transposase of the piggyBac DNA transposon, which is found in insects and has the same characteristic TTAA target-site duplications[210] as MER85. The ORF is actively transcribed in fetal brain and in cancer cells. That it has not been lost to mutation in 40–50 Myr of evolution (whereas the flanking, noncoding, MER85-like termini show the typical divergence level of such elements) and is actively transcribed provides strong evidence that it has been adopted by the human genome as a gene. Its function is unknown.

LINE1 activity clearly has also had fringe benefits. We mentioned above the possibility of exon reshuffling by cotranscription of neighbouring DNA. The LINE1 machinery can also cause reverse transcription of genic mRNAs, which typically results in nonfunctional processed pseudogenes but can, occasionally, give rise to functional processed genes. There are at least eight human and eight mouse genes for which evidence strongly supports such an origin[211] (see http://www-ifi.uni-muenster.de/exapted-retrogenes/tables.html). Many other intronless genes may have been created in the same way.

Transposons have made other creative contributions to the genome. A few hundred genes, for example, use transcriptional terminators donated by LTR retroposons (data not shown). Other genes employ regulatory elements derived from repeat elements[211].

Simple sequence repeats

Simple sequence repeats (SSRs) are a rather different type of repetitive structure that is common in the human genome—perfect or slightly imperfect tandem repeats of a particular k-mer. SSRs with a short repeat unit ($n = 1$–13 bases) are often termed microsa-

---

Table 13 Human genes derived from transposable elements

GenBank ID*	Gene name	Related transposon family†	Possible fusion gene§	Newly recognized derivation‖
nID 3150436	BC200	FLAM Alu‡		
pID 2330017	Telomerase	non-LTR retrotransposon		
pID 1196425	HERV-3 env	Retroviridae/HERV-R‡		
pID 4773880	Syncytin	Retroviridae/HERV-W‡		
pID 131827	RAG1 and 2	Tc1-like		
pID 29863	CENP-B	Tc1/Pogo		
EST 2529718		Tc1/Pogo		+
PID 10047247		Tc1/Pogo/Pogo		+
EST 4524463		Tc1/Pogo/Pogo		+
pID 4504807	Jerky	Tc1/Pogo/Tigger		
pID 7513096	JRKL	Tc1/Pogo/Tigger		
EST 5112721		Tc1/Pogo/Tigger		+
EST 11097233		Tc1/Pogo/Tigger		+
EST 6986275	Sancho	Tc1/Pogo/Tigger		
EST 8616450		Tc1/Pogo/Tigger		+
EST 8750408		Tc1/Pogo/Tigger		+
EST 5177004		Tc1/Pogo/Tigger		+
PID 3413884	KIAA0461	Tc1/Pogo/Tc2	+	
PID 7959287	KIAA1513	Tc1/Pogo/Tc2		+
PID 2231380		Tc1/Mariner/Hsmar1‡	+	
EST 10219887		hAT/Hobo	+	+
PID 6581095	Buster1	hAT/Charlie	+	
PID 7243087	Buster2	hAT/Charlie	+	
PID 6581097	Buster3	hAT/Charlie		
PID 7662294	KIAA0766	hAT/Charlie	+	
PID 10439678		hAT/Charlie		+
PID 7243087	KIAA1353	hAT/Charlie		+
PID 7021900		hAT/Charlie/Charlie3‡		+
PID 4263748		hAT/Charlie/Charlie8‡	+	
EST 8161741		hAT/Charlie/Charlie9‡		+
pID 4758872	DAP4,pP52^rIPK	hAT/Tip100/Zaphod		
EST 10990063		hAT/Tip100/Zaphod		+
EST 10101591		hAT/Tip100/Zaphod		
pID 7513011	KIAA0543	hAT/Tip100/Tip100	+	
pID 10439744		hAT/Tip100/Tip100		+
pID 10047247	KIAA1586	hAT/Tip100/Tip100		+
pID 10439762		hAT/Tip100	+	
EST 10459804		hAT/Tip100		+
pID 4160548	Tramp	hAT/Tam3		+
BAC 3522927		hAT/Tam3		+
pID 3327088	KIAA0637	hAT/Tam3	+	
EST 1928552		hAT/Tam3		+
pID 6453533		piggyBac/MER85‡	+	
EST 3594004		piggyBac/MER85‡		+
BAC 4309921		piggyBac/MER85‡		+
EST 4073914		piggyBac/MER75‡		+
EST 1963278		piggyBac		+

The Table lists 47 human genes, with a likely origin in up to 38 different transposon copies.
* Where available, the GenBank ID numbers are given for proteins, otherwise a representative EST or a clone name is shown. Six groups (two or three genes each) have similarity at the DNA level well beyond that observed between different DNA transposon families in the genome; they are indicated in italics, with all but the initial member of each group indented. This could be explained if the genes were paralogous (derived from a single inserted transposon and subsequently duplicated).
† Classification of the transposon.
‡ Indicates that the transposon from which the gene is derived is precisely known.
§ Proteins probably formed by fusion of a cellular and transposon gene; many have acquired zinc-finger domains.
‖ Not previously reported as being derived from transposable element genes. The remaining genes can be found in refs 142, 209.

Table 14 SSR content of the human genome

Length of repeat unit	Average bases per Mb	Average number of SSR elements per Mb
1	1,660	36.7
2	5,046	43.1
3	1,013	11.8
4	3,383	32.5
5	2,686	17.6
6	1,376	15.2
7	906	8.4
8	1,139	11.1
9	900	8.6
10	1,576	8.6
11	770	8.7

SSRs were identified by using the computer program Tandem Repeat Finder with the following parameters: match score 2, mismatch score 3, indel 5, minimum alignment 50, maximum repeat length 500, minimum repeat length 1.

tellites, whereas those with longer repeat units ($n = 14–500$ bases) are often termed minisatellites. With the exception of poly(A) tails from reverse transcribed messages, SSRs are thought to arise by slippage during DNA replication[212,213].

We compiled a catalogue of all SSRs over a given length in the human draft genome sequence, and studied their properties (Table 14). SSRs comprise about 3% of the human genome, with the greatest single contribution coming from dinucleotide repeats (0.5%). (The precise criteria for the number of repeat units and the extent of divergence allowed in an SSR affect the exact census, but not the qualitative conclusions.)

There is approximately one SSR per 2 kb (the number of non-overlapping tandem repeats is 437 per Mb). The catalogue confirms various properties of SSRs that have been inferred from sampling approaches (Table 15). The most frequent dinucleotide repeats are AC and AT (50 and 35% of dinucleotide repeats, respectively), whereas AG repeats (15%) are less frequent and GC repeats (0.1%) are greatly under-represented. The most frequent trinucleotides are AAT and AAC (33% and 21%, respectively), whereas ACC (4.0%), AGC (2.2%), ACT (1.4%) and ACG (0.1%) are relatively rare. Overall, trinucleotide SSRs are much less frequent than dinucleotide SSRs[214].

SSRs have been extremely important in human genetic studies, because they show a high degree of length polymorphism in the human population owing to frequent slippage by DNA polymerase during replication. Genetic markers based on SSRs—particularly $(CA)_n$ repeats—have been the workhorse of most human disease-mapping studies[101,102]. The availability of a comprehensive catalogue of SSRs is thus a boon for human genetic studies.

The SSR catalogue also allowed us to resolve a mystery regarding mammalian genetic maps. Such genetic maps in rat, mouse and human have a deficit of polymorphic $(CA)_n$ repeats on chromosome X[30,101]. There are two possible explanations for this deficit. There may simply be fewer $(CA)_n$ repeats on chromosome X; or $(CA)_n$ repeats may be as dense on chromosome X but less polymorphic in

Table 15 SSRs by repeat unit

Repeat unit	Number of SSRs per Mb
AC	27.7
AT	19.4
AG	8.2
GC	0.1
AAT	4.1
AAC	2.6
AGG	1.5
AAG	1.4
ATG	0.7
CGG	0.6
ACC	0.4
AGC	0.3
ACT	0.2
ACG	0.0

SSRs were identified as in Table 14.

the population. In fact, analysis of the draft genome sequence shows that chromosome X has the same density of $(CA)_n$ repeats per Mb as the autosomes (data not shown). Thus, the deficit of polymorphic markers relative to autosomes results from population genetic forces. Possible explanations include that chromosome X has a smaller effective population size, experiences more frequent selective sweeps reducing diversity (owing to its hemizygosity in males), or has a lower mutation rate (owing to its more frequent passage through the less mutagenic female germline). The availability of the draft genome sequence should provide ways to test these alternative explanations.

Segmental duplications

A remarkable feature of the human genome is the segmental duplication of portions of genomic sequence[215–217]. Such duplications involve the transfer of 1–200-kb blocks of genomic sequence to one or more locations in the genome. The locations of both donor and recipient regions of the genome are often not tandemly arranged, suggesting mechanisms other than unequal crossing-over for their origin. They are relatively recent, inasmuch as strong sequence identity is seen in both exons and introns (in contrast to regions that are considered to show evidence of ancient duplications, characterized by similarities only in coding regions). Indeed, many such duplications appear to have arisen in very recent evolutionary time, as judged by high sequence identity and by their absence in closely related species.

Segmental duplications can be divided into two categories. First, interchromosomal duplications are defined as segments that are duplicated among nonhomologous chromosomes. For example, a 9.5-kb genomic segment of the adrenoleukodystrophy locus from Xq28 has been duplicated to regions near the centromeres of chromosomes 2, 10, 16 and 22 (refs 218, 219). Anecdotal observations suggest that many interchromosomal duplications map near the centromeric and telomeric regions of human chromosomes[218–233].

The second category is intrachromosomal duplications, which occur within a particular chromosome or chromosomal arm. This category includes several duplicated segments, also known as low copy repeat sequences, that mediate recurrent chromosomal structural rearrangements associated with genetic disease[215,217]. Examples on chromosome 17 include three copies of a roughly 200-kb repeat separated by around 5 Mb and two copies of a roughly 24-kb repeat separated by 1.5 Mb. The copies are so similar (99% identity) that paralogous recombination events can occur, giving rise to contiguous gene syndromes: Smith–Magenis syndrome and Charcot–Marie–Tooth syndrome 1A, respectively[34,234]. Several other examples are known and are also suspected to be responsible for recurrent microdeletion syndromes (for example, Prader–Willi/Angelman,

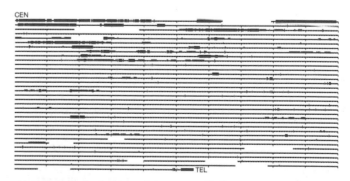

Figure 30 Duplication landscape of chromosome 22. The size and location of intrachromosomal (blue) and interchromosomal (red) duplications are depicted for chromosome 22q, using the PARASIGHT computer program (Bailey and Eichler, unpublished). Each horizontal line represents 1 Mb (ticks, 100-kb intervals). The chromosome sequence is oriented from centromere (top left) to telomere (bottom right). Pairwise alignments with > 90% nucleotide identity and > 1 kb long are shown. Gaps within the chromosomal sequence are of known size and shown as empty space.

velocardiofacial/DiGeorge and Williams' syndromes[215,235–240]).

Until now, the identification and characterization of segmental duplications have been based on anecdotal reports—for example, finding that certain probes hybridize to multiple chromosomal sites or noticing duplicated sequence at certain recurrent chromosomal breakpoints. The availability of the entire genomic sequence will make it possible to explore the nature of segmental duplications more systematically. This analysis can begin with the current state of the draft genome sequence, although caution is required because some apparent duplications may arise from a failure to merge sequence contigs from overlapping clones. Alternatively, erroneous

assembly of closely related sequences from nonoverlapping clones may underestimate the true frequency of such features, particularly among those segments with the highest sequence similarity. Accordingly, we adopted a conservative approach for estimating such duplication from the available draft genome sequence.

Pericentromeres and subtelomeres. We began by re-evaluating the finished sequences of chromosomes 21 and 22. The initial papers on these chromosomes[93,94] noted some instances of interchromosomal duplication near each centromere. With the ability now to compare these chromosomes to the vast majority of the genome, it is apparent that the regions near the centromeres consist almost entirely of interchromosomal duplicated segments, with little or no unique sequence. Smaller regions of interchromosomal duplication are also observed near the telomeres.

Chromosome 22 contains a region of 1.5 Mb adjacent to the centromere in which 90% of sequence can now be recognized to consist of interchromosomal duplication (Fig. 30). Conversely, 52% of the interchromosomal duplications on chromosome 22 were located in this region, which comprises only 5% of the chromosome. Also, the subtelomeric end consists of a 50-kb region consisting almost entirely of interchromosomal duplications.

Chromosome 21 presents a similar landscape (Fig. 31). The first 1 Mb after the centromere is composed of interchromosomal repeats, as well as the largest (> 200 kb) block of intrachromosomally duplicated material. Again, most interchromosomal duplications on the chromosome map to this region and the most subtelomeric region (30 kb) shows extensive duplication among nonhomologous chromosomes.

Figure 31 Duplication landscape of chromosome 21. The size and location of intrachromosomal (blue) and interchromosomal (red) duplications are depicted along the sequence of the long arm of chromosome 21. Gaps between finished sequence are denoted by empty space but do not represent actual gap size.

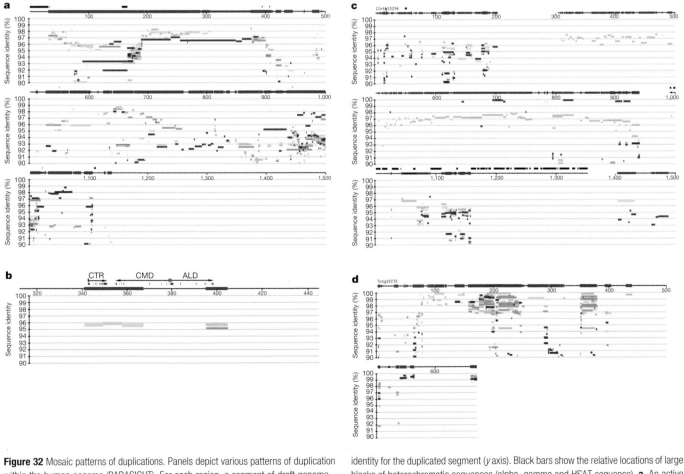

Figure 32 Mosaic patterns of duplications. Panels depict various patterns of duplication within the human genome (PARASIGHT). For each region, a segment of draft genome sequence (100–500 kb) is shown with both interchromosomal (red) and intrachromosomal (blue) duplications displayed along the horizontal line. Below the line, each separate sequence duplication is indicated (with a distinct colour) relative to per cent nucleotide identity for the duplicated segment (y axis). Black bars show the relative locations of large blocks of heterochromatic sequences (alpha, gamma and HSAT sequence). **a**, An active pericentromeric region on chromosome 21. **b**, An ancestral region from Xq28 that has contributed various 'genic' segments to pericentromeric regions. **c**, A pericentromeric region from chromosome 11. **d**, A subtelomeric region from chromosome 7p.

The pericentromeric regions are structurally very complex, as illustrated for chromosome 21 in Fig. 32a. The pericentromeric regions appear to have been bombarded by successive insertions of duplications; the insertion events must be fairly recent because the degree of sequence conservation with the genomic source loci is fairly high (90–100%, with an apparent peak around 96%). Distinct insertions are typically separated by AT-rich or GC-rich minisatellite-like repeats that have been hypothesized to have a functional role in targeting duplications to these regions[233,241].

A single genomic source locus often gives rise to pericentromeric copies on multiple chromosomes, with each having essentially the same breakpoints and the same degree of divergence. An example of such a source locus on Xq28 is shown in Fig. 32b. Phylogenetic analysis has suggested a two-step mechanism for the origin and dispersal of these segments, whereby an initial segmental duplication in the pericentromeric region of one chromosome occurs and is then redistributed as part of a larger cassette to other such regions[242].

A comprehensive analysis for all chromosomes will have to await complete sequencing of the genome, but the evidence from the draft genome sequence indicates that the same picture is likely to be seen throughout the genome. Several papers have analysed finished segments within pericentromeric regions of chromosomes 2 (160 kb), 10 (400 kb) and 16 (300 kb), all of which show extensive interchromosomal segmental duplication[215,219,232,233]. An example from another pericentromeric region on chromosome 11 is shown in Fig. 32c. Interchromosomal duplications in subtelomeric regions also appear to be a fairly general phenomenon, as illustrated by a large tract (~500 kb) of complex duplication on chromosome 7 (Fig. 32d).

The explanation for the clustering of segmental duplications may be that the genome has a damage-control mechanism whereby chromosomal breakage products are preferentially inserted into pericentromeric and, to a lesser extent, subtelomeric regions. The possibility of a specific mechanism for the insertion of these sequences has been suggested on the basis of the unusual sequences found flanking the insertions. Although it is also possible that these regions simply have greater tolerance for large insertions, many large gene-poor 'deserts' have been identified[93] and there is no accumulation of duplicated segments within these regions. Along with the fact that transitions between duplicons (from different regions of the genome) occur at specific sequences, this suggests that active recruitment of duplications to such regions may occur. In any case, the duplicated regions are in general young (with many duplications showing <6% nucleotide divergence from their source loci) and in constant flux, both through additional duplications and by large-scale exchange among similar chromosomal environments. There is evidence of structural polymorphism in the human population, such as the presence or absence of olfactory receptor segments located within the telomeric regions of several human chromosomes[226,227].

Genome-wide analysis of segmental duplications. We also performed a global genome-wide analysis to characterize the amount of segmental duplication in the genome. We 'repeat-masked' the known interspersed repeats in the draft genome sequence and compared the remaining draft genomic sequence with itself in a massive all-by-all BLASTN similarity search. We excluded matches in which the sequence identity was so high that it might reflect artefactual duplications resulting from a failure to overlap sequence contigs correctly in assembling the draft genome sequence. Specifically, we considered only matches with less than 99.5% identity for finished sequence and less than 98% identity for unfinished sequence.

We took several approaches to avoid counting artefactual duplications in the sequence. In the first approach, we studied only finished sequence. We compared the finished sequence with itself, to identify segments of at least 1 kb and 90–99.5% sequence identity. This analysis will underestimate the extent of segmental

duplication, because it requires that at least two copies of the segment are present in the finished sequence and because some true duplications have over 99.5% identity.

The finished sequence consists of at least 3.3% segmental duplication (Table 16). Interchromosomal duplication accounts for about 1.5% and intrachromosomal duplication for about 2%, with some overlap (0.2%) between these categories. We analysed the lengths and divergence of the segmental duplications (Fig. 33). The duplications tend to be large (10–50 kb) and highly homologous, especially for the interchromosomal segments. The sequence divergence for the interchromosomal duplications appears to peak between 96.5% and 97.5%. This may indicate that interchromosomal duplications occurred in a punctuated manner. It will be intriguing to investigate whether such genomic upheaval has a role in speciation events.

In a second approach, we compared the entire human draft genome sequence (finished and unfinished) with itself to identify duplications with 90–98% sequence identity (Table 17). The draft genome sequence contains at least 3.6% segmental duplication. The actual proportion will be significantly higher, because we excluded many true matches with more than 98% sequence identity (at least 1.1% of the finished sequence). Although exact measurement must await a finished sequence, the human genome seems likely to contain about 5% segmental duplication, with most of this sequence in large blocks (> 10 kb). Such a high proportion of large duplications clearly distinguishes the human genome from other sequenced genomes, such as the fly and worm (Table 18).

The structure of large highly paralogous regions presents one of the 'serious and unanticipated challenges' to producing a finished sequence of the genome[46]. The absence of unique STS or fingerprint signatures over large genomic distances (~1 Mb) and the high degree of sequence similarity makes the distinction between paralogous sequence variation and allelic polymorphism problematic. Furthermore, the fact that such regions frequently harbour intron–exon structures of genuine unique sequence will complicate efforts to generate a genome-wide SNP map. The data indicate that a modest portion of the human genome may be relatively recalcitrant to genomic-based methods for SNP detection. Owing to their repetitive nature and their location in the genome, segmental

Table 16 Fraction of finished sequence in inter- and intrachromosomal duplications

Chromosome	Intrachromosomal (%)	Interchromosomal (%)	All (%)
1	1.4	0.5	1.9
2	0.1	0.6	0.7
3	0.3	1.1	1.1
4	0.0	1.0	1.0
5	0.6	0.3	0.9
6	0.8	0.4	1.1
7	3.4	1.3	4.1
8	0.3	0.1	0.3
9	0.8	2.9	3.7
10	2.1	0.8	2.9
11	1.2	2.1	2.3
12	1.5	0.3	1.8
13	0.0	0.5	0.5
14	0.6	0.4	1.0
15	3.0	6.9	6.9
16	4.5	2.0	5.8
17	1.6	0.3	1.8
18	0.0	0.7	0.7
19	3.6	0.3	3.8
20	0.2	0.3	0.5
21	1.4	1.6	3.0
22	6.1	2.6	7.5
X	1.8	3.2	5.0
Y	12.1	16.0	27.4
Un	0.0	0.5	0.5
Total	2.0	1.5	3.3

Excludes duplications with identities >99.5% to avoid artefactual duplication due to incomplete merger in the assembly process. Calculation was performed on the finished sequence available in September 2000 and reflects the duplications found within the total amount of finished sequence then. Note that there is some overlap between the interchromosomal and intrachromosomal sets.

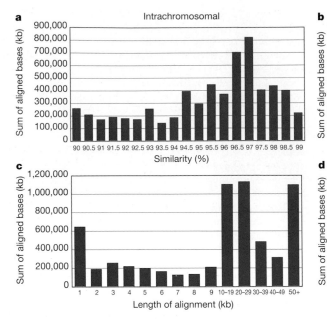
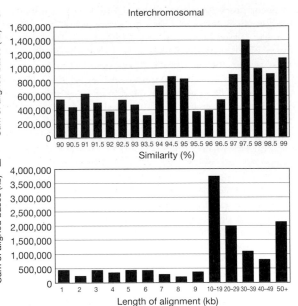
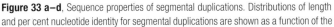

Figure 33 a–d, Sequence properties of segmental duplications. Distributions of length and per cent nucleotide identity for segmental duplications are shown as a function of the number of aligned bp, for the subset of finished genome sequence. Intrachromosomal, red; interchromosomal, blue.

duplications may well be underestimated by the current analysis. An understanding of the biology, pathology and evolution of these duplications will require specialized efforts within these exceptional regions of the human genome. The presence and distribution of such segments may provide evolutionary fodder for processes of exon shuffling and a general increase in protein diversity associated with domain accretion. It will be important to consider both genome-wide duplication events and more restricted punctuated events of genome duplication as forces in the evolution of vertebrate genomes.

Gene content of the human genome

Genes (or at least their coding regions) comprise only a tiny fraction of human DNA, but they represent the major biological function of the genome and the main focus of interest by biologists. They are also the most challenging feature to identify in the human genome sequence.

The ultimate goal is to compile a complete list of all human genes and their encoded proteins, to serve as a 'periodic table' for biomedical research[243]. But this is a difficult task. In organisms with small genomes, it is straightforward to identify most genes by the presence of long ORFs. In contrast, human genes tend to have small exons (encoding an average of only 50 codons) separated by long introns (some exceeding 10 kb). This creates a signal-to-noise problem, with the result that computer programs for direct gene prediction have only limited accuracy. Instead, computational prediction of human genes must rely largely on the availability of cDNA sequences or on sequence conservation with genes and proteins from other organisms. This approach is adequate for strongly conserved genes (such as histones or ubiquitin), but may be less sensitive to rapidly evolving genes (including many crucial to speciation, sex determination and fertilization).

Here we describe our efforts to recognize both the RNA genes and protein-coding genes in the human genome. We also study the properties of the predicted human protein set, attempting to discern how the human proteome differs from those of invertebrates such as worm and fly.

Noncoding RNAs

Although biologists often speak of a tight coupling between 'genes

Table 17 Fraction of the draft genome sequence in inter- and intrachromosomal duplications

Chromosome	Intrachromosomal (%)	Interchromosomal (%)	All (%)
1	2.1	1.7	3.4
2	1.6	1.6	2.6
3	1.8	1.4	2.7
4	1.5	2.2	3.0
5	1.0	0.9	1.8
6	1.5	1.4	2.7
7	3.6	1.8	4.5
8	1.2	1.5	2.1
9	2.1	2.3	3.8
10	3.3	2.0	4.7
11	2.7	1.4	3.7
12	2.1	1.2	2.8
13	1.7	1.6	3.0
14	0.6	0.6	1.2
15	4.1	4.4	6.7
16	3.4	3.4	5.5
17	4.4	1.7	5.7
18	0.9	1.0	1.9
19	5.4	1.6	6.3
20	0.8	1.4	2.0
21	1.9	4.0	4.8
22	6.8	7.7	11.9
X	1.2	1.1	2.2
Y	10.9	13.1	20.8
NA	2.3	7.8	8.3
UL	11.6	20.8	22.2
Total	2.3	2.0	3.6

Excludes duplications with identities >98% to avoid artefactual duplication due to incomplete merger in the assembly process. Calculation was performed on an earlier version of the draft genome sequence based on data available in July 2000 and reflects the duplications found within the total amount of finished sequence then. Note that there is some overlap between the interchromosomal and intrachromosomal sets.

Table 18 Cross-species comparison for large, highly homologous segmental duplications

	Percentage of genome (%)		
	Fly	Worm	Human (finished)*
> 1 kb	1.2	4.25	3.25
> 5 kb	0.37	1.50	2.86
> 10 kb	0.08	0.66	2.52

* This is an underestimate of the total amount of segmental duplication in the human genome because it only reflects duplication detectable with available finished sequence. The proportion of segmental duplications of > 1 kb is probably about 5% (see text).

and their encoded protein products', it is important to remember that thousands of human genes produce noncoding RNAs (ncRNAs) as their ultimate product[244]. There are several major classes of ncRNA. (1) Transfer RNAs (tRNAs) are the adapters that translate the triplet nucleic acid code of RNA into the amino-acid sequence of proteins; (2) ribosomal RNAs (rRNAs) are also central to the translational machinery, and recent X-ray crystallography results strongly indicate that peptide bond formation is catalysed by rRNA, not protein[245,246]; (3) small nucleolar RNAs (snoRNAs) are required for rRNA processing and base modification in the nucleolus[247,248]; and (4) small nuclear RNAs (snRNAs) are critical components of spliceosomes, the large ribonucleoprotein (RNP) complexes that splice introns out of pre-mRNAs in the nucleus. Humans have both a major, U2 snRNA-dependent spliceosome that splices most introns, and a minor, U12 snRNA-dependent spliceosome that splices a rare class of introns that often have AT/AC dinucleotides at the splice sites instead of the canonical GT/AG splice site consensus[249].

Other ncRNAs include both RNAs of known biochemical function (such as telomerase RNA and the 7SL signal recognition particle RNA) and ncRNAs of enigmatic function (such as the large Xist transcript implicated in X dosage compensation[250], or the small vault RNAs found in the bizarre vault ribonucleoprotein complex[251], which is three times the mass of the ribosome but has unknown function).

ncRNAs do not have translated ORFs, are often small and are not polyadenylated. Accordingly, novel ncRNAs cannot readily be found by computational gene-finding techniques (which search for features such as ORFs) or experimental sequencing of cDNA or EST libraries (most of which are prepared by reverse transcription using a primer complementary to a poly(A) tail). Even if the complete finished sequence of the human genome were available, discovering novel ncRNAs would still be challenging. We can, however, identify genomic sequences that are homologous to known ncRNA genes, using BLASTN or, in some cases, more specialized methods.

It is sometimes difficult to tell whether such homologous genes are orthologues, paralogues or closely related pseudogenes (because inactivating mutations are much less obvious than for protein-coding genes). For tRNA, there is sufficiently detailed information about the cloverleaf secondary structure to allow true genes and pseudogenes to be distinguished with high sensitivity. For many other ncRNAs, there is much less structural information and so we employ an operational criterion of high sequence similarity ($>95\%$ sequence identity and $>95\%$ full length) to distinguish true genes from pseudogenes. These assignments will eventually need to be reconciled with experimental data.

Transfer RNA genes. The classical experimental estimate of the number of human tRNA genes is 1,310 (ref. 252). In the draft genome sequence, we find only 497 human tRNA genes (Tables 19, 20). How do we account for this discrepancy? We believe that the original estimate is likely to have been inflated in two respects. First, it came from a hybridization experiment that probably counted closely related pseudogenes; by analysis of the draft genome sequence, there are in fact 324 tRNA-derived putative pseudogenes

(Table 20). Second, the earlier estimate assumed too high a value for the size of the human genome; repeating the calculation using the correct value yields an estimate of about 890 tRNA-related loci, which is in reasonable accord with our count of 821 tRNA genes and pseudogenes in the draft genome sequence.

The human tRNA gene set predicted from the draft genome sequence appears to include most of the known human tRNA species. The draft genome sequence contains 37 of 38 human tRNA species listed in a tRNA database[253], allowing for up to one mismatch. This includes one copy of the known gene for a specialized selenocysteine tRNA, one of several components of a baroque translational mechanism that reads UGA as a selenocysteine codon in certain rare mRNAs that carry a specific *cis*-acting RNA regulatory site (a so-called SECIS element) in their 3′ UTRs. The one tRNA gene in the database not found in the draft genome sequence is DE9990, a tRNAGlu species, which differs in two positions from the most related tRNA gene in the human genome. Possible explanations are that the database version of this tRNA contains two errors, the gene is polymorphic or this is a genuine functional tRNA that is missing from the draft genome sequence. (The database also lists one additional tRNA gene (*DS9994*), but this is apparently a contaminant, most similar to bacterial tRNAs; the parent entry (*Z13399*) was withdrawn from the DNA database, but the tRNA entry has not yet been removed from the tRNA database.) Although the human set appears substantially complete by this test, the tRNA gene numbers in Table 19 should be considered tentative and used with caution. The human and fly (but not the worm) are known to be missing significant amounts of heterochromatic DNA, and additional tRNA genes could be located there.

With this caveat, the results indicate that the human has fewer tRNA genes than the worm, but more than the fly. This may seem surprising, but tRNA gene number in metazoans is thought to be related not to organismal complexity, but more to idiosyncrasies of the demand for tRNA abundance in certain tissues or stages of embryonic development. For example, the frog *Xenopus laevis*, which must load each oocyte with a remarkable 40 ng of tRNA, has thousands of tRNA genes[254].

The degeneracy of the genetic code has allowed an inspired economy of tRNA anticodon usage. Although 61 sense codons need to be decoded, not all 61 different anticodons are present in tRNAs. Rather, tRNAs generally follow stereotyped and conserved wobble rules[255–257]. Wobble reduces the number of required anticodons substantially, and provides a connection between the genetic code and the hybridization stability of modified and unmodified RNA bases. In eukaryotes, the rules proposed by Guthrie and Abelson[256] predict that about 46 tRNA species will be sufficient to read the 61 sense codons (counting the initiator and elongator methionine tRNAs as two species). According to these rules, in the codon's third (wobble) position, U and C are generally decoded by a single tRNA species, whereas A and G are decoded by two separate tRNA species.

In 'two-codon boxes' of the genetic code (where codons ending with U/C encode a different amino acid from those ending with A/G), the U/C wobble position should be decoded by a G at position 34 in the tRNA anticodon. Thus, in the top left of Fig. 34, there is no tRNA with an AAA anticodon for Phe, but the GAA anticodon can recognize both UUU and UUC codons in the mRNA. In 'four-codon boxes' of the genetic code (where U, C, A and G in the wobble position all encode the same amino acid), the U/C wobble position is almost always decoded by I34 (inosine) in the tRNA, where the inosine is produced by post-transcriptional modification of an adenine (A). In the bottom left of Fig. 34, for example, the GUU and GUC codons of the four-codon Val box are decoded by a tRNA with an anticodon of AAC, which is no doubt modified to IAC. Presumably this pattern, which is strikingly conserved in eukaryotes, has to do with the fact that IA base pairs are also possible; thus

Table 19 Number of tRNA genes in various organisms

Organism	Number of canonical tRNAs	SeCys tRNA
Human	497	1
Worm	584	1
Fly	284	1
Yeast	273	0
Methanococcus jannaschii	36	1
Escherichia coli	86	1

Number of tRNA genes in each of six genome sequences, according to analysis by the computer program tRNAscan-SE. Canonical tRNAs read one of the standard 61 sense codons; this category excludes pseudogenes, undetermined anticodons, putative supressors and selenocysteine tRNAs. Most organisms have a selenocysteine (SeCys) tRNA species, but some unicellular eukaryotes do not (such as the yeast *S. cerevisiae*).

893 105

the IAC anticodon for a Val tRNA could recognize GUU, GUC and even GUA codons. Were this same I34 to be utilized in two-codon boxes, however, misreading of the NNA codon would occur, resulting in translational havoc. Eukaryotic glycine tRNAs represent a conserved exception to this last rule; they use a GCC anticodon to decode GGU and GGC, rather than the expected ICC anticodon.

Satisfyingly, the human tRNA set follows these wobble rules almost perfectly (Fig. 34). Only three unexpected tRNA species are found: single genes for a tRNATyr-AUA, tRNAIle-GAU, and tRNAAsn-AUU. Perhaps these are pseudogenes, but they appear to be plausible tRNAs. We also checked the possibility of sequencing errors in their anticodons, but each of these three genes is in a region of high sequence accuracy, with PHRAP quality scores higher than 70 for every base in their anticodons.

As in all other organisms, human protein-coding genes show codon bias—preferential use of one synonymous codon over another[258] (Fig. 34). In less complex organisms, such as yeast or bacteria, highly expressed genes show the strongest codon bias. Cytoplasmic abundance of tRNA species is correlated with both codon bias and overall amino-acid frequency (for example, tRNAs for preferred codons and for more common amino acids are more abundant). This is presumably driven by selective pressure for efficient or accurate translation[259]. In many organisms, tRNA abundance in turn appears to be roughly correlated with tRNA gene copy number, so tRNA gene copy number has been used as a proxy for tRNA abundance[260]. In vertebrates, however, codon bias is not so obviously correlated with gene expression level. Differing codon biases between human genes is more a function of their location in regions of different GC composition[261]. In agreement with the literature, we see only a very rough correlation of human tRNA gene number with either amino-acid frequency or codon bias (Fig. 34). The most obvious outliers in these weak correlations are

the strongly preferred CUG leucine codon, with a mere six tRNA-Leu-CAG genes producing a tRNA to decode it, and the relatively rare cysteine UGU and UGC codons, with 30 tRNA genes to decode them.

The tRNA genes are dispersed throughout the human genome. However, this dispersal is nonrandom. tRNA genes have sometimes been seen in clusters at small scales[262,263] but we can now see striking clustering on a genome-wide scale. More than 25% of the tRNA genes (140) are found in a region of only about 4 Mb on chromosome 6. This small region, only about 0.1% of the genome, contains an almost sufficient set of tRNA genes all by itself. The 140 tRNA genes contain a representative for 36 of the 49 anticodons found in the complete set; and of the 21 isoacceptor types, only tRNAs to decode Asn, Cys, Glu and selenocysteine are missing. Many of these tRNA genes, meanwhile, are clustered elsewhere; 18 of the 30 Cys tRNAs are found in a 0.5-Mb stretch of chromosome 7 and many of the Asn and Glu tRNA genes are loosely clustered on chromosome 1. More than half of the tRNA genes (280 out of 497) reside on either chromosome 1 or chromosome 6. Chromosomes 3, 4, 8, 9, 10, 12, 18, 20, 21 and X appear to have fewer than 10 tRNA genes each; and chromosomes 22 and Y have none at all (each has a single pseudogene).

Ribosomal RNA genes. The ribosome, the protein synthetic machine of the cell, is made up of two subunits and contains four rRNA species and many proteins. The large ribosomal subunit contains 28S and 5.8S rRNAs (collectively called 'large subunit' (LSU) rRNA) and also a 5S rRNA. The small ribosomal subunit contains 18S rRNA ('small subunit' (SSU) rRNA). The genes for LSU and SSU rRNA occur in the human genome as a 44-kb tandem repeat unit[264]. There are thought to be about 150–200 copies of this repeat unit arrayed on the short arms of acrocentric chromosomes 13, 14, 15, 21 and 22 (refs 254, 264). There are no true complete

AA	Freq	Codon	Wobble	Anticodon	Genes
Phe	171	UUU	\	AAA	0
Phe	203	UUC	/	GAA	14
Leu	73	UUA	—	UAA	8
Leu	125	UUG	—	CAA	6
Ser	147	UCU	/	AGA	10
Ser	172	UCC	/	GGA	0
Ser	118	UCA	—	UGA	5
Ser	45	UCG	—	CGA	4
Tyr	124	UAU	\	AUA	1
Tyr	158	UAC	\	GUA	11
stop	0	UAA	—	UUA	0
stop	0	UAG	—	CUA	0
Cys	99	UGU	\	ACA	0
Cys	119	UGC	\	GCA	30
stop	0	UGA	—	UCA	0
Trp	122	UGG	—	CCA	7
Leu	127	CUU	/	AAG	13
Leu	187	CUC		GAG	0
Leu	69	CUA	—	UAG	2
Leu	392	CUG	—	CAG	6
Pro	175	CCU	/	AGG	11
Pro	197	CCC	/	GGG	0
Pro	170	CCA	—	UGG	10
Pro	69	CCG	—	CGG	4
His	104	CAU	\	AUG	0
His	147	CAC	\	GUG	12
Gln	121	CAA	—	UUG	11
Gln	343	CAG	—	CUG	21
Arg	47	CGU	/	ACG	9
Arg	107	CGC		GCG	0
Arg	63	CGA	—	UCG	7
Arg	115	CGG	—	CCG	5
Ile	165	AUU	/	AAU	13
Ile	218	AUC		GAU	1
Ile	71	AUA	—	UAU	5
Met	221	AUG	—	CAU	17
Thr	131	ACU	/	AGU	8
Thr	192	ACC	/	GGU	0
Thr	150	ACA	—	UGU	10
Thr	63	ACG	—	CGU	7
Asn	174	AAU	\	AUU	1
Asn	199	AAC	\	GUU	33
Lys	248	AAA	—	UUU	16
Lys	331	AAG	—	CUU	22
Ser	121	AGU	\	ACU	0
Ser	191	AGC	\	GCU	7
Arg	113	AGA	—	UCU	5
Arg	110	AGG	—	CCU	4
Val	111	GUU	/	AAC	20
Val	146	GUC		GAC	0
Val	72	GUA	—	UAC	5
Val	288	GUG	—	CAC	19
Ala	185	GCU	/	AGC	25
Ala	282	GCC	/	GGC	0
Ala	160	GCA	—	UGC	10
Ala	74	GCG	—	CGC	5
Asp	230	GAU	\	AUC	0
Asp	262	GAC	\	GUC	10
Glu	301	GAA	—	UUC	14
Glu	404	GAG	—	CUC	8
Gly	112	GGU	\	ACC	0
Gly	230	GGC	\	GCC	11
Gly	168	GGA	—	UCC	5
Gly	160	GGG	—	CCC	8

Figure 34 The human genetic code and associated tRNA genes. For each of the 64 codons, we show: the corresponding amino acid; the observed frequency of the codon per 10,000 codons; the codon; predicted wobble pairing to a tRNA anticodon (black lines); an unmodified tRNA anticodon sequence; and the number of tRNA genes found with this anticodon. For example, phenylalanine is encoded by UUU or UUC; UUC is seen more frequently, 203 to 171 occurrences per 10,000 total codons; both codons are expected to be decoded by a single tRNA anticodon type, GAA, using a G/U wobble; and there are 14 tRNA genes found with this anticodon. The modified anticodon sequence in the mature tRNA is not shown, even where post-transcriptional modifications can be confidently predicted (for example, when an A is used to decode a U/C third position, the A is almost certainly an inosine in the mature tRNA). The Figure also does not show the number of distinct tRNA species (such as distinct sequence families) for each anticodon; often there is more than one species for each anticodon.

copies of the rDNA tandem repeats in the draft genome sequence, owing to the deliberate bias in the initial phase of the sequencing effort against sequencing BAC clones whose restriction fragment fingerprints showed them to contain primarily tandemly repeated sequence. Sequence similarity analysis with the BLASTN computer program does, however, detect hundreds of rDNA-derived sequence fragments dispersed throughout the complete genome, including one 'full-length' copy of an individual 5.8S rRNA gene not associated with a true tandem repeat unit (Table 20).

The 5S rDNA genes also occur in tandem arrays, the largest of which is on chromosome 1 between 1q41.11 and 1q42.13, close to the telomere[265,266]. There are 200–300 true 5S genes in these arrays[265,267]. The number of 5S-related sequences in the genome, including numerous dispersed pseudogenes, is classically cited as 2,000 (refs 252, 254). The long tandem array on chromosome 1 is not yet present in the draft genome sequence because there are no EcoRI or HindIII sites present, and thus it was not cloned in the most heavily utilized BAC libraries (Table 1). We expect to recover it during the finishing stage. We do detect four individual copies of 5S rDNA by our search criteria ($\geq 95\%$ identity and $\geq 95\%$ full length). We also find many more distantly related dispersed sequences (520 at $P \leq 0.001$), which we interpret as probable pseudogenes (Table 20).

Small nucleolar RNA genes. Eukaryotic rRNA is extensively processed and modified in the nucleolus. Much of this activity is directed by numerous snoRNAs. These come in two families: C/D box snoRNAs (mostly involved in guiding site-specific 2′-O-ribose methylations of other RNAs) and H/ACA snoRNAs (mostly involved in guiding site-specific pseudouridylations)[247,248]. We compiled a set of 97 known human snoRNA gene sequences; 84 of these (87%) have at least one copy in the draft genome sequence (Table 20), almost all as single-copy genes.

It is thought that all 2′-O-ribose methylations and pseudouridylations in eukaryotic rRNA are guided by snoRNAs. There are 105–107 methylations and around 95 pseudouridylations in human rRNA[268]. Only about half of these have been tentatively assigned to known guide snoRNAs. There are also snoRNA-directed modifications on other stable RNAs, such as U6 (ref. 269), and the extent of this is just beginning to be explored. Sequence similarity has so far proven insufficient to recognize all snoRNA genes. We therefore expect that there are many unrecognized snoRNA genes that are not detected by BLAST queries.

Spliceosomal RNAs and other ncRNA genes. We also looked for copies of other known ncRNA genes. We found at least one copy of 21 (95%) of 22 known ncRNAs, including the spliceosomal snRNAs. There were multiple copies for several ncRNAs, as expected; for example, we find 44 dispersed genes for U6 snRNA, and 16 for U1 snRNA (Table 20).

For some of these RNA genes, homogeneous multigene families that occur in tandem arrays are again under-represented owing to the restriction enzymes used in constructing the BAC libraries and, in some instances, the decision to delay the sequencing of BAC clones with low complexity fingerprints indicative of tandemly repeated DNA. The U2 RNA genes are located at the RNU2 locus, a tandem array of 10–20 copies of nearly identical 6.1-kb units at 17q21–q22 (refs 270–272). Similarly, the U3 snoRNA genes (included in the aggregate count of C/D snoRNAs in Table 20) are clustered at the RNU3 locus at 17p11.2, not in a tandem array, but in a complex inverted repeat structure of about 5–10 copies per haploid genome[273]. The U1 RNA genes are clustered with about 30 copies at the RNU1 locus at 1p36.1, but this cluster is thought to be loose and irregularly organized; no two U1 genes have been cloned on the same cosmid[271]. In the draft genome sequence, we see six copies of U2 RNA that meet our criteria for true genes, three of which appear to be in the expected position on chromosome 17. For U3, so far we see one true copy at the correct place on chromosome 17p11.2. For U1, we see 16 true genes, 6 of which are loosely clustered within 0.6 Mb at 1p36.1 and another 6 are elsewhere on chromosome 1. Again, these and other clusters will be a matter for the finishing process.

Table 20 Known non-coding RNA genes in the draft genome sequence

RNA gene*	Number expected†	Number found‡	Number of related genes§	Function
tRNA	1,310	497	324	Protein synthesis
SSU (18S) rRNA	150–200	0	40	Protein synthesis
5.8S rRNA	150–200	1	11	Protein synthesis
LSU (28S) rRNA	150–200	0	181	Protein synthesis
5S rRNA	200–300	4	520	Protein synthesis
U1	~30	16	134	Spliceosome component
U2	10–20	6	94	Spliceosome component
U4	??	4	87	Spliceosome component
U4atac	??	1	20	Component of minor (U11/U12) spliceosome
U5	??	1	31	Spliceosome component
U6	??	44	1,135	Spliceosome component
U6atac	??	4	32	Component of minor (U11/U12) spliceosome
U7	1	1	3	Histone mRNA 3′ processing
U11	1	0	6	Component of minor (U11/U12) spliceosome
U12	1	1	0	Component of minor (U11/U12) spliceosome
SRP (7SL) RNA	4	3	773	Component of signal recognition particle (protein secretion)
RNAse P	1	1	2	tRNA 5′ end processing
RNAse MRP	1	1	6	rRNA processing
Telomerase RNA	1	1	4	Template for addition of telomeres
hY1	1	1	353	Component of Ro RNP, function unknown
hY3	1	25	414	Component of Ro RNP, function unknown
hY4	1	3	115	Component of Ro RNP, function unknown
hY5 (4.5S RNA)	1	1	9	Component of Ro RNP, function unknown
Vault RNAs	3	3	1	Component of 13-MDa vault RNP, function unknown
7SK	1	1	330	Unknown
H19	1	1	2	Unknown
Xist	1	1	0	Initiation of X chromosome inactivation (dosage compensation)
Known C/D snoRNAs	81	69	558	Pre-rRNA processing or site-specific ribose methylation of rRNA
Known H/ACA snoRNAs	16	15	87	Pre-rRNA processing or site-specific pseudouridylation of rRNA

* Known ncRNA genes (or gene families, such as the C/D and H/ACA snoRNA families); reference sequences were extracted from GenBank and used to probe the draft genome sequence.
† Number of genes that were expected in the human genome, based on previous literature (note that earlier experimental techniques probably tend to overestimate copy number, by counting closely related pseudogenes).
‡ The copy number of 'true' full-length genes identified in the draft genome sequence.
§ The copy number of other significantly related copies (pseudogenes, fragments, paralogues) found. Except for the 497 true tRNA genes, all sequence similarities were identified by WashU BLASTN 2.0MP (W. Gish, unpublished; http://blast.wustl.edu), with parameters '-kap wordmask = seg B = 50000 W = 8' and the default +5/−4 DNA scoring matrix. True genes were operationally defined as BLAST hits with $\geq 95\%$ identity over $\geq 95\%$ of the length of the query. Related sequences were operationally defined as all other BLAST hits with P-values ≤ 0.001.

Table 21 Characteristics of human genes

	Median	Mean	Sample (size)
Internal exon	122 bp	145 bp	RefSeq alignments to draft genome sequence, with confirmed intron boundaries (43,317 exons)
Exon number	7	8.8	RefSeq alignments to finished sequence (3,501 genes)
Introns	1,023 bp	3,365 bp	RefSeq alignments to finished sequence (27,238 introns)
3' UTR	400 bp	770 bp	Confirmed by mRNA or EST on chromosome 22 (689)
5' UTR	240 bp	300 bp	Confirmed by mRNA or EST on chromosome 22 (463)
Coding sequence	1,100 bp	1,340 bp	Selected RefSeq entries (1,804)
(CDS)	367 aa	447 aa	
Genomic extent	14 kb	27 kb	Selected RefSeq entries (1,804)

Median and mean values for a number of properties of human protein-coding genes. The 1,804 selected RefSeq entries were those that could be unambiguously aligned to finished sequence over their entire length.

Our observations also confirm the striking proliferation of ncRNA-derived pseudogenes (Table 20). There are hundreds or thousands of sequences in the draft genome sequence related to some of the ncRNA genes. The most prolific pseudogene counts generally come from RNA genes transcribed by RNA polymerase III promoters, including U6, the hY RNAs and SRP-RNA. These ncRNA pseudogenes presumably arise through reverse transcription. The frequency of such events gives insight into how ncRNA genes can evolve into SINE retroposons, such as the tRNA-derived SINEs found in many vertebrates and the SRP-RNA-derived Alu elements found in humans.

Protein-coding genes

Identifying the protein-coding genes in the human genome is one of the most important applications of the sequence data, but also one of the most difficult challenges. We describe below our efforts to create an initial human gene and protein index.

Exploring properties of known genes. Before attempting to identify new genes, we explored what could be learned by aligning the cDNA sequences of known genes to the draft genome sequence. Genomic alignments allow one to study exon–intron structure and local GC content, and are valuable for biomedical studies because they connect genes with the genetic and cytogenetic map, link them with regulatory sequences and facilitate the development of polymerase chain reaction (PCR) primers to amplify exons. Until now, genomic alignment was available for only about a quarter of known genes.

The 'known' genes studied were those in the RefSeq database[110], a manually curated collection designed to contain nonredundant representatives of most full-length human mRNA sequences in GenBank (RefSeq intentionally contains some alternative splice forms of the same genes). The version of RefSeq used contained 10,272 mRNAs.

The RefSeq genes were aligned with the draft genome sequence, using both the Spidey (S. Wheelan, personal communication) and Acembly (D. Thierry-Mieg and J. Thierry-Mieg, unpublished; http://www.acedb.org) computer programs. Because this sequence is incomplete and contains errors, not all genes could be fully aligned and some may have been incorrectly aligned. More than 92% of the RefSeq entries could be aligned at high stringency over at least part of their length, and 85% could be aligned over more than half of their length. Some genes (16%) had high stringency alignments to more than one location in the draft genome sequence owing, for example, to paralogues or pseudogenes. In such cases, we considered only the best match. In a few of these cases, the assignment may not be correct because the true matching region has not yet been sequenced. Three per cent of entries appeared to be alternative splice products of the same gene, on the basis of their alignment to the same location in the draft genome sequence. In all, we obtained at least partial genomic alignments for 9,212 distinct known genes and essentially complete alignment for 5,364 of them.

Previous efforts to study human gene structure[116,274,275] have been hampered by limited sample sizes and strong biases in favour of compact genes. Table 21 gives the mean and median values of some basic characteristics of gene structures. Some of the values may be

underestimates. In particular, the UTRs given in the RefSeq database are likely to be incomplete; they are considerably shorter, for example, than those derived from careful reconstructions on chromosome 22. Intron sizes were measured only for genes in finished genomic sequence, to mitigate the bias arising from the fact that

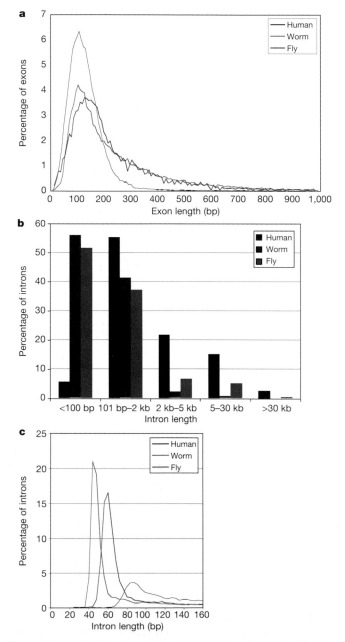

Figure 35 Size distributions of exons, introns and short introns, in sequenced genomes. **a**, Exons; **b**, introns; **c**, short introns (enlarged from **b**). Confirmed exons and introns for the human were taken from RefSeq alignments and for worm and fly from Acembly alignments of ESTs (J. and D. Thierry-Mieg and, for worm, Y. Kohara, unpublished).

long introns are more likely than short introns to be interrupted by gaps in the draft genome sequence. Nonetheless, there may be some residual bias against long genes and long introns.

There is considerable variation in overall gene size and intron size, with both distributions having very long tails. Many genes are over 100 kb long, the largest known example being the dystrophin gene (DMD) at 2.4 Mb. The variation in the size distribution of coding sequences and exons is less extreme, although there are still some remarkable outliers. The titin gene[276] has the longest currently known coding sequence at 80,780 bp; it also has the largest number of exons (178) and longest single exon (17,106 bp).

It is instructive to compare the properties of human genes with those from worm and fly. For all three organisms, the typical length of a coding sequence is similar (1,311 bp for worm, 1,497 bp for fly and 1,340 bp for human), and most internal exons fall within a common peak between 50 and 200 bp (Fig. 35a). However, the worm and fly exon distributions have a fatter tail, resulting in a larger mean size for internal exons (218 bp for worm versus 145 bp for human). The conservation of preferred exon size across all three species supports suggestions of a conserved exon-based component of the splicing machinery[277]. Intriguingly, the few extremely short human exons show an unusual base composition. In 42 detected

human exons of less than 19 bp, the nucleotide frequencies of A, G, T and C are 39, 33, 15 and 12%, respectively, showing a strong purine bias. Purine-rich sequences may enhance splicing[278,279], and it is possible that such sequences are required or strongly selected for to ensure correct splicing of very short exons. Previous studies have shown that short exons require intronic, but not exonic, splicing enhancers[280].

In contrast to the exons, the intron size distributions differ substantially among the three species (Fig. 35b, c). The worm and fly each have a reasonably tight distribution, with most introns near the preferred minimum intron length (47 bp for worm, 59 bp for fly) and an extended tail (overall average length of 267 bp for worm and 487 bp for fly). Intron size is much more variable in humans, with a peak at 87 bp but a very long tail resulting in a mean of more than 3,300 bp. The variation in intron size results in great variation in gene size.

The variation in gene size and intron size can partly be explained by the fact that GC-rich regions tend to be gene-dense with many compact genes, whereas AT-rich regions tend to be gene-poor with many sprawling genes containing large introns. The correlation of gene density with GC content is shown in Fig. 36a, b; the relative density increases more than tenfold as GC content increases from

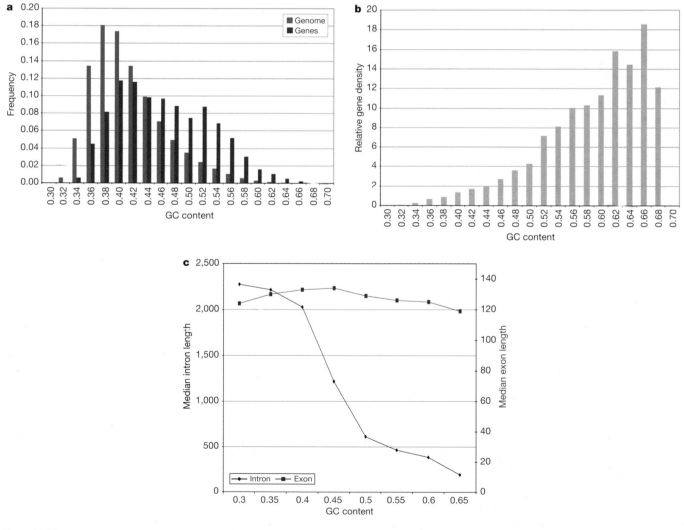

Figure 36 GC content. **a**, Distribution of GC content in genes and in the genome. For 9,315 known genes mapped to the draft genome sequence, the local GC content was calculated in a window covering either the whole alignment or 20,000 bp centred around the midpoint of the alignment, whichever was larger. Ns in the sequence were not counted. GC content for the genome was calculated for adjacent nonoverlapping 20,000-bp windows across the sequence. Both the gene and genome distributions have been normalized to sum to one. **b**, Gene density as a function of GC content, obtained by taking the ratio of the data in **a**. Values are less accurate at higher GC levels because the denominator is small. **c**, Dependence of mean exon and intron lengths on GC content. For exons and introns, the local GC content was derived from alignments to finished sequence only, and were calculated from windows covering the feature or 10,000 bp centred on the feature, whichever was larger.

30% to 50%. The correlation appears to be due primarily to intron size, which drops markedly with increasing GC content (Fig. 36c). In contrast, coding properties such as exon length (Fig. 36c) or exon number (data not shown) vary little. Intergenic distance is also probably lower in high-GC areas, although this is hard to prove directly until all genes have been identified.

The large number of confirmed human introns allows us to analyse variant splice sites, confirming and extending recent reports[281]. Intron positions were confirmed by applying a stringent criterion that EST or mRNA sequence show an exact match of 8 bp in the flanking exonic sequence on each side. Of 53,295 confirmed introns, 98.12% use the canonical dinucleotides GT at the 5′ splice site and AG at the 3′ site (GT–AG pattern). Another 0.76% use the related GC–AG. About 0.10% use AT–AC, which is a rare alternative pattern primarily recognized by the variant U12 splicing machinery[282]. The remaining 1% belong to 177 types, some of which undoubtedly reflect sequencing or alignment errors.

Finally, we looked at alternative splicing of human genes. Alternative splicing can allow many proteins to be produced from a single gene and can be used for complex gene regulation. It appears to be prevalent in humans, with lower estimates of about 35% of human genes being subject to alternative splicing[283–285]. These studies may have underestimated the prevalence of alternative splicing, because they examined only EST alignments covering only a portion of a gene.

To investigate the prevalence of alternative splicing, we analysed reconstructed mRNA transcripts covering the entire coding regions of genes on chromosome 22 (omitting small genes with coding regions of less than 240 bp). Potential transcripts identified by alignments of ESTs and cDNAs to genomic sequence were verified by human inspection. We found 642 transcripts, covering 245 genes (average of 2.6 distinct transcripts per gene). Two or more alternatively spliced transcripts were found for 145 (59%) of these genes. A similar analysis for the gene-rich chromosome 19 gave 1,859 transcripts, corresponding to 544 genes (average 3.2 distinct transcripts per gene). Because we are sampling only a subset of all transcripts, the true extent of alternative splicing is likely to be greater. These figures are considerably higher than those for worm, in which analysis reveals alternative splicing for 22% of genes for which ESTs have been found, with an average of 1.34 (12,816/9,516) splice variants per gene. (The apparently higher extent of alternative splicing seen in human than in worm was not an artefact resulting from much deeper coverage of human genes by ESTs and mRNAs. Although there are many times more ESTs available for human than worm, these ESTs tend to have shorter average length (because many were the product of early sequencing efforts) and many match no human genes. We calculated the actual coverage per bp used in the analysis of the human and worm genes; the coverage is only modestly higher (about 50%) for the human, with a strong bias towards 3′ UTRs which tend to show much less alternative splicing. We also repeated the analysis using equal coverage for the two organisms and confirmed that higher levels of alternative splicing were still seen in human.)

Seventy per cent of alternative splice forms found in the genes on chromosomes 19 and 22 affect the coding sequence, rather than merely changing the 3′ or 5′ UTR. (This estimate may be affected by the incomplete representation of UTRs in the RefSeq database and in the transcripts studied.) Alternative splicing of the terminal exon was seen for 20% of 6,105 mRNAs that were aligned to the draft genome sequence and correspond to confirmed 3′ EST clusters. In addition to alternative splicing, we found evidence of the terminal exon employing alternative polyadenylation sites (separated by > 100 bp) in 24% of cases.

Towards a complete index of human genes. We next focused on creating an initial index of human genes and proteins. This index is quite incomplete, owing to the difficulty of gene identification in human DNA and the imperfect state of the draft genome sequence.

Nonetheless, it is valuable for experimental studies and provides important insights into the nature of human genes and proteins.

The challenge of identifying genes from genomic sequence varies greatly among organisms. Gene identification is almost trivial in bacteria and yeast, because the absence of introns in bacteria and their paucity in yeast means that most genes can be readily recognized by ab initio analysis as unusually long ORFs. It is not as simple, but still relatively straightforward, to identify genes in animals with small genomes and small introns, such as worm and fly. A major factor is the high signal-to-noise ratio—coding sequences comprise a large proportion of the genome and a large proportion of each gene (about 50% for worm and fly), and exons are relatively large.

Gene identification is more difficult in human DNA. The signal-to-noise ratio is lower: coding sequences comprise only a few per cent of the genome and an average of about 5% of each gene; internal exons are smaller than in worms; and genes appear to have more alternative splicing. The challenge is underscored by the work on human chromosomes 21 and 22. Even with the availability of finished sequence and intensive experimental work, the gene content remains uncertain, with upper and lower estimates differing by as much as 30%. The initial report of the finished sequence of chromosome 22 (ref. 94) identified 247 previously known genes, 298 predicted genes confirmed by sequence homology or ESTs and 325 ab initio predictions without additional support. Many of the confirmed predictions represented partial genes. In the past year, 440 additional exons (10%) have been added to existing gene annotations by the chromosome 22 annotation group, although the number of confirmed genes has increased by only 17 and some previously identified gene predictions have been merged[286].

Before discussing the gene predictions for the human genome, it is useful to consider background issues, including previous estimates of the number of human genes, lessons learned from worms and flies and the representativeness of currently 'known' human genes.

Previous estimates of human gene number. Although direct enumeration of human genes is only now becoming possible with the advent of the draft genome sequence, there have been many attempts in the past quarter of a century to estimate the number of genes indirectly. Early estimates based on reassociation kinetics estimated the mRNA complexity of typical vertebrate tissues to be 10,000–20,000, and were extrapolated to suggest around 40,000 for the entire genome[287]. In the mid-1980s, Gilbert suggested that there might be about 100,000 genes, based on the approximate ratio of the size of a typical gene ($\sim 3 \times 10^4$ bp) to the size of the genome (3×10^9 bp). Although this was intended only as a back-of-the-envelope estimate, the pleasing roundness of the figure seems to have led to it being widely quoted and adopted in many textbooks. (W. Gilbert, personal communication; ref. 288). An estimate of 70,000–80,000 genes was made by extrapolating from the number of CpG islands and the frequency of their association with known genes[129].

As human sequence information has accumulated, it has been possible to derive estimates on the basis of sampling techniques[289]. Such studies have sought to extrapolate from various types of data, including ESTs, mRNAs from known genes, cross-species genome comparisons and analysis of finished chromosomes. Estimates based on ESTs[290] have varied widely, from 35,000 (ref. 130) to 120,000 genes[291]. Some of the discrepancy lies in differing estimates of the amount of contaminating genomic sequence in the EST collection and the extent to which multiple distinct ESTs correspond to a single gene. The most rigorous analyses[130] exclude as spurious any ESTs that appear only once in the data set and carefully calibrate sensitivity and specificity. Such calculations consistently produce low estimates, in the region of 35,000.

Comparison of whole-genome shotgun sequence from the pufferfish *T. nigroviridis* with the human genome[292] can be used to estimate the density of exons (detected as conserved sequences between fish and human). These analyses also suggest around 30,000 human genes.

Extrapolations have also been made from the gene counts for chromosomes 21 and 22 (refs 93, 94), adjusted for differences in gene densities on these chromosomes, as inferred from EST mapping. These estimates are between 30,500 and 35,500, depending on the precise assumptions used[286].

Insights from invertebrates. The worm and fly genomes contain a large proportion of novel genes (around 50% of worm genes and 30% of fly genes), in the sense of showing no significant similarity to organisms outside their phylum[293–295]. Such genes may have been present in the original eukaryotic ancestor, but were subsequently lost from the lineages of the other eukaryotes for which sequence is available; they may be rapidly diverging genes, so that it is difficult to recognize homologues solely on the basis of sequence; they may represent true innovations developed within the lineage; or they may represent acquisitions by horizontal transfer. Whatever their origin, these genes tend to have different biological properties from highly conserved genes. In particular, they tend to have low expression levels as assayed both by direct studies and by a paucity of corresponding ESTs, and are less likely to produce a visible phenotype in loss-of-function genetic experiments[294,296].

Gene prediction. Current gene prediction methods employ combinations of three basic approaches: direct evidence of transcription provided by ESTs or mRNAs[297–299]; indirect evidence based on sequence similarity to previously identified genes and proteins[300,301]; and *ab initio* recognition of groups of exons on the basis of hidden Markov models (HMMs) that combine statistical information about splice sites, coding bias and exon and intron lengths (for example, Genscan[275], Genie[302,303] and FGENES[304]).

The first approach relies on direct experimental data, but is subject to artefacts arising from contaminating ESTs derived from unspliced mRNAs, genomic DNA contamination and nongenic transcription (for example, from the promoter of a transposable element). The first two problems can be mitigated by comparing transcripts with the genomic sequence and using only those that show clear evidence of splicing. This solution, however, tends to discard evidence from genes with long terminal exons or single exons. The second approach tends correctly to identify gene-derived sequences, although some of these may be pseudogenes. However, it obviously cannot identify truly novel genes that have no sequence similarity to known genes. The third approach would suffice alone if one could accurately define the features used by cells for gene recognition, but our current understanding is insufficient to do so. The sensitivity and specificity of *ab initio* predictions are greatly affected by the signal-to-noise ratio. Such methods are more accurate in the fly and worm than in human. In fly, *ab initio* methods can correctly predict around 90% of individual exons and can correctly predict all coding exons of a gene in about 40% of cases[303]. For human, the comparable figures are only about 70% and 20%, respectively[94,305]. These estimates may be optimistic, owing to the design of the tests used.

In any collection of gene predictions, we can expect to see various errors. Some gene predictions may represent partial genes, because of inability to detect some portions of a gene (incomplete sensitivity) or to connect all the components of a gene (fragmentation); some may be gene fusions; and others may be spurious predictions (incomplete specificity) resulting from chance matches or pseudogenes.

Creating an initial gene index. We set out to create an initial integrated gene index (IGI) and an associated integrated protein index (IPI) for the human genome. We describe the results obtained from a version of the draft genome sequence based on the sequence data available in July 2000, to allow time for detailed analysis of the gene and protein content. The additional sequence data that has since become available will affect the results quantitatively, but are unlikely to change the conclusions qualitatively.

We began with predictions produced by the Ensembl system[306]. Ensembl starts with *ab initio* predictions produced by Genscan[275] and then attempts to confirm them by virtue of similarity to proteins, mRNAs, ESTs and protein motifs (contained in the Pfam database[307]) from any organism. In particular, it confirms introns if they are bridged by matches and exons if they are flanked by confirmed introns. It then attempts to extend protein matches using the GeneWise computer program[308]. Because it requires confirmatory evidence to support each gene component, it frequently produces partial gene predictions. In addition, when there is evidence of alternative splicing, it reports multiple overlapping transcripts. In total, Ensembl produced 35,500 gene predictions with 44,860 transcripts.

To reduce fragmentation, we next merged Ensembl-based gene predictions with overlapping gene predictions from another program, Genie[302]. Genie starts with mRNA or EST matches and employs an HMM to extend these matches by using *ab initio* statistical approaches. To avoid fragmentation, it attempts to link information from 5′ and 3′ ESTs from the same cDNA clone and thereby to produce a complete coding sequence from an initial ATG to a stop codon. As a result, it may generate complete genes more accurately than Ensembl in cases where there is extensive EST support. (Genie also generates potential alternative transcripts, but we used only the longest transcript in each group.) We merged 15,437 Ensembl predictions into 9,526 clusters, and the longest transcript in each cluster (from either Genie or Ensembl) was taken as the representative.

Next, we merged these results with known genes contained in the RefSeq (version of 29 September 2000), SWISSPROT (release 39.6 of 30 August 2000) and TrEMBL databases (TrEMBL release 14.17 of 1 October 2000, TrEMBL_new of 1 October 2000). Incorporating these sequences gave rise to overlapping sequences because of alternative splice forms and partial sequences. To construct a nonredundant set, we selected the longest sequence from each overlapping set by using direct protein comparison and by mapping the gene predictions back onto the genome to construct the overlapping sets. This may occasionally remove some close paralogues in the event that the correct genomic location has not yet been sequenced, but this number is expected to be small.

Finally, we searched the set to eliminate any genes derived from contaminating bacterial sequences, recognized by virtue of near identity to known bacterial plasmids, transposons and chromosomal genes. Although most instances of such contamination had been removed in the assembly process, a few cases had slipped through and were removed at this stage.

The process resulted in version 1 of the IGI (IGI.1). The composition of the corresponding IPI.1 protein set, obtained by translating IGI.1, is given in Table 22. There are 31,778 protein predictions, with 14,882 from known genes, 4,057 predictions from Ensembl merged with Genie and 12,839 predictions from Ensembl alone. The average lengths are 469 amino acids for the known proteins, 443 amino acids for protein predictions from the Ensembl–Genie merge, and 187 amino acids for those from Ensembl alone. (The smaller average size for the predictions from Ensembl alone reflects its tendency to predict partial genes where there is supporting evidence for only part of the gene; the remainder of the gene will often not be predicted at all, rather than included as part of another prediction. Accordingly, the smaller size cannot be used to estimate the rate of fragmentation in such predictions.)

The set corresponds to fewer than 31,000 actual genes, because some genes are fragmented into more than one partial prediction and some predictions may be spurious or correspond to pseudogenes. As discussed below, our best estimate is that IGI.1 includes about 24,500 true genes.

Evaluation of IGI/IPI. We used several approaches to evaluate the sensitivity, specificity and fragmentation of the IGI/IPI set.

Comparison with 'new' known genes. One approach was to examine

Table 22 Properties of the IGI/IPI human protein set

Source	Number	Average length (amino acids)	Matches to nonhuman proteins	Matches to RIKEN mouse cDNA set	Matches to RIKEN mouse cDNA set but not to nonhuman proteins
RefSeq/SwissProt/TrEMBL	14,882	469	12,708 (85%)	11,599 (78%)	776 (36%)
Ensembl–Genie	4,057	443	2,989 (74%)	3,016 (74%)	498 (47%)
Ensembl	12,839	187	81,126 (63%)	7,372 (57%)	1,449 (31%)
Total	31,778	352	23,813 (75%)	219,873 (69%)	2,723 (34%)

The matches to nonhuman proteins were obtained by using Smith-Waterman sequence alignment with an E-value threshold of 10^{-3} and the matches to the RIKEN mouse cDNAs by using TBLASTN with an E-value threshold of 10^{-6}. The last column shows that a significant number of the IGI members that do not have nonhuman protein matches do match sequences in the RIKEN mouse cDNA set, suggesting that both the IGI and the RIKEN sets contain a significant number of novel proteins.

newly discovered genes arising from independent work that were not used in our gene prediction effort. We identified 31 such genes: 22 recent entries to RefSeq and 9 from the Sanger Centre's gene identification program on chromosome X. Of these, 28 were contained in the draft genome sequence and 19 were represented in the IGI/IPI. This suggests that the gene prediction process has a sensitivity of about 68% (19/28) for the detection of novel genes in the draft genome sequence and that the current IGI contains about 61% (19/31) of novel genes in the human genome. On average, 79% of each gene was detected. The extent of fragmentation could also be estimated: 14 of the genes corresponded to a single prediction in the IGI/IPI, three genes corresponded to two predictions, one gene to three predictions and one gene to four predictions. This corresponds to a fragmentation rate of about 1.4 gene predictions per true gene.

Comparison with RIKEN mouse cDNAs. In a less direct but larger-scale approach, we compared the IGI gene set to a set of mouse cDNAs sequenced by the Genome Exploration Group of the RIKEN Genomic Sciences Center[309]. This set of 15,294 cDNAs, subjected to full-insert sequencing, was enriched for novel genes by selecting cDNAs with novel 3′ ends from a collection of nearly one million ESTs from diverse tissues and developmental timepoints. We determined the proportion of the RIKEN cDNAs that showed sequence similarity to the draft genome sequence and the proportion that showed sequence similarity to the IGI/IPI. Around 81% of the genes in the RIKEN mouse set showed sequence similarity to the human genome sequence, whereas 69% showed sequence similarity to the IGI/IPI. This suggests a sensitivity of 85% (69/81). This is higher than the sensitivity estimate above, perhaps because some of the matches may be due to paralogues rather than orthologues. It is consistent with the IGI/IPI representing a substantial fraction of the human proteome.

Conversely, 69% (22,013/31,898) of the IGI matches the RIKEN cDNA set. Table 22 shows the breakdown of these matches among the different components of the IGI. This is lower than the proportion of matches among known proteins, although this is expected because known proteins tend to be more highly conserved (see above) and because the predictions are on average shorter than known proteins. Table 22 also shows the numbers of matches to the RIKEN cDNAs among IGI members that do not match known proteins. The results indicate that both the IGI and the RIKEN set contain a significant number of genes that are novel in the sense of not having known protein homologues.

Comparison with genes on chromosome 22. We also compared the IGI/IPI with the gene annotations on chromosome 22, to assess the proportion of gene predictions corresponding to pseudogenes and to estimate the rate of overprediction. We compared 477 IGI gene predictions to 539 confirmed genes and 133 pseudogenes on chromosome 22 (with the immunoglobulin lambda locus excluded owing to its highly atypical gene structure). Of these, 43 hit 36 annotated pseudogenes. This suggests that 9% of the IGI predictions may correspond to pseudogenes and also suggests a fragmentation rate of 1.2 gene predictions per gene. Of the remaining hits, 63 did not overlap with any current annotations. This would suggest a rate of spurious predictions of about 13% (63/477), although the true rate is likely to be much lower because many of these may correspond to unannotated portions of existing gene predictions or to currently unannotated genes (of which there are estimated to be about 100 on this chromosome[94]).

Chromosomal distribution. Finally, we examined the chromosomal distribution of the IGI gene set. The average density of gene predictions is 11.1 per Mb across the genome, with the extremes being chromosome 19 at 26.8 per Mb and chromosome Y at 6.4 per Mb. It is likely that a significant number of the predictions on chromosome Y are pseudogenes (this chromosome is known to be rich in pseudogenes) and thus that the density for chromosome Y is an overestimate. The density of both genes and Alus on chromosome 19 is much higher than expected, even accounting for the high GC content of the chromosome; this supports the idea that Alu density is more closely correlated with gene density than with GC content itself.

Summary. We are clearly still some way from having a complete set of human genes. The current IGI contains significant numbers of partial genes, fragmented and fused genes, pseudogenes and spurious predictions, and it also lacks significant numbers of true genes. This reflects the current state of gene prediction methods in vertebrates even in finished sequence, as well as the additional challenges related to the current state of the draft genome sequence. Nonetheless, the gene predictions provide a valuable starting point for a wide range of biological studies and will be rapidly refined in the coming year.

The analysis above allows us to estimate the number of distinct genes in the IGI, as well as the number of genes in the human genome. The IGI set contains about 15,000 known genes and about 17,000 gene predictions. Assuming that the gene predictions are subject to a rate of overprediction (spurious predictions and pseudogenes) of 20% and a rate of fragmentation of 1.4, the IGI would be estimated to contain about 24,500 actual human genes. Assuming that the gene predictions contain about 60% of previously unknown human genes, the total number of genes in the human genome would be estimated to be about 31,000. This is consistent with most recent estimates based on sampling, which suggest a gene number of 30,000–35,000. If there are 30,000–35,000 genes, with an average coding length of about 1,400 bp and average genomic extent of about 30 kb, then about 1.5% of the human genome would consist of coding sequence and one-third of the genome would be transcribed in genes.

The IGI/IPI was constructed primarily on the basis of gene predictions from Ensembl. However, we also generated an expanded set (IGI+) by including additional predictions from two other gene prediction programs, Genie and GenomeScan (C. Burge, personal communication). These predictions were not included in the core IGI set, because of the concern that each additional set will provide diminishing returns in identifying true genes while contributing its own false positives (increased sensitivity at the expense of specificity). Genie produced an additional 2,837 gene predictions not overlapping the IGI, and GenomeScan produced 6,534 such gene predictions. If all of these gene predictions were included in the IGI, the number of the 31 new 'known' genes (see above) contained in the IGI would rise from 19 to 24. This would amount to an increase of about 26% in sensitivity, at the expense of increasing the number of predicted genes (excluding knowns) by 55%. Allowing a higher overprediction rate of 30% for gene predictions in this expanded set, the analysis above suggests that IGI+ set contains about 28,000 true genes and yields an estimate of about 32,000 human genes. We are investigating ways to filter the expanded set, to produce an IGI with the advantage of the increased sensitivity resulting from combining multiple gene prediction programs without the corresponding loss of specificity. Meanwhile, the IGI+ set can be used by researchers searching for genes that cannot be found in the IGI.

Some classes of genes may have been missed by all of the gene-finding methods. Genes could be missed if they are expressed at low levels or in rare tissues (being absent or very under-represented in EST and mRNA databases) and have sequences that evolve rapidly (being hard to detect by protein homology and genome comparison). Both the worm and fly gene sets contain a substantial number of such genes[293,294]. Single-exon genes encoding small proteins may also have been missed, because EST evidence that supports them cannot be distinguished from genomic contamination in the EST dataset and because homology may be hard to detect for small proteins[310].

The human thus appears to have only about twice as many genes as worm or fly. However, human genes differ in important respects from those in worm and fly. They are spread out over much larger regions of genomic DNA, and they are used to construct more alternative transcripts. This may result in perhaps five times as many primary protein products in the human as in the worm or fly.

The predicted gene and protein sets described here are clearly far from final. Nonetheless, they provide a valuable starting point for experimental and computational research. The predictions will improve progressively as the sequence is finished, as further confirmatory evidence becomes available (particularly from other vertebrate genome sequences, such as those of mouse and *T. nigroviridis*), and as computational methods improve. We intend to create and release updated versions of the IGI and IPI regularly, until they converge to a final accurate list of every human gene. The gene predictions will be linked to RefSeq, HUGO and SWISSPROT identifiers where available, and tracking identifiers between versions will be included, so that individual genes under study can be traced forwards as the human sequence is completed.

Comparative proteome analysis

Knowledge of the human proteome will provide unprecedented opportunities for studies of human gene function. Often clues will be provided by sequence similarity with proteins of known function in model organisms. Such initial observations must then be followed up by detailed studies to establish the actual function of these molecules in humans.

For example, 35 proteins are known to be involved in the vacuolar protein-sorting machinery in yeast. Human genes encoding homologues can be found in the draft human sequence for 34 of these yeast proteins, but precise relationships are not always clear. In nine cases there appears to be a single clear human orthologue (a gene that arose as a consequence of speciation); in 12 cases there are matches to a family of human paralogues (genes that arose owing to intra-genome duplication); and in 13 cases there are matches to specific protein domains[311–314]. Hundreds of similar stories emerge from the draft sequence, but each merits a detailed interpretation in context. To treat these subjects properly, there will be many following studies, the first of which appear in accompanying papers[315–323].

Here, we aim to take a more global perspective on the content of the human proteome by comparing it with the proteomes of yeast, worm, fly and mustard weed. Such comparisons shed useful light on the commonalities and differences among these eukaryotes[294,324,325]. The analysis is necessarily preliminary, because of the imperfect nature of the human sequence, uncertainties in the gene and protein sets for all of the multicellular organisms considered and our incomplete knowledge of protein structures. Nonetheless, some general patterns emerge. These include insights into fundamental mechanisms that create functional diversity, including invention of protein domains, expansion of protein and domain families, evolution of new protein architectures and horizontal transfer of genes. Other mechanisms, such as alternative splicing, post-translational modification and complex regulatory networks, are also crucial in generating diversity but are much harder to discern from the primary sequence. We will not attempt to consider the effects of alternative splicing on proteins; we will consider only a single splice form from each gene in the various organisms, even when multiple splice forms are known.

Functional and evolutionary classification. We began by classifying the human proteome on the basis of functional categories and evolutionary conservation. We used the InterPro annotation protocol to identify conserved biochemical and cellular processes. InterPro is a tool for combining sequence-pattern information from four databases. The first two databases (PRINTS[326] and Prosite[327]) primarily contain information about motifs corresponding to specific family subtypes, such as type II receptor tyrosine kinases (RTK-II) in particular or tyrosine kinases in general. The second two databases (Pfam[307] and Prosite Profile[327]) contain information (in the form of profiles or HMMs) about families of structural domains—for example, protein kinase domains. InterPro integrates the motif and domain assignments into a hierarchical classification system; so a protein might be classified at the most detailed level as being an RTK-II, at a more general level as being a kinase specific for tyrosine, and at a still more general level as being a protein kinase. The complete hierarchy of InterPro entries is described at http://www.ebi.ac.uk/interpro/. We collapsed the InterPro entries into 12 broad categories, each reflecting a set of cellular functions.

The InterPro families are partly the product of human judgement and reflect the current state of biological and evolutionary knowledge. The system is a valuable way to gain insight into large collections of proteins, but not all proteins can be classified at present. The proportions of the yeast, worm, fly and mustard weed protein sets that are assigned to at least one InterPro family is, for each organism, about 50% (Table 23; refs 307, 326, 327).

About 40% of the predicted human proteins in the IPI could be assigned to InterPro entries and functional categories. On the basis of these assignments, we could compare organisms according to the number of proteins in each category (Fig. 37). Compared with the two invertebrates, humans appear to have many proteins involved in cytoskeleton, defence and immunity, and transcription and translation. These expansions are clearly related to aspects of vertebrate physiology. Humans also have many more proteins that are classified as falling into more than one functional category (426 in human versus 80 in worm and 57 in fly, data not shown). Interestingly, 32% of these are transmembrane receptors.

We obtained further insight into the evolutionary conservation of proteins by comparing each sequence to the complete nonredundant database of protein sequences maintained at NCBI, using the BLASTP computer program[328] and then breaking down the matches according to organismal taxonomy (Fig. 38). Overall, 74% of the proteins had significant matches to known proteins.

Such classifications are based on the presence of clearly detectable homologues in existing databases. Many of these genes have surely evolved from genes that were present in common ancestors but have since diverged substantially. Indeed, one can detect more distant relationships by using sensitive computer programs that can recognize weakly conserved features. Using PSI-BLAST, we can recognize probable nonvertebrate homologues for about 45% of the 'vertebrate-specific' set. Nonetheless, the classification is useful for gaining insights into the commonalities and differences among the proteomes of different organisms.

Probable horizontal transfer. An interesting category is a set of 223 proteins that have significant similarity to proteins from bacteria, but no comparable similarity to proteins from yeast, worm, fly and

Table 23 Properties of genome and proteome in essentially completed eukaryotic proteomes

	Human	Fly	Worm	Yeast	Mustard weed
Number of identified genes	~32,000*	13,338	18,266	6,144	25,706
% with InterPro matches	51	56	50	50	52
Number of annotated domain families	1,262	1,035	1,014	851	1,010
Number of InterPro entries per gene	0.53	0.84	0.63	0.6	0.62
Number of distinct domain architectures	1,695	1,036	1,018	310	–
Percentage of 1-1-1-1	1.40	4.20	3.10	9.20	–
% Signal sequences	20	20	24	11	–
% Transmembrane proteins	20	25	28	15	–
% Repeat-containing	10	11	9	5	–
% Coiled-coil	11	13	10	9	–

The numbers of distinct architectures were calculated using SMART[339] and the percentages of repeat-containing proteins were estimated using Prospero[452] and a *P*-value threshold of 10⁻⁵. The protein sets used in the analysis were taken from http://www.ebi.ac.uk/proteome/ for yeast, worm and fly. The proteins from mustard weed were taken from the TAIR website (http:// www.arabidopsis.org/) on 5 September 2000. The protein set was searched against the InterPro database (http://www.ebi.ac.uk/interpro/) using the InterProscan software. Comparison of protein sequences with the InterPro database allows prediction of protein families, domain and repeat families and sequence motifs. The searches used Pfam release 5.2[307], Prints release 26.1[326], Prosite release 16[327] and Prosite preliminary profiles. InterPro analysis results are available as Supplementary Information. The fraction of 1-1-1-1 is the percentage of the genome that falls into orthologous groups composed of only one member each in human, fly, worm and yeast.
* The gene number for the human is still uncertain (see text). Table is based on 31,778 known genes and gene predictions.

mustard weed, or indeed from any other (nonvertebrate) eukaryote. These sequences should not represent bacterial contamination in the draft human sequence, because we filtered the sequence to eliminate sequences that were essentially identical to known bacterial plasmid, transposon or chromosomal DNA (such as the host strains for the large-insert clones). To investigate whether these were genuine human sequences, we designed PCR primers for 35 of these genes and confirmed that most could be readily detected directly in human genomic DNA (Table 24). Orthologues of many of these genes have also been detected in other vertebrates (Table 24).

A more detailed computational analysis indicated that at least 113 of these genes are widespread among bacteria, but, among eukaryotes, appear to be present only in vertebrates. It is possible that the genes encoding these proteins were present in both early prokaryotes and eukaryotes, but were lost in each of the lineages of yeast, worm, fly, mustard weed and, possibly, from other nonvertebrate eukaryote lineages. A more parsimonious explanation is that these genes entered the vertebrate (or prevertebrate) lineage by horizontal transfer from bacteria. Many of these genes contain introns, which presumably were acquired after the putative horizontal transfer event. Similar observations indicating probable lineage-specific horizontal gene transfers, as well as intron insertion in the acquired genes, have been made in the worm genome[329].

We cannot formally exclude the possibility that gene transfer occurred in the opposite direction—that is, that the genes were invented in the vertebrate lineage and then transferred to bacteria. However, we consider this less likely. Under this scenario, the broad distribution of these genes among bacteria would require extensive horizontal dissemination after their initial acquisition. In addition, the functional repertoire of these genes, which largely encode intracellular enzymes (Table 24), is uncharacteristic of vertebrate-specific evolutionary innovations (which appear to be primarily extracellular proteins; see below).

We did not identify a strongly preferred bacterial source for the putative horizontally transferred genes, indicating the likelihood of multiple independent gene transfers from different bacteria (Table 24). Notably, several of the probable recent acquisitions have established (or likely) roles in metabolism of xenobiotics or stress response. These include several hydrolases of different specificities, including epoxide hydrolase, and several dehydrogenases (Table 24). Of particular interest is the presence of two paralogues of monoamine oxidase (MAO), an enzyme of the mitochondrial outer membrane that is central in the metabolism of neuromediators and is a target of important psychiatric drugs[330–333]. This example shows that at least some of the genes thought to be horizontally transferred into the vertebrate lineage appear to be involved in important physiological functions and so probably have been fixed and maintained during evolution because

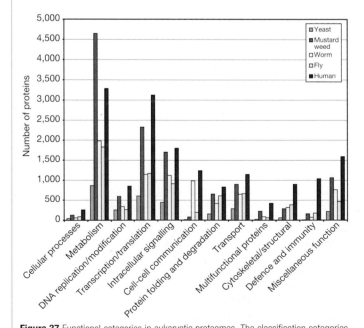

Figure 37 Functional categories in eukaryotic proteomes. The classification categories were derived from functional classification systems, including the top-level biological function category of the Gene Ontology project (GO; see http://www.geneontology.org).

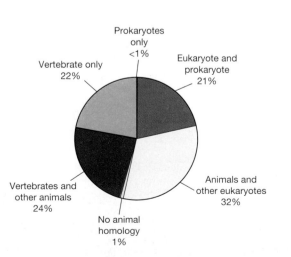

Figure 38 Distribution of the homologues of the predicted human proteins. For each protein, a homologue to a phylogenetic lineage was considered present if a search of the NCBI nonredundant protein sequence database, using the gapped BLASTP program, gave a random expectation (*E*) value of ≤ 0.001. Additional searches for probable homologues with lower sequence conservation were performed using the PSI-BLAST program, run for three iterations using the same cut-off for inclusion of sequences into the profile[328].

of the increased selective advantage(s) they provide.

Genes shared with fly, worm and yeast. IPI.1 contains apparent homologues of 61% of the fly proteome, 43% of the worm proteome and 46% of the yeast proteome. We next considered the groups of proteins containing likely orthologues and paralogues (genes that arose from intragenome duplication) in human, fly, worm and yeast.

Briefly, we performed all-against-all sequence comparison[334] for the combined protein sets of human, yeast, fly and worm. Pairs of sequences that were one another's best matches in their respective genomes were considered to be potential orthologues. These were then used to identify orthologous groups across three organisms[335]. Recent species-specific paralogues were defined by using the all-against-all sequence comparison to cluster the protein set for each organism. For each sequence found in an orthologous group, the recent paralogues were defined to be the largest species-specific cluster including it. The set of paralogues may be inflated by unrecognized splice variants and by fragmentation.

We identified 1,308 groups of proteins, each containing at least one predicted orthologue in each species and many containing additional paralogues. The 1,308 groups contained 3,129 human proteins, 1,445 fly proteins, 1,503 worm proteins and 1,441 yeast proteins. These 1,308 groups represent a conserved core of proteins that are mostly responsible for the basic 'housekeeping' functions of the cell, including metabolism, DNA replication and repair, and translation.

In 564 of the 1,308 groups, one orthologue (and no additional paralogues) could be unambiguously assigned for each of human, fly, worm and yeast. These groups will be referred to as 1-1-1-1 groups. More than half (305) of these groups could be assigned to the functional categories shown in Fig. 37. Within these functional categories, the numbers of groups containing single orthologues in each of the four proteomes was: 19 for cellular processes, 66 for metabolism, 31 for DNA replication and modification, 106 for transcription/translation, 13 for intracellular signalling, 24 for protein folding and degradation, 38 for transport, 5 for

Table 24 Probable vertebrate-specific acquisitions of bacterial genes

Human protein (accession)	Predicted function	Known orthologues in other vertebrates	Bacterial homologues		Human origin confirmed by PCR
			Range	Best hit	
AAG01853.1	Formiminotransferase cyclodeaminase	Pig, rat, chicken	*Thermotoga, Thermoplasma, Methylobacter*	*Thermotoga maritima*	Yes
CAB81772.1	Na/glucose cotransporter	Rodents, ungulates	Most bacteria	*Vibrio parahaemolyticus*	Yes (CAB81772, AAC41747.1)
AAB59448.1					NT* (AAB59448.1, AAA36608.1)
AAA36608.1					
AAC41747.1					
BAA1143.21	Epoxide hydrolase (α/β-hydrolase)	Mouse, *Danio*, fugu fish	Most bacteria	*Pseudomonas aeruginosa*	Yes
CAB59628.1	Protein-methionine-*S*-oxide reductase	Cow	Most bacteria	*Synechocystis sp.*	Yes
BAA91273.1	Hypertension-associated protein SA/ acetate-CoA ligase	Mouse, rat, cow	Most bacteria	*Bacillus halodurans*	NT*
CAA75608.1	Glucose-6-phosphate transporter/ glycogen storage disease type 1b protein	Mouse, rat	Most bacteria	*Chlamydophila pneumoniae*	Yes
AAA59548.1	Monoamine oxidase	Cow, rat, salmon	Most bacteria	*Mycobacterium tuberculosis*	Yes
AAB27229.1					
AAF12736.1	Acyl-CoA dehydrogenase, mitochondrial protein	Mouse, rat, pig	Most bacteria	*P. aeruginosa*	Yes
AAA51565.1					
IGI_M1_ctg19153_147	Aldose-1-epimerase	Pig (also found in plants)	*Streptomyces, Bacillus*	*Streptomyces coelicolor*	Yes
BAA92632.1	Predicted carboxylase (C-terminal domain, N-terminal domain unique)	None	*Streptomyces, Rhizobium, Bacillus*	*S. coelicolor*	Yes
BAA34458.1	Uncharacterized protein	None	Gamma-proteobacteria	*Escherichia coli*	Yes
AAF24044.1	Uncharacterized protein	None	Most bacteria	*T. maritima*	Yes
BAA34458.1	β-Lactamase superfamily hydrolase	None	Most bacteria	*Synechocystis sp.*	Yes
BAA91839.1	Oxidoreductase (Rossmann fold) fused to a six-transmembrane protein	None (several human paralogues of both parts)	*Actinomycetes, Leptospira*; more distant homologues in other bacteria	*S. coelicolor*	Yes
BAA92073.1	Oxidoreductase (Rossmann fold)	None	*Synechocystis, Pseudomonas*	*Synechocystis sp.*	Yes
BAA92133.1	α/β-hydrolase	None	*Rickettsia*; more distant homologues in other bacteria	*Rickettsia prowazekii*	Yes
BAA91174.1	ADP-ribosylglycohydrolase	None	*Streptomyces, Aquifex, Archaeoglobus* (archaeon), *E. coli*	*S. coelicolor*	Yes
AAA60043.1	Thymidine phosporylase/endothelial cell growth factor	None	Most bacteria	*Bacillus stearothermophilus*	Yes
BAA86552.1	Ribosomal protein S6-glutamic acid ligase	None	Most bacteria and archaea	*Haemophilus influenzae*	Yes
IGI_M1_ctg12741_7	Ribosomal protein S6-glutamic acid ligase (paralogue of the above)	None	Most bacteria and archaea	*H. influenzae*	Yes
IGI_M1_ctg13238_61	Hydratase	None	*Synechocystis, Sphingomonas*	*Synechocystis sp.*	Yes
IGI_M1_ctg13305_116	Homologue of histone macro-2A C-terminal domain, predicted phosphatase	None (several human paralogues, RNA viruses)	*Thermotoga, Alcaligenes, E. coli*, more distant homologues in other bacteria	*T. maritima*	Yes
IGI_M1_ctg14420_10	Sugar transporter	None	Most bacteria	*Synechocystis sp.*	Yes
IGI_M1_ctg16010_18	Predicted metal-binding protein	None	Most bacteria	*Borrelia burgdorferi*	Yes
IGI_M1_ctg16227_58	Pseudouridine synthase	None	Most bacteria	*Zymomonas mobilis*	Yes
IGI_M1_ctg25107_24	Surfactin synthetase domain	None	Gram-positive bacteria, Actinomycetes, Cyanobacteria	*Bacillus subtilis*	Yes

* NT, not tested.
Representative genes confirmed by PCR to be present in the human genome. The similarity to a bacterial homologue was considered to be 'significantly' greater than that to eukaryotic homologues if the difference in alignment scores returned by BLASTP was greater than 30 bits (~9 orders of magnitude in terms of *E*-value). A complete, classified and annotated list of probable vertebrate-specific horizontal gene transfers detected in this analysis is available as Supplementary Information. cDNA sequences for each protein were searched, using the SSAHA algorithm, against the draft genome sequence. Primers were designed and PCR was performed using three human genomic samples and a random BAC clone. The predicted genes were considered to be present in the human genome if a band of the expected size was found in all three human samples but not in the control clone.

multifunctional proteins and 3 for cytoskeletal/structural. No such groups were found for defence and immunity or cell–cell communication.

The 1-1-1-1 groups probably represent key functions that have not undergone duplication and elaboration in the various lineages. They include many anabolic enzymes responsible for such functions as respiratory chain and nucleotide biosynthesis. In contrast, there are few catabolic enzymes. As anabolic pathways branch less frequently than catabolic pathways, this indicates that alternative routes and displacements are more frequent in catabolic reactions. If proteins from the single-celled yeast are excluded from the analysis, there are 1,195 1-1-1 groups. The additional groups include many examples of more complex signalling proteins, such as receptor-type and src-like tyrosine kinases, likely to have arisen early in the metazoan lineage. The fact that this set comprises only a small proportion of the proteome of each of the animals indicates that, apart from a modest conserved core, there has been extensive elaboration and innovation within the protein complement.

Most proteins do not show simple 1-1-1 orthologous relationships across the three animals. To illustrate this, we investigated the nuclear hormone receptor family. In the human proteome, this family consists of 60 different 'classical' members, each with a zinc finger and a ligand-binding domain. In comparison, the fly proteome has 19 and the worm proteome has 220. As shown in Fig. 39, few simple orthologous relationships can be derived among these homologues. And, where potential subgroups of orthologues and

paralogues could be identified, it was apparent that the functions of the subgroup members could differ significantly. For example, the fly receptor for the fly-specific hormone ecdysone and the human retinoic acid receptors cluster together on the basis of sequence similarity. Such examples underscore that the assignment of functional similarity on the basis of sequence similarities among these three organisms is not trivial in most cases.

New vertebrate domains and proteins. We then explored how the proteome of vertebrates (as represented by the human) differs from those of the other species considered. The 1,262 InterPro families were scanned to identify those that contain only vertebrate proteins. Only 94 (7%) of the families were 'vertebrate-specific'. These represent 70 protein families and 24 domain families. Only one of the 94 families represents enzymes, which is consistent with the ancient origins of most enzymes[336]. The single vertebrate-specific enzyme family identified was the pancreatic or eosinophil-associated ribonucleases. These enzymes evolved rapidly, possibly to combat vertebrate pathogens[337].

The relatively small proportion of vertebrate-specific multicopy families suggests that few new protein domains have been invented in the vertebrate lineage, and that most protein domains trace at least as far back as a common animal ancestor. This conclusion must be tempered by the fact that the InterPro classification system is incomplete; additional vertebrate-specific families undoubtedly exist that have not yet been recognized in the InterPro system.

The 94 vertebrate-specific families appear to reflect important physiological differences between vertebrates and other eukaryotes. Defence and immunity proteins (23 families) and proteins that function in the nervous system (17 families) are particularly enriched in this set. These data indicate the recent emergence or rapid divergence of these proteins.

Representative human proteins were previously known for nearly all of the vertebrate-specific families. This was not surprising, given the anthropocentrism of biological research. However, the analysis did identify the first mammalian proteins belonging to two of these families. Both of these families were originally defined in fish. The first is the family of polar fish antifreeze III proteins. We found a human sialic acid synthase containing a domain homologous to polar fish antifreeze III protein (BAA91818.1). This finding suggests that fish created the antifreeze function by adaptation of this domain. We also found a human protein (CAB60269.1) homologous to the ependymin found in teleost fish. Ependymins are major glycoproteins of fish brains that have been claimed to be involved in long-term memory formation[338]. The function of the mammalian ependymin homologue will need to be elucidated.

New architectures from old domains. Whereas there appears to be only modest invention at the level of new vertebrate protein domains, there appears to be substantial innovation in the creation of new vertebrate proteins. This innovation is evident at the level of domain architecture, defined as the linear arrangement of domains within a polypeptide. New architectures can be created by shuffling, adding or deleting domains, resulting in new proteins from old parts.

We quantified the number of distinct protein architectures found in yeast, worm, fly and human by using the SMART annotation resource[339] (Fig. 40). The human proteome set contained 1.8 times as many protein architectures as worm or fly and 5.8 times as many as yeast. This difference is most prominent in the recent evolution of novel extracellular and transmembrane architectures in the human lineage. Human extracellular proteins show the greatest innovation: the human has 2.3 times as many extracellular architectures as fly and 2.0 times as many as worm. The larger number of human architectures does not simply reflect differences in the number of domains known in these organisms; the result remains qualitatively the same even if the number of architectures in each organism is normalized by dividing by the total number of domains (not shown). (We also checked that the larger number of human

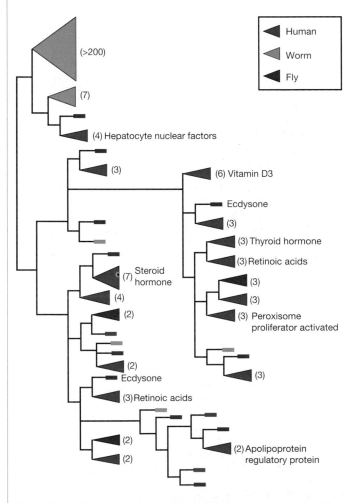

Figure 39 Simplified cladogram (relationship tree) of the 'many-to-many' relationships of classical nuclear receptors. Triangles indicate expansion within one lineage; bars represent single members. Numbers in parentheses indicate the number of paralogues in each group.

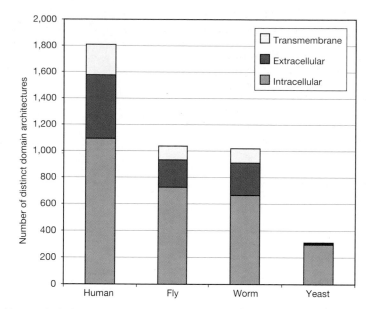

Figure 40 Number of distinct domain architectures in the four eukaryotic genomes, predicted using SMART[339]. The number of architectures is split into three cellular environments: intracellular, extracellular and membrane-associated. The increase in architectures for the human, relative to the other lineages, is seen when these numbers are normalized with respect to the numbers of domains predicted in each phylum. To avoid artefactual results from the relatively low detection rate for some repeat types, tandem occurrences of tetratricopeptide, armadillo, EF-hand, leucine-rich, WD40 or ankyrin repeats or C2H2-type zinc fingers were treated as single occurrences.

architectures could not be an artefact resulting from erroneous gene predictions. Three-quarters of the architectures can be found in known genes, which already yields an increase of about 50% over worm and fly. We expect the final number of human architectures to grow as the complete gene set is identified.)

A related measure of proteome complexity can be obtained by considering an individual domain and counting the number of different domain types with which it co-occurs. For example, the trypsin-like serine protease domain (number 12 in Fig. 41) co-occurs with 18 domain types in human (including proteins involved in the mammalian complement system, blood coagulation, and fibrinolytic and related systems). By contrast, the trypsin-like serine protease domain occurs with only eight other domains in fly, five in worm and one in yeast. Similar results for 27 common domains are shown in Fig. 41. In general, there are more different co-occurring domains in the human proteome than in the other proteomes.

One mechanism by which architectures evolve is through the fusion of additional domains, often at one or both ends of the proteins. Such 'domain accretion'[340] is seen in many human proteins when compared with proteins from other eukaryotes. The effect is illustrated by several chromatin-associated proteins (Fig. 42). In these examples, the domain architectures of human proteins differ from those found in yeast, worm and fly proteins only by the addition of domains at their termini.

Among chromatin-associated proteins and transcription factors, a significant proportion of domain architectures is shared between the vertebrate and fly, but not with worm (Fig. 43a). The trend was even more prominent in architectures of proteins involved in another key cellular process, programmed cell death (Fig. 43b). These examples might seem to bear upon the unresolved issue of the evolutionary branching order of worms, flies and humans, suggesting that worms branched off first. However, there were other cases in which worms and humans shared architectures not present in fly. A global analysis of shared architectures could not conclusively distinguish between the two models, given the possibility of lineage-specific loss of architectures. Comparison of protein architectures may help to resolve the evolutionary issue, but it will require more detailed analyses of many protein families.

New physiology from old proteins. An important aspect of

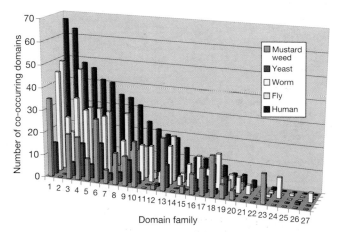

Figure 41 Number of different Pfam domain types that co-occur in the same protein, for each of the 10 most common domain families in each of the five eukaryotic proteomes. Because some common domain families are shared, there are 27 families rather than 50. The data are ranked according to decreasing numbers of human co-occurring Pfam domains. The domain families are: (1) eukaryotic protein kinase [IPR000719]; (2) immunoglobulin domain [IPR003006]; (3) ankyrin repeat [IPR002110]; (4) RING finger [IPR001841]; (5) C2H2-type zinc finger [IPR000822]; (6) ATP/GTP-binding P-loop [IPR001687]; (7) reverse transcriptase (RNA-dependent DNA polymerase) [IPR000477]; (8) leucine-rich repeat [IPR001611]; (9) G-proteinβ WD-40 repeats [IPR001680]; (10) RNA-binding region RNP-1 (RNA recognition motif) [IPR000504]; (11) C-type lectin domain [IPR001304]; (12) serine proteases, trypsin family [IPR001254]; (13) helicase C-terminal domain [IPR001650]; (14) collagen triple helix repeat [IPR000087]; (15) rhodopsin-like GPCR superfamily [IPR000276]; (16) esterase/lipase/thioesterase [IPR000379]; (17) Myb DNA-binding domain [IPR001005]; (18) F-box domain [IPR001810]; (19) ATP-binding transport protein, 2nd P-loop motif [IPR001051]; (20) homeobox domain [IPR001356]; (21) C4-type steroid receptor zinc finger [IPR001628]; (22) sugar transporter [IPR001066]; (23) PPR repeats [IPR002885]; (24) seven-helix G-protein-coupled receptor, worm (probably olfactory) family [IPR000168]; (25) cytochrome P450 enzyme [IPR001128]; (26) fungal transcriptional regulatory protein, N terminus [IPR001138]; (27) domain of unknown function DUF38 [IPR002900].

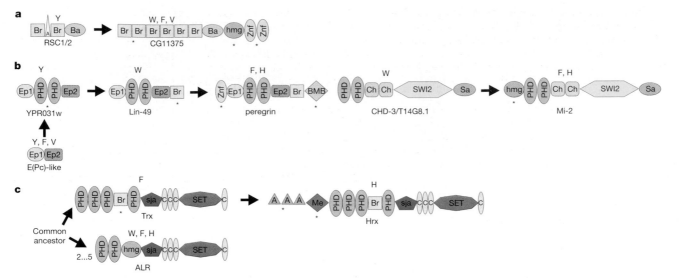

Figure 42 Examples of domain accretion in chromatin proteins. Domain accretion in various lineages before the animal divergence, in the apparent coelomate lineage and the vertebrate lineage are shown using schematic representations of domain architectures (not to scale). Asterisks, mobile domains that have participated in the accretion. Species in which a domain architecture has been identified are indicated above the diagram (Y, yeast; W, worm; F, fly; V, vertebrate). Protein names are below the diagrams. The domains are SET, a chromatin protein methyltransferase domain; SWI2, a superfamily II helicase/ATPase domain; Sa, sant domain; Br, bromo domain; Ch, chromodomain; C, a cysteine triad motif associated with the Msl-2 and SET domains; A, AT hook motif; EP1/EP2, enhancer of polycomb domains-1 and 2; Znf, zinc finger; sja, SET-JOR-associated domain (L. Aravind, unpublished); Me, DNA methylase/Hrx-associated DNA binding zinc finger; Ba, bromo-associated homology motif. **a–c**, Different examples of accretion.

vertebrate innovation lies in the expansion of protein families. Table 25 shows the most prevalent protein domains and protein families in humans, together with their relative ranks in the other species. About 60% of families are more numerous in the human than in any of the other four organisms. This shows that gene duplication has been a major evolutionary force during vertebrate evolution. A comparison of relative expansions in human versus fly is shown in Fig. 44.

Many of the families that are expanded in human relative to fly and worm are involved in distinctive aspects of vertebrate physiology. An example is the family of immunoglobulin (IG) domains, first identified in antibodies thirty years ago. Classic (as opposed to divergent) IG domains are completely absent from the yeast and mustard weed proteomes and, although prokaryotic homologues exist, they have probably been transferred horizontally from metazoans[341]. Most IG superfamily proteins in invertebrates are cell-surface proteins. In vertebrates, the IG repertoire includes immune functions such as those of antibodies, MHC proteins, antibody receptors and many lymphocyte cell-surface proteins. The large expansion of IG domains in vertebrates shows the versatility of a single family in evoking rapid and effective response to infection.

Two prominent families are involved in the control of development. The human genome contains 30 fibroblast growth factors (FGFs), as opposed to two FGFs each in the fly and worm. It contains 42 transforming growth factor-βs (TGFβs) compared with nine and six in the fly and worm, respectively. These growth factors are involved in organogenesis, such as that of the liver and the lung. A fly FGF protein, branchless, is involved in developing respiratory organs (tracheae) in embryos[342]. Thus, developmental triggers of morphogenesis in vertebrates have evolved from related but simpler systems in invertebrates[343].

Another example is the family of intermediate filament proteins, with 127 family members. This expansion is almost entirely due to 111 keratins, which are chordate-specific intermediate filament proteins that form filaments in epithelia. The large number of human keratins suggests multiple cellular structural support roles for the many specialized epithelia of vertebrates.

Finally, the olfactory receptor genes comprise a huge gene family of about 1,000 genes and pseudogenes[344,345]. The number of olfactory receptors testifies to the importance of the sense of smell in vertebrates. A total of 906 olfactory receptor genes and pseudogenes could be identified in the draft genome sequence, two-thirds of which were not previously annotated. About 80% are found in about two dozen clusters ranging from 6 to 138 genes and encompassing about 30 Mb (~1%) of the human genome. Despite the importance of smell among our vertebrate ancestors, hominids

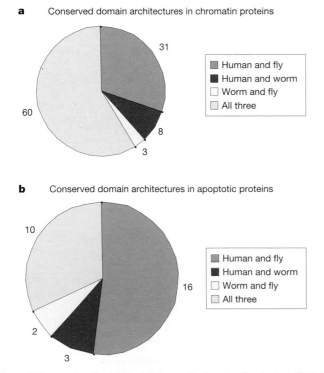

a Conserved domain architectures in chromatin proteins

31, 8, 3, 60

Human and fly
Human and worm
Worm and fly
All three

b Conserved domain architectures in apoptotic proteins

10, 16, 2, 3

Human and fly
Human and worm
Worm and fly
All three

Figure 43 Conservation of architectures between animal species. The pie charts illustrate the shared domain architectures of apparent orthologues that are conserved in at least two of the three sequenced animal genomes. If an architecture was detected in fungi or plants, as well as two of the animal lineages, it was omitted as ancient and its absence in the third animal lineage attributed to gene loss. **a**, Chromatin-associated proteins. **b**, Components of the programmed cell death system.

appear to have considerably less interest in this sense. About 60% of the olfactory receptors in the draft genome sequence have disrupted ORFs and appear to be pseudogenes, consistent with recent reports[344,346] suggesting massive functional gene loss in the last 10 Myr[347,348]. Interestingly, there appears to be a much higher proportion of intact genes among class I than class II olfactory receptors, suggesting functional importance.

Vertebrates are not unique in employing gene family expansion. For many domain types, expansions appear to have occurred independently in each of the major eukaryotic lineages. A good example is the classical C2H2 family of zinc finger domains, which have expanded independently in the yeast, worm, fly and human lineages (Fig. 45). These independent expansions have resulted in numerous C2H2 zinc finger domain-containing proteins that are specific to each lineage. In flies, the important components of the C2H2 zinc finger expansion are architectures in which it is combined with the POZ domain and the C4DM domain (a metal-binding domain found only in fly). In humans, the most prevalent expansions are combinations of the C2H2 zinc finger with POZ (independent of the one in insects) and the vertebrate-specific KRAB and SCAN domains.

The homeodomain is similarly expanded in all animals and is present in both architectures that are conserved and lineage-specific architectures (Fig. 45). This indicates that the ancestral animal probably encoded a significant number of homeodomain proteins, but subsequent evolution involved multiple, independent expansions and domain shuffling after lineages diverged. Thus, the most prevalent transcription factor families are different in worm, fly and human (Fig. 45). This has major biological implications because transcription factors are critical in animal development and differ-

entiation. The emergence of major variations in the developmental body plans that accompanied the early radiation of the animals[349] could have been driven by lineage-specific proliferation of such transcription factors. Beyond these large expansions of protein families, protein components of particular functional systems such as the cell death signalling system show a general increase in diversity and numbers in the vertebrates relative to other animals. For example, there are greater numbers of and more novel architectures in cell death regulatory proteins such as BCL-2, TNFR and NFκB from vertebrates.

Conclusion. Five lines of evidence point to an increase in the complexity of the proteome from the single-celled yeast to the multicellular invertebrates and to vertebrates such as the human. Specifically, the human contains greater numbers of genes, domain and protein families, paralogues, multidomain proteins with multiple functions, and domain architectures. According to these measures, the relatively greater complexity of the human proteome is a consequence not simply of its larger size, but also of large-scale protein innovation.

An important question is the extent to which the greater phenotypic complexity of vertebrates can be explained simply by two- or threefold increases in proteome complexity. The real explanation may lie in combinatorial amplification of these modest differences, by mechanisms that include alternative splicing, post-translational modification and cellular regulatory networks. The potential numbers of different proteins and protein–protein interactions are vast, and their actual numbers cannot readily be discerned from the genome sequence. Elucidating such system-level properties presents one of the great challenges for modern biology.

Table 25 The most populous InterPro families in the human proteome and other species

InterPro ID	Human		Fly		Worm		Yeast		Mustard weed		
	No. of genes	Rank	No. of genes	Rank	No. of genes	Rank	No. of genes	Rank	No. of genes	Rank	
IPR003006	765	(1)	140	(9)	64	(34)	0	(na)	0	(na)	Immunoglobulin domain
PR000822	706	(2)	357	(1)	151	(10)	48	(7)	115	(20)	C2H2 zinc finger
IPR000719	575	(3)	319	(2)	437	(2)	121	(1)	1049	(1)	Eukaryotic protein kinase
IPR000276	569	(4)	97	(14)	358	(3)	0	(na)	16	(84)	Rhodopsin-like GPCR superfamily
IPR001687	433	(5)	198	(4)	183	(7)	97	(2)	331	(5)	P-loop motif
IPR000477	350	(6)	10	(65)	50	(41)	6	(36)	80	(35)	Reverse transcriptase (RNA-dependent DNA polymerase)
IPR000504	300	(7)	157	(6)	96	(21)	54	(6)	255	(8)	rrm domain
IPR001680	277	(8)	162	(5)	102	(19)	91	(3)	210	(10)	G-protein β WD-40 repeats
IPR002110	276	(9)	105	(13)	107	(17)	19	(23)	120	(18)	Ankyrin repeat
IPR001356	267	(10)	148	(7)	109	(15)	9	(33)	118	(19)	Homeobox domain
IPR001849	252	(11)	77	(22)	71	(31)	27	(17)	27	(73)	PH domain
IPR002048	242	(12)	111	(12)	81	(25)	15	(27)	167	(12)	EF-hand family
IPR000561	222	(13)	81	(20)	113	(14)	0	(na)	17	(83)	EGF-like domain
IPR001452	215	(14)	72	(23)	62	(35)	25	(18)	3	(97)	SH3 domain
IPR001841	210	(15)	114	(11)	126	(12)	35	(12)	379	(4)	RING finger
IPR001611	188	(16)	115	(10)	54	(38)	7	(35)	392	(2)	Leucine rich repeat
IPR001909	171	(17)	0	(na)	0	(na)	0	(na)	0	(na)	KRAB box
IPR001777	165	(18)	63	(27)	51	(40)	2	(40)	4	(96)	Fibronectin type III domain
IPR001478	162	(19)	70	(24)	66	(33)	2	(40)	15	(85)	PDZ domain
IPR001650	155	(20)	87	(17)	78	(27)	79	(4)	148	(13)	Helicase C-terminal domain
IPR001440	150	(21)	86	(18)	46	(43)	36	(11)	125	(17)	TPR repeat
IPR002216	133	(22)	65	(26)	99	(20)	2	(40)	31	(69)	Ion transport protein
IPR001092	131	(23)	84	(19)	41	(46)	7	(35)	106	(24)	Helix–loop–helix DNA-binding domain
IPR000008	123	(24)	43	(34)	36	(49)	9	(33)	82	(34)	C2 domain
IPR001664	119	(25)	4	(71)	22	(63)	1	(41)	2	(98)	SH2 domain
IPR001254	118	(26)	210	(3)	12	(73)	1	(41)	15	(85)	Serine protease, trypsin family
IPR002126	114	(27)	19	(56)	16	(69)	0	(na)	0	(na)	Cadherin domain
IPR000210	113	(28)	78	(21)	117	(13)	1	(41)	54	(50)	BTB/POZ domain
IPR000387	112	(29)	35	(40)	108	(16)	12	(30)	21	(79)	Tyrosine-specific protein phosphatase and dual specificity protein phosphatase family
IPR000087	106	(30)	18	(57)	169	(9)	0	(na)	5	(95)	Collagen triple helix repeat
IPR000379	94	(31)	141	(8)	134	(11)	40	(10)	194	(11)	Esterase/lipase/thioesterase
IPR000910	89	(32)	38	(38)	18	(67)	8	(34)	18	(82)	HMG1/2 (high mobility group) box
IPR000130	87	(33)	56	(29)	92	(22)	8	(34)	12	(88)	Neutral zinc metallopeptidase
IPR001965	84	(34)	37	(39)	24	(61)	16	(26)	71	(39)	PHD-finger
IPR000636	83	(35)	32	(43)	24	(61)	1	(41)	14	(86)	Cation channels (non-ligand gated)
IPR001781	81	(36)	38	(38)	36	(49)	4	(38)	8	(92)	LIM domain
IPR002035	81	(36)	8	(67)	45	(44)	3	(39)	17	(83)	VWA domain
IPR001715	80	(37)	33	(42)	30	(55)	3	(39)	18	(82)	Calponin homology domain
IPR000198	77	(38)	20	(55)	20	(65)	10	(32)	9	(91)	RhoGAP domain

Forty most populous Interpro families found in the human proteome compared with equivalent numbers from other species. na, not applicable (used when there are no proteins in an organism in that family).

Segmental history of the human genome

In bacteria, genomic segments often convey important information about function: genes located close to one another often encode proteins in a common pathway and are regulated in a common operon. In mammals, genes found close to each other only rarely have common functions, but they are still interesting because they have a common history. In fact, the study of genomic segments can shed light on biological events as long as 500 Myr ago and as recently as 20,000 years ago.

Conserved segments between human and mouse

Humans and mice shared a common ancestor about 100 Myr ago. Despite the 200 Myr of evolutionary distance between the species, a significant fraction of genes show synteny between the two, being preserved within conserved segments. Genes tightly linked in one mammalian species tend to be linked in others. In fact, conserved segments have been observed in even more distant species: humans show conserved segments with fish[350,351] and even with invertebrates such as fly and worm[352]. In general, the likelihood that a syntenic relationship will be disrupted correlates with the physical distance between the loci and the evolutionary distance between the species.

Studying conserved segments between human and mouse has several uses. First, conservation of gene order has been used to identify likely orthologues between the species, particularly when investigating disease phenotypes. Second, the study of conserved segments among genomes helps us to deduce evolutionary ancestry.

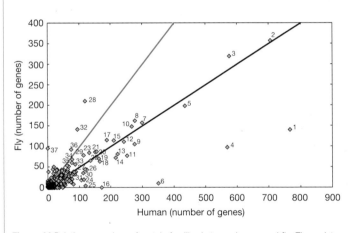

Figure 44 Relative expansions of protein families between human and fly. These data have not been normalized for proteomic size differences. Blue line, equality between normalized family sizes in the two organisms. Green line, equality between unnormalized family sizes. Numbered InterPro entries: (1) immunoglobulin domain [IPR003006]; (2) zinc finger, C2H2 type [IPR000822]; (3) eukaryotic protein kinase [IPR000719]; (4) rhodopsin-like GPCR superfamily [IPR000276]; (5) ATP/GTP-binding site motif A (P-loop) [IPR001687]; (6) reverse transcriptase (RNA-dependent DNA polymerase) [IPR000477]; (7) RNA-binding region RNP-1 (RNA recognition motif) [IPR000504]; (8) G-protein β WD-40 repeats [IPR001680]; (9) ankyrin repeat [IPR002110]; (10) homeobox domain [IPR001356]; (11) PH domain [IPR001849]; (12) EF-hand family [IPR002048]; (13) EGF-like domain [IPR000561]; (14) Src homology 3 (SH3) domain [IPR001452]; (15) RING finger [IPR001841]; (16) KRAB box [IPR001909]; (17) leucine-rich repeat [IPR001611]; (18) fibronectin type III domain [IPR001777]; (19) PDZ domain (also known as DHR or GLGF) [IPR001478]; (20) TPR repeat [IPR001440]; (21) helicase C-terminal domain [IPR001650]; (22) ion transport protein [IPR002216]; (23) helix–loop–helix DNA-binding domain [IPR001092]; (24) cadherin domain [IPR002126]; (25) intermediate filament proteins [IPR001664]; (26) C2 domain [IPR000008]; (27) Src homology 2 (SH2) domain [IPR000980]; (28) serine proteases, trypsin family [IPR001254]; (29) BTB/POZ domain [IPR000210]; (30) tyrosine-specific protein phosphatase and dual specificity protein phosphatase family [IPR000387]; (31) collagen triple helix repeat [IPR000087]; (32) esterase/lipase/thioesterase [IPR000379]; (33) neutral zinc metallopeptidases, zinc-binding region [IPR000130]; (34) ATP-binding transport protein, 2nd P-loop motif [IPR001051]; (35) ABC transporters family [IPR001617]; (36) cytochrome P450 enzyme [IPR001128]; (37) insect cuticle protein [IPR000618].

And third, detailed comparative maps may assist in the assembly of the mouse sequence, using the human sequence as a scaffold.

Two types of linkage conservation are commonly described[353]. 'Conserved synteny' indicates that at least two genes that reside on a common chromosome in one species are also located on a common chromosome in the other species. Syntenic loci are said to lie in a 'conserved segment' when not only the chromosomal position but the linear order of the loci has been preserved, without interruption by other chromosomal rearrangements.

An initial survey of homologous loci in human and mouse[354] suggested that the total number of conserved segments would be about 180. Subsequent estimates based on increasingly detailed comparative maps have remained close to this projection[353,355,356] (http://www.informatics.jax.org). The distribution of segment lengths has corresponded reasonably well to the truncated negative exponential curve predicted by the random breakage model[357].

The availability of a draft human genome sequence allows the first global human–mouse comparison in which human physical distances can be measured in Mb, rather than cM or orthologous gene counts. We identified likely orthologues by reciprocal comparison of the human and mouse mRNAs in the LocusLink database, using megaBLAST. For each orthologous pair, we mapped the location of the human gene in the draft genome sequence and then checked the location of the mouse gene in the Mouse Genome Informatics database (http://www.informatics.jax.org). Using a conservative threshold, we identified 3,920 orthologous pairs in which the human gene could be mapped on the draft genome sequence with high confidence. Of these, 2,998 corresponding mouse genes had a known position in the mouse genome. We then searched for definitive conserved segments, defined as human regions containing orthologues of at least two genes from the same mouse chromosome region (< 15 cM) without interruption by segments from other chromosomes.

We identified 183 definitive conserved segments (Fig. 46). The average segment length was 15.4 Mb, with the largest segment being 90.5 Mb and the smallest 24 kb. There were also 141 'singletons', segments that contained only a single locus; these are not counted in the statistics. Although some of these could be short conserved segments, they could also reflect incorrect choices of orthologues or problems with the human or mouse maps. Because of this conservative approach, the observed number of definitive segments is likely be lower than the correct total. One piece of evidence for this conclusion comes from a more detailed analysis on human chromosome 7 (ref. 358), which identified 20 conserved segments, of which three were singletons. Our analysis revealed only 13 definitive segments on this chromosome, with nine singletons.

The frequency of observing a particular gene count in a conserved segment is plotted on a logarithmic scale in Fig. 47. If chromosomal breaks occur in a random fashion (as has been proposed) and differences in gene density are ignored, a roughly straight line should result. There is a clear excess for $n = 1$, suggesting that 50% or more of the singletons are indeed artefactual. Thus, we estimate that true number of conserved segments is around 190–230, in good agreement with the original Nadeau–Taylor prediction[354].

Figure 48 shows a plot of the frequency of lengths of conserved segments, where the x-axis scale is shown in Mb. As before, there is a fair amount of scatter in the data for the larger segments (where the numbers are small), but the trend appears to be consistent with a random breakage model.

We attempted to ascertain whether the breakpoint regions have any special characteristics. This analysis was complicated by imprecision in the positioning of these breaks, which will tend to blur any relationships. With 2,998 orthologues, the average interval within which a break is known to have occurred is about 1.1 Mb. We compared the aggregate features of these breakpoint intervals with the genome as a whole. The mean gene density was lower in breakpoint regions than in the conserved segments (13.8 versus

18.6 per Mb). This suggests that breakpoints may be more likely to occur or to undergo fixation in gene-poor intervals than in gene-rich intervals. The occurrence of breakpoints may be promoted by homologous recombination among repeated sequences[359]. When the sequence of the mouse genome is finished, this analysis can be revisited more precisely.

A number of examples of extended conserved segments and syntenies are apparent in Fig. 46. As has been noted, almost all human genes on chromosome 17 are found on mouse chromosome 11, with two members of the placental lactogen family from mouse 13 inserted. Apart from two singleton loci, human chromosome 20 appears to be entirely orthologous to mouse chromosome 2, apparently in a single segment. The largest apparently contiguous conserved segment in the human genome is on chromosome 4, including roughly 90.5 Mb of human DNA that is orthologous to mouse chromosome 5. This analysis also allows us to infer the likely location of thousands of mouse genes for which the human orthologue has been located in the draft genome sequence but the mouse locus has not yet been mapped.

With about 200 conserved segments between mouse and human and about 100 Myr of evolution from their common ancestor[360], we obtain an estimated rate of about 1.0 chromosomal rearrangement being fixed per Myr. However, there is good evidence that the rate of chromosomal rearrangement (like the rate of nucleotide substitutions; see above) differs between the two species. Among mammals, rodents may show unusually rapid chromosome alteration. By comparison, very few rearrangements have been observed among primates, and studies of a broader array of mammalian orders, including cats, cows, sheep and pigs, suggest an average rate of chromosome alteration of only about 0.2 rearrangements per Myr

in these lineages[361]. Additional evidence that rodents are outliers comes from a recent analysis of synteny between the human and zebrafish genomes. From a study of 523 orthologues, it was possible to project 418 conserved segments[350]. Assuming 400 Myr since a common vertebrate ancestor of zebrafish and humans[362], we obtain an estimate of 0.52 rearrangements per Myr. Recent estimates of rearrangement rates in plants have suggested bimodality, with some pairs showing rates of 0.15–0.41 rearrangements per Myr, and others showing higher rates of 1.1–1.3 rearrangements per Myr[363]. With additional detailed genome maps of multiple species, it should be possible to determine whether this particular molecular clock is truly operating at a different rate in various branches of the evolutionary tree, and whether variations in that rate are bimodal or continuous. It should also be possible to reconstruct the karyotypes of common ancestors.

Ancient duplicated segments in the human genome

Another approach to genomic history is to study segmental duplications within the human genome. Earlier, we discussed examples of recent duplications of genomic segments to pericentromeric and subtelomeric regions. Most of these events appear to be evolutionary dead-ends resulting in nonfunctional pseudogenes; however, segmental duplication is also an important mode of evolutionary innovation: a duplication permits one copy of each gene to drift and potentially to acquire a new function.

Segmental duplications can occur through unequal crossing over to create gene families in specific chromosomal regions. This mechanism can create both small families, such as the five related genes of the β-globin cluster on chromosome 11, and large ones, such as the olfactory receptor gene clusters, which together contain nearly 1,000 genes and pseudogenes.

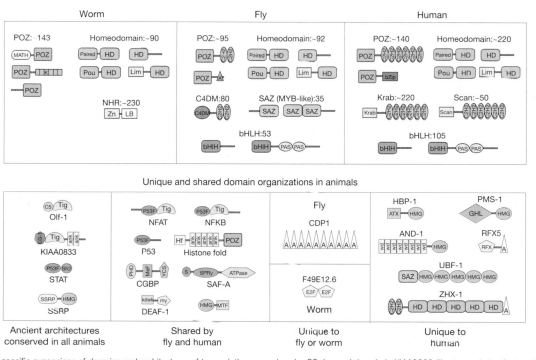

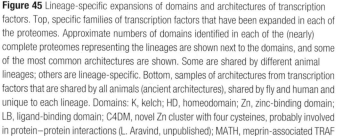

Figure 45 Lineage-specific expansions of domains and architectures of transcription factors. Top, specific families of transcription factors that have been expanded in each of the proteomes. Approximate numbers of domains identified in each of the (nearly) complete proteomes representing the lineages are shown next to the domains, and some of the most common architectures are shown. Some are shared by different animal lineages; others are lineage-specific. Bottom, samples of architectures from transcription factors that are shared by all animals (ancient architectures), shared by fly and human and unique to each lineage. Domains: K, kelch; HD, homeodomain; Zn, zinc-binding domain; LB, ligand-binding domain; C4DM, novel Zn cluster with four cysteines, probably involved in protein–protein interactions (L. Aravind, unpublished); MATH, meprin-associated TRAF

domain; CG-1, novel domain in KIAA0909-like transcription factors (L. Aravind, unpublished); MTF, myelin transcription factor domain; SAZ, specialized Myb-like helix-turn-helix (HTH) domain found in Stonewall, ADF-1 and Zeste (L. Aravind, unpublished); A, AT-hook motif; E2F, winged HTH DNA-binding domain; GHL, gyraseB-histidine kinase-MutL ATPase domain; ATX, ATaXin domain; RFX, RFX winged HTH DNA binding domain; My, MYND domain; KDWK, KDWK DNA-binding domain; POZ, Pox zinc finger domain; S, SAP domain; P53F, P53 fold domain; HF, histone fold; ANK, ankyrin repeat; TIG, transcription factor Ig domain; SSRP, structure-specific recognition protein domain; C5, 5-cysteine metal binding domain; C2H2, classic zinc finger domain; WD, WD40 repeats.

The most extreme mechanism is whole-genome duplication (WGD), through a polyploidization event in which a diploid organism becomes tetraploid. Such events are classified as autopolyploidy or allopolyploidy, depending on whether they involve hybridization between members of the same species or different species. Polyploidization is common in the plant kingdom, with many known examples among wild and domesticated crop species. Alfalfa (*Medicago sativa*) is a naturally occurring autotetraploid[364], and *Nicotiana tabacum*, some species of cotton (*Gossypium*) and several of the common brassicas are allotetraploids containing pairs of 'homeologous' chromosome pairs.

In principle, WGD provides the raw material for great bursts of innovation by allowing the duplication and divergence of entire pathways. Ohno[365] suggested that WGD has played a key role in evolution. There is evidence for an ancient WGD event in the ancestry of yeast and several independent such events in the ancestry of mustard weed[366–369]. Such ancient WGD events can be hard to detect because only a minority of the duplicated loci may be retained, with the result that the genes in duplicated segments cannot be aligned in a one-to-one correspondence but rather require many gaps. In addition, duplicated segments may be subsequently rearranged. For example, the ancient duplication in the yeast genome appears to have been followed by loss of more than 90% of the newly duplicated genes[366].

One of the most controversial hypotheses about vertebrate evolution is the proposal that two WGD events occurred early in the vertebrate lineage, around the time of jawed fishes some 500 Myr ago. Some authors[370–373] have seen support for this theory in the fact that many human genes occur in sets of four homologues—most notably the four extensive HOX gene clusters on chromosomes 2, 7, 12 and 17, whose duplication dates to around the correct time. However, other authors have disputed this interpretation[374], suggesting that these cases may reflect unrelated duplications of specific regions rather than successive WGD.

We analysed the draft genome sequence for evidence that might bear on this question. The analysis provides many interesting observations, but no convincing evidence of ancient WGD. We looked for evidence of pairs of chromosomal regions containing many homologous genes. Although we found many pairs containing a few homologous genes, the human genome does not appear to contain any pairs of regions where the density of duplicated genes approaches the densities seen in yeast or mustard weed[366–369].

We also examined human proteins in the IPI for which the orthologues among fly or worm proteins occur in the ratios 2:1:1, 3:1:1, 4:1:1 and so on (Fig. 49). The number of such families falls smoothly, with no peak at four and some instances of five or more homologues. Although this does not rule out two rounds of WGD followed by extensive gene loss and some unrelated gene duplication, it provides no support for the theory. More probatively, if two successive rounds of genome duplication occurred, phylogenetic analysis of the proteins having 4:1:1 ratios between human, fly and worm would be expected to show more trees with the topology (A,B)(C,D) for the human sequences than (A,(B,(C,D)))[375]. However, of 57 sets studied carefully, only 24% of the trees constructed from the 4:1:1 set have the former topology; this is not significantly different from what would be expected under the hypothesis of random sequential duplication of individual loci.

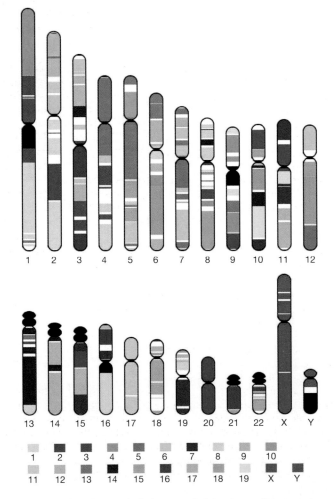

Figure 46 Conserved segments in the human and mouse genome. Human chromosomes, with segments containing at least two genes whose order is conserved in the mouse genome as colour blocks. Each colour corresponds to a particular mouse chromosome. Centromeres, subcentromeric heterochromatin of chromosomes 1, 9 and 16, and the repetitive short arms of 13, 14, 15, 21 and 22 are in black.

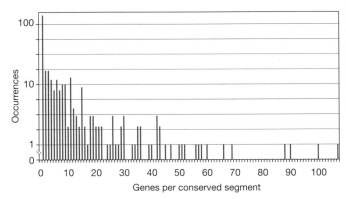

Figure 47 Distribution of number of genes per conserved segment between human and mouse genomes.

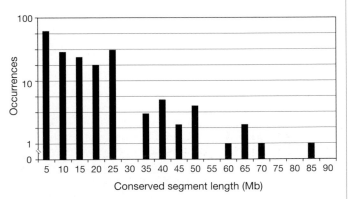

Figure 48 Distribution of lengths (in 5-Mb bins) of conserved segments between human and mouse genomes, omitting singletons.

We also searched for sets of four chromosomes where there are multiple genes with homologues on each of the four. The strongest example was chromosomes 2, 7, 12 and 17, containing the HOX clusters as well as additional genes. These four chromosomes appear to have an excess of quadruplicated genes. The genes are not all clustered in a single region; this may reflect intrachromosomal rearrangement since the duplication of these genes, or it may indicate that they result from several independent events. Of the genes with homologues on chromosomes 2, 12 and 17, many of those missing on chromosome 7 are clustered on chromosome 3, suggesting a translocation. Several additional examples of groups of four chromosomes were found, although they were connected by fewer homologous genes.

Although the analyses are sensitive to the imperfect quality of the gene predictions, our results so far are insufficient to settle whether two rounds of WGD occurred around 500 Myr ago. It may be possible to resolve the issue by systematically estimating the time of each of the many gene duplication events on the basis of sequence divergence, although this is beyond the scope of this report. Another approach to determining whether a widespread duplication occurred at a particular time in vertebrate evolution would be to sequence the genomes of organisms whose lineages diverged from vertebrates at appropriate times, such as amphioxus.

Recent history from human polymorphism

The recent history of genomic segments can be probed by studying the properties of SNPs segregating in the current human population. The sequence information generated in the course of this project has yielded a huge collection of SNPs. These SNPs were extracted in two ways: by comparing overlapping large-insert clones derived from distinct haplotypes (either different individuals or different chromosomes within an individual) and by comparing random reads from whole-genome shotgun libraries derived from multiple individuals. The analysis confirms an average heterozygosity rate in the human population of about 1 in 1,300 bp (ref. 97).

More than 1.42 million SNPs have been assembled into a genome-wide map and are analysed in detail in an accompanying paper[97]. SNP density is also displayed across the genome in Fig. 9. The SNPs have an average spacing of 1.9 kb and 63% of 5-kb intervals contain a SNP. These polymorphisms are of immediate utility for medical genetic studies. Whereas investigators studying a gene previously had to expend considerable effort to discover polymorphisms across the region of interest, the current collection now provides them with about 15 SNPs for gene loci of average size.

The density of SNPs (adjusted for ascertainment—that is, polymorphisms per base screened) varies considerably across the

genome[97] and sheds light on the unique properties and history of each genomic region. The average heterozygosity at a locus will tend to increase in proportion to the local mutation rate and the 'age' of the locus (which can be defined as the average number of generations since the most recent common ancestor of two randomly chosen copies in the population). For example, positive selection can cause a locus to be unusually 'young' and balancing selection can cause it to be unusually 'old'. An extreme example is the HLA region, in which a high SNP density is observed, reflecting the fact that diverse HLA haplotypes have been maintained for many millions of years by balancing selection and greatly predate the origin of the human species.

SNPs can also be used to study linkage disequilibrium in the human genome[376]. Linkage disequilibrium refers to the persistence of ancestral haplotypes—that is, genomic segments carrying particular combinations of alleles descended from a common ancestor. It can provide a powerful tool for mapping disease genes[377,378] and for probing population history[379-381]. There has been considerably controversy concerning the typical distance over which linkage disequilibrium extends in the human genome[382-387]. With the collection of SNPs now available, it should be possible to resolve this important issue.

Applications to medicine and biology

In most research papers, the authors can only speculate about future applications of the work. Because the genome sequence has been released on a daily basis over the past four years, however, we can already cite many direct applications. We focus on a handful of applications chosen primarily from medical research.

Disease genes

A key application of human genome research has been the ability to find disease genes of unknown biochemical function by positional cloning[388]. This method involves mapping the chromosomal region containing the gene by linkage analysis in affected families and then scouring the region to find the gene itself. Positional cloning is powerful, but it has also been extremely tedious. When the approach was first proposed in the early 1980s[9], a researcher wishing to perform positional cloning had to generate genetic markers to trace inheritance; perform chromosomal walking to obtain genomic DNA covering the region; and analyse a region of around 1 Mb by either direct sequencing or indirect gene identification methods. The first two barriers were eliminated with the development in the mid-1990s of comprehensive genetic and physical maps of the human chromosomes, under the auspices of the Human Genome Project. The remaining barrier, however, has continued to be formidable.

All that is changing with the availability of the human draft genome sequence. The human genomic sequence in public databases allows rapid identification in silico of candidate genes, followed by mutation screening of relevant candidates, aided by information on gene structure. For a mendelian disorder, a gene search can now often be carried out in a matter of months with only a modestly sized team.

At least 30 disease genes[55,389-422] (Table 26) have been positionally cloned in research efforts that depended directly on the publicly available genome sequence. As most of the human sequence has only arrived in the past twelve months, it is likely that many similar discoveries are not yet published. In addition, there are many cases in which the genome sequence played a supporting role, such as providing candidate microsatellite markers for finer genetic linkage analysis.

The genome sequence has also helped to reveal the mechanisms leading to some common chromosomal deletion syndromes. In several instances, recurrent deletions have been found to result from homologous recombination and unequal crossing over between large, nearly identical intrachromosomal duplications. Examples

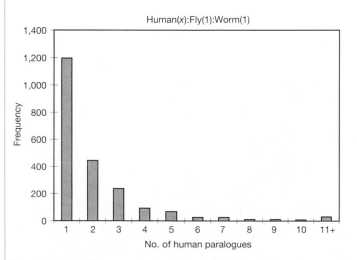

Figure 49 Number of human paralogues of genes having single orthologues in worm and fly.

include the DiGeorge/velocardiofacial syndrome region on chromosome 22 (ref. 238) and the Williams–Beuren syndrome recurrent deletion on chromosome 7 (ref. 239).

The availability of the genome sequence also allows rapid identification of paralogues of disease genes, which is valuable for two reasons. First, mutations in a paralogous gene may give rise to a related genetic disease. A good example, discovered through use of the genome sequence, is achromatopsia (complete colour blindness). The *CNGA3* gene, encoding the α-subunit of the cone photoreceptor cyclic GMP-gated channel, had been shown to harbour mutations in some families with achromatopsia. Computational searching of the genome sequences revealed the paralogous gene encoding the corresponding β-subunit, *CNGB3* (which had not been apparent from EST databases). The *CNGB3* gene was rapidly shown to be the cause of achromatopsia in other families[407,408]. Another example is provided by the presenilin-1 and presenilin-2 genes, in which mutations can cause early-onset Alzheimer's disease[423,424]. Second, the paralogue may provide an opportunity for therapeutic intervention, as exemplified by attempts to reactivate the fetally expressed haemoglobin genes in individuals with sickle cell disease or β-thalassaemia, caused by mutations in the β-globin gene[425].

We undertook a systematic search for paralogues of 971 known human disease genes with entries in both the Online Mendelian Inheritance in Man (OMIM) database (http://www.ncbi.nlm.nih.gov/Omim/) and either the SwissProt or TrEMBL protein databases. We identified 286 potential paralogues (with the requirement of a match of at least 50 amino acids with identity greater than 70% but less than 90% if on the same chromosome, and less than 95% if on a different chromosome). Although this analysis may have identified some pseudogenes, 89% of the matches showed homology over more than one exon in the new target sequence, suggesting that many are functional. This analysis shows the potential for rapid identification of disease gene paralogues *in silico*.

Drug targets

Over the past century, the pharmaceutical industry has largely depended upon a limited set of drug targets to develop new therapies. A recent compendium[426,427] lists 483 drug targets as accounting for virtually all drugs on the market. Knowing the complete set of human genes and proteins will greatly expand the search for suitable drug targets. Although only a minority of human genes may be drug targets, it has been predicted that the number will exceed several thousand, and this prospect has led to a massive expansion of genomic research in pharmaceutical research and development. A few examples will illustrate the point.

(1) The neurotransmitter serotonin (5-HT) mediates rapid excitatory responses through ligand-gated channels. The previously identified 5-HT$_{3A}$ receptor gene produces functional receptors, but with a much smaller conductance than observed *in vivo*. Cross-hybridization experiments and analysis of ESTs failed to reveal any other homologues of the known receptor. Recently, however, by searching the human draft genome sequence at low stringency, a putative homologue was identified within a PAC clone from the long arm of chromosome 11 (ref. 428). The homologue was shown to be expressed in the amygdala, caudate and hippocampus, and a full-length cDNA was subsequently obtained. The gene, which codes for a serotonin receptor, was named 5-HT$_{3B}$. When assembled in a heterodimer with 5-HT$_{3A}$, it was shown to account for the large-conductance neuronal serotonin channel. Given the central role of the serotonin pathway in mood disorders and schizophrenia, the discovery of a major new therapeutic target is of considerable interest.

(2) The contractile and inflammatory actions of the cysteinyl leukotrienes, formerly known as the slow reacting substance of anaphylaxis (SRS-A), are mediated through specific receptors. The second such receptor, CysLT$_2$, was identified using the combination of a rat EST and the human genome sequence. This led to the cloning of a gene with 38% amino-acid identity to the only other receptor that had previously been identified[429]. This new receptor, which shows high-affinity binding to several leukotrienes, maps to a region of chromosome 13 that is linked to atopic asthma. The gene is expressed in airway smooth muscles and in the heart. As the leukotriene pathway has been a significant target for the development of drugs against asthma, the discovery of a new receptor has obvious and important consequences.

(3) Abundant deposition of β-amyloid in senile plaques is the hallmark of Alzheimer's disease. β-Amyloid is generated by proteolytic processing of the amyloid precursor protein (APP). One of the enzymes involved is the β-site APP-cleaving enzyme (BACE), which is a transmembrane aspartyl protease. Computational searching of the public human draft genome sequence recently identified a new sequence homologous to BACE, encoding a protein now named BACE2[430,431]. BACE2, which has 52% amino-acid sequence identity to BACE, contains two active protease sites and maps to the obligatory Down's syndrome region of chromosome 21, as does APP. This raises the question of whether the extra copies of both BACE2 and APP may contribute to accelerated deposition of β-amyloid in the brains of Down's syndrome patients. The development of antagonists to BACE and BACE2 represents a promising approach to preventing Alzheimer's disease.

Given these examples, we undertook a systematic effort to identify paralogues of the classic drug target proteins in the draft genome sequence. The target list[427] was used to identify 603 entries in the SwissProt database with unique accession numbers. These were then searched against the current genome sequence database, using the requirement that a match should have 70–100% identity to at least 50 amino acids. Matches to named proteins were ignored, as we assumed that these represented known homologues.

We found 18 putative novel paralogues (Table 27), including apparent dopamine receptors, purinergic receptors and insulin-like growth factor receptors. In six cases, the novel paralogue matches at least one EST, adding confidence that this search process can identify novel functional genes. For the remaining 12 putative paralogues without an EST match, all have long ORFs and all but

Table 26 Disease genes positionally cloned using the draft genome sequence

Locus	Disorder	Reference(s)
BRCA2	Breast cancer susceptibility	55
AIRE	Autoimmune polyglandular syndrome type 1 (APS1 or APECED)	389
PEX1	Peroxisome biogenesis disorder	390, 391
PDS	Pendred syndrome	392
XLP	X-linked lymphoproliferative disease	393
DFNA5	Nonsyndromic deafness	394
ATP2A2	Darier's disease	395
SEDL	X-linked spondyloepiphyseal dysplasia tarda	396
WISP3	Progressive pseudorheumatoid dysplasia	397
CCM1	Cerebral cavernous malformations	398, 399
COL11A2/DFNA13	Nonsyndromic deafness	400
LGMD 2G	Limb-girdle muscular dystrophy	401
EVC	Ellis-Van Creveld syndrome, Weyer's acrodental dysostosis	402
ACTN4	Familial focal segmental glomerulosclerosis	403
SCN1A	Generalized epilepsy with febrile seizures plus type 2	404
AASS	Familial hyperlysinaemia	405
NDRG1	Hereditary motor and sensory neuropathy-Lom	406
CNGB3	Total colour-blindness	407, 408
MUL	Mulibrey nanism	409
USH1C	Usher type 1C	410, 411
MYH9	May-Hegglin anomaly	412, 413
PRKAR1A	Carney's complex	414
MYH9	Nonsyndromic hereditary deafness DFNA17	415
SCA10	Spinocerebellar ataxia type 10	416
OPA1	Optic atrophy	417
XLCSNB	X-linked congenital stationary night blindness	418
FGF23	Hypophosphataemic rickets	419
GAN	Giant axonal neuropathy	420
AAAS	Triple-A syndrome	421
HSPG2	Schwartz-Jampel syndrome	422

one show similarity spanning multiple exons separated by introns, so these are not processed pseudogenes. They are likely to represent interesting new candidate drug targets.

Basic biology

Although the examples above reflect medical applications, there are also many similar applications to basic physiology and cell biology. To cite one satisfying example, the publicly available sequence was used to solve a mystery that had vexed investigators for several decades: the molecular basis of bitter taste[432]. Humans and other animals are polymorphic for response to certain bitter tastes. Recently, investigators mapped this trait in both humans and mice and then searched the relevant region of the human draft genome sequence for G-protein coupled receptors. These studies led, in quick succession, to the discovery of a new family of such proteins, the demonstration that they are expressed almost exclusively in taste buds, and the experimental confirmation that the receptors in cultured cells respond to specific bitter substances[433–435].

The next steps

Considerable progress has been made in human sequencing, but much remains to be done to produce a finished sequence. Even more work will be required to extract the full information contained in the sequence. Many of the key next steps are already underway.

Finishing the human sequence

The human sequence will serve as a foundation for biomedical research in the years ahead, and it is thus crucial that the remaining gaps be filled and ambiguities be resolved as quickly as possible. This will involve a three-step program.

The first stage involves producing finished sequence from clones spanning the current physical map, which covers more than 96% of the euchromatic regions of the genome. About 1 Gb of finished sequence is already completed. Almost all of the remaining clones are already sequenced to at least draft coverage, and the rest have been selected for sequencing. All clones are expected to reach 'full shotgun' coverage (8–10-fold redundancy) by about mid-2001 and finished form (99.99% accuracy) not long thereafter, using established and increasingly automated protocols.

The next stage will be to screen additional libraries to close gaps between clone contigs. Directed probing of additional large-insert clone libraries should close many of the remaining gaps. Unclosed gaps will be sized by FISH techniques or other methods. Two chromosomes, 22 and 21, have already been assembled in this 'essentially complete' form in this manner[93,94], and chromosomes 20, Y, 19, 14 and 7 are likely to reach this status in the next few

months. All chromosomes should be essentially completed by 2003, if not sooner.

Finally, techniques must be developed to close recalcitrant gaps. Several hundred such gaps in the euchromatic sequence will probably remain in the genome after exhaustive screening of existing large-insert libraries. New methodologies will be needed to recover sequence from these segments, and to define biological reasons for their lack of representation in standard libraries. Ideally, it would be desirable to obtain complete sequence from all heterochromatic regions, such as centromeres and ribosomal gene clusters, although most of this sequence will consist of highly polymorphic tandem repeats containing few protein-coding genes.

Developing the IGI and IPI

The draft genome sequence has provided an initial look at the human gene content, but many ambiguities remain. A high priority will be to refine the IGI and IPI to the point where they accurately reflect every gene and every alternatively spliced form. Several steps are needed to reach this ambitious goal.

Finishing the human sequence will assist in this effort, but the experiences gained on chromosomes 21 and 22 show that sequence alone is not enough to allow complete gene identification. One powerful approach is cross-species sequence comparison with related organisms at suitable evolutionary distances. The sequence coverage from the pufferfish *T. nigroviridis* has already proven valuable in identifying potential exons[292]; this work is expected to continue from its current state of onefold coverage to reach at least fivefold coverage later this year. The genome sequence of the laboratory mouse will provide a particularly powerful tool for exon identification, as sequence similarity is expected to identify 95–97% of the exons, as well as a significant number of regulatory domains[436–438]. A public-private consortium is speeding this effort, by producing freely accessible whole-genome shotgun coverage that can be readily used for cross-species comparison[439]. More than onefold coverage from the C57BL/6J strain has already been completed and threefold is expected within the next few months. In the slightly longer term, a program is under way to produce a finished sequence of the laboratory mouse.

Another important step is to obtain a comprehensive collection of full-length human cDNAs, both as sequences and as actual clones. The Mammalian Gene Collection project has been underway for a year[18] and expects to produce 10,000–15,000 human full-length cDNAs over the coming year, which will be available without restrictions on use. The Genome Exploration Group of the RIKEN Genomic Sciences Center is similarly developing a collection of cDNA clones from mouse[309], which is a valuable complement

---

Table 27 New paralogues of common drug targets identified by searching the draft human genome sequence

Drug target	HGM symbol	SwissProt accession	Chromosome	Novel match IGI number	Chromosome containing paralogue	Per cent identity	dbEST GenBank accession
Aquaporin 7	AQP7	O14520	9	IGI_M1_ctg15869_11	2	92.3	AW593324
Arachidonate 12-lipoxygenase	ALOX12	P18054	17	IGI_M1_ctg17216_23	17	70.1	
Calcitonin	CALCA	P01258	11	IGI_M1_ctg14138_20	12	93.6	
Calcium channel, voltage-dependent, γ-subunit	CACNG2	Q9Y698	22	IGI_M1_ctg17137_10	19	70.7	
DNA polymerase-δ, small subunit	POLD2	P49005	7	IGI_M1_ctg12903_29	5	86.8	
Dopamine receptor, D1-α	DRD1	P21728	5	IGI_M1_ctg25203_33	16	70.7	
Dopamine receptor, D1-β	DRD5	P21918	4	IGI_M1_ctg17190_14	1	88.0	AI148329
Eukaryotic translation elongation factor, 1δ	EEF1D	P29692	2	IGI_M1_ctg16401_37	17	77.6	BE719683
FKBP, tacrolimus binding protein, FK506 binding protein	FKBP1B	Q16645	2	IGI_M1_ctg14291_56	6	79.4	
Glutamic acid decarboxylase	GAD1	Q99259	2	IGI_M1_ctg12341_103	18	70.5	
Glycine receptor, α1	GLRA1	P23415	5	IGI_M1_ctg16547_14	X	85.5	
Heparan N-deacetylase/N-sulphotransferase	NDST1	P52848	5	IGI_M1_ctg13263_18	4	81.5	
Insulin-like growth factor-1 receptor	IGF1R	P08069	15	IGI_M1_ctg18444_3	19	71.8	
Na,K-ATPase, α-subunit	ATP1A1	P05023	1	IGI_M1_ctg14877_54	1	83	
Purinergic receptor 7 (P2X), ligand-gated ion channel	P2RX7	Q99572	12	IGI_M1_ctg15140_15	12	80.3	H84353
Tubulin, ε-chain	TUBE*	Q9UJT0	6	IGI_M1_ctg13826_4	5	78.5	AA970498
Tubulin, χ-chain	TUBG1	P23258	17	IGI_M1_ctg12599_5	7	84.0	
Voltage-gated potassium channel, KV3.3	KCNC3	Q14003	19	IGI_M1_ctg13492_5	12	80.1	H49142

* HGM symbol unknown.

because of the availability of tissues from all developmental time points. A challenge will be to define the gene-specific patterns of alternative splicing, which may affect half of human genes. Existing collections of ESTs and cDNAs may allow identification of the most abundant of these isoforms, but systematic exploration of this problem may require exhaustive analysis of cDNA libraries from multiple tissues or perhaps high-throughput reverse transcription–PCR studies. Deep understanding of gene function will probably require knowledge of the structure, tissue distribution and abundance of these alternative forms.

Large-scale identification of regulatory regions

The one-dimensional script of the human genome, shared by essentially all cells in all tissues, contains sufficient information to provide for differentiation of hundreds of different cell types, and the ability to respond to a vast array of internal and external influences. Much of this plasticity results from the carefully orchestrated symphony of transcriptional regulation. Although much has been learned about the cis-acting regulatory motifs of some specific genes, the regulatory signals for most genes remain uncharacterized. Comparative genomics of multiple vertebrates offers the best hope for large-scale identification of such regulatory sites[440]. Previous studies of sequence alignment of regulatory domains of orthologous genes in multiple species has shown a remarkable correlation between sequence conservation, dubbed 'phylogenetic footprints'[441], and the presence of binding motifs for transcription factors. This approach could be particularly powerful if combined with expression array technologies that identify cohorts of genes that are coordinately regulated, implicating a common set of cis-acting regulatory sequences[442–445]. It will also be of considerable interest to study epigenetic modifications such as cytosine methylation on a genome-wide scale, and to determine their biological consequences[446,447]. Towards this end, a pilot Human Epigenome Project has been launched[448,449].

Sequencing of additional large genomes

More generally, comparative genomics allows biologists to peruse evolution's laboratory notebook—to identify conserved functional features and recognize new innovations in specific lineages. Determination of the genome sequence of many organisms is very desirable. Already, projects are underway to sequence the genomes of the mouse, rat, zebrafish and the pufferfishes T. nigroviridis and Takifugu rubripes. Plans are also under consideration for sequencing additional primates and other organisms that will help define key developments along the vertebrate and nonvertebrate lineages.

To realize the full promise of comparative genomics, however, it needs to become simple and inexpensive to sequence the genome of any organism. Sequencing costs have dropped 100-fold over the last 10 years, corresponding to a roughly twofold decrease every 18 months. This rate is similar to 'Moore's law' concerning improvements in semiconductor manufacture. In both sequencing and semiconductors, such improvement does not happen automatically, but requires aggressive technological innovation fuelled by major investment. Improvements are needed to move current dideoxy sequencing to smaller volumes and more rapid sequencing times, based upon advances such as microchannel technology. More revolutionary methods, such as mass spectrometry, single-molecule sequencing and nanopore approaches[76], have not yet been fully developed, but hold great promise and deserve strong encouragement.

Completing the catalogue of human variation

The human draft genome sequence has already allowed the identification of more than 1.4 million SNPs, comprising a substantial proportion of all common human variation. This program should be extended to obtain a nearly complete catalogue of common variants and to identify the common ancestral haplotypes present in the population. In principle, these genetic tools should make it possible to perform association studies and linkage disequilibrium studies[376] to identify the genes that confer even relatively modest risk

for common diseases. Launching such an intense era of human molecular epidemiology will also require major advances in the cost efficiency of genotyping technology, in the collection of carefully phenotyped patient cohorts and in statistical methods for relating large-scale SNP data to disease phenotype.

From sequence to function

The scientific program outlined above focuses on how the genome sequence can be mined for biological information. In addition, the sequence will serve as a foundation for a broad range of functional genomic tools to help biologists to probe function in a more systematic manner. These will need to include improved techniques and databases for the global analysis of: RNA and protein expression, protein localization, protein–protein interactions and chemical inhibition of pathways. New computational techniques will be needed to use such information to model cellular circuitry. A full discussion of these important directions is beyond the scope of this paper.

Concluding thoughts

The Human Genome Project is but the latest increment in a remarkable scientific program whose origins stretch back a hundred years to the rediscovery of Mendel's laws and whose end is nowhere in sight. In a sense, it provides a capstone for efforts in the past century to discover genetic information and a foundation for efforts in the coming century to understand it.

We find it humbling to gaze upon the human sequence now coming into focus. In principle, the string of genetic bits holds long-sought secrets of human development, physiology and medicine. In practice, our ability to transform such information into understanding remains woefully inadequate. This paper simply records some initial observations and attempts to frame issues for future study. Fulfilling the true promise of the Human Genome Project will be the work of tens of thousands of scientists around the world, in both academia and industry. It is for this reason that our highest priority has been to ensure that genome data are available rapidly, freely and without restriction.

The scientific work will have profound long-term consequences for medicine, leading to the elucidation of the underlying molecular mechanisms of disease and thereby facilitating the design in many cases of rational diagnostics and therapeutics targeted at those mechanisms. But the science is only part of the challenge. We must also involve society at large in the work ahead. We must set realistic expectations that the most important benefits will not be reaped overnight. Moreover, understanding and wisdom will be required to ensure that these benefits are implemented broadly and equitably. To that end, serious attention must be paid to the many ethical, legal and social implications (ELSI) raised by the accelerated pace of genetic discovery. This paper has focused on the scientific achievements of the human genome sequencing efforts. This is not the place to engage in a lengthy discussion of the ELSI issues, which have also been a major research focus of the Human Genome Project, but these issues are of comparable importance and could appropriately fill a paper of equal length.

Finally, it is has not escaped our notice that the more we learn about the human genome, the more there is to explore.

"We shall not cease from exploration. And the end of all our exploring will be to arrive where we started, and know the place for the first time."—T. S. Eliot[450]

Received 7 December 2000; accepted 9 January 2001.

1. Correns, C. Untersuchungen über die Xenien bei Zea mays. *Berichte der Deutsche Botanische Gesellschaft* **17**, 410–418 (1899).
2. De Vries, H. Sur la loie de disjonction des hybrides. *Comptes Rendue Hebdemodaires, Acad. Sci. Paris* **130**, 845–847 (1900).
3. von Tschermack, E. Uber Künstliche Kreuzung bei Pisum sativum. *Berichte der Deutsche Botanische Gesellschaft* **18**, 232–239. (1900).
4. Sanger, F. et al. Nucleotide sequence of bacteriophage Φ X174 DNA. *Nature* **265**, 687–695 (1977).
5. Sanger, F. et al. The nucleotide sequence of bacteriophage ΦX174. *J Mol Biol* **125**, 225–246 (1978).

6. Sanger, F., Coulson, A. R., Hong, G. F., Hill, D. F. & Petersen, G. B. Nucleotide-sequence of bacteriophage Lambda DNA. *J. Mol. Biol.* **162,** 729–773 (1982).

7. Fiers, W. *et al.* Complete nucleotide sequence of SV40 DNA. *Nature* **273,** 113–120 (1978).

8. Anderson, S. *et al.* Sequence and organization of the human mitochondrial genome. *Nature* **290,** 457–465 (1981).

9. Botstein, D., White, R. L., Skolnick, M. & Davis, R. W. Construction of a genetic linkage map in man using restriction fragment length polymorphisms. *Am. J. Hum. Genet.* **32,** 314–331 (1980).

10. Olson, M. V. *et al.* Random-clone strategy for genomic restriction mapping in yeast. *Proc. Natl Acad. Sci. USA* **83,** 7826–7830 (1986).

11. Coulson, A., Sulston, J., Brenner, S. & Karn, J. Toward a physical map of the genome of the nematode *Caenorhabditis elegans. Proc. Natl Acad. Sci. USA* **83,** 7821–7825 (1986).

12. Putney, S. D., Herlihy, W. C. & Schimmel, P. A new troponin T and cDNA clones for 13 different muscle proteins, found by shotgun sequencing. *Nature* **302,** 718–721 (1983).

13. Milner, R. J. & Sutcliffe, J. G. Gene expression in rat brain. *Nucleic Acids Res.* **11,** 5497–5520 (1983).

14. Adams, M. D. *et al.* Complementary DNA sequencing: expressed sequence tags and human genome project. *Science* **252,** 1651–1656 (1991).

15. Adams, M. D. *et al.* Initial assessment of human gene diversity and expression patterns based upon 83 million nucleotides of cDNA sequence. *Nature* **377,** 3–174 (1995).

16. Okubo, K. *et al.* Large scale cDNA sequencing for analysis of quantitative and qualitative aspects of gene expression. *Nature Genet.* **2,** 173–179 (1992).

17. Hillier, L. D. *et al.* Generation and analysis of 280,000 human expressed sequence tags. *Genome Res.* **6,** 807–828 (1996).

18. Strausberg, R. L., Feingold, E. A., Klausner, R. D. & Collins, F. S. The mammalian gene collection. *Science* **286,** 455–457 (1999).

19. Berry, R. *et al.* Gene-based sequence-tagged-sites (STSs) as the basis for a human gene map. *Nature Genet.* **10,** 415–423 (1995).

20. Houlgatte, R. *et al.* The Genexpress Index: a resource for gene discovery and the genic map of the human genome. *Genome Res.* **5,** 272–304 (1995).

21. Sinsheimer, R. L. The Santa Cruz Workshop—May 1985. *Genomics* **5,** 954–956 (1989).

22. Palca, J. Human genome—Department of Energy on the map. *Nature* **321,** 371 (1986).

23. National Research Council *Mapping and Sequencing the Human Genome* (National Academy Press, Washington DC, 1988).

24. Bishop, J. E. & Waldholz, M. *Genome* (Simon and Schuster, New York, 1990).

25. Kevles, D. J. & Hood, L. (eds) *The Code of Codes: Scientific and Social Issues in the Human Genome Project* (Harvard Univ. Press, Cambridge, Massachusetts, 1992).

26. Cook-Deegan, R. *The Gene Wars: Science, Politics, and the Human Genome* (W. W. Norton & Co., New York, London, 1994).

27. Donis-Keller, H. *et al.* A genetic linkage map of the human genome. *Cell* **51,** 319–337 (1987).

28. Gyapay, G. *et al.* The 1993–94 Genethon human genetic linkage map. *Nature Genet.* **7,** 246–339 (1994).

29. Hudson, T. J. *et al.* An STS-based map of the human genome. *Science* **270,** 1945–1954 (1995).

30. Dietrich, W. F. *et al.* A comprehensive genetic map of the mouse genome. *Nature* **380,** 149–152 (1996).

31. Nusbaum, C. *et al.* A YAC-based physical map of the mouse genome. *Nature Genet.* **22,** 388–393 (1999).

32. Oliver, S. G. *et al.* The complete DNA sequence of yeast chromosome III. *Nature* **357,** 38–46 (1992).

33. Wilson, R. *et al.* 2.2 Mb of contiguous nucleotide sequence from chromosome III of *C. elegans. Nature* **368,** 32–38 (1994).

34. Chen, E. Y. *et al.* The human growth hormone locus: nucleotide sequence, biology, and evolution. *Genomics* **4,** 479–497 (1989).

35. McCombie, W. R. *et al.* Expressed genes, Alu repeats and polymorphisms in cosmids sequenced from chromosome 4p16.3. *Nature Genet.* **1,** 348–353 (1992).

36. Martin-Gallardo, A. *et al.* Automated DNA sequencing and analysis of 106 kilobases from human chromosome 19q13.3. *Nature Genet.* **1,** 34–39 (1992).

37. Edwards, A. *et al.* Automated DNA sequencing of the human HPRT locus. *Genomics* **6,** 593–608 (1990).

38. Marshall, E. A strategy for sequencing the genome 5 years early. *Science* **267,** 783–784 (1995).

39. Project to sequence human genome moves on to the starting blocks. *Nature* **375,** 93–94 (1995).

40. Shizuya, H. *et al.* Cloning and stable maintenance of 300-kilobase-pair fragments of human DNA in *Escherichia coli* using an F-factor-based vector. *Proc. Natl Acad. Sci. USA* **89,** 8794–8797 (1992).

41. Burke, D. T., Carle, G. F. & Olson, M. V. Cloning of large segments of exogenous DNA into yeast by means of artificial chromosome vectors. *Science* **236,** 806–812 (1987).

42. Marshall, E. A second private genome project. *Science* **281,** 1121 (1998).

43. Marshall, E. NIH to produce a 'working draft' of the genome by 2001. *Science* **281,** 1774–1775 (1998).

44. Pennisi, E. Academic sequencers challenge Celera in a sprint to the finish. *Science* **283,** 1822–1823 (1999).

45. Bouck, J., Miller, W., Gorrell, J. H., Muzny, D. & Gibbs, R. A. Analysis of the quality and utility of random shotgun sequencing at low redundancies. *Genome Res.* **8,** 1074–1084 (1998).

46. Collins, F. S. *et al.* New goals for the U. S. Human Genome Project: 1998–2003. *Science* **282,** 682–689 (1998).

47. Sanger, F. & Coulson, A. R. A rapid method for determining sequences in DNA by primed synthesis with DNA polymerase. *J. Mol. Biol.* **94,** 441–448 (1975).

48. Maxam, A. M. & Gilbert, W. A new method for sequencing DNA. *Proc. Natl Acad. Sci. USA* **74,** 560–564 (1977).

49. Anderson, S. Shotgun DNA sequencing using cloned DNase I-generated fragments. *Nucleic Acids Res.* **9,** 3015–3027 (1981).

50. Gardner, R. C. *et al.* The complete nucleotide sequence of an infectious clone of cauliflower mosaic virus by M13mp7 shotgun sequencing. *Nucleic Acids Res.* **9,** 2871–2888 (1981).

51. Deininger, P. L. Random subcloning of sonicated DNA: application to shotgun DNA sequence analysis. *Anal. Biochem.* **129,** 216–223 (1983).

52. Chissoe, S. L. *et al.* Sequence and analysis of the human ABL gene, the BCR gene, and regions involved in the Philadelphia chromosomal translocation. *Genomics* **27,** 67–82 (1995).

53. Rowen, L., Koop, B. F. & Hood, L. The complete 685-kilobase DNA sequence of the human beta T cell receptor locus. *Science* **272,** 1755–1762 (1996).

54. Koop, B. F. *et al.* Organization, structure, and function of 95 kb of DNA spanning the murine T-cell receptor C alpha/C delta region. *Genomics* **13,** 1209–1230 (1992).

55. Wooster, R. *et al.* Identification of the breast cancer susceptibility gene BRCA2. *Nature* **378,** 789–792 (1995).

56. Fleischmann, R. D. *et al.* Whole-genome random sequencing and assembly of *Haemophilus influenzae* Rd. *Science* **269,** 496–512 (1995).

57. Lander, E. S. & Waterman, M. S. Genomic mapping by fingerprinting random clones: a mathematical analysis. *Genomics* **2,** 231–239 (1988).

58. Weber, J. L. & Myers, E. W. Human whole-genome shotgun sequencing. *Genome Res.* **7,** 401–409 (1997).

59. Green, P. Against a whole-genome shotgun. *Genome Res.* **7,** 410–417 (1997).

60. Venter, J. C. *et al.* Shotgun sequencing of the human genome. *Science* **280,** 1540–1542 (1998).

61. Venter, J. C. *et al.* The sequence of the human genome. *Science* **291,** 1304–1351 (2001).

62. Smith, L. M. *et al.* Fluorescence detection in automated DNA sequence analysis. *Nature* **321,** 674–679 (1986).

63. Ju, J. Y., Ruan, C. C., Fuller, C. W., Glazer, A. N. & Mathies, R. A. Fluorescence energy-transfer dye-labeled primers for DNA sequencing and analysis. *Proc. Natl Acad. Sci. USA* **92,** 4347–4351 (1995).

64. Lee, L. G. *et al.* New energy transfer dyes for DNA sequencing. *Nucleic Acids Res.* **25,** 2816–2822 (1997).

65. Rosenblum, B. B. *et al.* New dye-labeled terminators for improved DNA sequencing patterns. *Nucleic Acids Res.* **25,** 4500–4504 (1997).

66. Metzker, M. L., Lu, J. & Gibbs, R. A. Electrophoretically uniform fluorescent dyes for automated DNA sequencing. *Science* **271,** 1420–1422 (1996).

67. Prober, J. M. *et al.* A system for rapid DNA sequencing with fluorescent chain-terminating dideoxynucleotides. *Science* **238,** 336–341 (1987).

68. Reeve, M. A. & Fuller, C. W. A novel thermostable polymerase for DNA sequencing. *Nature* **376,** 796–797 (1995).

69. Tabor, S. & Richardson, C. C. Selective inactivation of the exonuclease activity of bacteriophage T7 DNA polymerase by in vitro mutagenesis. *J. Biol. Chem.* **264,** 6447–6458 (1989).

70. Tabor, S. & Richardson, C. C. DNA sequence analysis with a modified bacteriophage T7 DNA polymerase—effect of pyrophosphorolysis and metal ions. *J. Biol. Chem.* **265,** 8322–8328 (1990).

71. Murray, V. Improved double-stranded DNA sequencing using the linear polymerase chain reaction. *Nucleic Acids Res.* **17,** 8889 (1989).

72. Guttman, A., Cohen, A. S., Heiger, D. N. & Karger, B. L. Analytical and micropreparative ultrahigh resolution of oligonucleotides by polyacrylamide-gel high-performance capillary electrophoresis. *Anal. Chem.* **62,** 137–141 (1990).

73. Luckey, J. A. *et al.* High-speed DNA sequencing by capillary electrophoresis. *Nucleic Acids Res.* **18,** 4417–4421 (1990).

74. Swerdlow, H., Wu, S., Harke, H. & Dovichi, N. J. Capillary gel-electrophoresis for DNA sequencing—laser-induced fluorescence detection with the sheath flow cuvette. *J. Chromatogr.* **516,** 61–67 (1990).

75. Meldrum, D. Automation for genomics, part one: preparation for sequencing. *Genome Res.* **10,** 1081–1092 (2000).

76. Meldrum, D. Automation for genomics, part two: sequencers, microarrays, and future trends. *Genome Res.* **10,** 1288–1303 (2000).

77. Ewing, B. & Green, P. Base-calling of automated sequencer traces using phred. II. Error probabilities. *Genome Res.* **8,** 186–194 (1998).

78. Ewing, B., Hillier, L., Wendl, M. C. & Green, P. Base-calling of automated sequencer traces using phred. I. Accuracy assessment. *Genome Res.* **8,** 175–185 (1998).

79. Bentley, D. R. Genomic sequence information should be released immediately and freely in the public domain. *Science* **274,** 533–534 (1996).

80. Guyer, M. Statement on the rapid release of genomic DNA sequence. *Genome Res.* **8,** 413 (1998).

81. Dietrich, W. *et al.* A genetic map of the mouse suitable for typing intraspecific crosses. *Genetics* **131,** 423–447 (1992).

82. Kim, U. J. *et al.* Construction and characterization of a human bacterial artificial chromosome library. *Genomics* **34,** 213–218 (1996).

83. Osoegawa, K. *et al.* Bacterial artificial chromosome libraries for mouse sequencing and functional analysis. *Genome Res.* **10,** 116–128 (2000).

84. Marra, M. A. *et al.* High throughput fingerprint analysis of large-insert clones. *Genome Res.* **7,** 1072–1084 (1997).

85. Marra, M. *et al.* A map for sequence analysis of the *Arabidopsis thaliana* genome. *Nature Genet.* **22,** 265–270 (1999).

86. The International Human Genome Mapping Consortium. A physical map of the human genome. *Nature* **409,** 934–941 (2001).

87. Zhao, S. *et al.* Human BAC ends quality assessment and sequence analyses. *Genomics* **63,** 321–332 (2000).

88. Mahairas, G. G. *et al.* Sequence-tagged connectors: A sequence approach to mapping and scanning the human genome. *Proc. Natl Acad. Sci. USA* **96,** 9739–9744 (1999).

89. Tilford, C. A. *et al.* A physical map of the human Y chromosome. *Nature* **409,** 943–945 (2001).

90. Bentley, D. R. *et al.* The physical maps for sequencing human chromosomes 1, 6, 9, 10, 13, 20 and X. *Nature* **409,** 942–943 (2001).

91. Montgomery, K. T. *et al.* A high-resolution map of human chromosome 12. *Nature* **409,** 945–946 (2001).

92. Brüls, T. *et al.* A physical map of human chromosome 14. *Nature* **409,** 947–948 (2001).

93. Hattori, M. *et al.* The DNA sequence of human chromosome 21. *Nature* **405,** 311–319 (2000).

94. Dunham, I. *et al.* The DNA sequence of human chromosome 22. *Nature* **402,** 489–495 (1999).

95. Cox, D. *et al.* Radiation hybrid map of the human genome. *Science* (in the press).

96. Osoegawa, K. *et al.* An improved approach for construction of bacterial artificial chromosome libraries. *Genomics* **52,** 1–8 (1998).

97. The International SNP Map Working Group. A map of human genome sequence variation containing 1.42 million single nucleotide polymorphisms. *Nature* **409,** 928–933 (2001).

98. Collins, F. S., Brooks, L. D. & Chakravarti, A. A DNA polymorphism discovery resource for research on human genetic variation. *Genome Res.* **8,** 1229–1231 (1998).

99. Stewart, E. A. *et al.* An STS-based radiation hybrid map of the human genome. *Genome Res.* **7,** 422–433 (1997).

100. Deloukas, P. *et al.* A physical map of 30,000 human genes. *Science* **282,** 744–746 (1998).

101. Dib, C. *et al.* A comprehensive genetic map of the human genome based on 5,264 microsatellites.

Nature **380,** 152–154 (1996).
102. Broman, K. W., Murray, J. C., Sheffield, V. C., White, R. L. & Weber, J. L. Comprehensive human genetic maps: individual and sex-specific variation in recombination. *Am. J. Hum. Genet.* **63,** 861–869 (1998).
103. The BAC Resource Consortium. Integration of cytogenetic landmarks into the draft sequence of the human genome. *Nature* **409,** 953–958 (2001).
104. Kent, W. J. & Haussler, D. GigAssembler: an algorithm for the initial assembly of the human working draft . Technical Report UCSC-CRL-00-17 (Univ. California at Santa Cruz, Santa Cruz, California, 2001).
105. Morton, N. E. Parameters of the human genome. *Proc. Natl Acad. Sci. USA* **88,** 7474–7476 (1991).
106. Podugolnikova, O. A. & Blumina, M. G. Heterochromatic regions on chromosomes 1, 9, 16, and Y in children with some disturbances occurring during embryo development. *Hum. Genet.* **63,** 183–188 (1983).
107. Lundgren, R., Berger, R. & Kristoffersson, U. Constitutive heterochromatin C-band polymorphism in prostatic cancer. *Cancer Genet. Cytogenet.* **51,** 57–62 (1991).
108. Lee, C., Wevrick, R., Fisher, R. B., Ferguson-Smith, M. A. & Lin, C. C. Human centromeric DNAs. *Hum. Genet.* **100,** 291–304 (1997).
109. Riethman, H. C. *et al.* Integration of telomere sequences with the draft human genome sequence. *Nature* **409,** 953–958 (2001).
110. Pruit, K. D. & Maglott, D. R. RefSeq and LocusLink: NCBI gene-centered resources. *Nucleic Acids Res.* **29,** 137–140 (2001).
111. Wolfsberg, T. G., McEntyre, J. & Schuler, G. D. Guide to the draft human genome. *Nature* **409,** 824–826 (2001).
112. Hurst, L. D. & Eyre-Walker, A. Evolutionary genomics: reading the bands. *Bioessays* **22,** 105–107 (2000).
113. Saccone, S. *et al.* Correlations between isochores and chromosomal bands in the human genome. *Proc. Natl Acad. Sci. USA* **90,** 11929–11933 (1993).
114. Zoubak, S., Clay, O. & Bernardi, G. The gene distribution of the human genome. *Gene* **174,** 95–102 (1996).
115. Gardiner, K. Base composition and gene distribution: critical patterns in mammalian genome organization. *Trends Genet.* **12,** 519–524 (1996).
116. Duret, L., Mouchiroud, D. & Gautier, C. Statistical analysis of vertebrate sequences reveals that long genes are scarce in GC-rich isochores. *J. Mol. Evol.* **40,** 308–317 (1995).
117. Saccone, S., De Sario, A., Della Valle, G. & Bernardi, G. The highest gene concentrations in the human genome are in telomeric bands of metaphase chromosomes. *Proc. Natl Acad. Sci. USA* **89,** 4913–4917 (1992).
118. Bernardi, G. *et al.* The mosaic genome of warm-blooded vertebrates. *Science* **228,** 953–958 (1985).
119. Bernardi, G. Isochores and the evolutionary genomics of vertebrates. *Gene* **241,** 3–17 (2000).
120. Fickett, J. W., Torney, D. C. & Wolf, D. R. Base compositional structure of genomes. *Genomics* **13,** 1056–1064 (1992).
121. Churchill, G. A. Stochastic models for heterogeneous DNA sequences. *Bull. Math. Biol.* **51,** 79–94 (1989).
122. Bird, A., Taggart, M., Frommer, M., Miller, O. J. & Macleod, D. A fraction of the mouse genome that is derived from islands of nonmethylated, CpG-rich DNA. *Cell* **40,** 91–99 (1985).
123. Bird, A. P. CpG islands as gene markers in the vertebrate nucleus. *Trends Genet.* **3,** 342–347 (1987).
124. Chan, M. F., Liang, G. & Jones, P. A. Relationship between transcription and DNA methylation. *Curr. Top. Microbiol. Immunol.* **249,** 75–86 (2000).
125. Holliday, R. & Pugh, J. E. DNA modification mechanisms and gene activity during development. *Science* **187,** 226–232 (1975).
126. Larsen, F., Gundersen, G., Lopez, R. & Prydz, H. CpG islands as gene markers in the human genome. *Genomics* **13,** 1095–1107 (1992).
127. Tazi, J. & Bird, A. Alternative chromatin structure at CpG islands. *Cell* **60,** 909–920 (1990).
128. Gardiner-Garden, M. & Frommer, M. CpG islands in vertebrate genomes. *J. Mol. Biol.* **196,** 261–282 (1987).
129. Antequera, F. & Bird, A. Number of CpG islands and genes in human and mouse. *Proc. Natl Acad. Sci. USA* **90,** 11995–11999 (1993).
130. Ewing, B. & Green, P. Analysis of expressed sequence tags indicates 35,000 human genes. *Nature Genet.* **25,** 232–234 (2000).
131. Yu, A. Comparison of human genetic and sequence-based physical maps. *Nature* **409,** 951–953 (2001).
132. Kaback, D. B., Guacci, V., Barber, D. & Mahon, J. W. Chromosome size-dependent control of meiotic recombination. *Science* **256,** 228–232 (1992).
133. Riles, L. *et al.* Physical maps of the 6 smallest chromosomes of *Saccharomyces cerevisiae* at a resolution of 2.6-kilobase pairs. *Genetics* **134,** 81–150 (1993).
134. Lynn, A. *et al.* Patterns of meiotic recombination on the long arm of human chromosome 21. *Genome Res.* **10,** 1319–1332 (2000).
135. Laurie, D. A. & Hulten, M. A. Further studies on bivalent chiasma frequency in human males with normal karyotypes. *Ann. Hum. Genet.* **49,** 189–201 (1985).
136. Roeder, G. S. Meiotic chromosomes: it takes two to tango. *Genes Dev.* **11,** 2600–2621 (1997).
137. Wu, T.-C. & Lichten, M. Meiosis-induced double-strand break sites determined by yeast chromatin structure. *Science* **263,** 515–518 (1994).
138. Gerton, J. L. *et al.* Global mapping of meiotic recombination hotspots and coldspots in the yeast *Saccharomyces cerevisiae. Proc. Natl Acad. Sci. USA* **97,** 11383–11390 (2000).
139. Li, W. -H. *Molecular Evolution* (Sinauer, Sunderland, Massachusetts, 1997).
140. Gregory, T. R. & Hebert, P. D. The modulation of DNA content: proximate causes and ultimate consequences. *Genome Res.* **9,** 317–324 (1999).
141. Hartl, D. L. Molecular melodies in high and low C. *Nature Rev. Genet.* **1,** 145–149 (2000).
142. Smit, A. F. Interspersed repeats and other mementos of transposable elements in mammalian genomes. *Curr. Opin. Genet. Dev.* **9,** 657–663 (1999).
143. Prak, E. L. & Haig, H. K. Jr Mobile elements and the human genome. *Nature Rev. Genet.* **1,** 134–144 (2000).
144. Okada, N., Hamada, M., Ogiwara, I. & Ohshima, K. SINEs and LINEs share common 3′ sequences: a review. *Gene* **205,** 229–243 (1997).
145. Esnault, C., Maestre, J. & Heidmann, T. Human LINE retrotransposons generate processed pseudogenes. *Nature Genet.* **24,** 363–367 (2000).
146. Wei, W. *et al.* Human L1 retrotransposition: cis-preference vs. trans-complementation. *Mol. Cell. Biol.* **21,** 1429–1439 (2001)
147. Malik, H. S., Henikoff, S. & Eickbush, T. H. Poised for contagion: evolutionary origins of the infectious abilities of invertebrate retroviruses. *Genome Res.* **10,** 1307–1318 (2000).
148. Smit, A. F. The origin of interspersed repeats in the human genome. *Curr. Opin. Genet. Dev.* **6,** 743–748 (1996).
149. Clark, J. B. & Tidwell, M. G. A phylogenetic perspective on P transposable element evolution in Drosophila. *Proc. Natl Acad. Sci. USA* **94,** 11428–11433 (1997).
150. Haring, E., Hagemann, S. & Pinsker, W. Ancient and recent horizontal invasions of Drosophilids by P elements. *J. Mol. Evol.* **51,** 577–586 (2000).
151. Koga, A. *et al.* Evidence for recent invasion of the medaka fish genome by the Tol2 transposable element. *Genetics* **155,** 273–281 (2000).
152. Robertson, H. M. & Lampe, D. J. Recent horizontal transfer of a mariner transposable element among and between Diptera and Neuroptera. *Mol. Biol. Evol.* **12,** 850–862 (1995).
153. Simmons, G. M. Horizontal transfer of hobo transposable elements within the *Drosophila melanogaster* species complex: evidence from DNA sequencing. *Mol. Biol. Evol.* **9,** 1050–1060 (1992).
154. Malik, H. S., Burke, W. D. & Eickbush, T. H. The age and evolution of non-LTR retrotransposable elements. *Mol. Biol. Evol.* **16,** 793–805 (1999).
155. Kordis, D. & Gubensek, F. Bov-B long interspersed repeated DNA (LINE) sequences are present in *Vipera ammodytes* phospholipase A2 genes and in genomes of Viperidae snakes. *Eur. J. Biochem.* **246,** 772–779 (1997).
156. Jurka, J. Repbase update: a database and an electronic journal of repetitive elements. *Trends Genet.* **16,** 418–420 (2000).
157. Sarich, V. M. & Wilson, A. C. Generation time and genome evolution in primates. *Science* **179,** 1144–1147 (1973).
158. Smit, A. F., Toth, G., Riggs, A. D., & Jurka, J. Ancestral, mammalian-wide subfamilies of LINE-1 repetitive sequences. *J. Mol. Biol.* **246,** 401–417 (1995).
159. Lim, J. K. & Simmons, M. J. Gross chromosome rearrangements mediated by transposable elements in *Drosophila melanogaster. Bioessays* **16,** 269–275 (1994).
160. Caceres, M., Ranz, J. M., Barbadilla, A., Long, M. & Ruiz, A. Generation of a widespread Drosophila inversion by a transposable element. *Science* **285,** 415–418 (1999).
161. Gray, Y. H. It takes two transposons to tango: transposable-element-mediated chromosomal rearrangements. *Trends Genet.* **16,** 461–468 (2000).
162. Zhang, J. & Peterson, T. Genome rearrangements by nonlinear transposons in maize. *Genetics* **153,** 1403–1410 (1999).
163. Smit, A. F. Identification of a new, abundant superfamily of mammalian LTR-transposons. *Nucleic Acids Res.* **21,** 1863–1872 (1993).
164. Cordonnier, A., Casella, J. F. & Heidmann, T. Isolation of novel human endogenous retrovirus-like elements with foamy virus-related pol sequence. *J. Virol.* **69,** 5890–5897 (1995).
165. Medstrand, P. & Mager, D. L. Human-specific integrations of the HERV-K endogenous retrovirus family. *J. Virol.* **72,** 9782–9787 (1998).
166. Myers, E. W. *et al.* A whole-genome assembly of Drosophila. *Science* **287,** 2196–2204 (2000).
167. Petrov, D. A., Lozovskaya, E. R. & Hartl, D. L. High intrinsic rate of DNA loss in *Drosophila. Nature* **384,** 346–349 (1996).
168. Li, W. H., Ellsworth, D. L., Krushkal, J., Chang, B. H. & Hewett-Emmett, D. Rates of nucleotide substitution in primates and rodents and the generation-time effect hypothesis. *Mol. Phylogenet. Evol.* **5,** 182–187 (1996).
169. Goodman, M. *et al.* Toward a phylogenetic classification of primates based on DNA evidence complemented by fossil evidence. *Mol. Phylogenet. Evol.* **9,** 585–598 (1998).
170. Kazazian, H. H. Jr & Moran, J. V. The impact of L1 retrotransposons on the human genome. *Nature Genet.* **19,** 19–24 (1998).
171. Malik, H. S. & Eickbush, T. H. NeSL-1, an ancient lineage of site-specific non-LTR retrotransposons from *Caenorhabditis elegans. Genetics* **154,** 193–203 (2000).
172. Casavant, N. C. *et al.* The end of the LINE?: lack of recent L1 activity in a group of South American rodents. *Genetics* **154,** 1809–1817 (2000).
173. Meunier-Rotival, M., Soriano, P., Cuny, G., Strauss, F. & Bernardi, G. Sequence organization and genomic distribution of the major family of interspersed repeats of mouse DNA. *Proc. Natl Acad. Sci. USA* **79,** 355–359 (1982).
174. Soriano, P., Meunier-Rotival, M. & Bernardi, G. The distribution of interspersed repeats is nonuniform and conserved in the mouse and human genomes. *Proc. Natl Acad. Sci. USA* **80,** 1816–1820 (1983).
175. Goldman, M. A., Holmquist, G. P., Gray, M. C., Caston, L. A. & Nag, A. Replication timing of genes and middle repetitive sequences. *Science* **224,** 686–692 (1984).
176. Manuelidis, L. & Ward, D. C. Chromosomal and nuclear distribution of the *Hin*dIII 1.9-kb human DNA repeat segment. *Chromosoma* **91,** 28–38 (1984).
177. Feng, Q., Moran, J. V., Kazazian, H. H. Jr & Boeke, J. D. Human L1 retrotransposon encodes a conserved endonuclease required for retrotransposition. *Cell* **87,** 905–916 (1996).
178. Jurka, J. Sequence patterns indicate an enzymatic involvement in integration of mammalian retroposons. *Proc. Natl Acad. Sci. USA* **94,** 1872–1877 (1997).
179. Arcot, S. S. *et al.* High-resolution cartography of recently integrated human chromosome 19-specific Alu fossils. *J. Mol. Biol.* **281,** 843–856 (1998).
180. Schmid, C. W. Does SINE evolution preclude Alu function? *Nucleic Acids Res.* **26,** 4541–4550 (1998).
181. Chu, W. M., Ballard, R., Carpick, B. W., Williams, B. R. & Schmid, C. W. Potential Alu function: regulation of the activity of double-stranded RNA-activated kinase PKR. *Mol. Cell. Biol.* **18,** 58–68 (1998).
182. Li, T., Spearow, J., Rubin, C. M. & Schmid, C. W. Physiological stresses increase mouse short interspersed element (SINE) RNA expression in vivo. *Gene* **239,** 367–372 (1999).
183. Liu, W. M., Chu, W. M., Choudary, P. V. & Schmid, C. W. Cell stress and translational inhibitors transiently increase the abundance of mammalian SINE transcripts. *Nucleic Acids Res.* **23,** 1758–1765 (1995).
184. Filipski, J. Correlation between molecular clock ticking, codon usage fidelity of DNA repair, chromosome banding and chromatin compactness in germline cells. *FEBS Lett.* **217,** 184–186 (1987).
185. Sueoka, N. Directional mutation pressure and neutral molecular evolution. *Proc. Natl Acad. Sci.*

USA **85**, 2653–2657 (1988).
186. Wolfe, K. H., Sharp, P. M. & Li, W. H. Mutation rates differ among regions of the mammalian genome. *Nature* **337**, 283–285 (1989).
187. Bains, W. Local sequence dependence of rate of base replacement in mammals. *Mutat. Res.* **267**, 43–54 (1992).
188. Mathews, C. K. & Ji, J. DNA precursor asymmetries, replication fidelity, and variable genome evolution. *Bioessays* **14**, 295–301 (1992).
189. Holmquist, G. P. & Filipski, J. Organization of mutations along the genome: a prime determinant of genome evolution. *Trends Ecol. Evol.* **9**, 65–68 (1994).
190. Eyre-Walker, A. Evidence of selection on silent site base composition in mammals: potential implications for the evolution of isochores and junk DNA. *Genetics* **152**, 675–683 (1999).
191. The International SNP Map Working Group. An SNP map of the human genome generated by reduced representation shotgun sequencing. *Nature* **407**, 513–516 (2000).
192. Bohossian, H. B., Skaletsky, H. & Page, D. C. Unexpectedly similar rates of nucleotide substitution found in male and female hominids. *Nature* **406**, 622–625 (2000).
193. Skowronski, J., Fanning, T. G. & Singer, M. F. Unit-length LINE-1 transcripts in human teratocarcinoma cells. *Mol. Cell. Biol.* **8**, 1385–1397 (1988).
194. Boissinot, S., Chevret, P. & Furano, A. V. L1 (LINE-1) retrotransposon evolution and amplification in recent human history. *Mol. Biol. Evol.* **17**, 915–928 (2000).
195. Moran, J. V. Human L1 retrotransposition: insights and peculiarities learned from a cultured cell retrotransposition assay. *Genetica* **107**, 39–51 (1999).
196. Kazazian, H. H. Jr *et al.* Haemophilia A resulting from *de novo* insertion of L1 sequences represents a novel mechanism for mutation in man. *Nature* **332**, 164–166 (1988).
197. Sheen, F.-m. *et al.* Reading between the LINEs: Human genomic variation introduced by LINE-1 retrotransposition. *Genome Res.* **10**, 1496–1508 (2000).
198. Dombroski, B. A., Mathias, S. L., Nanthakumar, E., Scott, A. F. & Kazazian, H. H. Jr Isolation of an active human transposable element. *Science* **254**, 1805–1808 (1991).
199. Holmes, S. E., Dombroski, B. A., Krebs, C. M., Boehm, C. D. & Kazazian, H. H. Jr A new retrotransposable human L1 element from the LRE2 locus on chromosome 1q produces a chimaeric insertion. *Nature Genet.* **7**, 143–148 (1994).
200. Sassaman, D. M. *et al.* Many human L1 elements are capable of retrotransposition. *Nature Genet.* **16**, 37–43 (1997).
201. Dombroski, B. A., Scott, A. F. & Kazazian, H. H. Jr Two additional potential retrotransposons isolated from a human L1 subfamily that contains an active retrotransposable element. *Proc. Natl Acad. Sci. USA* **90**, 6513–6517 (1993).
202. Kimberland, M. L. *et al.* Full-length human L1 insertions retain the capacity for high frequency retrotransposition in cultured cells. *Hum. Mol. Genet.* **8**, 1557–1560 (1999).
203. Moran, J. V. *et al.* High frequency retrotransposition in cultured mammalian cells. *Cell* **87**, 917–927 (1996).
204. Moran, J. V., DeBerardinis, R. J. & Kazazian, H. H. Jr Exon shuffling by L1 retrotransposition. *Science* **283**, 1530–1534 (1999).
205. Pickeral, O. K., Makalowski, W., Boguski, M. S. & Boeke, J. D. Frequent human genomic DNA transduction driven by LINE-1 retrotransposition. *Genome Res.* **10**, 411–415 (2000).
206. Miki, Y. *et al.* Disruption of the APC gene by a retrotransposal insertion of L1 sequence in a colon cancer. *Cancer Res.* **52**, 643–645 (1992).
207. Branciforte, D. & Martin, S. L. Developmental and cell type specificity of LINE-1 expression in mouse testis: implications for transposition. *Mol. Cell. Biol.* **14**, 2584–2592 (1994).
208. Trelogan, S. A. & Martin, S. L. Tightly regulated, developmentally specific expression of the first open reading frame from LINE-1 during mouse embryogenesis. *Proc. Natl Acad. Sci. USA* **92**, 1520–1524 (1995).
209. Jurka, J. & Kapitonov, V. V. Sectorial mutagenesis by transposable elements. *Genetica* **107**, 239–248 (1999).
210. Fraser, M. J., Ciszczon, T., Elick, T. & Bauser, C. Precise excision of TTAA-specific lepidopteran transposons piggyBac (IFP2) and tagalong (TFP3) from the baculovirus genome in cell lines from two species of Lepidoptera. *Insect Mol. Biol.* **5**, 141–151 (1996).
211. Brosius, J. Genomes were forged by massive bombardments with retroelements and retrosequences. *Genetica* **107**, 209–238 (1999).
212. Kruglyak, S., Durrett, R. T., Schug, M. D. & Aquadro, C. F. Equilibrium distribution of microsatellite repeat length resulting from a balance between slippage events and point mutations. *Proc. Natl Acad. Sci. USA* **95**, 10774–10778 (1998).
213. Toth, G., Gaspari, Z. & Jurka, J. Microsatellites in different eukaryotic genomes: survey and analysis. *Genome Res.* **10**, 967–981 (2000).
214. Ellegren, H. Heterogeneous mutation processes in human microsatellite DNA sequences. *Nature Genet.* **24**, 400–402 (2000).
215. Ji, Y., Eichler, E. E., Schwartz, S. & Nicholls, R. D. Structure of chromosomal duplicons and their role in mediating human genomic disorders. *Genome Res.* **10**, 597–610 (2000).
216. Eichler, E. E. Masquerading repeats: paralogous pitfalls of the human genome. *Genome Res.* **8**, 758–762 (1998).
217. Mazzarella, R. & D. Schlessinger, D. Pathological consequences of sequence duplications in the human genome. *Genome Res.* **8**, 1007–1021 (1998).
218. Eichler, E. E. *et al.* Interchromosomal duplications of the adrenoleukodystrophy locus: a phenomenon of pericentromeric plasticity. *Hum. Mol. Genet.* **6**, 991–1002 (1997).
219. Horvath, J. E., Schwartz, S. & Eichler, E. E. The mosaic structure of human pericentromeric DNA: a strategy for characterizing complex regions of the human genome. *Genome Res.* **10**, 839–852 (2000).
220. Brand-Arpon, V. *et al.* A genomic region encompassing a cluster of olfactory receptor genes and a myosin light chain kinase (MYLK) gene is duplicated on human chromosome regions 3q13-q21 and 3p13. *Genomics* **56**, 98–110 (1999).
221. Arnold, N., Wienberg, J., Ermert, K. & Zachau, H. G. Comparative mapping of DNA probes derived from the V kappa immunoglobulin gene regions on human and great ape chromosomes by fluorescence in situ hybridization. *Genomics* **26**, 147–150 (1995).
222. Eichler, E. E. *et al.* Duplication of a gene-rich cluster between 16p11.1 and Xq28: a novel pericentromeric-directed mechanism for paralogous genome evolution. *Hum. Mol. Genet.* **5**, 899–912 (1996).
223. Potier, M. *et al.* Two sequence-ready contigs spanning the two copies of a 200-kb duplication on human 21q: partial sequence and polymorphisms. *Genomics* **51**, 417–426 (1998).
224. Regnier, V. *et al.* Emergence and scattering of multiple neurofibromatosis (NF1)-related sequences during hominoid evolution suggest a process of pericentromeric interchromosomal transposition. *Hum. Mol. Genet.* **6**, 9–16 (1997).
225. Ritchie, R. J., Mattei, M. G. & Lalande, M. A large polymorphic repeat in the pericentromeric region of human chromosome 15q contains three partial gene duplications. *Hum. Mol. Genet.* **7**, 1253–1260 (1998).
226. Trask, B. J. *et al.* Members of the olfactory receptor gene family are contained in large blocks of DNA duplicated polymorphically near the ends of human chromosomes. *Hum. Mol. Genet.* **7**, 13–26 (1998).
227. Trask, B. J. *et al.* Large multi-chromosomal duplications encompass many members of the olfactory receptor gene family in the human genome. *Hum. Mol. Genet.* **7**, 2007–2020 (1998).
228. van Deutekom, J. C. *et al.* Identification of the first gene (FRG1) from the FSHD region on human chromosome 4q35. *Hum. Mol. Genet.* **5**, 581–590 (1996).
229. Zachau, H. G. The immunoglobulin kappa locus—or—what has been learned from looking closely at one-tenth of a percent of the human genome. *Gene* **135**, 167–173 (1993).
230. Zimonjic, D. B., Kelley, M. J., Rubin, J. S., Aaronson, S. A. & Popescu, N. C. Fluorescence in situ hybridization analysis of keratinocyte growth factor gene amplification and dispersion in evolution of great apes and humans. *Proc. Natl Acad. Sci. USA* **94**, 11461–11465 (1997).
231. van Geel, M. *et al.* The FSHD region on human chromosome 4q35 contains potential coding regions among pseudogenes and a high density of repeat elements. *Genomics* **61**, 55–65 (1999).
232. Horvath, J. E. *et al.* Molecular structure and evolution of an alpha satellite/non-alpha satellite junction at 16p11. *Hum. Mol. Genet.* **9**, 113–123 (2000).
233. Guy, J. *et al.* Genomic sequence and transcriptional profile of the boundary between pericentromeric satellites and genes on human chromosome arm 10q. *Hum. Mol. Genet.* **9**, 2029–2042 (2000).
234. Reiter, L. T., Murakami, T., Koeuth, T., Gibbs, R. A. & Lupski, J. R. The human COX10 gene is disrupted during homologous recombination between the 24 kb proximal and distal CMT1A-REPs. *Hum. Mol. Genet.* **6**, 1595–1603 (1997).
235. Amos-Landgraf, J. M. *et al.* Chromosome breakage in the Prader-Willi and Angelman syndromes involves recombination between large, transcribed repeats at proximal and distal breakpoints. *Am. J. Hum. Genet.* **65**, 370–386 (1999).
236. Christian, S. L., Fantes, J. A., Mewborn, S. K., Huang, B. & Ledbetter, D. H. Large genomic duplicons map to sites of instability in the Prader-Willi/Angelman syndrome chromosome region (15q11-q13). *Hum. Mol. Genet.* **8**, 1025–1037 (1999).
237. Edelmann, L., Pandita, R. K. & Morrow, B. E. Low-copy repeats mediate the common 3-Mb deletion in patients with velo-cardio-facial syndrome. *Am. J. Hum. Genet.* **64**, 1076–1086 (1999).
238. Shaikh, T. H. *et al.* Chromosome 22-specific low copy repeats and the 22q11.2 deletion syndrome: genomic organization and deletion endpoint analysis. *Hum. Mol. Genet.* **9**, 489–501 (2000).
239. Francke, U. Williams-Beuren syndrome: genes and mechanisms. *Hum. Mol. Genet.* **8**, 1947–1954 (1999).
240. Peoples, R. *et al.* A physical map, including a BAC/PAC clone contig, of the Williams-Beuren syndrome-deletion region at 7q11.23. *Am. J. Hum. Genet.* **66**, 47–68 (2000).
241. Eichler, E. E., Archidiacono, N. & Rocchi, M. CAGGG repeats and the pericentromeric duplication of the hominoid genome. *Genome Res.* **9**, 1048–1058 (1999).
242. O'Keefe, C. & Eichler, E. in *Comparative Genomics: Empirical and Analytical Approaches to Gene Order Dynamics, Map Alignment and the Evolution of Gene Families* (eds Sankoff, D. & Nadeau, J.) 29–46 (Kluwer Academic, Dordrecht, 2000).
243. Lander, E. S. The new genomics: Global views of biology. *Science* **274**, 536–539 (1996).
244. Eddy, S. R. Noncoding RNA genes. *Curr. Op. Genet. Dev.* **9**, 695–699 (1999).
245. Ban, N., Nissen, P., Hansen, J., Moore, P. B. & Steitz, T. A. The complete atomic structure of the large ribosomal subunit at 2.4 angstrom resolution. *Science* **289**, 905–920 (2000).
246. Nissen, P., Hansen, J., Ban, N., Moore, P. B. & Steitz, T. A. The structural basis of ribosome activity in peptide bond synthesis. *Science* **289**, 920–930 (2000).
247. Weinstein, L. B. & Steitz, J. A. Guided tours: from precursor snoRNA to functional snoRNP. *Curr. Opin. Cell Biol.* **11**, 378–384 (1999).
248. Bachellerie, J.-P. & Cavaille, J. in *Modification and Editing of RNA* (ed. Benne, H. G. a. R.) 255–272 (ASM, Washington DC, 1998).
249. Burge, C. & Sharp, P. A. Classification of introns: U2-type or U12-type. *Cell* **91**, 875–879 (1997).
250. Brown, C. J. *et al.* The Human Xist gene—analysis of a 17 kb inactive X-specific RNA that contains conserved repeats and is highly localized within the nucleus. *Cell* **71**, 527–542 (1992).
251. Kickhoefer, V. A., Vasu, S. K. & Rome, L. H. Vaults are the answer, what is the question? *Trends Cell Biol.* **6**, 174–178 (1996).
252. Hatlen, L. & Attardi, G. Proportion of the HeLa cell genome complementary to the transfer RNA and 5S RNA. *J. Mol. Biol.* **56**, 535–553 (1971).
253. Sprinzl, M., Horn, C., Brown, M., Ioudovitch, A. & Steinberg, S. Compilation of tRNA sequences and sequences of tRNA genes. *Nucleic Acids Res.* **26**, 148–153 (1998).
254. Long, E. O. & Dawid, I. B. Repeated genes in eukaryotes. *Annu. Rev. Biochem.* **49**, 727–764 (1980).
255. Crick, F. H. Codon–anticodon pairing: the wobble hypothesis. *J. Mol. Biol.* **19**, 548–555 (1966).
256. Guthrie, C. & Abelson, J. in *The Molecular Biology of the Yeast Saccharomyces: Metabolism and Gene Expression* (eds Strathern, J. & Broach J.) 487–528 (Cold Spring Harbor Laboratory Press, Cold Spring Harbor, New York, 1982).
257. Soll, D. & RajBhandary, U. (eds) *tRNA: Structure, Biosynthesis, and Function* (ASM, Washington DC, 1995).
258. Ikemura, T. Codon usage and tRNA content in unicellular and multicellular organisms. *Mol. Biol. Evol.* **2**, 13–34 (1985).
259. Bulmer, M. Coevolution of codon usage and transfer-RNA abundance. *Nature* **325**, 728–730 (1987).
260. Duret, L. tRNA gene number and codon usage in the *C. elegans* genome are co-adapted for optimal translation of highly expressed genes. *Trends Genet.* **16**, 287–289 (2000).
261. Sharp, P. M. & Matassi, G. Codon usage and genome evolution. *Curr. Opin. Genet. Dev.* **4**, 851–860 (1994).
262. Buckland, R. A. A primate transfer-RNA gene cluster and the evolution of human chromosome 1. *Cytogenet. Cell Genet.* **61**, 1–4 (1992).
263. Gonos, E. S. & Goddard, J. P. Human tRNA-Glu genes: their copy number and organization. *FEBS Lett.* **276**, 138–142 (1990).
264. Sylvester, J. E. *et al.* The human ribosomal RNA genes: structure and organization of the complete repeating unit. *Hum. Genet.* **73**, 193–198 (1986).

265. Sorensen, P. D. & Frederiksen, S. Characterization of human 5S ribosomal RNA genes. *Nucleic Acids Res.* **19**, 4147–4151 (1991).

266. Timofeeva, M. *et al.* [Organization of a 5S ribosomal RNA gene cluster in the human genome]. *Mol. Biol. (Mosk.)* **27**, 861–868 (1993).

267. Little, R. D. & Braaten, D. C. Genomic organization of human 5S rDNA and sequence of one tandem repeat. *Genomics* **4**, 376–383 (1989).

268. Maden, B. E. H. The numerous modified nucleotides in eukaryotic ribosomal RNA. *Prog. Nucleic Acid Res. Mol. Biol.* **39**, 241–303 (1990).

269. Tycowski, K. T., You, Z. H., Graham, P. J. & Steitz, J. A. Modification of U6 spliceosomal RNA is guided by other small RNAs. *Mol. Cell* **2**, 629–638 (1998).

270. Pavelitz, T., Liao, D. Q. & Weiner, A. M. Concerted evolution of the tandem array encoding primate U2 snRNA (the RNU2 locus) is accompanied by dramatic remodeling of the junctions with flanking chromosomal sequences. *EMBO J.* **18**, 3783–3792 (1999).

271. Lindgren, V., Ares, A., Weiner, A. M. & Francke, U. Human genes for U2 small nuclear RNA map to a major adenovirus 12 modification site on chromosome 17. *Nature* **314**, 115–116 (1985).

272. Van Arsdell, S. W. & Weiner, A. M. Human genes for U2 small nuclear RNA are tandemly repeated. *Mol. Cell. Biol.* **4**, 492–499 (1984).

273. Gao, L. I., Frey, M. R. & Matera, A. G. Human genes encoding U3 snRNA associate with coiled bodies in interphase cells and are clustered on chromosome 17p11. 2 in a complex inverted repeat structure. *Nucleic Acids Res.* **25**, 4740–4747 (1997).

274. Hawkins, J. D. A survey on intron and exon lengths. *Nucleic Acids Res.* **16**, 9893–9908 (1988).

275. Burge, C. & Karlin, S. Prediction of complete gene structures in human genomic DNA. *J. Mol. Biol.* **268**, 78–94 (1997).

276. Labeit, S. & Kolmerer, B. Titins: giant proteins in charge of muscle ultrastructure and elasticity. *Science* **270**, 293–296 (1995).

277. Sterner, D. A., Carlo, T. & Berget, S. M. Architectural limits on split genes. *Proc. Natl Acad. Sci. USA* **93**, 15081–15085 (1996).

278. Sun, Q., Mayeda, A., Hampson, R. K., Krainer, A. R. & Rottman, F. M. General splicing factor SF2/ASF promotes alternative splicing by binding to an exonic splicing enhancer. *Genes Dev.* **7**, 2598–2608 (1993).

279. Tanaka, K., Watakabe, A. & Shimura, Y. Polypurine sequences within a downstream exon function as a splicing enhancer. *Mol. Cell. Biol.* **14**, 1347–1354 (1994).

280. Carlo, T., Sterner, D. A. & Berget, S. M. An intron splicing enhancer containing a G-rich repeat facilitates inclusion of a vertebrate micro-exon. *RNA* **2**, 342–353 (1996).

281. Burset, M., Seledtsov, I. A. & Solovyev, V. V. Analysis of canonical and non-canonical splice sites in mammalian genomes. *Nucleic Acids Res.* **28**, 4364–4375 (2000).

282. Burge, C. B., Padgett, R. A. & Sharp, P. A. Evolutionary fates and origins of U12-type introns. *Mol. Cell* **2**, 773–785 (1998).

283. Mironov, A. A., Fickett, J. W. & Gelfand, M. S. Frequent alternative splicing of human genes. *Genome Res.* **9**, 1288–1293 (1999).

284. Hanke, J. *et al.* Alternative splicing of human genes: more the rule than the exception? *Trends Genet.* **15**, 389–390 (1999).

285. Brett, D. *et al.* EST comparison indicates 38% of human mRNAs contain possible alternative splice forms. *FEBS Lett.* **474**, 83–86 (2000).

286. Dunham, I. The gene guessing game. *Yeast* **17**, 218–224 (2000).

287. Lewin, B. *Gene Expression* (Wiley, New York, 1980).

288. Lewin, B. *Genes IV* 466–481 (Oxford Univ. Press, Oxford, 1990).

289. Smaglik, P. Researchers take a gamble on the human genome. *Nature* **405**, 264 (2000).

290. Fields, C., Adams, M. D., White, O. & Venter, J. C. How many genes in the human genome? *Nature Genet.* **7**, 345–346 (1994).

291. Liang, F. *et al.* Gene index analysis of the human genome estimates approximately 120,000 genes. *Nature Genet.* **25**, 239–240 (2000).

292. Roest Crollius, H. *et al.* Estimate of human gene number provided by genome-wide analysis using *Tetraodon nigroviridis* DNA sequence. *Nature Genet.* **25**, 235–238 (2000).

293. The C. elegans Sequencing Consortium. Genome sequence of the nematode *C. elegans*: A platform for investigating biology. *Science* **282**, 2012–2018 (1998).

294. Rubin, G. M. *et al.* Comparative genomics of the eukaryotes. *Science* **287**, 2204–2215 (2000).

295. Green, P. *et al.* Ancient conserved regions in new gene sequences and the protein databases. *Science* **259**, 1711–1716 (1993).

296. Fraser, A. G. *et al.* Functional genomic analysis of *C. elegans* chromosome I by systematic RNA interference. *Nature* **408**, 325–330 (2000).

297. Mott, R. EST_GENOME: a program to align spliced DNA sequences to unspliced genomic DNA. *Comput. Appl. Biosci.* **13**, 477–478 (1997).

298. Florea, L., Hartzell, G., Zhang, Z., Rubin, G. M. & Miller, W. A computer program for aligning a cDNA sequence with a genomic DNA sequence. *Genome Res.* **8**, 967–974 (1998).

299. Bailey, L. C. Jr, Searls, D. B. & Overton, G. C. Analysis of EST-driven gene annotation in human genomic sequence. *Genome Res.* **8**, 362–376 (1998).

300. Birney, E., Thompson, J. D. & Gibson, T. J. PairWise and SearchWise: finding the optimal alignment in a simultaneous comparison of a protein profile against all DNA translation frames. *Nucleic Acids Res.* **24**, 2730–2739 (1996).

301. Gelfand, M. S., Mironov, A. A. & Pevzner, P. A. Gene recognition via spliced sequence alignment. *Proc. Natl Acad. Sci. USA* **93**, 9061–9066 (1996).

302. Kulp, D., Haussler, D., Reese, M. G. & Eeckman, F. H. A generalized hidden Markov model for the recognition of human genes in DNA. *ISMB* **4**, 134–142 (1996).

303. Reese, M. G., Kulp, D., Tammana, H. & Haussler, D. Genie—gene finding in *Drosophila melanogaster*. *Genome Res.* **10**, 529–538 (2000).

304. Solovyev, V. & Salamov, A. The Gene-Finder computer tools for analysis of human and model organisms genome sequences. *ISMB* **5**, 294–302 (1997).

305. Guigo, R., Agarwal, P., Abril, J. F., Burset, M. & Fickett, J. W. An assessment of gene prediction accuracy in large DNA sequences. *Genome Res.* **10**, 1631–1642 (2000).

306. Hubbard, T. & Birney, E. Open annotation offers a democratic solution to genome sequencing. *Nature* **403**, 825 (2000).

307. Bateman, A. *et al.* The Pfam protein families database. *Nucleic Acids Res.* **28**, 263–266 (2000).

308. Birney, E. & Durbin, R. Using GeneWise in the Drosophila annotation experiment. *Genome Res.* **10**, 547–548 (2000).

309. The RIKEN Genome Exploration Research Group Phase II Team and the FANTOM Consortium. Functional annotation of a full-length mouse cDNA collection. *Nature* **409**, 685–690 (2001).

310. Basrai, M. A., Hieter, P. & Boeke, J. D. Small open reading frames: beautiful needles in the haystack. *Genome Res.* **7**, 768–771 (1997).

311. Janin, J. & Chothia, C. Domains in proteins: definitions, location, and structural principles. *Methods Enzymol.* **115**, 420–430 (1985).

312. Ponting, C. P., Schultz, J., Copley, R. R., Andrade, M. A. & Bork, P. Evolution of domain families. *Adv. Protein Chem.* **54**, 185–244 (2000).

313. Doolittle, R. F. The multiplicity of domains in proteins. *Annu. Rev. Biochem.* **64**, 287–314 (1995).

314. Bateman, A. & Birney, E. Searching databases to find protein domain organization. *Adv. Protein Chem.* **54**, 137–157 (2000).

315. Futreal, P. A. *et al.* Cancer and genomics. *Nature* **409**, 850–852 (2001).

316. Nestler, E. J. & Landsman, D. Learning about addiction from the human draft genome. *Nature* **409**, 834–835 (2001).

317. Tupler, R., Perini, G. & Green, M. R. Expressing the human genome. *Nature* **409**, 832–835 (2001).

318. Fahrer, A. M., Bazan, J. F., Papathanasiou, P., Nelms, K. A. & Goodnow, C. C. A genomic view of immunology. *Nature* **409**, 836–838 (2001).

319. Li, W. -H., Gu, Z., Wang, H. & Nekrutenko, A. Evolutionary analyses of the human genome. *Nature* **409**, 847–849 (2001).

320. Bock, J. B., Matern, H. T., Peden, A. A. & Scheller, R. H. A genomic perspective on membrane compartment organization. *Nature* **409**, 839–841 (2001).

321. Pollard, T. D. Genomics, the cytoskeleton and motility. *Nature* **409**, 842–843 (2001).

322. Murray, A. W. & Marks, D. Can sequencing shed light on cell cycling? *Nature* **409**, 844–846 (2001).

323. Clayton, J. D., Kyriacou, C. P. & Reppert, S. M. Keeping time with the human genome. *Nature* **409**, 829–831 (2001).

324. Chervitz, S. A. *et al.* Comparison of the complete protein sets of worm and yeast: orthology and divergence. *Science* **282**, 2022–2028 (1998).

325. Aravind, L. & Subramanian, G. Origin of multicellular eukaryotes—insights from proteome comparisons. *Curr. Opin. Genet. Dev.* **9**, 688–694 (1999).

326. Attwood, T. K. *et al.* PRINTS-S: the database formerly known as PRINTS. *Nucleic Acids Res.* **28**, 225–227 (2000).

327. Hofmann, K., Bucher, P., Falquet, L. & Bairoch, A. The PROSITE database, its status in 1999. *Nucleic Acids Res.* **27**, 215–219 (1999).

328. Altschul, S. F. *et al.* Gapped BLAST and PSI-BLAST: a new generation of protein database search programs. *Nucleic Acids Res.* **25**, 3389–3402 (1997).

329. Wolf, Y. I., Kondrashov, F. A. & Koonin, E. V. No footprints of primordial introns in a eukaryotic genome. *Trends Genet.* **16**, 333–334 (2000).

330. Brunner, H. G., Nelen, M., Breakefield, X. O., Ropers, H. H. & van Oost, B. B. A. Abnormal behavior associated with a point mutation in the structural gene for monoamine oxidase A. *Science* **262**, 578–580 (1993).

331. Cases, O. *et al.* Aggressive behavior and altered amounts of brain serotonin and norepinephrine in mice lacking MAOA. *Science* **268**, 1763–1766 (1995).

332. Brunner, H. G. *et al.* X-linked borderline mental retardation with prominent behavioral disturbance: phenotype, genetic localization, and evidence for disturbed monoamine metabolism. *Am. J. Hum. Genet.* **52**, 1032–1039 (1993).

333. Deckert, J. *et al.* Excess of high activity monoamine oxidase A gene promoter alleles in female patients with panic disorder. *Hum. Mol. Genet.* **8**, 621–624 (1999).

334. Smith, T. F. & Waterman, M. S. Identification of common molecular subsequences. *J. Mol. Biol.* **147**, 195–197 (1981).

335. Tatusov, R. L., Koonin, E. V. & Lipman, D. J. A genomic perspective on protein families. *Science* **278**, 631–637 (1997).

336. Ponting, C. P., Aravind, L., Schultz, J., Bork, P. & Koonin, E. V. Eukaryotic signalling domain homologues in archaea and bacteria. Ancient ancestry and horizontal gene transfer. *J. Mol. Biol.* **289**, 729–745 (1999).

337. Zhang, J., Dyer, K. D. & Rosenberg, H. F. Evolution of the rodent eosinophil-associated Rnase gene family by rapid gene sorting and positive selection. *Proc. Natl Acad. Sci. USA* **97**, 4701–4706 (2000).

338. Shashoua, V. E. Ependymin, a brain extracellular glycoprotein, and CNS plasticity. *Ann. NY Acad. Sci.* **627**, 94–114 (1991).

339. Schultz, J., Copley, R. R., Doerks, T., Ponting, C. P. & Bork, P. SMART: a web-based tool for the study of genetically mobile domains. *Nucleic Acids Res.* **28**, 231–234 (2000).

340. Koonin, E. V., Aravind, L. & Kondrashov, A. S. The impact of comparative genomics on our understanding of evolution. *Cell* **101**, 573–576 (2000).

341. Bateman, A., Eddy, S. R. & Chothia, C. Members of the immunoglobulin superfamily in bacteria. *Protein Sci.* **5**, 1939–1941 (1996).

342. Sutherland, D., Samakovlis, C. & Krasnow, M. A. Branchless encodes a Drosophila FGF homolog that controls tracheal cell migration and the pattern of branching. *Cell* **87**, 1091–1101 (1996).

343. Warburton, D. *et al.* The molecular basis of lung morphogenesis. *Mech. Dev.* **92**, 55–81 (2000).

344. Fuchs, T., Glusman, G., Horn-Saban, S., Lancet, D. & Pilpel, Y. The human olfactory subgenome: from sequence to structure to evolution. *Hum. Genet.* **108**, 1–13 (2001).

345. Glusman, G. *et al.* The olfactory receptor gene family: data mining, classification and nomenclature. *Mamm. Genome* **11**, 1016–1023 (2000).

346. Rouquier, S. *et al.* Distribution of olfactory receptor genes in the human genome. *Nature Genet.* **18**, 243–250 (1998).

347. Sharon, D. *et al.* Primate evolution of an olfactory receptor cluster: Diversification by gene conversion and recent emergence of a pseudogene. *Genomics* **61**, 24–36 (1999).

348. Gilad, Y. *et al.* Dichotomy of single-nucleotide polymorphism haplotypes in olfactory receptor genes and pseudogenes. *Nature Genet.* **26**, 221–224 (2000).

349. Gearhart, J. & Kirschner, M. *Cells, Embryos, and Evolution* (Blackwell Science, Malden, Massachusetts, 1997).

350. Barbazuk, W. B. *et al.* The syntenic relationship of the zebrafish and human genomes. *Genome Res.* **10**, 1351–1358 (2000).

351. McLysaght, A., Enright, A. J., Skrabanek, L. & Wolfe, K. H. Estimation of synteny conservation and genome compaction between pufferfish (Fugu) and human. *Yeast* **17**, 22–36 (2000).

352. Trachtulec, Z. *et al.* Linkage of TATA-binding protein and proteasome subunit C5 genes in mice and humans reveals synteny conserved between mammals and invertebrates. *Genomics* **44**, 1–7 (1997).

353. Nadeau, J. H. Maps of linkage and synteny homologies between mouse and man. *Trends Genet.* **5**, 82–86 (1989).

354. Nadeau, J. H. & Taylor, B. A. Lengths of chromosomal segments conserved since divergence of man and mouse. *Proc. Natl Acad. Sci. USA* **81**, 814–818 (1984).

355. Copeland, N. G. *et al.* A genetic linkage map of the mouse: current applications and future prospects. *Science* **262**, 57–66 (1993).

356. DeBry, R. W. & Seldin, M. F. Human/mouse homology relationships. *Genomics* **33**, 337–351 (1996).

357. Nadeau, J. H. & Sankoff, D. The lengths of undiscovered conserved segments in comparative maps. *Mamm. Genome* **9**, 491–495 (1998).

358. Thomas, J. W. *et al.* Comparative genome mapping in the sequence-based era: early experience with human chromosome 7. *Genome Res.* **10**, 624–633 (2000).

359. Pletcher, M. T. *et al.* Chromosome evolution: The junction of mammalian chromosomes in the formation of mouse chromosome 10. *Genome Res.* **10**, 1463–1467 (2000).

360. Novacek, M. J. Mammalian phylogeny: shaking the tree. *Nature* **356**, 121–125 (1992).

361. O'Brien, S. J. *et al.* Genome maps 10. Comparative genomics. Mammalian radiations. Wall chart. *Science* **286**, 463–478 (1999).

362. Romer, A. S. *Vertebrate Paleontology* (Univ. Chicago Press, Chicago and New York, 1966).

363. Paterson, A. H. *et al.* Toward a unified genetic map of higher plants, transcending the monocot-dicot divergence. *Nature Genet.* **14**, 380–382 (1996).

364. Jenczewski, E., Prosperi, J. M. & Ronfort, J. Differentiation between natural and cultivated populations of *Medicago sativa* (Leguminosae) from Spain: analysis with random amplified polymorphic DNA (RAPD) markers and comparison to allozymes. *Mol. Ecol.* **8**, 1317–1330 (1999).

365. Ohno, S. *Evolution by Gene Duplication* (George Allen and Unwin, London, 1970).

366. Wolfe, K. H. & Shields, D. C. Molecular evidence for an ancient duplication of the entire yeast genome. *Nature* **387**, 708–713 (1997).

367. Blanc, G., Barakat, A., Guyot, R., Cooke, R. & Delseny, M. Extensive duplication and reshuffling in the arabidopsis genome. *Plant Cell* **12**, 1093–1102 (2000).

368. Paterson, A. H. *et al.* Comparative genomics of plant chromosomes. *Plant Cell* **12**, 1523–1540 (2000).

369. Vision, T., Brown, D. & Tanksley, S. The origins of genome duplications in *Arabidopsis*. *Science* **290**, 2114–2117 (2000).

370. Sidow, A. & Bowman, B. H. Molecular phylogeny. *Curr. Opin. Genet. Dev.* **1**, 451–456 (1991).

371. Sidow, A. & Thomas, W. K. A molecular evolutionary framework for eukaryotic model organisms. *Curr. Biol.* **4**, 596–603 (1994).

372. Sidow, A. Gen(om)e duplications in the evolution of early vertebrates. *Curr. Opin. Genet. Dev.* **6**, 715–722 (1996).

373. Spring, J. Vertebrate evolution by interspecific hybridisation—are we polyploid? *FEBS Lett.* **400**, 2–8 (1997).

374. Skrabanek, L. & Wolfe, K. H. Eukaryote genome duplication—where's the evidence? *Curr. Opin. Genet. Dev.* **8**, 694–700 (1998).

375. Hughes, A. L. Phylogenies of developmentally important proteins do not support the hypothesis of two rounds of genome duplication early in vertebrate history. *J. Mol. Evol.* **48**, 565–576 (1999).

376. Lander, E. S. & Schork, N. J. Genetic dissection of complex traits. *Science* **265**, 2037–2048 (1994).

377. Horikawa, Y. *et al.* Genetic variability in the gene encoding calpain-10 is associated with type 2 diabetes mellitus. *Nature Genet.* **26**, 163–175 (2000).

378. Hastbacka, J. *et al.* The diastrophic dysplasia gene encodes a novel sulfate transporter: positional cloning by fine-structure linkage disequilibrium mapping. *Cell* **78**, 1073–1087 (1994).

379. Tischkoff, S. A. *et al.* Global patterns of linkage disequilibrium at the CD4 locus and modern human origins. *Science* **271**, 1380–1387 (1996).

380. Kidd, J. R. *et al.* Haplotypes and linkage disequilibrium at the phenylalanine hydroxylase locus PAH, in a global representation of populations. *Am. J. Hum. Genet.* **63**, 1882–1899 (2000).

381. Mateu, E. *et al.* Worldwide genetic analysis of the CFTR region. *Am. J. Hum. Genet.* **68**, 103–117 (2001).

382. Abecasis, G. R. *et al.* Extent and distribution of linkage disequilibrium in three genomic regions. *Am. J. Hum. Genet.* **68**, 191–197 (2001).

383. Taillon-Miller, P. *et al.* Juxtaposed regions of extensive and minimal linkage disequilibrium in Xq25 and Xq28. *Nature Genet.* **25**, 324–328 (2000).

384. Martin, E. R. *et al.* SNPing away at complex diseases: analysis of single-nucleotide polymorphisms around APOE in Alzheimer disease. *Am. J. Hum. Genet.* **67**, 383–394 (2000).

385. Collins, A., Lonjou, C. & Morton, N. E. Genetic epidemiology of single-nucleotide polymorphisms. *Proc. Natl Acad. Sci. USA* **96**, 15173–15177 (1999).

386. Dunning, A. M. *et al.* The extent of linkage disequilibrium in four populations with distinct demographic histories. *Am. J. Hum. Genet.* **67**, 1544–1554 (2000).

387. Rieder, M. J., Taylor, S. L., Clark, A. G. & Nickerson, D. A. Sequence variation in the human angiotensin converting enzyme. *Nature Genet.* **22**, 59–62 (1999).

388. Collins, F. S. Positional cloning moves from perditional to traditional. *Nature Genet.* **9**, 347–350 (1995).

389. Nagamine, K. *et al.* Positional cloning of the APECED gene. *Nature Genet.* **17**, 393–398 (1997).

390. Reuber, B. E. *et al.* Mutations in PEX1 are the most common cause of peroxisome biogenesis disorders. *Nature Genet.* **17**, 445–448 (1997).

391. Portsteffen, H. *et al.* Human PEX1 is mutated in complementation group 1 of the peroxisome biogenesis disorders. *Nature Genet.* **17**, 449–452 (1997).

392. Everett, L. A. *et al.* Pendred syndrome is caused by mutations in a putative sulphate transporter gene (PDS). *Nature Genet.* **17**, 411–422 (1997).

393. Coffey, A. J. *et al.* Host response to EBV infection in X-linked lymphoproliferative disease results from mutations in an SH2-domain encoding gene. *Nature Genet.* **20**, 129–135 (1998).

394. Van Laer, L. *et al.* Nonsyndromic hearing impairment is associated with a mutation in DFNA5. *Nature Genet.* **20**, 194–197 (1998).

395. Sakuntabhai, A. *et al.* Mutations in ATP2A2, encoding a Ca2+ pump, cause Darier disease. *Nature Genet.* **21**, 271–277 (1999).

396. Gedeon, A. K. *et al.* Identification of the gene (SEDL) causing X-linked spondyloepiphyseal dysplasia tarda. *Nature Genet.* **22**, 400–404 (1999).

397. Hurvitz, J. R. *et al.* Mutations in the CCN gene family member WISP3 cause progressive pseudorheumatoid dysplasia. *Nature Genet.* **23**, 94–98 (1999).

398. Laberge-le Couteulx, S. *et al.* Truncating mutations in CCM1, encoding KRIT1, cause hereditary cavernous angiomas. *Nature Genet.* **23**, 189–193 (1999).

399. Sahoo, T. *et al.* Mutations in the gene encoding KRIT1, a Krev-1/rap1a binding protein, cause cerebral cavernous malformations (CCM1). *Hum. Mol. Genet.* **8**, 2325–2333 (1999).

400. McGuirt, W. T. *et al.* Mutations in COL11A2 cause non-syndromic hearing loss (DFNA13). *Nature Genet.* **23**, 413–419 (1999).

401. Moreira, E. S. *et al.* Limb-girdle muscular dystrophy type 2G is caused by mutations in the gene encoding the sarcomeric protein telethonin. *Nature Genet.* **24**, 163–166 (2000).

402. Ruiz-Perez, V. L. *et al.* Mutations in a new gene in Ellis-van Creveld syndrome and Weyers acrodental dysostosis. *Nature Genet.* **24**, 283–286 (2000).

403. Kaplan, J. M. *et al.* Mutations in ACTN4, encoding alpha-actinin-4, cause familial focal segmental glomerulosclerosis. *Nature Genet.* **24**, 251–256 (2000).

404. Escayg, A. *et al.* Mutations of SCN1A, encoding a neuronal sodium channel, in two families with GEFS+2. *Nature Genet.* **24**, 343–345 (2000).

405. Sacksteder, K. A. *et al.* Identification of the alpha-aminoadipic semialdehyde synthase gene, which is defective in familial hyperlysinemia. *Am. J. Hum. Genet.* **66**, 1736–1743 (2000).

406. Kalaydjieva, L. *et al.* N-myc downstream-regulated gene 1 is mutated in hereditary motor and sensory neuropathy-Lom. *Am. J. Hum. Genet.* **67**, 47–58 (2000).

407. Sundin, O. H. *et al.* Genetic basis of total colourblindness among the Pingelapese islanders. *Nature Genet.* **25**, 289–293 (2000).

408. Kohl, S. *et al.* Mutations in the CNGB3 gene encoding the beta-subunit of the cone photoreceptor cGMP-gated channel are responsible for achromatopsia (ACHM3) linked to chromosome 8q21. *Hum. Mol. Genet.* **9**, 2107–2116 (2000).

409. Avela, K. *et al.* Gene encoding a new RING-B-box-coiled-coil protein is mutated in mulibrey nanism. *Nature Genet.* **25**, 298–301 (2000).

410. Verpy, E. *et al.* A defect in harmonin, a PDZ domain-containing protein expressed in the inner ear sensory hair cells, underlies usher syndrome type 1C. *Nature Genet.* **26**, 51–55 (2000).

411. Bitner-Glindzicz, M. *et al.* A recessive contiguous gene deletion causing infantile hyperinsulinism, enteropathy and deafness identifies the usher type 1C gene. *Nature Genet.* **26**, 56–60 (2000).

412. The May-Hegglin/Fetchner Syndrome Consortium. Mutations in MYH9 result in the May-Hegglin anomaly, and Fechtner and Sebastian syndromes. *Nature Genet.* **26**, 103–105 (2000).

413. Kelley, M. J., Jawien, W., Ortel, T. L. & Korczak, J. F. Mutation of MYH9, encoding non-muscle myosin heavy chain A, in May-Hegglin anomaly. *Nature Genet.* **26**, 106–108 (2000).

414. Kirschner, L. S. *et al.* Mutations of the gene encoding the protein kinase A type I-α regulatory subunit in patients with the Carney complex. *Nature Genet.* **26**, 89–92 (2000).

415. Lalwani, A. K. *et al.* Human nonsyndromic hereditary deafness DFNA17 is due to a mutation in non-muscle myosin MYH9. *Am. J. Hum. Genet.* **67**, 1121–1128 (2000).

416. Matsuura, T. *et al.* Large expansion of the ATTCT pentanucleotide repeat in spinocerebellar ataxia type 10. *Nature Genet.* **26**, 191–194 (2000).

417. Delettre, C. *et al.* Nuclear gene OPA1, encoding a mitochondrial dynamin-related protein, is mutated in dominant optic atrophy. *Nature Genet.* **26**, 207–210 (2000).

418. Pusch, C. M. *et al.* The complete form of X-linked congenital stationary night blindness is caused by mutations in a gene encoding a leucine-rich repeat protein. *Nature Genet.* **26**, 324–327 (2000).

419. The ADHR Consortium. Autosomal dominant hypophosphataemic rickets is associated with mutations in FGF23. *Nature Genet.* **26**, 345–348 (2000).

420. Bomont, P. *et al.* The gene encoding gigaxonin, a new member of the cytoskeletal BTB/kelch repeat family, is mutated in giant axonal neuropathy. *Nature Genet.* **26**, 370–374 (2000).

421. Tullio-Pelet, A. *et al.* Mutant WD-repeat protein in triple-A syndrome. *Nature Genet.* **26**, 332–335 (2000).

422. Nicole, S. *et al.* Perlecan, the major proteoglycan of basement membranes, is altered in patients with Schwartz-Jampel syndrome (chondrodystrophic myotonia). *Nature Genet.* **26**, 480–483 (2000).

423. Rogaev, E. I. *et al.* Familial Alzheimer's disease in kindreds with missense mutations in a gene on chromosome 1 related to the Alzheimer's disease type 3 gene. *Nature* **376**, 775–778 (1995).

424. Sherrington, R. *et al.* Cloning of a gene bearing missense mutations in early-onset familial Alzheimer's disease. *Nature* **375**, 754–760 (1995).

425. Olivieri, N. F. & Weatherall, D. J. The therapeutic reactivation of fetal haemoglobin. *Hum. Mol. Genet.* **7**, 1655–1658 (1998).

426. Drews, J. Research & development. Basic science and pharmaceutical innovation. *Nature Biotechnol.* **17**, 406 (1999).

427. Drews, J. Drug discovery: a historical perspective. *Science* **287**, 1960–1964 (2000).

428. Davies, P. A. *et al.* The 5-HT3B subunit is a major determinant of serotonin-receptor function. *Nature* **397**, 359–363 (1999).

429. Heise, C. E. *et al.* Characterization of the human cysteinyl leukotriene 2 receptor. *J. Biol. Chem.* **275**, 30531–30536 (2000).

430. Fan, W. *et al.* BACE maps to chromosome 11 and a BACE homolog, BACE2, reside in the obligate Down Syndrome region of chromosome 21. *Science* **286**, 1255a (1999).

431. Saunders, A. J., Kim, T.-W. & Tanzi, R. E. BACE maps to chromosome 11 and a BACE homolog, BACE2, reside in the obligate Down Syndrome region of chromosome 21. *Science* **286**, 1255a (1999).

432. Firestein, S. The good taste of genomics. *Nature* **404**, 552–553 (2000).

433. Matsunami, H., Montmayeur, J. P. & Buck, L. B. A family of candidate taste receptors in human and mouse. *Nature* **404**, 601–604 (2000).

434. Adler, E. *et al.* A novel family of mammalian taste receptors. *Cell* **100**, 693–702 (2000).

435. Chandrashekar, J. *et al.* T2Rs function as bitter taste receptors. *Cell* **100**, 703–711 (2000).

436. Hardison, R. C. Conserved non-coding sequences are reliable guides to regulatory elements. *Trends Genet.* **16**, 369–372 (2000).

437. Onyango, P. *et al.* Sequence and comparative analysis of the mouse 1-megabase region orthologous to the human 11p15 imprinted domain. *Genome Res.* **10**, 1697–1710 (2000).

438. Bouck, J. B., Metzker, M. L. & Gibbs, R. A. Shotgun sample sequence comparisons between mouse and human genomes. *Nature Genet.* **25**, 31–33 (2000).

439. Marshall, E. Public-private project to deliver mouse genome in 6 months. *Science* **290**, 242–243 (2000).

440. Wasserman, W. W., Palumbo, M., Thompson, W., Fickett, J. W. & Lawrence, C. E. Human-mouse genome comparisons to locate regulatory sites. *Nature Genet.* **26**, 225–228 (2000).

441. Tagle, D. A. *et al.* Embryonic epsilon and gamma globin genes of a prosimian primate (*Galago crassicaudatus*). Nucleotide and amino acid sequences, developmental regulation and phylogenetic footprints. *J. Mol. Biol.* **203**, 439–455 (1988).

442. McGuire, A. M., Hughes, J. D. & Church, G. M. Conservation of DNA regulatory motifs and discovery of new motifs in microbial genomes. *Genome Res.* **10**, 744–757 (2000).

articles

443. Roth, F. P., Hughes, J. D., Estep, P. W. & Church, G. M. Finding DNA regulatory motifs within unaligned noncoding sequences clustered by whole-genome mRNA quantitation. *Nature Biotechnol.* **16**, 939–945 (1998).

444. Cheng, Y. & Church, G. M. Biclustering of expression data. *ISMB* **8**, 93–103 (2000).

445. Cohen, B. A., Mitra, R. D., Hughes, J. D. & Church, G. M. A computational analysis of whole-genome expression data reveals chromosomal domains of gene expression. *Nature Genet.* **26**, 183–186 (2000).

446. Feil, R. & Khosla, S. Genomic imprinting in mammals: an interplay between chromatin and DNA methylation? *Trends Genet.* **15**, 431–434 (1999).

447. Robertson, K. D. & Wolffe, A. P. DNA methylation in health and disease. *Nature Rev. Genet.* **1**, 11–19 (2000).

448. Beck, S., Olek, A. & Walter, J. From genomics to epigenomics: a loftier view of life. *Nature Biotechnol.* **17**, 1144–1144 (1999).

449. Hagmann, M. Mapping a subtext in our genetic book. *Science* **288**, 945–946 (2000).

450. Eliot, T. S. in *T. S. Eliot. Collected Poems 1909–1962* (Harcourt Brace, New York, 1963).

451. Soderland, C., Longden, I. & Mott, R. FPC: a system for building contigs from restriction fingerprinted clones. *Comput. Appl. Biosci.* **13**, 523–535 (1997).

452. Mott, R. & Tribe, R. Approximate statistics of gapped alignments. *J. Comp. Biol.* **6**, 91–112 (1999).

Supplementary Information is available on *Nature*'s World-Wide Web site (http://www.nature.com) or as paper copy from the London editorial office of *Nature*.

Acknowledgements

Beyond the authors, many people contributed to the success of this work. E. Jordan provided helpful advice throughout the sequencing effort. We thank D. Leja and J. Shehadeh for their expert assistance on the artwork in this paper, especially the foldout figure; K. Jegalian for editorial assistance; J. Schloss, E. Green and M. Seldin for comments on an earlier version of the manuscript; P. Green and F. Ouelette for critiques of the submitted version; C. Caulcott, A. Iglesias, S. Renfrey, B. Skene and J. Stewart of the Wellcome Trust, P. Whittington and T. Dougans of NHGRI and M. Meugnier of Genoscope for staff support for meetings of the international consortium; and the University of Pennsylvania for facilities for a meeting of the genome analysis group.

We thank Compaq Computer Corporations's High Performance Technical Computing Group for providing a Compaq Biocluster (a 27 node configuration of AlphaServer ES40s, containing 108 CPUs, serving as compute nodes and a file server with one terabyte of secondary storage) to assist in the annotation and analysis. Compaq provided the systems and implementation services to set up and manage the cluster for continuous use by members of the sequencing consortium. Platform Computing Ltd. provided its LSF scheduling and loadsharing software without license fee.

In addition to the data produced by the members of the International Human Genome Sequencing Consortium, the draft genome sequence includes published and unpublished human genomic sequence data from many other groups, all of whom gave permission to include their unpublished data. Four of the groups that contributed particularly significant amounts of data were: M. Adams *et al.* of the Institute for Genomic Research; E. Chen *et al.* of the Center for Genetic Medicine and Applied Biosystems; S.-F. Tsai of National Yang-Ming University, Institute of Genetics, Taipei, Taiwan, Republic of China; and Y. Nakamura, K. Koyama *et al.* of the Institute of Medical Science, University of Tokyo, Human Genome Center, Laboratory of Molecular Medicine, Minato-ku, Tokyo, Japan. Many other groups provided smaller numbers of database entries. We thank them all; a full list of the contributors of unpublished sequence is available as Supplementary Information.

This work was supported in part by the National Human Genome Research Institute of the US NIH; The Wellcome Trust; the US Department of Energy, Office of Biological and Environmental Research, Human Genome Program; the UK MRC; the Human Genome Sequencing Project from the Science and Technology Agency (STA) Japan; the Ministry of Education, Science, Sport and Culture, Japan; the French Ministry of Research; the Federal German Ministry of Education, Research and Technology (BMBF) through Projektträger DLR, in the framework of the German Human Genome Project; BEO, Projektträger Biologie, Energie, Umwelt des BMBF und BMWT; the Max-Planck-Society; DFG—Deutsche Forschungsgemeinschaft; TMWFK, Thüringer Ministerium für Wissenschaft, Forschung und Kunst; EC BIOMED2—European Commission, Directorate Science, Research and Development; Chinese Academy of Sciences (CAS), Ministry of Science and Technology (MOST), National Natural Science Foundation of China (NSFC); US National Science Foundation EPSCoR and The SNP Consortium Ltd. Additional support for members of the Genome Analysis group came, in part, from an ARCS Foundation Scholarship to T.S.F., a Burroughs Wellcome Foundation grant to C.B.B. and P.A.S., a DFG grant to P.B., DOE grants to D.H., E.E.E. and T.S.F., an EU grant to P.B., a Marie-Curie Fellowship to L.C., an NIH-NHGRI grant to S.R.E., an NIH grant to E.E.E., an NIH SBIR to D.K., an NSF grant to D.H., a Swiss National Science Foundation grant to L.C., the David and Lucille Packard Foundation, the Howard Hughes Medical Institute, the University of California at Santa Cruz and the W. M. Keck Foundation.

Correspondence and requests for materials should be addressed to E. S. Lander (e-mail: lander@genome.wi.mit.edu), R. H. Waterston (e-mail: bwaterst@watson.wustl.edu), J. Sulston (e-mail: jes@sanger.ac.uk) or F. S. Collins (e-mail: fc23a@nih.gov).

Affiliations for authors: 1, Whitehead Institute for Biomedical Research, Center for Genome Research, Nine Cambridge Center, Cambridge, Massachusetts 02142, USA; 2, The Sanger Centre, The Wellcome Trust Genome Campus, Hinxton, Cambridgeshire CB10 1RQ, United Kingdom; 3, Washington University Genome Sequencing Center, Box 8501, 4444 Forest Park Avenue, St. Louis, Missouri 63108, USA; 4, US DOE Joint Genome Institute, 2800 Mitchell Drive, Walnut Creek, California 94598, USA; 5, Baylor College of Medicine Human Genome Sequencing Center, Department of Molecular and Human Genetics, One Baylor Plaza, Houston, Texas 77030, USA; 6, Department of Cellular and Structural Biology, The University of Texas Health Science Center at San Antonio, 7703 Floyd Curl Drive, San Antonio, Texas 78229-3900, USA; 7, Department of Molecular Genetics, Albert Einstein College of Medicine, 1635 Poplar Street, Bronx, New York 10461, USA; 8, Baylor College of Medicine Human Genome Sequencing Center and the Department of Microbiology & Molecular Genetics, University of Texas Medical School, PO Box 20708, Houston, Texas 77225, USA; 9, RIKEN Genomic Sciences Center, 1-7-22 Suehiro-cho, Tsurumi-ku Yokohama-city, Kanagawa 230-0045, Japan; 10, Genoscope and CNRS UMR-8030, 2 Rue Gaston Cremieux, CP 5706, 91057 Evry Cedex, France; 11, GTC Sequencing Center, Genome Therapeutics Corporation, 100 Beaver Street, Waltham, Massachusetts 02453-8443, USA; 12, Department of Genome Analysis, Institute of Molecular Biotechnology, Beutenbergstrasse 11, D-07745 Jena, Germany; 13, Beijing Genomics Institute/Human Genome Center, Institute of Genetics, Chinese Academy of Sciences, Beijing 100101, China; 14, Southern China National Human Genome Research Center, Shanghai 201203, China; 15, Northern China National Human Genome Research Center, Beijing 100176, China; 16, Multimegabase Sequencing Center, The Institute for Systems Biology, 4225 Roosevelt Way, NE Suite 200, Seattle, Washington 98105, USA; 17, Stanford Genome Technology Center, 855 California Avenue, Palo Alto, California 94304, USA; 18, Stanford Human Genome Center and Department of Genetics, Stanford University School of Medicine, Stanford, California 94305-5120, USA; 19, University of Washington Genome Center, 225 Fluke Hall on Mason Road, Seattle, Washington 98195, USA; 20, Department of Molecular Biology, Keio University School of Medicine, 35 Shinanomachi, Shinjuku-ku, Tokyo 160-8582, Japan; 21, University of Texas Southwestern Medical Center at Dallas, 6000 Harry Hines Blvd., Dallas, Texas 75235-8591, USA; 22, University of Oklahoma's Advanced Center for Genome Technology, Dept. of Chemistry and Biochemistry, University of Oklahoma, 620 Parrington Oval, Rm 311, Norman, Oklahoma 73019, USA; 23, Max Planck Institute for Molecular Genetics, Ihnestrasse 73, 14195 Berlin, Germany; 24, Cold Spring Harbor Laboratory, Lita Annenberg Hazen Genome Center, 1 Bungtown Road, Cold Spring Harbor, New York 11724, USA; 25, GBF - German Research Centre for Biotechnology, Mascheroder Weg 1, D-38124 Braunschweig, Germany; 26, National Center for Biotechnology Information, National Library of Medicine, National Institutes of Health, Bldg. 38A, 8600 Rockville Pike, Bethesda, Maryland 20894, USA; 27, Department of Genetics, Case Western Reserve School of Medicine and University Hospitals of Cleveland, BRB 720, 10900 Euclid Ave., Cleveland, Ohio 44106, USA; 28, EMBL European Bioinformatics Institute, Wellcome Trust Genome Campus, Hinxton, Cambridge CB10 1SD, United Kingdom; 29, Max Delbrück Center for Molecular Medicine, Robert-Rossle-Strasse 10, 13125 Berlin-Buch, Germany; 30, EMBL, Meyerhofstrasse 1, 69012 Heidelberg, Germany; 31, Dept. of Biology, Massachusetts Institute of Technology, 77 Massachusetts Ave., Cambridge, Massachusetts 02139-4307, USA; 32, Howard Hughes Medical Institute, Dept. of Genetics, Washington University School of Medicine, Saint Louis, Missouri 63110, USA; 33, Dept. of Computer Science, University of California at Santa Cruz, Santa Cruz, California 95064, USA; 34, Affymetrix, Inc., 2612 8th St, Berkeley, California 94710, USA; 35, Genome Exploration Research Group, Genomic Sciences Center, RIKEN Yokohama Institute, 1-7-22 Suehiro-cho, Tsurumi-ku, Yokohama, Kanagawa 230-0045, Japan; 36, Howard Hughes Medical Institute, Department of Computer Science, University of California at Santa Cruz, California 95064, USA; 37, University of Dublin, Trinity College, Department of Genetics, Smurfit Institute, Dublin 2, Ireland; 38, Cambridge Research Laboratory, Compaq Computer Corporation and MIT Genome Center, 1 Cambridge Center, Cambridge, Massachusetts 02142, USA; 39, Dept. of Mathematics, University of California at Santa Cruz, Santa Cruz, California 95064, USA; 40, Dept. of Biology, University of California at Santa Cruz, Santa Cruz, California 95064, USA; 41, Crown Human Genetics Center and Department of Molecular Genetics, The Weizmann Institute of Science, Rehovot 71600, Israel; 42, Dept. of Genetics, Stanford University School of Medicine, Stanford, California 94305, USA; 43, The University of Michigan Medical School, Departments of Human Genetics and Internal Medicine, Ann Arbor, Michigan

48109, USA; 44, MRC Functional Genetics Unit, Department of Human Anatomy and Genetics, University of Oxford, South Parks Road, Oxford OX1 3QX, UK; 45, Institute for Systems Biology, 4225 Roosevelt Way NE, Seattle, WA 98105, USA; 46, National Human Genome Research Institute, US National Institutes of Health, 31 Center Drive, Bethesda, Maryland 20892, USA; 47, Office of Science, US Department of Energy, 19901 Germantown Road, Germantown, Maryland 20874, USA; 48, The Wellcome Trust, 183 Euston Road, London, NW1 2BE, UK.

† Present addresses: Genome Sequencing Project, Egea Biosciences, Inc., 4178 Sorrento Valley Blvd., Suite F, San Diego, CA 92121, USA (G.A.E.); INRA, Station d'Amélioration des Plantes, 63039 Clermont-Ferrand Cedex 2, France (L.C.).

DNA sequence databases

GenBank, National Center for Biotechnology Information, National Library of Medicine, National Institutes of Health, Bldg. 38A, 8600 Rockville Pike, Bethesda, Maryland 20894, USA

EMBL, European Bioinformatics Institute, Wellcome Trust Genome Campus, Hinxton, Cambridge CB10 1SD, UK

DNA Data Bank of Japan, Center for Information Biology, National Institute of Genetics, 1111 Yata, Mishima-shi, Shizuoka-ken 411-8540, Japan

Correction

International Human Genome Sequencing Consortium

Nature 409, 860–921 (2001)
Published 2 August 2001

Nature 409, 860–921 (2001).

We have identified several items requiring correction or clarification in our paper on the sequencing of the human genome.

• Six additional authors should have been included: Pieter de Jong, Joseph J. Catanese, and Kazutoyo Osoegawa (Department of Cancer Genetics, Roswell Park Cancer Institute, Buffalo, New York 14263, USA; present address: Children's Hospital Oakland Research Institute, 747 52nd Street Oakland, California 94609, USA) and Hiroaki Shizuya, Sangdun Choi and Yu-Juin Chen (Division of Biology, California Institute of Technology, Pasadena, California 91125, USA). These investigators and their laboratories constructed the high-quality BAC libraries that were crucial in sequencing the genome, as described in Table 1. These libraries were not previously published. We apologize to our colleagues for this omission.

• The Supplementary Information on *Nature*'s website has been revised. Changes to the original Supplementary Information are available in the Supplementary Information to this Correction. We have added 7 additional investigators to the full list of authors. We have also added 79 additional references, citing previously published sequences that were included in the draft genome sequence.

• Table 27 reported 18 instances of apparently novel paralogues of genes encoding drug targets. We have carefully reviewed these 18 cases and found that two are incorrect: a paralogue of an insulin-like growth factor-1 receptor gene and a paralogue of the calcitonin-related polypeptide alpha gene. In both cases, we had incorrectly recorded the chromosomal location sequence of the known gene, thereby erroneously giving rise to an apparent paralogue (the first instance was identified by J. Englebrecht and C. Kristensen (personal communication)). Of the 16 remaining apparent paralogues, two (calcium channel paralogue IGI_M1_ctg17137_10 and heparan N-deacetylase/N-sulphotransferase paralogue IGI_M1_ctg13263_18) have so far been confirmed as bona fide genes[1–2].

• Several correspondents have written to point out that a handful of clones listed as human sequence in the HTG division of GenBank (established to house 'unfinished' sequence data) are actually mouse sequence (about two dozen out of 30,000 clones). They asked whether these clones give rise to contamination in the human draft sequence. As noted in the paper, we used computer programs to identify and eliminate instances of such contamination (with mouse sequence, vector sequence, and so on) before assembling the draft genome sequence. In reviewing the work, we identified one mouse clone that slipped through the filter. This clone has been eliminated in subsequent assemblies (http://genome.cse.ucsc.edu/). Because the draft sequence remains an imperfect partial product, we welcome additional comments that could help in improving it.

• The discussion of possible horizontal gene transfer from bacterial genomes to vertebrate genomes has provoked considerable discussions[3–5]. We reported 113 instances of human genes that had reasonably close homologues in bacteria, but either had no homologue or only a weaker homologue in non-vertebrate eukaryotes for which extensive genomic sequence was available. We suggested two hypotheses to explain these data: horizontal gene transfer (HGT) from bacteria to human or gene loss in the other lineages. We had no data to distinguish between these hypotheses, although we suggested that the latter was a more "parsimonious" explanation as it involved fewer independent events. In the introduction we stated that this seemed "likely".

Several correspondents have undertaken more comprehensive analyses and have argued that a significant proportion of the cases can be explained by gene loss[3–5]. We agree. We believe that the two hypotheses cannot be distinguished on the basis of parsimony, because too little is known about the relative rates of HGT and gene loss in evolution. Instead, extensive sequence data from many additional organisms will be required to assess definitively the provenance of each gene.

We note that the process of HGT into the vertebrate genome from other organisms has clearly occurred on multiple occasions, as seen from the sudden arrival of many DNA transposons with strong similarities to other organisms. The most recent documented cases occurred subsequent to the eutherian radiation (see Fig. 19).

• A key reference concerning 3'-transduction by LINE elements was omitted on page 887. The sentence citing references 205 and 206 should also have cited Goodier et al[6].

• In Fig. 33, the unit on the y axis should be bp, not kb. The legend should read "Sequence properties of segmental duplications. Distributions of length and per cent nucleotide identity are shown as a function of the number of aligned bp from the finished vs finished human genomic sequence dataset. Intrachromosomal (blue), interchromosomal (red)".

• In Fig. 41, the legend should begin: "For each of the 27 common domain families, the number of different Pfam domain types that co-occur with the family in each of the five eukaryotic proteomes. The 27 families were chosen to include the 10 most common domain families in each proteome. The data are ranked ..."

• In Table 22, the entry 81,126 should be 8,126.

• On page 898, line 31, the final phrase of the sentence ("... and the representativeness of currently 'known' human genes") should be deleted. The sentence should read: "Before discussing the gene predictions for the human genome, it is useful to consider background issues, including previous estimates of the number of human genes and lessons learned from worms and flies".

• On page 900, line 38, remove "(see above)".

• We failed to acknowledge the crucial role of sequence editing software, which has been widely used for inspection and subsequent finishing of the sequence assemblies. The two principal programs used were CONSED[7] and GAP4[8].

1. Burgess, D. L. *et al.* A cluster of three novel (Ca(2+)) channel gamma subunit genes on chromosome 19q13.4: Evolution and expression–profile of the gamma subunit gene family. *Genomics* **71**, 339–350 (2001).
2. Aikawa, J. *et al.* Multiple isozymes of heparan sulfate/heparin GlcNAc N-deacetylase/GlcN N-sulfotransferase. Structure and activity of the fourth member, NDST4. *J. Biol. Chem.* **276**, 5876–5882 (2001).
3. Salzberg, S. L *et al.* Microbial genes in the human genome: Lateral transfer or gene loss? *Science* **292**, 1903–1906 (2001).
4. Stanhope, M. J. *et al.* Phylogenetic analyses do not support horizontal gene transfers from bacteria to vertebrates. *Nature* **411**, 940–944 (2001).
5. Reelofs, J. & Van Haastert, P. J. M. Genes lost during evolution. *Nature* **411**, 1013–1014 (2001).
6. Goodier, J. L., Ostertag, E. M. & Kazazian, H. H. Transduction of 3'-flanking sequences is common in L1 retrotransposition. *Hum. Mol. Genet.* **9**, 653–657 (2000).
7. Gordon, D., Abajian, C. & Green, P. Consend: a graphical tool for sequence finishing. *Genome Res.* **3**, 195–202 (1998).
8. Staden, R., Beal, K. F. & Bonfield, J. K. The Staden package. 1998. *Methods Mol. Biol.* **132**, 115–130 (2001).

Supplementary information (with changes to the original Supplementary Information) is available on *Nature*'s World-Wide Web site (http://www.nature.com).

Genome speak

Allele Alternative version of a particular gene. Humans carry two sets of most genes, one inherited from each parent, so a single allele for each locus is inherited separately from each parent.

Amino acid Any of a class of 20 molecules that are combined to form proteins in living things.

Annotation Identification of the locations and coding regions of genes in a genome and the prediction of functions for these regions.

Autosome A chromosome not involved in sex determination. The diploid human genome contains 22 pairs of autosomes, and 1 pair of sex chromosomes. Compare with **sex chromosome**.

BAC (bacterial artificial chromosome) A chromosome-like structure, constructed by genetic engineering, that is used as a vector to clone DNA fragments of genome (100 to 300 kb insert size) in cells of the bacterium *Escherichia coli.*

Base pair (bp) Two nitrogenous bases (adenine and thymine or guanine and cytosine) held together by weak bonds. See **DNA, nucleotide**.

Bioinformatics The study of genetic and other biological information using computer and statistical techniques. In genome projects, bioinformatics includes the development of methods to search databases, to analyse DNA sequence information, and to predict protein sequence and structure from DNA sequence data.

BLAST (Basic Local Alignment Search Tool) A computer-search program that searches for sequence similarity to identify homologous genes.

Centromere The compact region at the centre of a chromosome.

Chromosome A rod-shaped structure inside the nucleus of a cell which contains a densely packed continuous strand of DNA. Different organisms have different numbers of chromosomes. The diploid human genome consists of 23 pairs of chromosomes, 46 in all: 22 pairs of autosomes and two sex chromosomes. See **autosome, sex chromosome**.

Clone An exact copy made of biological material, such as a DNA segment (a gene or other region).

Cloning The process of generating multiple, exact copies of a particular piece of DNA to allow it to be sequenced or studied in some other way.

cDNA (complementary DNA) A DNA sequence made from a messenger RNA molecule. cDNAs can be used experimentally to determine the sequence of messenger RNAs after their introns (non-protein-coding sections) have been spliced out.

Conserved sequence A sequence of DNA (or an amino-acid sequence in a protein) that has remained essentially unchanged throughout evolution, usually because of functional constraints.

Contig A contiguous sequence of DNA created by assembling overlapping sequenced fragments.

DNA (deoxyribonucleic acid) The molecule that encodes genetic information. The four nucleotides in DNA contain the bases: adenine (A), guanine (G), cytosine (C) and thymine (T). Two strands of DNA are held together in the shape of a double helix by bonds between base pairs of nucleotides, where A pairs with T and G with C. See **nucleotide, base pair**.

Diploid A full set of genetic material, consisting of paired chromosomes, one from each parental set. Most animal cells except the gametes have a diploid set of chromosomes. Compare with **haploid**.

Draft sequence DNA sequence in which the order of bases is sequenced at least four to five times (an accuracy of 99.9%), which enables the reassembling of DNA fragments in their original order. Some segments can be missing or in the wrong order or orientation. Compare with **finished sequence**.

Euchromatin The gene-rich regions of a genome. Compare with **heterochromatin**.

Eukaryote An organism whose cells have a complex internal structure, including a nucleus. Animals, plants and fungi are all eukaryotes. Compare with **prokaryotes**.

Exon The protein-coding DNA sequence of a gene. Compare with **intron**.

EST (expressed sequence tag) A short sequence from a coding region of a gene that identifies the gene.

Finished sequence DNA sequence in which bases are identified to an accuracy of 99.99% and are placed in the right order and orientation along a chromosome with almost no gaps.

FISH (fluorescence in situ hybridization) A process that vividly paints chromosomes or portions of chromosomes with fluorescent molecules. This technique is useful for identifying chromosomal abnormalities and gene mapping.

Gamete Mature male or female reproductive cell (sperm or egg) with a haploid set of chromosomes.

Gene The fundamental physical and functional unit of heredity. A gene is an ordered sequence of nucleotides located in a particular position on a particular chromosome that encodes a specific functional product.

Gene mapping Determination of the relative positions of genes on a DNA molecule (chromosome or plasmid) and of the distance, in linkage units or physical units, between them.

Genetic code The sequence of nucleotides, coded in triplets (codons) along the messenger RNA, that determines the sequence of amino acids in protein synthesis. The DNA sequence of a gene can be used to predict the messenger RNA sequence, and the genetic code can in turn be used to predict the amino-acid sequence.

Genome The complete genetic material of an organism; the entire DNA sequence.

Genomic library A collection of clones made from a set of randomly generated overlapping DNA fragments representing the entire genome of an organism.

Genomics The study of genomes and their sets of genes.

Genotype The set of genes that an individual carries; usually refers to the particular pair of alleles (alternative forms of a gene) that a person has at a given region of the genome. Genotype refers to what is inherited (for example, an allele for brown eyes), whereas phenotype refers to what is expressed (brown eyes in this case).

Haploid A single set of chromosomes (half the full set of genetic material) present in the egg and sperm cells of animals and in the egg and pollen cells of plants. Compare with **diploid**.

Haplotype A particular combination of alleles (alternative forms of genes) or sequence variations that are closely linked – that is, are likely to be inherited together – on the same chromosome.

Heterochromatin Compact, gene-poor regions of a genome, which are enriched in simple sequence repeats. Compare with **euchromatin**.

Intron The DNA sequence interrupting the protein-coding sequence of a gene; this sequence is transcribed into RNA but is cut out before the RNA is transcribed. Compare with **exon**.

Karyotype A photomicrograph of an individual's chromosomes arranged in a standard format showing the number, size and shape of each chromosome type; used in low-resolution physical mapping to correlate gross chromosomal abnormalities with the characteristics of specific diseases.

Kilobase (kb) Unit of length of DNA fragments equal to 1000 nucleotides.

Library An unordered collection of clones whose relationship to each other can be established by physical mapping.

Linkage The proximity of two or more markers (for example, genes) on a chromosome.

Long and short arms The regions either side of the centromere, a compact part of a chromosome, are known as arms. As the centromere is not in the centre of the chromosome, one arm is longer than the other.

Marker An identifiable physical location or landmark on a chromosome (for example, a restriction enzyme cleavage site) whose inheritance through generations can be monitored.

Megabase (Mb) Unit of length for DNA fragments equal to 1 million nucleotides.

Meiosis The process of two consecutive cell divisions in the diploid progenitors of sex cells, which results in four progeny cells, each with a haploid set of chromosomes.

mRNA (messenger RNA) RNA that serves as a template for protein synthesis.

Mitosis The process of nuclear division in cells that produces two daughter cells that are genetically identical to each other and to the parent cell.

Mutation An alteration in a genome compared to some reference state.

Nucleotide A subunit of DNA or RNA comprised of a nitrogenous base (adenine, guanine, thymine or cytosine in DNA; adenine, guanine, uracil or cytosine in RNA), a phosphate molecule and a sugar molecule (deoxyribose in DNA and ribose in RNA). Nucleotides are linked to form the strands of a DNA or RNA molecule. See **base pair**.

Phenotype The observable properties and physical characteristics of an organism.

Physical map The localization of identifiable landmarks on DNA.

Plasmid An autonomously replicating, extra-chromosomal circular DNA molecule, distinct from the normal bacterial genome and non-essential for cell survival under non-selective conditions. Artificially constructed plasmids are used as cloning vectors.

Polymorphism A difference in DNA sequence among individuals. To be called a polymorphism, a variant should be present in a significant number of people in the population.

Prokaryote A cell or organism lacking a membrane-bound, structurally discrete nucleus and other subcellular compartments. Bacteria are prokaryotes. Compare with **eukaryote**.

Protein A large molecule composed of one or more chains of amino acids in a specific order; the order is determined by the base sequence of nucleotides in the gene coding for the protein.

Proteome The complete set of proteins encoded by the genome.

Pseudogene A region of DNA that shows extensive similarity to a known gene, but does not function.

Recombinant DNA A combination of DNA molecules of different origin that are joined using recombinant DNA technologies.

Recombination The process by which DNA is exchanged between pairs of equivalent chromosomes during egg and sperm formation.

Recombination has the effect of making the chromosomes of the offspring distinct from those of the parents.

RNA (ribonucleic acid) A molecule with a similar structure to DNA that plays an important role in protein synthesis and other chemical activities of the cell. There are several types of RNA molecules, including messenger RNA, which acts as an intermediary molecule between DNA and protein. See **nucleotide, mRNA**.

STS (sequence tagged site) A short (200 to 500 base pairs) DNA sequence that has a single occurrence in the human genome and whose location and base sequence are known.

Sex chromosome The X or Y chromosome in humans. Determines the sex of an individual. Females have two X chromosomes in diploid cells; males have an X and a Y chromosome. The sex chromosomes comprise the 23rd chromosome pair of a human genome. Compare with **autosome**.

SNP (single-nucleotide polymorphism) A polymorphism caused by the change of a single nucleotide. Most genetic variation between individuals is due to SNPs.

Splicing The process that removes introns (non-protein-coding portions) from transcribed RNAs. Exons (protein-coding portions) can also be removed. Depending on which exons are removed, different proteins can be made from the same initial RNA or gene. Different proteins created in this way are 'splice variants' or 'alternatively spliced'.

Telomere The end of a chromosome. This specialized structure is involved in the replication and stability of linear DNA molecules.

Transcription The process of copying a gene into RNA. This is the first step in turning a gene into a protein, although not all transcripts generate proteins. Compare **translation**.

Transcriptome The complete set of RNAs transcribed from a genome in a particular tissue at a particular time.

Translation The process of using a messenger RNA sequence to build a protein. The messenger RNA serves as a template on which transfer RNA molecules, carrying amino acids, are lined up. The amino acids are then linked together to form a protein chain.

YAC (yeast artificial chromosome) A type of vector used to clone DNA fragments inside yeast cells. It is constructed from the telomeric, centromeric and replication origin sequences needed for replication in yeast cells.

Index

DO IT YOURSELF

Keeping Fit

Body Systems

Carol Ballard

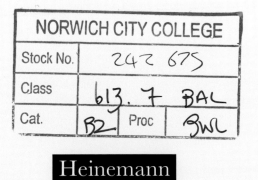

Heinemann
LIBRARY

www.heinemann.co.uk/library

Visit our website to find out more information about Heinemann Library books.

To order:

☎ Phone 44 (0) 1865 888066

📄 Send a fax to 44 (0) 1865 314091

💻 Visit the Heinemann bookshop at www.heinemann.co.uk/library to browse our catalogue and order online.

First published in Great Britain by Heinemann Library, Halley Court, Jordan Hill, Oxford OX2 8EJ, part of Pearson Education.

Heinemann is a registered trademark of Pearson Education Ltd.

© Pearson Education Ltd 2008
First published in paperback in 2008
The moral right of the proprietor has been asserted.

Editorial: Louise Galpine and Catherine Veitch
Design: Richard Parker and Tinstar Design Ltd
Illustrations: ODI
Picture Research: Mica Brancic and Elaine Willis
Production: Victoria Fitzgerald

Originated by Chroma Graphics (Overseas) Pte. Ltd
Printed and bound in China by Leo Paper Group.

ISBN 978 0 4311 1 119 3 (hardback)
12 11 10 09 08
10 9 8 7 6 5 4 3 2 1

ISBN 978 0 4311 1 135 3 (paperback)
12 11 10 09 08
10 9 8 7 6 5 4 3 2 1

British Library Cataloguing in Publication Data
Ballard, Carol
Keeping fit : body systems - (Do it yourself)
613.7'1

A full catalogue record for this book is available from the British Library.

Acknowledgements
The publishers would like to thank the following for permission to reproduce photographs: ©Corbis pp. **4** (Steve Chenn), **8** (Bettmann), **27** (Duomo), **29** (Richard T. Nowitz), **43** (Roy Morsch); ©Getty Images pp. **5** (John Kelly), **7** (Tara Moore), **11** (Nick Veasy), **13** (Brad Rickerby), **15** (Allsport Concepts/Mike Powell), **17** (Photographer's Choice/Karl Weatherly), **19** (Taxi/Michael Malyszko), **21** (Johner Images), **30** (Stone/Christel Rosenfeld), **31** (Simon Weller), **32** (Joe McBride), **33** (Allsport Concepts/Pascal Rondeau), **36** (Chris McGrath), **37** (Juergen Stein), **38** (Digital Vision/Roy McMahon), **39** (Vince Michaels), **42** (PhotoDisc); ©PhotoLibrary p. **41**; ©Science Photo Library pp. **9** (D. Roberts), **23** left and right (ISM), **24** (Biophoto Associates), **25** (Susumu Nishinaga).

Cover photograph of woman stretching leg on track, reproduced with permission of Getty Images/Digital Vision.

Every effort has been made to contact copyright holders of any material reproduced in this book. Any omissions will be rectified in subsequent printings if notice is given to the publishers.

The publishers would like to thank Nick Lapthorn for his help in the preparation of this book.

Contents

Any words appearing in the text in bold, **like this**, are explained in the glossary.

Get moving!

Imagine you have just got a new bicycle. You could treat it in one of two ways:

1. Not use it very much, dump it carelessly on the ground, and never clean or oil it.

2. Use it often, put it away carefully, keep it clean and oiled.

Which would keep it looking best and working most efficiently? It would obviously be the second. If you didn't look after your bicycle, you could buy a new one – although it would be expensive. Now think about your body. You can treat it badly or you can take care of it, just as you could a bicycle. But could you go to a shop and buy a new body if it wore out? No! It makes sense to take very good care of your body. You have to keep it in good working condition for the whole of your lifetime.

Swimming is really good for your body – if you cannot swim yet, why not take some lessons and learn?

What sort of exercise?

"Keeping fit" really means looking after your body properly. One of the most important things you can do for your body is to exercise it often. That does not just mean at school in sports lessons, it means being active outside school too. There are all sorts of fun things you can do to keep fit – almost anything that gets your body moving is going to be good for it!

An active body

This book shows you what is happening in your body when you move around and exercise. It explains how your body moves and what your **heart** and **lungs** do. It also shows you how to take care of yourself when you exercise. Read on – and then get moving!

Warning!

Check with an adult before you try any of the activities described in this book to make sure it is safe for you to do them. You should also check with a doctor if you have any illness or medical condition that might affect your safety or your ability to exercise. Stop immediately if you feel unwell and seek medical advice.

Cycling over rough ground like this makes every part of the body work hard – but it is important to follow every safety precaution!

Warming up

Bend and stretch

You do not need any equipment for these exercises, but make sure you are in a space big enough to swing your arms and legs freely.

1

Waist twists

Stand with your feet about the same distance apart as your shoulders. Put your hands on your hips. Now slowly move your hips round in a circle. Do five circles clockwise then five circles anti-clockwise.

2

Shoulder rolls

Stand as you did for waist twists. Lift your right arm with your hand pointing upwards as high as you can. Now swing your arm backwards, down, forwards, and up to where you started, to draw a complete circle. Do this five times with your right arm then five times with your left arm. Then repeat, but circling your arms in the opposite direction – forwards, down, backwards, and up. Can you move each arm in a different direction at the same time?

3

Leg stretch

Lie on your back on the floor. Keeping your head on the floor, lift your right leg and bring your knee as close to your chest as you can. Then lower your leg to the floor again. Do the same with your left leg. Repeat five times for each leg.

Prepare your body

It is important to prepare your body gently for exercise, rather than giving it a nasty shock! You can do this by spending a few minutes doing some bending and stretching exercises like the ones described here. Gentle activities like this are called "warming up" because as you do them your **muscles** get warmer.

Warming up ideas

Other good warming up activities include:

- gentle jogging
- running on the spot
- hopping
- jumping.

Have you seen professional sportsmen and women doing stretches like this before they begin? Their bodies need to warm up just as yours does.

Avoiding injury

Warming up can help to avoid injury. If your body is cold and stiff when you do something very energetic, you can easily damage muscles and **joints**. Warming up helps muscles and joints to get ready for whatever you need them to do and reduces the chance of damage or injury.

Bones and muscles

To understand how warming up before you exercise can reduce the risk of injury, you need to know how your **bones** and muscles work.

Bone facts

A baby has about 300 bones when it is born. During childhood, some bones join together. An adult skeleton is made up of 206 bones of all sorts of shapes and sizes. The smallest bones are in the ear. The longest bone is the **thigh** bone.

This gymnast needs a flexible spine to bend her body into this shape!

Bones

Your bones provide a framework for the rest of your body — without your bony **skeleton**, you would be a jelly-like lump! The backbone (**spine**) is made up of 33 separate bones. These all link together to make a **flexible** central support. Because the backbone is flexible, you can bend over and touch your toes. Some of your bones protect delicate parts of your body. The skull protects your brain. The **ribcage** protects the **heart** and **lungs**.

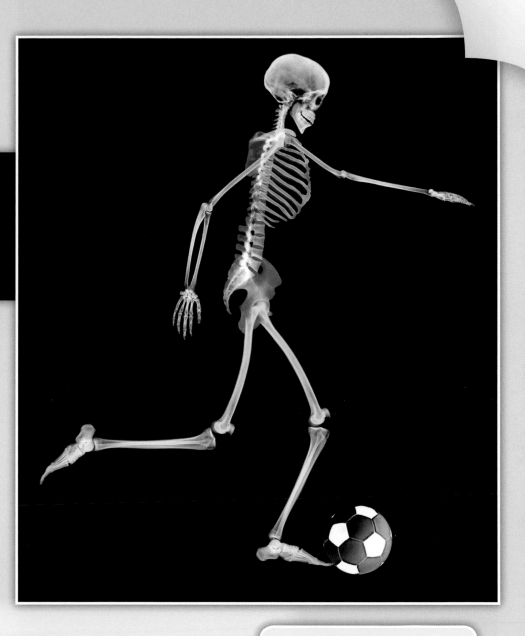

If you could see your skeleton when you kick a ball, it would look like this.

Muscles

Muscles are important too. Without them, we would not be able to move at all. They are like stretchy **elastic** bands and most are attached to bones. The muscles pull the bones into new positions, allowing us to move. Sometimes you want to move part of your body while the rest stays still, such as when you hit a ball. At other times you want to move all of your body, such as when you run. It does not matter what type of movement it is – every movement needs muscles!

Muscle facts

Humans have around 650 muscles! The smallest muscle is in the ear. The longest muscle is at the front of the thigh. One of the strongest muscles moves the hip and thigh when you jump or climb.

Cold muscles

Before you begin exercising your muscles are cold. They are not very elastic, which means they are not very stretchy. If you start to exercise vigorously when your muscles are like this, you can easily stretch them too much. This can tear them. A torn muscle is a painful injury and the damage can take a long time to heal. This is one good reason for warming up gently before you start your exercise activity. Gentle stretching exercises help to warm the muscles up slowly. This means they are ready to stretch a lot when you begin to be very active.

This picture shows how the parts of the elbow joint all fit together.

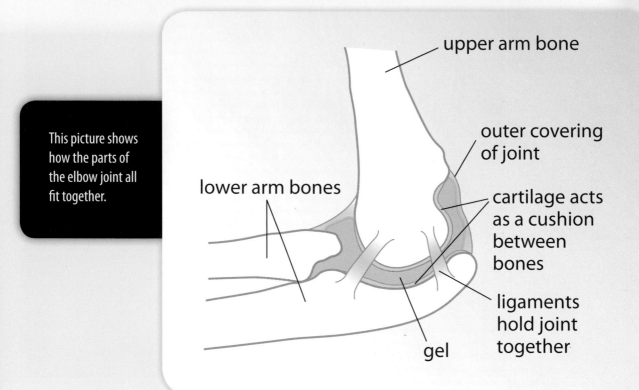

upper arm bone

outer covering of joint

lower arm bones

cartilage acts as a cushion between bones

ligaments hold joint together

gel

Inside a joint

Caring for your joints is another good reason for warming up before you exercise.
If you could look inside a joint, you would see that it has several parts:

* an outer covering
* the ends of the two bones that meet at the joint
* **cartilage** covering the ends of each bone to stop them rubbing against each other
* tough bands called **ligaments** that hold the joint together
* a jelly that acts like lubricating oil in an engine.

Joints

A joint is the place where two bones meet. Elbows, wrists, knees, and ankles are all joints. You cannot bend a bone itself, but you can bend at the joint between two bones. Without joints you would be very stiff. Imagine how difficult it would be to walk without bending your knee or ankle. Some joints only allow movement in one direction. Your knee is like this – you can only bend it backwards and forwards. Other joints allow movement in all sorts of directions. Your shoulder is like this – you can move your upper arm in almost any direction you want to.

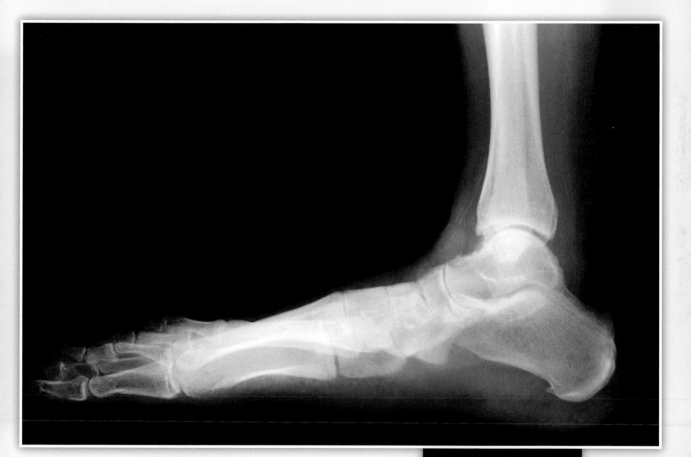

This X-ray shows the bones in an ankle joint.

Loosening up

Before you exercise, the jelly inside your joints is quite firm and your joints are stiff. As you get warmer the jelly gets runnier and your joints can move more easily. Gentle warming-up exercises before you begin help to warm the jelly making your joints feel loose and supple.

Move around, have fun

Steps to follow

Skip!

For this activity you will need:

* a skipping rope
* plenty of space.

Before you start, check your rope is the right length for you. Stand on the middle of it and hold each end up. The ends should just come to your armpits. If your rope is shorter than this, you need a different one. If it is longer than this, tie a knot in one or both ends to shorten it.

 Hold the end of your skipping rope in each hand. As you turn the rope, step over it with your right foot on one turn and then your left foot on the next turn. You can do this on the spot or can travel over a distance.

 Now turn the rope and jump over it with both feet together every time. You can vary this by doing an extra little bounce between each jump, or by jumping with your feet together on one turn then feet apart on the next turn.

 Do the same as in 1 or 2 but turn the rope backwards instead of forwards.

Keeping fit on your own

There are many different things you can do on your own to keep fit and have fun. Here are some ideas:

- Go for a walk – this is so simple but walking briskly is really good for you. For a change try walking 50 paces then jogging 50 paces.

- Go swimming – it exercises most of the **muscles** in your body.

- Ride your bicycle – why not cycle to local places instead of going by bus or car?

- Dance – put your favourite music on and make up your own dance steps.

- Hula hoop – how many times can you spin a hula hoop around your waist before it falls to the floor?

- Ball games – find a wall, practise throwing a ball against it and catching it. Make it harder by turning round in between throwing and catching, or try clapping your hands behind your back.

- Basketball – shoot a ball through a basketball net and jump to catch it.

Spinning a hula hoop around your waist is an excellent way of keeping fit.

This activity is good for improving catching and throwing skills and you have to stay alert all the time!

 Stand in a circle, spacing yourselves by spreading your arms out so that your fingertips touch the fingertips of the person on each side of you.

 One person holds the ball. They throw it quickly to somebody else, shouting that person's name as they throw.

 The person whose name is called must catch the ball and then throw it quickly to somebody else, shouting that person's name as they throw. If the catcher drops the ball, they are out.

 The game continues until only two people are left.

 The aim is to keep the ball moving as quickly as you can, for as long as you can.

Circle ball game

For this activity you will need:

* a ball
* five or more people.

Keeping fit with friends

You and your friends can have great fun keeping fit together! Team games such as basketball, football, and hockey are played at many schools. There are lots of sports clubs to join out of school, too, where you can improve your basic skills and play in matches and tournaments.

Have you ever tried running in a relay race like this? Organized sports are great fun and can help you to keep fit.

As well as organized sports, there are other ways of keeping fit with your friends. Set yourself these challenges:

Activity	What you need	What you do
Set a challenge, such as how far can you travel without putting your feet on the floor	Place such as gymnasium, activity centre, or adventure playground	See if you can achieve the challenges
Skip rope together	Long skipping rope	Two people turn a long rope, others take it in turns to skip
Make up a series of simple exercises, such as touch your toes, do star jumps, sit down and stand up	Space large enough to move around freely	All start together and see who can complete the series fastest, or do the most repeats in a set time
Play a game such as tag	Plenty of space for running around	One person is "It", and tries to catch somebody else; everybody else runs away to avoid being caught – but if you are caught you become "It" instead

Feel your muscles work

1 Hold your right arm out straight. Make the hand into a fist with the palm upwards.

2 Lightly rest the fingers of your left hand on the front of your right upper arm.

3 Slowly bend your right arm at the elbow and then lower it again. Your left hand should be able to feel the muscles inside your right arm moving as you raise and lower it.

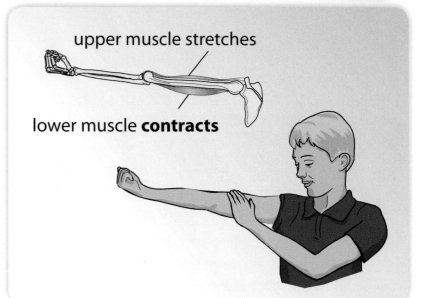

upper muscle stretches

lower muscle **contracts**

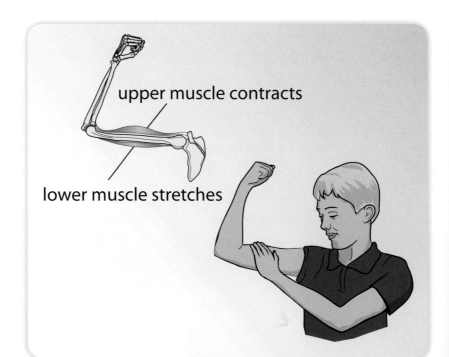

upper muscle contracts

lower muscle stretches

What happens inside your arm?

What is happening inside your arm when you raise and lower it? Two muscles work as a pair, doing opposite jobs.

Raising your arm

When you want to raise your arm your brain sends a signal to the muscle at the front of your upper arm. The signal travels from the brain to the muscle via nerves. When the muscle receives the signal it responds by contracting (getting shorter). The muscle is attached to the **bones** in the lower arm. When it contracts, these bones are pulled up. This also stretches the muscle at the back of the upper arm.

Lowering your arm

When you lower your arm, your brain sends a signal to the muscle at the back of your upper arm. When the muscle receives the signal it responds by contracting (getting shorter). The muscle is attached to the back of the bones in the lower arm. When it contracts, it pulls these bones downwards. This also stretches the muscle at the front of the upper arm.

Cycle races can last a long time and cover great distances. Cyclists' leg muscles are very strong and powerful.

Pairs of muscles

Muscles work in pairs like this to move all the bones in your body. If one muscle pulls a bone in one direction there will be another muscle to pull it back again. When one muscle in a pair contracts to pull the bone the other muscle is stretched.

Pumping blood

Steps to follow

1 Hold your right hand out with your palm facing up.

2 Gently rest the index and middle fingers of your left hand on the inside of your arm, in line with your thumb and a little above your wrist.

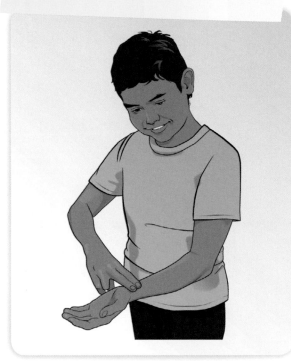

3 Your left hand fingers should be able to feel a regular "beat" in your arm. If you cannot feel anything at first, try moving your left hand fingers around a little until you can. Each beat you feel is one push from your **heart** as it pumps blood round your body.

When you can feel the beat, count how many beats you feel in one minute. This is called your **pulse rate**.

Heartbeats

Your heart beats about 70 times every minute when you are resting, and more when you are moving around and exercising. That makes about:

- 4,000 beats every hour
- 100,000 beats every day
- 40 million beats every year!

18

The heart

Your heart is mainly made of **muscle**. It is in the middle of your chest, inside your **ribcage**. Your heart's job is to pump blood around your body. It starts pumping even before you are born, and does not stop until you die. You do not have to think about it — your heart keeps on pumping every minute of the day and night.

Blood vessels

Blood travels through a network of tubes called **blood vessels**. The biggest tubes are called **arteries** and **veins**. The tiniest tubes are called **capillaries**.

Medical staff often measure a patient's pulse rate. This can help them to see how well the patient is.

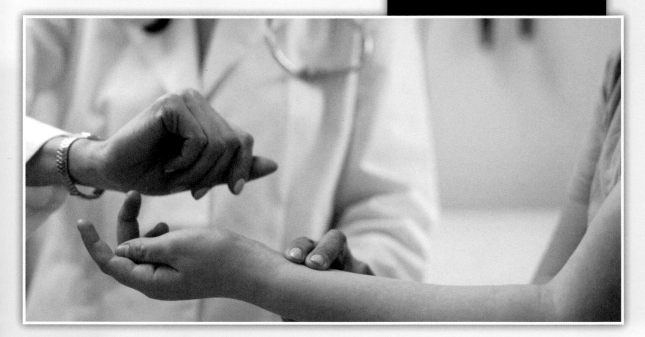

The movement of blood

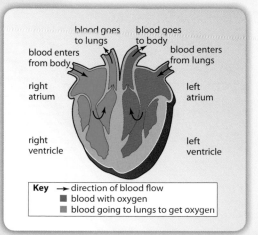

blood goes to lungs   blood goes to body
blood enters from body   blood enters from lungs
right atrium   left atrium
right ventricle   left ventricle

Key → direction of blood flow
■ blood with oxygen
■ blood going to lungs to get oxygen

Your heart is really like two separate pumps. Veins bring blood from the rest of your body to the right side of your heart. The right side of the heart pumps this blood to the **lungs**. The blood travels through the lungs, where it gets rid of **carbon dioxide** and picks up **oxygen**. It then travels back to the left side of the heart. The left side of the heart then pumps the blood out to the rest of the body. This movement of blood around the body is called **circulation**.

Does your heart rate change when you exercise?

You need a clock or watch that shows minutes and seconds.

 1 Begin by sitting quietly and still for five minutes, then measure your pulse rate. Write it down. This is your **resting rate**.

 2 Exercise energetically for two minutes. Star jumps or running on the spot are both ideal.

 3 As soon as your two minutes are up, measure your pulse rate again. Write it down. This is your after-exercise rate.

 4 Sit quietly and measure your pulse rate after another two minutes, and then another five minutes.

 5 You can show your results on a graph like this. Get your friends to do the same and add their results to your graph.

You should find that your after-exercise pulse rate was a lot faster than your resting rate. After resting for a while, it should go back to the resting rate again.

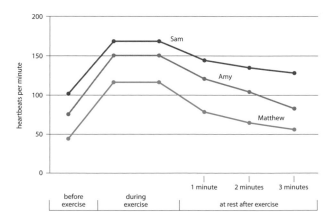

Exercise and pulse rate

Why does this happen? It's all to do with the body supplying your muscles with what they need to work. Blood carries oxygen, energy, and important chemicals around your body. It also collects waste gases and waste chemicals so they can be broken down and removed from the body.

When you are sitting quietly your heart beats just fast enough to give your muscles as much oxygen and energy as they need. When you begin to move or exercise your muscles need more oxygen and energy. They also make more waste gas and chemicals. Your heart pumps faster to make the blood circulate more quickly. This supplies the muscles with extra oxygen and energy, and takes away the waste products.

When you are really active like this girl your heart has to beat faster to pump blood more quickly around your body.

When you rest your muscles need less oxygen and energy. They make less waste. The whole process slows down again. After a few minutes everything is back to normal. The fitter you are, the quicker your pulse rate will return to its normal resting rate.

Breathing

Steps to follow

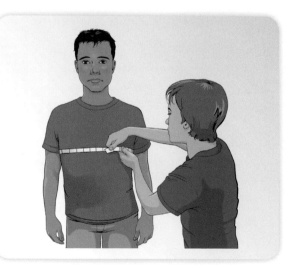

How much does your chest expand?

For this activity you will need:
* a tape measure
* a friend to help you.

1 Ask a friend to put a tape measure around your chest just below your armpits. It should be quite tight around your body but should not squash you at all. Breathe out as much as you can. Your friend should write down the measurement given on the tape measure.

2 Now take the biggest breath you can. Your friend should write down the measurement given on the tape measure again.

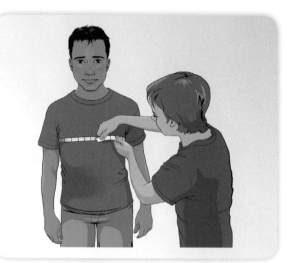

3 Take your first measurement away from your second measurement. This tells you how much your chest expanded when you breathed in.

4 Here is an example of what your results might look like:

First measurement – breathing out 76 cm (30 in)

Second measurement – breathing in 84 cm (33 in)

Take 76 cm (30 in) away from 84 cm (33 in): answer = 8 cm (3 in).

Where are your lungs?

Your **lungs** are in your chest protected by your **ribcage**. When you breathe in they **expand** as they fill up with air. When you breathe out they **contract** as air leaves them. Your lungs cannot do this all by themselves – **muscles** have to help. A big sheet of muscle called the **diaphragm** stretches across the lower part of your chest. Other muscles are attached to your ribs.

The blue areas on this X-ray show a person's lungs. In the first picture, the lungs look big because the person is breathing in. In the second picture, the lungs look smaller because the person is breathing out.

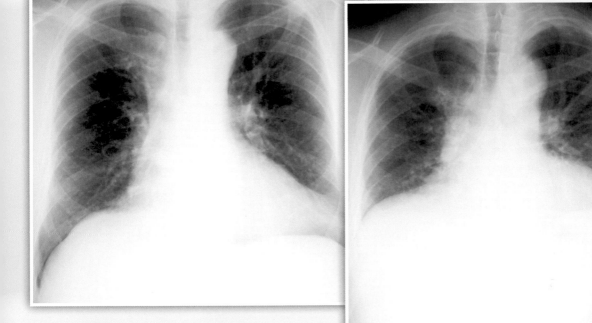

When you breathe in the muscles make the space in your chest bigger. Air is pulled into your body through your mouth and nose. It moves into a tube called the **windpipe** and travels down to the top of your chest. Here, the windpipe branches into two smaller tubes – one carrying air to your left lung and the other carrying air to your right lung.

When you breathe out the opposite happens. The muscles make the space in your chest smaller. This pushes waste air out of your lungs. It is forced out of your lungs into the tubes, then into the windpipe. It leaves your body through your mouth and nose.

A lungful of air

An adult's lungs can hold about 6 litres (11–12 pints) of air. A child's lungs do not hold quite as much as this. Each time you breathe in and out, about 0.5 litres (1 pint) of air enters, then leaves, your lungs.

23

Inside your lungs

Have you ever wondered what your lungs are like inside? It might seem strange, but try to imagine an upside-down tree. From the top you have a single trunk. This splits into two big branches, then each of the branches splits again and again, into smaller and smaller branches until you come to the tiniest twigs. Your windpipe is like a hollow tree trunk. It splits into two main tubes. Then each of these splits again and again into narrower and narrower tubes. Eventually they form tiny little groups like hollow bunches of grapes. The "grapes" are called **alveoli**. They have very thin walls that gases can pass through. The alveoli are surrounded by tiny **blood vessels**.

This photograph shows part of the inside of a lung. In the centre of the picture is a **bronchiole**. The spaces around it are alveoli.

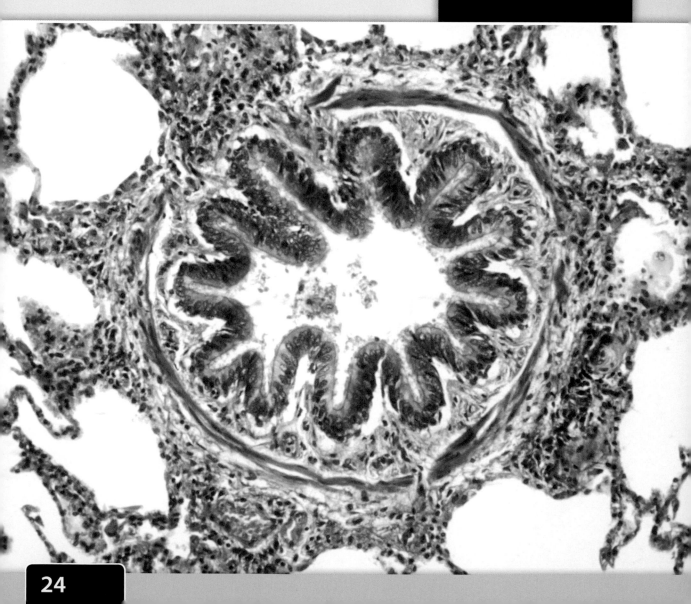

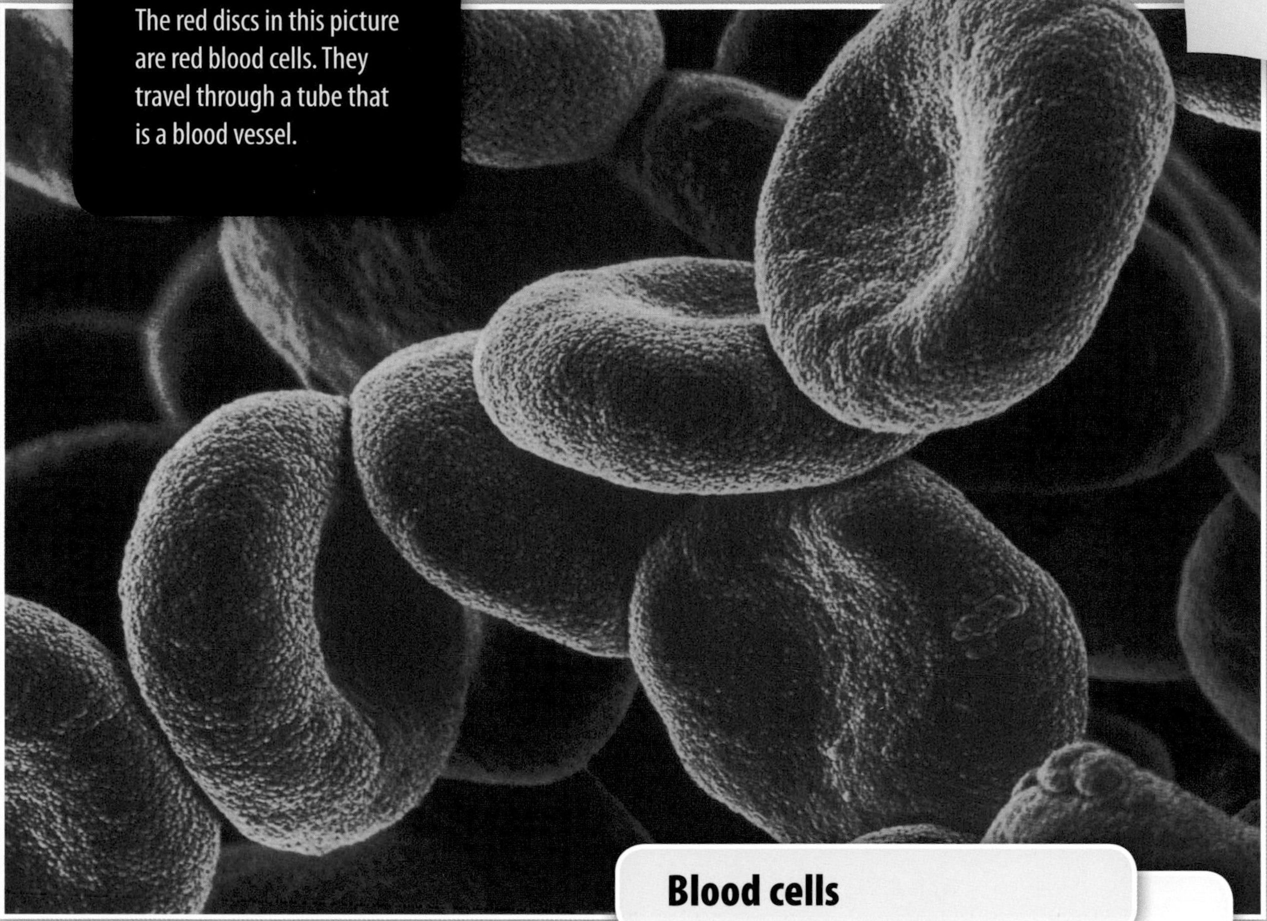

The red discs in this picture are red blood cells. They travel through a tube that is a blood vessel.

Blood cells

How do lungs work?

What actually happens inside your lungs when you breathe in and out?

Breathing in:

Air rushes into the windpipe through the narrower and narrower tubes until it reaches the alveoli. Here, **oxygen** moves through the alveoli walls and into the blood vessels. The blood then carries the oxygen away.

Breathing out:

How does oxygen travel in the blood? If you looked at a drop of blood under a microscope, you would see lots of tiny objects floating around in a clear liquid. These are blood **cells**. Some are colourless, but others are red. The red blood cells are what make your blood look red. They are really important because they carry the oxygen around. Carbon dioxide travels around in the liquid.

Your muscles and other parts of your body make a waste gas called **carbon dioxide**. Your body has to get rid of this somehow. As blood travels around your body it collects waste carbon dioxide. When it reaches the lungs, the carbon dioxide leaves the blood and moves into the alveoli. When you breathe out the waste carbon dioxide is forced out of your body.

Making the most of your lungs

You do not need any equipment for this deep-breathing exercise. It is a good way to begin and end an exercise session.

 Stand with your feet about the same distance apart as your shoulders. Look straight ahead and let your arms hang down loosely by your sides. Take a very slow, deep breath in while you count to five.

 Hold your breath for a slow count of two.

 Let your breath out very slowly as you count to five.

 Slowly count to two.

Repeat ten times from the beginning.

Automatic or controlled?

Most of the time, you breathe in and out without thinking about it. Your brain automatically controls how fast you breathe. When you are doing some activities, though, it can be important to control your breathing. Swimmers need to breathe in a rhythm that matches their swimming strokes. In breaststroke, when the hands push forwards the head dips under the water. When the hands push back the head lifts out of the water. The swimmer can only take a breath when their head is out of the water.

This swimmer is taking a quick breath as she raises her arm. If she gets the timing wrong she'll get a mouth full of water instead of air!

Slow or fast?

Slow, deep breathing is much more efficient than fast, shallow breathing. This is because, when you breathe slowly and deeply, most of the air taken in gets right down into your lungs. Your body can make full use of the oxygen in every breath. If your breaths are quick and shallow, much of the air does not get any further than your nose or windpipe – so your body cannot get any oxygen from it!

Hold your breath!

Have you ever tried to see how long you can hold your breath for? Take a deep breath in and hold it for as long as you can. Eventually you have to breathe out. This is because your body needs a regular oxygen supply. If you try to stop it by holding your breath, your brain makes you breathe whether you want to or not!

Look after yourself!

Mixing it up

You need a step that will make your **heart** and **lungs** work hard for this activity:

 1 Use a bottom stair or step. Step on to it with your right foot first then bring your left foot up too. Then step back down, again with your right foot first.

 2 Repeat five times.

 3 Repeat five more times using your left foot first.

 4 If you can, repeat all this again.

You do not need any equipment for this stretching activity:

 1 Stand with your feet about the same distance apart as your shoulders. Hold your hands together straight above your head. Keeping your eyes fixed ahead of you, very slowly bring your arms and upper body down and right round in a big circle until you are back in your starting position.

 2 Repeat, but make the circle in the opposite direction.

 3 Repeat steps 1 and 2 four more times.

Interval training

Most sportsmen and women combine two different types of exercise in a training session:

- a fast, energetic exercise that really makes the heart work hard
- a slower exercise that doesn't make the body work too hard.

Putting two contrasting exercises together like this is called **interval training**. A simple type of interval training is to sprint 20 paces then walk 20 paces.

While your body is growing and developing, it is a good idea to try to sleep for at least eight hours every night.

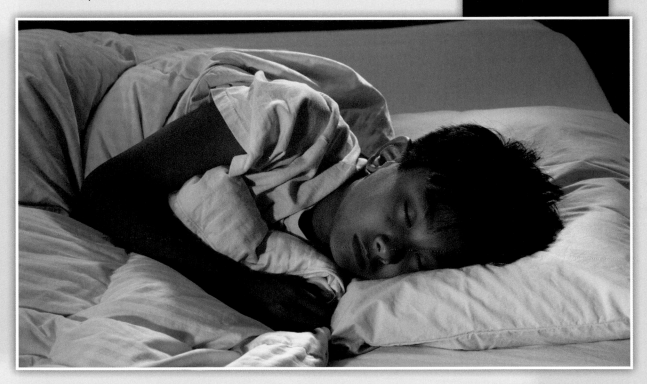

How much exercise?

Everybody is different so it is difficult to give an exact figure for how much exercise you need to do. For most children, an hour of exercise a day is a good starting amount. If you try to do too much exercise your body will get too tired.

Rest and sleep

Rest is important. A good night's sleep will help you to be at your best the next day. If you have too little sleep you will be tired the next day. Your reactions will be slow and your movements will not be as fast and strong as they are when you are properly rested.

Why do you need food?

Whatever you do to keep fit you will use up energy. You get your energy from your food, so it is important to make sure that your food provides enough energy for everything you do. The parts of your food that give you energy are called **carbohydrates** and **fats**. Your food also provides the **proteins** that your body needs to grow and repair, and **vitamins** and **minerals** that keep you healthy.

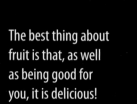

The best thing about fruit is that, as well as being good for you, it is delicious!

What is in your food?

Different foods provide different things. This table shows you some foods that are good sources of each type of **nutrient**:

Nutrient	Needed for	Found in
Carbohydrates (sugars and starches)	Energy	Bread, pasta, cereal, rice, potatoes
Fats	Energy	Dairy products, nuts, oils, meat
Proteins	Growing and repairing	Meat, fish, eggs, nuts, dairy products
Vitamins and minerals	Staying healthy	Fruit, vegetables

Healthy eating

To stay fit and healthy, and to have plenty of energy for activities, you should try to eat something from each of the groups of food opposite every day. The main part of a meal should be bread, pasta, or cereal, with lots of vegetables or fruit. We should have less protein-rich food, and even less fatty or sugary food.

If you eat more energy-rich food than your body uses up, your body will store the extra food as fat. If you get fat you will find it harder to run around and be active. It is also not good for your **heart**. If you eat less energy-rich food than your body uses up, your body will use the fat it has stored. This can make you feel tired and weak.

Junk food

You have probably heard people talking about "junk foods". Most junk foods contain far more fat, salt, or sugar than your body can use. You should only eat foods such as burgers, chips, and chocolate as a treat every now and then.

Eating junk food like this every day is not good for your body.

Take care of yourself

There are some basic steps you can take to look after yourself, whatever activity you choose to do:

- Protective clothing: Make sure you always wear the right protective clothing for your activity. It is designed to prevent you hurting yourself. For example, cycle helmets protect your head when you are cycling.

- Other clothing: Try to dress sensibly for your activity. Ask yourself questions such as: Are my shoes suitable? Am I likely to be too hot or too cold?

- Equipment: If you have special equipment for your activity check it carefully to make sure it is safe to use. For example, check your bicycle's tyres, brakes, and lights before you set off.

It is easy to tumble when you are skateboarding. The protective clothing this boy is wearing should save him from hurting his head, elbows, or knees.

- Rules and instructions: Most activities have rules or instructions that you should follow. These are for your safety as well as the safety of other people. Breaking the rules or ignoring instructions can put you and others in danger. For example, a bad tackle in a football match can injure your opponent and result in you being sent off!

- Safety notices: Always look for safety notices before you begin. These can give you important information such as where the fire exit is or which is the deep end of the swimming pool.

Oh dear! Because he has broken the rules, this footballer is going to miss the rest of the match.

- Avoid risks: It might sound obvious, but try not to take any unnecessary risks!

- Medical: Some illnesses or conditions mean that you must keep your medicine with you. For example, many people with asthma must keep their inhaler with them. If this applies to you, make sure you do as you have been told to. It is a good idea to also tell an adult who is with you so that they know what to do if you become ill.

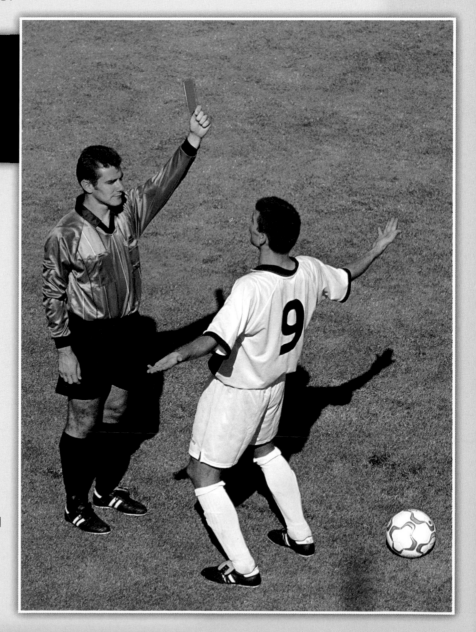

Drugs and sport

Steps to follow

Practise your skills

For these activities you will need:

* a football
* several markers
* a tennis racket
* a tennis ball
* a basketball.

Whatever your sport, you do not need **drugs** to improve your performance. Instead, you should practise your skills and be proud of your achievements. Here are some activities to help you improve your skills. These activities are useful in many different sports.

1 Set up several markers in a straight line with spaces between them. Dribble a ball in and out between the markers. Try to keep the ball under your control all the time. Now vary the distance between the markers.

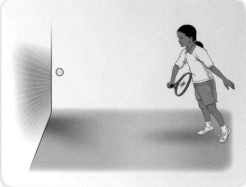

2 Stand several paces back from a wall. Use a tennis racket to hit a tennis ball at the wall. Keep hitting it back when it bounces back to you. How many times can you do it without missing? Use forehand, backhand, and alternate the two. Now try hitting the ball before it bounces each time.

3 Bounce a basketball on the ground several times. How many bounces can you do without losing control of the ball? Now try bouncing using alternate hands. You can make the practice harder by bouncing the ball under one leg, under the other leg, or behind you.

Banned drugs

Newspapers and television news programmes often have reports about sportsmen or women taking drugs or failing drug tests. There are very strict rules about taking drugs in sport and competitors are tested regularly. In many sports, if someone is found to have taken a banned substance they are not allowed to compete again for a long time.

Taking drugs is cheating!

Taking drugs is really just cheating. The person thinks they are not good enough to win by their own skills so they rely on a drug to help them. This is not fair on the other competitors who have not taken drugs.

Dangers of drugs

Taking drugs to improve your performance is not only unfair it is also very dangerous. Many drugs can damage your body causing health problems for the rest of your life.

Temperature control

When you are active, your **muscles** work hard. They get warm and generate heat. This makes your whole body feel warm. This is fine, but you cannot keep on getting hotter and hotter! Your body has to maintain a constant, safe temperature.

One way your body loses unwanted heat is by sweating. Sweat is a salty liquid made in **sweat glands** in your skin. When you start to get hot, sweat trickles out through tiny holes in the skin called **pores**. As air passes over your skin the sweat evaporates. This helps to cool your skin down. When you stop exercising your muscles stop generating heat. Your body slowly cools down and your skin stops releasing sweat.

This tennis player is wearing a towelling band around his wrist. It will soak up his sweat and stop it dripping on to his racket and making his hand slippery.

Water loss

If you lose a lot of water as sweat your body can become short of water. This is called **dehydration**. It makes your body start to overheat and you might get a headache, feel tired, and thirsty. You might also feel a bit dizzy and faint. You can avoid becoming dehydrated by drinking plenty of water before, during, and after exercise. During exercise you should try to have a drink of water about every 20 minutes, even if you do not feel very thirsty.

Sweating

You have about 3 million sweat glands in your body!

An adult who is very active in a hot environment can lose 2–3 litres (4–6 pints) of sweat in 1 hour!

When you have been exercising hard like this girl, a drink of cold water will cool you down. It will also replace some of the water lost by sweating.

Blood and temperature

Your blood also helps to control your body temperature. A network of tiny blood **capillaries** runs throughout your skin. Some are close to the surface. Others are deep inside the skin.

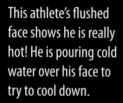

This athlete's flushed face shows he is really hot! He is pouring cold water over his face to try to cool down.

Getting hot

When your body is resting, blood flows evenly through the skin capillaries. When you start to get hot, more blood flows through capillaries just below the surface of your skin. Heat passes from the blood, through the skin, and into the air. This explains why you often have a red face when you have been exercising hard. There is more blood than usual near the surface of the skin and so it looks red.

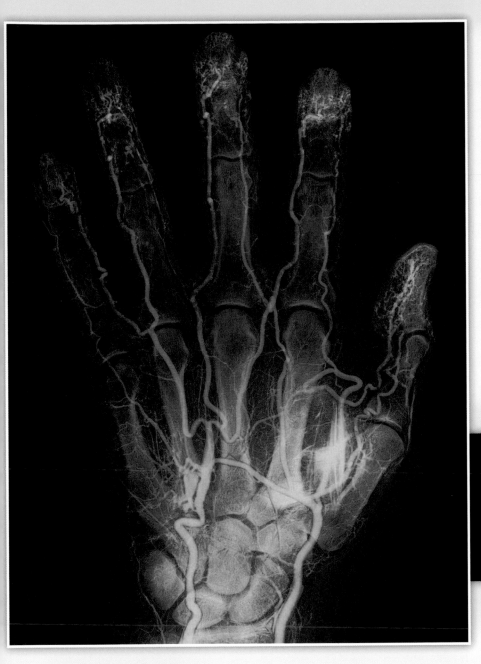

Cooling down

When your body cools down the opposite happens. More blood flows through capillaries deeper in the skin. There is less blood flowing just below the skin's surface so less heat is lost through the skin. If you get very cold, your skin can start to look blue. This is because you cannot see the red colour of the blood as it flows deeper within the skin.

In this X-ray, you can see some of the blood vessels in a hand.

Help your body!

It makes sense to help your body to control its temperature. You can do this by wearing more than one layer of clothes. This will mean you are warm enough when you begin exercising. When you get hot you can take off the top layer. Splashing cold water on your skin or running your wrists (where **blood vessels** are near to the surface of the skin) under a cold tap will help you cool down too. Taking a short break and resting for a few minutes also gives your body a chance to cool down.

When your activity is over...

It is a good idea to cool down slowly rather than to stop suddenly. You do not need any equipment for these activities:

Side bends:
Stand with your feet about the same distance apart as your shoulders. Put your hands on your hips. Now slowly bend to your left from your waist, letting your hips move to your right a little. Straighten up and then slowly bend to your right. Repeat several times.

Walking around:
It may sound very simple, but walking around slowly for a few minutes can help your body to cool down.

Jogging:
If you have been running fast, jogging can be a good way to finish your activity session. You can jog slowly and gently on the spot or over a short distance.

Avoiding muscle stiffness

Cooling down properly after an activity session is as important as warming up before you begin! If you stop exercising suddenly and simply rest, your **muscles** will probably feel stiff and tired the next day. This is because of a substance called **lactic acid**. Your muscles produce lactic acid when they work hard. If your muscles stop exercising suddenly, they cannot get rid of the lactic acid. Some gets trapped in your muscles making them feel tired and heavy. If you do some gentle cooling down exercises, your muscles can slowly get rid of the lactic acid so you feel fine later.

Gentle stretching and bending can help your muscles to cool down after exercise.

Tracksuit time

While you are active, your body will be quite hot. As soon as you stop it will cool down. Try to pull on some warm clothing such as a tracksuit to avoid cooling too much and feeling shivery.

Hygiene

Don't forget about personal hygiene! If you have been active, you will probably have been sweating. A warm shower will get rid of this and clean your skin. It will also help to relax your muscles.

Conclusion

You should now know that keeping active really matters! Being active is one of the best ways of keeping your body fit and healthy.

Strong heart

Exercising a **muscle** makes it stronger. Your **heart** is a muscle, and the more exercise you take the stronger it gets. This means that the more active you are the stronger and healthier your heart will be. You will be able to run faster and keep going for longer.

Have fun!

Exercise and activity should be fun! There are lots of great ways to exercise – both on your own or with friends. This book gives some suggestions, but you will probably have some favourites of your own as well. It is a good idea to vary what you do. Mixing activities that make you run and jump with others that make you bend and stretch will help every part of your body.

The 4 "S's"

A good mix of exercises and activities will help you develop the "4 S's" – Speed, **Stamina**, Strength, and Skills. Together these will help you do well in just about every sport or activity you can think of!

Eating healthy food like this provides your body with everything it needs to be active and fit.

Be sensible

Being sensible about your exercise is important. Before you start, check with an adult that your planned activity is safe for you. Also try to remember to:

- warm up before you exercise
- cool down when you finish
- wear protective clothing if necessary
- obey signs, rules, and instructions.

These young basketball players need the "4 S's" to play well.

Eat, drink, and sleep

Keeping fit is not only about exercise, though. Other things are involved, too, including:

- eating healthy food with plenty of fresh fruit and vegetables
- drinking plenty of water
- getting a good night's sleep.

If you can combine exercise, rest, and a healthy diet you are well on the way to having a fit, healthy body. Your hair will shine, your skin will be clear and fresh, your eyes will be bright, and you will feel ready for anything!

Glossary

alveoli very tiny part of your lungs. Several alveoli together look like a very, very small bunch of grapes.

artery type of blood vessel. Arteries are the strongest blood vessels.

blood vessel name for part of the network of tubes through which blood travels round your body. All your blood vessels together make up a complicated network that reaches every part of you.

bone part of your skeleton. Your bones give your body its shape.

bronchiole small branch of air tube in the lungs. Bronchioles look like the roots of a tree.

capillary type of blood vessel. Capillaries are the smallest blood vessels.

carbohydrate type of food chemical or food group. Carbohydrates contain a lot of energy and provide fuel for the body. Pasta, rice, and bread all contain carbohydrates.

carbon dioxide waste gas made by your body. Carbon dioxide leaves your body when you breathe out.

cartilage material similar to bone but flexible. Cartilage covers and cushions the ends of bones at joints.

cell one of the tiny building blocks that all living things are made from. Your cells need energy to make them work.

circulation movement of blood. The network of blood vessels means your blood can circulate to every part of your body.

contract get smaller or shorter. A stretched rubber band contracts when you stop pulling it.

dehydration not having enough water. Dehydration can make you feel thirsty, sick, and headachy.

diaphragm sheet of muscle across the bottom of your chest. Your diaphragm helps you to breathe.

drug substance that affects the way your body works. Taking drugs is banned in many sports.

elastic can be stretched. A rubber band is elastic.

expand get bigger or longer. A balloon expands when you blow it up.

fat type of food chemical or food group. Butter, oil, and fried foods all contain fats.

flexible can be bent. A training shoe is flexible.

heart organ that pumps blood around your body. Your heart pumps non-stop, even when you are asleep.

interval training swapping between two different types of exercise. If you run, walk, run, walk, run, walk you are doing interval training.

joint place where two bones meet. Your joints allow your body to bend.

lactic acid substance that your muscles make when they work hard. Cooling down lets your muscles get rid of lactic acid.

ligament strong band that holds a joint together. Without ligaments your joints would be weak and wobbly.

lungs organs that you use for breathing. Your lungs take in air and let out waste gases.

mineral useful chemical found in food. Iron and salt are both minerals.

muscle part of your body that can move bones. Without muscles you would not be able to move at all.

nutrient part of your food that your body can use. Proteins and vitamins are both nutrients.

oxygen gas that your body needs to work. You get oxygen from the air when you breathe in.

pore tiny hole. Pores in your skin let sweat trickle out.

protein type of food chemical or food group. Proteins help to build body parts and repair our bodies. Meat, fish, eggs, and nuts all contain proteins.

pulse rate how fast your heart is beating. You can measure your pulse rate at your wrist.

resting rate your pulse rate when you are resting. It should be slow and steady.

ribcage bony cage in your chest. Your ribcage protects your heart and lungs.

skeleton all your bones together. Your skeleton is the framework for the rest of your body.

spine bones in your back. Your spine is flexible and lets you twist and bend.

stamina being able to keep going for a long time. It takes a lot of stamina to run a marathon.

sweat glands parts of your skin that make you sweat. You have about 3 million sweat glands in your body!

thigh part of your leg between your hip and your knee. The thigh bone is the longest in your body.

vein type of blood vessel. Veins are bigger than capillaries but not as strong as arteries.

vitamin type of useful chemical found in food. For example, vitamin C is found in oranges.

windpipe tube that connects your mouth and nose to your lungs. Air passes through your windpipe when you breathe in and out.

Find out more

Books

Body Matters: Why Should I Get Off the Sofa? And Other Questions About Health and Exercise, Louise Spilsbury (Heinemann Library, 2004)

Get Fit! Eat Right! Be Active!: Girls Guide to Health & Fitness, Michelle H. Nagler (Scholastic, 2001)

Healthy Body: Exercise and Your Body, Polly Goodman (Hodder Wayland, 2005)

Keeping Healthy: Exercise, Carol Ballard (Hodder Wayland , 2007)

Kid Power: Active Kids, Bobbie Kalman (Crabtree Publishing Co, 2003)

Training for the Top: Nutrition and Energy, Paul Mason (Raintree, 2005)

What About Health: Exercise, Fiona Waters (Hodder Wayland, 2004)

Websites

http://news.bbc.co.uk/cbbcnews/hi/specials/sport/sportsround/default.stm

Read up-to-date news on different sports, and find out how you can get involved.

www.kidshealth.org

You can find the answers to many questions about keeping fit and healthy on this website.

Organizations

British Gymnastics

British Gymnastics, Ford Hall, Lillehall NSC, Newport, Shropshire, TF10 9NB
www.british-gymnastics.org

British Swimming and Amateur Swimming Association

The ASA is involved with swimming at every level, from beginners to Olympic standard.
ASA, Harold Fern House, Derby Square, Loughborough, Leicestershire, LE11 5AL
www.britishswimming.org

England Athletics

England Athletics, Athletics House, Central Boulevard, Blythe Valley Park,
Solihull, West Midlands, B90 8AJ
www.british-athletics.co.uk

English Federation of Disability Sport

The national body responsible for developing sport for disabled people in England.
English Federation of Disability Sport, Manchester Metropolitan University,
Alsager Campus, Hassall Road, Alsager, Stoke on Trent, ST7 2H
www.efds.net

Index

SAVAGE
EARTH

SAVAGE

ALWYN SCARTH

EARTH

HarperCollins*Publishers*

In association with Granada Television

HarperCollins*Publishers*
77–85 Fulham Palace Road
London W6 8JB

02 01 00 99 98 97
10 9 8 7 6 5 4 3 2 1

I am very pleased to record
my most sincere thanks
(in alphabetical order) to
Anthony Newton, Francine
Ozanne, Katie Piper, Jean-
Louis Renaud, Henri Rouvier
and Jean-Claude Tanguy, for all
their valuable help while I
was preparing this book.

Educated at St Catharine's
College, Cambridge where he
was awarded a PhD, Alwyn
Scarth was for 30 years a
Lecturer in Geography at
Dundee University. He is now
based mainly in Paris where
he continues his writing and
research. His previous works
include *Volcanoes* (UCL Press,
London).

Adapted from the Granada
Television series SAVAGE
EARTH. The production team
behind SAVAGE EARTH was:
Series Producer: Bill Jones;
Producers: Liz McLeod, Bill
Lyons; Directors Chris Malone,
Bill Lyons; Assistant Producers:
Kate Coombes, Emma Hawley,
Debra Prinselaar, Ann-Marie
Burnham; Film Research:
Maggi Cook; Production Co-
ordinator: Del Bowen-Hayes;
Production Finance: Tim
Hynes; Cameras: Lawrence
Jones, Tim Pollard; Sound:
Mark Atkinson; Film Editors:
David Creswell, Kim Horton;
Music: Howard Davidson;
Graphic Design: Paul Kearton.

ISBN 0 00 220106 2

Designed by Clare Baggaley

Colour reproduction by
Colourscan, Singapore
Printed and bound by
Graficas Estella, Spain

CONTENTS

1

2

3

4

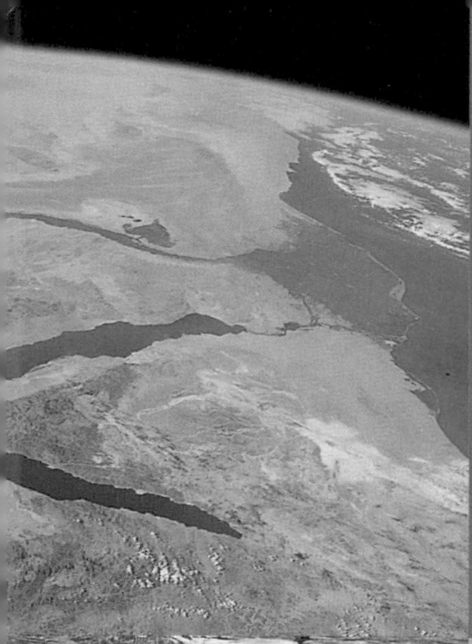

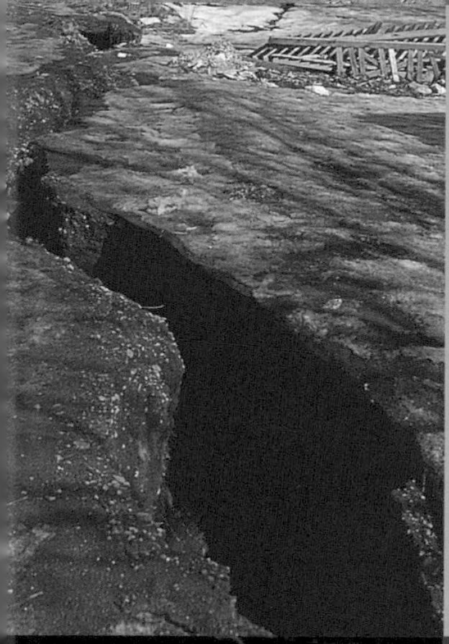

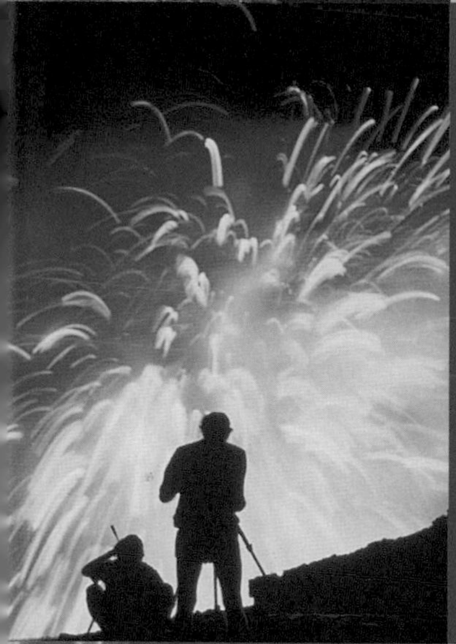

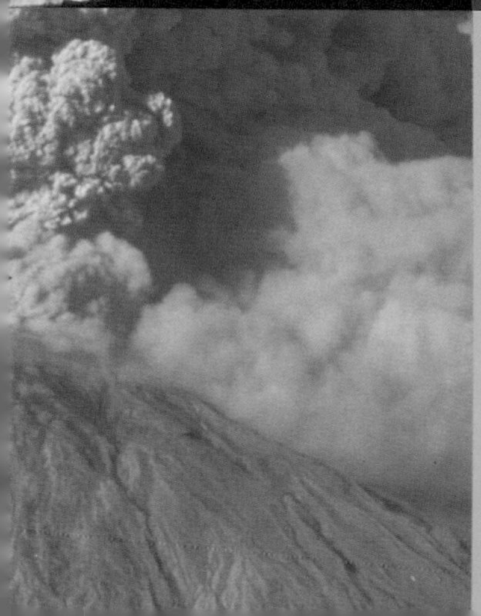

the Earth in perspective

THE EARTH IS A DYNAMIC PLANET: IT IS CONSTANTLY CHANGING. THE IMMENSE ENERGY THAT LIES BENEATH THE SURFACE MOVES CONTINENTS, CREATES ISLANDS AND CAN OPEN UP GREAT CRACKS IN THE GROUND. FOR EXAMPLE, WHILE THE ATLANTIC OCEAN IS WIDENING AT ITS CENTRE, THE FLOOR OF THE PACIFIC OCEAN IS PLUNGING BENEATH THE SURROUNDING LAND MASSES, WHERE IT MELTS AND FORMS THE MOST SPECTACULAR SYSTEM OF VOLCANOES IN THE WORLD: THE 'RING OF FIRE'. EARTHQUAKES ACCOMPANY MANY OF THESE DYNAMIC CHANGES, AS WELL AS VOLCANIC ERUPTIONS, AND TOGETHER THEY COMPRISE THE MOST SPECTACULAR EXAMPLES OF THE EARTH'S POWER.

On a day-to-day basis, we are aware only of the catastrophic manifestations of the changes that are occurring beneath the Earth's crust, and as a result it has taken scientists many years to discover the reasons for these dramatic events. The true picture unfolds over millions of years with the movement of the plates that make up the land-masses and ocean floors at an average annual rate of around 10cm (4in). This, however, is fast enough to have opened up the whole Atlantic Ocean between Europe and North America within 180 million  years. The Earth is 4,600 million years old – there has been plenty of time for slow changes to produce vast results.

From the human point of view, the powers unleashed when a movement takes place – perhaps a slip of just 5m (16½ft) in rocks 10km (6¼ miles) deep – can cause a devastating earthquake. Molten rock, rising through a narrow chimney in the crust, can explode and bury an entire city.

On 23 January 1973 Helgafell erupted on the island of Heimaey, off the coast of Iceland, threatening the town of Vestmannaeyjar

Volcanic activity produces volcanoes, hot springs and geysers, such as this one at Yellowstone National Park, United States

4.6 thousand million years ago
Earth formed. Core, Mantle and Crust develop. First 'granitic' continents. Outgassing of Carbon dioxide, nitrogen and water. Then atmosphere and oceans

4.0 thousand million years ago
Oldest rocks discovered to date laid down (were sediments eroded from older rocks)

3.5 thousand million years ago
Very earliest forms of bacteria and algae

This geological timebar plots the occurrence of some significant events in the history of the Earth. Geological time refers to the entire history of the Earth revealed by study of the rocks composing the crust, and is distinct from historical time, which refers to events that have been recorded by observers. The length of historical time varies around the world

2.5 thousand million years ago
Increase in free oxygen in atmosphere

2.0–1.5 thousand million years ago
Early super-continent. Mountain ranges in Scotland, Canada and central Africa created

700 million years ago
Early multicellular life

570 million years ago
Super-continent breaks up. Organisms with shells; fossils

500 million years ago
Early fish

450 million years ago

350 million years ago

300 million years ago

225 million years ago

180 million years ago

140 million years ago

65 million years ago

50 million years ago
Early horses

350 million years ago
Early trees. Main coal measures. 'Hercynian' mountains in central France, central Germany, Poland

225 million years ago
Super-continent splits in two: 'Laurasia' in north; 'Gondwanaland' in south

140 million years ago
Early flowering plants
Andean mountains begin to form

10,000 years ago
'Modern' Man

450 million years ago
Early land plants. 'Caledonian' mountains in Scotland, Norway, eastern United States

300 million years ago
New super-continent 'Pangaea' Early reptiles

180 million years ago
Laurasia splits; Atlantic Ocean starts opening Gondwanaland splits; Indian Ocean starts opening Early birds and mammals

65 million years ago
Extinction of dinosaurs
Early primates
Rocky Mountains begin to form

40–50 million years ago
India starts to collide with Asia; Himalayan mountains begin to form
Africa colliding with Europe; Pyrenees and Alps begin to form

15 million years ago
Arabia separates from Africa; Red Sea opens

11 million years ago
Mediterranean Sea closed at Straits of Gibraltar, dries up for a time

100,000 years ago
Neanderthal Man

1.8 million years ago
Start of widespread glaciations

c.3 million years ago
Stone tools used by human-like beings

the Earth's surface

THE DIFFERENT WAYS IN WHICH SECTIONS OF THE EARTH'S CRUST BEHAVE ARE ESSENTIAL TO AN UNDERSTANDING OF EARTHQUAKES AND VOLCANOES. HERE WE OUTLINE THE DIFFERENT TYPES OF INTERACTION BETWEEN THE CRUSTAL PLATES THAT COMPRISE THE OCEAN FLOORS AND THE CONTINENTS ON WHICH WE LIVE, AND WHAT IS HAPPENING BENEATH THE EARTH'S SURFACE.

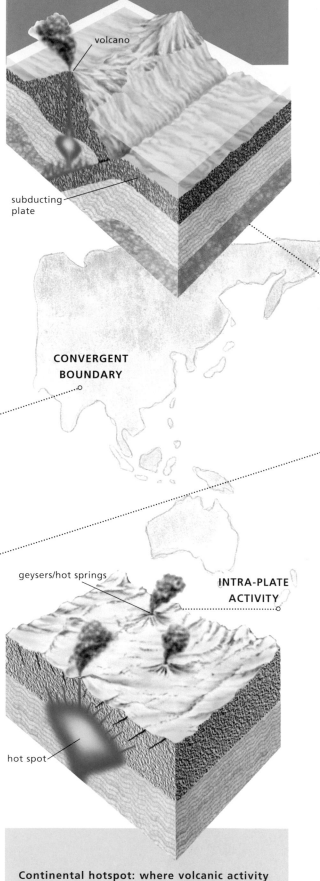

Subduction: where one oceanic plate plunges underneath another, volcanic islands such as the Aleutian Islands, off the coast of Alaska, may form; also produces earthquakes

volcano

subducting plate

CONVERGENT BOUNDARY

INTRA-PLATE ACTIVITY

geysers/hot springs

volcanic seamount

hot spot

hot spot

Collision: where one continental plate plunges underneath another. This process forms ranges of high, folded mountains such as the Himalayas. Continuing pressures cause frequent earthquakes along cracks or faults in the rocks

Oceanic hotspot: where volcanic activity in the form of hotspots creates volcanic seamounts that may build up above sea-level as in Hawaii

Continental hotspot: where volcanic activity producess hot springs, geysers and other forms of mild volcanic activity, as seen on North Island, New Zealand

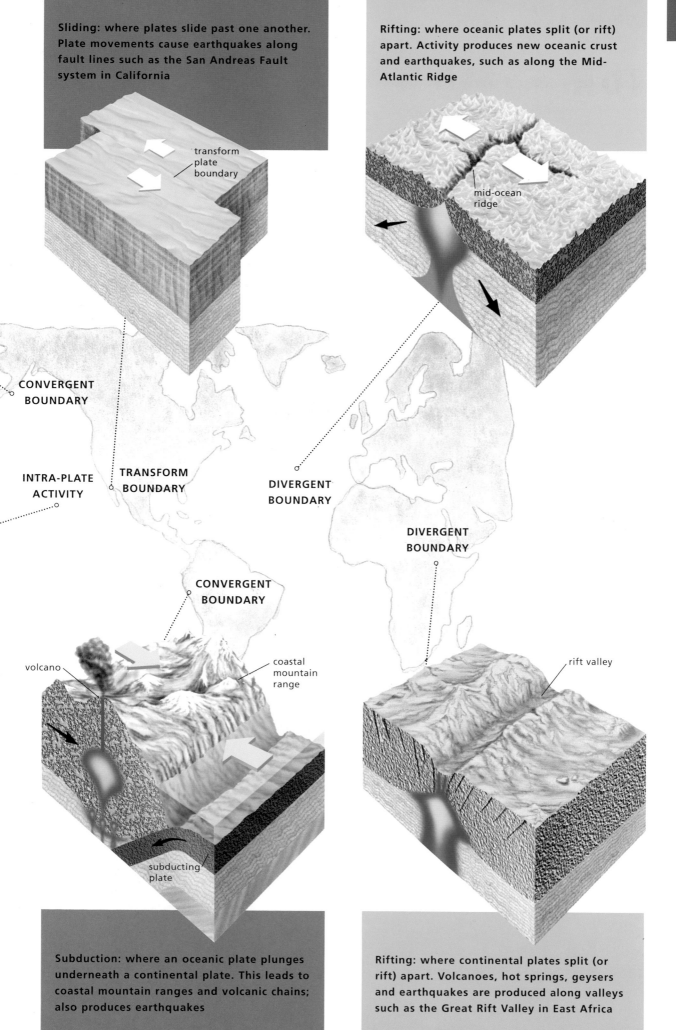

Sliding: where plates slide past one another. Plate movements cause earthquakes along fault lines such as the San Andreas Fault system in California

transform plate boundary

Rifting: where oceanic plates split (or rift) apart. Activity produces new oceanic crust and earthquakes, such as along the Mid-Atlantic Ridge

mid-ocean ridge

CONVERGENT BOUNDARY

INTRA-PLATE ACTIVITY

TRANSFORM BOUNDARY

DIVERGENT BOUNDARY

DIVERGENT BOUNDARY

CONVERGENT BOUNDARY

volcano

coastal mountain range

rift valley

subducting plate

Subduction: where an oceanic plate plunges underneath a continental plate. This leads to coastal mountain ranges and volcanic chains; also produces earthquakes

Rifting: where continental plates split (or rift) apart. Volcanoes, hot springs, geysers and earthquakes are produced along valleys such as the Great Rift Valley in East Africa

introduction

summary

THE AIM OF THIS BOOK IS TO EXAMINE ALL ASPECTS OF EARTHQUAKES AND VOLCANIC ERUPTIONS IN TERMS OF THE SIX QUESTIONS ESSENTIAL TO ANY INVESTIGATION: WHY? HOW? WHERE? WHAT? WHO? AND WHEN?

Why?
The answer to this question is dependent on the nature of the Earth's interior.

How?
Here we need to look at the results of the movements of the crustal plates.

A bleak view showing the aftermath of the 1906 earthquake in San Francisco, California

Where?
The location of earthquake and volcanic activity is directly linked to the growth, conflict and destruction of these plates.

What?
This is the question that receives the closest attention in this book. Earthquakes vary in magnitude and in their destructive intensity. Volcanic eruptions display over a dozen different styles, producing anything from hot water to molten lava and the finest ash. Both earthquakes and eruptions generate important secondary effects, which can be just as calamitous: huge sea-waves or tsunamis, mudflows, landslides, fires, famines, diseases and vast destruction.

Who?
Here we must focus attention on the victims of these natural disasters. The numbers involved depend on a range of factors including the density of population, the style of building, and the extent of awareness and emergency training.

When?
Since the Earth behaves with a certain consistency, careful study of the past encourages scientists to forecast its future behaviour. It is possible to make long-term forecasts in terms of say, ten or 100 or 1,000 years, especially after an area has been closely monitored. But the Earth functions in long time-spans, and short-term predictions are extremely difficult to make for both eruptions and earthquakes. The millions of people living in the dangerous belts of the Earth's surface, however, desperately need to know exactly when the next eruption or earthquake will happen. There has been significant progress, but until such time that accurate predictions can be made, we will have to rely on the speedy communication of information, advances in building technology and populations that are well-equipped to deal with disasters when they strike.

Trees flattened by the blast produced by the eruption of Mount St Helens in 1980

Old Faithful, a geyser at Yellowstone National Park, United States, erupts about once every 67 minutes and its timetable is posted daily for visitors. Other geysers may erupt much less regularly

the composition of the Earth

THE REASONS THAT EARTHQUAKES AND VOLCANIC ERUPTIONS TAKE PLACE DEPEND ON THE NATURE OF THE EARTH'S INTERIOR. THE DIAGRAM (RIGHT) SHOWS HOW THE DIFFERENT ELEMENTS THAT COMPRISE OUR PLANET ARE ARRANGED, AND THE INDIVIDUAL SECTIONS OF THE STRUCTURE OF THE EARTH ARE DESCRIBED BELOW.

The core

The globe is made up of a core surrounded by concentric shells. The core itself comprises nearly one third of the global mass. The inner core, 5,100–6,400km (3,169–3,977 miles) deep has a temperature of about 4,300°C. It is apparently composed of iron, kept solid in spite of its heat by the tremendous pressures confining it.

The outer core

The surrounding outer core, 2,885–5,100km (1,793–3,170 miles) deep is also composed largely of iron, but with some nickel and a few lighter elements. This outer core is fluid and convection currents keep it in slow but constant motion. These currents and the rotation of the globe make the outer core a self-exciting dynamo that has developed the Earth's magnetic field.

The Earth is a dipole, ie. it has two magnetic poles, North and South. During the planet's history, however, the poles have, at different times, become reversed. These magnetic reversals have been used to date rocks and have proved to be vitally important in demonstrating the movement of crustal plates (see pp.18–19).

The mantle

The outer core is enveloped by the mantle which comprises the lower mantle and the upper mantle. The lower mantle is 2,235km (1,390 miles) thick and 650–2,885km (404–1,793 miles) deep. It is solid, hot and held under great pressure. Nevertheless, stresses and strains and convection currents and creep have developed within it. Surrounding the lower mantle is a shell about 500km (311 miles) thick, lying between 60–150km (37–93 miles) and 650km (404 miles) deep. This shell is composed of a transition zone and the more plastic layers of the upper mantle. Together, they form the asthenosphere (from the Greek *asthenos* meaning 'weak') which reacts to stresses and strains in a fluid way, although it is only partly molten. Convection currents keep the asthenosphere in slow, but continuous, motion and they are thus probably a major driving force behind the movement of the plates across the Earth's surface.

An eruption on Stromboli, an island off the coast of Sicily in the Mediterranean

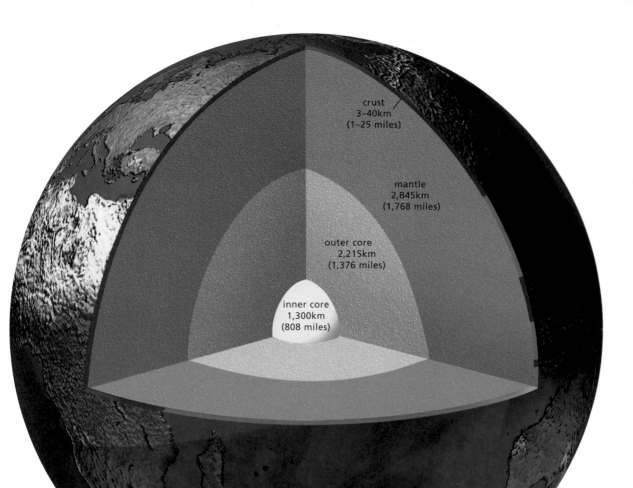

crust
3–40km
(1–25 miles)

mantle
2,845km
(1,768 miles)

outer core
2,215km
(1,376 miles)

inner core
1,300km
(808 miles)

The lithosphere

The outermost shell of the globe is the lithosphere (from the Greek *lithos* meaning 'stone'), which can be as little as 60km (37 miles) thick below the oceans, but can reach as much as 150km (93 miles) thick beneath the continents. Like the other shells, the lithosphere is divided into two layers: the lower layer is the solid upper mantle; the upper, outermost layer is the Earth's crust. The thickness of the crust varies from about 70km (43½ miles) under the main mountain ranges to only 3km (1¾ miles) along the crests of the mid-ocean ridges. It is an average of 40km (25 miles) thick on the continents, where it is pale in colour, generally granitic in character, with a low density. Under the oceans, on the other hand, it is dense, dark-coloured and basaltic, and averages no more than 6km (3¾ miles) in

The shells that comprise the earth. The upper part of the mantle comprises the plastic asthenosphere, 150–650km (93–404 miles) deep, and the cooler, more solid lithosphere, 60–150km (37–93 miles) thick. The thickness of the outermost layer, the crust, has been exaggerated on this diagram

thickness. This crust that seems so firm to us is thin, brittle and fragile. It accounts for just one thousandth of the volume of the globe.

There is a constant interchange and interaction between the global shells – and especially between the outermost layers. The main results are the growth, movement and consumption of the global plates; and their most obvious manifestations are earthquakes and volcanic eruptions.

chapter 1

PLATE
TECTONICS

plate growth at the mid-ocean ridges

THE GROWTH, MOVEMENT, COLLISION AND CONSUMPTION OF THE PLATES THAT COMPRISE THE EARTH'S CRUST ARE THE BASIC CAUSES OF EARTHQUAKES AND VOLCANIC ERUPTIONS. HERE WE LOOK AT THE DIFFERENT WAYS IN WHICH PLATES INTERACT, A STUDY KNOWN AS PLATE TECTONICS. THE FIRST OF THESE IS PLATE GROWTH.

The best example of plate growth can be seen along the Mid-Atlantic Ridge. Although it rises about 4,000m (13,000ft) above the oceanic plains, most of the ridge is submerged. The crest of the ridge only rises above sea-level in Iceland, but volcanic islands also emerge from its flanks in Jan Mayen, the Azores, Ascension Island, and Tristan da Cunha. The ridge rises to two parallel crests that face each other across a long central depression. This is the point at which the plates are growing and diverging. Here the Atlantic Ocean is actively widening at an average rate of just a few centimetres a year. Thus New York is moving further away from London.

upwelling under ocean creates a spreading ridge

mid-ocean ridge

The Mid-Atlantic Ridge is a submerged mountain range rising about 4,000m (13,000ft) above the ocean floor and only emerges above sea-level in a few places along its length

It seems that the plates are being pulled apart along the mid-ocean ridge by diverging convection currents operating in the asthenosphere and upper mantle. This process is also known as rifting. The divergence causes the solid basaltic plates to split open along many parallel cracks or fissures that trend along the ridge. The cracks can be as little as 1m (3¼ft) or as long as 1km (⅔ mile). Whatever their lengths, they have the same effects. They cause mild earthquakes and mild eruptions. The earthquakes rarely exceed magnitude 6.0 but have shallow sources around 5km (3 miles) deep. So little land is exposed on or near the mid-ocean ridge that the earthquakes usually pass unnoticed, but the earthquake that shook the Azores on 1

hotspot

convergent zone: downwelling subducts dense oceanic crust into the mantle

descending ocean plate

January 1980 was intense enough to cause serious damage in Angra do Heroísmo in Terceira.

Once the plates have cracked and rifted apart, the pressures on the zone directly below are immediately reduced. The asthenosphere is only 3km (1¾ miles) beneath the crest of the ridge and the lower pressure allows some of the minerals within it to melt out. Together these minerals form what is often called primary basalt, which is less dense than the materials of the asthenosphere as a whole. Thus, the primary basalt rises into cracks as they develop and become available and makes its way towards the surface of the ridge. This activity is enormously important in the Earth's dynamic growth. It accounts for three-quarters of the annual production of volcanic rock on Earth. Every year 3km³ (¾ cubic mile) of new volcanic rock is added to the diverging plate margins. Most of it solidifies in the cracks en route and becomes welded

Lava erupted underwater forms characteristic 'pillow lavas' as it cools

to one or other of the diverging plates. The primary basalt that succeeds in reaching the surface is changed a little on the way into a form of basalt lava. From diving machines, it can be seen emerging as pillow-like lumps that glow red-hot in the murky water. The cold water quickly quenches them into their characteristic shapes as they ooze out, one after the other, and pile up in masses of solidified 'pillow lavas' on the surface of each diverging plate. The pressure of the water also ensures that there are no explosions. The growth of oceanic plates is marked therefore, by mild, continued activity, rather than savage outbursts.

Earth scientists have noted that as each crack in the ocean floor becomes choked with solidified basalt lava, new cracks rift open alongside them. Piles of basalt congeal on the edges of each plate as they move apart. The newest basalts, therefore, occupy the crests of the ridges while increasingly older basalts form the flanks of the ridge. Scientists studying Paleomagnetism (see pp.18–19) have succeeded in dating and identifying different bands of basalt on either side of the diverging ridge. It shows that the bands alternate in exactly the same way on either side of the ridge crest, and the older the bands of basalts, the farther away they were from the crest of the mid-ocean ridge. The oldest bands occurred on the outer fringes of the ocean, near the continental shelves. Thus the ocean floor must have spread out from the mid-ocean ridges. In addition, as the basalts cooled, they become denser. Therefore, where the basalts are new and hot they are high, and form a mid-ocean ridge. As they cool, become denser, and move further from the mid-ocean ridge, they sink. Thus the mid-ocean ridges are flanked by abyssal plains over 4,000m (13,000ft) deep.

One theory put forward to explain the apparent movement of the Earth's crust is the existence of upward and downward convection currents in the mantle

lithosphere

mantle

upwelling: mid-ocean ridge

outer core

core

paleomagnetism

THE EXISTENCE OF PLATE GROWTH AT OCEAN RIDGES AND THEREBY THE CREATION OF THE ATLANTIC OCEAN OVER THE PAST 180 MILLION YEARS HAVE BEEN CONFIRMED BY AN AREA OF STUDY KNOWN AS PALEOMAGNETISM (MEANING 'FOSSIL MAGNETISM').

The Earth acts like a giant magnet with poles at points to the north and south. Although these correspond roughly with the geographical poles (the top and bottom of the imaginary axis of the rotation of the Earth), they do not occur at exactly the same points. At present the magnetic north pole is 1,900km (1,180 miles) from the North Pole; the magnetic south pole is about 2,600km (1,615 miles) from the South Pole. The magnetic poles move slowly around the geographical poles, and over several thousands of years their *mean* positions coincide. In accordance with our normal polarity (ie. the magnetism that exists at present), a freely swinging compass needle points to the magnetic north pole, and as it is moved it will dip at different angles according to its latitude.

Over time, the poles have, at irregular intervals, and for different lengths of time, become reversed (known as 'reverse polarity'). When rocks form, eg. as sediments or cooled solidified volcanic rocks, they often contain minerals that become magnetized and will point, like compass needles, to the magnetic pole of the day. Analysis of carefully-chosen, uncontaminated rock specimens, shows their latitude and position in relation to the magnetic pole that existed when they were formed. A pattern of magnetic reversals has now been worked out for the last several hundred million years.

These tests have been vital in establishing how plates grow and move. For example, when the results are plotted on maps of mid-ocean ridges, a simple general pattern emerges: stripes of normal magnetism alternate with stripes of reverse magnetism. This pattern is mirrored on either side of the ridge, with the stripes of rock increasing in age, the further they are away from the ridge crest on both plates. This discovery, made in the 1960s, formed one of the foundations of the theory of plate tectonics, because it showed how plates grow at the mid-ocean ridges.

Paleomagnetic studies from rocks on the continental crust also demonstrate the way in which the plates have moved to reach their present positions. If magnetism is not lost or changed once it is attained, rocks magnetized at the same time should point to the same

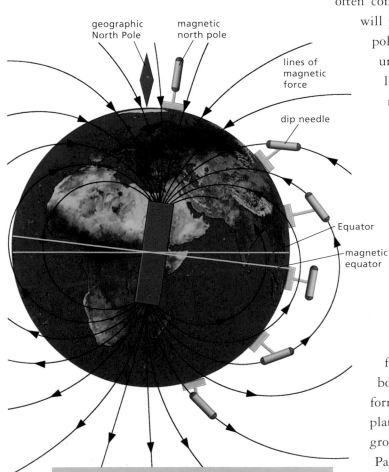

geographic
North Pole

magnetic
north pole

lines of
magnetic
force

dip needle

Equator

magnetic
equator

The angle of a dip needle (a compass in a vertical plane) determines lines of latitude as it moves through the Earth's magnetic field. It can thus indicate the position of rocks at the time they became magnetized, helping us to track the movement of the continents

apparent polar wandering path for North America

apparent polar wandering path for Eurasia

EURASIA

NORTH AMERICA

500 my
400 my

500 my
400 my
300 my
200 my

300 my

200 my

apparent polar wandering path for Eurasia

100 my

100 my

NORTH AMERICA

EURASIA

apparent polar wandering path for North America

AFRICA

The map (below left) plots apparent polar wandering for rocks magnetized over the past 500 million years. The map (above left) shows that the paths converge when the land masses are placed in their correct positions at the time the rocks were magnetized

magnetic north pole. Scientists, however, soon found that uncontaminated magnetized rocks of exactly the same age in different continents did not point to the same north pole. Similarly, magnetized rocks of different ages on the same continent also pointed to different north poles.

Scientists plotted and mapped the poles to which the various magnetized rocks on different continents seemed to be pointing. In general, specimens from the most recent rocks pointed most closely to the present north pole. The older the specimens the more they diverged – suggesting that the continents and the plates carrying them must have moved in relation to the pole. Some plates had moved more than others and in different directions. Also, when continents had been joined together (as India and Asia are today), the plots of their apparent poles ran parallel. And, when continents split apart (as North America separated from Europe), the divergence increased.

By conducting worldwide tests, it became a relatively simple matter to discover where the various rocks (and their continents) had been situated when they were magnetized: place the specimens of the same age in their correct original location and they all point to the same magnetic pole. Soon it becomes apparent that the outlines of the continental masses resemble pieces of a jigsaw that were once locked together.

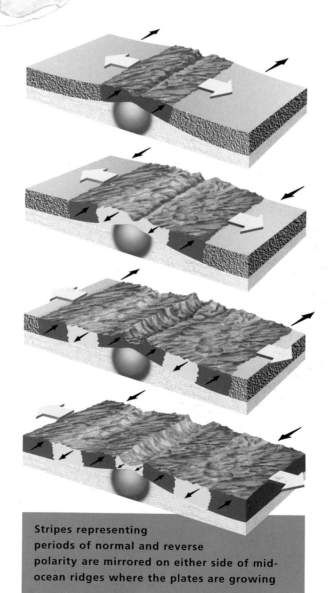

Stripes representing periods of normal and reverse polarity are mirrored on either side of mid-ocean ridges where the plates are growing

continental movement

EARTH SCIENTISTS HAVE SHOWN THAT FEATURES FOUND ON MANY SEPARATE CONTINENTS ORIGINALLY LAY NEXT TO EACH OTHER. THROUGHOUT HISTORY AND PRE-HISTORY CONTINENTS HAVE JOINED AND SEPARATED AS THE GLOBAL PLATES HAVE CARRIED THEM ACROSS THE FACE OF THE EARTH.

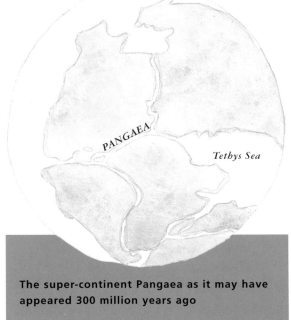

The last time the continents were all joined was about 300 million years ago in the super-continent called 'Pangaea'. About 225 million years ago, it split into a southern continent 'Gondwanaland', and a northern continent, 'Laurasia'. Soon afterwards both these large continents began to split into the continents that are recognizable today. Take the present continents (and their shelves) and put them in their positions of 225 million years ago. Many independent features then match closely. In old Laurasia, the outlines of the edge of the continental shelves, about 1,000m (3,280ft) deep, fit neatly together in the Atlantic Ocean. Eastern Canada, southern Greenland and Ireland

The super-continent Pangaea as it may have appeared 300 million years ago

lie together. Brazil fits equally well into the Gulf of Guinea, off Africa. The continents of old 'Gondwanaland' group around Antarctica. South America, South Africa, Madagascar and India fit to one side of Antarctica. Australia and New Zealand joined Antarctica too along the Great Australian Bight.

This movement is illustrated by many of today's geological features. A physical map of the world shows how structures and rock types run from one continent to another, although they are now widely separated. Thus, the old Caledonian Mountains of Scotland continue both to Norway and Greenland and the Appalachians in the United States. The present ocean floor between these fragments is comprised of younger basalts formed when the plates carried the continental masses apart (see pp.18–19).

The world's coal and oil deposits were formed in a humid tropical climate. Now, they are not only widely scattered across the globe, but they almost all lie far from the latitudes of their origin. Similarly, when 'Laurasia' had a tropical climate, 'Gondwanaland' was experiencing a period of glaciation. All the southern continents,

The fit of the southern continents and India around Antarctica 225 million years ago

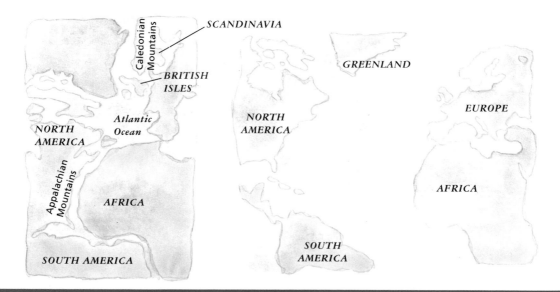

How the continents around the Atlantic Ocean used to fit together. it has taken 180 million years for the Atlantic Ocean to open up to its present size

together with the Indian sub-continent, must have been near the ice-covered South Pole at that time. Since that period, India, however, has crossed the equator and crashed into Asia.

The continental movements can thus be demonstrated by matching geological structures, rock types, fossil remains of flora and fauna, as well as the fit of many continental shelf outlines. Paleomagnetic evidence corroborates the matching fits and their subsequent separation.

Volcanic hotspots also reveal the movement of the plates. They are caused by convectional plumes of hot material that burn through the mantle like blowtorches, breaking through the lithosphere and forming large volcanoes. These plumes seem to be stationary. If the plates above them were also stationary then each plume would have formed one enormous volcano. As it is, hotspot volcanoes, such as those in Réunion in the Indian Ocean and the Hawaiian Islands in the Pacific Ocean, are amongst the world's largest volcanoes. But these active hotspot volcanoes lie at the end of a line of extinct volcanoes, the oldest of which lie furthest from those that are presently active: those at the far north-western end of the Hawaiian line, are 75 million years old. Thus, the Hawaiian Islands stand at the south-eastern end of submerged volcanoes forming the Hawaiian and Emperor lines of seamounts. Even within the Hawaiian Islands, activity is concentrated on their south-eastern parts at Mauna Loa and Kilauea on Hawaii. This process is continuing at this moment as a new volcanic island, Loihi, is building up to the south-east beneath the surface of the Pacific Ocean.

Mountains of comparable age and structure are found in North America, the British Isles and Scandinavia. When the landmasses are reassembled they show the mountains as a continuous range that was formed around 300 million years ago

plate consumption at the subduction zones

SUBDUCTION OCCURS WHEN ONE PLATE SLIDES UNDERNEATH ANOTHER, AND THE AREAS IN WHICH IT OCCURS ARE EXTREMELY UNSTABLE. MOST OF THE EARTH'S SUBDUCTION TAKES PLACE AROUND THE PACIFIC OCEAN, THE FLOOR OF WHICH COMPRISES SEVERAL DIFFERENT CRUSTAL PLATES. THE PACIFIC PLATE IS BY FAR THE LARGEST, AND IS MOVING NORTH-WESTWARDS AND PLUNGING BENEATH BOTH THE NORTH AMERICAN PLATE AND THE EURASIAN PLATE. IT ALSO INTERACTS WITH THE PHILIPPINE PLATE AND THE INDIAN-AUSTRALIAN PLATE.

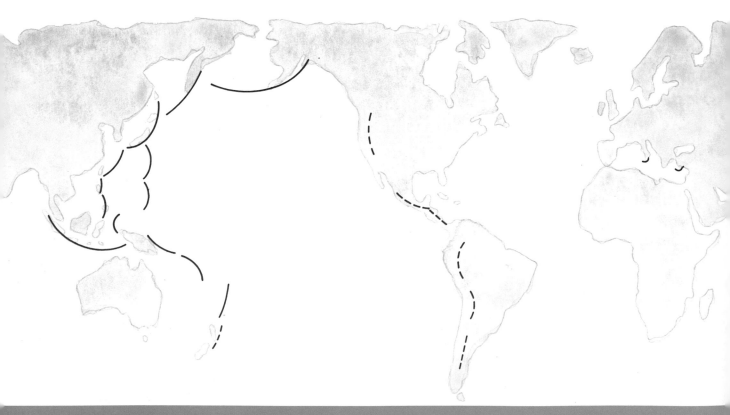

Subduction zones form volcanic chains on land and arcs of volcanic islands in the sea. This pattern is particularly clear along the subduction zones that surround the Pacific Ocean, and gives it its name, the 'Ring of Fire'

Elsewhere in the eastern Pacific the Nazca Plate is sinking below the South American Plate, the Cocos Plate is plunging under Central America and the small Juan de Jura Plate has been almost completely overridden by the North American Plate. Where the Indian-Australian Plate is composed of oceanic crust it plunges beneath the Eurasian Plate alongside Indonesia, but where it carries the Indian continental mass, it is thrust under the Eurasian continental mass in Tibet. The main topographical results of subduction are dramatic: highly folded mountains, chains of large volcanoes on land, and arcs of volcanic islands in the ocean. Thus the Andes and Cascade Range in the Americas, and Japan, Indonesia and the Aleutian Islands all have the

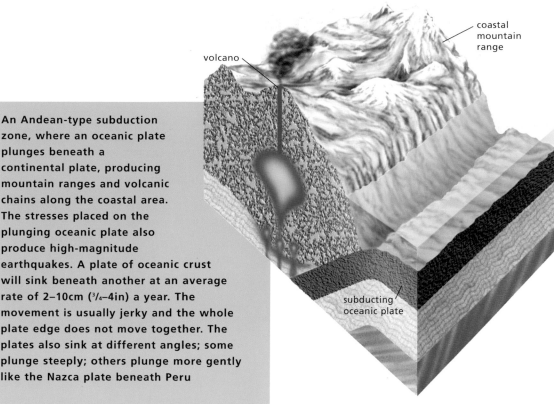

volcano

coastal
mountain
range

subducting
oceanic plate

An Andean-type subduction
zone, where an oceanic plate
plunges beneath a
continental plate, producing
mountain ranges and volcanic
chains along the coastal area.
The stresses placed on the
plunging oceanic plate also
produce high-magnitude
earthquakes. A plate of oceanic crust
will sink beneath another at an average
rate of 2–10cm (³/₄–4in) a year. The
movement is usually jerky and the whole
plate edge does not move together. The
plates also sink at different angles; some
plunge steeply; others plunge more gently
like the Nazca plate beneath Peru

same fundamental cause. These narrow bands contain some of the most active and unstable ground on Earth.

Subduction

A plate of oceanic crust sinks beneath another plate at an average rate of 2–10cm (³/₄–4in) a year. The movement is usually jerky and the whole plate edge does not move together. The plates also sink at different angles; some plunge steeply like the Marianas subduction zone, others plunge more gently like the Nazca plate beneath Peru.

Subduction starts at the ocean trenches which range from 5,000–11,000m (16,400–36,100ft) deep. The subducted plate forms one wall of the trench, the outer edge of the overriding plate forms the opposite wall. As the plate is subducted, the edge of the overriding plate scrapes the sediments from it and they are added, folded and smashed, into the overriding plate. Such movements mean that these areas are prone to severe earthquakes. The stresses and strains on the plunging oceanic plate are even

greater: energy accumulates until the plate jerks downward again and generates a high magnitude earthquake.

The Benioff Zone

Most of these earthquakes are shallow and occur in the first 20–30km (12½–18½ miles) of the plunging plate. However, research carried out by the American scientist H. Benioff had shown that intermediate and deep focus earthquakes also occurred quite frequently. These sometimes reached a depth of 700km (435 miles) but no more. Benioff had also discovered that these earthquakes were not arranged vertically below the trench, but sloped down at an angle under the overriding plate. The deepest earthquakes were furthest from the trench. In fact Benioff made his discovery before subduction became a recognized feature of global dynamics. Indeed the distribution of these earthquakes played a major role in first formulating ideas about plate subduction. For this reason the plunging band of earthquakes on the subducting plate is called the Benioff Zone.

THE FORMATION OF VOLCANOES IN SUBDUCTION ZONES

When it sinks, the subducing plate which has a coating of wet sediments, disturbs the hot asthenosphere of the mantle. At a depth of about 80km (50 miles), the once-solid plate starts to melt, and this releases water from the hydrous minerals within the oceanic plate. The water rises into the asthenosphere in the wedge between the sinking and the overriding plate. The addition of water is one of the main factors

volcano

subducting
oceanic plate

Volcanic island arcs are generated were two oceanic plates converge. This type of subduction has produced the Aleutian Islands off the coast of Alaska

that cause some of the minerals to melt from the asthenosphere. As the plate sinks further it is subject to greater pressures. Other minerals melt from it, and join the asthenosphere, and also produce more water. Other changes take place until the subducted plate melts completely and becomes assimilated into the asthenosphere at a depth of about 700km (435 miles). It is for this reason that there are no earthquakes on the

Benioff Zone at a depth greater than 700km (435 miles).

The freshly melted minerals derived from the asthenosphere, and probably also from the subducting plate, are less dense than the surrounding asthenosphere. The melt is therefore more buoyant and slowly begins to rise, but before it reaches the surface, it undergoes many changes and may spend centuries underground. The melted minerals in the asthenosphere are often called primary magma, which, at first, is very similar to the primary basalts that rise up in the mid-ocean ridges (see pp.16–17). But in subduction zones, the thickness of the overriding crustal plate blocks easy access to the landsurface, and the molten rocks therefore rise much more slowly. The magma is also often trapped either just under or within the overriding plate where it collects in a magma reservoir. These reservoirs are often 25–50km (15½–31 miles) deep and could hold up to 20km³ (4¾ cubic miles) of magma. Smaller reservoirs sometimes even form above them, closer to the surface.

The temperature of the primary magma entering the reservoir is probably approaching 1400°C. It soon starts to cool and some of the minerals begin to crystallize out. Those with the highest melting (or solidification) points are the first to do so. These also happen to be denser than the primary magma and settle towards the bottom of the reservoir. The proportion of silica-rich minerals increases in the upper part of the reservoir because they have lower melting points. The upper parts of the reservoir also retain their gases and water. This partial crystallization means that distinct layers develop in the reservoir: the dense basic magma containing few gases lies at the bottom, with silicious magma containing more gas and water occupying the top. The lower layers are more fluid, whereas the upper layers are viscous. The hot magma may also melt some of the cool plate forming the walls of the reservoir. If the plate contains continental rocks, they are usually broadly granitic (and therefore silicic) in character. Thus when the walls melt they contaminate the magma and can increase further the silicic content of the reservoir's upper layers.

ash cloud
column of gas and finer fragments
explosion
strato volcano
Benioff Zone
subduction of plate
crustal melting
magma reservoir
new magma injection
partial melting
water release

The formation of subduction volcanoes. Magma produced as the subducting plate descends rises up through the mantle towards the surface where it may become trapped in a magma reservoir before erupting on the surface

The final important change is the dilation or expansion of the magma, which may be enough to set the magma on its journey to the surface. Many experts, however, now believe that the eruption process is precipitated when a further batch of primary magma is injected into the reservoir from below. This appears to be true of the eruptions of Pinatubo in the Philippines in

1991 and Mount St Helens in 1980. The injection of new magma causes the old magma to force its way out of the reservoir, usually in a narrow chimney or vent that pierces the crust. As the magma rises up the vent the pressures upon it from the surrounding rock are reduced, but the rising magma itself builds up considerable pressure, expanding fractures, pushes rock aside and generating thousands of shallow, low magnitude earthquakes.

The next critical point is about 2km (1¼ miles) below the surface, a point that occurs just below small volcanoes, but that is well within the body of their larger counterparts. At this depth the confining pressures are now so low that gas and water bubbles start to separate out from the magma and begin to rise, and these in turn push the magma upwards. Its uppermost layers become a frothy foaming liquid which quickly approaches the top of the vent. Suddenly the water and gas bubbles overcome the viscosity of the magma, the bubbles explode, and the volcano erupts. The magma is smashed into fine dust, ash or pumice that can tower 30km (18½ miles) into the air and can plunge a 200km (124 mile) area into total darkness. The upper, silicic layers of magma evacuate the reservoir, and the denser, more basic layers may follow them in more docile lava flows. About 500 volcanoes have erupted from subduction zones within the past 10,000 years.

There are of course, many complications to this scenario, but the basic outline of subduction zones is remarkably simple. They are made up of parallel bands comprising an ocean trench, a plunging plate with shallow, intermediate and deep earthquakes, and a volcanic chain or island arc, rising parallel to the trench and 150–200km (93–124 miles) away.

when continents collide

India, Africa, Australia and Antarctica were joined together in the southern continental mass of Gondwanaland about 225 million years ago. When Gondwanaland began to disintegrate, India began its northward journey, travelling at a rate of 5–10cm (2–4in) per year. The Indian continental mass first crashed into the Tibetan edge of southern Asia about 50 million years ago. But the plate has continued to move north, crumpling the sediments scraped from the sea-floor into enormous folds, thrusting the edge of the Indian continent under the shattered and sliced southern edges of Asia. A few million years later the result was the Himalayas.

The Asian collision zone

The Himalayan range of mountains is 8,000m (26,250ft) high, 300km (186 miles) wide and 4,000km (2,490 miles) long, and stretches from Afghanistan in the east to Myanmar (Burma) in the west. Sections of India became rammed under Tibet, practically doubling the normal thickness of continental crust, and making Tibet, at over 3,000m (9,840 ft), the highest and largest plateau in the world. The collision has compressed the continental crust by about 2,000km (1,243 miles). In response to this assault the Asian continent simply cracked under the strain. Great blocks of Mongolia, China and south-east Asia were forced to slip sideways, chiefly towards the South China Sea. Tibet, for instance, is being pushed south-eastwards at a rate of about 2–3cm (1in) per year. Huge blocks of Asia are sliding past each other along cracks, or major faults, such as the 2,000km (1,243 mile) long Altyn Tagh fault in north Tibet, and the Red River fault in Vietnam. Vietnam has slipped at least 600km (373 miles) south-east on this fault at a rate of between 3cm and 5cm (1¼–2in) a year. But in fact there are many thousands of such faults, most of which seem to

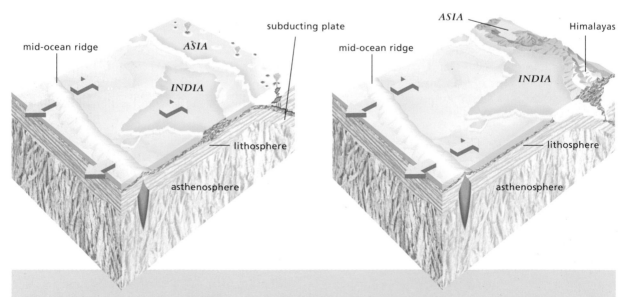

When the Indian sub-continent first broke free from Gondwanaland it travelled northwards at 5–10cm (2–4in) per year. About 50 million years ago it collided with southern Asia forming the Himalayas. This movement continues today as the Indo-Australian plate pushes northwards at a rate of about 5cm (2in) a year

slip sideways, but many also move up and down.

One of the chief results of this tremendous collision has been violent and frequent earthquakes. The cracks, or faults, might stay locked together for centuries, but eventually the pressures exerted on them cause them to give way. One slight movement is enough to shake the ground for a minute or two over 500km (311 miles) or more. In a highly-populated area like China, this could cause the deaths of 100,000 people. The pressure thrusting India under the Himalayas also generates powerful earthquakes there. Fortunately, most happen in sparsely-populated areas and only a few, such as those at Quetta in 1935 and Assam in 1896, have caused large numbers of deaths.

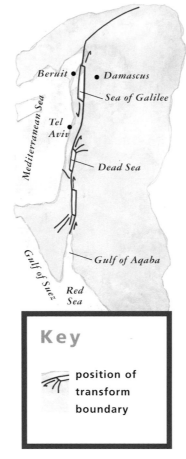

Key

position of transform boundary

The Middle East collision zone

A few million years after India began its contest with Asia, the Red Sea and the Gulf of Aden opened up. A small plate carrying Arabia, gradually drifted away from Egypt and Somalia, areas that stayed with the rest of the African plate. The Arabian continental mass has acted much like India, but on a smaller scale, crumpling mountain ranges in Iran, the Caucasus, and Turkey.

As it advanced northwards, it slid past Palestine, Israel and western Syria, along a great lateral fault-crack marked by the River Jordan valley. Arabia has also pushed Turkey westwards towards Greece, along one of its main cracks, the North Anatolian fault. In this area too, frequent, violent, and lethal earthquakes are caused by thrusting, crumpling, or sliding, and have caused extensive damage in Iran, north-eastern Turkey, and Armenia at different times over the past few decades.

The Himalayas began to form when the Indian plate collided with, and dipped underneath, the Asian plate. The resulting thickness of the continental crust accounts for the great height of the mountains

The Mediterranean collision zone

The predominant legacy of the collision zones described above has been earthquakes. Volcanic eruptions do occur, notably Hassan Dag in central Turkey, but they usually play a subordinate role. Volcanoes are much more important, however, in the Mediterranean collision zone.

When the African plate split from Gondwanaland, it began travelling northwards more slowly than the Indian-Australian plate. Nevertheless, it soon also began to crush the floor of the ocean between old Gondwanaland to the south and old Laurasia to the north. The part of this ocean lying between Europe and Africa may be regarded as an early prototype of the Mediterranean Sea. Eventually the northward push of Arabia against Asia blocked off the eastern exit of this ocean. About 70 million years ago, the African Plate began crushing its oceanic crust up against the Eurasian Plate. The story is made complicated because both plates were broken into smaller microplates, one of which lies under the Aegean Sea, another under Apulia and the Adriatic Sea east of Italy, and a third in northern Morocco. In addition, Africa and Europe did not always close up together in the same direction. The final major complication is that the Bay of Biscay swung open, detached Spain from Brittany and turned it south-eastwards between Africa and Europe. In addition, Turkey is being squeezed westwards towards Greece as Arabia is pushed northwards.

In the past 70 million years these movements have produced an extremely complicated pattern of crumpled, folded mountains and intermittent subduction zones. This provides some explanation for the way that the mountain ranges around the Mediterranean curve across the map. The Pyrenees run west-east. The Sierra Nevada in Spain curves around the edges of a microplate almost to join the Atlas Mountains in North Africa. They, in turn, are relayed by the Pelitorani Mountains of northern Sicily into Calabria and follow the edge of the Adriatic microplate up the Apennines. They join the Alps curving around the Adriatic plate and then turn eastwards into the Carpathians and also bend southwards into a mass of smaller ranges in the Balkans extending into Greece. Then the mountains broaden into their wider bands; as they cross Turkey, one follows the south coast, the other the north coast. And off they continue into Iran to join the Himalayas.

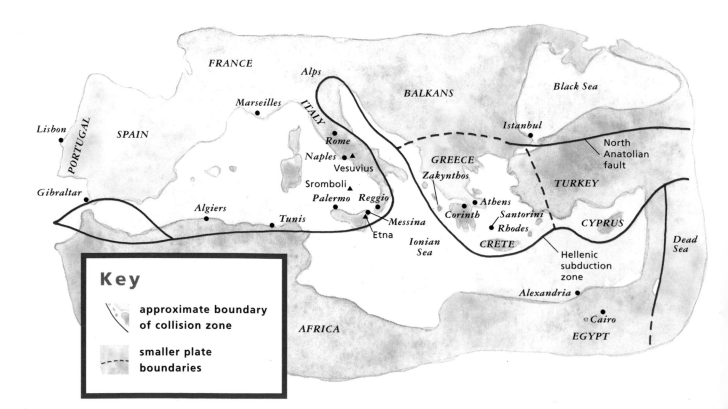

Key

approximate boundary of collision zone

smaller plate boundaries

Lava-flows on Etna, one of many volcanoes that have grown up within the complex pattern of plate boundaries in the Mediterranean

In all this area, there is only one subduction zone approaching the clarity of those in the Pacific Ocean. This is the Hellenic Arc, where the African Plate plunges beneath the Aegean Plate, and the last chains of the Balkan Mountains. It causes the main active volcanoes of the Aegean Sea: Santorini, Nisyros, Milos and Kos in particular. In Italy, the Aeolian Islands, north of Sicily, are probably also related to subduction of the African plate east of Sicily. Vesuvius and the volcanoes around Naples may be a result of subduction where the African plate and the Adriatic microplate plunge below Europe. Etna, however, appears to rise on deep secondary cracks in the crust caused by the impact of the two major plates. Other volcanoes have arisen along cracks within the Atlas Mountains of Morocco, whereas active volcanoes only occur in Catalonia in the Iberian Peninsula. The very irregularity of the volcanic pattern is a symptom of the almost chaotic history of this region. A few examples pin-point their extraordinary story. Southern Sicily belongs to the African plate, as does the top of the Matterhorn in the Alps. Its base, however, belongs to the European plate. The collision has also forced rocks up from the upper mantle, so that they now form the Troodos Mountains in Cyprus. The rocks of most of the mountain ranges around the Mediterranean Sea are crumpled, folded and thrust over each other in great slices, but the crust is also stretching in parts of the Apennines, in the Aegean Sea and in the Vienna Basin. The Gulf of Corinth is widening and Sicily is moving further from Calabria.

All these complicated contortions produce one simple result: the area around the Mediterranean is riddled with earthquakes that are small manifestations of these movements. But, even here, their distribution is not entirely straightforward. Peninsular Greece has by far the most earthquakes every year. On the other hand, southern Italy, especially Calabria and Eastern Sicily, has perhaps the highest incidence of severe earthquakes in the world for such a small area. The Balkans and north Africa experience severe earthquakes quite often, but there have relatively few in the Alps in recorded history, and the Iberian Peninsula has had even fewer.

plate sliding and rifting

THE PLATES THAT COMPRISE THE EARTH'S SURFACE ARE NOT ALWAYS IN DIRECT CONFRONTATION, THEY MAY ALSO SLIDE PAST EACH OTHER, OR RIFT AND SPLIT APART. THESE ARE NOT BENIGN PROCESSES, HOWEVER, AS THE PEOPLE OF LOS ANGELES AND SAN FRANCISCO IN THE UNITED STATES, AND THE GREAT RIFT VALLEY IN EAST AFRICA CAN TESTIFY.

Plate sliding

In some cases certain plates meet each other at an oblique angle thus avoiding subduction or collision altogether, such as San Andreas Fault system in southern California (see right), and the River Jordan-Dead Sea Fault system in the Middle East (see p.27). In such conditions there is little chance for volcanic eruptions to develop. But the plates do not glide past each other as if they had been well-oiled. As on all other fault-cracks, the dislocation is jerky. Each horizontal slip can cause earthquakes just as powerful as their counterparts in subduction zones.

Plate splitting

The Atlantic Ocean developed when the North and South American plates split from Eurasia and Africa respectively. Plates probably start to split when conditions in the mantle change. For example, an alteration in the convection currents could start stretching a new zone of oceanic or continental crust in a new zone.

As the crust stretches, it gets thinner and eventually cracks under the strain into a long furrow. Both edges of the furrow also crack and form blocks of crust that drop down like steps towards the central trough. These cracks are faults, which cut through the whole crust. Thus, when the crust is pulled apart and becomes thinner, the result is downward vertical displacements in a long band. Because of the depth of the faults, molten rock can sometimes rise and form volcanoes at the surface. Each displacement on the faults also causes an earthquake. This process is called rifting and is how the Atlantic Ocean first started to open up. As the Atlantic Ocean rifted open, volcanic rocks spewed out, and their remains form the lavas of Skye and Mull and other Hebridean Islands. In the Great Rift Valley system of East Africa massive eruptions have formed great volcanic piles.

In north-eastern Africa, the extension and rifting has been even greater: the Arabian plate has already split off. On land, great piles of volcanic rocks have erupted in the Afar Triangle near Djibouti. The Red Sea and the Gulf of Aden have opened up as rifting has allowed erup-tions to create new oceanic crust. In the future, the eastern fringe of the African plate (Somalia, Tanzania and Kenya) could also split off.

California

Hayward fault
Calaveras fault
San Francisco
San Andreas fault
Garlock fault

Los Angeles

Once a mid-ocean ridge develops and the ocean crust begins to spread outwards from it, the separation of the two diverging plates is complete. The Atlantic Ocean has long been in this position. The faulted step-like blocks that bordered its original trough are a long way apart. Thick sediments eroded from both the American and European continents now bury most of them along the Atlantic fringe. But these old faults are not wholly dead. They can still quake: on 31 August 1886, an earthquake damaged Charleston, South Carolina, when one of these ancient buried blocks slipped again. The edges of the 300 million year-old rift forming the Midland Valley in Scotland still also produce a flurry of tremors every year.

A view to the west showing Asia in the foreground and Africa in the background as photographed by the crew of the Space

Shuttle Columbia. The Red Sea is widening, as rifting produces new oceanic crust, pushing Saudi Arabia further from Africa

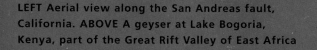

LEFT Aerial view along the San Andreas fault, California. ABOVE A geyser at Lake Bogoria, Kenya, part of the Great Rift Valley of East Africa

chapter 2

EARTHQUAKES

earthquakes in history

A MAJOR EARTHQUAKE IS ONE OF THE MOST SUDDEN, UNPREDICTABLE AND TERRIFYING EVENTS ON EARTH, SHATTERING OUR ASSUMPTION THAT WE LIVE ON 'SOLID GROUND'. EARTHQUAKES ARE LETHAL BECAUSE THEY HAPPEN WITHOUT WARNING, AND WHILE LONG-TERM FORECASTS CAN BE MADE, ACCURATE SHORT-TERM PREDICTION IS EXTREMELY DIFFICULT. THUS EARTHQUAKES HAVE CLAIMED OVER 1.5 MILLION VICTIMS SINCE 1900 – INCLUDING AN ESTIMATED 600,000–850,000 IN TANGSHAN, CHINA, IN 1976. A FURTHER 3,000,000 PEOPLE WERE KILLED AS A RESULT OF EARTHQUAKES BETWEEN 1600 AND 1900.

It is little wonder that such catastrophes have been recorded for centuries. Archives in China date back to 2300 BC while Japanese records start from AD 416. In contrast, North American reports only began in the early 19th Century. Thus on the world scale, records are incomplete and sporadic, and have often become distorted by exaggeration. The most active area in Europe, the area around the Mediterranean Sea, has preserved the longest records, going back – albeit incompletely – for 2,500 years.

Greece experiences the most earthquakes in Europe. On average, a small earthquake happens there once every three days, but not many are as devastating as the one that hit Argostoli in the Ionian Islands in 1953. In Ancient Greece the cities of Corinth and Sparta, for instance, were destroyed, and rebuilt several times. The people associated the torments of earthquakes with their god Poseidon, the 'Earth-shaker'. However, Ancient Greece also provides a rare example of some benefit resulting from earthquakes. When an earthquake occurred during their frequent inter-city wars, the armies declared a truce, and returned home until the following summer!

In Italy, earthquakes tend to be less frequent, but are sometimes stronger and usually more devastating than in Greece. The toe of Italy, Calabria, and eastern Sicily (see above), have had some of the most savage earthquakes recorded in Europe – notably in 1783 and 1908. These big earthquakes seem to happen once every 90–125 years, but in between, other earthquakes have also cost hundreds of lives. The last major earthquake in the area devastated Messina in Sicily and Reggio in Calabria on 28 December 1908 – the Feast of the Massacre of the Innocents – when about 160,000 people died, and many towns were left in ruins.

The Romans suffered earthquakes too. On 5 February AD 62 an earthquake severely damaged Pompeii; repairs were not complete by the time Vesuvius erupted in AD 79. In Naples, an earthquake rocked the theatre where the Emperor Nero was making his stage debut as a musician, thereby bringing his performance to an abrupt end. Typically, Nero was upset by the Gods' apparent slight to his talents.

The Greek god of the sea Poseidon, the 'Earth-shaker', was believed to control earthquakes. He was also depicted as a charging bull because of the power he was able to unleash

the earthquake at Lisbon

1 November 1755

SPAIN AND PORTUGAL ARE AMONG THE MOST SEISMICALLY STABLE COUNTRIES IN SOUTHERN EUROPE, BUT THE EARTHQUAKE THAT DESTROYED LISBON IN 1755 WAS PROBABLY THE MOST POWERFUL RECORDED IN THE LAST 2,000 YEARS. AT 10.00 ON 1 NOVEMBER, ALL SAINTS' DAY, THE GROUND SHOOK VIOLENTLY FOR SEVEN TERRIFYING MINUTES. ALL OF PORTUGAL, MOST OF SPAIN AND MUCH OF MOROCCO VIBRATED. FURTHER AFIELD, CHANDELIERS IN THE CASTLES AND CHATEAUX OF WESTERN EUROPE STARTED TO SWING, CHURCH BELLS BEGAN TO PEAL, WAVES APPEARED ON THE SURFACE OF LOCH NESS IN SCOTLAND, AND BOATS WERE RIPPED FROM THEIR MOORINGS IN THE CANALS OF AMSTERDAM.

Although well-documented, it is quite difficult to piece together exactly what happened, as reports range from the exaggerated to the understated. Probably well over 100,000 people were killed. Even King José Manuel and his family had a narrow escape, leaving their palace in Belem, outside Lisbon, just before it collapsed.

A British surgeon in Lisbon, Richard Wolsall, described his experiences in a letter to the Royal Society of London. In his detailed account, he wrote that the first shock seemed to last:

'about the tenth part of a minute, and then came down every church and convent in town, together with the King's palace and the magnificent opera-house ... there was not a large building in town that escaped ... The shocking sight of the dead bodies, together with the shrieks of those who were half-buried in the ruins ... far exceeds all description ... the most resolute person durst not stay a moment to remove a few stones off the friend he loved most, though many might have been saved by so doing: but nothing was thought of but self-preservation; getting into open places, and into the middle of streets, was the most probable security'.

Then, about noon, fires broke out, 'occasioned from the goods and the kitchen fires being all jumbled together.' There must have been an immense 'fire-storm.' Mr Wolsall reported that a gale

An artist's impression of the view of Lisbon from the sea as seen before the earthquake of 1755

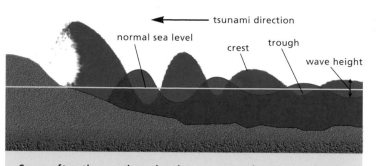

tsunami direction ←

normal sea level

crest trough

wave height

Soon after the earthquake the sea surged up into a huge
12m (39½ft) tsunami that flooded lower Lisbon

suddenly blew up on what had previously been a perfectly calm day, and 'made the fire rage with such fury, that, at the end of three days, all the city was reduced to cinders'. Thus many of those who had survived the falling masonry were burnt to death a few hours later. In spite of this terrible loss of life the cremation of the dead bodies was a source of some relief to the surgeon because, at least, it stopped the spread of disease.

The earthquake also produced a huge wave or tsunami. 'Every element seemed to conspire to our destruction.' Soon after the devastating shock, the sea surged up 12m (39½ft) and flooded lower Lisbon. Thousands of people who had assembled for safety on the vast quays alongside the River Tagus were drowned and sucked out into the Atlantic Ocean when the wave subsided. The victims included the

Spanish Ambassador and 35 of his servants. Less than an hour later, the tsunami crashed over the walls of the Spanish port of Cádiz and swept on to Gibraltar, the Moroccan coast, and Madeira.

By the evening of All Saints' Day, Lisbon was a heap of burning rubble. Three-quarters of the buildings were damaged beyond repair. In the centre of the city, it was impossible to make out the old pattern of the streets. Many people fled the city, but for those that remained, there were additional hazards: food was scarce, there were powerful aftershocks, and the bewildered inhabitants were easy prey for thieves.

The terrible news sent shock-waves throughout Europe's intellectual community, that had longer-lasting effects than those generated by the earthquake. Prompted by these events the French philosopher Voltaire began his most famous book, *Candide*, published in 1759. The work analyzed the idea of divine justice, and questioned the prevailing notion of the time, that Man was living in 'the best of all possible worlds'. Thanks to Voltaire, the Lisbon earthquake changed the intellectual climate, helping to pave the way for a new revolutionary age.

Following the Lisbon earthquake, three-quarters of the city's buildings were thrown to the ground, or destroyed by fire

earthquake features

AN EARTHQUAKE IS A SUDDEN AND VIOLENT MOVEMENT OF THE EARTH'S SURFACE CAUSED BY THE SLOW MOVEMENTS OF THE CRUSTAL PLATES EXERTING A VARIETY OF FORCES ON THE ROCKS ABOVE.

The rocks themselves are elastic and can store mechanical energy in the same way as a compressed spring. When the stresses and strains are exerted slowly, over long periods of time, the rocks bend and crumple to accommodate them, forming enormous, complicated folds. These folds form the basic features of the rocks in the world's younger mountain ranges such as the Alps and the Himalayas, and the remnants of older ranges such as the Appalachians.

FAULTS

When forces are applied more strongly, or if they finally exceed the strength of the weakest part of the solid rock, then the rock gives way and cracks. The strain energy is relieved and the forces are accommodated by a sudden dislocation of the rocks on either side of the crack. This is

called 'elastic rebound'. The movement may be over in a few seconds at its source, but the vast amount of energy released travels through the rocks of the crust in earthquake (seismic) waves, that travel outwards for a distance of up to 1,000km (621 miles), and can be registered on sensitive earthquake-measuring equipment (seismographs), all over the world. The crack marking the dislocation is called a fault. Following an earthquake the rocks on either side of the fault come to rest in new positions. The degree of displacement varies but occasionally can be visible on the land surface as a fault scarp.

The rock masses on either side of the fault soon become locked together in new positions due to forces exerted upon them from the crust: friction is perhaps the most important of these. The stresses and strains that caused the original dislocation continue, and eventually break the 'frictional lock', causing another earthquake.

Faults rarely exist in isolation, but tend to cluster in parallel sheaves. Within this arrangement one fault may be dislocated while the others stay locked. In addition displacements do not necessarily occur along the whole length

> When rocks crack in response to the strain along a fault, energy is released producing a dislocation. This is called 'elastic rebound'

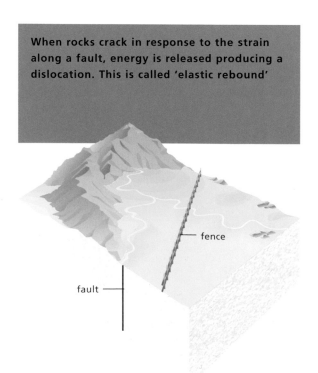

fence

fault

Original position of rocks

Build-up of strain

of a given fault. Most faults are apparently divided into segments; one or more segments may jolt, whilst others remain still. Eventually, it seems, those segments that have been locked for a long time will move and 'catch up' with their neighbours. The San Andreas fault system in California provides probably the most famous example of different movements along different

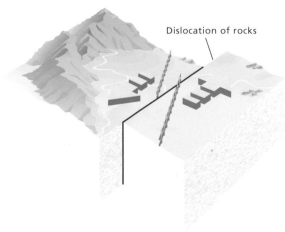

Dislocation produced by the Californian earthquake at San Fernando in 1971 is visible in this picture

segments. The southern segment of the fault has not dislocated since 1857, whereas one of the central segments (see right) moves every 20 or 30 years. Such varied displacements are valuable because they can provide a basis for the difficult task of predicting earthquakes. Segments along active faults that have not generated earthquakes for an abnormal length of time in relation to the fault as a whole, often attract particular attention, and are known as 'seismic gaps'.

Dislocation of rocks

Strain released

Allan Lindh

Geologist with the United States Geological Survey, Allan Lindh is one member of the team responsible for establishing the Parkfield Experiment (see also pp.168–169). In their centre at Menlo Park, just outside San Francisco, California, they are aiming to solve the mystery of earthquake prediction by constantly analyzing seismic activity, deformation of the earth's surface, water levels and magnetic fields.

'Parkfield is unique in a lot of ways ... the reason we are here is that in the past it has produced magnitude 6 earthquakes ... every 20–30 years.'

He explains seismic gap theory as follows:

'As people noticed around the world that there were other places where earthquakes seemed to be regular they developed something called seismic gap theory. The idea is since the plates are moving all the time at a steady rate and since that is what causes the earthquakes, you look at one place, look at how fast the plates are moving, look when the earthquake last occurred, and see, given how fast the plates are moving, how soon it can happen again.'

Parkfield lies between two major sections of the San Andreas fault. The northern part is constantly slipping and does not produce large earthquakes. The southern part, however, produces powerful earthquakes. The 'transitional' area around Parkfield experiences relatively regular magnitude 6 earthquakes, although at the time of writing, it has been just over 30 years since the last one. Allan is fairly confident that the next one will come within the next five years.

types of fault

THERE ARE THREE BROAD GROUPS OF FAULTS THAT ARE ALL BASICALLY RELATED TO THE CRUSTAL MOVEMENTS WHICH PREDOMINATED DURING THEIR FORMATION. NORMAL FAULTS ARE CAUSED WHEN THE CRUST IS STRETCHED; REVERSE FAULTS ARE CAUSED WHEN IT IS COMPRESSED; WRENCH FAULTS FORM BETWEEN BLOCKS THAT SLIDE HORIZONTALLY PAST EACH OTHER. MOVEMENTS ALONG ALL THREE TYPES OF FAULTS ARE LIKELY TO PRODUCE SEVERE EARTHQUAKES.

Faults cut through the solid rocks of the crust at different angles known as the dip of the fault-plane. Successive movements along the fault-plane can polish the rocks in such a way that they will glisten if erosion exposes them on the Earth's surface. At other times, the friction caused by the dislocation crushes and shatters the rocks along the fault-plane, so that they form lines of weakness called shear-zones, that might be exploited by surface streams and carved into valleys.

Normal faults

When the crust is stretched, the rocks are gradually pulled apart until they fracture and form a 'normal fault'. Here a rock mass moves relatively downwards, down the dip of the fault-plane. The surface area of the land is slightly increased as a result. The Wasatch Front near Salt Lake City in Utah is an example of a normal fault.

Reverse faults

When the crust is compressed as two rock masses are forced together, then a 'reverse fault' can develop. Here a rock mass moves up the dip of the fault-plane. In this case the area of the land surface is slightly reduced. The El Asnam fault in Algeria is an example of this type of fault. When the angle of such a fault-plane is very low, the resulting feature is often called a

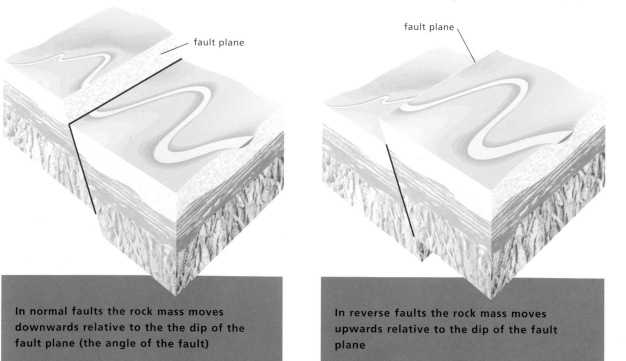

fault plane

fault plane

In normal faults the rock mass moves downwards relative to the the dip of the fault plane (the angle of the fault)

In reverse faults the rock mass moves upwards relative to the dip of the fault plane

'thrust fault', where one block has been thrust over another. These reverse and thrust faults are typical of mountain ranges which are, of course, predominantly zones of collision and compression.

Horizontal faults

When the crust is subjected to horizontal or lateral forces the faults dislocate the rock masses sideways. Faults produced in this way have been given many names, including 'wrench faults' and 'lateral faults'. These are no less destructive than other types of faults, and they have caused a great deal of damage in California, China and Turkey within the last 25 years. The effects of the lateral wrenching can be seen in displaced fences, culverts or even streams, for instance, along the San Andreas Fault in California. These horizontal displacements are described as 'dextral', or right-lateral, when they move to the right in relation to the observer, and 'sinistral', or left-lateral, when they move to the left. For example, when an observer faces the San Andreas Fault, the land beyond the fault-line appears to have moved to the right. Thus it is a dextral wrench fault. There is no stretching or compression directly associated with wrench faults although they may contain certain segments that move up or down.

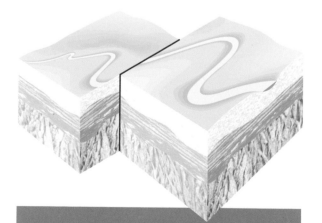

In horizontal faults forces dislocate the rock masses sideways (also known as wrench or lateral faults)

This aerial view north-west along the San Andreas fault shows scarps formed by displacements along the fault. An uplifted block on the right gives way to a similarly uplifted block on the left in the distance

earthquake waves

THE SOURCE OF EARTHQUAKE WAVES IS KNOWN AS THE FOCUS AND REPRESENTS THE EXACT POINT WITHIN THE EARTH'S CRUST WHERE DISLOCATION BEGINS. THE FOCUS OF MOST EARTHQUAKES IS LESS THAN 30KM (18½ MILES) DEEP. ON THE SURFACE, DIRECTLY ABOVE THE FOCUS, IS THE EPICENTRE OF THE EARTHQUAKE. THIS IS WHERE THE GREATEST DAMAGE USUALLY OCCURS.

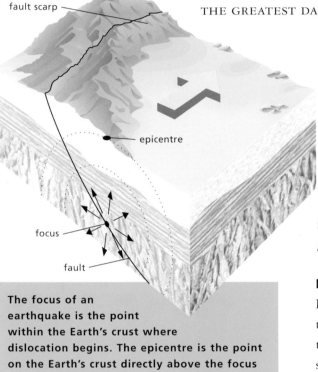

fault scarp

epicentre

focus

fault

The focus of an earthquake is the point within the Earth's crust where dislocation begins. The epicentre is the point on the Earth's crust directly above the focus

Waves produced by the earthquake spread through the Earth. Initially, they cause powerful vibrations but they grow weaker as they spread out from the focus. There are two groups of earthquake waves, body waves and surface waves, each travelling at different speeds and causing different types of vibration. In general terms, body waves travel faster than surface waves, but surface waves cause greater damage.

Body waves

Body waves are so-called because they travel through the body of the Earth. There are two types of body waves: primary waves and secondary waves.

Primary, or 'P-waves', can pass through both solids and liquids, including water and molten rocks, in the Earth's interior. They travel fastest of all, and give the first indication on earthquake-registering seismographs, as well as in the streets, that an earthquake is imminent. They are longitudinal, or compressional waves, and cause the rocks to vibrate forwards and backwards in the direction of the wave movement. As the P-wave passes, the rock particles are squeezed together. Then, once the wave has passed through, the rock particles return more or less to their original state. P-waves travel at about 6km (3¾ miles) per second through continental crust, and at about 8km (5 miles) per second through oceanic crust. Sometimes P-waves can be transmitted into the atmosphere as booming sound waves.

Secondary, or 'S-waves' only travel at about half the speed of P-waves – 3.6km (2¼ miles) per second through continental crust and about 4.7km (3 miles) per second through oceanic crust. Secondary waves cannot pass through

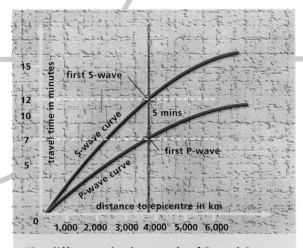

first S-wave

travel time in minutes

15

12

10

7

5

0

S-wave curve

P-wave curve

5 mins

first P-wave

distance to epicentre in km

1,000 2,000 3,000 4,000 5,000 6,000

The difference in the speeds of P- and S-waves can be used to plot the distance of seismic stations from earthquake epicentres

fluids, such as water, or the liquid outer core of the Earth. They are shear, or transverse waves: as they pass through the rock, they disturb the particles by moving them both side-to-side and up-and-down, at right angles to the direction in which they are travelling.

Surface waves

The second group of waves are known as surface waves. These travel around the Earth just underneath the surface. Within this group there are two different types, Love waves and Rayleigh waves, named after the scientists who first described them.

Surface waves arrive shortly after the body waves. They can cause extensive damage in built-up areas, in part because they take longer to pass through a given spot. They are, of course, restricted to the crust close to the Earth's surface. Love waves travel faster than Rayleigh waves. Love waves push the rocks horizontally sideways at right angles to the direction in which they are travelling. They shear buildings rather like secondary body waves, but unlike S-waves, Love waves cause no vertical motion. Rayleigh waves are the slowest moving earthquake waves. Rather like water travelling in an ocean wave, Rayleigh waves push the rock particles upwards and backwards as they advance. The particles move in a vertical plane following an elliptical path as the wave passes by.

In practice there are some complications to these intricate patterns. Waves can be bent, or refracted when they pass from one rock type to

Surface waves: longitudinal Rayleigh waves produce ripples like sea-waves. Transverse Love waves cause a shearing motion which causes much of the surface damage

another, or from one shell of the globe to another. Also, when body waves reach the Earth's surface much of their energy is reflected back down into the ground. This can vastly increase the amount of vibration that takes place near the landsurface. Thus, miners working deep in the solid rock beneath Tangshan in July 1976 survived whilst violent shaking destroyed much of the city above them.

The type of underlying rock is an important factor in the amount of damage caused by an earthquake. Good, solid granite and massive layers of sandstone, for instance, vibrate much less than silty, sandy alluvium that occurs alongside rivers and in coastal areas. Thus, in 1908, the beautiful waterfront built on alluvium at Messina in Sicily was wrecked, whilst buildings on the solid rock west of the city survived. A similar pattern was revealed at San Francisco in 1906, Tokyo in 1923, and at Kobe in 1995.

measuring earthquakes

THERE ARE TWO DIFFERENT WAYS OF MEASURING AN EARTHQUAKE. THE FIRST IS A CALCULATION OF ITS MAGNITUDE OR STRENGTH. THE SECOND IS A JUDGEMENT OF INTENSITY MADE BY EVALUATION OF REPORTS OF THE EXTENT OF SURFACE DAMAGE.

Seismographs

The great earthquake that devastated Lisbon in 1755 (see pp.36–37) caused chandeliers to swing in many of the great houses of western Europe. This effect, produced when a free mass (in this case the chandelier) remains at rest, while a fixed object (the house) moves in response to the ground's vibrations, forms the basis of the way in which modern seismographs work. If the movements of the chandelier could have been traced on the floor of the room in which it was situated it could have recorded the vibrations of the earthquake. Modern seismographs record both horizontal and vertical vibrations. These are registered on a paper trace over a drum, calibrated to a clock, which rotates with the passage of time. Thus seismographs register the size, or amplitude, of the vibrations caused by the shock waves, and the time at which they occur.

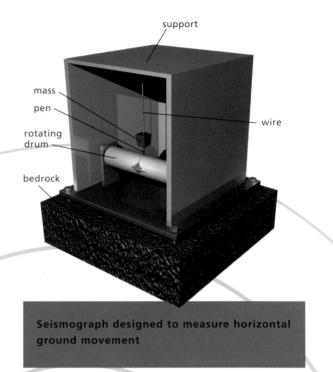

Seismograph designed to measure horizontal ground movement

A seismograph consists of a freely-pivoting horizontal strut, fixed to an upright support, that is firmly anchored to the ground. The horizontal strut has a heavy mass at the far end, to which a pen is attached. The pen traces a continuous line onto the paper, which is wrapped around a rotating drum lying on its side on a horizontal axle, which is also anchored to the ground like the upright support. If no ground movements take place the pen would trace a straight line. When the earthquake shock waves arrive the pen swings up and down. This is because the waves vibrate the vertical support and the drum that are both fixed to the ground. The horizontal strut vibrates much less due to the inertia of the heavy mass at its far end. Thus the paper on the drum shifts backwards and forwards under the pen, tracing the movement on the paper. The rotation of the drum is calibrated to a clock so that these vibrations can be timed accurately. To record all horizontal movements caused by waves

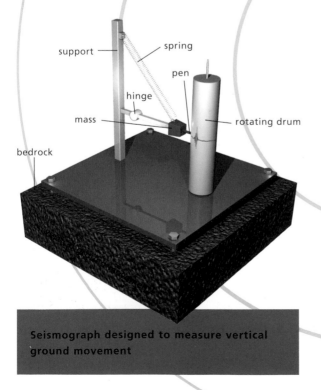

Seismograph designed to measure vertical ground movement

two seismographs are used; one to record waves travelling north or south; the other east or west.

A third seismograph registers vertical movements. In this case, a solid horizontal support is fixed firmly in place and the drum rotates about a vertical axle. The heavy mass and the pen are suspended vertically by a fine spring from the well-anchored horizontal support.

Seismographs throughout the world

The number of seismographs in operation has vastly increased since the World-wide Standardized Seismographic Network, (WWSSN), was first established in 1962. The earthquake waves reach many stations in less than ten minutes. The network transmits the data to central computers and the focus, epicentre and size of the earthquake are known well within the hour. Many more earthquakes are registered than ever make the headlines – about one million earthquakes happen every year – fortunately major earthquakes are rare.

Books were shaken from the shelves of this book shop in Los Gatos, California, during the Loma Prieta earthquake in 1989

earthquake scales

ALTHOUGH THE MAJORITY OF EARTHQUAKES PASS VIRTUALLY UNNOTICED, SEVERAL TIMES A DECADE, VIOLENT EARTHQUAKES DEVASTATE ENTIRE AREAS. THERE IS, HOWEVER, NO SINGLE WAY OF MEASURING THESE LARGE VARIATIONS IN EARTHQUAKES AND THEIR EFFECTS. THE TWO MOST COMMON WAYS OF MEASURING AND ANALYZING EARTHQUAKES ARE IN TERMS OF THEIR MAGNITUDE AND INTENSITY.

The magnitude and intensity scales were devised in an attempt to establish an absolute scale of earthquake values. Both have since been modified to take into account modern technological advances. The magnitude scale is based on calculations of the vigour of earthquakes at their source. The intensity scale describes informed, but subjective, assessments of the varying effects of earthquakes on the landsurface.

Magnitude

The scale of earthquake magnitudes was devised by the American seismologist Charles Richter in 1935. At first, his aim was simply to compare earthquakes in different areas of California, but his method soon spread all over the world. Consequently it is now usually known as the Richter Scale of magnitude. It is based on the size, or amplitude, of the waves traced by the pen on the seismograph, and on the distance between the instrument, and the focus of the earthquake. The seismographs had to be standardized so that waves of equal length traced out lines of equal size on all the instruments. The waves weaken as they spread out from the focus of the earthquake and Richter therefore had to make allowance for the distance between the focus and the instrument. This distance could be calculated by measuring the time interval between the arrivals of the P-waves and S-waves. Adjustments could then also be made to standardize for the effect of distance – as if all the instruments were 100km (62 miles) from the focus.

The magnitude 8.1 earthquake that struck Mexico City in 1985 destroyed hundreds of buildings, and damaged many more

Richter devised a formula using the maximum vibration actually measured on the seismograph standardized for the effect of its distance from the focus. The size and strength of any earthquake could then be calculated in absolute terms as its magnitude. The values were then placed on a logarithmic scale. While it is generally held that earthquake magnitudes of between 1.0 and 10.0 can be measured on the Richter Scale, in fact the scale is open-ended, and a very large earthquake could, in theory, exceed magnitude 10.0. To compare, the Messina earthquake of 1908 measured 7.5, the Anchorage (Alaska) earthquake in 1964 measured 8.4, while the Moroccan earthquake that destroyed the town of Agadir in 1960 reached only 5.8. The Lisbon earthquake of 1755 could have exceeded 9.0.

The Richter Scale is logarithmic, thus a rise of one unit of magnitude represents a ten-fold increase in the measurement of earthquake waves on the seismograph: a magnitude 5.0 earthquake is ten times greater than one of magnitude 4.0. The differences in the energy released are much greater. For each unit of magnitude, the energy released at the focus increases by 30–32 times.

Magnitude tells us little about the effect of earthquakes on human lives, and does not necessarily correlate with intensity (see pp. 48–49), even near the epicentre. The Anchorage earthquake (magnitude 8.4) killed a relatively small number of people (131) in part because the area was sparsely populated. The Agadir earthquake (magnitude 5.8) claimed 12,000–14,000 lives mainly because the focus of the earthquake was particularly shallow – just 2–3km (1¼–1¾ miles) deep – and was situated directly beneath the town.

the Richter scale of magnitude

Magnitude	Qualitative Description	Average number per year	Approx. intensity equivalent near epicentre (Mercalli scale)	
0–1.9	-	700,000	I–V	Recorded but not felt
2–2.9	-	300,000	I–V	Recorded but not felt
3–3.9	Minor	40,000	I–V	Felt by some
4–4.9	Light	6,200	I–V	Felt by many
5–5.9	Moderate	800	VI–VII	Slight damage
6–6.9	Strong	120	VIII	Damaging
7–7.9	Major	18	IX–XI	Destructive
8–8.9	Great	1 every 10–20 years	XII	Widely devastating

Note. Recent advances in earthquake studies have brought modifications to the original scale, and seismologists use more refined methods of comparing earthquakes, although the principles of operation remain much the same.

This bridge, destroyed during the Alaska earthquake of 1964, lay a short distance from the epicentre. The Alaskan earthquake measured 8.4 on the Richter scale

intensity

IN GENERAL, THE MOST SEVERE EFFECTS OF AN EARTHQUAKE OCCUR AT AND AROUND THE EPICENTRE, WITH THE SHOCK WAVES BECOMING WEAKER AS THEY SPREAD OUT FROM THAT POINT. AS NOTED EARLIER (SEE PP.36–37), WHILE THE LISBON EARTHQUAKE OF 1755 DEVASTATED THE CITY, IT WAS FELT AS A MILD SHUDDER ON THE STREETS OF BORDEAUX, AND CAUSED RIPPLES ON THE WATER AT LOCH NESS, SCOTLAND, 1,750KM (1,090 MILES) AWAY. ALL EARTHQUAKES HAVE VARIABLE EFFECTS, AND DIFFERENT TYPES OF UNDERLYING ROCK RESPOND IN DIFFERENT WAYS TO THE SHOCK WAVES PASSING THROUGH THEM. IT IS THESE VARYING EFFECTS THAT THE SCALE OF EARTHQUAKE INTENSITY TRIES TO EVALUATE.

The intensity of an earthquake is assessed by subjective, qualitative observations of its effects on the landscape; unlike the Richter scale it is not based on mathematical calculations. The degree of damage in built-up areas and changes in the natural landscape have been put in a scale ranging from I–XII. The scale then allows the effects of new earthquakes to be quickly placed in the appropriate category. It is also possible to assess the intensity of earthquakes that happened before the development of seismographs.

Intensity has been evaluated ever since the Calabrian earthquakes in Italy in 1783 caused such widespread and variable devastation. The basis of the present scale was devised by the Italian geologist, Mercalli, in 1902 and modified versions are still in use. A modified Mercalli Scale, developed in 1931, is used in the United States; slightly different versions are used in Japan and Europe. In Europe the MSK Intensity Scale is used, named after the scientists who derived it: Medvedev, Sponheuer and Karnik. Their aim was to quantify degrees of damage to structures, and classify the types of building affected, more clearly.

The basis of intensity evaluation is what witnesses saw or felt, as well as reports, and responses to questionnaires in each area affected. The timing and, especially, the site of these descriptions is significant primarily because the intensity of an earthquake can vary within a small area. Nowadays, after an earthquake in the United States, for example, the National Earthquake Information Centre sends out questionnaires to government officials, police officers, fire officers and other volunteers. Thus, the variable pattern of damage and earthquake intensity is built up and mapped, and this serves not merely an historical record, but also to evaluate earthquake risk for the future.

For instance, the pattern of intensity during the San Francisco earthquake of 1906 varied from VI–X, even within the city itself. The most intensely affected areas were built on coastal silts, and those least affected on compact hard rocks. Eighty-three years later, the most serious damage caused by the the Loma Prieta earthquake also occurred around the coast and on recent land-fill sites in the Bay area.

Occasionally the most intense damage can happen a long way from the epicentre. For example, during the Michoacán earthquake in Mexico in 1985, some of the greatest – and certainly the most lethal – damage happened 360km (224 miles) away in Mexico City. The Mexican capital is built partly on silt on the drained floor of Lake Texcoco. These silts amplified the ground motion by 75 times. The result was losses of US$4 billion and up to 35,000 lives. Intensity assessments thus have a practical and vital, application that magnitude evaluations cannot match. A further advantage of an intensity scale is that it provides a ready summary of what earthquakes can do.

ABOVE The mansions on Nob Hill were devastated by fire following the 1906 San Francisco earthquake. Here a stone fireplace and chimney are all that remain standing
BELOW Forward ground movement during the earthquake caused this railway track to buckle

modified Mercalli Intensity Scale of 1931

I Felt only rarely. Sometimes dizziness or nausea; birds and animals uneasy; trees, structures, liquids, doors sway.

II Felt indoors by a few, especially on upper floors. Same other effects as I, but more noticeably; delicately suspended objects may swing.

III Felt indoors, especially on upper floors, by several people. Usually rapid vibration, as if lightly loaded lorries passing. Hanging objects and standing motor cars rock slightly.

IV Felt indoors by many, outside by few. Some awakened, no-one usually frightened. Sensation of heavy object striking building. Vibration as of heavy lorries passing. Crockery, windows and doors rattle; walls and frames creak; hanging objects and standing motor cars sway.

The Loma Prieta earthquake 1989 damaged many roads. This is a collapsed section of the San Francisco-Oakland Bay Bridge

V Felt indoors by almost everyone, outdoors by most people. Many awakened, a few frightened and run outdoors. Buildings tremble, crockery and windows sometimes break and some vases fall. Pictures and doors clatter, small objects move. Some liquids spilt; clocks stopped; trees shaken; animals anxious.

This 21-storey steel apartment building collapsed during the Mexico earthquake in 1985

VI Felt by all indoors and outdoors. Many frightened and some alarmed. All awakened. People, trees and bushes shaken. Liquids set in motion; small bells set ringing. Crockery broken; plaster cracks and falls; books, vases fall over. Some furniture moved. Domestic animals try to escape. Minor landslides on steep slopes.

VII All frightened, run outdoors, general alarm. Some people thrown to ground. Trees shaken quite strongly; waves and mud stirred up in lakes; sandbanks collapse. Large bells ring. Suspended objects quiver. Much damage in badly-built buildings, old walls; slight in well-built buildings. Chimneys crack, much plaster, tiles and loose bricks fall. Heavy furniture overturned. Concrete ditches damaged.

VIII Alarm approached panic. Vehicle drivers disturbed. Trees shaken and broken. Sand and mud spurt from ground, marked changes in springs and wells. Much damage to ordinary and older buildings; walls, chimneys, pillars, towers, statues and gravestones crack or fall. Very heavy furniture overturned.

IX General panic. Ground cracked open 10cm (4in). Much damage to structures built to withstand earthquakes. Frequent partial or total collapse in other buildings, and reservoirs, underground pipes broken; buildings dislodged from foundations. Rockfalls.

X Widely-cracked ground, fissures up to 1m (3¼ft) wide. Frequent river-bank and coastal landslides and shifted sands. Water-levels change; water thrown onto riversides, etc. Serious damage to dams, embankments, bridges. Severe damage to well-built wooden structures, masonry structures destroyed along with their foundations. Rails bent; open cracks and waves on roads. Pipes torn apart.

XI Widespread serious ground disturbance, broad fissures, landslips and landslides. Muddy water spurts upward. Tsunamis develop. Severe damage to all wooden structures, great damage to dams. Few masonry structures remain upright, pillars of bridges and viaducts wrecked. All pipelines wrecked. Rails badly bent. Main roads impassable.

XII Total damage to all constructions, great disturbance to ground with many shearing cracks. Many large landslides on slopes, rockfalls common, rock masses dislocated, water channels altered and dammed. Ground surface waves like water and remains undulating. Objects thrown into the air.

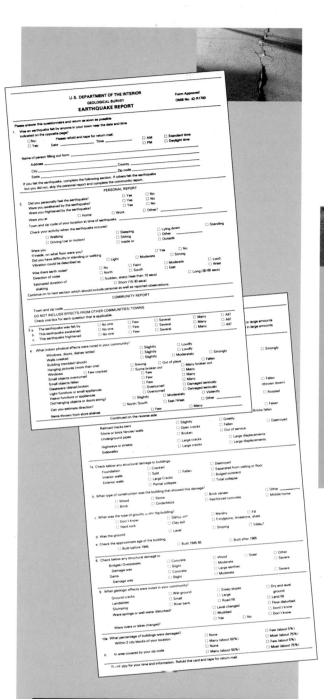

In 1976 a magnitude 7.9 earthquake devastated the town of Joyabaj, Guatemala

earthquake report

This earthquake report questionnaire is sent out by the US Geological Survey to those affected by earthquakes, and helps to map the intensity of the earthquake, by asking people what they saw and felt. It is also a way of assessing the types of damage sustained by different types and ages of building. It asks people to describe damage to their own homes as well as to other buildings in their area.

the effects
of earthquakes

PEOPLE, ANIMALS AND MAN-MADE STRUCTURES ARE THE MOST VULNERABLE TO EARTHQUAKES; WIDE OPEN SPACES ARE MUCH LESS VULNERABLE. THE DIRECT EFFECTS OF EARTHQUAKES ARE ALSO OFTEN FAR LESS DEVASTATING AND LIFE-THREATENING THAN THE SECONDARY CATASTROPHES THAT THEY CAUSE: FIRES, TSUNAMIS, LANDSLIDES, FAMINES AND EPIDEMICS. IT IS THEREFORE MUCH MORE DANGEROUS TO BE IN A CITY THAN IN THE SURROUNDING COUNTRYSIDE BOTH DURING AND AFTER AN EARTHQUAKE.

PRIMARY EFFECTS

In open country, the shocks can form small scarps, about 1m (3¼ft) high, for distances of 3km (1¾ miles) or more. The Armenian earthquake of 1988 formed a fine example. Where great fault-scarps have already formed, further uplift of the block can take place, forming a fresh scarp along the base of the slope. This is common on active faults in Utah and Nevada. Elsewhere the ground cracks, throwing down trees or precipitating landslides. Thus the 1906 San Francisco earthquake felled some redwood trees in northern California. The Calabrian earthquake of 1783, and the earthquakes

The magnitude 7.8 Peruvian earthquake of 1970 caused the beach sediments underneath this road, along the bay in western Chimbote, to slump and fissure

at Anchorage in 1964 and Loma Prieta in 1989, all caused massive landslides.

Historical reports of earthquakes often claimed that the ground had cracked open and swallowed up entire buildings or settlements. A more logical explanation, however, is that landslides or rock falls were responsible. Even in open country, some places are clearly safer than others. The foot of a sandy sea-cliff is no place to seek refuge from an earthquake: even if there is no landslide the earthquake may well cause a tsunami. Solid, hard rock such as granite is more stable than the sandy-clays of a damp alluvial plain where liquefaction may occur.

When you stamp repeatedly on a patch of wet sand on a beach, it immediately becomes wet, loses its cohesion, and the area around the point of impact becomes a miniature quicksand: the sand has liquefied in response to the vibrations caused by the stamping. Shock waves produced by earthquakes cause liquefaction on a grand scale – with spectacular effects on buildings. Elsewhere, different grain-sizes or different types of shock wave vibration can cause sand and

water to spurt out in little cones called 'sand boils' that look like little volcanoes and may reach up to 30cm (12in) high.

In relatively rare cases streams can be diverted. The El Asnam earthquake in Algeria in 1980 pushed back a small lake when land was jerked upwards across a stream. In California many streams crossing the San Andreas Fault system bend to the right as a result of its right-lateral displacement.

The general nature of the underlying rocks may also play a role in the area over which earthquakes are felt. The effects of the San Francisco earthquake in 1906 were restricted to a relatively narrow belt of California, 200km (124 miles) wide, possibly because the notably faulted rocks to the east quickly weakened the shock waves. In contrast, the New Madrid earthquakes in Missouri occurred in broad, gently sloping, less fractured rocks. Consequently shocks were clearly felt 1,200km (746 miles) away from the epicentre.

During urban earthquakes the vibrations of the shock waves often dislodge cornices,

Following the 1989 Loma Prieta earthquake many homeowners in the area buttressed their foundations to prevent further damage from aftershocks

decorative statues, concrete panels, or cause floors or façades or whole buildings to collapse. Pillars supporting bridges and roads are often sheared at their base or where they join the superstructure.

These effects can also be exacerbated by the type of soil underlying the buildings in a city. In damp alluvium, shaking increases the underground water pressure and water invades all the interstices in the sandy silt. The whole mass shudders and liquefies. The ground liquefied during the earthquake at Niigata in Japan in 1964. Several blocks of flats stayed intact but keeled over at a steep angle and sank about 5m (16½ft): some grateful inhabitants escaped from their homes by walking down the outside walls of the blocks. During the Alaskan earthquake, also in 1964, liquefaction of frost-ridden ground at Turnagain Heights in Anchorage sent suburban homes sliding sideways. A relatively small number of people were killed in these two earthquakes, but in general, liquefaction is probably one of the main direct causes of earthquake fatalities: it was a major contributor to the numbers of lives lost in San Francisco in 1906, Messina and Reggio di Calabria in 1908, Tokyo in 1923 and Kobe in 1995.

SECONDARY EFFECTS

The main secondary effects of earthquakes are fire, tsunamis, landslides, epidemics, famine, changes in the level of the land, and their cost in human lives.

Fire

Historically, movements produced by earthquakes knocked inflammable material into open hearths, causing fires to break out within a few minutes. Poor quality housing and wooden buildings were soon destroyed. When earthquakes wrecked the Cretan Palaces about 1750 BC, excavations have revealed ample evidence of the fires that followed. More recently it was fire, starting in the slums, spreading to Chinatown and onto the wealthier areas of the city, that caused most of the damage to San Francisco in 1906. Fire devastated the wooden homes of Tokyo after the Kanto earthquake in 1923: 25–30 per cent of the 143,000 victims met their deaths as a result of fire.

In modern cities, earthquakes compound the effects of fire by cutting gas and water pipes. The former adds to the combustion and explosions, while the latter removes the most effective means of stopping it. When the water

The Sherman Glacier as it appeared before the 1964 earthquake. The picture (right) shows the glacier partially covered by a rockslide caused by the earthquake

Sand boils, such as this caused by the Peruvian earthquake in 1970, can reach up to 30cm (12in) in height

supply was cut in San Francisco, whole streets were blown up to stop the fire consuming the whole city. Similarly, severed electric cables can be very dangerous. In Kobe, in 1995, for example, cables dangled, sparkling in the narrow streets for days afterwards.

Disease

Burst water pipes provide a further hazard, especially where the water can become infected. Diseases such as cholera and typhoid fever can become rife. There is always the danger that disease can reach epidemic proportions in a devastated city because communications and medical supplies may be cut off by damaged roads, railways or bridges.

Landslides

Earthquakes often cause landslides, especially in steep river valleys, and coastal cliffs. In weak sands or clays, in particular, the slightest vibration can bring down a whole slope. In Calabria in 1783, continual shocks swept through the country from 5 February until the

end of May. This earthquake probably caused more physical damage to open country than any recorded in Europe. There was a landslide in practically every ravine in western Calabria, and it was common for entire fields to be transported over 500m (1,640ft) downslope.

A magnitude 7.8 earthquake 70km (43½ miles) off the coast of Peru on 31 May 1970, caused the most spectacular landslide of modern times, high up in the Andes, causing at least 20,000 of the 66,000 recorded fatalities. The earthquake itself killed about 25,000 people in the Andean town of Huaraz, and destroyed most of the houses in the Rio Santa Valley. Severe vibrations disturbed the steep, glacier-covered flanks of Huascaran (6,768m, 22,205ft), dislodging about 1 million m³ (35 million ft³) of ice from its summit, which fell onto a mass of rock and ice 800m (2,625ft) below. Shortly afterwards 50 million m³ (1,766 million ft³) of rock and melting ice began to move down the Rio Santa Valley at nearly 350km/h (217mph).

About 14km (8¾ miles) from Huascaran, the earthquake had devastated the small town of Yungay. Two survivors saw the landslide advancing. They ran to the cemetery knoll and, moments later, they watched a flow of rock, ice and mud, 3m (9¾ft) high, swamp the ruins of Yungay and seal the fate of 20,000 people.

The peak of a mountain to the right of the picture collapsed to form this rockslide

The 1923 earthquake and the fires that followed caused devastation in Tokyo. This photograph was taken from the top of the Imperial Hotel, one of the few buildings to survive the earthquake

tsunamis

The most widespread of the secondary effects of earthquakes are huge, and frequently devastating, sea-waves or tsunamis. The word comes from the Japanese 'tsu', meaning harbour, and 'nami' meaning wave; 'a wave breaking into a harbour'. In fact they are so powerful that they can cross the Pacific Ocean with ease.

When an earthquake epicentre is on the sea-floor, or very near the coast, the faulting can cause the Earth's crust to sag and generate large submarine landslides. The water falls into the subsidence, so that the sea often retreats soon after the earthquake. About 10–15 minutes later the water returns as a huge wave that crashes onto the shore. Meanwhile, the tsunami spreads very quickly out to sea but is virtually undetectable until it reaches shallow coastal waters again. The great Chilean earthquake on 21–22 May 1960 generated three tsunamis that reached Japan, 16,000km (9,950 miles) away, 22 hours later. Over 3,000 houses and 250 bridges were destroyed, 2,500 ships damaged and 165 people killed. During its journey, the tsunami toppled the huge statues on Easter Island, drowned 50 people and caused US$50 million worth of damage in Hawaii. Ships on the open sea, however, were not affected.

The basic reason for this apparent anomaly is that in deep water, the wave length (the distance between the wave crests) of the tsunamis can be over 500km (311 miles), but the amplitude (height from crest to trough) may be less than 10m (33ft). The waves thus have imperceptible slopes. However, they do move fast, up to 800km/h (497mph), where the waters are 5,000m (16,400ft) deep over the abyssal plains

The tsunamis that followed the Alaskan earthquake of 1964 wrecked the sea front at Kodiak as seen here

of the oceans. As they approach shallow water, the friction of the sea-floor slows down the wave but increases its height. The tsunami can then form walls of water 30m (98ft) high that break and then crash upon the shore at speeds of about 80km/h (50mph). Narrowing, funnel-shaped, bays increase wave height even further which helps explain why devastation has often been very severe on heavily indented coasts such as Japan, Chile and Alaska. The highest recorded tsunami was caused by the Japanese earthquake of 24 April 1771. It reached a height of 85m (280ft) and caused 9,313 deaths in Japan alone.

Most tsunamis do most of their damage near

sea level   displacement

their source and only about 10 per cent devastate areas more than 8,000km (4,970 miles) away. Nevertheless, at such a distance they are still much more destructive than earthquake shock waves. Earthquakes cause most tsunamis; volcanic eruptions account for only 5 per cent.

The Pacific Ocean accounts for about 75 per cent of damaging tsunamis, with 12 per cent in

Ships and debris were also washed up along the shore at the port of Seward

the Mediterranean. Both areas experience violent earthquakes (and eruptions). Less seismically active areas produce fewer tsunamis: the Atlantic Ocean 9 per cent, the Indian Ocean 3 per cent.

The Lisbon earthquake of 1755 caused possibly the largest recorded European tsunami, reaching 15m (49ft) high in Portugal, Spain and Morocco. Following the Calabrian earthquake of 1783, tsunamis swept up and down the Straits of Messina. The Prince of Scilla and 2,473 of his people were swept out to sea. There was one survivor: a woman, 'four months gone with child' was rescued after nine hours. Miraculously both mother and child were unharmed.

Tsunamis, Simoda Bay, Japan, 23 December 1854. Extracts from the log of Russian frigate *Diana*

'The first earthquake shock was at 9.15 [am] and lasted 2–3 minutes. At 10.00 [am] a huge wave entered the bay and swamped the whole town and its houses and temples in a few minutes. Masses of debris started to float about ... Then the water began to rise up and boil ... and crashed onto the town ... There were innumerable whirlpools that turned the frigate round and round ... She was buffeted so much that the cannons were dislodged and one man was killed and several injured.'

'At 10.30 [am] a junk was thrown up against the frigate. It smashed open and sank. Only two men were saved because they had been thrown ropes. The rest were drowned down below where they had sought refuge. At 11.15 [am] the frigate lost two anchors and was sent twirling round again. By then the whole town was a flattened, empty space. Only 17 houses out of about 1,000 were still upright ... The waters kept on rising and falling until noon and the sea-level varied from minus 8¾ft [2.65m] to plus 39½ft [12m].'

'At 2.00 [pm] the sea-floor rose up again so violently that it threw the frigate onto its side several times. When calm returned, it took four whole hours to disentangle the ... mess of the ship's ropes and anchor-chains ... the bay was no more than a mass of ruins.'

increasing wave height

decreasing water depth

changing land levels and human cost

THE FINAL SECONDARY EFFECTS OF EARTHQUAKES ARE THEIR TERRIBLE COST IN HUMAN LIVES AND CHANGES IN THE LEVEL OF THE LAND.

Changing land levels

Usually the least devastating secondary effect of earthquakes is that the level of the land can rise or fall over a wide area. Such displacements are small and are most clearly visible in coastal areas. Darwin reported that the Chilean earthquake on 20 February 1835 raised the land by about 1m (3¼ft) around the Bay of Concepción. Captain Fitzroy, the commander of the Beagle 'found beds of putrid mussel-shells, still adhering to the rocks' some 3m (9¾ft) above the high-water mark, whereas before the earthquake they had always lived below low water. Older seashells were scattered over the land to a height of 200m (656ft), which showed that the uplift of 1835 was only the last of many during the preceding centuries. The Alaskan earthquake in 1964 displaced about 160,000km² (61,776 square miles) of land. In and around Prince William Sound, a long hump was upraised – in places by over 10m (33ft). Alongside it ran a trough marked by some 2m (6½ft) of subsidence. Both ran from north-east to south-west parallel to the fault-line that had generated the earthquake. Lines of dead barnacles underlined the old raised coastline all around Prince William Sound and the Kenai Peninsula nearby.

Human cost

The final secondary effect of earthquakes is loss of human life. As has already been discussed, earthquakes themselves pose very little threat. Serious injury or death is caused mainly by the

Mexico 1985. Many buildings were left as heaps of rubble

collapse of buildings or other man-made structures, such as roads and bridges, or when the earthquakes provoke other catastrophic events already outlined. The death-toll resulting from an earthquake bears little direct relationship to its magnitude, but is more closely related to its intensity, because this is in part a measure of damage caused by the shock-waves. Other factors include the density of population, the style of building that predominates in the area affected and the time of day when the shock occurs.

Chance was one of the reasons for the difference in death-toll between the earthquakes in Tokyo in 1923 and Anchorage in 1964. In Anchorage it was Good Friday, and public buildings were empty. Moreover the area was, and still is, much less densely populated. The earthquake that badly damaged Kalamata in Greece in 1986, fortunately occurred in the early evening, when everyone was outside. Similarly many people were outside enjoying the sunny holiday weather on 1 January 1980, when an earthquake struck Terceira in the Azores, damaging the beautiful city of Angra do Heroísmo. The empty apartments and other buildings meant there were few casualties.

It is usually better to be inside a wooden hut than an old, hurriedly-built block of flats, during an earthquake. Survival, however, is frequently a matter of chance. There was a remarkable example of lucky escape during the Calabrian earthquake in 1783. At Terra Nuova, the first shock on 5 February buried the priest

As many as 35,000 people could have been killed by the Mexico earthquake although the official figure is 9,500. 30,000 people were injured and 100,000 left homeless

with some of his flock alive under a huge pile of rubble. The second 'shock' came just in time. It disturbed the ruins, and they scrambled to safety. During the Mexican earthquake in 1985, a young French couple were on their honeymoon in an hotel in the centre of Mexico. The hotel was wrecked. In bed at the time the earthquake struck, the floor of the couple's room collapsed and, together with their bed, they fell nine storeys. The couple were later rescued, astonished, but otherwise unharmed.

Sir William Hamilton – husband of Admiral Lord Nelson's mistress Emma Hamilton – who provided a report of the Calabrian disaster, described apparent differences in the positions of bodies found when the rubble was cleared away. The men, he claimed, tended to be found in an attitude of struggle. In contrast the women often had their hands clasped over their heads, as if they had given up in despair. Mothers, however, always had their arms clutched tightly around their children.

Amongst those who are trapped, rates of survival vary greatly according to how seriously they are injured, the time taken for them to be rescued and how determined the individual is to survive. The age of the victim is also another important factor: older people tend to be weaker and lack the strength necessary to survive for long periods without food or water, or to dig their way out. Babies, however, seem to be remarkably robust and can survive even after being trapped for several days. In addition, the fact that babies are unaware of the dangers they face, means that they do not suffer from shock or stress.

For those who survive relatively unscathed, additional stress is caused by the frantic search for friends and family, something that is seen in all television footage following such disasters. Shock, panic, fear, hunger, illness, bereavement and even robbery may be suffered by many, if not all, survivors before normality can be restored. The statistics of death-tolls from earthquakes, therefore, cover a wide range of calamities.

Statistics themselves cannot always be taken at face value. Death-tolls figures must be regarded as estimates and, in some cases, they can only be guesses. Until the last century, there were no accurate census returns. The population before and after an earthquake, and thus the total death-toll, could only be an estimate. Even today, after the earthquakes in Tangshan, China in 1976 and in Mexico City in 1985, for example, some estimates of fatalities were four or five times greater than others. This may be due to the availability of accurate census information, different ways of interpreting information, or other, financial or politically motivated reasons.

Uplifted sea floor at Cape Cleare, Montague Island, Prince William Sound following the 1964 Alaska earthquake

some important earthquakes

Date	Magnitude	Site	Est. deaths
464 BC		Sparta, Greece	20,000
AD 342		Antioch, Turkey	40,000
565		Antioch, Turkey	30,000
856 Dec		Corinth, Greece	45,000
893		Armenia	20,000
1038 9 Jan		Shansi, China	23,000
1057		Chihli, China	25,000
1169		Sicily, Italy	25,000
1183		Syria-Lebanon	20,000
1201		Aegean Sea	100,000
1268		Silicia, Asia Minor	60,000
1290 27 Sept		Chihli, China	100,000
1293 20 May		Kamekura, Japan	30,000
1456 5 Dec		Naples, Italy	30–60,000
1531 26 Jan		Lisbon, Portugal	30,000
1556 23 Jan	8.3?	Shansi, China	830,000
1641 5 Feb		Tabriz, Persia	30,000
1653 23 Feb		Smyrna, Turkey	15,000
1667 Nov		Shemaka, Caucasus	80,000
1693 9–11 Jan		Catania, Italy	60,000
1715 May		Algeria	20,000
1727 18 Nov		Tabriz, Persia	77,000
1731		Peking, China	100,000
1737 11 Oct		Calcutta, India	300,000
1755 7 June		Kashan, Persia	40,000
1755 1 Nov	9.0?	Lisbon, Portugal	100,000+
1759 30 Oct		Jordan Valley	20,000
1783 5 Feb		Calabria, Italy	80,000
1797 4 Feb		Quito, Ecuador	41,000
1822 5 Sept		Aleppo, Syria	22,000
1828		Echigo, Japan	30,000
1835 20 Feb	8.5	Concepcion, Chile	35
1847 8 May		Zenkoji, Japan	12–34,000
1853 21 April		Shiraz, Persia	12,000
1853 11 July		Ispahan, Persia	10,000
1857 9 Jan	8.3	Fort Tejon, California	1

1857 16 Dec	6.5	Italy	12,000
1861 21 Mar		Mendoza, Argentina	18,000
1868 13 Aug		Peru-Ecuador	25,000
1868 16 Aug		Ecuador-Colombia	70,000
1896 15 June		Sanriku, Japan	27,000
1897 12 June	8.7	Assam, India	1,500
1905 4 April	8.6	Kangra, India	19,000
1906 18 April	8.25	San Francisco, USA	700
1906 17 Aug	8.6	Valparaiso, Chile	20,000
1907 21 Oct	7.7	Afghanistan	12,000
1908 28 Dec	7.5	Messina-Calabria, Italy	160,000
1915 13 Jan	7.0	Avezzano, Italy	32,000
1920 16 Dec	8.6	Kansu, China	200,000
1923 1 Sept	8.3	Tokyo, Japan	143,000
1927 22 May	8.3	Nan-Shan, China	200,000
1932 26 Dec	8.5	Kansu, China	70,000
1934 15 Jan	8.4	Bihar India-Nepal	10,700
1935 30 May	7.5	Quetta, India (Pakistan)	35–60,000
1939 25 Jan	8.3	Chillan, Chile	28,000
1939 26 Dec	7.9	Erzincan, Turkey	30,000
1948 5 Oct		Soviet-Iranian border	19,800
1949 5 Aug	6.8	Ambato-Ecuador	6,000
1954 9 Sept	6.8	Orleansville (El Asnam), Algeria	1,500
1960 29 Feb	5.8	Agadir, Morocco	14,000
1960 21–30 May	9.5 (3.5)	Southern Chile	5,700
1962 1 Sept	6.9	Qazvin, Iran	12,000
1963 26 July	6.0	Skopje, Yugoslavia	1,200
1964 27 Mar	8.4	Anchorage, Alaska	131
1968 31 Aug	7.3	Dashye Bayaz, Iran	12,000
1970 31 May	7.8	Ancash, Peru	66,000
1972 23 Dec	6.2	Managua, Nicaragua	5,000
1975 4 Feb	7.5	Haicheng, China	1,328
1976 4 Feb	7.9	Guatemala	22,000
1976 6 May	6.5	Friuli, Italy	1,000
1976 28 July	7.9	Tangshan, China	850,000
1978 16 Sept	7.4	Iran	15,000
1980 10 Oct	7.2	El Asnam, Algeria	20,000
1980 23 Nov	7.0	Irpinia, Italy	4,000
1985 19 Sept	8.1	Michoacan, Mexico	20,000
1988 7 Dec	6.8	Armenia	25,000
1989 17 Oct	7.1	Loma Prieta, California	62
1990 21 June	7.7	North-west Iran	50,000
1993 30 Sept		Maharashtra, India	15,000
1995 17 Jan	7.2	Kobe, Japan	5,500
1997 May	7.1	E. Iran	1,560

earthquake distribution

ONE OF THE FEW BENEFITS RESULTING FROM THE COLD WAR PERIOD WAS THAT THE ACCURATE INFORMATION ABOUT THE WORLD DISTRIBUTION OF EARTHQUAKES WAS AVAILABLE FOR THE FIRST TIME. THE TEST BAN TREATY, AGREED BETWEEN THE NUCLEAR POWERS IN THE EARLY 1960S, LIMITED OPEN-AIR NUCLEAR TESTS, BUT UNDERGROUND TRIALS CONTINUED. UNDERGROUND NUCLEAR EXPLOSIONS GENERATE SMALL EARTHQUAKES THAT CAN BE MONITORED USING SEISMOGRAPHS. ALMOST OVERNIGHT, WESTERN GOVERNMENTS RELEASED FUNDS TO ESTABLISH A WORLD-WIDE NETWORK OF 120 SEISMOLOGICAL STATIONS, EACH EQUIPPED WITH THREE STANDARDIZED SEISMOGRAPHS. THERE ARE NOW OVER 1,000.

The seismographs not only record any earthquake, but they also reveal the place where it happened, whether it was generated by the Earth itself, or by a bomb. The vibrations are timed on the seismographs with the shock waves taking longer to reach the more distant stations. P-waves travel faster than S-waves (see pp.42–43), therefore, the further a station is from the source of the earthquake, the greater will be the time delay between the arrival of the P-waves and the arrival of the S-waves. Because the general speed of both kinds of waves is known, it is possible to calculate the distance between the seismograph and the source of the earthquake. For example, if the calculated distance was 1,000km (621 miles), then the earthquake could have occurred anywhere on a circle with a radius of 1,000km (621 miles). If several stations have registered the shocks, and scientists have calculated their own distances from the source of the earthquake, the radii of these circles, when drawn on a map, should all intersect at one point. This point represents the epicentre of the earthquake or nuclear explosion.

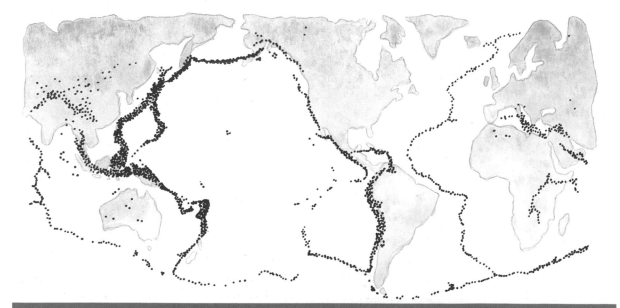

This map illustrates the distribution of earthquakes with magnitudes greater than or equal to 5 recorded 1980–1990

The epicentre of an earthquake can be located by drawing circles representing the distance of three or more seismic stations from the epicentre. The epicentre occurs where the lines intersect

In fact, as with triangulation surveys used for land-mapping, measurements from only three different stations are needed to plot the epicentre of an earthquake accurately.

Once it was possible to calculate earthquake epicentres quickly they could then be mapped. A standardized map of the main earthquakes during the previous few years was published in 1967. Their distribution was even more strikingly limited to long narrow zones than had ever been imagined. The lines formed by plotting the locations of earthquake epicentres were to give a major clue to the existence of the plates that make up the Earth's crust. The sites of the earthquakes virtually marked out the plate boundaries. Thereafter, earthquakes were seen in their true light as an important manifestation of the way in which the Earth works.

The earthquakes occurred in three main lines: first, around the Pacific Ocean (on the subduction zones); second, in a broad, complex belt stretching from the Azores and Gibraltar, via the Alps, the Mediterranean Sea and the Himalayas, to south-east Asia, (where the plates with continents upon them are colliding); and third, on the ridges in the Atlantic, Indian and Pacific Oceans. In these mid-ocean ridges, where the plates are separating, the earthquakes tend to be relatively small. But, in the areas of subduction and collision, they are often extremely violent. Subduction and collision zones account for 90 per cent of earthquakes.

The foci of most earthquakes are shallow. About 70 per cent of earthquakes begin at depths of less than 70km (43½ miles) – and most of those start in the brittle rocks less than about 30km (18½ miles) deep. About 25 per cent of earthquakes have foci between 70km (43½ miles) and 300km (186 miles) deep. These are called 'intermediate'. The remaining five per cent of earthquakes are called 'deep focus' and they occur at depths between 300km (186 miles) and 700km (435 miles). All earthquakes occurring below 70km (43½ miles), in fact, have their source on crustal slabs undergoing subduction. No earthquakes are generated below a depth of 700km (435 miles) because the crustal slabs have then become 'assimilated' into the plastic asthenosphere. But, even in the subduction zones, deep earthquakes are uncommon: relatively shallow earthquake foci are the norm all over the world.

In general terms, subduction zones and collision zones have the most frequent high magnitude and high intensity earthquakes; these are linked in turn to high death-tolls in heavily-populated areas. Earthquakes caused by lateral displacements such as those in China, southern California and northern Turkey tend to have similar characteristics. Earthquakes on mid-ocean ridges are lower in magnitude and less intense. In addition only small areas of the ridges actually rise above sea-level. There is also a category of earthquakes that are associated with the rise of molten rock that is usually the prelude to volcanic eruptions (see pp.90–93). These tend to be weak and very shallow.

However, whatever their location, most earthquakes of similar magnitudes and intensities that occur in similar human environments have roughly similar physical effects.

the San Francisco earthquake

18 April 1906

THE SAN ANDREAS FAULT ON CALIFORNIA MUST BE THE MOST FAMOUS AND MOST CAREFULLY-STUDIED IN THE WORLD BECAUSE ITS EARTHQUAKES THREATEN MILLIONS OF PEOPLE IN ONE OF THE WORLD'S WEALTHIEST AREAS. THE 'BIG ONE', A HIGH-MAGNITUDE EARTHQUAKE, IS BUILDING UP SOMEWHERE ALONG THE FAULT LINE, AND THIS IS WHY SCIENTISTS ARE WATCHING AND PONDERING ITS EVERY WHIM.

Debris produced by the earthquake litters Mission Street while the fire rages

In fact, the San Andreas fault comprises a system of branching faults stretching almost the length of California. The system marks the boundary where the Pacific Plate on the west has been sliding past the North American Plate on the east for about 30 million years and has caused a horizontal displacement totalling 300km (186½ miles – the distance from London to Manchester). The faults are often locked together until the pressures force the rocks apart again. The earthquake that results may displace the rocks by a few metres in seconds.

There has been a number of serious earthquakes in California in recent years, including those at Loma Prieta in 1989 and Northridge in 1994, but the scale and location of the 1906 San Francisco earthquake meant that it became the foundation of present-day seismology. It also illustrates the devastating effects of the fires caused by earthquakes.

On the morning of 18 April 1906 the northernmost 430km (267 miles) of the San Andreas fault system ruptured, from near San Juan Bautista in the south, to Cape Mendocino in the north; no other recorded Californian earthquake has sprung from such a long dislocation. The magnitude has been estimated at 8.3 although some believe it may have been as low as 6.9. The lateral displacements were visible in the north where they exceeded 6m (19½ft) around the epicentre at Olema, north-west of San Francisco.

In terms of the damage caused by

San Francisco ablaze. The elegant mansions built on the solid rocks of Nob Hill survived the earthquake but were destroyed by the fire

the earthquake, there was a distinct correlation between the intensity of the damage, and the nature of the buildings' foundations. Well-constructed buildings on solid rock stood reasonably firm, whilst houses built on sands and silts vibrated much more, and destruction was therefore greater. In a valley at the seaward end of the main thoroughfare, Market Street, small wooden houses and brick blocks of flats inhabited largely by the poor, and many wharves near the ferry station, were flung down into the cracked streets. Land reclaimed from mudflats, especially alongside the Bay, suffered the most. Buildings on the unstable infilled land vibrated so wildly that they collapsed completely. The water pipes and the gas mains broke all over the city.

On the other hand poor construction methods were to blame for the destruction of the expensive and newly finished City Hall: all that remained was the grand dome surrounded by rubble and twisted girders. Nearby, however, well-built steel-caged 'skyscrapers' were left practically unscathed. Throughout the city the tramlines and railway lines were twisted in all directions and the roads were cracked and subsided. Three-quarters of the headstones and monuments in the cemeteries were broken, twisted and displaced.

No sooner had the shocks of the main earthquake stopped than the fires started. The shocks threw furniture and beams into open hearths, flames spread from cracked chimneys and shattered stoves, gas hissed from broken pipes and was set alight. By noon on 18 April the badly-destroyed wooden houses of the poor south of Market Street were an inferno. The earthquake had severed the water pipes and there was no water to combat the flames. The fire spread northwards. It engulfed the commercial area and gutted many skyscrapers that had withstood the shocks. It went on spreading northward to Chinatown and the homes of the wealthy on the hills nearby. Then it turned westward. To stop its advance, they had to blow up buildings alongside Van Ness Avenue, one of the main arteries of the city. The fire burnt more than 28,000 buildings and made 350,000 people homeless. The officials admitted a death toll of about 700 but there must have been at least four times as many – notably among the unregistered immigrants in the areas near Market Street and Chinatown.

The aftermath. The ruins stretch as far as the eye can see in this picture taken after the fires were finally extinguished

Largely spared by the earthquake, the steel-caged skyscrapers in the financial district were also badly damaged by fire. Here the fire is still burning; it was many days before the flames were finally brought under control

the Loma Prieta earthquake

17 October 1989

ON 17 OCTOBER 1989 ABOUT 40KM (25 MILES) OF THE SAN ANDREAS FAULT MOVED BETWEEN LOS GATOS AND SAN JUAN BAUTISTA. THE FOCUS WAS 17KM (10½ MILES) DEEP. IT CAUSED A MAGNITUDE 7.1 EARTHQUAKE WITH AN EPICENTRE NEAR LOMA PRIETA PEAK IN THE SANTA CRUZ MOUNTAINS, ABOUT 100KM (62 MILES) SOUTH-EAST OF SAN FRANCISCO.

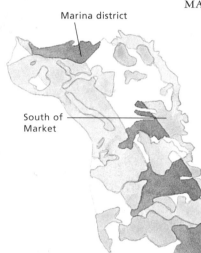

Marina district

South of Market

Predicted intensity of ground shaking in San Francisco during major earthquakes

Key

- weak
- strong
- very strong
- violent

In 1988, the US Geological Survey had forecast that this particular zone of the San Andreas Fault had a 30 per cent chance of suffering an earthquake above magnitude 6.5 in the next 30 years, but they could not predict exactly when it would happen. It happened, most inconveniently, at 17.04, just before an important baseball game was due to start in San Francisco. The earthquake shook the stadium and its 60,000 fans and was probably the first ever to be shown live on network television. The game, on the other hand, was cancelled, and some of the fans soon discovered that there were no roads fit to drive over, and no homes to go to. It was the third largest earthquake (in terms of magnitude) to hit the United States since 1906. It was also the most costly because it caused about US$6 billion damage to property, destroyed 414 houses and 97 businesses, damaged 18,306 homes and 97 businesses, made 18,892 people homeless, injured 3,757 and killed 62 people. Although the city of Santa Cruz was damaged, the Santa Cruz mountains, near the epicentre, are sparsely populated.

An aerial view of a collapsed section of the Cypress Viaduct in Oakland, California. The earthquake struck at 17.04 when the roads were busy; many people were trapped by falling concrete blocks

A right-hand displacement occurred, and the Pacific Plate slipped about 1.9m (6¼ft) north-west. The fault did not reach the surface, but the earthquake caused millions of surface cracks. But, very unusually for the San Andreas system, there was a distinct movement of about 1.3m (4¼ft) upwards over the North American Plate, causing, for instance, 25cm (10in) of crustal compression in the town of Los Gatos.

The earthquake caused damage reaching VIII on the modified Mercalli Scale in the area around the epicentre between Los Gatos, Santa Cruz and Watsonville, where wooden and non-reinforced buildings were damaged. But

Fires and gas explosions in the Marina district of San Francisco added to the dangers faced by the inhabitants

intensities of IX occurred away on Interstate roads 880 in Oakland and 280 in San Francisco and also in the marine area of north San Francisco. There were thousands of landslides and rockfalls, especially in the Santa Cruz Mountains.

The most intense damage occurred where land infill liquefied along the shores of San Francisco Bay about 80km (50 miles) from the epicentre. On the eastern shores of the Bay, the sandy fill liquefied and sand boils spurted out on the runways at Oakland airport. But the worst liquefaction, and the worst damage, occurred in the Marina area on the northern shore of San Francisco, opposite old Alcatraz. Much of this area had been an old lagoon, and had been filled with sand and rubble from the buildings damaged in 1906 to make the site of the International Panama-Pacific Exposition in 1915. By 1989 it had been built over. The earthquake liquefied the ground and heavily damaged many buildings. Sand boils even brought up pieces of charred wood from the earthquake in 1906.

An apartment block slumped on its foundations; huge quantities of debris were created by falling buildings

The most spectacular damage occurred to motorways on stilts: the pillars sheared and sections of their upper decks dropped onto passing traffic on the lower decks. The most dramatic collapse took place on the Cypress Viaduct on the Nimitz Freeway in Oakland where inadequate design was compounded by ground liquefaction. The shock rolled on like a wave causing section after section of the upper deck to collapse onto the deck below. Three viaducts in San Francisco itself were also very badly damaged along with hundreds of bridges throughout the area.

The Marina area also experienced a terrible fire, but it was brought under control within 12 hours, thanks to the help of many volunteer fire-fighters. As all the district's water pipes were broken and useless they compensated by pumping water straight from the Bay.

INTERVIEW

LOMA PRIETA, 1989

Sherra Cox

An aerial view of earthquake and fire damage in the Marina district of San Francisco

Sherra Cox had a busy afternoon planned for October 17 1989:

 'I had left my office a little early that day in order to get home and perhaps unpack some boxes – I just moved into the apartment – and to watch the World Series. When I got there, however, I decided I was too lazy and took a little nap and just as I got up at 5 o'clock, I turned on the TV and the building started to shake ... it very quickly turned into a big wave-type motion. The building seemed to tilt to one side so you couldn't stand ... so I just automatically went to a door to hold on to be able to stand up but ... the building fell down on itself. It was a four storey building and it fell to the street and it tilted from the front towards the back'.

During the earthquake Sherra was conscious of a deep roar; before the building collapsed she was conscious of the structural changes that were going on around her:

 'The first thing I saw was the ceiling dropping and the walls just like an accordion ... I sort of turned back towards the entrance door in the hallway and that's when the door popped out ... the ceiling dropping caused the door to buckle and come out.'

Sherra's heavy front door knocked her down, pinning her to the floor. At that moment she heard a voice.

 'I heard someone say "Is anyone in there?" ... and I shouted "Yes, I'm here" ... Whoever it was did not hear me ... I reached back and ... there was a pipe ... and I could bang on the door with it and make a definite sound ...'

Sherra's quick thinking meant that she was found relatively quickly. After being alerted by passers-by a fireman crawled into the debris to see whether there was indeed a survivor trapped in the rubble.

 'I heard them say "Is anybody there?" again. I was shouting as loud as I could because they couldn't hear my voice, but they said "We hear a tapping. Tap louder, as loud

as you can if you can hear our voice." So I tapped as loud as I could. They said "We hear you ... we're coming to get you ... just keep shouting."'

It took about an hour for the fireman to locate Sherra but finally he got close enough for them to talk.

 'He told me his name was Gerry [Shannon, San Francisco Fire Department]. I said "I'm very glad to know you Gerry".'

Eventually he reached her but soon realized that any further progress was blocked by huge beams that had fallen in the bedroom.

 '... he told me that he had to go out and get some chain saws ... but it was getting dark and he put his hand under this one beam and I could see his fingers ... I saw him and I grabbed hold of him and I begged him not to leave me, and he said he had to go but he would be back.'

Inadequately built garage walls meant that this apartment block was in danger of collapsing following the earthquake

Meanwhile the situation outside in the street was getting worse: broken gas pipes meant there was a high risk of explosions. Sherra could hear

people warning Gerry not to go back into the building but she was unaware that sparks from the chain saw could possibly trigger a gas explosion.

 'When he started back in he said he ... was going to start a chain saw and it would be very loud and just to be calm ... he started it and nothing happened and he was able to cut through quite a few beams ... then he had to get another chain saw ... when he went out the second time he said there was just no way he could not come back even though ... they were really shouting even more so not to come back in.'

Finally all that lay between Gerry and Sherra was the door. It took several men to lift it, and even then they were only able to shift it slightly. By this time the building was already on fire. Salt water was being used to control the flames but in the final stages of the rescue these had to be turned off to stop the building collapsing further under the weight of the water. At last the men began to pull Sherra clear of the rubble. A large crowd of photographers and camera crews began to applaud as she finally emerged.

 'I wanted to know where Gerry was because ... there was no way I was going to let this fireman get away without knowing who he was. There was an ambulance they put me in right away, and some of the other people followed and asked for Gerry, and he came over to the stretcher and I just put my arms around him and kissed him on the cheek.'

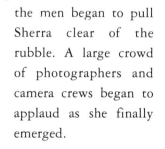

the Alaskan earthquake
27 March 1964

ALASKA IS 'BIG COUNTRY' AND EXPERIENCES BIG EARTHQUAKES TO MATCH. EIGHT EARTHQUAKES EXCEEDING MAGNITUDE 8.0, AND ABOUT 70 OVER MAGNITUDE 7.0, HAVE STRUCK SOUTHERN ALASKA AND THE ALEUTIAN ISLANDS DURING THIS CENTURY ALONE. ONE OF THE LARGEST EARTHQUAKES EVER RECORDED IN NORTH AMERICA STRUCK SOUTHERN ALASKA AT 17.36 ON GOOD FRIDAY, 27 MARCH 1964. ITS EPICENTRE WAS NEAR THE NORTHERN SHORE OF PRINCE WILLIAM SOUND, 130KM (81 MILES) EAST OF ANCHORAGE, AND ITS FOCUS WAS 20KM (12½ MILES) DEEP.

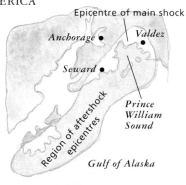

It measured magnitude 8.4 on the Richter scale, caused damage over an area of 80,000km² (31,000 square miles), was felt over an area of more than 800,000km² (310,000 square miles) and caused water levels to fluctuate in wells as far away as Florida by as much as 5m (16½ft). The level of the land and sea-floor changed over 160,000km² (62,000 square miles). A long trough, running north-east to south-west and including most of the Kenai Peninsula subsided by as much as 2m (6½ft). Parallel to it, a long hump like an upturned boat rose by as much as 15m (49ft), especially near Montague Island.

Anchorage, the largest town in Alaska, had 100,000 inhabitants, half the population of the largely empty, wilderness state. The earthquake tossed the buildings in the city about like ships in a storm for nearly four minutes. It was just the same in the smaller towns in the district, including Seward, Kenai and Valdez. These primary effects were then followed by secondary effects.

Anchorage is built on sands and clays left behind when the glaciers melted. The vibrations

One span of the 'Million-dollar' truss bridge was dropped into the Copper River by the earthquake; the other truss spans were shifted on their piers

liquefied these water-laden terrains – and sand sometimes spouted from the ground. Shops and bars in central Anchorage subsided, landslide after landslide began to slip downslope, taking their crown of buildings with them. A fashionable suburb slid 600m (1,970ft), leaving behind a chaos of homes and gardens as if they had suddenly frozen on a stormy sea. A school split in two, fissures formed in the playground and supplied another landslide that swamped the railway yard. A radio-announcer broadcast and recorded his own vivid 'Anchorage Experience' as it was happening. It is a striking contrast to the written accounts of other earthquakes (see panel p.72).

A similar pattern was repeated throughout the district. The communications system suffered badly. Embankments, bridges, roads, railways and harbours cracked, subsided and

These rails were buckled by lateral ground movement

sometimes even rose up. It was to cost US$22 million to repair the damage to the Alaska Railroad and its harbour alone. Cracks and subsidence made many roads impassable. Harbours were lifted out of the water: the quayside at Cordova rose 3m (9¾ft), but other areas were flooded.

Submarine subsidence and landslides then produced a number of tsunamis. They washed ships up onto land at Kodiak and Seward and dumped them amidst the tangle of wrecked harbour installations. The tsunamis swept down the Canadian and American coasts as far as northern California.

A whole range of shocks and secondary effects struck the port of Valdez. The earthquake damaged the buildings, cracked the oil-storage tanks, and liquefied the sands of the old delta where the town was built. The resulting landslide swept the quayside – and 30 people

Alaska's communication system was badly damaged by the earthquake. Cracks and subsidence made many roads impassable and many bridges collapsed into the water. In this picture the road bridge over the River Kenai Pen has been broken in several places

Testimony of R Pate, KHAR Radio announcer, Anchorage, Alaska

'Hey, boy – Oh-wee, that's a good one! Hey – boy oh boy oh boy! Man, that's an earthquake! Hey, that's an earthquake for sure! ... Man – everything's moving – you know, all that stuff in all the cabinets have come up loose ... I've never lived through anything like this before in my life! And it hasn't even shown signs of stopping yet, either ... the whole place is shaking ... Hold it, I'd better put the television on the floor. Just a minute – Boy! Let me tell you that sure scared the hell out of me, and it's still shaking. I'm telling you! I wonder if I should get outside? Oh boy! Man, I'm telling you that's the worst thing I've ever lived through! I wonder if that's the last one of 'em? Oh man! Oh – Oh boy, I'm telling you that's something I hope I don't go through very often. Maa-uhn! ... I'm telling you, the whole place just moved like somebody had taken it by the nape of the neck and was shaking it ... I wonder if the KHAR radio tower is still standing up. Man! You sure can't hear it, but I wonder what they have to say on the air about it? ... Man, that could very easily have knocked the tower down – I don't get anything on the air – from any of the stations – I can't even think! I wonder what it did to the tower. We may have lost the tower, I'll see if any of the stations come on – No, none of them do. I assume the radio is okay – Boy! The place is still moving! You couldn't even stand up when that thing was going like that I was falling all over the place here. I turned this thing on and started talking just after the thing started, and man! I'm telling you, this house was shaking like a leaf! The picture frames – all the doors were opened – the dishes were falling out of the cabinets – and it's still swaying back and forth – I've got to go through and make a check to make sure that none of the water lines are ruptured or anything. Man, I hope I don't live through one of those things again.'

waiting for a boat – into the sea. Then tsunamis wrecked the waterfront, fire broke out in the broken oil-storage tanks and spread through the remains of the harbour area. Valdez was so badly damaged that the town had to be moved to a new site altogether at a cost of US$37.5 million.

How could anyone have survived such an onslaught in southern Alaska? Many taller buildings of heavy materials suffered badly, but well-made wooden framed buildings often survived, if not exactly on an even keel, or in their original positions. The tsunamis wrecked

The business area of Anchorage was very badly damaged. The cracks in the foreground were caused by lateral ground spreading

the coasts as much as the earthquake shocks. But even for such a sparsely-populated area, the number of deaths was remarkably small. Many more people would have died had the earthquake not taken place on a holiday evening when schools and businesses were empty. The earthquake claimed 131 lives, 122 of which resulted from tsunamis in Alaska, British Columbia, Oregon and California.

ABOVE Tsunamis washed ships up onto the
waterfront at Seward and dumped them among
wrecked harbour installations

BELOW This truck was bent around a tree by the
surge waves generated by underwater landslides
along the Seaward waterfront

the Kobe earthquake

17 January 1995

IN 1978, THE JAPANESE EARTHQUAKE PREDICTION PROGRAMME CHOSE TEN AREAS FOR SPECIAL MONITORING. KOBE WAS ON THE EDGE OF ONE OF THESE SELECTED AREAS THAT STRETCHED ACROSS HYOGO PROVINCE, AND EASTWARDS THROUGH OSAKA TO NAGOYA. THIS IS A HEAVILY-INDUSTRIALIZED, HIGHLY-POPULATED REGION, AND IT WAS CLEAR THAT AN EARTHQUAKE WOULD CAUSE A HIGH DEGREE OF COSTLY DAMAGE. AT THE TIME, HOWEVER, THE TOKYO AREA IN KANTO PROVINCE, AND THE NEARBY PROVINCE OF TOKAI, WERE JUDGED TO BE AT GREATER RISK. SEVENTEEN YEARS LATER KOBE WAS STRUCK BY A HIGH-MAGNITUDE EARTHQUAKE WHICH PROVIDED A GRAPHIC ILLUSTRATION OF WHAT COULD HAPPEN IN TOKYO IN THE FUTURE.

The magnitude 7.2 earthquake caused the Kobe intersection of the Hanshin Motorway to topple sideways

Therefore, the experts thought that there could be an earthquake in the Kobe area, but had no real reason to expect one. The shocks came as a surprise and also occurred along a fault that had previously been obscured by a blanket of coastal alluvium. It is a fairly short fault, one of many branching from a much longer, well-known fault called the Median Tectonic Line. This fault line has developed because the Philippine plate is squeezing up against southern Japan. The pressure has produced a crack that is forcing some of the blocks of crust to slide horizontally out of the way with a right-handed horizontal movement. Gradually, the block to the north of the fault is carrying Kobe and Osaka towards the east, whilst the block to the south of the line is moving intermittently westwards. This kind of movement has built up energy which has been released periodically, not only on the main fault, but also on the many parallel faults that these forces have created.

At 05.46 on 17 January 1995 one of these smaller faults was producing a right-lateral movement, ie. when the observer faces the fault-line, the block on the other side moves to the right. In all, between 40km (25 miles) and 60km (37 miles) of the fault moved. The focus of the magnitude 7.2 earthquake was 19km (12 miles) below the Akashi Straits. The epicentre lay in the channel between Kobe and Awaji Island. In seconds, Kobe moved 1.7m (5½ft) further away from Awaji Island, as the fault jerked to the right and also thrust a maximum of 1.3m (4¼ft) upwards.

The Hanshin trains were thrown off the collapsed railway viaduct; buildings in the surrounding area were crushed

The fault gave out two warning foreshocks about 12 hours before the main earthquake and it produced 6,000 aftershocks. These ranged from a magnitude 4.9 earthquake, two hours after the main shock, to hundreds of little tremors during the following month. There had also been some ground deformation beforehand and on Awaji Island some strange animal behaviour had been noted. In spite of these warnings, the people of Kobe were totally unprepared for what was to happen next.

The earthquake cut a swathe of devastation across Kobe. It stretched 25km (15½ miles) north-westwards from Awaji Island in a band 500m (1,640ft) wide. In this corridor, the intensity of damage reached the maximum of 7 on the Japanese intensity scale – the equivalent of XI on the modified Mercalli Scale. Elsewhere, the damage was less severe.

There were many small, and a few moderate, landslides of up to 100m (328ft) in length, and all occurred within 4km (2½ miles) of the fault. Where the soil liquefied, the results were altogether more disastrous. It naturally affected the coastal sediment and the vast areas of reclaimed land used for additional harbour space and, unfortunately, for housing. Within minutes, the port of Kobe was useless, hundreds of houses collapsed and sand spurted out onto

The fires that followed the earthquake caused huge amounts of damage. Some smoke is still visible in this picture taken on 18 January 1995

the surface. On Port Island, the weathered, granitic infilling liquefied and not only subsided about 50cm (19³/₄in), but also pushed the concrete walls of the container quays about 2m (6½ft) into the sea.

Meanwhile, amplified by the alluvial ground, the earthquake shocks powered through central Kobe, Ashiya and on to Nishinomiya. More than 100,000 houses collapsed. Within two hours, 234 fires had broken out. Eventually, about 1km² (⅓ square mile) of closely spaced, compact, largely wooden buildings burnt down in the Kobe metropolitan area – the equivalent of a century of accidental fires.

Ten per cent of the infrastructure of the area was lost (roads, railways, electricity, gas, sewerage), 10 per cent of educational facilities, 5 per cent of housing, 12 per cent of the raw materials industrial sector and 14 per cent of the wholesale-retail trade sector. The disaster cost 0.2 per cent of GNP. In contrast, damage caused by the Tokyo earthquake of 1923 cost 7 per cent of GNP.

Around 5,500 people were killed, about 36,500 were injured and 188,000 houses badly damaged or completely destroyed in the Kobe metropolitan area. 52,000 people were left homeless, and there were 350,000 refugees at the height of the crisis. 316,000 out of 3,021,091 people living in the Kobe area were evacuated to refugee camps in the days after the calamity.

The earthquake destroyed several bridges and the Hanshin Expressway viaduct collapsed for a distance of 600m (1,968ft). All the lifeline services were shut down over 150km² (58 square miles). The electricity supply was cut when half the substations in the zone of severe damage were destroyed: 2,000,000 homes were left without power. Underground cables were more vulnerable than aerial cables. Many gas pipes failed at the screw joints but the polyethylene pipes resisted. Many water pipes cracked at the joints – especially the smaller service pipes inside buildings. Repairs were handicapped when the Water Works office collapsed and buried the maps of pipeline networks! Over 1 million homes had no water for ten days. Telecommunications were badly damaged too and were not fully restored until the end of January – except where buildings had collapsed. The earthquake severely damaged the railways, but happened before the 'bullet' train began its daily service. Although there were no railway injuries, many railway viaducts and bridges collapsed and several stations were damaged. The bullet train was fully restored to service after 81 days on 8 April, but many commuter lines were closed until June. The roads, of course, also lost many bridges.

The ports suffered most of all: 30 per cent of Japan's container trade operated from Kobe and the disaster badly damaged 234 out of the 240 container berths.

The earthquake caused Daikai Street to cave in; the Daikai station of the Kobe Express Underground lies beneath the central subsided section of this road

ABOVE At night fires raged, devastating the densely populated areas of Hyogo and Nagata

BELOW The main street of North Sannomiya. The buildings seen here show varying degrees of earthquake damage

INTERVIEW

KOBE, 1995

Mrs Komazawa and Mrs Iio

Hokkaido

Sapporo ●

Pacific
Ocean

Sea of Japan

Tokyo ●
Kobe ● ● Kyoto ● Yokohama
● Osaka

Shikoku

Kyushu

Mrs Komazawa was working in an office in Yokohama when the earthquake of 1923 struck the Kanto province of Tokyo.

'During the earthquake I was hiding under the desk ... Then I was trapped among fallen objects and could not move at all. A man ... tried to save me by pulling ... with all his might, then at last all my body could move and I was taken out of the building and carried outside.'

She lay under a tree in Yokohama Park for a day and a night, before a kindly passer-by sent word to her family of her plight, and her aunt came to find her. It was some time before Mrs Komazawa recovered from her injuries. Shortly afterwards, her husband was transferred by his company from Yokohama to Kobe, 440km (273 miles) away. Although sad to leave her home, Mrs Komazawa was relieved to have moved from the earthquake danger zone around Tokyo.

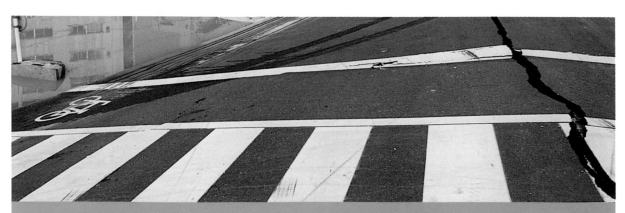

A detail showing damage to Daikai Street. Huge cracks appeared all along the road as it simply caved in when the ground started to shake

'I never thought I would have such an earthquake in Kobe.'

Sixty years later, on 16 January 1995, Mrs Komazawa and her friend Mrs Iio were preparing for the New Year Tea Ceremony. Mrs Iio did not go to bed until 03.00 on the morning of 17 January. She remembers,

'... I saw the moon shining extraordinarily bright in the sky ...'

She woke again at around 05.40, it was pitch black. Then at 05.46 the earthquake struck.

'... at the moment of the jerk, the shelf of the home shrine fell off ... and then the home shrine fell nearly squashing me but narrowly missing my head ... I was caught under the shrine at my back ... and I was lying there helplessly.'

Mrs Komazawa was not trapped, and began to crawl towards Mrs Iio, who reached out to hold her friend's hand. For the first time she noticed the scene around her.

'I looked around the room ... paintings, scrolls on the wall were hanging off the wall or fallen on the debris ... I told Mrs Komazawa "Don't panic! Someone is looking for us from the fallen roof." ... they were calling "Are you all right?" ... The people saved us by pulling off the room slate, and broke into the ceiling and pulled us out.'

The rescuers had to work carefully when they pulled out Mrs Komazawa so as not to cause further damage that would crush Mrs Iio.

'They managed to lift and hand down Mrs Komazawa on the ground and I crawled down the roof with bare feet and took rest at the house across the road ... We stayed there until 4pm or so, then we moved to the temporary shelter placed on the parking lot.'

The scene that greeted them was terrible,

'It was the end of the world ... The road in front of our house was covered up by the collapsed houses ... the only thing left to us was our own lives.'

Mrs Komazawa is fatalistic. Although she is 90 years old and has survived two earthquakes, she knows that another could strike at any moment, and that this time she may not be so lucky.

Large areas of the city were devastated by the earthquake and later by fire. This aerial view gives an idea of the extent of the damage

the Northridge earthquake

17 January 1994

ON 17 JANUARY 1994 A MAGNITUDE 6.7 EARTHQUAKE SHOOK THE SAN FERNANDO VALLEY 30KM (18½ MILES) NORTH OF LOS ANGELES IN CALIFORNIA. ITS FOCUS WAS 19KM (12 MILES) DEEP, THE FAULT SLIPPED AN AVERAGE OF 2M (6½FT), AND ITS EPICENTRE WAS AT NORTHRIDGE. FIFTY-SEVEN PEOPLE DIED, A FURTHER 9,000 WERE INJURED, AND DAMAGE WAS ESTIMATED AT OVER US$13 BILLION.

Some railway crew members saw the earthquake rush towards them in their engine headlights. The rails twisted from the ground, 'exploded' into the air, and the train was then thrown off the tracks. In this densely-populated area, 1,600 buildings were declared unsafe and 7,300 others were damaged; freeway bridges collapsed, and broken gas pipes caused explosions and fires. Fortunately, the 10–20 seconds of violent shaking took place at 04.30 in the morning, when many roads and bridges were empty. If the earthquake had happened during the day then lists of casualties would have been far longer. Improved building techniques since the nearby San Fernando earthquake of 1971 also limited damage and loss of life, but nevertheless, the intricate network of Los Angeles freeways collapsed in seven places.

In southern California the San Andreas Fault system and its associated faults bend round so that they trend east to west around Los Angeles. The Pacific Plate is moving towards the north-west, and tends to push against this bend rather than slide past the North American Plate, as it does along the rest of the San Andreas system. The area around Los Angeles and San Diego is continually being forced up against this bend, and the rocks of the crust are squeezed, folded or broken into slices, and pushed upwards along reverse or thrust faults. This is also what happened in the earthquakes at San Fernando in

At California State University, Northridge, shaking knocked the contents of the shelves in the pharmacy to the floor

These sections of Interstate 5 at Gavin Canyon were sheared apart during the earthquake

1971 and at Whittier Narrows in 1987.

The Northridge earthquake took place on a fault in the bedrock that was completely hidden by sediments. It was a 'blind' or 'masked' fault. No-one knew that it even existed. Such events demonstrate just how difficult it is to predict earthquakes in extremely mobile zones of the Earth's crust – the very places where prediction is needed most. The Northridge fault remains hidden because the displacement along the fault took place 19km (12 miles) underground and did not break through to the landsurface. It did, however, cause the greatest earthquake damage in the United States since San Francisco was devastated in 1906.

During the Northridge earthquake there was a great deal of ground movement. Damage recorded on the modified Mercalli Intensity Scale reached between VIII and IX in the San Fernando valley. Nevertheless, many houses survived mainly because they had been built after earthquake-resistant design and building codes had been enforced. What happened inside the houses, however, was a different matter: pictures were thrown from walls, refrigerators and cupboards were emptied onto the floor, furniture was moved, pipes were broken, some fires were started, and there were many landslides out in the country. Bricks and masonry fell from buildings and damaged parked cars, and some wooden homes were shaken from their foundations, and flopped over onto the crawl-space between the foundations and their ground floors. More than 50km (31 miles) from the epicentre, damage was only slight, although the score-board did fall down at Anaheim Stadium, 75km (46½ miles) away.

West central Los Angeles suffered some of the worst damage, because it lay within 20km (12½ miles) of the epicentre, and because its buildings were constructed

Like many specially designed, low rise buildings the Holy Cross Medical Centre suffered little damage

before earthquake-resistant provisions were incorporated into the building codes. Raised sections of freeways produced the most spectacular failures. On the Santa Monica freeway (Interstate Highway 10) at Venice Boulevard in Los Angeles, the circular steel 'ties' or belts wrapped around the columns were meant to reinforce them and hold them together. But they were too thin and the spaces between them too great. The earthquake broke them apart, and the weight of the concrete freeway crushed the columns

and whole sections collapsed. The columns, however, which had been properly strengthened after the San Fernando earthquake in 1971, remained intact. Similarly, most buildings that were designed and built to resist known earthquake forces survived with little or no damage. The Olive View Hospital at Sylmar, 16km (10 miles) from the epicentre, survived intact except that its fire-sprinkler system was damaged. It had been designed to resist earthquake forces, with a steel-framed structure with concrete and steel load-bearing walls, and proved to be a successful replacement for its predecessor that had collapsed during the San Fernando earthquake of 1971.

Buildings with a 'soft' ground floor (called the first floor in the United States) were damaged more than those around them. 'Soft' ground floors are those with large open areas such as garages and shops, which have little lateral strength and, therefore, cannot withstand strong vibrations. At Reseda in Northridge, 14 people were killed when a block of flats dropped onto the ground floor garage, crushing all the cars. The car-park of California State University at Northridge – full of soft storeys – collapsed inwards in a tangled wreckage. As expected, many steel-frame buildings withstood the earthquake well, but many of them developed cracks after six months that would weaken them in any future earthquake.

Tall buildings are particularly vulnerable during earthquakes because shaking is usually several times greater on upper floors than at ground level – hence tall buildings are more likely to collapse. In some cases the problem can be overcome by placing base-isolators (huge rubber pads) between the building and its foundations. One seven-storey building with base-isolators on the UCLA campus in central Los Angeles, 37km (23 miles) from the epicentre, survived the earthquake relatively unscathed.

Most structural damage occurred to the following types of construction: older buildings that had not been built to post-1971 seismic provisions; recent garages with weakly-

Reseda was one of the areas in Northridge that was badly affected by the earthquake

ABOVE Damage to the 'soft' lower storeys of the car park at California State University, Northridge
BELOW This five-storey building partially collapsed

connected, load-bearing columns; buildings with a 'soft' ground floor storey; and tall buildings. Buildings of 18 or more storeys with a natural swaying motion of 2 secs or more were particularly vulnerable. The natural period of such buildings matches the seismic surface waves that are propagated in areas of highly-populated sedimentary basins in southern California.

On the plus side, by far the majority of buildings in the area resisted the earthquake extremely well. About 90,000 buildings were inspected in Los Angeles following the earthquake: only two per cent were deemed unsafe to enter; ten per cent could be entered only to a limited extent; and 88 per cent were judged to be safe enough for unlimited access and use. The survival of so many buildings in the area illustrates the immense value of well-conceived building codes and modern, earthquake-resistant design and construction practices.

Although reinforced, the frame of this 15-storey building cracked

The third and fourth storeys of this unreinforced masonry building were damaged while the floors below were left relatively unscathed

the Messina-Calabria earthquake

28 December 1908

THE AREA AROUND THE MEDITERRANEAN HAS BEEN SHAPED BY THE COLLISION BETWEEN THE EUROPEAN PLATE IN THE NORTH AND THE AFRICAN PLATE IN THE SOUTH. ONE OF THE MAIN RESULTS OF THIS COLLISION IS THAT GREECE AND ITALY SUFFER THE MOST FREQUENT EARTHQUAKES IN THE WHOLE OF EUROPE. EARTHQUAKES CAUSED BY PLATE COLLISION ARE OFTEN THE MOST VIOLENT OF ALL.

The relatively small area in eastern Sicily and nearby Calabria, the toe of Italy, experiences some of the most destructive earthquakes on Earth. The whole area is riddled with major active faults, different sections of which have moved at various times in recent years. These displacements have been happening ever since Africa and Europe began to collide about 40 million years ago. The result is that the crust of Calabria has been broken into blocks that have risen up to form the Sila and Aspromonte uplands. The Peloritani mountains form a similarly upraised block in northern Sicily. The area between them, however, has collapsed and has been flooded to form the Straits of Messina. It is in this area that the most savage earthquakes are concentrated.

Particularly destructive earthquakes seem to occur in this area about once every 90–125 years. In 1908 the epicentre lay in the Straits of Messina itself, between Messina in Sicily (population then 150,000) and Reggio in Calabria (population then 45,000), two of the most populous cities in the region. If this pattern persists there could be another earthquake in the area within the next 30 years.

The Messina earthquake has thus far been the most deadly natural disaster to occur in Europe in the 20th Century. It happened at 05.21 on the morning of 28 December 1908, the Feast of the Massacre of the Innocents. The focus of the earthquake was relatively shallow, perhaps only 10km (6¼ miles) deep, and its magnitude was 7.5. For an earthquake of such magnitude the shocks were felt over a relatively small area – 1,000km (621 miles) – as far away as Palermo, Naples, Tunis, and Joanina in Greece.

ITALY

Milazzo •
Messina • • Reggio di Calabria

SICILY

Etna ▲

Tyrrhenian Sea

Straits of Messina

Messina
• Bagnara
• Villa San Giovanni
XI • Reggio di Calabria
X • Pellaro

IX

VII

Ionian Sea

Key

) Intensity
) value

The search for survivors in the aftermath of the earthquake

84

earthquakes

Soldiers had to police the ruined buildings the protect them from looters

There was just a single foreshock, a light tremor lasting for 20 secs that increased in intensity and then declined. This was followed by a 7.5 magnitude earthquake that rocked the ground for over 30 secs. The Feast of the Massacre of the Innocents claimed 160,000 lives.

The most serious damage was concentrated along the shores of the Straits of Messina where the buildings had been constructed on alluvium soil. Here the seismic waves were greatly magnified and liquefaction also occurred. These areas included the centres of Messina, Reggio, Villa San Giovanni, and most of the towns along the neighbouring coast. The fish market in Messina sank below sea-level, the railway station foundered and the façade of the cathedral crashed into the Piazza del Duomo and the roof fell into the nave. In Reggio, the city centre, the harbour and the cathedral met the same fate. In a 40km (25 mile) zone along the Straits scarcely a single building remained undamaged. In the 30km (18½ mile) wide band around the coastal area the

destruction was less severe, but damage did occur throughout most of southern Calabria and northeast Sicily. Tsunamis 3–6m (9¾–19¾ft) in height caused additional devastation.

The stricken area was isolated. News of the disaster filtered out only slowly. The trains from Palermo and Catania, for example, were unable to reach Messina because landslides had blocked the tracks. Roads were destroyed and telegraph cables were severed. The sea appeared to be the only point of access. Several Italian naval vessels had survived in the harbour at Messina. The Captain of the *Serpente* set sail to find a place where the telegraph cables were intact: he had to sail a distance of 70km (43½ miles) up the Calabrian coast to the town of Marina di Nicótera. That evening Roman newspapers released the first reports of the earthquake.

In Messina and Reggio the survivors and the first Red Cross workers to reach the area began to pull the bodies from the wreckage and line them up on the shores. On 30 December King Vittorio Emmanuele III visited the scene of the disaster. He was horrified by what he saw and immediately sent a personal telegram to Rome 'There is complete havoc here: fire, blood and death; send ships, ships, ships and more ships'. Even when the rescue operation was complete, it was many years before the villages were rebuilt.

This makeshift hospital was set up amongst the wreckage to treat those wounded by the earthquake

the Mexico earthquake

19 September 1985

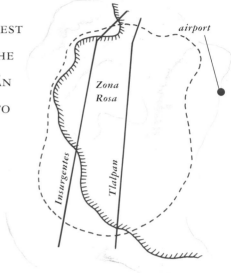

MEXICO CITY IS ONE OF THE LARGEST AND OLDEST SETTLEMENTS IN THE AMERICAS. ORIGINALLY THE SITE OF THE GREAT AZTEC CAPITAL OF TÉNOCHTITLAN, WHEN HERNÁN CORTÉS LED THE SPANISH CONQUISTADORS INTO TÉNOCHTITLAN IN 1519, HE DECLARED THAT HE HAD NEVER SET EYES ON ANYTHING SO SPLENDID.

The Aztecs had built their capital on islands in the midst of Lake Texcoco which were joined to the shore by impressive causeways. Within five years, the Spaniards had overthrown the Aztec Empire, reduced all its 'pagan' public buildings to rubble, and started to build Mexico City, their own Christian capital, upon the ruins. It quickly became a flourishing city but soon the islands began to restrict expansion. In the demand for building space, the waters that surrounded the island were filled with rubble, rocks and soil. Lake Texcoco was drained and buildings were constructed on the weak sands and clays of its floor. Mexico City was then free to grow and soon attracted a huge, densely-packed population.

This brief summary of the city's history helps to explain why the 1985 earthquake caused much more damage in Mexico City than at its epicentre, 380km (236 miles) away in the province of

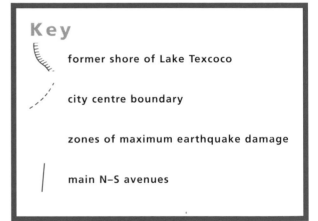

Key

〰️   **former shore of Lake Texcoco**

- - -   **city centre boundary**

| **zones of maximum earthquake damage**

| **main N–S avenues**

Michoacán. The rocks of Michoacán were volcanic and solid and withstood the ground movement well. The weak infilling and lake-floor sediments

Many buildings in Mexico City were reduced to rubble by the earthquake that reached 8.1 on the Richter scale. Few people survived in buildings that were as badly damaged as this one

In the aftermath of the earthquake debris littered the streets

beneath Mexico City increased the effects of the seismic waves: foundations shook far more violently. Liquefaction was common.

At 07.18 on 19 September 1985, the Cocos Plate on the floor of the Pacific Ocean pushed further into its subduction zone under Mexico, unleashing an earthquake of magnitude 8.1. The seismic waves reverberated throughout the world and reached Mexico City within 1 min. Many people were getting up, or were already on their way to work, and there were no warning foreshocks. The earthquake waves threw down buildings, burying and killing thousands under the masonry. Many old, 1–2 storey buildings managed to remain upright. Larger, more modern buildings collapsed like packs of cards. This was especially common in some of the more recently-constructed public buildings such as blocks of flats, hotels and hospitals. The fashionable Zona Rosa area, in the centre of town, was particularly badly affected.

The combination of poor construction and an unconsolidated substratum once again proved lethal. It was calculated that 412 major buildings had collapsed and that a further 3,124 were very badly damaged. Controversy has raged over the number of people killed in the disaster. Official figures suggest that at least 9,500 people died, but according to unconfirmed reports, the death-toll could have been as high as 35,000. About 30,000 people were injured and over 100,000 were left homeless. Damage occurred over an area of nearly 1 million km^2 (386 square miles), and the earthquake was felt by 20 million people.

Still standing, but badly damaged, this apartment block was one of many left unfit for habitation by the earthquake

INTERVIEW
MEXICO, 1985

Elizabeth, Cielo and Roberto Marquez

On 19 September 1985 Cielo Marquez was on her way to work. At 07.19 she felt the earthquake that shook the city but it was only later that she became aware of its strength.

 'I could hear the radio in the bus station and it said that buildings were destroyed in the Zona Rosa and Colonia Roma areas. The most affected area was the Juarez complex where we used to live, so I immediately went back but it took me four hours to reach the place. They were cordoning off the area to stop people going back into the danger zones, but when I saw the collapsed buildings I thought the worst, that my family was already dead.'

Cielo was soon joined by other members of her family, her brother and sister, and they looked on appalled at the tangle of metal and glass that confronted them.

'The building where we used to live twisted and leaned to the side and the upper floors were sandwiched together ... But the rest of the buildings collapsed into dust, all of them were totally destroyed, you could smell gas, hear screams ...'

Cielo's parents and her children were all inside the apartment. The earthquake caught her daughter, Elizabeth, completely by surprise.

 'Suddenly I felt the ground moving ... We ... tried to open the door and it slammed shut by itself and it opened again and at that moment we felt the building shake and the structure sank ... my sister and I jumped under the table and the walls fell down. The building remained standing but inside the apartment the walls and ceiling fell down and the floor cracked. The building split and suddenly there was this noise like an explosion. The windows blew out and at that moment the building came away from the pavement.'

Like the building above, the General Hospital was badly affected by the earthquake.

The members of the Marquez family were injured by the flying debris, their eyes were irritated by the dust, there was a terrible smell of gas, and they were all in shock.

'We were afraid of not being rescued and that another earthquake would happen ... There were 14 floors and we were on the ground floor and with all that weight on us we believed ... we would be crushed and would die here.'

Elizabeth's brother Roberto was also in the apartment.

 'I was sleeping when the earthquake happened. My sister ... pulled me by the hair and she said "There is an earthquake, wake up", and she pulled me under the bed because the ceiling started to fall down ... The structure of the building shook and sank ... Thankfully the building didn't collapse and

Miraculously, live babies were still being rescued from the wreckage several days later

there were some holes which protected us from the collapsed upper floors.'

Already a large number of people had arrived at the scene to begin pulling people from the rubble. The priority for the Marquez family was now to make themselves heard.

Unstable debris and weakened buildings made rescues particularly dangerous

 'There was very little oxygen because of the gas and we didn't have much space inside. My sisters couldn't shout really loud, [our] parrot was the one who started screaming really loud, asking for help, "Mama, mama, take me out of here. Help, help". It was thanks to the parrot that we were rescued and those were words the parrot had never said before.'

Elizabeth says that the parrot must have been mimicking their cries for help. She adds:

 'There was even a moment when the parrot's screams hurt our ears so we told him to shut up but at the same time we wanted him to continue screaming because we couldn't do it ... When [the rescuers] got close to the parrot, they discovered that we were there as well.'

It was about eight hours before the Marquez family were finally rescued. Although physically they escaped relatively unscathed, the psychological wounds inflicted by their ordeal have taken longer to heal.

 'Every time there's an earthquake we get really ill, we get really nervous, we feel despair and believe the building will collapse at any minute. But we have got through it. Thanks to our effort and some other help we have got over this.'

volcanic earthquakes

EARTHQUAKES THAT OCCUR ON OR AROUND VOLCANOES CAN ACT AS WARNING SIGNS OF IMPENDING ERUPTIONS. THEY CAN ALSO HAVE DEVASTATING CONSEQUENCES, OR MAY EVEN BE FALSE ALARMS. HERE ARE FOUR VERY DIFFERENT STORIES.

Iceland

Time: Sunday morning, 7 April 1727. Place: Sandfell Church, at the foot of Öraefajökull volcano in south-east Iceland. Rev. Jón Thorláksson has just started his sermon. Suddenly, the building begins to rock and the congregation stops listening. An old man rushes out of the church, throws himself to the ground, and starts to listen. People laugh nervously at his peculiar behaviour. The old man hurries back to the minister, shouting 'Be on your guard, sir. The Earth is on fire!' Then a second earthquake threatens to cause the church to collapse on top of them. Rev. Thorláksson abandons the service and they all hurry home. The earthquakes are already making the shimmering ice-cap heave up and down on the crest of Öraefajökull. That afternoon, the shocks become more violent, overturning furniture and throwing loose utensils and ornaments to the ground in every house in every hamlet at the foot of the volcano. The ground begins to rumble. At 09.00 on Monday 8 August, Öraefajökull erupts for the first time since 1362, showering the district with ash, blacking out the daylight for three days, and flooding the villages with water melted from the ice-cap. The earthquakes had acted as a warning system but unfortunately people were not aware of the signs.

Volcanic earthquakes shook Pompeii during the eruption of Vesuvius

Such warnings are common. The magma has a consistency something like molten glass. It rises into the volcano, invading the chimney and neighbouring cracks in the rock. As it moves upwards, each surge causes displacements of the solid rock, thereby generating earthquakes. These are shallow, usually less than magnitude 5.0; their effects are usually limited to within 25km (15½ miles) of the volcano. Only rarely do they reach destructive intensities.

Vesuvius

Volcanic earthquakes also continue during violent eruptions, not just because of rising magma, but also because gases explode from it and cause the ground to shake. During the climax of the eruption of Vesuvius in AD 79, Pliny the Younger described the effects of the earthquakes at home in Misenum, 32km (20 miles) from the volcano. 'The buildings around were already tottering and we would have been in danger in our confined space if our house had collapsed.'

He and his mother climbed to the safety of the hill above Misenum. The earthquakes continued. 'The carriages we had ordered began to lurch to and fro although the ground was flat, and we could not keep them still, even when we wedged their wheels with stones.' Both Pliny and his mother survived.

Mount St Helens

There are times, too, when volcanic earthquakes can have even more disastrous consequences. Rising magma caused Mount St Helens to tremble for a week before its first eruption on 27 March 1980. Then there were far more earthquakes than eruptions during the following 52 days. Meanwhile the rising magma had caused the north flank of the cone to swell out by over 150m (492ft), so that it became unstable.

The magnitude 5.1 earthquake that took place at 08.32 on 18 May 1980 was unusually large. It shook loose the top of the north flank of Mount St Helens. Half the summit swept down the side of the volcano in a huge landslide. The magma was then exposed and, in a matter of seconds, it exploded outwards and upwards in one of the largest recorded eruptions in North America.

This great eruption was inevitable, but the earthquake had brought it forward by several days and had perhaps increased its violence by wrecking the summit of the volcano. Thus Mount St Helens showed that earthquakes and eruptions are not only related, they can also be inter-related: earthquakes could warn of eruptions and – sometimes at least – provoke them.

The Old Roman Market, Pozzuoli. Originally thought to be a temple dedicated to the Egyptian goddess Serapis, because of an inscription found there, it is often incorrectly called the 'Temple of Serapis'

Pozzuoli

Unfortunately, the pattern is not invariably simple and direct, otherwise predicting eruptions would be much easier. There are false alarms, and sometimes no alarms at all. One example is the entrance to the Underworld of the Ancient Romans, the area around Pozzuoli, west of Naples, in the Phlegraean, or 'Burning' Fields. It is pock-marked with old volcanoes but only La Solfatara is still fuming sulphurous smoke and steam. However, the ancient Roman gods Pluto and Vulcan have not been entirely idle, because upsurging magma has shaken the ground, and made the land swell up, and then subside again, four times in the past 3,000 years. Only once has the magma erupted onto the landsurface – for a single week in 1538. The first changes in ground level were registered on the columns of the Old Roman Market, incorrectly called the 'Temple of Serapis' (see caption above). No sooner had it been built in about 100 BC than the land started to sink, sea-water soon flooded in, and a new pavement had to be built 2m (6½ft) higher than the previous one. After the Roman Empire fell, the market was abandoned, but the land continued to subside.

Stone-boring molluscs began to eat into the columns and the holes they made show that the building had sunk at least 5.8m (19ft) by about AD 1000.

Then, sometime before 1500, the land began to jerk upwards again in a series of earthquakes that were caused by rising magma. The land probably rose by as much as 8m (26ft) at Pozzuoli in the 50 years before 1538. The ruined 'Temple of Serapis' was on dry land again. But all the houses in the district were being shaken to their very foundations. The earthquakes reached a climax in the area on 27 and 28 September 1538. At 18.00 on 28 September the land at Pozzuoli suddenly rose by about 5m (16½ft) and exposed a band of sea-floor, 350m (1,150ft) wide, that was covered with stranded fish. The accompanying shocks had ruined practically every building in Pozzuoli. At 20.00 on Sunday 29 September, the ground cracked open at the village of Tripergole, 4.5km (2¾ miles) west of Pozzuoli and molten rock exploded out. The terrified citizens fled to Naples. When the eruption ended a week later, on Sunday 6 October 1538, one eyewitness, Francesco Marchesino, claimed that 'there were

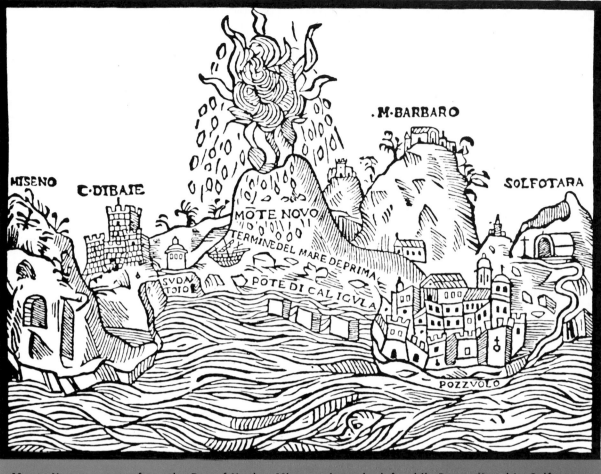

Monte Nuovo as seen from the Bay of Naples. Misenum is to the left while Pozzuoli and La Sulfatara are to the right

not ten houses still intact, most were crushed or ruined... hardly one stone remained standing above another ... and half the Cathedral had collapsed.' The earthquakes had done most of this damage. The eruption had merely coated the empty ruins of Pozzuoli in ash. It had also completely buried Tripergole beneath a cone 130m (426ft) high that they christened Monte Nuovo.

Southern Italy was in Spanish hands at the time. Luckily the Viceroy, Pedro de Toledo, was a passionate builder and he soon restored Pozzuoli. In the following centuries the land subsided again, but generally without intensely damaging earthquakes. Monte Nuovo fell silent.

Then, in 1969, the earthquakes started again at Pozzuoli, cracking masonry and terrifying its citizens. Little by little the city jerked upwards by about 1.7m (5½ft) as magma rose towards the surface. But, just as suddenly, the earthquakes stopped and the land began to subside again. There was no eruption.

But the crisis was not over for long. In August 1982, the earthquakes began again and the land started to rise. The centre of the swelling was at the harbour in the very heart of Pozzuoli. The people were even more terrified and the buildings even more damaged than before. The shocks continued for more than two years and over 500 were recorded on 1 April 1984. At that time 40,000 people had been evacuated from the city centre and panic was widespread. Then, once again, the earthquakes stopped, as if the magma had halted. There was no eruption. But the harbour quaysides had been carried too high to be used by the local boats and another set of quays had to be built in front of them and 2m (6½ft) lower.

chapter**3**

VOLCANOES

volcanic eruptions

VOLCANIC ERUPTIONS CAN BE SPECTACULAR AS THE PHOTOGRAPHS IN THIS BOOK ILLUSRATE ONLY TOO CLEARLY. CONSEQUENTLY MOST PEOPLE HAVE HEARD OF VESUVIUS, ETNA AND MOUNT ST HELENS. EARTHQUAKES, ON THE OTHER HAND, ARE FRIGHTENINGLY ANONYMOUS, SUDDEN, DESTRUCTIVE AND DEADLY, AND HAVE NONE OF THE SAVAGE BEAUTY OF THEIR EXPLOSIVE COUNTERPARTS.

It is easy to assume that all volcanoes erupt only sporadically, producing huge lava flows, and billowing clouds of ash. However, volcanic eruptions are far more varied than earthquakes, and volcanoes throw out much more than just molten lava and ash. Eruptions last far longer than earthquakes and often tend to build up to a climax over a period of several months of activity. Volcanoes can, therefore, be watched and studied in detail, and familiarity with their behaviour has produced a worldwide network of devotees.

major volcanic eruptions

Date	Volcano and location	Deaths	Date	Volcano and location	Deaths
1500 BC	Santorini, Greece	unknown	1892	Awu, Indonesia	1,532
AD 79	Vesuvius, Italy	c. 5,000	1902	Soufrière, St Vincent	1,565
1006	Merapi, Indonesia	unknown	1902	Montagne Pelée, Martinique	29,000
1362	Öraefajökull, Iceland	c. 200	1902	Santa María, Guatemala	7,000
1586	Kelut, Indonesia	10,000	1906	Vesuvius, Italy	200
1631	Vesuvius, Italy	4,000	1911	Taal, Philippines	1,335
1638	Raung, Indonesia	1,000	1919	Kelut, Indonesia	5,110
1669	Etna, Sicily	0	1929	Santiaguito (Santa María)	5,000
1672	Merapi, Indonesia	3,000		Guatemala	
1711	Awu, Indonesia	3,000	1930	Merapi, Indonesia	1,369
1727	Öraefajökull, Iceland	2	1937	Rabaul, Papua New Guinea	505
1730–6	Lanzarote, Canary Islands	0	1943	Parícutin, Mexico	3
1760	Makian, Indonesia	2,000	1951	Mount Lamington,	2,942
1772	Papandajan, Indonesia	2,957		Papua New Guinea	
1783	Laki, Iceland	9,350	1951	Hibok-Hibok, Philippines	500
1783	Asama, Japan	1,377	1953	Ruapehu, New Zealand	151
1792	Unzen, Japan	14,524	1963	Agung, Indonesia	983
1794	Vesuvius, Italy	18	1966	Kelut, Indonesia	212
1812	Awu, Indonesia	963	1968	Arenal, Costa Rica	78
1814	Mayon, Philippines	1,200	1979	Etna, Sicily	9
1815	Tambora, Indonesia	60,000+	1980	Mount St Helens, USA	57
1822	Galunggung, Indonesia	4,011	1981	Semeru, Indonesia	265
1835	Cosegüina, Nicaragua	7	1982	El Chichón, Mexico	2,000+
1843	Etna, Sicily	59	1985	Nevado del Ruiz, Colombia	23,000
1845	Nevado del Ruiz, Colombia	1,000	1986	Lake Nyos, Cameroon	1,742
1856	Awu, Indonesia	2,806	1990	Kelut, Indonesia	35
1877	Cotopaxi, Ecuador	400	1991	Unzen, Japan	43
1883	Krakatau, Indonesia	36,417	1991	Pinatubo, Philippines	1,202
1886	Tarawera, New Zealand	153	1993	Mayon, Phillipines	75
1888	Bandai San, Japan	461	1994	Merapi, Indonesia	61

eruption styles

Here we provide a summary of they way in which volcanic eruptions have been categorized in this book.

A. MILD ERUPTIONS
Hotsprings and pools: usually no lava
Geyser: small extent
Mudpot: short-lived
Fumaroles: fragile
Solfataras: not threatening

B. MODERATE ERUPTIONS
Strombolian eruptions: cinders, ash, lava-flows, cinder cones
Icelandic eruptions: lava-flows and cinder cones on fissures
Deepwater eruptions: pillow lavas
Subglacial eruptions: glacier bursts
Hawaiian eruptions: cinders, ash, lava-flows, huge shields
Basaltic floods: massive lava-flows

C. VIGOROUS ERUPTIONS
Vulcanian eruptions: ash, cinders, blocks, noise, ash cones

Surtseyan eruptions: tuffs, noise, tuff-cones
Steam-blast eruptions: fine fragments, blocks, maars
Volcanic gas eruptions: gas only

D. VIOLENT ERUPTIONS
Ash and pumice floods: ash and pumice, ash-plains
Blasts and debris avalanches: landslides, shattered rock, hummocky land
Peléan eruptions: nuées ardentes, ash, domes
Plinian eruptions: ash, nuées ardentes, pumice, strato-volcanoes
Caldera collapse: ash, pumice, calderas
Stratospheric aerosols: atmospheric cooling, jet problems, sunsets

E. MAJOR SIDE-EFFECTS OF ERUPTIONS
Volcanic mudflows: mud, mud plains
Volcanic tsunamis: large devastating on-shore sea-waves

97

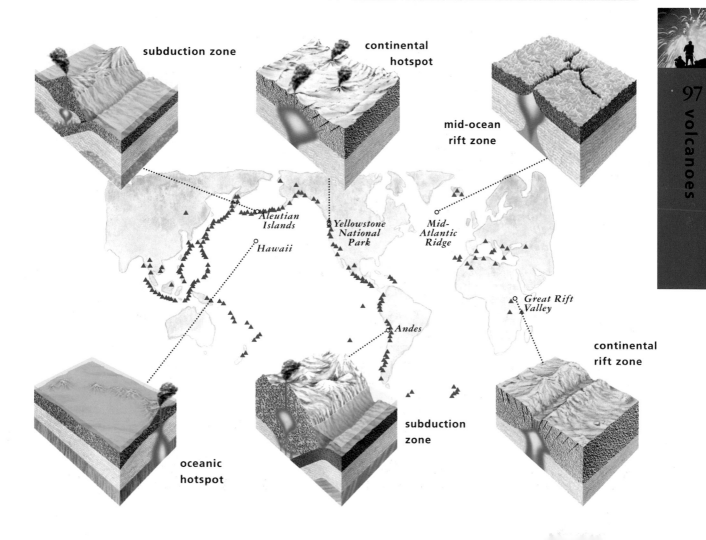

subduction zone

continental hotspot

mid-ocean rift zone

Aleutian Islands

Yellowstone National Park

Mid-Atlantic Ridge

Hawaii

Great Rift Valley

Andes

continental rift zone

oceanic hotspot

subduction zone

what is an eruption?

IN BASIC TERMS A VOLCANO IS A HOLE IN THE EARTH'S CRUST, ON LAND OR ON THE SEA FLOOR, FROM WHICH MATERIALS ARE EXPELLED NATURALLY FROM BELOW. THESE MATERIALS MAY INCLUDE HOT LAVA, COMMONLY IN THE FORM OF FLOWS, CINDERS, BLOCKS, ASH OR PUMICE, COLD ROCK FRAGMENTS OF ALL SIZES, GASES, AEROSOLS, STEAM AND WATER. SOME MATERIALS COOL AND PILE UP AROUND THE HOLE, OR CHIMNEY, AND OFTEN FORM A CONE-SHAPED HILL. OTHER FINE MATERIALS CAN BE BLASTED INTO THE STRATOSPHERE, CARRIED AROUND THE WORLD WITHIN ABOUT 15 DAYS, AND THEN REMAIN AS AEROSOLS THAT VEIL THE SUN FOR SEVERAL YEARS.

Volcanoes, therefore, can eject a variety of different materials, and can erupt in a number of ways. A few of the main reasons for this variation are discussed here.

1. TYPE OF MAGMA

The material that rises to the surface inside the volcano is called magma (see pp.24–25). When the volcano erupts, the magma usually breaks up into lava and gases. The lava either runs across the surface as flows, piles up as domes, or, underwater, oozes out to form pillow-like lumps. Depending on the strength of the explosion, the gases that are released can break the lava into fragments that can be as small as dust. The dust aerosols described above can be responsible for producing cooler weather than normal for a period of several years, and can also produce spectacular, coloured sunsets. The chemical composition of the magma is a fundamental factor in the variability of volcanic eruptions, because it influences the fluidity of the lava, the way in which gases escape from it, and also the degree of shattering of both the magma itself, and the surrounding rock.

The top layer of this slow-moving Hawaiian lava-flow has started to solidify, but the red-heat of the lava is visible around the edges, where it is setting fire to vegetation as it

Basic magma

Basic magma, with less than about 55 per cent silica, is hot – about 1200°C – and fluid enough to flow easily. Gases can usually escape without causing huge explosions. The molten lava flows out, often in great fountains, and then forms long flows before it solidifies. Greater concentrations of gas tear the molten lava into clots and droplets that solidify into smaller particles. These volcanic fragments pile up in layers around the volcanic chimney and build a cone about 100–200m (328–656ft) high.

Silicic magma

Silicic magma behaves differently. It contains between 55 per cent and 70 per cent silica, its temperature is commonly between 700 and 900°C, and it

which solidifies as pumice that can float across oceans. Coarser ash and pumice, and the occasional lava-flow, accumulate in large cones such as Vesuvius or Mount St Helens. As the eruption ends, the remaining viscous lava often oozes out of the volcanic chimney and piles up in a dome above it. This dome then becomes the first victim of the violent explosions of the next eruption. These violent eruptions of silicic magma are concentrated in the subduction zones (see pp.22–25), and the calmer, more effusive eruptions of basic magma are characteristic of other plate edges and many hotspots such as the Hawaiian chain of volcanic islands (see pp.114–115).

moves along the ground. Solidified flows can be seen towards the back of the photograph

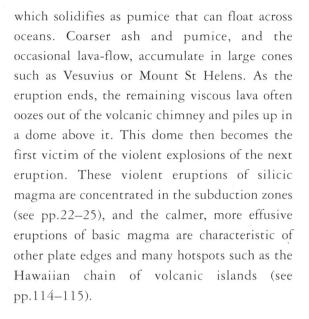

2. WATER

A second agent of variability in volcanic eruptions is their relation to the depth and quantity of water surrounding them. The pressure of deep water stifles explosions, but shallow water greatly intensifies the vigour of an eruption. Each upsurge of red-hot magma suddenly changes the cold water into steam and explosions shatter the magma into fine ash. These are called Surtseyan eruptions. On land, stream waters or ice meltwater can filter down to meet a rising hot magma. This meeting in a confined space produces a few vigorous explosions before the water supply is exhausted. These eruptions are called steam-blast, or 'phreatic' from the Greek word *phreatos* meaning 'well', and are amongst the shortest-lived of all eruptions. Longer-lasting eruptions occur when the downward-percolating water reaches rocks heated by red-hot magma below. This generates convectional water circulation below ground and causes geysers and mud-volcanoes to erupt at regular intervals.

is viscous. As the magma approaches the surface, gases can only escape from their bubbles by causing vast explosions. Hence the lava may be shattered into dust or fine ash that can mix with escaping sulphur dioxide, for example, to form aerosols that can travel around the world. Other lavas can be changed into froth like a meringue,

Mauna Loa, Hawaii

Krakatau, Indonesia

Etna, Sicily

Vesuvius, Italy

3. SUPPLY OF MAGMA

Another general factor is the supply of the magma. At the mid-ocean ridges it is practically continuous and so are the eruptions. Almost everywhere else on Earth, the magma only surges upwards from time to time, and, even then, much of it solidifies in the crust before it can erupt onto the surface. Stromboli has probably erupted at least a dozen times nearly every day for the past 2,500 years. Some volcanoes, like Sakurajima in Japan, Izalco in El Salvador and the north-east crater of Etna, have erupted frequently for several decades this century. They, too, are exceptional. Most volcanoes only erupt for brief and irregular periods, separated by long interludes of silence, and may be dormant for most of their active lives. Many smaller volcanoes are active only briefly, with magma rising intermittently for less than a decade before it stops, or finds a better path to the surface elsewhere. Thus, many of the cones in the Chain of Puys in central France were probably active for only a few years before they fell silent. However, it is never safe to assume that any volcano is dormant or extinct; several apparently extinct volcanoes, including Bezymianny in Kamchatka, Pinatubo in the Philippines, and El Chichón in Mexico, have erupted with some force since 1956 alone.

4. SIDE EFFECTS

A final feature that makes volcanic eruptions so variable is their side effects which can sometimes be more life-threatening than the eruptions themselves. Eruptions near the sea sometimes unleash great tsunamis. These were the major cause of death following the eruption of Krakatau in 1883. Eruptions can also cause ice to melt on the crests of volcanoes and generate mudflows, such as the one from Armero, Colombia, in 1985, that killed 23,000 people. In Iceland, meltwater produced by sub-glacial eruptions can match the discharge of the River Amazon. Luckily, floods such as this occur in sparsely-populated areas. Lakes on the summits of volcanoes can also cause mudflows. The lake in the crater of Kelut, Indonesia, produced three devastating mudflows since 1586 before efforts were made to drain it. Many volcanoes also develop secondary mudflows. Pinatubo provides the best recent example. The 1991 eruption blanketed the slopes of Mt Pinatubo in the Philippines with fine ash, and killed the tropical vegetation that bound the soil together. Now, every year, the rainy season storms generate mudflows on its flanks that have so far killed almost as many people as the main eruption itself. Famine is another major secondary effect of eruptions. Volcanic ash and gas kill crops and animals, and aid may not arrive in time to prevent famine. After Tambora erupted in 1815, 60,000 or more people are said to have died in the resulting famine.

volcanic materials

Type	% Silica content by weight	Typical temperature on emission	Typical forms	Comments
Basalt	50	1200°C	Ocean floors, flows, cinder cones	Fluid. By far the most common volcanic rock
Andesite	60	1000°C	Flows, cinder cones, domes	Fairly fluid; subduction zones (e.g. Andes)
Dacite	60-65	800°C–900°C	Ash, pumice, domes	Viscous; subduction zones
Rhyolite	70+	700°C–800°C	Ash, pumice, domes	Very viscous; volcanic glass (Obsidian) is often rhyolitic Rare
Trachyte	65	1000°C	Flows, domes, ash, pumice	Viscous; rich in sodium and potassium
Phonolite	55–60	1000°C	Pumice, flows, domes, ash	Viscous; rich in sodium and potassium

volcanic flows

	Origin	Danger level	Av. speed + temperature
Lava-flows	Basaltic and Andesitic effusions	Not lethal	Soon slow to 500m (1,640ft) a day or less
Mud flows	Secondary features: ice meltwater or lake water + loose surface soil and rock	Lethal	30–50km/h (18½–31mph); usually cold
Glacier burst	Ice and ice meltwater + loose glacial materials first accumulating under ice-cap	Lethal	50km/h (31mph); vast discharge. Cold
Nuée ardente	Ash, pumice, gas, lava fragments in ground hugging mass and aerosols	Extremely lethal	500km/h (311mph); hot: 500°C

airborne volcanic fragments

Type	Size	Comments
Dust	0.5mm	Impalpable, often like flour
Ash	0.5–2mm	Sand-like, often called sand in older descriptions
Lapilli	2–64mm (¹/₁₂–2½in)	Rough, rounded nut-sized (from the Italian meaning 'little stones')
Cinders	6.4–30cm (2½–12in)	Very rough chunks, like clinker
Blocks	0.5–1m+ (20–40in+)	Angular, like masonry. Often old material blown from a volcano
Bomb	0.5–1m+ (20–40in+)	Twirled and rounded often almond-shaped.
Pumice	1–10cm+ (½–4in+)	Solidified 'foam' of silicic magma. Floats on water
Tuff	2–64mm (¹/₁₂–2½in)	Yellowish fragments shattered by magma-water interaction. Thin beds

eruption styles

VOLCANOES ERUPT IN SO MANY DIFFERENT WAYS, AND EJECT SUCH A VARIETY OF MATERIALS, THAT IT SEEMS IMPOSSIBLE TO GROUP THEIR ACTIVITY INTO PARTICULAR STYLES. IT IS, HOWEVER, AN EXERCISE THAT EARTH SCIENTISTS HAVE PRACTISED FOR A LONG TIME. AT THE TURN OF THE CENTURY, FOR INSTANCE, THE GREAT FRENCH VOLCANOLOGIST, LACROIX, DESCRIBED FOUR MAIN ERUPTION STYLES: HAWAIIAN, STROMBOLIAN, VULCANIAN AND PELÉAN, AFTER THE BEST-KNOWN VOLCANOES TYPICAL OF EACH GROUP.

Scientists soon realized that there were types of eruption that did not easily fit into these groups, and many more were subsequently described. At present, more than 12 different styles are commonly distinguished, and even these groups are not exclusive. Here we will place eruption styles into four broad groups: mild, moderate, vigorous and violent. Each group contains smaller sub-groups, depending, for example, on what is expelled from the volcano, or whether the eruption takes place on land or underwater.

Mild eruptions

On land, mild eruptions are limited to emissions of gas, steam, hot water, sulphurous fumes and bubbling mud from geysers, hissing holes and fissures. They are the glory of Yellowstone Park in Wyoming, United States, central Iceland and the North Island of New Zealand. They are also common on dormant or dying volcanoes that have had a much more violent past, such as Lassen Peak in California and Teide in Tenerife.

Such activity is termed hydrothermal, and heated water is one of its basic components. The water comes from the rain and melting snows and percolates down into the crust. In many volcanic areas, magma still lies in relatively shallow masses long after violent eruptions have ceased. The rocks above it remain hot and they heat the water that filters into them to temperatures of over 200°C without boiling. In the simplest case, this now less dense water returns to the surface and forms hot-water pools.

Probably more often, steam bubbles and hisses continuously from the rising water and forms more typical hot springs such as those at Furnas in São Miguel in the

ABOVE Organ terraces at Mammoth Hot Springs, Yellowstone National Park, formed when hot waters stream downslope.
BELOW Mud-pots at Yellowstone

ABOVE Steam from La Solfatara (named after the Italian word for sulphur), near Pozzuoli, Italy
BELOW Yellowstone's world-famous geyser, Old Faithful

Azores, or in Bumpas Hell on Lassen Peak, California. Towns in several countries have tapped these hot waters for heating and power, including Larderello in Italy, Chaudes-Aigues in France and Reykjavík and Hveragerdi in Iceland.

In some cases steam from the percolated water mixes with sulphurous fumes produced by the magma. These fumes are called solfataras and fumaroles, names derived from the Italian. The Ancient Romans believed their Underworld lay below the volcano known as La Solfatara, near Pozzuoli. The poet Virgil compared these wispy fumes to ghosts; 'bodiless, airy, flitting behind an empty figment of a form'. Steam and fume emissions are common on many dormant or declining volcanoes, where holes hissing with escaping hydrogen sulphide or sulphur dioxide are surrounded by halos of yellow sulphur crystals.

If the hot water cannot circulate freely underground, or rise to the surface easily, then two things may happen: the water only gushes out intermittently and/or it becomes contaminated and muddy. The restricted circulation means that, as the water becomes hotter, the steam is placed under great pressure and forces the water to spurt out onto the surface in a geyser. These fountains can reach as much as 20m (65½ft) high and last for over 5 mins. The interval between eruptions varies from geyser to geyser. Old Faithful in Yellowstone Park now erupts about once every 67 mins, and its timetable is posted daily for visitors, but Beehive nearby only erupts about once a year.

The hot waters often dissolve various chemicals as they circulate through the rocks. They then precipitate them again on the surface, where they can form cowls or cones around the fissure. Where the hot waters stream downslope they form magnificent organ-pipe terraces such as Mammoth Springs in Yellowstone Park.

Where the water lingers longer underground and the rocks are easily weathered or dissolved, boiling, bubbling mud erupts at the surface in mud-pots that sometimes reach 20m (65½ft) across. A mud-pot on Vulcano in the Aeolian Islands is reputed to cure rheumatism.

Many of these mild eruptions are products of fragile systems that can be disrupted by earth-tremors, changes in rainfall patterns or human intervention, for example. As a result their activity is often short-lived. The Great Geyser in Iceland has been active for 8,000 years. Now, however, it has to be stimulated into action using soap-powder.

During Icelandic eruptions, lava erupts along fissures or cracks in the Earth's crust, producing red-hot fountains that can reach 100m (328ft) in height

Moderate eruptions

Moderate eruptions expel lava and some gases. The lava is nearly always of the basic, basaltic kind that emerges in a hot, fluid form from the chimney, and streams away in lava-flows. At the same time, moderate gas explosions can also shatter some of the basalts into clots and droplets that solidify into cinders and ash that pile up in cones around the crater hole. Columns of gas and ash might also rise about 2km (1¼ miles) above the crater. The eruptions often happen on fissures that can be anything from 5–50km (3–31 miles) long. Away from the chimney, however, they are rarely dangerous because flowing lava predominates over the explosions. Nevertheless, 'moderate' does not necessarily mean small, because such eruptions are by far the most common form of volcanic activity, and have piled up some of the largest lava accumulations on the planet. Strombolian eruptions are the most common in the moderate group. The two main variants are Icelandic eruptions which extend along fissures, and Hawaiian activity which is concentrated on a central hub. Basaltic flood eruptions are an extreme case brought about when vast volumes of lava are expelled. Eruptions in deep water and under ice-caps are other special cases.

Etna in Sicily erupts its lavas, on average, at rates of 25m³ (883ft³) per second, forming flows reaching 7.5km (4½ miles) long and 12m (39½ft) thick

Hawaiian eruptions are characterized by slow-moving, wide-spreading lava-flows. These lava-flows build up into huge, shield-like volcanoes

Stromboli

STROMBOLI BEGAN LIFE ABOUT 1 MILLION YEARS AGO, 2,000M (6,560FT) DOWN ON THE SEABED NORTH OF SICILY IN THE MEDITERRANEAN. CONSTANT MODERATE ACTIVITY HAS PRODUCED A VOLCANIC ISLAND THAT NOW RISES 926M (3038FT) ABOVE SEA-LEVEL. THREE, AND SOMETIMES AS MANY AS SIX, CRATERS ERUPT APPROXIMATELY EVERY 20 MINS, AS THEY HAVE USUALLY DONE FOR THE PAST 2,500 YEARS.

lapilli and cinders

thin, windblown ash layers

lava-flows

A Strombolian eruption

The first warning of an impending eruption is a low, shuddering rumble. A red glow then brightens in the necks of the craters. The chimneys begin to hiss like old steam engines, rumble like thunder, or explode like shells. Soon the gases explode and shatter the molten lava into red and orange clots and droplets that curl about 200m (656ft) into the air. Gas and steam swirl around them. The fragments then fall back and cool on the cones they are forming around the craters. Meanwhile, the wind scatters fine ash and sulphurous steam. These explosions continue for perhaps 5 mins until the craters can manage no more than a dull groan. The red-hot molten fragments settle on the cones and the colour gradually fades as the embers cool. Then there is silence until the whole process begins again.

Occasionally the molten lava pours out in continuous streams on the Sciara del Fuoco (the 'Scar of Fire') on the northern flank of the volcano below the craters. But the steep slope causes the lavas to cascade and shatter as they career down the Sciara and head straight into the sea.

Sometimes Stromboli remains quiet for a day or two. On most volcanoes such periods of repose represent a good time to visit the crater. But not on Stromboli. The rest period only means that the volcano is preparing a more vigorous eruption which is usually unleashed without warning.

Strombolian eruptions

Strombolian eruptions epitomise moderate activity and Stromboli, appropriately enough, is the best place to see them. However, although the eruptions on Stromboli are typical of the style, they have not produced a typical Strombolian volcano. Stromboli has grown far too big for that, because it has been erupting for at least 2,500 years. In fact, elsewhere, most Strombolian eruptions only last for a year or two at most before they become extinct. Usually, there is never time for them to build up cinder cones more than 250m (820ft) high, or send out lava-flows over 10km (6¼ miles) long. The cones have a shallow, bowl-shaped crater directly above the chimney,

key features

Strombolian eruptions are characterized by:
- constant, but usually short lived, moderate activity
- cinder cones with a shallow, bowl-shaped crater
- dust and ash
- lava-flows; Initially fast-moving, soon slow down

Strombolian eruptions are usually short-lived. The prolonged activity exhibited by Stromboli itself is exceptional and has produced a strato-volcano that rises 3,000m (9,840ft) from the sea floor

which stays open during the eruption, but is plugged with solidified lava when it stops. Sometimes lava gushes out from one side of the chimney so fast that it carries away all the fragments that have fallen on it. In this case, the cinders never pile up in that sector and the cone is 'breached' and forms a crescent in plan rather than a perfect circle. The main problem caused by the fragments is that the wind sends the dust and ash swirling for as much as 5km (3 miles) from the volcano. The lava-flows are more dangerous at first, because the molten basalt at temperatures between 1000 and 1200°C can travel at up to 50km/h (31mph). Fortunately this does not continue for long as edges of the flow soon solidify until it resembles a red-hot molten river that moves forward between solid lava walls. In some cases, the surface solidifies too, but the molten lava continues to press forward within a tube of lava that also feeds the advancing snout of the flow. In either case the flows travel forward fastest immediately after they are erupted and soon slow down to walking pace. As a result, lava-flows often reach three-quarters of their ultimate length after only a

quarter of the eruption period has elapsed.

Thus, Strombolian eruptions are only potentially dangerous for those within about 1km (⅔ mile) of the chimney. In fact, they rarely kill anybody except by odd quirks of fate. In 1843, the people of Bronte, Sicily, were watching a flow approaching their town from a Strombolian eruption on the western flank of Etna. The hot lava tongue encroached upon a marshy field and the heat suddenly converted the water to steam that exploded from the confined space under the flow. Molten clots of lava showered onto the startled spectators, killing 59 people. Three people were killed whilst Parícutin was erupting in Mexico between 1943 and 1952. They were struck by lightning generated in the column of ash and gas rising above the volcano.

Strombolian cones and lava-flows are the most common volcanic forms on land in the world. There are, for instance, over 75 in the Chain of Puys in central France; over 200 decorate the flanks of Etna; and over 1,000 Strombolian cones are scattered around Parícutin in Mexico.

the eruption of Etna

11 March 1669

THE FAMOUS ERUPTION ON THE SOUTHERN FLANKS OF ETNA IN 1669 SHOWS THE LIMITS OF
WHAT STROMBOLIAN ERUPTIONS CAN ACHIEVE. IT BEGAN AT NICOLOSI, 2,000M (6,560FT)
AND 14KM (8¾ MILES) BELOW THE SUMMIT OF ETNA. IN EARLY MARCH 1669, THE EARTH
BEGAN TO QUAKE WITH INCREASING VIOLENCE. ON 11 MARCH A FISSURE 12KM (7½ MILES)
LONG RIPPED OPEN ON THE FLANKS OF ETNA AND REVEALED A WOUND LIVID WITH MOLTEN
LAVA. THE VILLAGERS LEFT EVERYTHING AND FLED.

That evening exploding gas began to throw ash and cinders into the air 'with a most terrible and vigorous din' (this was the birth of the Monti Rossi cone). Almost at once, a bright orange stream of lava surged out nearby. Within three days it had buried most of Monpilieri, La Guardia, Malpasso, Mascalucia, San Pietro and Camporotondo, whose people had only time to pack up their valuables before they left. By this time, however, the flow was slowing down markedly so that the snout was advancing at no more than 100m (328ft) an hour, but the tongue was already 6km (3¾ miles) long by 16 March. By the end of March the flow stretched 10km (6¼ miles) from Nicolosi and was strong enough to shift aside fields of both wheat and vines. In early April, the snout of the flow was poised outside the walls of Catania and 13km (8 miles) from its source. On 14 April, the lavas wrapped around the western city wall and turned south-eastwards towards the Ursino Castle. The following day the lava pushed down a sector of the western wall – and halted for Easter week. On 23 April, the Tuesday after Easter, the lava

The origin of Etna's activity is something of a mystery: it lies neither on a subduction zone nor on a large crustal fissure. Instead it seems to be located on an intersection of secondary fractures produced by the collision of the African and Eurasian Plates

This painting, depicting the lava-flows invading the west side of Catania in 1669, hangs in the Cathedral at Catania. It was painted shortly after the eruption

uninhabitable. It was so thick that trees and crops had burnt, animals were starving, and there was 'great store of a strong sulfureous smoak, wherewith some of our company were at first almost stifled through inadvertency.' The wind was blowing the finest ash to Catania, and 100km (62 miles) away to Calabria; it even reached Zante (Zakynthos) across the Ionian Sea.

Most terrifying of all was the current of molten lava issuing from the foot of Monti Rossi. At night the glow from the lavas was so bright in Catania that 'books and writings printed in the smallest characters could be read with ease.' At times, the lavas surged forward without warning and then stopped again equally quickly. On 8 June lava swamped the ground floor of Ursino Castle, and built a terrace, 1km (⅔ mile) wide, between the fortress and the sea. The final burst came on 26 June when a brilliant red torrent rushed southwards, straight into the sea, for a period of four hours. The Catanians were amazed and mesmerized by the spectacle and thanked their lucky stars, Saint Agatha or any other protector they could invoke, that this lava had not chosen to travel over Catania.

Then, on 11 July 1669 the eruption near Nicolosi stopped. By then, the Monti Rossi formed a cone 250m (820ft) high and the area 3km (1¼ miles) around was blanketed in thick ash a century later. The lava flow formed a great rugged black scar all the way down to Catania. Nearly 1,000m³ (35,300ft³) of lava had erupted and now covered 37.5km² (14½ square miles). About 27,000 people had been made homeless and only 3,000 out of 20,000 citizens were still in Catania. Over a dozen villages were destroyed or badly damaged. Nobody had been killed.

also entered the sea south of the city, causing 'a superb and terrifying spectacle' full of hissing, crashing, black and red-hot rocks.

The lava-flows were now advancing much more slowly than a month before but this time a large city was in the way. On 30 April, the lavas started to spill once again over the western walls. The panic-stricken Catanians turned to their protecting patron, Saint Agatha, whose veil had stopped many lava-flows in the past. This time the veil was presented to the advancing snout in vain, and soon the lavas piled up against the Church of San Nicolo, but were making only slow progress. The citizens had time to remove all their property from their homes. As some English merchants of Messina commented, the citizens 'not only, at good leisure, removed their goods, but the very tiles, and beams, and what else was moveable.' They also took the brass cannons from Ursino Castle and church bells from their steeples; and they barricaded the streets with the masonry from already ruined houses to arrest the flow.

Meanwhile, the explosions of gas cinders and ash were continuing at the Monti Rossi. The swirling ash made Nicolosi completely

Icelandic eruptions

ICELANDIC ERUPTIONS OCCUR WHERE FISSURES IN THE EARTH'S CRUST DOMINATE VOLCANIC ACTIVITY. THE BEST PLACE TO SEE THEM IS ICELAND, WHOSE ERUPTIONS HAVE BUILT UP A SECTION OF THE MID-ATLANTIC RIDGE ABOVE SEA-LEVEL. THE BASALTIC PLATEAUX OF WESTERN ICELAND BELONG TO THE NORTH AMERICAN PLATE AND ARE MOVING TO THE WEST; EASTERN ICELAND BELONGS TO THE EURASIAN PLATE AND IS MOVING TO THE EAST.

Modern activity is centred on the ridge crest, a broad band, 70km (43½ miles) wide and 400km (249 miles) long, that curves diagonally across the country from north-east to south-west. Thousands of fissures spring from the volcanoes dotted along this band, that run at right angles to the direction of plate divergence. They form when the crust cracks in response to the stretching caused by the strains of the separation of the plates. Basaltic magma moves up towards the surface, but most of it fails to reach the open air, and solidifies below ground. The basalt that does reach the surface, erupts along the fissure in fountains reaching 100m (328ft) into the air. After a few days, the eruptions are concentrated in many individual chimneys where they build up cinder cones as the lavas spread outwards. These eruptions are strongest during their early weeks, and become

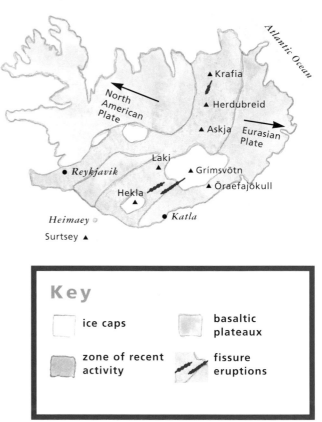

Key

- ice caps
- zone of recent activity
- basaltic plateaux
- fissure eruptions

key features

Icelandic eruptions are characterized by:

- ◆ lava fountains
- ◆ cinder cones on fissures
- ◆ vast lava-flows
- ◆ fine ash
- ◆ sulphur dioxide emissions

less powerful over time. They leave behind rows of 50–100 cinder cones, commonly less than 100m (328ft) high, and vast lava-flows. The magma that solidifies below ground welds the walls of the fissure strongly together. As crustal stretching continues, the basalt-choked fissure resists the pressure and cracks, and eruptions thus occur alongside it. The result is that Icelandic fissures only erupt for one episode and then become extinct. In this way they differ from fissures that produce Strombolian eruptions, which can be active at different points, and at different intervals.

The Laki eruption in Iceland

At 09.00 on Whit Sunday, 8 June 1783, the south-east side of Laki mountain split open. From 8 June until 25 July 1783, the fissure became increasingly wide on the south-western flanks of Laki. Fluid basalt, as hot as 1250°C, spurted 1km (⅔ mile) into the air in swishing fountains, and surged into the River Skaftà gorge. Gas explosions built cone after cone of ash and cinders and hurled ash and dust 12km (7½ miles) into the air. The basalts gushed out at about 5,000m³ (177,000ft³) per second – double the discharge of the Rhine. In a few days they had filled the River Skaftà gorge to the brim and spread out onto the coastal plain. On 11 July, woodcutters working in the gorge had to run for their lives when the molten lava charged down the gorge. The next day, the farmers on the plain had just enough time to drive off their stock, load their valuables onto their carts and flee.

Then, from 25 July until 30 October, the north-eastern flank of Laki burst open. This time lavas gushed into the River Hverfisfljót gorge, filled it, and spread out over the coastal plain.

By the end of October 1783, 90 per cent of the lava had erupted, and activity slowed down and stopped altogether on 7 February 1784. In all, the fissures were then 27km (16¾ miles) long, they had erupted 140 cones and 14.7km³ (3½ cubic miles) of lavas that covered an area of 599km² (231 square miles). Perhaps as many as 21 farming hamlets were swamped.

Although no-one was killed directly as a result of the advancing lava-flows this was to be the worst human disaster in Iceland since it was first settled in AD 875. The fine ash stunted the growth of the summer grazing lands, sulphur dioxide contaminated the rain producing sulphuric acid, and fluorine poisoned the animals. Half the Icelandic stock of cattle, three-quarters of the horses and three-quarters of the sheep, all perished. Fish catches were vastly reduced. The famine spread quickly and caused at least 9,300 of the 10,521 deaths registered in Iceland before the end of 1785: nearly a quarter of the population.

It was called the 'Haze Famine' because it was associated with a mysterious, dry blue fog that spread over Europe and beyond during the summer of 1783. The haze irritated the eyes, reeked of sulphur and persisted through storms and changes of winds. It killed trees and crops in Iceland, and scorched leaves and new growth throughout much of Europe. It also produced huge variations in weather conditions: in July 1883 the weather was cold in Iceland, there was snow in Poland and Russia, but there were high temperatures and mighty thunderstorms in western Europe. In Japan, frost and high rainfall ruined the rice harvest in 1783 causing a terrible famine.

The acid and dust aerosol lingered in the lower stratosphere and reduced the amount of the Sun's heat reaching the Earth's surface for 1–2 years. The winters of 1784, 1785 and 1786 were amongst the coldest of the latter half of the century. Annual temperatures from 1783–86 were probably 1–3°C below average. The winter of 1783–84 ranks as the coldest in Europe and North America during the last 250 years.

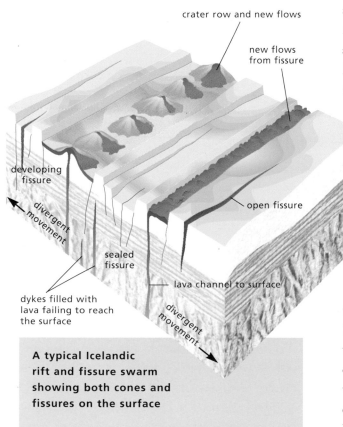

crater row and new flows

new flows from fissure

developing fissure

divergent movement

sealed fissure

open fissure

dykes filled with lava failing to reach the surface

lava channel to surface

divergent movement

A typical Icelandic rift and fissure swarm showing both cones and fissures on the surface

deepwater and sub-glacial eruptions

NOT ALL VOLCANIC ERUPTIONS ARE CHARACTERIZED BY FOUNTAINS OF RED-HOT LAVA. DEEPWATER AND SUB-GLACIAL ERUPTIONS ARE TWO CASES WHERE MAGMA DOES NOT REACH THE LANDSURFACE. THE HEAT THAT IS GENERATED PRODUCES SOME DRAMATIC EFFECTS.

Deepwater eruptions

Deepwater eruptions take place in the sea where the water pressure prevents any explosions. They occur especially along the crests of all mid-ocean ridges and from ocean floors where they are often linked to volcanic seamounts related to hotspots. When the eruptions are more than 100m (328ft) deep, the lavas ooze out, and solidify in piles of pillow-shaped lumps. Gases such as hydrogen sulphide and carbon dioxide bubble up in 'black smokers'. All these eruptions were virtually unknown until the 1960s, but they are the most voluminous in the world, and generate new oceanic crust. Their remote location and the cushion of the water means that we are protected from the power of these eruptions. If they were to take place on land, mid-ocean ridge eruptions would probably adopt the Icelandic style. If they were to occur on emerged seamounts, they would probably follow the Hawaiian style.

Sub-glacial eruptions

Eruptions that occur underneath glaciers also can be almost stifled by thick ice-caps. In Iceland, when Grímsvötn erupts beneath the Vatnajökull ice-cap, the hot basalt melts some of the ice, and the water accumulates until it suddenly bursts from beneath the ice-cap. This is called a 'jökulhlaup' or glacier burst. Sub-glacial eruptions may also form table mountains (see right).

Glacier-burst from Vatnajökull

Vatnajökull, 'the water glacier', the largest ice-cap in Iceland, is aptly named because the eruptions that occur beneath it have generated a succession of brief, but formidable, floods. Grímsvötn is the largest of the volcanic fissure systems in Iceland. At its summit is a huge, ice-filled hollow, probably a volcanic caldera. This is where meltwater accumulates whenever eruptions melt some of the ice, thus forming a lake which eventually lifts up the 500m (1,640ft) of covering ice and makes it float. Within a few days water breaks through the now buoyant ice-barrier. It drains southwards under the ice and cascades out from its edge in an enormous flood of meltwater, ice-blocks, mud, sand and boulders: the glacier bursts.

Water pressure prevents explosions during deepwater eruptions; lava oozes out in pillow-shaped lumps

The latest volcanic eruption beneath Vatnajökull occurred in 1996. At 10.48 on Sunday 29 September, a magnitude 5.0 earthquake shook Vatnajökull. Almost 30 hours of volcanic tremors followed. By the morning of 1 October, lava was erupting from a fissure under the ice. It soon began to melt the ice until several lakes formed across the surface of Vatnajökull. At first the explosions were stifled, but increased lava emissions soon built up a ridge above the fissure, bringing the volcanic chimneys closer to the surface. Explosions were then able to blast fine fragments into the atmosphere. At 05.18 on 2 October, Surtseyan explosions began, firing out block plumes of ash 500m (1,640ft) into the air, while a white column of steam rose into the sky.

About 10km (6¼ miles) to the south, meltwater was pouring into the Grímsvötn hollow. On 4 October, 2km³ (½ cubic mile) of water had accumulated and reached levels 20m (66ft) higher than ever previously recorded. All the authorities could do was dig trenches and raise dykes on the coastal plains to try to concentrate the flow into channels.

On 13 October, the eruption stopped. It had built up a long ridge of tuff and ash, and a Surtseyan cone rising 40m (131ft) above the open-air lake where the main activity had been. The heat from the rocks, however, continued to melt the ice, and meltwater kept accumulating under the ice on the summit of Grímsvötn. On 2 November the water level reached 1,509m (4,950ft) – 60m (197ft) above the level when glacier-bursts were usually unleashed.

Eventually, at about 08.30 on Tuesday 5 November, the River Skeidar clouded with mud and began to smell of sulphur. Suddenly it flooded, its discharge increasing by 100 times in less than two hours. It swept across the coastal plain with a frontal wave, 4m (13ft) high. Ice, rocks, water and mud ripped away 10km (6¼ miles) of the Icelandic coastal ring-road, damaged bridges and tore down electricity and telephone cables. No-one was killed. But the long-delayed onset and unusually quick climax are still a puzzle.

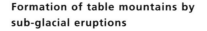

Formation of table mountains by sub-glacial eruptions

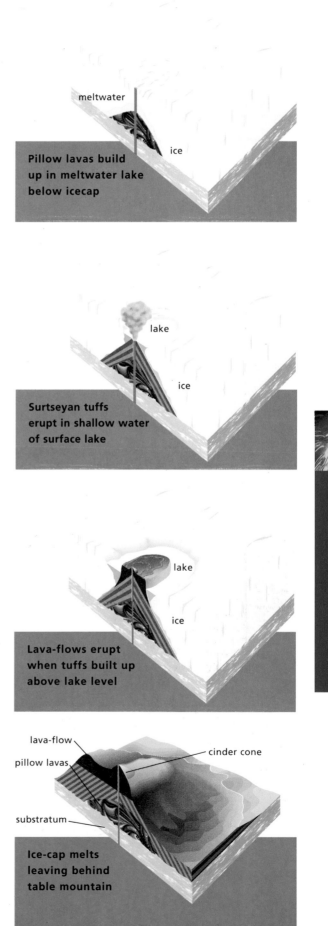

meltwater

ice

Pillow lavas build up in meltwater lake below icecap

lake

ice

Surtseyan tuffs erupt in shallow water of surface lake

lake

ice

Lava-flows erupt when tuffs built up above lake level

lava-flow

pillow lavas

cinder cone

substratum

Ice-cap melts leaving behind table mountain

Hawaiian eruptions

According to Hawaiian mythology the spectacular volcanic activity seen in Hawaii is caused by the fire goddess Pelé, who was chased from her home in Tahiti, and settled in the crater of Kilauea. The scientific explanation may be less poetic but it is certainly no less dramatic.

The volcanic islands of Hawaii are situated over a hotspot in the Pacific Ocean where the Pacific Plate is sliding north-west at a rate of 10cm (4in) per year. The diagram (right) shows how they were formed. Magma rises in a central vent from which thin flows of basalt emerge and spread over a wide area. As the layers accumulate and the volcano grows larger, lava flows may also emerge from vents on either side of the summit, in flank eruptions. The characteristic, broad-based shape of this type of volcano has given them the name 'shield volcanoes'.

Five shields join to make the islands of Hawaii, three of which are still active: Kilauea, Mauna Loa and Hualalai. Mauna Loa is probably the largest active volcano in the world, rising 9km (5½ miles) from the floor of the Pacific Ocean, with a diameter of 100km (62 miles). Another example is Réunion Island in the Indian Ocean, which is composed of two huge shields.

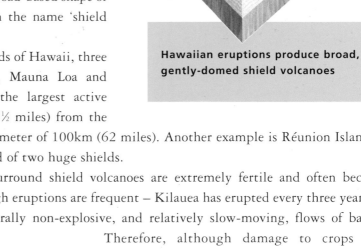

Hawaiian eruptions produce broad, gently-domed shield volcanoes

The weathered lava-flows that surround shield volcanoes are extremely fertile and often become highly populated. In Hawaii, although eruptions are frequent – Kilauea has erupted every three years on average since 1830 – they are generally non-explosive, and relatively slow-moving, flows of basalt.

Therefore, although damage to crops and property can be immense, the number of human lives claimed by eruptions is relatively low; even when fluid lava flows into narrow valleys, people usually have time to pack their bags and leave.

The Piton de la Fournaise in Réunion is also extremely active, erupting once every ten months on average. But in contrast to Hawaii, most of the active craters lie on the barren, sparsely populated, eastern part of the island.

Volcanic activity in this part of the world is continuing with a new Hawaiian island, Loihi, lurking beneath the surface. It will be many centuries, however, before the crest rises above the Pacific: at present eruptions are still taking place 1,000m (3,280ft) below sea-level.

key features

Hawaiian eruptions are characterized by:

◆ frequency
◆ hot, fluid, wide-spreading emissions of basalt
◆ relatively non-explosive nature
◆ destructive but slow-moving lava-flows
◆ shield volcano

The islands of Hawaii are part of a long chain of volcanic islands, known as seamounts, stretching from Siberia. New volcanic islands are now being formed to the south of Hawaii, and in thousands of years, Kilauea (above) will become extinct

INTERVIEW

KALAPANA, HAWAII

Todd and Mary Dressler

Todd and Mary Dressler were living in Kalapana, a small town in the shadow of Kilauea, when a new fissure on the volcano's side began erupting in 1983. On that day they received a phone call from Todd's mother:

'... it was dark, maybe 3 o'clock in the morning ... she asked me to look out of the window ... there was this huge glow in the mountain, like a nuclear glow. And then I realized that there was a major eruption, so all of us got in the car ... we drove all the way around to realize that the eruption was happening really close to us, because we couldn't see it better than in our own back yard.'

The eruption began along a crack in the side of the volcano 6.5km (4 miles) in length, in an area of forest, east of the summit caldera. The Dresslers went to have a closer look at the area.

'We flew up in an airplane with a friend of ours ... and took a look at it and realized where the crack was and it really didn't look that scary ... but as the months went on ... and the mountain then really started erupting, when there were 1,500ft [457m] fountains ... then it started really coming to us, that something serious was going to happen.'

The eruptive phases consisted of lava fountains lasting up to a few days, followed by a period of inactivity, that averaged about a month. Fifty phases were recorded between 1983 and 1986.

' ... the mountain would expand and then it would erupt for like ten days. And they would have these incredible fountains on the mountain that ... were so alluring ... and then the mountain would ... stop. And the lava flow would stop. And it would just come down through the forest and burn lots of forest and maybe catch a few houses, and then it would go away ... And then the mountain would inflate again and then it would do the same thing again, over and over for years.'

The eruptions continued without respite until, ominously, the mountain and the type of lava flow began to change.

The lava-flows at Kalapana spread out over the land and began to run off into the sea.

'... this went on for seven years ... it was many phases of eruption, many different flows came down the mountain, and when Kupaianaha was born ... that is when it finally took everything out, because the volcano had changed into a shield, which meant that there was much volume every day, 500,000 cubic yards [382,300m^3] a day coming into the area ...'

On 1 April 1990 the Dresslers finally began to move out of the house they had lived in for 15 years:

 'And from that moment until April 22, when our house was actually taken down, ... those were the most threatening days of my life. It would come close to the house and then it would subside and stop. But April Fool's Day was the last day my girls were able to be at their home, they went to school never to return.'

In the last few days before their house was engulfed Todd and Mary watched the approach of the lava.

The slow-moving lava-flows produced by Kilauea destroyed everything in their path

 '... it is really interesting because you look down ... and you see all the ants leaving, all the roaches leaving, all the insects leaving and one day the birds aren't there. And ... the explosions [caused by methane gas released by the lava] get closer and closer ... one night I watched my wife get blown 5ft [1.5m] off the ground ... from a methane explosion. Some think we were crazy for hanging out as long as we did but ... you become one with the area for so long you just want to be there till the end.'

Todd made a video of the final moments.

 '... it was devastating, ... each little sparkle and each little crackling, ... watching the house getting gutted took about 35–45 minutes, ... what really kept me sane through that 45 minutes was knowing that ... we can rebuild again and ... that my children were safe and we were safe ... but it was very emotional ... we thought this was where we would always be.'

Here we can see steam produced as the red-hot lava is cooled by the water

INTERVIEW

VOLCANO CHASERS

Steve and Donna O'Meara

Steve and Donna O'Meara are passionate about volcanoes. They live in Hawaii, a group of islands created entirely by volcanic activity, in a village called Volcano. Their second date was on a volcano; they got married on a volcano and they spend their holidays chasing volcanoes.

'... we travel all over the world photographing volcanoes and mainly having fantastic adventures ... the first time I saw an erupting volcano ... it just gives you a sense of awe ... what we do is embrace the fact that we know our lives are short and make the most of every moment ... I'd rather have ten minutes of something wonderful than a lifetime of nothing special'.

Steve had been Donna's astronomy teacher and for their second date it seems that he was determined to make an impression:

'... it was the day before Christmas Eve and Steve called me at my office ... and he said "how would you like to see an erupting volcano?" and I said "sure" ... 18 hours later we were hovering in

a helicopter over Kupaianaha which is a Hawaiian lava lake that was about 700ft [213m] wide and it was churning and bubbling and I was screaming ... I guess that was it, I was hooked, and it was the most incredible experience I ever had in my life.'

'... I never forget my first eruption, it was a large fire fountain ... 1km [²/₃ mile] long, and these fire fountains going up 100 sometimes 200ft [30–60m] high ... it went from sounding like a waterfall – its liquid lava sounded just like a waterfall – but then more gas started coming out than lava and it was breathing, it was choking ... it was inhaling ... and then it could cough and all this molten phlegm would fly out, spat all over the ground, and you're in awe and the sounds echoing off the cold air, all the phlegm would fall back in the throat, the stuff would go flying out, and it would fall back into the throat. Ultimately the volcano made its last gasp and that was it ... it just died ...'

For two people with such a fascination with volcanoes, as well as nature and science in general, it is no surprise that they have settled in

The characteristic shield-shaped profile of Mauna Loa, Hawaii

Lava fountains produced by Stromboli in the Mediterranean are among the most spectacular, and the most regular, on Earth

Hawaii. Hawaiian volcanoes have both a characteristic form and style of eruption.

 '... it is called a shield volcano, so it looks like an overturned saucer. The eruptions are very gentle ... the molten rock is fed almost directly from the centre of the Earth ... [the Pacific Ocean floor is on] a moving plate under which is there is a hotspot [like] a blow-torch, and it blows right through and makes a hole in the plate ... now the plate is moving, it moves off the hotspot and a new blow-torch hole comes up and that's another island ... this continues and you get [a] chain of islands.'

In keeping with their courtship, when Steve and Donna decided to get married, they were both keen for the ceremony to take place on a volcano. After gaining permission from the Hawaii National Park, they flew out to a vent on Kilauea, made an offering of lilies to Pelé, the goddess of the volcano, and exchanged vows.

 'We were married on a lava flow that was about three hours old ...'

 'And then it was covered over so no-one will ever step on it again.'

In spite of their love-affair with volcanoes the O'Mearas are very aware of their dangers.

 'There is always a dark side to volcanoes ... so we always respect them. When we visit volcanoes we go to the experts ... we just go up with the geologists, they know the land best ... it is when you do not respect the volcano ... if you have no fear ... that's when you'll die.'

 'But even then, every year photographers, journalists, vulcanologists, geologists ... who know these volcanoes very well, die, ... their sheer unpredictability is always a factor ...'

basalt floods

BASALT FLOODS ARE THE MOST SPECTACULAR AND POSSIBLY THE MOST DEADLY OF ALL LAVA ERUPTIONS. MODERATE ONLY IN TERMS OF THEIR LOW LEVEL OF EXPLOSIVITY, VAST QUANTITIES OF HOT, FLUID BASALTS GUSH OUT FROM LONG FISSURES, FORMING SHEETS THAT MOVE SO FAST THEY CAN TRAVEL 150KM (93 MILES) BEFORE THEY STOP AND SOLIDIFY. THE COLUMBIA VOLCANIC PLATEAU OF OREGON AND WASHINGTON HAVE INDIVIDUAL FLOWS COVERING 1,000KM² (386 SQUARE MILES) AND THEY FLOODED A TOTAL AREA OF 130,000KM² (50,000 SQUARE MILES) ABOUT 12 MILLION YEARS AGO. THE ROZA ERUPTION IN OREGON WAS ONE OF THE MIGHTIEST, DISCHARGING BASALT AT OVER 1 MILLION M³ (35.3 MILLION FT³) PER SECOND.

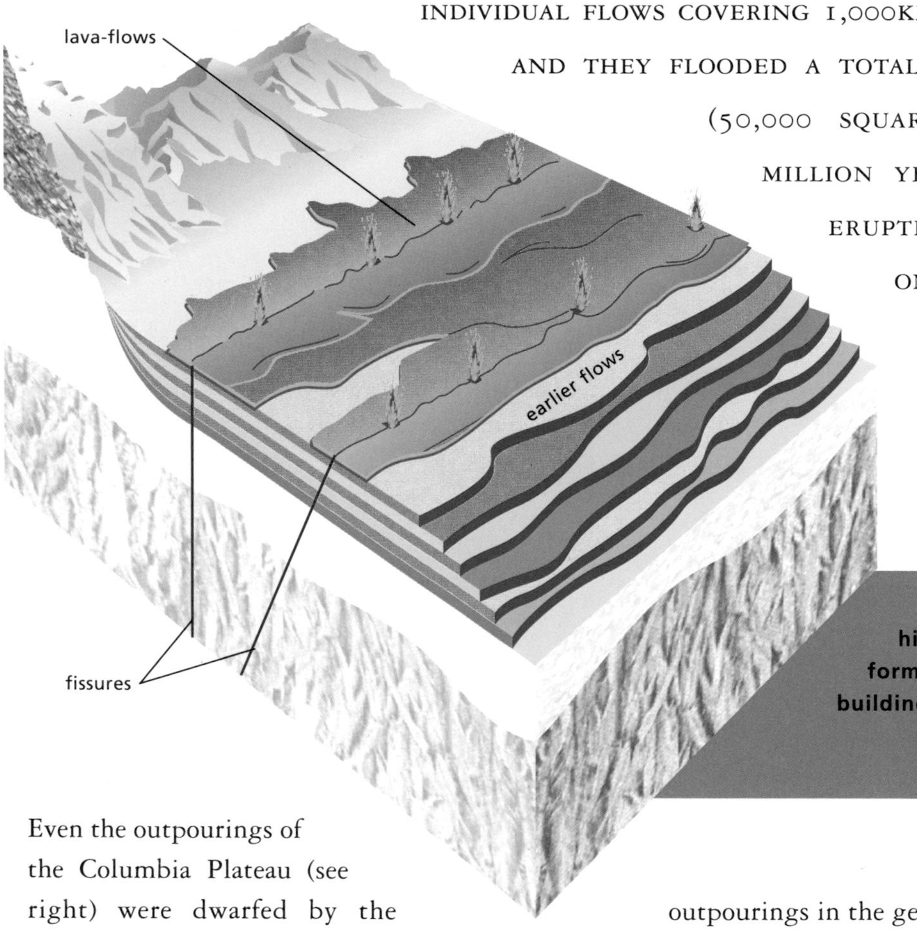

lava-flows

earlier flows

fissures

A fissure eruption of highly fluid basalt. Lava forms layers rather than building volcanic cones

volcanoes

Even the outpourings of the Columbia Plateau (see right) were dwarfed by the eruptions that formed the Deccan Plateau in India, about 65 million years ago. These lava-flows cover 500,000km² (193,000 square miles). Many scientists believe that these eruptions shut out the sunlight and produced poisonous gases that between them killed off the dinosaurs. There are similar vast basaltic plateaux in the Karoo of South Africa, central Siberia and southern Brazil. There are also smaller basaltic plateaux in Northern Ireland and in the Isle of Skye in western Scotland. Luckily, there have been no remotely comparable basaltic floods since the evolution of man. It is not clear what exactly caused these outpourings in the geological past, so predicting the next one is indeed hazardous. It would, however, be extremely difficult to run away from liquid basalts gushing out at a rate of 5km³ (1¼ cubic miles) an hour, especially if they were also producing huge quantities of noxious gases. This is the only type of basaltic eruption that is really to be feared on a world scale. It is just as well that so far there are no signs of another.

Death of the dinosaurs

About 65 million years ago, a cataclysmic event killed off many different species, both on land and at sea. It was so widespread and significant that it is recognized as marking the end of the

Secondary and the beginning of the Tertiary Era. Although scientists have resisted attributing this to a single, abrupt event, evidence suggests that, by geological standards, it took place within a relatively short period of time.

Some scientists believe that a huge meteorite hit the Earth, its impact scattering rock fragments over such a wide area that a freezing darkness persisted until many species starved or died of cold. The geological beds laid down at this time apparently support this theory as they are rich in particles of the metal iridium, common in meteorites, but usually very rare on Earth. A possible culprit could be the large meteorite that formed the huge Chicxulub crater on the edge of the Yucatán Peninsula in Mexico. This meteorite was perhaps 10km (6¼ miles) across. Its impact made a crater 200km (124 miles) in diameter and released energy equivalent to a million eruptions of Mount St Helens in 1980. In addition, tests have also shown that this particular meteorite did hit the Earth 65 million years ago.

Other scientists have proposed that eruptions of the flood basalts forming the Deccan Plateau in India caused the demise of the dinosaurs and their companions. Like all volcanic rocks the Deccan basalts were magnetized at the time they were created (see pp.18–19). At this time the Earth was experiencing magnetic reversals once or twice every million years. The vast volume of the Deccan basalts only registers two changes of magnetic polarity, so, they must have all erupted within less than a million years. It is possible that the eruptions were not continuous throughout that period but it is a fact that between 10–100km³ (2½–24 cubic miles) of basalt gushed onto the continental mass of India each year. The lavas have also been dated and results show that they are also 65 million years old. The cause of this volcanic outburst seems to have been the sudden development of a hotspot under part of the Indian plate.

The noxious quality of these basalt flows lies in their gas content. The lavas were abnormally rich in sulphur dioxide and carbon dioxide, which together would form sulphuric acid,

thereby killing the vegetation upon which the dinosaurs depended. The carbon dioxide would have spread far enough to kill animals in nearby valleys but could also have had a profound effect on the cycle that delivers carbon dioxide to marine sediments. Hence many marine species would have suffered just as much as those on land. Scientists have also discovered that hotspot volcanoes such as Réunion in the Indian Ocean, also give off iridium, and that it is not just present in meteorites.

Therefore, although there is evidence to support either theory, no direct link has yet been demonstrated between the death of the dinosaurs and the impact of the Chicxulub meteorite or the Deccan eruption.

Basalt flood lavas at Columbia Volcanic Plateau, Picture Gorge, Oregon, United States

vigorous eruptions

VIGOROUS ERUPTIONS ARE MORE EXPLOSIVE THAN MODERATE ERUPTIONS AS THEY OFTEN CONTAIN A STRONG ELEMENT OF GAS OR STEAM, PRODUCED WHEN MAGMA COMES INTO CONTACT WITH WATER, EITHER ON THE SURFACE OR UNDERGROUND. THE AMOUNT OF WATER AND THE SITE OF THE EXPLOSIONS DETERMINE THE ERUPTION STYLE. MOST TYPES OF MAGMA INVOLVED ARE BASALTIC, AND THE CONFLICT WITH WATER GIVES THEM FAR MORE VIGOUR THAN THEY WOULD OTHERWISE ACHIEVE. WITHOUT WATER THEY WOULD PRODUCE MODERATE, USUALLY STROMBOLIAN, ACTIVITY. VULCANIAN ERUPTIONS BELONG TO THIS VIGOROUS GROUP, BUT THEIR EXPLOSIONS MAINLY OCCUR WHEN GASES ESCAPE FROM RISING MAGMAS THAT ARE VISCOUS AND SILICIC.

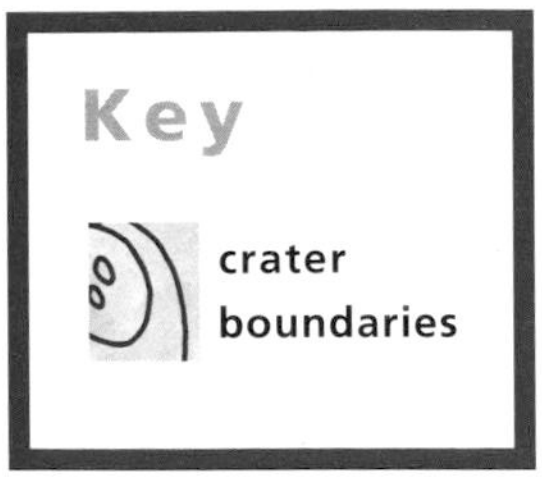

Key

crater boundaries

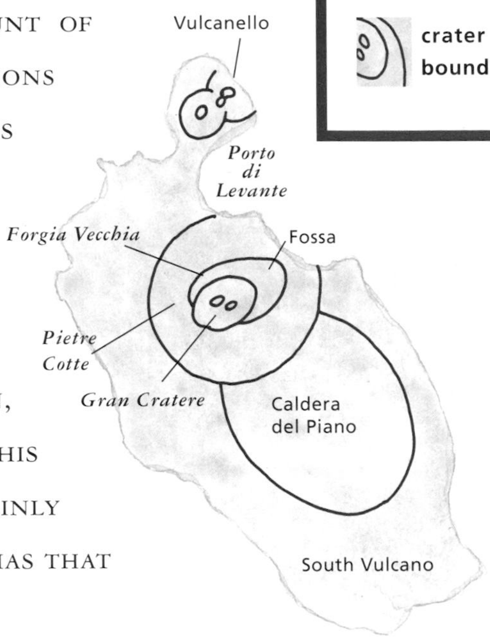

Vulcanello

Porto di Levante

Forgia Vecchia

Fossa

Pietre Cotte

Gran Cratere

Caldera del Piano

South Vulcano

ocean

tuffs

A Surtseyan eruption.
Fragments known as tuffs
are expelled by repeated
explosions caused when magma
rises into water less than 100m (328ft) deep

All vigorous eruptions produce cones and blankets of finely-shattered fragments. Lava-flows are small and usually rare; if they occur at all, it is towards the end of the vigorous activity. The main threat from vigorous eruptions comes from falling ash and larger fragments. Vigorous eruptions can be alarming, as the explosions they produce are loud and abrupt, but they pose little danger to those more than 2km (1¼ miles) away.

Vulcanian eruptions

Vulcanian eruptions are named after the activity of Fossa cone at Vulcano in the Aeolian Islands off Sicily. The Ancient Romans believed that Vulcano was the site of the forges of Vulcan, armourer to the Gods. The eruptions start suddenly: quick successions of explosions shatter new magma and old fragments of the volcano and shoot them from the chimney as if they had been fired from a gun. The noise is deafening. A black cloud of ash and steam rises 5km (3 miles) into the air. Volcanic fragments rain down on and around the cone. Several days of these explosions can be followed by several days of total calm until the eruptive spasm is over. Vulcano last erupted between 2 August 1888 and 22 March 1890 and Arenal, in Costa Rica, produced a Vulcanian eruption in 1968. Sakurajima in Japan has produced over 5,000 Vulcanian eruptions since 1955.

Vulcanian eruptions tend to produce bigger cones than their Strombolian counterparts, often 500m (1,640ft) high and about 2km (1¼ miles) across. Craters are large and deep. If they produce lava-flows they are often remarkably viscous.

Surtseyan eruptions

Surtseyan eruptions are named after Surtsey, the island that formed in the sea off the coast of Iceland between 1963 and 1967. They occur when

The crater of Vulcano looking towards two of the other Aeolian islands, Lipari and Salina

basaltic magmas rise into areas of shallow water less than 100m (328ft) deep, and are thus quite common in coasts surrounding volcanic areas, such as Iceland, the Azores and Hawaii. Hot basalt at 1200°C that meets water at less than 20°C, suddenly produces steam that expands rapidly, shatters the magma into fine fragments, and fires them out in pointed jets of black fragments. The explosions are repeated every minute or so for several months at least. Each explosion expels a thin layer of fine fragments called tuffs, that accumulate in a tuff-cone, that can reach 500m (1,640ft) in height. Billowing clouds of ash and steam also rise in a column 5km (3 miles) above the crater. Sometimes this column collapses and surges out from the volcano like the collar around the base of a nuclear explosion. Like Vulcanian eruptions, Surtseyan activity is less dangerous than it first appears, and presents no threat (except from wind-blown ash) at distances of over 2km (1¼ miles). But the eruptions are disconcerting: the water appears to explode and looks as if it is 'on fire'.

The tuff-cones are fragile and a few days of Atlantic storms, for instance, can sweep them away. This is what happened to Sabrina tuff-cone that formed off São Miguel, in the Azores, in 1811. When the tuffs accumulate in such quantity that water can no longer reach the magma in the chimney, the eruptions change to the Strombolian style. The Strombolian lava-flows that emerge form an armour-plate around the cone, and often create an apron that protects the cone from attack by waves. This change is what saved Surtsey from destruction on 4 April 1964.

A fumerole on Vulcano. Yellow sulphur produced by the volcano can be seen in the foreground

the eruption of Surtsey

ERUPTIONS REPEATED OVER MILLIONS OF YEARS PRODUCED THE MID-ATLANTIC RIDGE AND FORMED ICELAND. THE RIDGE CONTINUES SOUTH-WEST OF ICELAND, AS A SHALLOW VOLCANIC PLATFORM, WHERE WEAKER ACTIVITY HAS CREATED THE SMALL AND SCATTERED VESTMANN ISLANDS JUST ABOVE SEA-LEVEL. THEY HAD BEEN QUIET FOR AT LEAST A THOUSAND YEARS WHEN, SUDDENLY, OUT OF A GREY NOVEMBER DAWN, AN ERUPTION STARTED TO CREATE AN ENTIRELY NEW ISLAND. IT MADE A FASCINATING NEW WORLD FOR THE EXPERTS TO STUDY AND A WONDERFUL SPECTACLE FOR EVERYBODY TO ADMIRE. THEY CALLED IT SURTSEY, AFTER THE NORSE GIANT SURTUR, WHO HAD FOUGHT FREYR, THE GOD OF FERTILITY AND PROSPERITY, IN THE BATTLE BEFORE THE END OF THE WORLD.

On Heimaey, the largest of the Vestmann Islands, people started to smell sulphur on 11 November 1963. Two days later, a research vessel measured sea water temperatures 2°C warmer than elsewhere off the south-western end of the Vestmann Islands. The eruptions had started a few days before, 130m (426ft) down on the submerged Mid-Atlantic Ridge, 33km (20½ miles) south-west of the Icelandic mainland. At that depth the pressure of the water stifled any explosions, and the molten rock poured out and formed piles of pillow lavas. As the piles grew, the water became shallower and its pressure decreased. As a result the water could be changed into steam, which shattered the lava into millions of fragments; these were then thrown high into the air thus revealing the existence of the eruptions.

On 14 November 1963, the *Isleifur II* was fishing south-west of the Vestmann Islands. Ólafur Vestmann, the cook, was on watch. At 07.15, he felt the ship swirl and roll, and, peering into the dawn half-light, he saw dark

smoke rising out of the sea about 1,500m (4,900ft) away. He awoke Captain Tómasson. Both thought another vessel was on fire, but radio enquiries revealed that there had been no S.O.S. signals. Captain Tómasson grabbed his binoculars and saw black columns erupting from the sea. He called the radio post on Heimaey to report that an eruption seemed to have started. For the next few hours, the captain sailed the *Isleifur II* around the growing eruption. At 08.00 the columns of ash and steam were 70m (230ft) high and, by 10.30, explosions every 30 secs sent columns 400m (1,312ft) skywards. The temperature of the sea nearby rose to 12°C – about 5°C above normal.

Soon explosions every few seconds were firing out shattered lava fragments in curved black plumes like a cockerel's tail. By the next morning they had piled up into an island 10m (33ft) high, which quickly increased in size. At first the eruptions came from a fissure, 500m (1,640ft) long, but then they concentrated on one spot and formed the crater and cone called

'The eruption was most vigorously active, the eruption column rushing continuously upwards.' Icelandic geologist, Sigurdur Thorarinsson, on the eruption of Surtsey in 1964

volcanoes

Once the eruption began the island grew quickly: within 24 hours the lava fragments contained within the plumes of smoke and ash had piled up to a height of 10m (33ft)

Surtur I. Even the experienced Icelandic geologist, Sigurdur Thorarinsson, was enthralled by the sight: 'The volcano was most vigorously active, the eruption column rushing … upwards, and, when darkness fell, it was a pillar of fire and the entire cone was aglow with bombs which rolled down the slopes into the white surf around the island. Flashes of lightning lit up the eruption cloud and peals of thunder cracked above our heads. The din from the thunderbolts, the rumble from the eruption cloud, and the bangs resulting from bombs crashing into the sea produced a most impressive symphony …'

Eruptions went on with the same vigour for some weeks. On 6 December, three Frenchmen made the first landing on Surtsey, to take photographs for *Paris Match*, but the volcano drove them back after 15 mins. Some Vestmann islanders landed on 13 December in an attempt to name the island Vesturey (West Island). Sigurdur Thorarinsson and another scientist landed on 16 December and collected lava samples that proved to be basalts just like those of Katla on the mainland nearby.

The new island needed the protection of solid lava-flows if it were to survive the attacking waves. These flows could only erupt, however, if the fragments piled up so thickly that the sea could no longer flood into the chimney. The Surtseyan eruption would thereby lose its character and become a Strombolian eruption. But the sea was fighting back all the time, eroding a cliff all around the accumulating cone of tuff fragments, and spreading them in a beach, 150m (490ft) wide at its base. On 29 December 1963, Surtsey started also erupting from a subsidiary chimney, 2km (1¼ miles) to the north-east. Activity went on until 6 January 1964, but never succeeded in building an island.

Then the eruptions on Surtsey abandoned their original chimney and broke out from another, just to the north-west, on 1 February 1964. Surtur Junior, as it was called, quickly built up another cone, alongside the first, that was 180m (590ft) high by the end of March. The waves found it harder and harder to penetrate into the new chimney. On 4 April, a lava lake welled up in the crater of Surtur Junior, lava fountains spurted 50m (164ft) into the air, and lava flows ran along the beach. These Strombolian eruptions gave Surtsey just the armour-plating that it needed to survive the onslaught of the Atlantic waves. Thereafter, activity continued on and off, until July 1967.

Meanwhile on 5 June 1965, another chimney began to erupt in the sea, 500m (1,640ft) north-west of Surtsey, forming an island called Syrtlingur. Throughout the summer, Surtseyan

Strombolian lava flows prevented Surtsey from being washed away by the powerful Atlantic seas

eruptions piled up fragments, and the Atlantic waves washed them away again. Syrtlingur reached its maximum height of 65m (213ft) on 15 September. It was last seen on 17 October 1965 before a week of bad weather. When it finally calmed on 24 October, the eruption had stopped, and Syrtlingur had vanished.

Another subsidiary chimney also started erupting on 28 December 1965, 500m (1,640ft) south-west of Surtsey, forming an islet called Jolnir. Jolnir lasted a little longer than Syrtlingur, and disappeared on 20 September 1966. Neither Jolnir nor Syrtlingur produced enough fragments to stop the sea entering the chimney, and therefore could erupt no lava-flows to defend them against the waves. Rapid creation and subsequent sea erosion characterizes most islands formed by Surtseyan eruptions. Surtsey itself only survived because it adopted a different style of eruption.

steam-blast and volcanic gas eruptions

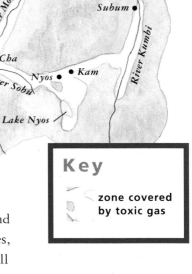

THE TWO FINAL CATEGORIES OF VIGOROUS ERUPTIONS ARE VERY DIFFERENT IN TERMS OF THE THREATS THAT THEY POSE. STEAM-BLAST ERUPTIONS PRODUCE SCARS IN THE LANDSCAPE BUT ARE SHORT-LIVED AND POSE RELATIVELY LITTLE DANGER IN THEMSELVES. VOLCANIC GAS, ON THE OTHER HAND, CAN BE DEADLY AND CAN ESCAPE PRACTICALLY UNNOTICED.

Steam-blast eruptions

Steam-blast or phreatic eruptions on land are broadly similar to Surtseyan eruptions, but much less water is available, and the explosive contact with the hot magma takes place in a confined space about 250m (820ft) underground. Water usually infiltrates the rocks from surface streams or melting ice and snow. Several big blasts will quickly exhaust such a water supply, and so steam-blast eruptions may last just a day, or even less than an hour. The blasts can, however, be vicious enough to blow huge holes in the landsurface and shoot fragments of rock for a distance of 5km (3 miles). Two such holes, Big Hole and Hole-in-the-Ground, in Oregon, United States, are still dry, but they soon fill with water in humid areas and form distinctive circular lakes. The most famous are the *maars* (*meers*) of the Eifel area in western Germany, and there are many more in central France.

Similar eruptions occur when magma is rising into large explosive volcanoes, where they often offer preliminary warnings of more violent activity. One of their major distinguishing characteristics is that the fragments expelled are cold because they are shattered from old rock, not from new magma. Such eruptions went on for almost a year before new magma reached the surface at Nevado del Ruiz on 13 November 1985, and they continued for two months at Mount St Helens from 27 March to 18 May 1980. Individual eruptions in this style produce limited threats because they are confined to a short time and a small space.

Volcanic gas eruptions

Volcanic gas escapes from most eruptions and plays an essential role in explosions. But it is nearly always accompanied by lava-flows or fragments or both. Thus the sulphur dioxide and fluorine expelled from Laki in 1783–84 were almost a by-product of the great lava-flows, although they indirectly caused huge losses of human and animal life.

Eruptions of volcanic gas alone are very rare; in fact, many scientists do not believe that they are produced directly by eruptions. They happen absolutely without warning and release lethal volumes of

Key

 zone covered by toxic gas

Lake Nyos where gas killed 1,700 people in 1986

invisible carbon dioxide. Since it was first identified in 1979 this type of eruption has caused more deaths than all other forms of vigorous eruption combined.

On 20 February 1979 on the Diëng Plateau in central Java, a sudden explosion of carbon dioxide from a dry crater killed 142 people. In Cameroon on 15 August 1984 carbon dioxide exploded from Lake Monoun causing 37 deaths. Neither eruption created much scientific interest. A third case, at Lake Nyos, Cameroon, in 1986, produced great controversy about the origin of the gas. Some scientists thought that the gas had gradually accumulated on the floor of the lake where it had remained trapped by dense layers of water until a landslide, earthquake or heavy rainfall had disturbed the layers, releasing the gas. Others believed that the gas was produced by a volcanic eruption.

The gas eruption from Lake Nyos, Cameroon

Lake Nyos is one of many lakes in the North-west Province of Cameroon that have been formed by steam-blast explosions. On 19 August 1986, a local healer became suspicious when herb leaves turned red near the lake, perhaps because some gas had escaped. At 16.00 on 21 August, some herdsmen heard the lake gurgling, and some strange bangs were audible between 21.30 and 22.00. About 20.30 Mr Malanjaï saw water begin to shoot upwards making sounds like gunshots. A cloud of water droplets and carbon dioxide covered his house, 120m (394ft) above the lake, at about 22.00. It gave him a headache and his children fell down as they tried to leave the house. Kalus Keituh in Upper Nyos village saw the water quickly spurt up and change colour from red to white. The cloud covered the house of his neighbour Mr Pakalé, about 100m (328ft) above the lake, killing one of his children and all his cows. Next morning it became clear that about 600 of the 606 inhabitants of Nyos village had been gassed.

About 1km³ (¼ cubic mile) of concentrated, almost pure carbon dioxide spread northwards from Lake Nyos about 23.30 on 21 August 1986. As the gas is denser than air, it moved along the ground in a long cloud about 40m (131ft) thick, travelling at 20–50km/h (12½–31mph). Human beings are asphyxiated if they breathe air containing more than 20–30 per cent carbon dioxide for more than 10 mins. The gas did not mix readily with the air and the cloud kept its lethal concentrations until it had spread 23km (14 miles) from the lake. Many people in villages in this area were also killed.

Many people in Nyos village died in their beds. Others tried to escape before they were overcome by fumes. The small number of survivors said that they had smelt something similar to rotten eggs (hydrogen sulphide) or gunpowder (sulphur dioxide). Both gases would only have come from a volcanic eruption.

Steam-blast or phreatic eruptions produced by the south-eastern crater of Etna, Sicily, during 1971

violent eruptions

VIOLENT ERUPTIONS ARE USUALLY PRODUCED BY LARGE, ACTIVE VOLCANOES. ALMOST ALL OF THESE VOLCANOES ARE MORE THAN 10,000 YEARS OLD AND MANY ARE OVER 1 MILLION YEARS OLD. THE MAJORITY HAVE GROWN UP OVER SUBDUCTION ZONES, WHICH IS WHY SO MANY OF THEM FORM THE IMPRESSIVE 'RING OF FIRE' THAT SURROUNDS THE PACIFIC OCEAN. THESE ERUPTIONS ARE FAR FROM CONTINUOUS, AND MANY OF THESE VOLCANOES ARE DORMANT FOR MOST OF THEIR ACTIVE LIVES, UNTIL SPORADICALLY, AND DRAMATICALLY, THEY BURST INTO ACTION.

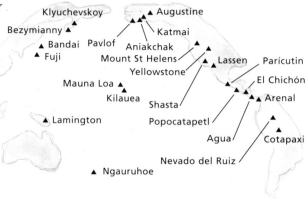

Violent volcanic activity is generally short-lived but is always highly destructive. Among the weapons at its disposal are ash clouds, nuées ardentes, mudflows, landslides, tsunamis and climatic changes. Due to the difficulties of studying such eruptions at close range their behaviour tends to be categorized according to the types of deposits that are left behind. The repetition of huge and violent eruptions over thousands of years creates large structures called strato-volcanoes, so-called because they are composed of many layers of material.

Ash and pumice floods

Ash and pumice floods are vast and rare, and lie on the boundary between vigorous and violent eruptions. Nobody has seen them happening, which is fortunate because they are wide-spreading and very fast-moving. They are composed mainly of rhyolite, and apparently emerge as fine, frothy, ashy, pumice, like milk boiling over from a pan at 700km/h (435 mph). At Yellowstone Park, USA and Taupo in New Zealand, they have volumes of 3,000km³ (720 cubic miles) and have blanketed nearly 20,000km² (7,700 square miles). Ash and pumice floods spread so quickly that they

occasionally trap masses of fossils: the 20 million year-old flood in Oregon, called the John Day Formation, has proved to be a paleontologist's treasure trove.

Only one ash and pumice flood has been recorded in recent times. It happened unobserved at the foot of Katmaï volcano in an unpopulated area of Alaska on 6 June 1912. Although it was relatively small, it was nevertheless one of the biggest eruptions of the

key features

Blasts and debris avalanches are characterized by:
- highly powerful blasts
- ash clouds
- landslides
- shattered rock
- hummocky land
- huge volcanic craters left by landslides

20th Century. About 35km³ (8½ cubic miles) of pumice, 200m (656ft) thick, covered the Ukak valley within 60 hours. Those who first saw it many months later called it 'The Valley of 10,000 Smokes', because the entire surface of the flood emitted wispy columns of gas and steam.

Blasts and debris avalanches

Blasts and debris avalanches have only just been fully recognized. In June 1956, a blast blew off the top of Bezymianny, and deposited an apron, covering 100km², (39 square miles) at its base. Although there had been months of preliminary eruptions, the blast occurred in the remote, inhospitable and inaccessible Kamchatka Peninsula off eastern Siberia. The volcano was hardly known (in fact its name means 'no name') and no-one was killed by the blast.

Then, on 18 May 1980, the same thing – but on a smaller scale – happened at Mount St Helens. Specialists had closely followed the volcano's two months of preliminary activity when journalists and television crews had often joined thousands of visitors. The climactic moment was actually photographed, but sadly 57 people were killed, including the geologist monitoring events that day. The blast blew off the crest and north flank of Mount St Helens and spread 3km³ (¾ cubic mile) of the volcano in a debris avalanche that covered 60km² (23 square miles) at its feet. Mount St Helens became world-famous, and has been studied every day since the eruption. Specialists have now found evidence of previously unsuspected blasts and debris avalanches on more than 150 other strato-volcanoes.

During the eruption of Mount St Helens a plume of ash erupted for more than nine hours, eventually reaching 19–24km (12–15 miles) above sea-level. The plume moved eastwards at an average speed of 97km/h (60mph)

the eruption of
Mount St Helens

IN WASHINGTON STATE, NATIVE AMERICAN LEGEND TELLS OF AN UGLY OLD WOMAN CALLED TAH-ONE-LAT-CLAH ('FIRE MOUNTAIN') WHO LIVED IN THE CASCADE RANGE. ONE DAY THE SPIRIT GOD TURNED HER INTO A BEAUTIFUL VIRGIN, AND TWO GREAT WARRIORS, WYEAST AND PAHTO, SOON BEGAN TO COMPETE FOR HER AFFECTIONS. SHE WAS UNABLE TO CHOOSE BETWEEN THEM, AND THE WARRIORS BEGAN A DUEL, HURLING FIRE, LIGHTNING, AND BURNING ROCKS AT EACH OTHER SO FIERCELY THAT THE EARTH SHOOK, THE SUN WAS BLACKED OUT, AND THE PEOPLE WERE TERRIFIED. THE SPIRIT GOD WAS SO DISGUSTED BY SUCH BEHAVIOUR THAT HE TURNED ALL THREE INTO MOUNTAINS NEAR THE RIVER COLUMBIA VALLEY: WYEAST BECAME MOUNT HOOD, PAHTO BECAME MOUNT ADAMS AND TAH-ONE-LAT-CLAH BECAME MOUNT ST HELENS.

Geologists have discovered that Mount St Helens is younger and more violent than any large volcano in the Cascade Range. It is only 30,000 years old, and it erupts violently about once every 3,000–4,000 years. In 1975, the geologists D.R. Crandell and D.R. Mullineaux declared that Mount St Helens could well erupt before the end of the present century. The beautiful virgin was turned back into an old woman on 18 May 1980.

Mount St Helens issued warnings for two months. Small earthquakes centred just under the volcano began at 15.37 on 20 March 1980. On 25 March the volcano was closed to climbers.

Mount St Helens is the smallest of five major volcanic peaks in the Cascade Range. It measured 2,950m (9,678ft) before the eruption in 1980

On 26 March an emergency co-ordination centre was set up at Vancouver, Washington. At 12.36 on 27 March the first gas-blast, phreatic eruption exploded cold black ash 3km (1¾ miles) into the air. Residents and forestry loggers were evacuated from the mountain area and roadblocks were placed around a restricted zone. It was also on 27 March that the northern sector of the cone began to bulge outwards. Geologists began to monitor the mountain.

By the beginning of April, and especially at weekends, the whole area swarmed with visitors. The eruptions continued, with spectators buying bags full of ash. Then the eruptions stopped between 22

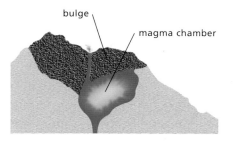
bulge
magma chamber

debris flow

lateral blast

The eruption of Mount St Helens. 1. Bulge on north side of mountain, 90m (295ft). 2. Magnitude 5.0 earthquake dislodges weakened rocks of north face causing huge landslide. 3. Pressure of carbon dioxide and water that has been building up over a period of months is finally released producing a lateral blast which blows out the north face of the mountain

As well as the main blast that took place on 18 May other eruptions followed. This one happened on 22 July, sending pumice and ash 10–18km (6¼–11 miles) into the air, and was visible 160km (100 miles) away in Seattle

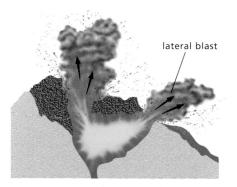

April and 7 May, but the earthquakes went on, and the north flank continued to swell alarmingly at a rate of 1.5m (5ft) a day. On 30 April, Governor Dixy Lee Ray of Washington State established a Red Zone, ranging from 5–13km (3–8 miles) around the volcano that was prohibited to all except appropriate scientists and officials. The Geological Survey moved its chief observation post to a new site, Coldwater II, 9km (5½ miles) from the volcano.

Meanwhile Harry Truman, 83, owner of 16 cats, refused to leave his Mount St Helens Lodge on Spirit Lake, north of the volcano. 'This damn mountain won't ever do me any harm. In any case, if it explodes, well then, I'll go up with it'. One local geologist thought that the Coldwater II observation post was badly placed, facing onto the bulging flank. 'It was like looking down the barrel of a loaded gun.'

Mount St Helens started erupting again on 7 May and the earthquakes and bulging continued. Then, on 14 May, the eruptions stopped again; earthquakes fell to their lowest levels for a month; and the rate of bulging stopped increasing.

Events over the next few days happened as follows:

15 May: bulging rate constant; fewer earthquakes; no eruptions.
16 May: bulging rate constant; fewer earthquakes; no eruptions. Scout leaders allowed to remove equipment from camps in restricted zone. Evacuated home-owners also granted permission to retrieve belongings after a protest.
17 May: bulging rate constant; fewer earthquakes; no eruptions. 30 car-loads of home-owners go in a police-escorted convoy to salvage belongings from their houses. Geologist David Johnston is on duty at Coldwater II observation point.
18 May: beautiful, cloudless morning; bulging rate constant; few earthquakes; no eruptions ... until 08.32.

At 08.32 on 18 May 1980, a magnitude 5.0 earthquake destabilized the bulging north flank of the volcano, and 3km³ (¾ cubic mile) of it shuddered and collapsed in a debris avalanche landslide that hurtled northwards at 250km/h (155mph). In an instant it buried Harry Truman, his lodge and his cats. Within a second the exposed magma exploded. The blast shot outwards and downwards at speeds approaching 500km/h (311mph) and burnt and devastated 600km² (232 square miles) within two minutes. David Johnston at Coldwater II just had time to radio his base at Vancouver: 'This is it! This is it!' Those were the last words he uttered. The blast knocked down the conifers on the nearby hills as if they were matchsticks. The explosions

Sunset over the eruption of 22 July 1980, three months after the main blast

This car was caught in the mudflow 16km (10 miles) north of the volcano

More than 200 homes and over 300km (186 miles) of roads were destroyed by mudflows during 1980

volcanoes

Mount St Helens and Spririt Lake were popular with tourists before the eruption, attracted by the tranquil surroundings and the natural beauty of the area

its own weather and there were streaks of lightning going horizontally across the sky instead of down to earth and the lightning was blue and pink and it was really quite pretty.'

Sue still remembers vividly what it felt like to walk through a cloud of volcanic ash:

 ... it was nearly a foot [30cm] deep in places and it was so hot underneath ... you could only stay in it for a short period of time and then we would have to get up on a stump and ... take our shoes off and dump [the ash] out and unroll our pants and ... within a few minutes it would be filled up ... like slogging through a huge field of talcum powder and it just smelled terrible ... it was the smell of rotten eggs.'

that there were trees all around them: they had fallen down into a hole left by the roots of a tree which was then covered over by other falling trees. Bruce started to climb out of the hole but was driven back by the heat. They waited until the air had cooled slightly and then tried again. Sue was met by a scene of total devastation.

 'It was completely destroyed. There were maybe a few trees standing, but halfway up they'd been snapped off and most of the trees were down ... it was silent ... it happened so fast ... it was too hard for us to even comprehend what had happened.'

Another ash cloud full of debris engulfed them. They tried to climb out of the valley because they were afraid that the ash contained poisonous gas from the eruption.

Bruce and Sue both survived but Terry and Karen were not so lucky. Just as the first cloud hit, Terry dived into the tent that he and Karen shared. Seconds later a tree fell on top of the tent killing them both. After a few days Bruce returned to the scene to find out what had happened to his friends.

 '... about a week later, Bruce went back in and they found them ... together, with their arms around each other, and they were dead'.

 '... it was so dark and so heavy with ash coming down that I felt we were going to asphyxiate ... so we took our shirts off and wrapped them around our head and so we couldn't see anyway, it was dark so it was like blindly climbing up and over and falling off the trees ... we started getting hit by bigger pieces and decided we'd better wait that part out and we climbed underneath a log and I remember ... the ash cloud made

After the eruption Mount St Helens was only 2,550m (8,364ft) high, with a crater 1.5km (1 mile) wide

Peléan eruptions

PELÉAN ERUPTIONS WERE ONLY FULLY APPRECIATED AFTER MONTAGNE PELÉE DESTROYED ST PIERRE, MARTINIQUE, ON 8 MAY 1902. THEY ARE A LETHAL AND DEVASTATING COMBINATION OF HOT SIDEWAYS BLASTS, NUÉES ARDENTES OR GLOWING AVALANCHES, AND LARGE LAVA DOMES. THE DORMANT VOLCANOES SHOW VIRTUALLY NO ACTIVITY FOR DECADES OR CENTURIES, THEN, FOR A FEW WARNING WEEKS, STEAM-BLAST ERUPTIONS SHATTER THE WALLS OF THE CHIMNEY, CRATER THE SUMMIT, AND SCATTER FRAGMENTS 10KM (6¼ MILES) OR MORE FROM THE VOLCANO.

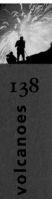

nuées ardentes

lava dome

beds of lava and ash

A Peléan eruption showing the creation of a large crater by repeated steam-blast eruptions

At the same time, the viscous, silicic magma rises towards the top of the chimney where pressures upon it are much reduced. The gases in the magma quickly separate out into bubbles that push the whole mass faster upwards. Near the top of the chimney, the gases explode and blow the magma into smithereens, forming a turmoil of fragments ranging from dust and gas to blocks of the old volcanic crest. The whole mass can be as hot as 700°C when it bursts out from the chimney. Sometimes a blast of hot air, gas and fine ash shoots out directly for 10km (6¼ miles) or more. At other times, the gases and fine ash mix with much larger fragments which surge downslope under gravity at speeds of 500km/h (311mph), smashing and picking up trees, buildings, bridges, and people on the way. These are nuées ardentes – incandescent clouds or glowing avalanches – that hug the ground as they move. There is no means of diverting or avoiding them and this is why they are the most lethal of volcanic eruptions. Blasts and nuées ardentes only last for two or three minutes, but this is enough time to devastate 50km² (19 square miles), and burn everything in their path.

Almost at the same time, magma surges up the chimney forming a lava dome. Spines of glowing lava can often rise up 100m (328ft) before they weather and crumble as they solidify. The solidified dome can withstand most of the weaker gas explosions that happen as the eruption wanes. In some cases, such as Merapi in Java, the dome remains at the summit throughout most eruptions, but one sector is not

An artist's impression of the aftermath of the eruption as viewed from the French Naval vessel *Suchet*, one of the first ships to reach the stricken area

supported by the crater wall. This collapses about every two years, releasing small blasts and nuées ardentes that career down the slopes.

The eruption of Montagne Pelée

In almost 300 years since the French first settled in St Pierre, Martinique in 1635, the volcano that dominated the area, Montagne Pelée, had only had two small eruptions, in 1792 and 1851. By the beginning of the 20th Century, St Pierre had become known as the 'pearl of the West Indies', and was the commercial and intellectual centre of the island. Its buildings were made

St Pierre with the dome of Montagne Pelée visible in the background. Le Prêcheur is around the bay to the north

of stone, it had a busy port, electricity, a piped water supply, many mechanized distilleries, fine squares, a Grand Hotel, a college, a chamber of commerce, a cathedral and an elegant theatre. It was the hub of the island's wealth, earned from the production of sugar and rum, that was controlled by the French colonial administrators and plantation owners.

Early in 1902, a sickly smell of hydrogen sulphide began to spread into Le Prêcheur and to St Pierre, 7km (4½ miles) from the volcano. A minor steam-blast eruption on 24 April expelled a small amount of ash – the first real indication of renewed activity. On 27 April the mountain was calm enough for groups to climb to the summit. The crater of the Étang Sec was no longer dry, but contained a lake that looked 'like quicksilver', and a new cinder cone was producing boiling water and the fumes tarnished the visitors' silver buttons. This was also the day of the French Parliamentary elections. None of the candidates won an overall majority and so a second ballot, between the two leading candidates, was set for 11 May.

Montagne Pelée burst into action on 1 May. The next day at 23.00, terrifying explosions

wakened the inhabitants of St Pierre. The first ash fell on the city since 1851, and was soon 3cm (1¼in) deep. On 3 May, Governor Mouttet arrived to visit St Pierre and Le Prêcheur. The Governor promised that the people of Le Prêcheur could shelter in the barracks in St Pierre, if conditions got worse, and many people from the slopes of Montagne Pelée had already crowded into St Pierre. One of the election candidates, Fernand Clerc, called for the evacuation of St Pierre. The mayor Raymond Fouché, however, issued a counter-call for calm, closed the schools, and ordered the firemen to hose away the ash.

Two days of relative calm followed and attention turned to the strange behaviour of the Rivière Blanche that drained from the crater rim to the coast between St Pierre and Le Prêcheur. For a week it had been flooding and drying up. On 5 May it was in full spate. At 12.45, the crater rim gave way, and the waters that had accumulated in the crater swirled into the Rivière Blanche and formed a mudflow 10m (33ft) high that rushed down the valley, threw the Guérin rum factory into the sea, and killed 23 people. The mudflow sent a small tsunami across the bay that crashed onto the Place Bertin 15 minutes later. Governor Mouttet made a second visit to St Pierre, and the day ended when ash clogged the generators, and cut off the electricity supply.

Montagne Pelée ▲

● *Le Prêcheur*

Morne Jacob ▲

● *St Pierre*

Caribbean Sea

Fort de France ●

The inhabitants of St Pierre and Le Prêcheur were becoming more and more frantic. On 6 May food supplies were provided by the Governor himself but no evacuation order was given. The same day, the mayor of St Pierre issued a poster to try and diffuse the tension, affirming that 'lava will not reach the city'. That evening, a glow from the crater lit up the eruption. Nobody realized that this showed that the molten rock had finally reached the surface. Throughout 7 May Montagne Pelée spewed ash over all north-western Martinique; in Le Prêcheur roofs began to collapse under its weight.

Finally on 7 May, the mayor of St Pierre asked the Governor to send troops to help distribute food to refugees, and patrol the city streets. Governor Mouttet arranged for them to go the following morning. He and his wife, and several senior administrators, went to spend the night in St Pierre to demonstrate his confidence in their future and calm the citizens. The Governor's Scientific Commission (apart from one member) met in St Pierre and concluded that the town was in no danger from earthquakes, landslides, or mudflows. The area's wildlife appeared not to share this opinion: reports claimed that the rats, cats, snakes and birds – even a boa constrictor from the town's Botanical Gardens – escaped and headed south.

There was a terrible thunderstorm during the night, and the rain washed the ash from St Pierre. 8 May, Ascension Day, dawned bright and sunny and, at 07.00, holiday-makers from Fort-de-France disembarked from the steamer Diamant. At 07.15 a skiff carrying Governor Mouttet and three members of the Scientific Commission left for Le Prêcheur. They were never seen again. From time to time dark clouds shot from Montagne Pelée right over St Pierre. The climax came at 08.02. It was not the most powerful eruption of the 20th Century, but it was the most deadly, killing 28,000 people.

At 08.00 the telegraph clerk at St Pierre signalled 'Go ahead' to his colleagues in Fort-de-France to start the day's work. At 08.01 (the times were calibrated on the international network) his colleague asked for the morning's news, and then at 08.02 he heard a 'short trill on the line. Then nothing more'. At the same time, a businessman was phoning a friend in St Pierre. 'He had just finished his sentence, when I heard a dreadful scream, then another much weaker groan, like a stifled death rattle. Then silence'. A blinding flash, a tremendous blast and a violet-red nuée ardente blasted straight down to St Pierre at 500km/h (311mph). The swirling mixture of gas, steam, scalding mud, scorching ash, glowing stones and boulders, and drops of

The ruins of St Pierre. Repeated blasts and nuées ardentes flattened most of the buildings in the town

molten rock, picked up and smashed buildings, trees and huts. In St Pierre a few walls parallel to the blast stayed upright, but nearly everything else was cut down: the theatre, hotel, chamber of commerce, the college, the bank and hundreds of shops and houses. The rum distilleries blasted apart, the rum casks ignited, and soon St Pierre had become a raging inferno. The cathedral collapsed upon the Ascension Day worshippers and its dome came to rest in the sea.

It is usually said that there were only two survivors in St Pierre: a cobbler and a prisoner. This story is untrue; there were, in fact, about 70 survivors in the city, on the edges of the nuée ardente, and on boats out to sea. The cobbler,

Le Petit Parisien

SUPPLÉMENT LITTÉRAIRE ILLUSTRÉ

DIRECTION: 18, rue d'Enghien (10ᵉ) PARIS

The cover of this issue of *Petit Parisien* featured an artist's impression of a family running from an approaching nuée ardente

A prisoner named Sylbaris (or Cyparis) was being held in this cell on the morning of 8 May. He was one of only 70 survivors

Léon Compère-Léandre, found himself covered in burns and was then plunged into darkness. When daylight returned he saw the mass destruction around him and fled. The prisoner, Louis-Auguste Sylbaris (or Cyparis), had been

jailed for disorderly conduct the previous day. He had been put in a stone cell, built like a bomb-shelter, in a hollow in the prison courtyard. Its only window faced away from the nuée ardente. 'All of a sudden, there was a terrifying noise', he said. 'Everybody was screaming "Help! Help! I'm burning! I'm dying!" Five minutes later nobody was crying out any more – except me'. He was rescued a few days later, badly burnt and extremely thirsty. Offshore, the nuée ardente destroyed or overturned all but one of a dozen large vessels, and smashed all the smaller craft. At sea, the survival rate was low, but better than on land, as there was slightly more warning and some people were able to rush to shelter below deck.

As far as the rest of the island and mainland France were concerned, after 08.02 St Pierre had fallen silent. A steamer set out from Fort-de-France and managed to reach St Pierre at 11.00. The city was blazing and it was impossible for the ship to land. That afternoon the steamer and a Naval vessel the *Suchet* were able to rescue the small number of burnt, incoherent survivors. At 21.55 on 8 May the captain of the *Suchet* telegraphed to the Navy Ministry in Paris. 'Back from St Pierre, city completely destroyed by mass of fire about 8 this morning. Suppose all population annihilated. Have brought back the few survivors, about thirty. All ships in roads burnt and lost. Eruption volcano continues. I am leaving for Guadeloupe to get supplies.'

During the next few days rescue operations concentrated on Le Prêcheur and the coastal villages to the north. At Le Prêcheur, a mudflow earlier that morning had already killed 400 villagers, so soon after dawn, about 400 others had climbed up to a hill south of the village to find refuge. Sadly they were then killed by the nuée ardente which missed the village by 500m (1,640ft).

For the rest of the month nuées ardentes were produced almost daily. Finally the explosive eruptions stopped and a huge dome arose in the old crater. A single spine of lava lasted for several months but it quickly weathered away when the eruption stopped in 1904.

Plinian eruptions

PLINIAN ERUPTIONS ARE NAMED AFTER PLINY THE ELDER, THE MOST FAMOUS VICTIM OF THE ERUPTION OF VESUVIUS IN AD 79, AND HIS NEPHEW PLINY THE YOUNGER, WHO DESCRIBED THE EVENT IN TWO LETTERS TO THE ROMAN HISTORIAN, TACITUS. THE MOST POWERFUL OF ALL VOLCANIC ERUPTIONS, THEY RELEASE HUGE AMOUNTS OF ENERGY, MUCH OF WHICH IS USED TO EXPEL A BILLOWING, ROARING COLUMN OF GAS, STEAM, ASH AND PUMICE FROM THE CHIMNEY INTO THE STRATOSPHERE.

This enormous, rising column is sustained by convection and incessant gas explosions for many hours. In its upper reaches, 25km (15½ miles) or more above the crater, the power wanes and the column branches out into a characteristic umbrella-pine shape. Vast areas are plunged into darkness as dust, ash and pumice rain down upon an area of as much as 500km² (193 square miles), choking streams, blocking roads, suffocating people and animals, destroying crops, defoliating forests and causing rooftops to collapse. Although the ash and pumice falls are dangerous, they build up gradually over several hours, and can allow time for evacuation. The most hazardous feature of a Plinian eruption is nuées ardentes.

The eruptive column may soar upwards for several hours or for as long as two or three days. From time to time its rising impetus may be checked by a decrease in the intensity of the gas explosions, or a sudden widening of the chimney. If this occurs, the column collapses and crumbles in a dark, fiery mass, and rushes down the volcano as nuées ardentes at a speed of 500km/h (311mph).

It is these nuées ardentes that often cause the greatest devastation and death-tolls in Plinian eruptions because it is impossible to escape from them. In AD 79, the column erupting from Vesuvius collapsed and generated nuées ardentes at least six times, and caused most of the deaths in Herculaneum and Pompeii. Similar nuées ardentes seared the slopes around El Chichón in Mexico on 3 April 1982 and killed over 2,000 villagers. As they are rarely observed first-hand

nuées ardentes

mudflow (lahar)

Plinian eruptions produce deadly nuées ardente: incandescent clouds of red-hot ash that can travel 500km/h (311mph)

142

'Lancaster Sands' by J.M.W. Turner, c.1816. During a tour of the north of England in 1816 Turner and his party were caught in a rain storm. Note the spectacular colours in the sky

the existence of nuées ardentes was frequently overlooked until scientists recently began to study more closely the deposits that were left behind by Plinian eruptions.

The tremendous release of energy in a Plinian eruption shakes and cracks the summit of the volcano, and the removal of huge quantities of magma from the reservoir destabilizes the whole structure. The summit can then collapse, with an enormous additional explosion, down into the spaces left behind when the magma departed. Within a few minutes, a vast fuming hole, or caldera, sinks into the old crest of the volcano which can be anything from 2–10km (1¼–6¼ miles) across. The volcano is decapitated and may lose perhaps 400m (1,312 ft) in height. Subsequently, small eruptions begin to fill the caldera with domes, cinder cones and lava-flows.

Many, but not all, Plinian eruptions expel enormous quantities of sulphur dioxide which combines with water condensed from rising steam to form sulphuric acid. The acid droplets and the finest dust particles make aerosols that

the high altitude winds blow around the world in about two weeks. They remain in the stratosphere for 2–3 years, reducing the amount of heat reaching the Earth from the sun, and causing cooler weather. Some sulphurous Plinian eruptions have reduced world temperatures by 1°C or more for about three years.

The most remarkable example of climatic effects followed the largest recorded Plinian eruption at Tambora, in Indonesia, on 10 and 11 April 1815. The eruptive column rose at least 40km (25 miles) high and about 125km³ (30 cubic miles) of fragments were expelled. The top 1,000m (3,280ft) of the volcano was blown to smithereens, and the crest was replaced with a caldera, 700m (2,296ft) deep and 6km (3¾ miles) across. The dust and acid aerosols circled the Earth for several years and reduced temperatures in 1816 so that it became known as 'the year without a summer', particularly in Europe and North America. The aerosols also produced brilliant sunsets that inspired many paintings by British artist J.M.W. Turner.

the Plinian eruption of Vesuvius in AD 79

THE EVENT THAT GAVE PLINIAN ERUPTIONS THEIR NAME, AND VESUVIUS ITS REPUTATION, LASTED FROM 24–26 AUGUST IN AD 79. IT LAID WASTE TO MUCH OF CAMPANIA, ONE OF THE MOST DAZZLING PROVINCES IN THE ROMAN EMPIRE. NAPLES WAS ITS CHIEF CENTRE, WITH A POPULATION OF ABOUT 50,000; POMPEII WAS A BUSY COUNTRY TOWN WITH 20,000 INHABITANTS, AND HERCULANEUM, OPLONTIS, STABIAE AND PUTEOLI (POZZUOLI) WERE ALL PROSPEROUS SEA-SIDE TOWNS, EACH WITH ABOUT 5,000 INHABITANTS.

A view of the Bay of Naples with Vesuvius dominating the skyline

The most famous victim of Vesuvius was Pliny the Elder, author of a vast *Natural History*, and commander of the Imperial Roman Fleet. He was 56. His nephew, Pliny the Younger, aged 17, was staying at Cape Misenum on the north shore of the Bay of Naples with his mother when Vesuvius erupted. A number of years later, the historian, Tacitus, invited Pliny the Younger to describe his uncle's death, and his own experiences at Misenum. The two letters he wrote are the oldest surviving detailed descriptions of a volcanic eruption – and recent geological research has also shown how remarkably accurate and perceptive they were. The only regret is that they do not describe events in the cities that were destroyed.

In his first letter Pliny describes the death of his uncle:

'At that time, my uncle was at Misenum in command of the fleet. On 24 August, about one in the afternoon, my mother pointed out a cloud of an odd size and appearance that had formed [over Vesuvius] ... The cloud could best be described as more like an umbrella pine than any other tree, because it rose up high in a kind of trunk and then divided

Soldier, scholar and naturalist, Pliny the Elder, who died during the eruption in AD 79

into branches ... Sometimes it looked light-coloured, sometimes it looked mottled and dirty with the earth and ash it had carried up. Like a true scholar, my uncle saw at once that it deserved closer study and ordered a boat to be prepared.'

'[He was about to leave when he got a message from his friend Rectina, begging him to rescue her.] He changed plan and ... ordered the large galleys {quadriremes} to be launched ... He steered bravely straight for the danger zone that everyone else was leaving in fear and haste, but still kept on noting his observations.'

'The ash already falling became hotter and thicker as the ships approached the coast, and it was soon superseded by pumice and blackened burnt stones shattered by the fire. Suddenly the sea shallowed where the shore was obstructed and choked by debris from the mountain. [Instead of turning back, as the Captain advised,

he decided to push on to Stabiae, across the bay where his friend Pomponianus lived.] Pomponianus had already put his belongings into a boat to escape as soon as the contrary, onshore wind changed ... My uncle calmed and encouraged his terrified friend'.

'Meanwhile, tall, broad flames blazed from several places on Vesuvius and glared out in the darkness of the night. My uncle ... went to bed and apparently fell asleep ... but, eventually, the courtyard outside began to fill with so much ash and pumice that, if he had stayed in his room, he would never have been able to get out. He was awakened, and joined Pomponianus and his servants who had stayed up all night. They wondered whether to stay indoors or go out into the open, because the buildings were now swaying back and forth and shaking with more violent tremors ... After weighing up the risks, they chose the open country, and tied pillows with cloths over their heads for protection.'

An artist's impression of the despair of the inhabitants of Herculaneum as the ash cloud from the volcano approaches

A view of Vesuvius from the excavated ruins of the Forum at Pompeii. Much of Pompeii and the surrounding towns buried during the eruption have yet to be excavated

'It was daylight everywhere else by this time, but they were still enveloped in a darkness that was blacker and denser than any night ... My uncle went down to the shore to see if there was any chance of escape by sea, but the waves were still running far too high. He lay down to rest on a sheet, and called for drinks of cold water. Then, suddenly, flames and a strong smell of sulphur giving warning of yet more flames to come, forced the others to flee. He himself stood up, with the support of two slaves, and then suddenly collapsed and died, because, I imagine, he was suffocated when the dense fumes choked him. When daylight returned the following day, his body was found intact and uninjured, still fully clothed and looking more like a man asleep than dead.'

The eruption was one of the greatest natural catastrophes ever to inflict Imperial Rome. As well the events at Cape Misenum, thousands more died in other settlements in the area, particularly Pompeii and Herculaneum. The ash and pumice buried the cities which are now among the best-known archaeological sites in the world. Their aggressor, Vesuvius, became the most famous volcano on Earth.

When Vesuvius exploded on 24 August, it hurled a huge column of ash and pumice more than 25km (15½ miles) into the air. The northwesterly winds carried the fragments directly over Pompeii, where they soon began piling up thickly in the streets. A suffocating, pitch-black darkness engulfed the area. Many people panicked and fled, including the baker Modestus who left 81 loaves in his oven, where they remained for 1,800 years. By late evening the fates of Pompeii and nearby Oplontis appeared to be sealed, but up to that point only a sprinkling of ash had fallen on Herculaneum, upwind to the west. Its inhabitants were, however, anxious to be evacuated. Many took to their boats and others waited on the shore for help.

In fact Herculaneum was the first town to be completely destroyed. At 01.00 on 25 August, a nuée ardente raced down the western slopes of the volcano at over 100km/h (62mph). It caught those on the shore waiting to escape. They died huddled together, and were soon entombed in 20m (65ft) of ash. This is how they were discovered by excavators in 1982.

Those who had stayed in Pompeii spent a terrible night of anguish. The bejewelled mistress of the House of the Faun died when the roof collapsed under the weight of the ash and pumice which was now 2.4m (8ft) deep in the streets. The first three nuées ardentes did not enter Pompeii. At 07.30, the fourth nuée swept rooftops and upper storeys away completely, burning and suffocating everyone still sheltering in the town. The nuée ardente caught some as they struggled to escape: a slave bent double under a sack of food, a woman with her handkerchief in her mouth, two boys, holding

hands, trying to protect themselves with a roof-tile, a priest clutching the treasure of a Temple of Isis, a doctor with his surgical instruments, an athlete with his bottle of body-oil, a noblewoman with her gladiator lover, and a dog on its chain. At 07.35 no-one was left alive in Pompeii. A fifth nuée completed the devastation of the town. The sixth, at 08.00, was the largest of all. It spread southwards as far as Stabiae and killed Pliny the Elder on the shore. It then spread westwards as far as Misenum where it lost its momentum, 32km (20km) away, in front of the eyes of Pliny the Younger.

Forgotten for 1,600 years, excavations began in the 18th Century, mainly for antiquities. More scientific excavations began after the unification of Italy in 1861. It was at this time that Giuseppe Fiorelli revealed the bodies of those who had died during the eruption. The fine dry ash from Vesuvius had encased the victims where they died. Over the years their bodies had decayed leaving a hollow encased by the ash. As soon as the excavators found one of these hollows, Fiorelli poured liquid plaster of Paris into it. When the plaster had set, the excavators scraped away the encasing ash to reveal a model of the victim, which often showed clearly their last expression as they tried desperately to keep the glowing ash from their eyes and lungs.

Excavations are still continuing because a quarter of Pompeii, two-thirds of Herculaneum, and nearly all of Oplontis and Stabiae, have still to be revealed.

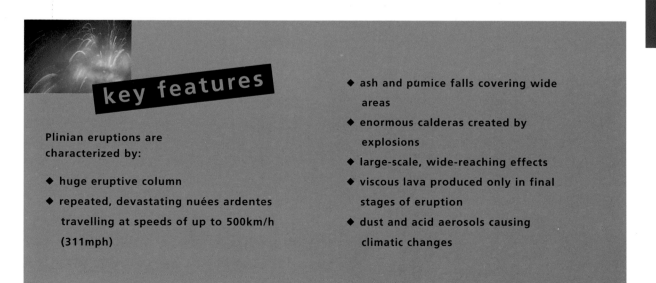

key features

Plinian eruptions are characterized by:

◆ huge eruptive column
◆ repeated, devastating nuées ardentes travelling at speeds of up to 500km/h (311mph)

◆ ash and pumice falls covering wide areas
◆ enormous calderas created by explosions
◆ large-scale, wide-reaching effects
◆ viscous lava produced only in final stages of eruption
◆ dust and acid aerosols causing climatic changes

secondary effects of volcanic eruptions

VOLCANIC MUDFLOWS AND TSUNAMIS ARE THE TWO CHIEF SECONDARY EFFECTS OF VIOLENT – AND PARTICULARLY PLINIAN – ERUPTIONS.

Volcanic mudflows

Volcanic mudflows are produced when huge volumes of volcanic fragments mix with water derived from melting summit ice-caps, crater-lakes, or even torrential rainstorms, and they therefore tend to be a feature of powerful eruptions on large volcanoes. Indonesia is particularly badly affected: since 1586 eleven major mudflows have killed about 30,000 people, and the Indonesian word 'lahar' has been adopted by scientists as the term for mudflows.

Nevado del Ruiz, 1985

On 13 November 1985, the mudflows that raced from the summit of Nevado del Ruiz in Colombia killed more people than any eruption since 1902. The Plinian eruption was relatively small and the volcano, although large (5,389m (17,680ft) high), was a long way from any settlements. The mudflows produced by the eruption travelled 60km (37 miles) to the east, destroying the small agricultural town of Armero in the valley of River Magdalena, and killing 23,000 people altogether.

There was plenty of warning of the impending eruption. Volcanic earthquakes and steam-blast eruptions shook the mountain for 51 weeks before the great catastrophe, producing columns of steam and ash and scattering cool fragments as much as 10km (6¼ miles) from the summit. The crater was located on the north-eastern edge of the ice-cap, just above the valley of the River Lagunillas and its main tributary, the River Azufrado. It was clear that this would be the route a mudflow from the volcano would take, but unfortunately maps of likely threats to the area were not widely available.

In addition geologists were not able to agree over the likely extent of the area that would be affected by an eruption. Some said a large eruption would only affect an area of about 10km² (4 square miles) around the volcano. Other visiting experts, however, affirmed that a larger eruption was imminent and finally convinced local geologists of its dangers. In October, a group of Italian experts recommended that evacuation plans be prepared and safe refuges designated. Several towns drew up well-planned contingency arrangements but no refuges were set up.

The eruption finally began at 15.06 on 13 November 1985. Ash started falling on Armero at 17.00 and soon turned into muddy rain. Ruiz erupted molten fragments for the first time at 21.08. Very little molten rock erupted, but this was enough to melt one tenth of the

Ice structures such as this one around the summit of Nevado del Ruiz were melted by the eruption in 1985 causing devastating mudflows

volcanoes

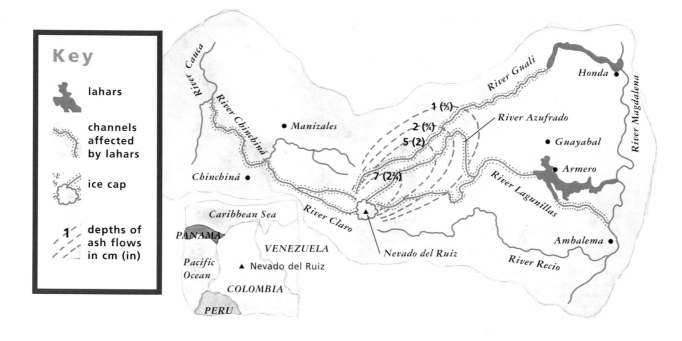

Key

- lahars
- channels affected by lahars
- ice cap
- 1 depths of ash flows in cm (in)

River Cauca

River Chinchiná

River Guali

Honda

River Magdalena

River Azufrado

1 (⅜)

2 (¾)

5 (2)

• Manizales

• Guayabal

• Armero

Chinchiná •

7 (2¾)

River Lagunillas

Caribbean Sea

River Claro

Ambalema •

PANAMA

VENEZUELA

Nevado del Ruiz

River Recio

Pacific Ocean

▲ Nevado del Ruiz

COLOMBIA

PERU

ice-cap, and form mudflows that picked up everything in their path. One of the flows raced west down the River Cauca. Immediately an order was given to evacuate Chinchiná, 50km (31 miles) downstream, but the mudflow arrived at 22.30, before the evacuation could be completed, and 1,927 people died.

The most lethal mudflow gathered impetus in the steep River Azufrado valley about 21.30. It was 30m (98ft) high and was travelling at 36km/h (22mph). This time, however, no evacuation order was given.

What happened when the mudflow finally reached Armero is unclear, but when it finally abated, it became apparent that it had damaged or destroyed two hospitals, 50 schools, 58 industrial plants, 343 commercial premises, 5,092 houses, 60 per cent of the livestock and 30 per cent of the area's rice crop. About 23,000 people and 15,000 animals died. Only 100 out of 5,000 houses in Armero remained intact, but the cemetery survived unscathed.

Arenas, the main active crater of Nevado del Ruiz

INTERVIEW

ARMERO, COLOMBIA, 1985

In November 1985 Juan Gaitan, a doctor who had been working overseas, was enjoying a vacation with his family in Armero, Colombia.

Dr Juan Gaitan

 'It was about 4.30 in the afternoon and ash started to fall ... I asked my father ... what was happening, and he explained to me ... that the Nevado del Ruiz was erupting and it was throwing ash and the wind was bringing it here. This was happening around four, five in the afternoon and it started to go dark and it started to rain, so the ash was mixing with the rain, so something like mud was forming.'

At about 20.30 Juan went to bed. He can remember the noise of the rain on the roof, part of which was made from corrugated iron. At 23.00 Juan's brother phoned to see if they knew what was happening. Shortly afterwards the lights went out and Juan, his wife, father and mother, took a torch out into the street to investigate.

 'What attracted my attention was the water that was coming down, as Armero is on an incline. The water that was

passing through the street was black. Normally when it rains the water is brown ...'

They went back inside and were just lifting the living room rug to save it from flood damage when they heard something.

 'Suddenly we heard a huge noise and we turned to look at the front of the house when it shattered and at that moment something came into the house, neither hot nor cold ... then I felt something fall through the roof ... the level kept on rising, rising, rising ... forcing me against the ceiling when suddenly, I don't know how, I came through the roof of the house.'

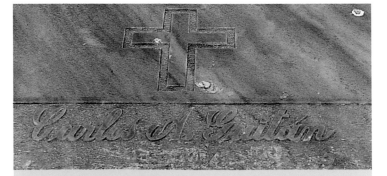

This grave is dedicated to the members of Juan Gaitan's family that died in the mudflow in 1985

'At that moment ... we started going down through the town. We'd get to walls and the same pressure would knock them down ... I remember that we went past the dome of the church. I was able to see the dome of the church and calculate that it measures 20–30m [66–98ft] ... we fell on the main park of the town. We were going to crash and I remember the colour – I don't know why I remember the colour – a grey wall ... it fell on me and I was trapped underneath ... I started to hold my breath ... I remember that something was squeezing my head ... and there came a point when I couldn't hold on any more ... I started to swallow that water ... there was some buzzing in my head and I saw some yellow stars and I lost consciousness ... In a little while I was breathing again ... we started again in that same wave that took us down through the whole town ...'

One of four views of Armero in a memorial dedicated to all those who died

During his terrifying journey down the hill Juan had been stabbed by a pole, but in spite of this, when he finally came to a standstill he began straight away to look around for some way to pull himself out.

 '... suddenly I saw the shadow of someone ... I lifted my arm and said "Here I am, help me out" ... The man pulled me and I got to where the man was, which was on a corrugated iron roof, and the man sat me down ... After a few minutes we began to talk. I asked him what his name was. He said "My name is Alfonso" and I told him "My name is Juan Gaitan ... I'm a doctor". "Yes" he said, "I know you are a doctor ... because I was a patient of yours when you were working here."'

Now he was out of the mud Juan became aware of the full extent of his injuries; the pole that had stabbed him was still embedded in his chest. Between them Juan and Alfonso managed to remove it. The deafening roar of the mud had given way to silence. Then people began to shout. Some were crying out in pain, others wanted to shout messages to loved ones, and find out the identities of those around them. Hours passed and the weather grew colder. Juan began

to throw mud on himself to try to keep warm. He also put mud inside his wound to try and stem the flow of blood. As the sun rose they became aware of the full extent of the damage.

 'As the dawn came we saw that the mountain was full of people ... We started to see around us and everything was grey, only grey ... And we could see around us that there were pieces of houses, of walls ... [I said] "Well we're sitting on what's left of Armero."'

It was many more hours before help arrived for Juan and the other survivors. Planes flew tantalizingly close but no rescuers appeared. Passers-by were too frightened to help. Many people died from their terrible injuries. Juan reflects on what it has taught him.

The memorial that houses the four views of Armero (see above left)

 'One learns to really live ... for the small things ... the real privilege of health, of your children, of the family ... these are good things that I learned from all these bad things that happened.'

tsunamis

Tsunamis are produced by violent eruptions that occur on volcanic islands or in coastal areas. Since many 'violent' volcanoes are located on or near the coast, particularly on the subduction zones around the Pacific Ocean, volcanic tsunamis can be frequent. Eruptions, however, cause only 5 per cent of all tsunamis.

The biggest and most frequent volcanic tsunamis occur when calderas and debris avalanches collapse into the sea. Those caused by nuées ardentes are smaller and less common, while mudflows and glacier-bursts produce the smallest and rarest of all. The largest tsunamis can be detected by equipment all over the world, whereas the smallest are noticed only within a localized area. The tsunami produced by Krakatau in 1883, for example, registered on tidal gauges in the English Channel, but the mudflow from Montagne Pelée caused a tsunami only 5m (16½ft) high. Volcanic tsunamis have long, imperceptible wave-lengths as they sweep across the deep oceans. In shallow water, the wave-length shortens, its height increases, and it curls over and crashes onto the shore at 80km/h (50mph) in a wall of water 30m (98ft) high.

One volcanic tsunami has been accused of destroying a civilization. The Bronze Age Minoan civilization in Crete came to an abrupt end c.1450 BC, when all but one of its palaces were destroyed. The Greek archaeologist, Marinatos, proposed that the Plinian eruption of Santorini, 125km (78 miles) to the north, was to blame. He suggested that a tsunami, generated when the great caldera collapsed, could have destroyed the palaces and towns. Although this theory initially attracted a lot of support, it became apparent that the eruption occurred about 50 years before the fall of the Cretan civilization. It also seems unlikely that a tsunami generated to the north of Crete could have destroyed palaces standing 200m (656ft) above its southern coast.

Anak Krakatau ('son of Krakatau'), the new cone that has grown up inside the water-filled caldera of Krakatau since the eruption of 1883

The eruption of Krakatau, 1883

Before it erupted, Krakatau was a small, uninhabited island, comprising three volcanoes, rising just 822m (2,697ft) out of sea. The events of 26 August, however, were shattering. The explosions were heard on Rodriguez Island, in the Indian Ocean, 4,653km (2,890 miles) away. Darkness fell for two days in southern Sumatra and western Java. Dust and acid aerosols circled the world for several years, reducing temperatures and producing brilliant sunsets and blue moons. Explosions and avalanches created a huge caldera and generated huge tsunamis which crashed onto the shores of Java and Sumatra. Falling ash and nuées ardentes

The *Berouw* was picked up by the tsunami and washed 2.6km (1½ miles) upriver in Teloeq Betoeng, southern Sumatra, killing all 28 crew members. The ship is still there today

claimed relatively few lives: most of the victims drowned 40km (25 miles) from Krakatau.

By the evening a huge column of ash and gas rose over 36km (22 miles) above Krakatau. Ash was falling thickly and explosions were shaking the ground. The first, small, tsunami (2m, 6½ft high), was recorded around 18.00. Gradually the waves became larger and began to travel further.

Monday, 27 August dawned clear. At 06.30 at Anjer, on the western coast of Java, telegraph-master Schruit was looking across the Sunda Straits to Krakatau. Suddenly he saw 'an enormous wave … like a mountain' rushing towards the town. 'Never have I run so fast in my life … death was at my heels … I fell, utterly exhausted … and, to my amazement, I saw the wave retreating'. The tsunami destroyed practically everything below 25m (82ft) above sea-level and many thousands were drowned. Moments later, probably the same tsunami smashed onto Semangka Bay and Teloeq Betoeng in southern Sumatra. All the low-lying areas were smashed and sucked into the sea.

For the next few hours, the waves in the Straits were mountainous, whipped up by hurricane-force winds and a series of enormous explosions from Krakatau. Another great tsunami was unleashed about 10.30 in the pitch darkness on Monday morning. Again it smashed the coasts of western Java and Sumatra.

One of the survivors was a rice-grower, working in the paddy-fields 8km (5 miles) inland from Merak in western Java, at 10.30 that morning.

'We saw a great black thing, a long way off, coming towards us. It was very high … and we soon saw that it was water. Trees and houses were washed away … Not far off was some steep, sloping ground. We all ran towards it and tried to climb out of the way of the water. It was too quick for most of them, and many were drowned at my side.'

In the Sunda Straits the population was decimated. Below the great tidemarks left by the tsunamis, about 30m (98ft) high, the coastal areas were a tangle of smashed houses, trees, animal carcasses and human bodies. In Java and Sumatra, 132 villages were damaged and 165 were completely destroyed. 36,417 people were killed. Smaller waves were registered on tidal gauges as far away as Britain and America.

chapter **4**

FORECASTING

forecasting and predicting earthquakes

MAKING SHORT-TERM PREDICTIONS STEMS FROM LONG-TERM FORECASTS WHICH ARE, IN TURN, DERIVED FROM A STUDY OF THE PAST BEHAVIOUR OF THE EARTH'S CRUST. EACH YEAR THERE ARE ABOUT 1 MILLION EARTHQUAKES, MOST OF THEM VERY SMALL. WHAT IS IMPORTANT, HOWEVER, IS THE ABILITY TO PREDICT HIGH MAGNITUDE EARTHQUAKES THAT MAY HIT HIGHLY POPULATED AREAS. SUCH EVENTS ARE MUCH LESS COMMON AND THEIR WARNING SIGNALS ARE MORE DIFFICULT TO DISTINGUISH.

low risk zones

high risk zones

Segments representing seismic gaps around the subduction zones of the Pacific Ocean

In general terms the subduction zones and areas of active horizontal displacement, such as parts of China and California, are the areas in which earthquakes are most likely to occur. However, plate movements are far from continuous from a human point of view; some segments of a fault or subduction zone move, whilst others stay still for decades or even centuries. Immobile segments of faults, or seismic gaps, represent zones that have not experienced earthquakes for abnormally long time compared to segments nearby.

These seismic gaps are the places to look for future earthquakes in the mobile zones of the globe. Unfortunately there are a large number of them. About half the subduction zones around the Pacific Ocean, for example, comprise seismic gaps. Those situated in highly populated areas, such as California, south-eastern Japan, and Java, tend to attract the most attention, and are the areas in which accurate prediction of an

Tokyo, Japan is still a high risk zone

impending earthquake would be the most valuable. Five earthquakes exceeding magnitude 8.5, have struck the United States Pacific coast north of Cape Mendocino in the past 1,700 years, with time intervals ranging from 90–560 years. It has been calculated that the last great earthquake occurred on 26 January 1700. Now the area is rising by 4mm (⅙in), and contracting by a significant amount each year. The crust is therefore being squeezed continuously and is bound to crack sooner or later.

Seismic gaps should reveal the areas where big earthquakes are possible, or likely, within several decades. Unfortunately scientists do not always know exactly what to look for. As earthquakes are caused when rocks crack along a fault, in response to strains that have built up over many years, it would be logical to expect some precursory signs before an earthquake takes place. However, just because one particular sort of change is recorded before an earthquake, this does not necessarily mean that it is a warning sign. The Romans, for example, believed earthquakes occurred when the wind came from a certain direction.

Because of these doubts, experts measure as many changes as possible. This systematic, empirical method proved very successful in the prediction of an earthquake at Haicheng, China. A modified version of this system is also being used in Kanto and Tokai provinces in Japan, and at the Parkfield pilot site on the San Andreas Fault in California. There has been considerable investment in measuring all kinds of ground deformations – based on repeated surveys accurate to 1mm ($^1/_{25}$in) or less – that might show the minute effects of stresses and strains before the rupture.

Changes in ground-water levels and content seem to be more significant than changes in rocks at the present time. Ground-water aquifers delicately reflect the state of underground fissures or other conditions and, therefore, reveal

The Kobe earthquake of 1995 devastated many areas of the city. It lay outside the official high-risk area designated by the Japanese authorities

changes in such factors as temperature, pH value, and particularly radon content. Radioactive decay of uranium in the rocks produces the gas radon-222 which reaches the ground-water. Radon is itself radioactive but it decays within a few days. Therefore changes in radon concentrations give a good, quick picture of the varying amounts of water entering an aquifer. These changes may be caused when fissures open or close as stresses alter in the rocks. These variations can be relayed to laboratories and recorded at once. radon-222 changes can, therefore, indicate an imminent earthquake. They are measured widely in Japan. At Kobe the radon increased fourfold between the end of October and the end of December 1994. By 8 January 1995, there was ten times as much Radon present as in October. On 17 January 1995 the earthquake hit Kobe (see pp.74–75). It has also been discovered since that mineral water taken from thermal springs near the epicentre of that earthquake showed great increases in chlorine and sulphur ions between August 1994 and January 1995.

An ancient Chinese seismometer: a tremor would make a ball fall into a frog's mouth

prediction and prevention of tsunamis

NEAR THEIR SOURCE AREAS TSUNAMIS OCCUR WITHIN ABOUT 15 MINS OF THE EARTHQUAKE OR ERUPTION FROM WHICH THEY ORIGINATED. WITHOUT PREDICTING THE CAUSE, IT IS IMPOSSIBLE TO GIVE ADEQUATE WARNING OF THE TSUNAMI NEAR ITS SOURCE. LONG-DISTANCE TSUNAMIS MAY TAKE UP TO 22 HRS TO CROSS THE PACIFIC OCEAN GIVING SUFFICIENT TIME TO TAKE EVASIVE ACTION. FOR EXAMPLE A TSUNAMI COULD REACH SAN FRANCISCO FROM JAPAN, 8,000KM (4,970 MILES) AWAY, IN ABOUT 10 HOURS. BUT THERE MAY BE MUCH LESS TIME AVAILABLE.

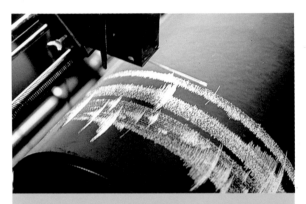

This smoke drum seismic record records earth tremors in the Hawaii Volcanoes National Park on the east rift of Kilauea

The Pacific Ocean experiences the most dangerous tsunamis and it is also fringed by some of the world's most densely-populated coastal plains. Hawaii is particularly at risk as tsunamis can reach the islands from all over the Pacific Ocean: about 100 have been recorded since 1813, and they often cause great coastal damage.

The Pacific Tsunami Warning System (PTSW) is an attempt to combat the potential destruction by quickly detecting earthquakes or eruptions that might produce tsunamis, and estimating their height and time of arrival at vulnerable places. The original American system was developed after a tsunami generated in the Aleutian Islands on 1 April 1946, swept away a 30m (98ft) lighthouse on Unimak Island and severely damaged Hilo in Hawaii a few hours later. It became an international organization after a powerful tsunami generated in Chile in May 1960 devastated Hawaii and Japan. There are now 23 member states, concentrated around the Pacific Ocean. The system is based on a network of 69 earthquake stations and 65 tide-stations to plot the course and likely size of the tsunamis, all co-ordinated from the Pacific Tsunami Warning Centre at Honolulu in Hawaii.

Tsunami, Hawaii 1957. This sequence of photographs shows the arrival of the Oahu tsunami at Laie Point, 9 March 1957. It was triggered by an earthquake in Alaska on this date

For example, the alert is raised after a magnitude 7.0 earthquake, the epicentre of which can be located in about 15 mins. If a tsunami develops, the warning is sent as quickly as possible to the threatened areas. By this time, however, the coastal fringes near the source of the tsunami would already have been inundated.

Under these circumstances, the safest place to be is onboard ship, and vessels should ideally be as far out to sea as possible (where the water depth is at a maximum). For those on land, if the sea starts to retreat after an earthquake, the most sensible places to head for are hills and valley sides at least 30m (98ft) above the old sea-level.

an earthquake and tsunami reaction timetable

19 September 1985

07.18	Earthquake, magnitude 8.1, strikes Michoacán, Mexico
07.19	Seismic waves reach Mexico City; eventually felt by 20 million people
07.19–c.07.24	412 buildings in Mexico City collapse, 3124 more badly damaged. Communication systems and Public Utility Systems put out of action, 30,000 injured, 9,500 (possibly up to 35,000) deaths and 100,000 left homeless in Mexico City. Estimated damage: US$3,000 million
07.23	Short-period alarms set off at National Earthquake Information Center (Golden, Colorado)
07.25	Interpretation of seismograms at NEIC begins
07.27	P-wave arrives at Honolulu
07.28	Surface wave arrives at NEIC in Golden
07.30	P-waves arrive in France and Italy
07.35	Preliminary estimate of epicentre: 17.8°N, 102.3°W
07.48	Pacific Tsunami Warning Center contacted. Estimated magnitude 7.8
07.49	U.S. National Warning Center notified of site and magnitude
07.52	Surface wave arrives at Shemya Island, Aleutian Islands
08.00	News Services informed
08.05	PTWC issues tsunami watch for Pacific region
08.18	World Organizations informed: eg. UN Disaster Relief Organisation; European-Mediterranean Seismological Centre in Strasbourg, France
08.20	Additional data received from Istituto Nazionale di Geofisica in Italy
08.30–Noon	Data exchanges with Seismic Stations in Central and South America
10.20	PTWC cancels tsunami watch: no dangerous tsunami
Noon	Additional data allows revision of site of earthquake: 18.13°N, 102.31°W

INTERVIEW

HAWAII, 1946

Marsue McShane

At 01.59 on 1 April 1946 the inhabitants of the north-east coast of Hawaii were unaware of the implications of an earthquake happening deep below sea-level, 3,700km (2,300) miles away. The earthquake took place on the ocean floor, on the northern slope of the Aleutian trench, off the coast of Alaska. Within 20 mins a lighthouse on Unimak Island, 96km (60 miles) to the northwest, was destroyed by waves 35m (115ft) high. At the same time, waves from the Aleutians were also heading south, towards Hawaii.

Marsue McShane arrived in Hawaii in 1945.

 'Before I came here I lived in Ohio, Cincinnati, and my first job was at Laupahoehoe ... I knew nothing about Hawaii but I wanted to teach around the world so I came here and I met my fellow teachers ... and the four of us shared a cottage ... and we couldn't believe the beauty of the place ... it was just an idyllic life.'

The waves caused by the earthquake took less than five hours to reach the capital of Hawaii, Honolulu, on the island of Oahu. They reached

Laupahoehoe about 30 mins later. Marsue remembers:

'... we were not quite up ... we were still in our bathrobes and things ... Danny Axiona ... knocked on our door and said "Come and see the tidal wave" ... first we ... couldn't see any tidal wave, but there was a place to observe the cove, and we went up to look and we were standing in our pyjamas and slippers and everything ... and the water sort of sucked out like you were emptying a bath tub, and went a little bit beyond where it is usually at low tide, and then it slowly came back in and up a bit higher than high tide ...'

This process was repeated a second time, and by the third, a large amount of debris, sand and fish from the ocean floor was deposited on the sea front where Marsue's school's athletics field was situated. The mood at this stage was almost light-hearted: some children were trying to catch the fish that had been stranded on the playing field, another group of students was being taught about tidal waves by one of the science teachers. Marsue hurried back to the house to dress and to fetch her camera.

A memorial to all those who died in the tsunami overlooks the harbour today

forecasting

'[I] focused the camera on the waves [and thought] "I hope it's a big one this time" ... Then it got bigger and bigger and never did dissolve and go back – and that was the first time it occurred to anybody that it was danger ... I dropped the camera and tried to run ... the cottage just dissolved ... the roof went "Boom" and so ... I crawled up and sat on the corner of the roof, and it sucked way in up to where the school was ... and then began to suck out again.'

Marsue and her friends decided they would try to run as far as they could before the wave returned, but it caught up with them, and they were pulled underneath the water and out to sea. Huge walls of water continued to crash over the shoreline. Although a strong swimmer Marsue was unable to battle against the huge power of the waves.

'... I came up a second time and my head was right by [a] lighthouse, the light was sticking up and there I was facing the light on the lighthouse'.

When she emerged for a third time it took Marsue a few moments before she realized she was still alive:

'... I thought well nothing's broken, I can move ... my shoes were gone, my socks were gone, my blue jeans were gone.'

She now tried to get away from the cliffs. It was very difficult to move through the water as it was full of rubbish but eventually she managed to find a door to hold on to. She realized that it may be sometime before she was rescued and willed herself to remain calm until help arrived.

'Finally I saw an airplane circling, he never buzzed his motor to let me know he saw me ... but finally he dropped a rubber raft, but now the sea was too rough and it was too far for me to get there with my door ... but then he dropped another one, and it was

ABOVE Marsue with her class, 1946
BELOW The teachers at Laupahoehoe 1946, some of whom died in the tsunami

now 5.30pm, starting to turn dark ... and I swam over to this rubber raft ... and I got into it ... then that's when the rescue boat came out.'

Marsue was one of the lucky ones; 159 people were killed by the 1946 tsunami, including 21 people in the tiny settlement of Laupahoehoe, and 96 in the neighbouring village Hilo. Almost 500 homes or businesses were completely destroyed and 1,000 more were badly damaged. If modern alarm systems had been in place in 1946 it is likely that nobody would have died. With 30 mins warning there should be plenty of time for people to move to high ground away from the shore. There are now sirens to let people know that a tsunami is approaching.

forecasting

success and failure in China

SEISMIC ACTIVITY IN CHINA IS DUE TO THE NORTHWARD PRESSURE OF THE INDIAN SUB-CONTINENT THAT IS SQUEEZING ASIA, AND PUSHING CHINA SIDEWAYS TOWARDS THE EAST. EARTHQUAKES PRODUCED BY SUCH MOVEMENTS ARE VIOLENT. THE AREA OF THE NORTH CHINA PLAIN, AROUND THE GULF OF CHIHLI EAST OF BEIJING, IS DENSELY POPULATED, AND ACCURATE PREDICTION OF EARTHQUAKES IN SUCH AN AREA IS VITAL.

In 1966 two earthquakes within as many weeks prompted the government to establish an earthquake bureau to investigate the possibility of prediction. Areas known to be prone to earthquakes were selected for intensive study, and 20,000 scientists and over 100,000 amateur assistants, were sent there. At the same time a public awareness and education programme was implemented.

As the general problem of prediction worldwide was a lack of knowledge of the vital signals of earthquakes, this labour-intensive, time-consuming, empirical method had undoubted merits. Local faults, tremors, ground tilt, changes in water levels in springs and wells, radon contents, magnetic field variations and unusual behaviour by animals, were all recorded. At the same time scientists mapped and analyzed faults and carried out precise levelling, gravity and magnetic studies.

By 1973 it was clear that the plain around the Gulf of Chihli was swelling, and that earth tremors had increased five times in the past year, and seemed to be moving north towards the Haicheng area. A major earthquake seemed likely but a more precise prediction was still needed. A network of seismic stations was set up in 1974. A 50 km- (31 mile-) long coastal area between Haicheng and Yingkow was the focus of 'abnormal features': water was seen shooting from the ground and animals were restless.

Around Haicheng in 1975, the water level began to alter in wells, implying that the ground might be starting to fissure in response

The focus of the earthquake in 1976 was directly under Tangshan and the epicentre was therefore in the town itself

forecasting

to the strains. In January 1975 experts said that an earthquake was imminent. A magnitude 4.8 earthquake struck the area 70km (43½ miles) north of Haicheng but this was not the high-magnitude earthquake they were expecting.

During the first three days of February 1975 over 500 tremors shook the area between Haicheng and Yingkow. On the morning of 4 February the tremors suddenly stopped. The scientists told the provincial government, who, at 10.00 issued the prediction that an earthquake of magnitude 6.0 would soon occur.

That Tuesday evening, a magnitude 7.5 earthquake devastated the Haicheng region. Thousands of buildings collapsed, but the people were already waiting outside, and a relatively small number were killed: 1,328. This was the first accurate short-term prediction of an earthquake based on scientific methods – albeit at enormous cost in man-hours.

Data collection continued and early in 1976 scientists forecast that the area between Haicheng and Beijing, where 'abnormal phenomena' had been apparent, would suffer a large earthquake at some time in the next five years. This was significant as the area included the large industrial city of Tangshan, 200km (124 miles) east of Beijing. However, there was no apparent major fault threatening the region and the city had not experienced an earthquake since records began. Magnetic and water level measurements varied slightly from their usual levels, but other than this, Tangshan seemed no more threatened than many other cities.

Tangled wreckage such as this proved lethal for most of those trapped inside

But if an earthquake were to happen, Tangshan was in a high-risk category as it was built on thick, silty sediment. The sediment was to have a two-fold effect in the disaster that hit the city: it obscured a major fault, and when the fault slipped, the sediment liquefied. Given the lack of apparent evidence of an impending earthquake, however, a decision was made not to evacuate the city.

The fault slipped for a length of 150km (93 miles), with a sideways dislocation of about 3m (9¾ft). The focus of the earthquake, with a magnitude of 7.6 or 7.9, was directly beneath Tangshan, and its epicentre was therefore in the city. It struck Tangshan at 03.43 on 28 July 1976. Half the brick buildings of more than one storey collapsed, only four remained undamaged. Roads and bridges in the area were shattered. The silts underlying the city had liquefied. In the wake of this disaster the official death toll was 240,000, but others have estimated fatalities at anywhere between 500,000 and 850,000.

Buildings near the epicentre of the earthquake were reduced to piles of rubble within seconds

INTERVIEW

TANGSHAN, 1976

Miner Wang Shu Bin was admitted to Kailuan Hospital in Tangshan on July 27 1976. The doctors decided to keep him in over night, he was put on a drip due to dehydration and his wife stayed to keep him company.

Wang Shu Bin

Wang Shu Bin and his family before the earthquake. Sadly his wife was killed

Wang Shu Bin had in fact experienced the most lethal earthquake of the 20th Century.

 'After the building collapsed there were 19 of us in the ward including doctors and patients ... I was trapped in the bed by a large piece of concrete ... The concrete above me was so close I could touch it just by stretching up ... A lot of people were crying for help, many people were still alive. After the building collapsed there was not even a chink of light.'

 'At 3.42 in the morning my head was especially clear, and from the room I could see outside. There was lightning ... Lots of lightning ... I thought it was going to rain. The weather that day was ... very

The hospital in which Wang Shu Bin was being treated at the time of the earthquake

muggy, very hot. Gloomy and heavy. At that moment I saw the fluorescent light on the ceiling swinging violently ... I did not realize it was an earthquake. In the blink of an eye, around five seconds later, the whole building collapsed.'

Wang Shu Bin's wife had been asleep on an empty hospital bed when the earthquake struck. Afterwards they were able to carry on a conversation. His wife was badly injured – crushed below the waist by a fallen piece of concrete. Wang Shu Bin tried to extricate himself from the tangle of metal, concrete and rubble.

 '... I used all my strength to push myself out with my feet and to pull out my hand that was trapped in the rubble ... After I pulled it out my wife was ... crying out, a lot of other people were calling for help. I felt

forecasting

that I was not injured very much and once I had saved myself I had to rescue my wife.'

In spite of what he believed Wang Shu Bin was quite badly hurt: his wounds were serious if superficial, but the dangers of infection were high; many people were already dead or dying. It is difficult to comprehend his painstaking progress as he first worked to free himself and then worked his way towards his wife.

 'From on my bed to under my bed [took] about two days. My hand was totally trapped. My leg was crushed – it felt like a wooden plank was on top of me. I felt later and realized it was a dead body.'

It took him another day to reach the concrete block that was the last obstacle separating him from his wife. This was to prove impossible to overcome. Only able to touch her fingertips, Wang Shu Bin and his wife talked about their family and their life together until she no longer responded. Wang Shu Bin remained underneath the rubble for a further four days as he dug his way out.

 'During that four days a lot of people were still crying out ... I touched a lot of dead bodies on the way digging myself out. Later when I got out, 19 people were in there, only I came out alive ... no matter what I did I couldn't find a way out ... big concrete pillars and blocks, and big bricks. Finally I found a bottle of glucose ... and a pillow stuffed with husks of grain ... Whenever I was hungry on my way out this was my food.'

Digging through the rubble to reach the outside was extremely hazardous work but the building skills Wang Shu Bin had learned as a miner helped to save his life.

 'I was crawling on my stomach through the filth, I had a lot of cuts on my body and the smell made me choke ... On the way digging myself out I ... ignored the pain. I

barely slept. I didn't rest ... I would stop and shore up my tunnel ... I reinforced the walls with pieces of brick, supporting the roof ... I dug a tunnel 12m [39ft] long.

Damaged roads and bridges made it difficult for rescue teams to move around the area

Finally, after seven days he collapsed, exhausted. And as he lay in the cramped tunnel he began to feel that perhaps it would be better to die with his wife in the rubble. Then he realized that he could hear noise from the road outside. He shouted to try to alert rescuers to his presence.

 '... I suddenly heard voices ... It was a military medical team from Shenyang. They were short of medicine and were looking for medicine in the ruins of this ... hospital ... I shouted upwards ... then they heard my shouts.'

 'They found me on August 4 at 9am, finally, at 6.50pm they got me out. It was very difficult. Then, when I saw the first beam of light it was like the first shaft of sunlight in my life ... The first thing I set eyes on was a blue sky and the big leaves of a tree and the face of the person that saved me ... I was very emotional. I clung to their heads and cried because I had been so lonely for the last eight days ... I couldn't believe that I was saved.'

Wang Shu Bin lost nine of his family in the Tangshan earthquake. He still mourns for all those that died, the people who were 'lost in a moment'.

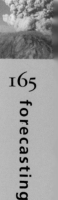

handling
earthquakes in Japan

JAPAN PROBABLY SUFFERS MORE NATURAL DISASTERS EVEN THAN CHINA. THE AREA AROUND TOKYO, IN KANTO AND TOKAI PROVINCES, IS ONE OF THE MOST VULNERABLE IN THE WHOLE COUNTRY, BECAUSE IT IS THE FOCUS OF TWO SUBDUCTION ZONES. JUST TO THE SOUTH-EAST OF THE CAPITAL, THE PACIFIC PLATE IS PLUNGING BOTH BENEATH JAPAN, ALONG THE JAPAN TRENCH, AND ALSO BENEATH THE PHILIPPINE PLATE, ALONG THE IZU-BONIN TRENCH. IN TURN, THE NORTHERNMOST POINT OF THE PHILIPPINE PLATE IS ALSO PLUNGING UNDER JAPAN AROUND THE IZU PENINSULA, WHICH IS IN FACT AN ISLAND ON THE PHILIPPINE PLATE THAT HAS BEEN CARRIED INTO COLLISION WITH THE REST OF JAPAN.

In addition, some scientists believe that Hokkaido Island and eastern Honshu belong to the American Plate rather than the Eurasian Plate, and this multiplicity of plate margins thereby increases the chances of violent earthquakes. About 12 million people live in the Tokyo conurbation. Kanto and Tokai provinces have experienced nine earthquakes exceeding magnitude 7.9 in the past 300 years and several earthquakes of over magnitude 6.0 hit the area every year.

The Seismological Society had already gathered together many historical records when an earthquake on 1 September 1923 devastated Tokyo and much of Kanto province. The earthquake started a huge fire, kindled by open hearths and wooden buildings. About 40 per cent of Tokyo was destroyed and 142,807 people died. Damage caused by the earthquake cost 7 per cent of GNP. The geological community was spurred into action.

In 1925, the world's first Earthquake Research Institute was founded, which studied the effects of earthquakes all over the world. The creation of the world-wide seismological station network and the formulation of the theory of

Kanto earthquake 1923. View from the roof of the Imperial Hotel, Tokyo. One of the few buildings in the

plate tectonics in the 1960s provided a boost, and a committee for predicting earthquakes was also established. The national threat to Japan from seismic activity means that, unlike in many other countries, there is a united political will to achieve accurate prediction, and a general recognition of the value of such a policy.

The Kanto earthquake, 1923

This initiative produced an early success: scientists discovered a seismic gap in the subduction zone along the Kuril Trench east of Hokkaido Island, in which one segment had remained still, whilst all its neighbours had produced major earthquakes since 1900. Accurate surveys then showed that eastern Hokkaido was contracting as if stresses were building up in the quiet segment. An earthquake was forecast, although not an exact date, and it duly arrived in 1973. Suitably encouraged, in 1978, the government designated eight highly-populated earthquake-prone areas for special monitoring, and two others – in Kanto and Tokai provinces – for the closest possible attention.

The most modern surveillance methods have been applied to the particularly vulnerable area of the Izu Peninsula, 100km (62 miles) south-west of Tokyo, which is still colliding with the rest of Japan. After 44 years of relative inactivity, a magnitude 6.9 earthquake shook the southern

end of Izu in 1974. From 1974–78, the eastern part of Izu swelled up by as much as 15cm (6in), accompanied by a swarm of earth tremors. In 1978, the radon content changed for five days, earth tremors increased for 15 hours, and then stopped dead. Three hours later there was a magnitude 7.0 earthquake offshore near Izu Island. Unfortunately, the monitoring network was not dense enough to predict this earthquake accurately. Conversely there were no such warning signs prior to a magnitude 6.7 earthquake off Izu in 1980.

West of Izu, the Philippine Plate is plunging under Tokai, producing magnitude 8.0 earthquakes every 100–150 years. There is a seismic gap, however, in the trench in Suruga Bay, west of Izu, which has not moved during the present century. The subducting Philippine Plate must, therefore, have built up stresses that should soon dislocate the rocks. There is some evidence of these stresses: the coast of Tokai has sunk by 60cm (23½in) since 1900 and Suruga Bay has narrowed by 1m (3¼ft). There are also not many earth tremors near the Bay but plenty around it and this so-called 'doughnut pattern' sometimes heralds a major earthquake. The whole area is now criss-crossed with monitoring equipment, and the hope is that, if all goes well, the experts may be able to issue a few days' warning of a future disaster.

city to remain standing, the hotel had been specially designed by American architect Frank Lloyd Wright

predictions on the San Andreas fault system

THERE ARE FOUR MAIN, AND A NUMBER OF MINOR, SEGMENTS ALONG THE SAN ANDREAS FAULT SYSTEM. THESE WILL ALL BREAK AT DIFFERENT TIMES IN RESPONSE TO DIFFERENT DEGREES OF STRAIN THAT BUILD UP AND, THEREFORE, THE FULL LENGTH OF EACH SEGMENT ONLY RARELY MOVES DURING ANY ONE EARTHQUAKE.

segment that slipped in the 1989 Loma Prieta earthquake

The northern, and longest, segment stretches about 480km (298 miles) from Cape Mendocino to Hollister, and appears to move once every 250 years, but not to the same extent along its whole length. During the San Francisco earthquake of 1906, the southern section moved much less than the northern section, and the southern section still has some ground to make up, even following the Loma Prieta earthquake in 1989. Between San Francisco Bay and Hollister there are three active branches of the fault system: the San Andreas fault proper going through San Francisco; the Hayward fault passing through Oakland on the east of the Bay; and the Calaveras fault, running alongside it, further inland. Each branch has moved independently in the past 160 years but magnitudes only exceeded 6.8 at San Francisco in 1906. On the Hayward and San Andreas branches, scientists believe that there is a 20 per cent chance of a magnitude 7.0 earthquake in the next 30 years.

A USGS scientist operates a two-colour laser geodimeter at a station near Parkfield

From Hollister to Parkfield, 150km (93 miles) south-east, the segment moves gradually, causing medium magnitude earthquakes asbout every 22 years. Between Parkfield and San Bernadino, north of Los Angeles, the fault system jerks more intensely, and at intervals of about 150 years. The southernmost segment of the San Andreas fault system, from San Bernadino south-east into Mexico, has been quiet over the past 250 years, but neighbouring faults have produced earthquakes of high magnitude.

Scientists have constructed a diagram of the probability of earthquakes occurring along the San Andreas system. The probability of a magnitude 7.5–8.0 earthquake within the next 30 years, in the southern segments of the fault, varies between 10 and 40 per cent. Los Angeles has a 60 per cent chance, and San Francisco a 50 per cent chance, of being shaken by a large earthquake in the next 30 years.

forecasting

The Parkfield prediction

In 1985 the US Geological Survey predicted that 'an earthquake of about magnitude 6.0 would occur before 1993 on the San Andreas Fault near Parkfield [California] ...' Never before had the time, place and magnitude of an earthquake been so precisely predicted on a scientific basis. The project has had a great deal of support, and has been funded by US$1 million from Californian state authorities and US$1 million from the Federal Government. The aim was to find out if specific, measurable, recognizable changes occurred just before an earthquake. Such observations could then be tested further at Parkfield, and may be applicable to earthquake zones elsewhere in the world.

The village of Parkfield is packed full of highly sensitive equipment. The scientists register seismicity, strain, water levels, water chemistry, heat flow, geomagnetism, ground acceleration, seismic velocities and animal behaviour. The data are transmitted to and monitored at Menlo Park, the western headquarters of the US Geological Survey. Parkfield was chosen because it has suffered fairly frequent, but relatively minor, magnitude 6.0 earthquakes: in 1881, 1901, 1922, 1934 and 1966. The average interlude is 22 years, with a five year margin for error on either side. The next quake could be due any time.

San Francisco: a 50 per cent chance of a high magnitude earthquake in the next 30 years

Duane Hamann

Duane Hamann is a the only teacher at the small primary school in Parkfield, California. He also has another, very important, part-time job: he checks ground deformation using laser equipment as part of the United States Geological Survey's Parkfield Experiment.

'... about 13 years ago Al Lindh (see p.39) from the USGS came by my house one day and he said "Would you like another part-time job?"'

(see p.39)

Although Duane had no formal training there were many reasons why USGS geologist, Allan Lindh, thought he was the right man for the job. First, he had the necessary time each day to devote to reading and adjusting the instruments. Second, he had already worked for the USGS prior to the introduction of specialist laser equipment. Third, the new equipment was being installed on land that had been owned by Duane's family for the past 100 years and he was involved with helping to set it up.

The machine he works with is known as a two-coloured geodimeter which is aimed at 19 different points on the horizon.

'The two-coloured geodimeter operates on the principle of how fast light travels ... we send a beam of light out and actually in this case we use two colours of light ... red and blue ... on the other end of the line that I'm measuring there's a reflector ... We send this beam of light out ... and it hits the reflector and it is returned to the instrument, and the amount of time that it takes ... in simple terms is how we get our measurement ... I can actually get an accurate measurement on a line that is (5.6km) 3½ miles away to within a fraction of a millimetre ...'

forecasting

INTERVIEW

EARTHQUAKE 'SENSITIVES'

Many people and animals are able to feel or 'sense' when earthquakes are about to happen. Strange behaviour by domestic pets is particularly noticeable and people may experience headaches, electric shocks and ground movement.

Linda Curtis is a seismological secretary at the United States Geological Survey in Pasadena, California. She takes calls from people who feel earthquakes coming but do not know what to do with their information. There is no funded research into sensitivity at present and so the scientists themselves are busy with other projects. Linda makes notes and keeps files on Rodolex cards on everyone that calls.

'We receive lots of calls, for example, here is one from a woman who has a Japanese Love Fish named Richter. He likes to jump out of his aquarium right before earthquakes ... another guy whose house creaks before it quakes ... another gentleman has a TV that gets interference right before earthquakes ... a miniature dachshund that does circles ... an African Grey Parrot called Dorian that likes to pick feathers out of his chest several weeks to a month prior to an earthquake... and a Rottweiler named King who makes circles right before earthquakes.'

The 1994 Northridge earthquake caused this landslide at Pacific Palisades

King's owner is Dan Farell, a dog trainer and police dog handler from Whittier, California. The first example of King's sensitive behaviour occurred in June 1992:

The Northridge earthquake also seriously damaged many roads and bridges. This is a

'... At 1 o'clock in the morning, just getting ready to go to sleep ... and my dog starts going really crazy ... he starts running around in circles in the house, running circles in the room, barking at me, jumping on the bed. Finally, I got him calmed down five or ten minutes after that, not knowing what the heck is going on with him. About 6am the next morning my dog ... starts jumping on my chest, barking at me, doing all sorts of crazy things, about five minutes after that an earthquake hit ... About five minutes after that, he starts barking at me again, to let me know another one's coming ... [we] got inside of a doorway and we had a very nice-sized after-shock after that.'

Since 1992 King's sensitive behaviour has continued, particularly when there are 'swarms' of small, repeated earthquakes.

forecasting

'When we start getting swarms of earthquakes King will actually look at the ground, he'll go in circles, he'll growl at it, he'll bark at the ground ... King really is a pretty happy-go-lucky dog.'

Linda knows there are a large number of people and their pets who sense something before earthquakes occur, and although she believes they all have something interesting to

collapsed span from a southbound intersection of Interstate 5

contribute, their information is not a priority for the scientists who are hard at work on quantitative research projects. Allan Lindh is a geologist with the USGS.

 'I've had a lot of people call me or talk to me over the years about whether or not they can sense earthquakes, and some of them have been very convincing, and it's very hard for me to dismiss their stories altogether. But all efforts to treat it as a scientific phenomenon have proven fruitless ... if a few people can sense something in the earth, before earthquakes, some of the time, that doesn't help you predict earthquakes, especially if it's not a stable feature of those people's make-up ... I wouldn't be surprised if things as strange as that someday might prove to be true, but scientifically the only way to approach it is to find things you can measure ...'

An unreinforced building in Santa Monica, Los Angeles, damaged in 1994

 'If people can sense something before earthquakes I think it ... has to do with some emotional state so that it is not repeatable. Science is based on repeatability. It is very hard to repeat experiments with earthquakes in the first place, if you throw in an additional variable like how people feel ... there's no evidence that it has come to anything trying to study that directly. I have over the years, asked people who believed they could predict earthquakes, to write down in a notebook every day ... I have told that to hundreds of people. Not one of them has ever brought me a log. So if people feel they can predict earthquakes they should write it down, keep a record, and we'll compare it to the list of earthquakes and see if they can.'

Linda Curtis also believes there are many more people able to sense earthquakes than are listed in her Rodolex.

'I think there's a lot more than I hear from. I think maybe for every call I get there could possibly be maybe 50 or 100 more people that are 'earthquake sensitives'. I know there's a whole network of sensitives that talk with each other and communicate with each other about sensing earthquakes on the World Wide Web.'

the Sicilian earthquakes of 1693 and 1968

AT INTERVALS OF 90–125 YEARS EASTERN SICILY AND CALABRIA EXPERIENCE SOME OF THE MOST INTENSE EARTHQUAKES IN THE WORLD. IN 1908 THE FOCUS OF THE EARTHQUAKE LAY BETWEEN MESSINA IN SICILY, AND REGGIO IN CALABRIA IN THE STRAITS OF MESSINA. IN 1783, THE FOCUS WAS SITUATED IN CALABRIA, AND IN 1693 IT WAS WEST OF SYRACUSE, IN SICILY. THESE EARTHQUAKES ALWAYS CAUSED A GREAT DEAL OF DAMAGE BUT EACH TIME THE INHABITANTS WOULD ALWAYS BEGIN REBUILDING ON TOP OF THE RUINS OF THEIR TOWNS AND VILLAGES.

In 1693, however, a particularly severe earthquake killed over 60,000 people, destroyed 49 towns and numerous villages. This time the citizens of the Sicilian town of Noto decided to transfer their whole settlement to what they hoped would be a safer place.

One of the survivors, a monk called Tortora, described what had happened in Noto. 'On 9 January, at 4 o'clock in the night [four hours after sunset, 22.00], a sharp earthquake was felt which destroyed a great number of structures and caused the death of over 200 persons. The following day, everyone went to the open spaces, both within and without the town, and they stayed there throughout the Saturday night, fearing lest such a great scourge should be repeated ... As soon as the twenty-first hour struck on Sunday [15.00 on 11 January], and 40 hours, therefore, having elapsed, there was such a terrifying and horrible earthquake that the ground swayed up and down like the sea, the mountains tottered and fell down, and the whole town crumbled piteously, bringing about the death of about 1,000 people'.

Noto was a mass of ruins. The survivors held a mass meeting, and decided to rebuild their

Palazzo Astuto, Noto. A splendid example of 18th-Century Baroque architecture

town about 16km (10 miles) away, on the plateau overlooking the coastal plain. The rebuilding took 50 years but is now one of the most beautiful small Baroque towns in the world. Built in a rich honey-coloured stone, and recently restored, it is an operatic succession of squares, mansions and churches, with elegant façades, porticoes and balconies. Thankfully this jewel of the Mediterranean has not been hit by an earthquake since.

The original cathedral in Noto was destroyed by the earthquake. This replacement is one of the town's centrepieces

Ruderi di Gibellina to Gibellina Nuova

The worst earthquake to hit Sicily since 1908 devastated the villages in the Belice valley in the rugged western mountains in January 1968. Most of the people were made homeless and were forced to sleep out in the open until aid agencies were able to provide wooden huts as temporary accommodation. A decade later the huts were still the only homes available.

Like the citizens of Noto nearly 300 years before, the villagers of Gibellina decided to rebuild their settlement 20km (12½ miles) away, on the plain, near the motorway and the railway. The result is Gibellina Nuova the vision of the mayor Ludovico Corrao. Built to limit casualties in any future calamity, Gibellina Nuova has wide streets, with buildings only two storeys high. The most talented artists in Italy contributed sculptures decorating practically every junction. Squares are enormous whilst shops and cafés seem rare. This is a long way from the close-knit intimacy, hubbub and twisting alleys of the old Gibellina, now called Ruderi di Gibellina – the 'wreckage of Gibellina', but it will be safer.

The earthquake needed two attempts to destroy Old Gibellina. The first quake killed about 200 people and the survivors fled to the safety of the open hills. Three days later, the second quake threw the tottering ruins to the ground, killing the policemen who were on guard.

The mayor decided that the Ruderi should be preserved forever in a great tomb of concrete, with furrows marking the old pattern of the streets. Only a few larger ruins that stayed upright now rise above the white blocks that are a memorial to the old village.

The remains of Old Gibellina. Concrete covers the damaged houses and trenches have been left along the old streets

forecasting and predicting volcanic eruptions

VOLCANIC ERUPTIONS ARE SLIGHTLY EASIER TO FORECAST THAN EARTHQUAKES BECAUSE THERE IS USUALLY MORE WARNING. SIGNS, HOWEVER, CAN BE AMBIGUOUS OR DIFFICULT TO INTERPRET, AND IN SOME CASES, MAY SIMPLY PROVE TO BE FALSE ALARMS.

Children around Mt Unzen, Japan, wear protective clothing

The situation is further complicated by the fact that the distinction between volcanoes that are active, dormant or extinct is not always straightforward. Active volcanoes might erupt fairly often but eruptions are rarely continuous. Etna, for instance, is active: the emission of gas and steam from the main summit is relatively constant; ash and cinders explode regularly from a crater at the base of the main cone; and lavas spew out every few years from fissures on its flanks. Vesuvius was active in every decade from 1631–1944, but has not erupted since, and could now be described as dormant. Mount St Helens on the other hand was dormant from 1857 until its great outburst in 1980. Its most recent eruption, a very mild one, took place in 1986. The question that scientists need to answer, therefore, is whether it is still active or has become dormant once again.

There are also many volcanoes that are clearly active and probably dangerous enough to merit scientific attention. In fact, there are more potentially dangerous volcanoes in the world than scientists to monitor them, or funds available to buy the equipment needed. Therefore, the volcanoes that seem most likely to pose a real threat are selected for special monitoring. The geological and historical records show up the most dangerous candidates. Only about 50 of the 89 selected volcanoes are already under this intensive care. Some are located in remote, unpopulated areas and therefore present little threat to the human population. Amongst these are the many active volcanoes bordering the northern Pacific Ocean from the Aleutian Islands through the Kuril Islands to Kamchatka. Others pose a direct threat to large cities. In Japan, volcanic bomb shelters have been built around Sakurajima, to provide shelter from volcanic bombs. Also in Japan, the town of Shimbara lies at the foot of Unzen, a volcano that caused the deaths of 14,524 people in 1792, and killed three geologists and over 30 journalists in 1991. About 1 million people in and around Naples could be in grave danger if Vesuvius were to erupt violently again. Volcanoes such as these have to be watched very carefully, and both are amongst those selected for special monitoring.

Shelters have been built around Sakurajima in Japan to prevent injuries from volcanic bombs

Dangers posed by volcanoes

The monitoring of volcanoes takes on many varied and increasingly sophisticated forms. When the magma is rising towards the surface it causes earthquakes of increasing magnitude. It will sometimes heat the surrounding rocks and will almost always increase the amount of gas and steam expelled. Once it enters the body of the volcano the magma can also sometimes deform the shape of the cone. The earthquakes are frequent, usually of fairly low magnitudes, and have a shallow focus near the volcano. Generally, but unfortunately not always, the earthquakes occur more often as the magma nears the crater. Volcanic earthquakes increased in number before Pinatubo erupted in 1991, but not before the eruption of Mount St Helens in 1980.

When the magma rises closer to the surface, some of the gases trapped within it can escape without exploding and form fumaroles and solfataras on the volcano which are collected and analyzed. The most significant changes are increases in temperature and especially in emissions of gases common in magma, such as hydrogen sulphide, carbon dioxide and sulphur dioxide: Nevado del Ruiz was producing considerable amounts of sulphur dioxide from October 1985 until it erupted in November. Teide and Vulcano, however, have been emitting sulphurous gases for years at varying rates without bursting into violent activity.

Once the magma has entered the volcano, it can sometimes cause the cone to swell or bulge outwards. These swellings can be measured by tiltmeters, arranged in a triangle, to indicate changes in different directions. Kilauea in Hawaii swells by about 1m (3¼ft) before it erupts. Unzen in Japan, bulged by about 50m (164ft) during the last three days before it erupted on 24 May 1991. There were even more

Lava-flows from Etna in 1971 engulfed this house in Fornazzo, Sicily, on the east flanks of the volcano

disastrous results when the magma rose off-centre at Mount St Helens and caused a bulge on its north face that was clearly visible. On this occasion, however, the rate of bulging was not increasing when the earthquake precipitated the landslide on 18 May 1980. On a broader scale, the satellite-based Global Positioning System is now used to monitor all kinds of changes of level and lateral displacements on volcanoes that have no thick network of monitoring devices set up either on or near them. Similarly, satellites can be used to monitor the most sensitive of heat changes on volcanoes where magma is rising towards the surface. These can give early indications of eruptions that are especially valuable on remote, or even unknown, volcanoes.

All these methods of monitoring are useful, but are best used together rather than in isolation, because individual indicators may prove unreliable. This degree of co-ordination requires teamwork and is costly, but, if it works well, an eruption could be forecast to within a week or so, and subsequently predicted to within a matter of days. In the case of volcanoes however, it is not simply the knowledge of when the eruption is to take place that is important. It is also necessary to know the type of eruption that is likely to occur, and what materials will be emitted, so that appropriate action can be taken.

175

forecasting

damage limitation in Sicily

ALTHOUGH IT IS IMPOSSIBLE TO STOP VOLCANIC ERUPTIONS, HISTORY CAN ILLUSTRATE MANY ATTEMPTS TO DO SO, USING BOTH NATURAL AND SUPERNATURAL MEANS. IN CENTRAL AMERICA ONE TRIBE USED TO OFFER HUMAN SACRIFICES TO THE CRATER OF MASAYA TO STOP ITS ERUPTIONS. THE NEAPOLITANS USED TO PARADE THE HEAD OF THEIR PATRON SAINT, ST JANUARIUS, IN FRONT OF THE TERRIFYING OUTBURSTS OF VESUVIUS. THE CATANIANS USED TO MEET THE ADVANCING LAVAS OF ETNA WITH THE VEIL OF THEIR OWN PATRON SAINT, ST AGATHA. THE VILLAGERS OF PARÍCUTIN, IN MEXICO, KNELT IN PRAYER IN FRONT OF THE ADVANCING LAVA-FLOW IN 1943 AND 1944. ATTEMPTS TO DIVERT LAVA-FLOWS FROM ETNA HAVE PRODUCED MIXED RESULTS.

Map labels:
Etna summit cone
north-east crater
south-east crater
Valle del Bove
barriers
Zafferana

Key

- lavas extending first barrier 1992
- lava overflowed from first barrier 1992
- lavas diverted on upper flow from 29 May 1992

Catania 1669

On 30 April 1669, when the lava-flow from the flanks of Etna threatened the walls of Catania and started to invade the city, most Catanians thought that the city would be swamped. Diego Pappalardo, priest of Pedara, had the idea of trying to divert the flow near its source, where it would have the greatest effect. He decided to make a hole in the solid wall of the flow to encourage the molten lava to flow out sideways, take up a new course, and starve the snout that was advancing into Catania, thus bringing it to a halt.

He chose 50 men and, on 6 May 1669, took them up to the edge of the flow near the newly-buried village of Malpasso. The solidified sidewall of the flow was thin enough to be opened up, but still strong enough not to give way and drown everyone in molten lava at 1000°C. Armed with sledge-hammers, iron crow-bars and hooks, and protected against the heat with wet animal skins, they then lined up and took turns to run up to the lava-wall and hit it as hard as they could. Little by little, they knocked a hole in the sidewall of the flow and revealed the molten lava within. Then came the most difficult part of all: causing the molten lava to leave its old course and

During the eruption of Etna in 1992 helicopters dropped concrete blocks to slow down lava-flows

begin to flow out sideways without engulfing anyone. Amazingly they succeeded; some were burnt and singed, but nobody was killed. The molten lava began to trickle, and then gush, sideways. Diego Pappalardo then directed his men to block the old molten channel with boulders as best they could. They also succeeded in this Herculean task. Most of the lava started to flow out westwards. Rumours of the success spread like wildfire to Catania. The news also spread to the town of Paternò whose citizens noticed that the flow was now making straight for their own town. A group of enraged citizens rode off up to the new diversion, threatened Diego Pappalardo and his men with instant death, and drove them away from the scene. Left to its own devices, the diverted branch solidified, and the molten lavas resumed their previous course. They soon started to feed the snout again that was advancing slowly through western Catania. Paternò was saved. In the event, most of Catania was saved too, initially because much of the lava flowed into the sea, and then because the eruption stopped before it could overwhelm the eastern part of the city. Following this attempt to interfere with the lava's natural course, such activities were then banned until 1983.

Etna 1983

In 1983, the solidified walls of the lava-flow were blown apart by explosives. The molten lava then began to flow sideways out from the breach. At the same time, bulldozers and lorries were used to pile up ramparts of ash and cinders to contain the flow and direct it into a harmless course away from seven villages that it had been threatening. It was a vast task and could only have been done out of the way of farms and settlements on a mountain the size of Etna. As it was, it took seven weeks to move 750,000m^3 (26½ million ft^3) of ash and cinders into place.

Zafferana 1992

A bigger eruption on Etna, starting on 14 December 1991, seemed likely to swamp the town of Zafferana. A rampart of ash and cinders,

21m (69ft) high, was thrown across the valley where the lavas were advancing. They poured over it on 7 April 1992. Three other dams were built lower down, and the lava destroyed every one. In early May, the advancing snout was within 700m (2,296ft) of Zafferana. Faced with

Earthen barriers comprising bulldozed cinders and lava blocks were also used to slow down the flows

the increasing emergency, the experts decided to take more practical measures, this time near the source of the flow, 8km (5 miles) up valley from Zafferana. Helicopters dropped concrete blocks onto the molten lava four times. Each time the bombardment slowed down the snout's advance on Zafferana, but, each time, it started to move forward again. More drastic measures had to be tried. On 29 May 1992, the Pappalardo technique was used again. The solidified walls of the flow were blasted open, and most of the molten lava entered a newly-dug channel alongside it. Then the original channel was blocked with boulders, which cut off the supply of molten lava to the snout threatening Zafferana. Next, they channelled the diverted flow back onto the solidified old flow so that it would do no collateral damage. This new flow was advancing 6,000m (19,685ft), rather than 600m (1,968ft) from Zafferana, giving many weeks in which to prepare further efforts to save the town. In the event they were not needed. The eruption declined suddenly in June 1992 and lava emerged only fitfully until it stopped altogether in March 1993. Zafferana was saved.

damage limitation in Iceland

THE VESTMANN ISLANDS IN ICELAND WERE JOINED BY A NEW MEMBER WHEN SURTSEY ERUPTED IN 1963. ON 23 JANUARY 1973 THE OLDEST AND LARGEST ISLAND IN THE GROUP, HEIMAEY, BURST INTO ACTIVITY. THIS POSED A REAL THREAT TO VESTMANNAEYJAR, THE MAIN TOWN ON THE ISLAND, WITH 5,300 INHABITANTS AND AN IMPORTANT FISHING PORT, LYING JUST 1KM (⅔ MILE) TO THE NORTH.

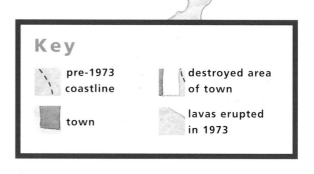

narrowed harbour entrance

Vestmannaeyjar

Eldfell s

Helgafell s

The authorities responded to the eruption first by evacuating the people and almost every moveable object of value from the town, and then by controlling the lava-flow advancing upon the harbour. These operations were aided by three factors. First, the fishing boats were in port sheltering from a storm, and were all therefore available for the evacuation. Second, the intensity of the eruption waned markedly after the first month, making its effects easier to control. Third, the eruption was a moderate Strombolian type: an outburst 1km (⅔ mile) further north on the same fissure would have caused a vigorous Surtseyan eruption in the harbour itself, that would have probably

Key

pre-1973 coastline	destroyed area of town
town	lavas erupted in 1973

destroyed the ships, the port and the town. The eruption was, however, a significant threat, and the action taken against it represents one of the very few successful operations ever accomplished against volcanic activity.

About 30 hours of increasing earthquakes warned everyone to prepare. At 01.55 on 23

The harbour at Vestmannaeyjar. Piles of volcanic ash reached 5m (16½ft) high in the eastern part of the town nearest to the volcano. Ash buried or burnt 80 houses in the area

178

forecasting

January, an orange curtain of lava, 200m (656ft) high, appeared from a fissure stretching 1,800m (5,900ft) from the old volcano, Helgafell. Within a couple of days, activity had concentrated on one chimney exploding ash and cinders, and oozing lava eastward into the sea. On 30 January, the new cone, named Eldfell, had reached 185m (607ft) high, the lava-flow had added 1km² (⅖ square mile) to the eastern coast, and hot ash had crushed and set fire to some of the wooden houses in Vestmannaeyjar. By this time, however, the inhabitants had long been evacuated.

Lava-flows engulf this house located near to the volcano

The evacuation was a victory for contingency planning and efficient organization. Seventy-seven fishing boats in Vestmannaeyjar harbour took most of the people to the mainland; the old and infirm were taken by air. Within seven hours, most of the 5,300 inhabitants had been installed in temporary accommodation. Only the police and those with special skills likely to be useful in the emergency stayed behind. They then evacuated the animal livestock, cars, deep-frozen fish, administrative files, and the cash in the bank. A seven-person committee directed operations.

In late January and early February 1973, those who had stayed on Heimaey continually fought the hot ash piling up as much as 5m (16½ft) deep in the eastern part of Vestmannaeyjar. Metal sheets were nailed over the windows to stop them from being broken by volcanic bombs and large cinders. They shovelled ash from the roofs to stop it crushing houses or setting them on fire. It was necessary to wear gas masks in the lower-lying areas and in cellars to guard against the dense, invisible and deadly carbon dioxide that sometimes erupted with the ash. No-one was killed. In spite of these efforts, ash buried or burnt about 80 houses, mainly in eastern Vestmannaeyjar, nearest the volcano. From mid-February, the explosions began to decline.

At night lava from the volcano illuminates the sky over Vestmannaeyjar

Then a new problem loomed: part of the crater wall of the new cone collapsed. The lavas were now free to flow northwards to Vestmannaeyjar harbour, instead of harmlessly eastwards. Officials considered the options. Bombing the crater might succeed, but there was always the danger that the west wall of the crater would also collapse, and direct even more lava straight onto the town. As the lava-flow could not be safely diverted near its source, volunteers began pouring seawater onto its snout, to make the flow solidify faster and slow down. As soon as it became apparent that this method was working the Icelandic government, and then the United States sent ships with powerful pumps to quench the lavas more effectively. Soon, 20,000m³ (706,300ft³) of lava was solidifying every hour and, at the same time, ash barriers were bulldozed up around the flow to protect the rest of Vestmannaeyjar.

In spite of these heroic efforts the lava flows still cut the electricity supply from the mainland and destroyed three fish-processing factories and over 300 houses before they were brought to a halt. Disaster was averted but at huge cost in terms of time and money.

damage limitation
in the Philippines

South
China
Sea

LUZON

Zambales
Range

Pinatubo
● *Clark Air Force Base*

● *Manila*

FORECASTING A VOLCANIC ERUPTION DEPENDS NOT ONLY ON VOLCANIC STUDIES AND ASSESSMENTS, COMMUNICATION, AND A CORRECT PERCEPTION OF THE DANGERS POSED, IT ALSO REQUIRES ACTION. THE ERUPTION OF MT PINATUBO IN 1991 CLEARLY SHOWS THE RESULTS OF AN EFFECTIVE OPERATION IN TERMS OF MONITORING, ASSESSING THE THREAT, AND THEN COMMUNICATING AND ACTING UPON THE DANGER.

On 1 April 1991 Mt Pinatubo, a volcano in the Zambales Range, 80km (50 miles) north of Manila, capital of the Philippines, was thought to be 'dormant' as there had been no eruptions in recorded history. About 500,000 people lived on the plains around Pinatubo and about 15,000 semi-nomadic Aeta people, growing coffee, bananas and root crops, lived on the thickly forested slopes. There were also some 16,000 US personnel at Clark Air Force Base nearby.

In the afternoon of 2 April 1991 the villagers of Patal Pinto saw ash and steam explode, 500m (1,640ft) high, from a crack on the upper northern slopes of Pinatubo. On 4 April the first report of this activity was made to the headquarters of the Philippine Institute of Volcanology and Seismology (PHIVOLCS). Five thousand people were immediately evacuated from the vulnerable area within 10km (6¼ miles) of the summit. Surveillance was set up, and 40–178 volcanic earthquakes were recorded per day. Close contact was established with the US Geological Survey and Clark Air Force Base.

In early May geological field studies were undertaken which revealed a history of violent eruptions stretching back 1 million years, with the latest outburst about 400–600 years ago. There had been frequent ash-falls, volcanic mudflows and nuées ardentes, which had spread 20km (12½ miles) from the crest. On 23 May a hazard map was published, showing the likely spread of ash-falls, volcanic mudflows, and nuées ardentes. The National Disaster Organizations distributed the map to all national and local civil and military authorities.

Over the next week Alert Levels assigned to the increasing possibility of a major eruption were issued. On 8 June molten rock reached the surface and formed a dome of viscous lava, north-west of the crest. On 9 June the first nuées ardentes erupted at 14.55, and raced 4km (2½ miles) down the valley. PHIVOLCS issued Alert Level 5 ('eruption in progress') at 15.15. About 25,000 people were evacuated from an area within 20km (12½ miles) of Pinatubo.

The climax of the eruption occurred between 12–15 June. A Plinian eruption at 08.51 on 12 June generated a column 19km (12 miles) high in 19 minutes. Several other outbursts followed. Nuées ardentes raced down the main valleys, devastating some villages already evacuated. There was a general evacuation of all within 30km (18½ miles) of the crest, making a total of 58,000 evacuees. The climax of the eruption on 15 June 1991 formed a column up to 40km (25 miles) high. Earthquakes caused the summit to collapse into a caldera, 2km (1¼ miles) across.

Pinatubo quickly calmed down from 16 June and Alert Levels were gradually reduced. Two cities and 61 municipalities were declared calamity areas. About 860km² (332 square miles) of agricultural land was covered in thick ash. The

Mudflows from Pinatubo as viewed from space. The abandoned Clark Air Force Base that housed 16,000 US personnel prior to the eruption is towards the upper left corner of the photograph

Key

☐ possible nuées ardentes

☐ possible ash fall

▨ nuées ardentes buffer zone

〰 possible lahars

Aeta tribes lost nearly all of their traditional homeland. The Office of Civil Defence listed 847 dead, 184 injured and 23 missing. Of these, 537 died from diseases caught at the evacuation centres, 29 were victims of volcanic mudflows, and 281 were killed when roofs collapsed under the weight of ash drenched by typhoon rains. Thus, deaths caused by the eruption itself were effectively minimized. Efficient organization and communication and prompt evacuation saved thousands of lives.

Hazard map published before the eruption

Areas affected following eruption

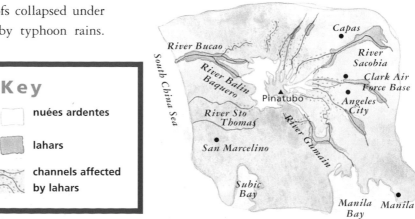

Key

☐ nuées ardentes

▨ lahars

〰 channels affected by lahars

the future

IN SPITE OF ALL THE DIFFICULTIES FACED BY SCIENTISTS AND THE AUTHORITIES WHEN THEY ARE CONFRONTED BY THE THREAT OF EARTHQUAKES OR ERUPTIONS, CONTINUED EFFORTS TOWARDS ACCURATE PREDICTION AND DAMAGE LIMITATION ARE ESSENTIAL.

There are several basic lessons to be learned from past events. First, we should try to avoid living in the most dangerous spots, such as valleys draining from violent active volcanoes, or on weak sands and clays along active fault-lines. Second, we should endeavour to construct the strongest possible buildings, which is costly, but not as costly as the damage that can otherwise ensue. Third, danger spots should be monitored so that real warning signals can be detected, predictions can be made, and threatened areas can be evacuated in time. Fourth, there should be adequate, clearly designated refuges and organized practice-evacuations, so that the people recognize the danger and know exactly what to do when the danger threatens.

In reality, not all these lessons can be applied: Tokyo, Los Angeles and San Francisco, for instance, cannot be moved, and are growing increasingly crowded and therefore more vulnerable to earthquakes. Thousands of houses have been built higher and higher up the slopes of Vesuvius, on ground devastated by eruptions in the past few centuries. Japan and the United States do, however, have the resources to fund extensive monitoring and to make use of costly building techniques. Less developed and/or less politically stable countries are unable to afford such schemes, and are also ill-equipped to organise and implement emergency plans in the event of a disaster.

There is always the hope, however, that scientific advances will produce increasingly accurate predictions thereby minimizing the number of casualties and the amount of damage caused. Nevertheless, even if a successful prediction can be made, it has no practical value in the absence of appropriate action. In recognition of both of past failures, and the inability of many countries to cope with the effects of natural disasters, the United Nations has named the 1990s the International Decade for Natural Disaster Reduction. It was calculated that, between 1970 and 1990, natural disasters in the world, ranging from floods and hurricanes to volcanic eruptions and earthquakes, had cost 2.8 million lives and billions of US dollars. The problem is exacerbated in developing countries, where population, industrialization and city crowding have expanded so fast, that increasingly lethal natural disasters are inevitable unless new measures are adopted. In 1985, the mudflow from Nevado del Ruiz killed 23,000 people, primarily because damage-limitation procedures were not properly implemented. In 1991, orderly evacuations from the zone of much greater danger around Pinatubo saved at least twice that number of lives. In 1988, the Armenian earthquake buried 25,000 people when badly-constructed buildings collapsed heaps of rubble, but an earthquake of a roughly similar magnitude at Northridge, California, in 1992 claimed only 57 lives.

If the examples given in this book tell us anything it is that we cannot attempt to contain our savage Earth. The tasks for the future are to discover more about it, learn how to live with it, and above all to respect it. Be warned and beware.

From top to bottom: Anak Krakatau, Indonesia; Nevado del Ruiz, Colombia; the cell of Sylbaris, St Pierre, Martinique; Tokyo at night

glossary

ash
Pulverized volcanic rock exploded violently from a vent in small fragments. It can form cones, widespread blankets on land, and the finest particles may remain in the stratosphere for years.

basalt
A dark, pasty-grey volcanic rock, poor in silica (about 50 per cent or less by weight) and relatively rich in iron, calcium and magnesium. By far the most common volcanic rock, forming the bulk of the ocean floors, and on land it occurs in many lava-flows, cinder cones, shield volcanoes and volcanic plateaux. On eruption it is usually hot and fluid, and flows 10km (6¼ miles) are common. It is chiefly erupted in effusive emissions without violent explosions, from fissures as well as single vents.

caldera
A large almost circular or horse-shoe shaped hollow, several kilometres across, formed mainly by collapse into the magma reservoir, but also by great volcanic explosions. Usually bounded by steep enclosing walls and formed most often on strato-volcanoes. The term is derived from the Spanish word for cauldron. The Portuguese spelling, 'caldeira', is sometimes used.

cinder cone
A steep conical hill, usually less than 250m (820ft) high, with straight slopes at the angle of rest of the loose materials composing the cone. Formed when moderate repeated explosions accumulate layers of cinders, lapilli and ash.

collision
Occurs when two plates carrying continental masses are pushed together, causing many faults and folds in the rocks and long, high mountain ranges in the continents.

convergent boundary
A boundary between two plates where they are moving together with the result that one plunges beneath the other and becomes assimilated into the mantle. This type of interaction can occur between two continental plates, two oceanic plates, or a continental and an oceanic plate.

crater
A bowl-shaped hollow in the summit of a volcano which lies directly above the vent from which fragments are ejected.

crust
The solid but brittle outer layer of the Earth forming the upper part of the lithosphere. It comprises continental crust composed of granitic types of rock, and oceanic crust, composed of denser, basaltic types of rock. The continental crust occupies relatively small areas resting on the continuous oceanic crust below.

divergent boundary
A boundary between two plates that are moving or rifting apart where volcanic activity creates new continental or oceanic crust.

earthquake
A sudden shaking of the Earth caused when a dislocation occurs along a fault. The pent-up energy released reverberates in waves from the point of dislocation.

earthquake epicentre
The point on the Earth's surface that is situated directly above the focus of an earthquake.

earthquake focus
The exact place in the Earth's crust where the dislocation causing an earthquake first occurs.

earthquake intensity
A scale of 12 degrees (I–XII), developed by Mercalli, and later modified, that describes the various amounts of surface damage caused by earthquakes.

earthquake magnitude
A scale developed by Richter, and later modified, designed to measure the energy released by an earthquake at its focus.

earthquake waves
Waves of energy that spread out through the Earth's crust from the focus of an earthquake. There are two types of body waves (P-waves and S-waves) that travel through the Earth, and two types of surface waves (Rayleigh waves and Love waves) that travel just beneath the Earth's surface.

elastic rebound
A sudden release of energy stored in rocks subjected to stresses and strains resulting in movement along a fault.

eruption
The way in which volcanic materials – gases, liquids and solids – are expelled onto the Earth's surface from a volcano.

fault
A crack in the Earth's crust caused

when the stresses and strains derived from plate movements dislocate the brittle rocks. Faults can be 'normal', 'reverse', or 'horizontal', depending on the direction of the dislocation. 'Blind' or 'masked' faults are covered by sediments and are thus invisible at the Earth's surface.

fault scarp
A cliff created by movement along a fault, representing the exposed surface of the fault before it is altered by weathering etc.

fissure
A crack, fault, fracture, or cluster of joints, cutting deep into the Earth's crust, up which magma may rise. Usually produces lava-flows with some cinder cones.

forecast
An informed estimate that an earthquake or eruption is most likely to take place within a period of several years, decades, or centuries.

fumarole
A vent giving off gases or steam and often surrounded by fragile precipitated crystals. Occurs on active and dormant volcanoes.

geological time
The entire history of the Earth, stretching back 4,600 million years, that is revealed by study of the rocks composing the crust.

geyser
A fountain of water, heated by volcanic activity, that spurts from the ground at intervals.

granite
A coarse-grained crystalline rock composed chiefly of quartz and feldspars. It forms when rhyolitic magma solidifies and crystallizes below the Earth's surface, and is only exposed by erosion.

historic time
The period during which events have been recorded by observers. It varies from about 3,000 years around the Mediterranean and in China, and 200 years in parts of the Americas.

hotspot
A stationary plume of rising mantle which generates chains of volcanoes as the plates move over it.

island arc
A gently curving chain of volcanic islands rising above sea-level from the ocean floor, formed when an oceanic plate is subducted beneath another. Volcanic chains are their equivalent on land.

landslide
A sudden, massive movement of rocks downslope under the influence of gravity, caused when earthquakes or eruptions make the bedrock unstable.

lava
Derived directly from magma, lava reaches the surface as molten rock or magma, but it soon cools and solidifies as flows, domes on land, and pillows under the sea. When shattered by gas explosions, it also forms fragments ranging in size from dust to blocks that are thrown through the air.

liquefaction
The invasion of rocks, sands and alluvium by groundwater when violent earthquakes greatly increase water pressure.

lithosphere
The brittle, solid outer shell of the Earth comprising both the crust and the solid upper part of the mantle. Broken up into plates, it is very thin at the mid-ocean ridges and thickest under the continents.

magma
Hot rock material formed by partial melting of the mantle below the lithosphere, usually at depths of 70–200km (43½–124 miles). It is a viscous liquid containing both gases and solid crystals. When it erupts on the Earth's surface, the gases explode and the molten materials form flows and fragments of lava.

magma reservoir
A large zone of ill defined fissures and cavities in the lithosphere where rising magma halts for varying lengths of time. Usually 2–50km (1¼–31 miles) deep.

mantle
The hot, but not wholly mobile layer of Earth situated below the Earth's crust and which envelops the Earth's core.

mid-ocean ridge
A large ridge on the ocean floor, where volcanic eruptions generate new oceanic crust, and where two plates diverge.

mudflow (lahar)
Fast-flowing and highly destructive currents of water, mud, sand, boulders or masonry, commonly formed when a volcanic eruption melts part of an ice-cap or disturbs a crater lake.

nuée ardente
A French term used to describe an incandescent cloud or glowing avalanche of hot gas and fragments

of all sizes, including ash, pumice rock debris in an aerosol-like emulsion expelled by explosive eruptions, which travels across the ground at very high speeds and gives off glowing, billowing clouds. It is, perhaps the most dangerous of all the forms of volcanic eruptions.

phreatic eruption
A sudden, violent eruption, chiefly of steam, that emits newly shattered fragments of older, solid rocks. Phreatic eruptions are caused when rising new magma meets water percolating downwards.

plate
Large, usually rigid slabs into which the lithosphere is broken. Their edges are the main zones where eruptions and earthquakes may occur, as the plates constantly diverge or converge, collide or plunge, or slide past each other.

prediction
An informed estimate that an earthquake or eruption is most likely to take place within a period of several hours or days.

rift
A long zone where the lithosphere is stretched, thinned and eventually broken so that areas on either side of it diverge. Rifting gives rise to faults, earthquakes and eruptions.

seamount
A volcanic mountain found below sea-level, and especially common in the Pacific Ocean. They often rise 2,000m (6,560ft) from the ocean floor. Active seamounts are being built up at present by submarine eruptions and could eventually form new volcanic islands. They may also be extinct, submerged remains of old volcanoes.

seismic gap
A sector of an earthquake-prone area where no earthquakes have taken place for an abnormally long time compared with sectors nearby. Such an area is deemed likely to experience an earthquake in the near future.

shield
A large, gently sloping volcano composed mainly of fluid basaltic lava-flows emitted from clustered vents, with relatively few fragmented layers.

silica
The molecule formed of silicon and oxygen (SiO_2) that is a fundamental component of volcanic rocks, and the most important factor in controlling the fluidity of magma. In general, the higher the silica content of a magma, the greater its viscosity.

solfatara
An Italian word used to describe the quiet emission of sulphurous gases from a fumarole.

strato-volcano
A large, often steep-sided volcanic cone composed of stratified, bedded layers of lava fragments and flows as well as many other volcanic products.

subduction zone
Where two plates converge and one sinks at an angle beneath the other into the mantle. The subducted slab stimulates melting in the mantle above it and helps form volcanoes. The slab's plunging action also generates violent earthquakes.

transform boundary
A boundary where two plates slide past one another without affecting the lithosphere

tsunami
A Japanese term used to describe huge, rapidly moving sea-waves generated by violent eruptions or earthquakes. Imperceptible in the open sea, tsunamis crash onto the shore at 80km/h (50mph) in waves reaching 30m (98ft) above sea-level. They are particularly common and dangerous in the Pacific Ocean.

vent
The conduit or pipe through which volcanic material travels through the crust to the Earth's surface.

volcanic chain
A series of volcanoes, arranged in a curve or straight line, erupted on the continents as a result of subduction. They are the land equivalents of island arcs.

volcanic fragments
Ash bombs, cinders, lapilli or pumice shattered by explosions during an eruption. They are the main constituent of cinder cones and many strato-volcanoes.

volcanic gas
Contained in small proportions within magma and commonly comprising, for example, steam, sulphur dioxide and carbon dioxide. As the magma closely approaches the Earth's surface, the gases are exsolved and can become a major factor in the violence of eruptions. Because several such gases are toxic, they can also be important contributors to volcanic death tolls.

volcano
A hill or mountain formed around and above a vent by accumulations of erupted materials, such as ash, pumice, cinders or lava-flows. The term refers both to the chimney or vent itself and to the often cone-shaped accumulation above it.

further reading

General

Levy, M. and Salvadori, M. (1995) *Why the Earth Quakes*. W.W. Norton & Company, New York, United States

Press, F. and Siever, R. (1986) *Earth*. W.H. Freeman, San Francisco, United States

Ritchie, D. (1994) *The Encyclopedia of Earthquakes and Volcanoes*. Facts on File, New York, United States

Tarbuck, Edward J. and Lutgens, Frederick K. (1996) *Earth: An Introduction to Physical Geology*. Prentice Hall, New Jersey, United States

Earthquakes

Aki, K. and Richard, P.G. (1981) *Quantitative Seismology*. W.H. Freeman, San Francisco, United States

Bolt, B.A. (1988) *Earthquakes*. W.H. Freeman, San Francisco, United States

Bolt, B.A. (1993) *Earthquakes and Geological Discovery*. Scientific American, New York, United States

Richter, C. (1958) *Elementary Seismology*. California Inst. of Technology, San Francisco, United States

Scholtz, C.M. (1980) *The Mechanics of Earthquakes and Faulting*. Cambridge University Press, Cambridge, United Kingdom

Yeats, R.S., Allen, C.R. and Sieh, K. (1996) *Geology of Earthquakes*. Oxford University Press, New York, United States

Volcanoes

Bullard, F.M. (1984) *Volcanoes of the Earth*. University of Texas Press, Austin, United States

Decker, R.W. and Decker, B.B. (1997) *Volcanoes*. W.H. Freeman, San Francisco, United States

Decker, R.W. and Decker, B.B. (1991) *Mountains of Fire*. Cambridge University Press, Cambridge, United Kingdom

Eyewitness Guide (1997) *Volcano*. Dorling Kindersley, London, United Kingdom

Fisher, R.V., Heiken, G. and Hulen, J.B. (1997) *Volcanoes: Crucibles of Change*. Princeton University Press, United States

Francis, P. (1976) *Volcanoes*. Penguin, United Kingdom

Green, J. and Short, N.M. (Eds) (1971) *Volcanic Landforms and Surface Features*. Springer, New York

Johnson, C. and Weisel, D. (1994) *Fire on the Mountain*. Chronicle Press, San Francisco, United States

Luhr, J.F. and Simkin, T. (Eds) (1993) *Parícutin: The Volcano Born in a Mexican Cornfield*. Geoscience Press, United States

Macdonald, G.A. (1972) *Volcanoes*. Prentice Hall, New Jersey, United States

Scarpa, R. and Tilling, R.I. (Eds) (1996) *Monitoring and Mitigation of Volcano Hazards*. Springer, Berlin, Germany

Scarth, A. (1994) *Volcanoes: An Introduction*. UCL Press, London, United Kingdom; Texas A. and M. University Press, Texas, United States

Simkin, T. and Siebert, L. (1994) *Volcanoes of the World*. Geoscience Press, United States

Periodicals and magazines

Fact Sheets, special reports and internet services are published by the Hazards Programs of the United States Geological Survey.

Also published by the United States Geological Survey, the periodical *Earthquakes & Volcanoes* was discontinued in 1995, but may still be held by some libraries.

Accessible articles may also occasionally appear in *Scientific American*, *Geographical Magazine* and *National Geographic*.

index

picture credits

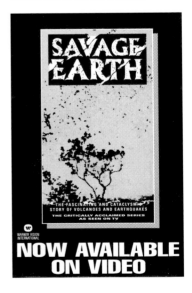